Managing

ALL-IN-ONE

FOR DUMMIES®

A Wiley Brand

by Marty Brounstein; Peter Economy;
Terry Hildebrandt, MA, MA, PCC;
Stephen Kindel; Ken Lloyd, PhD;
Marshall Loeb; Bob Nelson, PhD;
Christina Tangora Schlachter, PhD;
Vivian Scott and The Dispute Resolution
Center of Snohomish & Island Counties;
Marilee Sprenger

Managing All-in-One For Dummies®

Published by:
John Wiley & Sons, Inc.,
111 River Street, Hoboken,
NJ 07030-5774,
www.wiley.com

Copyright © 2014 by John Wiley & Sons, Inc., Hoboken, New Jersey

Published simultaneously in Canada

No part of this publication may be reproduced, stored in a retrieval system or transmitted in any form or by any means, electronic, mechanical, photocopying, recording, scanning or otherwise, except as permitted under Sections 107 or 108 of the 1976 United States Copyright Act, without the prior written permission of the Publisher. Requests to the Publisher for permission should be addressed to the Permissions Department, John Wiley & Sons, Inc., 111 River Street, Hoboken, NJ 07030, (201) 748-6011, fax (201) 748-6008, or online at http://www.wiley.com/go/permissions.

Trademarks: Wiley, For Dummies, the Dummies Man logo, Dummies.com, Making Everything Easier, and related trade dress are trademarks or registered trademarks of John Wiley & Sons, Inc., and may not be used without written permission. All other trademarks are the property of their respective owners. John Wiley & Sons, Inc., is not associated with any product or vendor mentioned in this book.

LIMIT OF LIABILITY/DISCLAIMER OF WARRANTY: WHILE THE PUBLISHER AND AUTHOR HAVE USED THEIR BEST EFFORTS IN PREPARING THIS BOOK, THEY MAKE NO REPRESENTATIONS OR WARRANTIES WITH RESPECT TO THE ACCURACY OR COMPLETENESS OF THE CONTENTS OF THIS BOOK AND SPECIFICALLY DISCLAIM ANY IMPLIED WARRANTIES OF MERCHANTABILITY OR FITNESS FOR A PARTICULAR PURPOSE. NO WARRANTY MAY BE CREATED OR EXTENDED BY SALES REPRESENTATIVES OR WRITTEN SALES MATERIALS. THE ADVISE AND STRATEGIES CONTAINED HEREIN MAY NOT BE SUITABLE FOR YOUR SITUATION. YOU SHOULD CONSULT WITH A PROFESSIONAL WHERE APPROPRIATE. NEITHER THE PUBLISHER NOR THE AUTHOR SHALL BE LIABLE FOR DAMAGES ARISING HEREFROM.

For general information on our other products and services, please contact our Customer Care Department within the U.S. at 877-762-2974, outside the U.S. at 317-572-3993, or fax 317-572-4002. For technical support, please visit www.wiley.com/techsupport.

Wiley publishes in a variety of print and electronic formats and by print-on-demand. Some material included with standard print versions of this book may not be included in e-books or in print-on-demand. If this book refers to media such as a CD or DVD that is not included in the version you purchased, you may download this material at http://booksupport.wiley.com. For more information about Wiley products, visit www.wiley.com.

Library of Congress Control Number: 2013954203

ISBN 978-1-118-78408-2 (pbk); ISBN 978-1-118-80814-6 (ebk); ISBN 978-1-118-80815-3 (ebk)

Manufactured in the United States of America

10 9 8 7 6 5 4 3

Contents at a Glance

Table of Contents

Introduction

Congratulations! As a result of your astute choice of material, you're about to read a completely fresh approach to the topic of management. If you've already read other books about management, you've surely noticed that most of them fall into one of two categories: (1) deadly boring snooze-o-ramas that make great paperweights; or (2) recycled platitudes glazed with a thin sugar coating of pop psychobabble, which sound great on paper but fail abysmally in the real world.

Managing All-in-One For Dummies is different. This book is fun. Its approach reflects a strong belief and experience that management can be fun, too. You can get the job done and have fun in the process.

On some days, you'll face challenges — perhaps pushing you to your limit or beyond. However, on many more days, the joys of managing — teaching a new skill to an employee, helping land a new customer, accomplishing an important assignment, and so on — can bring you a sense of fulfillment that you never imagined possible.

Managing All-in-One For Dummies provides a comprehensive overview of the fundamentals of effective management, presented in a fun and interesting format. It's six books in one, drawing from a wealth of information across ten management-focused titles, compiled to support your efforts without giving you more than you want or need.

Managing can be an intimidating job. New managers — especially ones promoted into the position for their technical expertise — often have trouble knowing what they need to do. Don't worry. Relax. Help is at your fingertips.

About This Book

Managing All-in-One For Dummies is perfect for all levels of management. If you're a new manager or a manager-to-be, you can find everything you need to know to be successful. If you're an experienced manager, challenge yourself to shift your perspective and take a fresh look at your management philosophies and techniques. Maybe you can't teach an old dog new tricks, but you can always incorporate changes that make your job (and the jobs of your employees) easier, resulting in more fun and effectiveness.

Whether you're new to the job or are facing a new task in your current job, all managers feel overwhelmed sometimes. The secret to dealing with stress is to discover what you can do better (or differently) to obtain your desired results. When you do make a mistake, pick yourself up, laugh it off, and learn from it. This book exists to make learning easier so that you won't have to make all the same mistakes and learn the hard way.

You can use this book as a reference; you aren't required to read it from front to back in order to understand what's being said. Feel free to jump into whatever chapter you need the most on a given day. If there's information in a different chapter that will aid your understanding of the subject at hand, we'll be sure to let you know.

One more thing: Within this book, you may note that some web addresses break across two lines of text. If you're reading this book in print and want to visit one of these web pages, simply key in the web address exactly as it's noted in the text, pretending as though the line break doesn't exist. If you're reading this as an e-book, you've got it easy: Just click the web address to be taken directly to the web page.

Foolish Assumptions

As we wrote this book, we made a couple assumptions about you, our reader:

- ✔ You're a manager or a manager-to-be, and you're truly motivated to discover some new approaches to managing organizations and leading people.
- ✔ You're ready, willing, and able to commit yourself to becoming a better manager.

Note that we don't assume you have an MBA or a specific level of experience with management. If you're new to your management role, you'll find this material completely accessible. If you've been in management for a while but need some ideas for refreshing your leadership style or getting out of an unproductive rut, this book can definitely help as well.

Icons Used in This Book

To guide you along the way and point out the information you really need to know, this book uses the following icons along its left margins:

This icon points to tips and tricks that make managing easier — little ideas that can make a big impact on how you do your job.

If you don't heed the advice next to these icons, the situation may blow up in your face. Watch out!

Some information is so important that it's worth repeating. Those tidbits get this icon to help you find them again easily.

Beyond the Book

In addition to the material in the print or e-book you're reading right now, this product comes with access-anywhere goodies on the web. Check out the free Cheat Sheet at `www.dummies.com/cheatsheet/managingaio` for articles on the following topics:

✔ Managing conflict actively and constructively

✔ Heading off performance problems before they require drastic action

✔ Laying the groundwork for terrific cross-group communication

✔ Unlocking the magic of delegation (so you can get a good night's sleep once in a while!)

Where to Go from Here

You can read any chapter in this book without having to read what comes before or after. Or you can read the whole book backward or forward. Or, if you've got a print copy, you can just carry it around with you to impress your friends. (It's quite thick, isn't it?)

If you're a new or aspiring manager and you want a crash course in management, you may want to start at the beginning and work your way through to the end. Forget about going back to school to get your MBA — save your money and take a trip to Hawaii instead. Simply turn the page and take your first step into the world of management.

If you're already a manager and are short on time (and what manager isn't short on time?), you may want to turn to a particular topic, such as delegating tasks or hiring employees, to address a specific need or question. The table of contents and index can direct you to the answers you seek.

Wherever you begin, we hope you enjoy your journey!

Book I
Getting Started

getting started
with

Managing

Contents at a Glance

Chapter 1

Now You're a Manager

*M*anaging is truly a calling. In the world of business, no other position allows you to have such a direct, dramatic, and positive impact on the lives of others and on the ultimate success of your enterprise.

This chapter provides an overview of the challenging and ever-changing world of management. Whether you're a manager or a manager-to-be, you can benefit from this inside look into the kinds of management techniques that can help you get the best from your employees every day of the week.

Identifying the Different Styles of Management

One definition describes *management* as "getting things done through others." Another definition more specifically defines management as "making something planned happen within a specific area through the use of available resources." Seems simple enough. So why do so many bright, industrious people have trouble managing well? And why do so many companies today seem to offer a flavor-of-the-month training program that changes each time some new management fad blows through the business scene?

Unfortunately, good management is a scarce commodity, both precious and fleeting. Despite years of changing management theory and countless management fads, many workers — and managers, for that matter — have developed a distorted view of management and its practice. Managers often don't know the right approach to take or exactly what to do. And as the saying goes, "If it's foggy in the pulpit, it'll be cloudy in the pew."

Do you ever hear any of the following remarks at your office or place of business?

- ✔ "We don't have the authority to make that decision."
- ✔ "She's in charge of the department, so fixing the problem is her responsibility, not ours."
- ✔ "Why do they keep asking us what we think when they never use anything we say?"
- ✔ "I'm sorry, but that's our policy. We're not allowed to make exceptions."
- ✔ "If my manager doesn't care, I don't, either."
- ✔ "It doesn't matter how hard you work. No one's going to notice anyway."
- ✔ "You can't trust those employees — they just want to goof off."

When you hear remarks like these at work, red lights should be flashing before your eyes, and alarm bells should be ringing loudly in your ears. Remarks like these indicate that managers and employees aren't communicating effectively — that managers don't trust their employees, and that employees lack confidence in their managers. If you're lucky, you find out about these kinds of problems while you still have a chance to do something about them. If you're not so lucky and you miss the clues, you may be stuck repeatedly making the same mistakes.

The expectations and commitments that employees carry with them on the job are largely a product of the way their managers treat them. Following are the most commonly adopted styles of management. Do you recognize your management style?

Tough guy (or gal) management

What's the best way to make something planned happen? Everyone seems to have a different answer to this question. Some people see management as something you do *to* people — not *with* them. Does this type of manager sound familiar? "We're going to do it my way. Understand?" Or perhaps the ever-popular threat: "It had better be on my desk by the end of the day — or else!" If worse comes to worst, a manager can unveil the ultimate weapon: "Mess up one more time, and you're out of here!"

This type of management is often known as *Theory X management,* which assumes that people are inherently lazy and need to be driven to perform. Managing by fear and intimidation is always guaranteed to get a response. The question is, do you get the kind of response you really want? When you closely monitor your employees' work, you usually end up with only short-term compliance. In other words, you never get the best from others by lighting a fire under them — you have to find a way to build a fire within them.

Of course, sometimes managers have to take command of the situation. If a proposal has to be shipped out in an hour and your customer just sent you some important changes, take charge of the situation to ensure that the right people are on the task.

 When you have to act quickly with perhaps not as much discussion as you'd like, it's important to apologize in advance and let people know why you're acting the way you are. Remember that the majority of employees leave their positions because of the actions (or lack thereof) of their direct supervisor or manager. So make sure you move quickly but with clear communication and respect for your staff.

Nice guy (or gal) management

At the other end of the spectrum, some people see management as a "nice guy" or "nice gal" kind of idea. *Theory Y management* assumes that people basically want to do a good job. In the extreme interpretation of this theory, managers are supposed to be sensitive to their employees' feelings and avoid disturbing their employees' tranquility and sense of self-worth.

The approach may come across like this: "Uh, there's this little problem with your report; none of the numbers are correct. Now, don't take this personally, but we need to consider our alternatives for taking a more careful look at these figures in the future."

This scenario also plays out when someone from the peer group is promoted into a management position. He sometimes can't easily transition from being a buddy into being the manager.

Again, managers may get a response with this approach (or they may choose to do the work themselves!), but are they likely to get the best possible response? No, the employees are likely to take advantage of the managers.

The right kind of management

Good managers realize that they don't have to be tough all the time. If your employees are diligently performing their assigned tasks and no business emergency requires your immediate intervention, you can step back and let them do their jobs. Not only do your employees learn to be responsible, but also you can concentrate your efforts on what is most important to the bottom-line success of your organization.

A manager's real job is to inspire employees to do their best and establish a working environment that allows them to reach their goals. The best managers make every possible effort to remove the organizational obstacles that prevent employees from doing their jobs and to obtain the resources and training that employees need to do their jobs effectively. All other goals — no matter how lofty or pressing — must take a back seat.

Bad systems, bad policies, bad procedures, and poor treatment of others are organizational weaknesses that managers must identify and repair or replace. Build a strong organizational foundation for your employees. Support your people, and they will support you. When given the opportunity to achieve, workers in all kinds of businesses, from factories to venture capital firms, have proven this rule to be true. If you haven't seen it at your place of business, you may be mistaking your employees for problems. Quit squeezing them and start squeezing your organization. The result is employees who want to succeed and a business that flourishes right along with them. Who knows? Your employees may even stop hiding when they see you coming their way!

Squeezing employees may be easier than fighting the convoluted systems and cutting through the bureaucratic barnacles that have grown on your organization. You may be tempted to yell, "It's your fault that our department didn't achieve its goals!" Yes, blaming your employees for the organization's problems may be tempting, but doing so isn't going to solve the problems. You may get a quick, short-lived response when you push your people, but ultimately, you're failing to deal with the organization's real problems.

Everyone wants to win. The difficult challenge of management is to define "winning" in such a way that it feels like winning for everyone in the organization. People are often competing with coworkers for a piece of the pie instead of trying to make the pie bigger. It's your job to help make a bigger pie.

Meeting the Management Challenge

When you're assigned a task in a nonmanagement position, completing it by yourself is fairly simple and straightforward. Your immediate results are in direct response to your effort. To accomplish your task, you review the task, decide how best to accomplish it, and set schedules and milestones for its successful completion. Assuming that you have access to the tools and resources necessary to accomplish your task, you can probably do it yourself quickly and easily. You're an expert doer — a bright, get-things-done type of person.

However, if you hold a management position, you were probably selected because you're skilled in the areas you're now responsible for managing. For example, John was a member of a team of software programmers developing a complex application for portable computers. When he was a team member, everything was fine. He came to work in a T-shirt and jeans — just like the rest of his teammates — and often spent time with his programmer friends after hours. The bond that the team shared changed, however, when John became the team's manager.

In his new role of manager, John first changed offices. Instead of sharing an open bay with the other programmers, he moved into his own office — one with four walls and a window looking out over the parking lot. A secretary guarded his door. Of course, the jeans and T-shirt had to go — they were replaced with a business suit and tie. Instead of having fun programming, John was suddenly concerned about more serious topics, such as cost overruns, schedule delays, percent direct, and days receivable.

As John's role changed, so did John. And as John changed, so did his relationship with his coworkers. He was no longer a coworker; he was The Boss. To achieve his goals, John quickly had to make the transition from a doer to a manager of doers.

When you want to get a task done through someone else, you employ a different set of skills than when you do the task yourself. This simple decision to pass the responsibility of completing a task to someone else introduces an interpersonal element into your equation. Being good technically at your job is no longer enough, no matter how good your technical skills are. Now you must have good planning, organization, leadership, and follow-up skills.

In other words, in addition to being a good doer, you have to be a good manager of doers. If you need some help in this area, keep reading: There's no time to waste!

Skipping quick fixes that don't stick

Despite what many people want you to believe, management isn't always a shoot-from-the-hip proposition. Sure, some managers may make decisions too quickly from time to time, but the most effective ones take the time they need to consider their options before making a decision. Being a manager isn't easy. Yes, the best management solutions seem to be common sense; however, turning common sense into common practice is often difficult.

Management is an attitude, a way of life. Management is a very real desire to work with people and help them succeed, as well as a desire to help your organization succeed. Management is a life-long learning process that doesn't end when you walk out of a one-hour seminar or finish viewing a 25-minute video. Management is like the old story about the unhappy home-owner who was shocked to receive a bill for $100 to fix a leaky faucet. When asked to explain the basis for this seemingly high charge, the plumber said, "Tightening the nut cost you $5. Knowing which nut to tighten cost you $95!"

Management is a people job. If you're not up to the task of working with people — helping them, listening to them, encouraging them, and guiding them — then you shouldn't be a manager.

Because management is such a challenge, an entire management training industry has sprung up, ready to help managers learn how to solve their problems. Unfortunately, some trainers focus on creating instant gratification among course attendees, many of whom have spent hundreds and even thousands of dollars to be there.

At one such touchy-feely offsite management meeting meant to build team-work and communication, a too-common example took place: Just after lunch, a big tray of leftover veggies, bagels, fruit, and such was sitting on a table at the side of the room. The facilitator rose from his chair, faced the group, and said, "Your next task is to split yourselves into four groups and construct a model of the perfect manager by using only the items on that tray of leftovers." A collective groan filled the room. "I don't want to hear any complaints," the trainer said. "I just want to see happy people doing happy things for the next half-hour."

The teams feverishly went about their task of building the perfect manager. With some managers barely throttling the temptation to engage each other in a massive food fight, the little figures began to take shape. A banana here, a carrot stick there . . . and, *voilá!* After a brief competition for dominance, the winners were crowned. The result? Thought you'd never ask. Check out Figure 1-1.

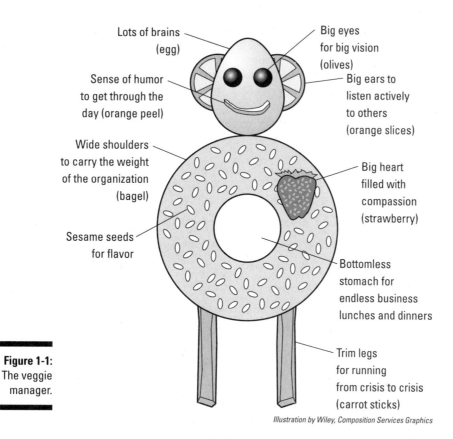

Lots of brains
(egg)

Big eyes
for big vision
(olives)

Sense of humor
to get through the
day (orange peel)

Big ears to
listen actively
to others
(orange slices)

Wide shoulders
to carry the weight
of the organization
(bagel)

Big heart
filled with
compassion
(strawberry)

Sesame seeds
for flavor

Bottomless
stomach for
endless business
lunches and dinners

Figure 1-1:
The veggie
manager.

Trim legs
for running
from crisis to crisis
(carrot sticks)

Illustration by Wiley, Composition Services Graphics

The result was kind of cute (and kind of tasty, too), but did it really make a difference in the way these managers managed their employees when they returned to the office the next day? Doubt it. Was the seminar a nice break from the day-to-day office routine? Yes. Was it a meaningful teaching tool with lasting impact? No.

Partnering with your employees

Managers today face yet another challenge — one that has shaken the foundations of modern business. The new reality is partnering managers and workers in the workplace.

Originally, management meant dividing the company's work into discrete tasks, assigning the work to individual workers, and then closely monitoring the workers' performance and steering them in the right direction to accomplish their tasks on time and within budget.

The old reality of management often relied on fear, intimidation, and power over people to accomplish goals. If things weren't going according to management's plan, management simply commanded its way out of the problem: "I don't care what you have to do to get it done — just get it done. Now!" The line between managers and workers was drawn clearly and drawn often.

In the new business environment, what's going on inside the organization is a reflection of what's going on outside the organization. The following factors are creating rapid and constant change in today's new business environment:

- ✔ A surge of global competition
- ✔ New technology and innovation
- ✔ The flattening of organizational hierarchies
- ✔ A global economic downturn, with widespread cost cutting and layoffs
- ✔ The rise of small business
- ✔ The changing values of today's workers
- ✔ A more diverse pool of employees
- ✔ Increasing demands for better customer service

Sure, managers still have to divide and assign work, but workers are taking on more of that responsibility. Most important, managers are finding out that they can't command their employees' best work — they have to create an environment that fosters their employees' desire to do their best work. In short, the new reality is the partnership of managers and workers in the workplace.

The landscape of business worldwide has changed dramatically during the past few decades. If you don't change with it, you're going to be left far behind your competitors. You may think that you can get away with treating your employees like "human assets" or children, but you can't. You can't, because your competitors are discovering how to unleash the hidden power of their employees. They're no longer just talking about it; they're doing it!

Being open to new ideas and procedures

A few years ago, one of this book's authors made a presentation to a group of high-tech managers. As he was wrapping up his presentation, he opened the floor to questions. A hand shot up. "With all the downsizing and layoffs we've endured, people are lucky to get a paycheck, much less anything else.

Why do we have to bother to empower and reward employees?" Before
he had a chance to respond, another manager in the audience shot back,
"Because it's a new army."

This response really sums it all up. In business, times are changing. Now
that employees have tasted the sweet nectar of empowerment, you can't
turn back. Companies that stick with the old way of doing business — the
hierarchical, highly centralized model — will lose employees and customers to companies that make the new ways of doing business a part of their
corporate culture. The best employees will leave the old-model companies in
droves, seeking employers who will treat them with respect and who are
willing to grant them greater autonomy and responsibility.

That leaves you with the employees who don't want to take risks or rock
the boat. You get the yes-men and yes-women. No one will challenge your
ideas — they'll be afraid to. No one will suggest better or more efficient ways
to do business because they know that you won't listen or care anyway. Your
employees won't bother to go out of their way to help a customer because
you don't trust them to make the most basic decisions — the ones that can
make the biggest difference to the satisfaction, or the lack thereof, of your
precious customers.

Imagine the difference between an employee who tells your key customer,
"Sorry, my hands are tied. I'm not allowed to make any exceptions to our
policies," and the employee who tells that customer, "Sure, I'll do everything in my power to get you your order by your deadline." Which type of
employee do you think your customers prefer to do business with? Which
type of employee do you prefer to do business with?

Managers used to rent behavior. Some workers were even called "hired
hands." Today hiring your hands isn't good enough. You must find a way to
engage their souls and bring their best efforts to the workplace each day.

Establishing two-way trust

Companies that provide exceptional customer service unleash their
employees from the constraints of an overly controlling hierarchy and
allow front-line workers to serve their customers directly and efficiently.
For many years, Nordstrom, Inc., devoted exactly one page to its employee
manual, shown in Figure 1-2.

> We're glad to have you with our Company. Our number one goal is to provide outstanding customer service.
>
> Set both your personal and professional goals high.
>
> Nordstrom Rules:
>
> Rule #1: Use your good judgement in all situations.
>
> There will be no additional rules. Please feel free to ask your department manager, store manager, or division general manager any question at any time.

Figure 1-2: Nordstrom's rules show an exceptional amount of trust in employees.

Source: *Business and Society Review, Spring 1993, n85*

Today employees also receive a standard employee handbook — the company's legal environment has changed considerably — but this one page still guides most employee behavior at the company. You may think that a *small* company with five or ten employees can get away with a similar policy, but certainly not a big company like yours. However, Nordstrom isn't a small business by any stretch of the imagination.

How does management at a large business like Nordstrom get away with such a policy? They do it through trust.

First, Nordstrom hires good people. Second, the company gives them the training and tools to do their jobs well. Then management gets out of the way and lets the employees do their work. Nordstrom knows that it can trust its employees to make the right decisions because the company knows that it has hired the right people for the job and has trained them well.

We're not saying that Nordstrom doesn't have problems — every company does. But Nordstrom has taken a proactive stance in creating the environment that employees most need and want.

Can you say the same for your organization?

When you trust your employees, they respond by being trustworthy. When you recognize them for being independent and responsive to their customers, they continue to be independent and responsive to their customers. And when you give them the freedom to make their own decisions, they more often than not make good ones. With a little training and a lot of support, these decisions back up the best interests of the company because the right people at the right level of the organization make them.

Mastering the New Functions of Management

Remember the four classic functions of management — plan, organize, lead, and control — that you learned in school? (Yeah, a lot of managers were asleep in that class, too.) These management functions form the foundation from which every manager works. Although these basic functions are fine for taking care of most of your day-to-day management duties, they fail to reflect the new reality of the workplace and the new partnership of managers and workers.

What today's managers need is a new set of functions that build upon the four classic functions of management. You're in luck. The sections that follow describe the functions of the manager in the 21st-century workplace.

Energize

Today's managers are masters of making things happen — starting with themselves. As the saying goes, "If it's to be, it's to begin with me."

Think of the best managers you know. What one quality sets them apart from the rest? Is it their organizational skills, their fairness, or their technical ability? Perhaps their ability to delegate or the long hours they keep set them apart.

All these traits may be important to a manager's success, but none of them is the unique quality that makes a good manager great. The most important management function is to get people excited and inspired — that is, to *energize* them.

Great managers create far more energy than they consume. The best managers are organizational catalysts. Instead of taking energy from an organization, they channel and amplify it to the organization. In every interaction, effective managers add to the natural energy of their employees and leave the employees in a higher energy state than when they started the interaction. Management becomes a process of transmitting the excitement that you feel about your organization and its goals to your employees in terms that they can understand and appreciate. And it's a process of getting their ideas and, where appropriate, their buy-in for even more success. Before you know it, your employees will be as excited about the organization as you are, and you can simply allow their energy to carry you forward.

A picture is worth a thousand words. This statement is as true for the pictures that you paint in the minds of others as for the pictures that people paint on canvas or print on the pages of magazines and books. Imagine taking a vacation with your family or friends. As the big day draws near, you keep the goal exciting and fresh in the minds of your family or friends by creating a vision of the journey that awaits you. Vivid descriptions of white-sand beaches, towering redwoods, glittering skylines, secluded lakes, hot food, and indoor plumbing paint pictures in the minds of each of your fellow travelers. With this vision in mind, everyone works toward a common goal of a successful vacation.

Successful managers create compelling visions — pictures of a future organization that inspire and compel employees to bring out their best performance.

Empower

Have you ever worked for someone who didn't let you do your job without questioning your every decision? Maybe you spent all weekend working on a special project, only to have your boss casually discard it: "What were you thinking when you did this? Our customers will never buy into that approach!" Or maybe you went out of your way to help a customer, accepting a return shipment of an item against company policy, and got a response like this: "Why do you think we have policies — because we enjoy killing trees? If we made exceptions for everyone, we'd go out of business!" How did it feel to have your sincere efforts at doing a great job disparaged? What was your reaction? Chances are you won't bother making the extra effort again.

Despite rumors to the contrary, when you empower your employees, you don't stop managing. What changes is the way you manage. Managers still provide vision, establish organizational goals, and determine shared values. However, managers must establish a corporate infrastructure — skills training, teams, and so on — that supports empowerment. And although all your employees may not want to be empowered, you still have to provide an environment that supports employees who are eager for a taste of the freedom to apply their personal creativity and expertise to your organization.

Great managers allow their employees to do great work. This role is a vital function of management because even the greatest managers in the world can't succeed all by themselves. To achieve the organization's goals, managers depend on their employees' skills. Effective management means leveraging the efforts of every member of a work unit to focus on a common purpose. If you're constantly doing your employees' work for them, not only have you lost the advantage of the leverage your employees can provide you, but also you're putting yourself on the path to stress, ulcers, and worse.

However, far worse than the personal loss that you suffer when you don't empower employees is that everyone in your organization loses. Your employees lose because you aren't allowing them to stretch themselves or to show creativity or initiative. Your organization loses the insights that its creative workforce brings with it. Finally, your customers lose because your employees are afraid to provide them with exceptional service. Why should they, if they're constantly worried that you will punish them for taking initiative or for pushing the limits of the organization to better serve your customers?

As William McKnight, former CEO of manufacturing giant 3M, put it, "The mistakes people make are of much less importance than the mistakes management makes if it tells people exactly what to do."

Support

A manager's job is not that of a watchdog, police officer, or executioner. Increasingly, managers must be coaches, colleagues, and cheerleaders for the employees they support. The main concern of today's managers needs to be shaping a more supportive work environment that enables each employee to feel valued and be more productive.

When the going gets tough, managers support their employees. Now, this doesn't mean that you do everything for your employees or make their decisions for them. It does mean that you give your employees the training, resources, and authority to do their jobs, and then you get out of the way. You're always there for your employees to help pick up the pieces if they fall, but fall they must if they're going to learn. The idea is the same as in learning to skate: If you're not falling, you're not learning.

The key to creating a supportive environment is establishing trust or *openness* throughout an organization. In an open environment, employees can bring up questions and concerns. In fact, they're encouraged to do so. When the environment is truly open, an individual can express concerns without fear of retribution. Hidden agendas don't exist, and people feel free to make the same remarks in business meetings that they'd say after work. When employees see that their managers are receptive to new ideas, they're more likely to feel invested in the organization and to think of more and better ways to improve systems, solve problems, save money, and better serve customers.

Managers also support each other. Guarding personal fiefdoms, fighting between departments, and withholding information have no place in the modern organization; companies cannot afford to support these dysfunctional behaviors. All members of the organization, from top to bottom, must realize that they play on the same team. To win, team members must support each other and keep their co-workers apprised of the latest information. Which team are you on?

Communicate

Without a doubt, communication is the lifeblood of any organization, and managers are the common element that connects different levels of employees. Almost everyone has experienced firsthand the positive effects on a business and its employees when managers communicate — and the negative effects when managers don't. Managers who don't communicate effectively are missing out on a vital role of management.

Information is power, and as the speed of business accelerates, information must be communicated to employees faster than ever. Constant change and increasing turbulence in the business environment necessitate more communication, not less. (The topic of change is the focus of Book VI.) Who's going to be around in five years: the manager who has mastered this function or the one who has not?

With the proliferation of e-mail, voicemail, text messages, tweets, and the other means of communication in modern business, managers simply have no excuse not to communicate with their employees. You can even use the telephone or try a little old-fashioned face-to-face talk with your employees and coworkers!

To meet the expectations you set for them, your employees have to be aware of your expectations. A goal is great on paper, but if you don't communicate it to employees and don't keep them up-to-date on their progress toward achieving that goal, how can you expect them to reach it? You can't. It's like training for the Olympics but never getting feedback on how you're doing against the competition.

Employees often appreciate the little things — an invitation to an upcoming meeting, praise for a job well done, or an insight into the organization's finances. Not only does sharing this kind of information make a business run better, but also it creates tremendous goodwill and cements the trust that bonds your employees to the organization and to the successful completion of the organization's goals.

Taking the First Steps toward Becoming a Manager

Many managers are never formally trained to be managers; it's just something that's added to their job description. One day you may be a computer programmer working on a hot new web browser, and the next day you may be in charge of the new development team. Before, you were expected only to show up to work and create a product. Now you're expected to lead and motivate a group of workers toward a common goal. Sure, you may get paid more to do the job, but the only training you may get for the task is in the school of hard knocks.

Managers (or managers-to-be) can easily discover how to become good managers by following the recommendations in the sections that follow. No one way is absolutely right or absolutely wrong; each has its pluses and minuses.

Look and listen

If you're fortunate enough to have had a skilled teacher or mentor during the course of your career, you've been treated to an education in management that's equal to or better than any MBA program. You've learned firsthand the right and wrong ways to manage people. You've learned what it takes to get things done in your organization, and you've learned that customer satisfaction involves more than simply giving your customers lip service.

Unfortunately, any organization with good management also has living, breathing examples of the wrong way to manage employees. You know the people we're talking about: the manager who refuses to make decisions, leaving employees and customers hanging. Or the boss who refuses to delegate even the simplest decision to employees. Or the supervisor who insists on managing every single aspect of a department, no matter how small or inconsequential. Examples of the right way to manage employees are, regrettably, still few and far between.

 You can benefit from the behaviors that poor managers model. When you find a manager who refuses to make decisions, for example, carefully note the impact that the management style has on workers, other managers, and customers. You feel your own frustration. Make a mental note: "I'll never, ever demotivate another person like that." Indecision at the top inevitably leads to indecision within all ranks of an organization — especially when employees are punished for filling the vacuum left by indecisive managers. Employees become confused, and customers become concerned as the organization drifts aimlessly.

Observe the manager who depends on fear and intimidation to get results. What are the real results of this style of management? Do employees look forward to coming to the office every day? Are they all pulling for a common vision and goal? Are they extending themselves to bring innovation to work processes and procedures? Or are they more concerned with just getting through the day without being yelled at? Think about what you would do differently to get the results you want.

You can always learn something from other managers, whether they're good managers or bad ones.

Do and learn

Perhaps you're familiar with this old saying (attributed to Lao Tze):

> Give a man a fish, and he eats for a day,
>
> Teach a man to fish, and he eats for a lifetime.

Such is the nature of managing employees. If you make all the decisions, do the work your employees are able to do when given the chance, and try to carry the entire organization on your own shoulders, you're harming your employees and your organization far more than you can imagine. Your employees never find out how to succeed on their own, and after a while, they quit trying. In your sincere efforts to bring success to your organization, you stunt your employees' growth and make your organization less effective and vital.

Simply reading a book (even this one) or watching someone else manage — or fail to manage — isn't enough. To take advantage of the lessons you learn, you have to put them into practice. Keep these key steps in mind:

1. **Take the time to assess your organization's problems.** Which parts of your organization work and which don't? Why or why not? You can't focus on all your problems at once. Concentrate on a few problems that are the most important, and solve them before you move on to the rest. If issues exist across client or business groups, schedule time to discuss them with key stakeholders and idea-share to resolve problems.

2. **Take a close look at yourself.** What do you do to help or hinder your employees when they try to do their jobs? Do you give them the author-ity to make decisions? Just as important, do you support them when they go out on a limb for the organization? Study your personal inter-actions throughout your business day. Do they result in positive or negative outcomes?

   If you haven't had a personality/management assessment done, consider it. If you decide to move forward with one, budget for it and schedule a follow-up meeting after it is conducted to discuss the results.

3. **Try out the techniques that you learn from reading or from observing other managers at work.** Nothing changes if you don't change first. "If it's to be, it's to begin with me."

4. **Step back and watch what happens.** You'll see a difference in the way you get tasks done and in the way your customers and employees respond to your organization's needs and goals — promise!

Chapter 2

Setting Goals as a Manager

· ·

In This Chapter

▶ Linking goals to your organization's vision

▶ Creating SMART goals

▶ Concentrating on fewer goals

▶ Publicizing your goals

▶ Following through with your employees

▶ Determining sources of power

· ·

*I*f you created a list of the most important duties of management, "setting goals" would likely be near the top. In most companies, senior management sets the overall purpose — the vision — of the organization. Middle managers then have the job of developing goals and plans for achieving the vision senior management sets. Managers and employees work together to set goals and develop schedules for attaining them.

As a manager, you're probably immersed in goals — not only for yourself, but also for your employees, your department, and your organization. This flood of goals can cause stress and frustration as you try to balance the relative importance of each one.

You're likely to find yourself struggling with questions of priorities, especially as you get accustomed to your new role: "Should I tackle my department's goal of improving turnaround time first, or should I get to work on my boss's goal of finishing the budget? Or maybe the company's goal of improving customer service is more important. Well, I think I'll just try to achieve my own personal goal of setting aside some time to eat lunch today."

As you discover in this chapter, sometimes having too many goals is as bad as not having any goals. This chapter helps you understand why setting strong, focused goals is essential to your success and that of your employees. We also guide you in communicating visions and goals and keeping both yourself and your employees on track to meet established goals.

Goals provide direction and purpose. If you can see it, you can achieve it. Goals help you see where you're going and how you can get there. And the *way* you set goals can impact how motivating they are to others.

Knowing Where You're Going

Believe it or not, Lewis Carroll's classic book *Alice in Wonderland* offers lessons that can enhance your business relationships. Consider the following passage, in which Alice asks the Cheshire Cat for advice on which direction to go.

> "Would you tell me, please, which way I ought to go from here?"
>
> "That depends a good deal on where you want to go," said the Cat.
>
> "I don't much care where — " said Alice.
>
> "Then it doesn't matter which way you go," said the Cat.
>
> " — so long as I get *somewhere,*" Alice added as an explanation.
>
> "Oh, you're sure to do that," said the Cat, "if you only walk long enough."

It takes no effort at all to get *somewhere.* Just do nothing, and you're there. However, if you want to get somewhere meaningful and succeed as a manager, you first have to know where you want to go. And after you decide where you want to go, you need to make plans for how to get there. This practice is as true in business as in your everyday life.

For example, suppose that you have a vision of starting up a new sales office in Prague so that you can better service your Eastern European accounts. How do you go about achieving this vision? You have three choices:

✔ An unplanned, non-goal-oriented approach

✔ A planned, goal-oriented approach

✔ A hope and a prayer

Which choice do you think is most likely to get you to your goal? Go ahead, take a wild guess!

If you guessed the unplanned, non-goal-oriented approach to reaching your vision, shame on you! Please report to study hall. Your assignment is to write 500 times, "A goal is a dream with a deadline." Now, no talking to your class-mates and no goofing off. We've got our eyes on you!

If you guessed the planned, goal-oriented approach, you've earned a big gold star and a place in the new-manager Hall of Fame. Congratulations!

Following are the main reasons to set goals whenever you want to accomplish something significant:

- ✔ **Goals provide direction.** For the preceding example (starting up a new sales office in Prague), you can probably find a million different ways to better serve your Eastern European business accounts. However, to get something done, you have to set a definite vision — a target to aim for and to guide the efforts of you and your organization. You can then translate this vision into goals that take you where you want to go.

  Without goals, you're doomed to waste countless hours going nowhere. With goals, you can focus your efforts and your team's efforts on only the activities that move you toward where you're going — in this case, opening a new sales office.

- ✔ **Goals tell you how far you've traveled.** Goals provide milestones to measure how effectively you're working toward accomplishing your vision. If you determine that you must accomplish several specific milestones to reach your final destination and you complete a few of them, you know exactly how many remain. You know right where you stand and how far you have yet to go.

- ✔ **Goals help make your overall vision attainable.** You can't reach your vision in one big step — you need many small steps to get there. If, again, your vision is to open a new sales office in Prague, you can't expect to proclaim your vision on Friday and walk into a fully staffed and functioning office on Monday. You must accomplish many goals — from shopping for office space, to hiring and relocating staff, to printing stationery and business cards — before you can attain your vision.

  Goals enable you to achieve your overall vision by dividing your efforts into smaller pieces that, when accomplished individually, add up to big results.

- ✔ **Goals clarify everyone's role.** When you discuss your vision with your employees, they may have some idea of where you want to go but no idea of how to go about getting there. As your well-intentioned employees head off to help you achieve your vision, some employees may duplicate the efforts of others, some employees may focus on the wrong strategies and ignore more important tasks, and some employees may simply do something else altogether (and hope that you don't notice the difference).

  Setting goals with your team clarifies what the tasks are, who handles which tasks, and what is expected from each employee and from the entire team.

✔ **Goals give people something to strive for.** People are typically more motivated when challenged to attain a goal that's beyond their normal level of performance — this is known as a *stretch goal*. Not only do goals give people a sense of purpose, but also they relieve the boredom that can come from performing a routine job day after day. Be sure to discuss a goal with your employees and seek feedback where appropriate to gain their commitment and buy-in.

For goals to be effective, they have to link directly to the manager's final vision. To stay ahead of the competition — or simply to maintain their current position in business — organizations create compelling visions, and then management and employees work together to set and achieve the goals to reach those visions. (If you're going to be involved in setting a vision for your organization, or if you're just curious how that process happens, be sure to check out Chapter 3 in Book II.)

Check out the following examples of compelling visions that drive the development of goals at several successful enterprises. (These visions are perhaps even more important as the companies fight for competitive advantage in the face of depressed telecommunications and technology sectors.)

✔ Samsung is a Korea-based manufacturer of electronics, chemicals, and heavy machinery, as well as a provider of architectural and construction services. Samsung's vision is to lead the digital convergence movement; this vision drives the organization's goals.

✔ Motorola, long known for its obsession with quality, has set a target of no more than two manufacturing defects per billion parts produced.

✔ A century ago, the chairman of AT&T created a vision for the organization comprising good, cheap, and fast worldwide telephone service. AT&T's vision today is "to be the most admired and valuable company in the world."

When it comes to goals, the best ones

✔ Are few in number but very specific and clear in purpose.

✔ Are stretch goals — they're attainable, but they aren't too easy or too hard.

✔ Involve people. When you involve others in a collaborative, team-based process, you get buy-in so it becomes their goal, not just yours.

Identifying SMART Goals

You can find all kinds of goals in all types of organizations. Some goals are short-term and specific ("Starting next month, we will increase production by two units per employee per hour"); others are long-term and vague ("Within the next five years, we will become a learning organization"). Employees easily understand some goals ("Line employees will have no more than 20 rejects per month"), but other goals can be difficult to measure and subject to much interpretation ("All employees are expected to show more respect to each other in the next fiscal year"). Still other goals can be accomplished relatively easily ("Reception staff will always answer the phone by the third ring"), whereas others are virtually impossible to attain ("All employees will master the five languages that our customers speak before the end of the fiscal year").

How do you know what kind of goals to set? The whole point of setting goals, after all, is to achieve them. It does you no good to go to the trouble of calling meetings, hacking through the needs of your organization, and burning up precious time only to end up with goals that aren't acted on or completed. Unfortunately, this scenario describes what far too many managers do with their time.

The best goals are *smart* goals — actually, *SMART* is the acronym to help you remember them. SMART refers to a handy checklist for the five characteristics of well-designed goals:

- ✔ **Specific:** Goals must be clear and unambiguous; broad and fuzzy thinking has no place in goal setting. When goals are specific, they tell employees exactly what's expected, when, and how much. Because the goals are specific, you can easily measure your employees' progress toward their completion.

- ✔ **Measurable:** What good is a goal that you can't measure? If your goals aren't measurable, you never know whether your employees are making progress toward their successful completion. Not only that, but your employees may have a tough time staying motivated to complete their goals when they have no milestones to indicate their progress.

- ✔ **Attainable:** Goals must be realistic and attainable by average employees. The best goals require employees to stretch a bit to achieve them, but they aren't extreme. That is, the goals are neither out of reach nor set too low. Goals that are set too high or too low become meaningless, and employees naturally come to ignore them.

✔ **Relevant:** Goals must be an important tool in the grand scheme of reaching your company's vision. You may have heard that 80 percent of workers' productivity comes from only 20 percent of their activities. You can guess where the other 80 percent of work activity ends up! This relationship comes from Italian economist Vilfredo Pareto's 80/20 rule. This rule, which states that 80 percent of the wealth of most countries is held by only 20 percent of the population, has been applied to many other fields since its discovery. Relevant goals address the 20 percent: the workers' activities that have such a great impact on performance and bring your organization closer to its vision, thereby making it, and you, a success.

✔ **Time-bound:** Goals must have starting points, ending points, and fixed durations. Commitment to deadlines helps employees manage competing priorities and focus their efforts on completing the goal on or before the due date. Goals without deadlines or schedules for completion tend to be overtaken by the day-to-day crises that invariably arise in an organization.

SMART goals make for smart organizations. Many supervisors and managers neglect to work with their employees to set goals together. And for the ones that do, goals are often unclear, ambiguous, unrealistic, immeasurable, uninspiring, and unrelated to the organization's vision. By developing SMART goals with your employees, you can avoid these traps while ensuring the progress of your organization and your team.

Although the SMART system of goal setting provides guidelines to help you frame effective goals, you have additional considerations to keep in mind. The following considerations help you ensure that anyone in your organization can easily understand and act on the goals you and your employees agree on.

✔ **Ensure that goals are related to your employees' role in the organization.** Pursuing an organization's goals is far easier for employees when those goals are a regular part of their jobs and they can see how their contributions support the company. For example, suppose that you set a goal for employees who solder circuit boards to raise production by 2 percent per quarter. These employees spend almost every working moment pursuing this goal because the goal is an integral part of their job. However, if you give the same employees a goal of "improving the diversity of the organization," what exactly does that have to do with your line employees' role? Nothing. The goal may sound lofty and may be important to your organization, but because your line employees don't make the hiring decisions, you're wasting both your time and theirs with that particular goal.

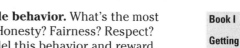

✓ **Whenever possible, use values to guide behavior.** What's the most important value in your organization? Honesty? Fairness? Respect? Whatever it is, ensure that leaders model this behavior and reward employees who live it.

✓ **Make your goals simple.** The easier your goals are to understand, the more likely the employees are to work to achieve them. Goals should be no longer than one sentence; make them concise, compelling, and easy to read and understand. Simple goals are better goals.

Goals that take more than a sentence to describe are actually multiple goals. When you find multiple-goal statements, break them into several individual, one-sentence goals. Goals that take a page or more to describe aren't really goals; they're books. File them away and try again.

Setting Goals: Less Is More

When one organization had determined that it needed to develop a long-range strategic plan — strategic planning was "in" at the time and seemed like a good thing to do — the entire management team was marshaled for this effort. The team scheduled several all-day planning sessions, retained a high-priced consultant, and announced to the staff that something major was brewing at the top.

The management team threw itself wholeheartedly into the planning effort. The managers wanted to answer questions like the following:

✓ Why did the organization exist?

✓ Who were its customers?

✓ What were its values?

✓ What was its mission?

✓ What were its goals?

✓ How could the organization know when it achieved the goals?

Session after session, they had great idea after great idea. Before long, they had more than 12 poster-sized flip chart pages taped to the walls of the meeting room, each brimming with goals for the organization. "Improve customer service." "Provide quicker project turnaround." "Fix the heating and air conditioning system at corporate headquarters." And many more — in all, more than 200!

When the last planning meeting ended, the managers congratulated each other over their collective accomplishment and went back to their regular office routines. Before long, the goals were forgotten, the pages on which they were recorded neatly folded and stored away in someone's file cabinet. Meanwhile, business went on as usual, and the long-range planning effort went into long-term hibernation. Soon the organization's employees who knew that the management team had embarked on a momentous process of strategic planning finally tired of asking about it.

Don't let all your hard work be in vain. When you go through the exercise of setting goals, keep them to a manageable number that can realistically be followed up on. And when you finish one goal, move on to the next.

When it comes to goal setting, less is more. The following guidelines can help you select the right goals — and the right number of goals — for your organization:

- ✔ **Pick two or three goals to focus on.** You can't do everything at once — at least, not well — and you can't expect your employees to, either. Attempt to complete only a few goals at any one time. Setting too many goals dilutes the efforts of you and your staff and can result in a complete breakdown in the process.

- ✔ **Pick the goals with the greatest relevance.** Certain goals bring you a lot closer to attaining your vision than do other goals. Because you have only so many hours in your workday, it clearly makes sense to concentrate your efforts on a few goals that have the biggest payoff rather than on a boatload of goals with relatively less impact to the business.

- ✔ **Focus on the goals that tie most closely to your organization's mission.** You may be tempted to take on goals that are challenging, interesting, and fun to accomplish but that are far removed from your organization's mission. Don't do it.

- ✔ **Regularly revisit the goals and update them as necessary.** Business is anything but static, and regularly assessing your goals is important in making sure that they're still relevant to the vision you want to achieve. Put in quarterly or midyear review schedules. If the goals remain important, great — carry on. If not, meet with your employees to revise the goals and the schedules for attaining them.

Avoid creating too many goals in your zeal to get as many things done as quickly as you can. Too many goals can overwhelm you — and they can overwhelm your employees, too. You're far better off setting a few significant goals and then concentrating your efforts on attaining them. Don't forget that management isn't measured by one huge success after another. Instead, it involves successfully meeting daily challenges and opportunities — gradually but inevitably improving the organization in the process.

Communicating Your Vision and Goals to Your Team

Having goals is great, but how do you get the word out to your employees? As you know, goals should align with the organization's vision. Establishing goals helps you ensure that employees focus on achieving the vision in the desired time frame and with the desired results. You have many possible ways to communicate goals to your employees, but some ways are better than others. In every case, you must communicate goals clearly, the receiver must understand the goals, and the relevant parties must follow through on achieving the goals.

Communicating your organization's vision is as important as communicating specific goals. You can communicate the vision in every way possible, as often as possible, throughout your organization and to significant others such as clients, customers, suppliers, and so forth. Be aware of possible obstacles, too: Often an organization's vision is pounded out in a series of grueling management meetings that leave the participants (you, the managers!) beaten and tired. By the time the managers reach their final goal of developing a company's vision, they're sick of it and ready to go on to the next challenge.

Many organizations drop the ball at this crucial point and are thereby slow to communicate the vision. Also, each succeeding layer of an organization tends to siphon off some of the vision's energy, so by the time it filters down to the front-line employees, the vision has become dull and lifeless.

When you communicate vision and goals, do it with energy and a sense of urgency and importance. You're talking about the future of your organization and your employees, not the score of last night's game! If your team doesn't think that you care about the vision, why should they? Simply put, they won't.

Companies usually announce their visions to employees — and the public — in ways that are designed to maximize the impact. Companies commonly communicate their vision in these ways:

- ✔ By conducting huge employee rallies where the vision is unveiled in inspirational presentations

- ✔ By branding their vision on anything possible — business cards, letterhead stationery, massive posters hung in the break rooms, newsletters, employee name tags, and more

- ✔ By proudly emblazoning their vision statements within corporate websites; on Facebook fan pages; and via electronic media campaigns, Twitter tweets, and other Internet-enabled methods of communication

- ✔ By mentioning the corporate vision in newspaper, radio, television, and other media interviews

- ✔ By encouraging managers to "talk up" the vision in staff meetings or other verbal interactions with employees and during recruiting

To avoid a cynical "fad" reaction from employees who may already be suspicious of management's motives when unveiling a new initiative, making consistent, casual, and genuine reference to it is much more effective than hosting a huge, impersonal event. Again, in this case, less is often better.

Unlike visions, goals are much more personalized to the department or individual employees, and you must use more formal and direct methods to communicate them. The following guidelines can help:

- ✔ **Write down your goals.**

- ✔ **Conduct one-on-one, face-to-face meetings with your employees to introduce, discuss, and assign goals.** If physical distance prohibits this or you can't conduct a face-to-face meeting, conduct your meeting over the phone. The point is to make sure that your employees hear the goals, understand them and your expectations, and have the opportunity to ask for clarifications.

- ✔ **Call your team together to introduce team-related goals.** You can assign goals to teams instead of solely to individuals. If this is the case, get the team together and explain the role of the team and each individual in the successful completion of the goal. Make sure that all team members understand exactly what they are to do and whether a leader or co-leaders are ultimately responsible for the goals' completion. Get employee buy-in and try to make the goals resonate with each person.

- ✔ **Gain the commitment of your employees, whether individually or on teams, to work toward the successful accomplishment of their goals.** Ask your employees to prepare and present plans and milestone schedules explaining how they can accomplish the assigned goals in the agreed-upon timeline. After your employees begin working on their goals, regularly monitor their progress to ensure that they're on track, and collaborate with them to resolve any problems.

Juggling Priorities: Keeping Your Eye on the Ball

After you decide what goals are important to you and your organization, you come to the difficult part. How do you, the manager, maintain the focus of your employees — and yourself, for that matter — on achieving the goals you've set?

The process of goal setting can generate excitement and engage employees in the inner workings of the business, whether the goals are set individually or by department or function. This excitement can quickly evaporate, though, when employees return to their desks. You, the manager, must take steps to ensure that the organization's focus remains centered on the agreed-upon goals, not on other matters (which are less important but momentarily more pressing). Of course, this task is much easier said than done.

Staying focused on goals can be extremely difficult — particularly when you're a busy person and the goals compound your regular responsibilities. Think about situations that demand your attention during a typical day at work:

✔ How often do you sit down at your desk in the morning to prioritize your day, only to have your priorities completely changed five minutes later when you get a call from your boss?

✔ How many times has an employee unexpectedly come to you with a problem?

✔ Have you ever gotten caught in a so-called quick meeting that lasts for several hours?

In unlimited ways, you or your employees can get derailed and lose the focus you need to get your organization's goals accomplished. One of the biggest problems employees face is confusing activity with tangible results. Do you know anyone who works incredibly long hours — late into the night and on weekends — but never seems to get anything done? These employees always seem busy, but they're working on the wrong things. This is called the *activity trap,* and it's easy for you and your employees to fall into.

Remember the general rule that 80 percent of workers' productivity comes from 20 percent of their activity? The flip side of this rule is that only 20 percent of workers' productivity comes from 80 percent of their activity. This statistic illustrates the activity trap at work. What do you do in an average day? More important, what do you do with the 80 percent of your time that produces so few clear results? You can get out of the activity trap and take control of your schedules and priorities. However, you have to be tough, and you have to single-mindedly pursue your goals.

Achieving your goals is all up to you. No one, not even your boss (perhaps *especially* not your boss), can make it any easier for you to concentrate on achieving your goals. You have to take charge and find an approach that works for you. If you aren't controlling your own schedule, you're simply letting everyone else control your schedule for you.

Following are some tips to help you and your employees get out of the activity trap:

- ✔ **Complete your top-priority task first.** With all the distractions that compete for your attention, with the constant temptation to work on the easy stuff first and save the tough stuff for last, and with people dropping into your office just to chat or to unload their problems on you, concentrating on your top-priority task is always a challenge. However, if you don't do your top priority first, you're almost guaranteed to find yourself caught in the activity trap. That is, you'll find the same priorities on your list of tasks to do day after day, week after week, and month after month. If your top-priority task is too large, divide it into smaller chunks and focus on the most important piece first.

- ✔ **Get organized.** Getting organized and managing your time effectively are both incredibly important pursuits for anyone in business. If you're organized, you can spend less time trying to figure out what you should be doing and more time just doing it.

- ✔ **Just say no.** If someone tries to make his problems your problems, just say no! If you're a manager, you probably like nothing more than taking on new challenges and solving problems. However, the conflict arises when solving somebody else's problems interferes with your own work. You have to fight the temptation to lose control of your day. Always ask yourself, "How does this help me achieve my goals?"

Using Your Power for Good: Making Your Goals Reality

After you create a set of goals with your employees, how do you make sure they get done? How do you turn your priorities into your employees' priorities? The best goals in the world mean nothing if they aren't achieved. You can choose to leave this critical step to chance or you can choose to get involved.

You have the power to make your goals happen. Power has gotten a bad rap lately. In reaction to the highly publicized leadership styles that signified greed and unethical behavior in American corporations, employees have increasingly demanded — and organizations are recognizing the need for — management that is principle centered and has a more compassionate, human face.

Nothing is inherently wrong with power — everyone has many sources of power. Not only do you have power, but you also exercise power to control or influence people and events around you on a daily basis (in a positive way, we hope). Generally, well-placed power is a positive thing. However, power can be a negative thing when abused or when someone acts in only self-interest. Manipulation, exploitation, and coercion have no place in the modern workplace.

You can use your positive power and influence to your advantage — and to the advantage of the people you lead — by tapping into it to help achieve your organization's goals. People and systems often fall into ruts or non-productive patterns of behavior that are hard to break. Power properly applied can redirect people and systems and move them in the right direction — the direction that leads to the accomplishment of goals.

Everyone has five primary sources of power, as well as specific strengths and weaknesses related to these sources. Recognize your strengths and weaknesses and use them to your advantage. As you review the five sources of power that follow, consider your own personal strengths and weaknesses.

- **Personal power:** This is the power that comes from within your character. Your passion for greatness, the strength of your convictions, your ability to communicate and inspire, your personal charisma, and your leadership skills all add up to personal power.

- **Relationship power:** Everyone has relationships with people at work. These interactions contribute to the relationship power that you possess in your organization. Sources of relationship power include close friendships with top executives, partners, owners, people who owe you favors, and coworkers who provide you with information and insights that you wouldn't normally receive.

- **Knowledge power:** To see knowledge power in action, just watch what happens the next time your organization's computer network goes down. You'll see who really has the power in your organization — in this case, your computer network administrator. Knowledge power comes from the special expertise and knowledge gained during the course of your career. Knowledge power also comes from obtaining academic degrees (think MBA) or special training.

✔ **Task power:** Task power is the power that comes from the job or process you perform at work. As you've probably witnessed, people can facilitate or impede the efforts of their coworkers and others by using their task power. For example, when you submit a claim for payment to your insurance company and months pass with no action ("Gee, we don't seem to have your claim in our computer — are you sure you submitted one? Maybe you should send us another one just to be safe!"), you're on the receiving end of task power.

✔ **Position power:** This kind of power derives strictly from your rank or title in the organization and is a function of the authority that you wield to command human and financial resources. Whereas the position power of the receptionist in your organization is probably quite low, the position power of the chairman, president, or owner is at the top of the position power chart. The best leaders seldom rely on position power to get things done today.

If you identify weakness in certain sources of power, you can strengthen them. For example, work on your weakness in relationship power by making a concerted effort to know your coworkers better and to cultivate relationships with higher-ranking managers or executives. Instead of passing on the invitations to get together with your coworkers after work, join them — have fun and strengthen your relationship power at the same time.

Be aware of the sources of your power and use your power in a positive way to help you and your employees accomplish the goals of your organization. For getting things done, a little power can go a long way.

Chapter 3

Embracing Corporate Social Responsibility

Corporate social responsibility — CSR, for short — is a way of doing business that's rapidly gaining popularity in the United States and around the world. *Corporate social responsibility* means conducting your business in a way that has a positive impact on the communities you serve. As you discover in this chapter, CSR affects many different aspects of operating a business — from recycling, to ethics, to environmental laws, and much more.

Ethics and office politics are powerful forces in any organization. *Ethics* is the framework of values that employees use to guide their behavior. You've seen the devastation that poor ethical standards can lead to — witness the string of business failures attributed to less than sterling ethics in more than a few large, seemingly upstanding businesses. Today more than ever, managers are expected to model ethical behavior, to ensure that their employees follow in their footsteps, and to purge the organization of employees who refuse to align their own standards with the standards of their employer.

At its best, *office politics* means the relationships that you develop with your coworkers — both up and down the chain of command — that enable you to get tasks done, stay informed about the latest goings-on in the business, and form a personal network of business associates for support throughout your career. Office politics help ensure that all employees work in the best interests of their coworkers and the organization. At its worst, office politics can degenerate into a competition, with employees concentrating their efforts on trying to increase their personal power at the expense of other employees — and their organizations.

This chapter looks at adopting a corporate social responsibility strategy, determining the nature and boundaries of your political environment, and building an ethical organization.

Understanding Socially Responsible Practices

CSR has been gaining traction within businesses of all kinds in recent years. At one time, CSR was the sole province of socially progressive companies like ice cream maker Ben & Jerry's and organic yogurt manufacturer Stonyfield Farm, but this is no longer the case. Today even the largest, most conservative companies — including Walmart, ExxonMobil, General Electric, and McKesson — have adopted CSR practices and strategies.

Depending on the exact approach you take and how you implement it, you may have to spend a significant amount of money to conduct your business in a socially responsible way, but the benefits nearly always outweigh the costs. People want to buy products and services from companies that are socially responsible and that are making a positive impact on their communities. What's more, they want to *work for* companies that are socially responsible and that are making a positive impact on their communities. Finally, becoming a socially responsible company can actually reduce costs. For these reasons and others like them, CSR is taking the business world by storm.

Figuring out how you can employ CSR

CSR involves conducting your business in a way that has a positive impact on the communities you serve. But what exactly does that look like in the real world? Consider some of the traits of a socially responsible business:

- ✔ It takes responsibility for the conditions in which its products are manufactured, whether in this country or internationally, and whether by the company itself or by subcontractors.

- ✔ It promotes recycling; environmental responsibility; and using natural resources in more efficient, productive, and profitable ways.

- ✔ It views employees as assets instead of costs and engages them in their jobs by involving them in decision-making. In the event of layoffs or job eliminations, it is viewed as a company that treats people fairly.

- ✔ It's committed to diversity in hiring and selection of vendors, board members, and advisers.

✔ It adopts strong internal management and financial controls.

✔ It meets or exceeds all applicable social and environmental laws and regulations.

✔ It supports its communities through volunteerism, philanthropy, and local hiring.

✔ It promotes sustainability — that is, meeting the needs of the present without compromising the ability of future generations to meet their needs.

As a manager, you may be tasked with helping to develop your company's CSR goals. If that's the case, the exact goals you select must be aligned with both your company's core business objectives and its core competencies. Some of the traits in the preceding list may or may not fit with your company's culture, objectives, or competencies. To be effective, your approach to CSR must make sense for your company and its employees, customers, and other stakeholders.

Consider for a moment the six Guiding Principles that coffee purveyor Starbucks embraces. As you can see, the company's Guiding Principles strongly influence its CSR strategy:

✔ Provide a great work environment and treat each other with respect and dignity.

✔ Embrace diversity as an essential component in the way we do business.

✔ Apply the highest standards of excellence to the purchasing, roasting, and fresh delivery of our coffee.

✔ Develop enthusiastically satisfied customers all the time.

✔ Contribute positively to our communities and our environment.

✔ Recognize that profitability is essential to our future success.

Enjoying net benefits of socially responsible practices

The best corporate social responsibility is tightly integrated into a company's business operations; this strong connection can have a positive impact on the bottom line. Many CSR activities can reduce the cost of doing business while drawing new customers into the company's orbit, increasing the top line. The younger generation of employees now entering the workplace wants to make a difference in the world, too. Companies that practice CSR are more attractive to these talented men and women, who will remain loyal to their employers as long as they continue to have an opportunity to make a difference.

Adopting a corporate social responsibility strategy offers benefits that include the following:

- ✔ **Attracting and retaining employees:** Providing employees avenues for greater satisfaction and higher engagement means that you create a more attractive workplace.

- ✔ **Promoting customer loyalty:** Given the option between a company that they view as responsible and one that makes no similar efforts, customers choose the company that shows good corporate citizenship.

- ✔ **Becoming more efficient:** Taking steps toward environmentally responsible measures like greater energy efficiency also reduces operating costs.

Long story short, adopting socially responsible business practices is a net benefit to the companies that adopt them. Why not try them in your organization and see what happens? You'll likely be pleasantly surprised with the results.

Developing a CSR strategy for implementation

Adopting corporate social responsibility in an effective manner requires developing a strategy for its implementation. The spectrum of possible CSR initiatives available to a company is mind-boggling. You can start with a barebones approach — say, replacing disposable (and environmentally unfriendly) Styrofoam coffee cups with washable and infinitely reusable porcelain coffee mugs — or you can go all the way to a multiphase international CSR strategy that touches every part of your organization and has a direct and significant impact on the world.

It's better to address the immediate needs of your customers before you try to solve all the problems of the world. Customer needs often boil down to the most basic of human needs: safety, love and belonging, self-esteem, and self-actualization. If you can address these needs, you'll have a customer for life.

When developing your own CSR strategy, consider that it must be

- ✔ **Authentic and in alignment with your goals.** Your CSR strategy must ring true for your organization. The best way to ensure that this is the case is to closely match it to your company's mission, vision, and values. Employees, customers, and others will know when it's not authentic, and your CSR strategy won't have the desired effect. And if it doesn't match what you do, it's off course. For example, if you're manufacturing children's clothing, supporting an organization that works to feed hungry children makes more sense than one that aids veterans.

✔ **Simple and easy to express.** Be sure that everyone in your organization knows what your CSR strategy and goals are and that they can express them consistently to one another — and to the general public. Your CSR efforts are multiplied when they're clear and straightforward and when everyone in your company has a clear understanding of their role.

✔ **Inclusive.** Your CSR strategy isn't worth the paper it's written on if you haven't engaged your employees in the process of developing and implementing it. Instead of forcing a CSR strategy on your employees, invite their active participation in creating it and then rolling it out. You'll get better results, and your employees will be pleased that you thought highly enough about them to involve them in the process.

✔ **Part of your company's story.** When you have your CSR strategy in place, don't be afraid to publicize your efforts to be socially responsible along with your successes. Again, many people (including prospective customers, clients, and employees) are attracted to companies that operate in a socially responsible way. If you don't get out the word about your programs, you'll lose this powerful advantage. So tell your story — as often as you can — to your employees and to the general public. Use company newsletters and brochures, your website, and social media.

 Above all, don't spend hours, days, or weeks laboring over a CSR strategy, only to file it away and forget all about it. Integrate your strategy into your everyday business operations. In this way, you'll gain the full benefit of corporate social responsibility — a benefit that can give you a distinct competitive advantage in the marketplace.

Evaluating the Political Side of Your Workplace

How political is your office or workplace? As a manager, having your finger on the political pulse of the organization is particularly important. Truth be told, although it may make perfect sense to do something new or different in an organization, you often have to convince a decision maker to make a change. This task is easier if you're politically savvy and have a good handle on your political environment.

Embarking on the path of corporate social responsibility may make good sense for a variety of different reasons, but you've got to sell it to your boss. And she has to sell it to her boss. Getting in touch with the office politics at play can make you more effective, and it can help your department and your employees have a greater impact within the organization.

Assessing your organization's political environment

Asking insightful questions of your coworkers is one of the best ways to quickly assess your organization's political environment. You can often get the inside scoop from coworkers who have been around for a while. You'll also quickly discover whether you need to avoid organizational taboos or hot buttons. Give these questions a try:

✔ "What's the best way to get a nonbudget item approved?"

✔ "How can I get a product from the warehouse that my client needs today when I don't have time to do the paperwork?"

✔ "Can I do anything else for you before I go home for the day?"

Although asking savvy questions gives you an initial indication of the political lay of the land in your organization, you can do more to assess the office politics. Watch for the following signs while you're getting a sense of how your organization really works:

✔ **Find out how others who seem to be effective get tasks done.** How much time do they spend preparing before sending through a formal request for a budget increase? Which items do they delegate and to whose subordinates? When you find people who are particularly effective at getting tasks done in your organization's political environment, model their behavior.

✔ **Observe how others are rewarded for the jobs they do.** Does management swiftly and enthusiastically bestow warm and personal rewards in a sincere manner to clearly show what behavior is important? Does management give credit to everyone who helped make a project successful, or does only the manager get his picture in the company newsletter? By observing your company's rewards, you can tell what behavior management expects of employees in your organization. Practice this behavior.

✔ **Observe how others are disciplined for the jobs they do.** Does management come down hard on employees for relatively small mistakes? Are employees criticized in public or in front of coworkers? Is everyone held accountable for decisions, actions, and mistakes even if they had no prior involvement? Such behavior indicates that management doesn't encourage risk taking. If your organization is risk averse, maintain an outwardly reserved political style as you work behind the scenes.

✔ **Consider how formal the people in the organization are.** When you're in a staff meeting, for example, you definitely show poor form if you blurt out, "That's a dumb idea. Why would we even consider doing such a thing?" Instead, buffer and finesse your opinions like so: "That's an interesting possibility. Could we explore the pros and cons of implementing that?" The degree of formality you find in your company indicates how you need to act to conform to the expectations of others.

Identifying key players

When you've discovered that you work in a political environment (did you really have any doubt in your mind?), you need to determine who the key players are. They are the individuals who can help you move your corporate social responsibility goals forward. They can also provide positive models of ethical behavior for you and your employees to follow and emulate. Key players are the politically astute individuals who make things happen in an organization.

Some key players are at the top of the organization, as you may expect. However, you'll find key players at every level — not just the top. For example, as the department head's assistant, Jack may initially appear to be nothing more than a gofer. However, you may later find out that Jack is responsible for scheduling all his boss's appointments, setting agendas for department meetings, and vetoing actions on his own authority. Jack is an informal leader in the organization, and because you can't get to your boss without going through Jack, you know that Jack has much more power in the organization than his title indicates.

All the following factors are indicators that can help you identify the key players in your organization:

- ✔ Which employees in your organization do others seek out for advice?

- ✔ Which employees do others consider to be indispensable?

- ✔ Whose office is located closest to those of the organization's top management, and whose office is located miles away?

- ✔ Who eats lunch with the president, the vice presidents, and other members of the upper management team?

As you figure out who the key players in your organization are, you start to notice that they have different office personalities. Use the following categories to figure out how to work with the different personality types of your organization's key players. Do you recognize any of these players in your organization?

- ✔ **Movers and shakers:** These individuals usually far exceed the boundaries of their office positions. For example, you may find a mover and shaker who's in charge of purchasing but who's also helping to negotiate a merger. Someone in charge of the physical plant may have the power to designate a wing of the building to the group of her choosing.

✔ **Corporate citizens:** These employees are diligent, hardworking, company-loving people who seek slow but steady, long-term advancement through dedication and hard work. Corporate citizens are great resources for getting information and advice about the organization. You can count on them for help and support, especially if your ideas are in the best interest of the organization.

✔ **The town gossips:** These employees always seem to know what's going on in the organization — usually before the individuals who are actually affected by the news know it. Assume that anything you say to these individuals will get back to the person about whom you say it.

✔ **Firefighters:** These individuals relish stepping into a potential problem with great fanfare at the last conceivable moment to save a project, client, deadline, or whatever. Keep these people well informed of your activities so that you aren't the subject of the next "fire."

✔ **Vetoers:** These people in your organization have the authority to kill your best ideas and ambitions with a simple comment such as, "We tried that and it didn't work." The best way to deal with vetoers is to keep them out of your decision loop. Try to find other individuals who can get your ideas approved, or rework the idea until you hit upon an approach that satisfies the vetoer.

✔ **Techies:** Every organization has technically competent workers who legitimately have a high value of their own opinions. Experts can take charge of a situation without taking over. Get to know your experts well — you can trust their judgments and opinions.

✔ **Whiners:** A few employees are never satisfied with whatever is done for them. Associating with them inevitably leads to a pessimistic outlook, which you can't easily turn around. Worse, your boss may think that you're a whiner, too. In addition, pessimistic people tend to be promoted less often than optimists. Be an optimist: Your optimism makes a big difference in your career and in your life.

Redrawing your organization chart

Your company's organization chart may be useful for determining who's who in the formal organization, but it really has no bearing on who's who in the informal political organization. What you need is the real organization chart.

Start by finding your organization's official organization chart — the one that looks like a pyramid; see Figure 3-1 for an example. Throw it away. Now, from your impressions and observations, start outlining the real relationships in your organization. Begin with the key players whom you've already identified. Indicate their relative power by level and relationships by approximation. Use the following questions as a guideline:

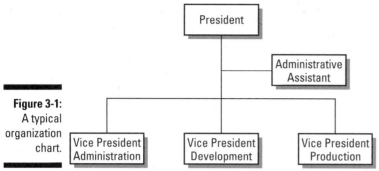

Figure 3-1:
A typical
organization
chart.

Illustration by Wiley, Composition Services Graphics

✓ **Whom do these influential people associate with?** Draw the associations on your chart and connect them with solid lines. Also connect friends and relatives.

✓ **Who makes up the office cliques?** Be sure that all members are connected because talking to one is like talking to them all.

✓ **Who are the office gossips?** Use dotted lines to represent communication without influence and solid lines for communication with influence.

✓ **Who's your competition?** Circle those employees likely to be considered for your next promotion. Target them for special attention.

✓ **Who's left off the chart?** Don't forget about these individuals. The way today's organizations seem to change every other day, someone who is off the chart on Friday may be on the chart on Monday. Always maintain positive relationships with all your coworkers, and never burn bridges between you and others within the company. Otherwise, you may find yourself left off the chart someday.

The result of this exercise is a chart of who really has political power in your organization and who doesn't. Figure 3-2 shows how the organization may really work. Update your organization chart as you find out more information about people. Of course, understand that you may be wrong. You can't possibly know the inner power relationships of every department. Sometimes individuals who seem to have power may have far less of it than people who have discovered how to exhibit their power more quietly.

Be genuine and respectful in your quest to understand your company's politics. If you're seen as someone who's two-faced or untrustworthy, someone who aligns with the power players for a while and then moves on, you ultimately won't be trusted or rewarded for your political savvy.

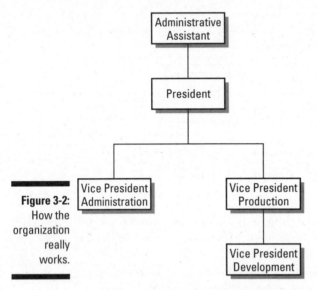

Figure 3-2:
How the
organization
really
works.

Illustration by Wiley, Composition Services Graphics

Doing the Right Thing: Ethics and You

Each year or two, the leaders of some company somewhere trigger a huge scandal due to some ethical lapse. These lapses are often so egregious that you wonder whether anyone in charge knows the difference between right and wrong — or, if they do know the difference, whether they really care.

Despite appearances to the contrary, many business leaders do know the difference between right and wrong. Now more than ever, businesses and the leaders who run them are trying to do the right thing, not just because the right thing is politically correct, but also because it's good for the bottom line.

Defining ethics on the job

Do you know what ethics are? In case you're a bit rusty on the correct response, the long answer is that ethics are standards of beliefs and values that guide conduct, behavior, and activities — in other words, a way of thinking that provides boundaries for our actions. The short answer is that ethics are simply doing the right thing.

Although all people come to a job with their own sense of ethical values — based on their upbringing and life experiences — organizations and leaders are responsible for setting clear ethical standards.

When you have high ethical standards on the job, you generally exhibit some or all of the following personal qualities and behaviors:

- ✔ Accountability
- ✔ Dedication
- ✔ Fairness
- ✔ Honesty
- ✔ Impartiality
- ✔ Integrity
- ✔ Loyalty
- ✔ Responsibility

Ethical behavior starts with you. As a manager, you're a leader in your organization, and you set an example — both for other managers and for the workers who are watching your every move. When others see you behaving unethically, you're sending the message loud and clear that ethics don't matter. The result? Ethics won't matter to them, either.

However, when you behave ethically, others follow your example and behave ethically, too. And if you practice ethical conduct, it also reinforces and perhaps improves your own ethical standards. As a manager, you have a responsibility to try to define, live up to, and improve your own set of personal ethics.

Creating a code of ethics

Although most people have a pretty good idea about what kinds of behavior are ethical and what kinds of behavior aren't, ethics are somewhat subjective and open to interpretation by the individual employee. For example, one worker may think that making unlimited personal phone calls from the office is okay, while another worker may consider that behavior to be inappropriate.

So what's the solution to ethics that vary from person to person in an organization? A code of ethics.

By creating and implementing a code of ethics, you clearly and unambiguously spell out for all employees — from the very top to the very bottom — your organization's ethical expectations. A code of ethics isn't a substitute for company policies and procedures; the code complements them. Instead of leaving your employees' definition of ethics on the job to chance — or someone's upbringing — you clearly spell out that stealing, sharing trade secrets, sexually harassing a coworker, and engaging in other unethical behavior is unacceptable and may be grounds for dismissal. And when you require your employees to read and sign a copy acknowledging their acceptance of the code, your employees can't very well claim that they didn't know what you expected of them. The ethics policy should be reviewed and agreed to annually so that it remains top-of-mind for all employees.

Four key areas form the foundation of a good code of ethics:

- ✔ Compliance with internal policies and procedures
- ✔ Compliance with external laws and regulations
- ✔ Direction from organizational values
- ✔ Direction from individual values

A code of ethics isn't worth the paper it's printed on if it doesn't address some very specific issues, as well as the more generic ones listed previously. The following are some of the most common issues addressed by typical codes of ethics:

- ✔ Conflicts of interest
- ✔ Diversity
- ✔ Employee health and safety
- ✔ Equal opportunity
- ✔ Gifts and gratuities
- ✔ Privacy and confidentiality
- ✔ Sexual harassment

In addition to working within an organization, a well-crafted code of ethics can be a powerful tool for publicizing your company's standards and values to people outside your organization, including vendors, clients, customers, investors, potential job applicants, the media, and the general public. Your code of ethics tells others that you value ethical behavior and that it guides the way you and your employees do business.

Of course, simply having a code of ethics isn't enough. You and your employees must also live it. Even the world's best code of ethics does you no good if you file it away and never use it.

Checking out a sample code of ethics

Because of the nature of the public trust they are charged with (they're spending our tax dollars, after all!), government workers have long been held to a higher standard of ethical behavior than employees in private industry. The U.S. Congress adopted this Code of Ethics for Government Service on July 11, 1958 (and it's still just as valid today).

Any person in government service should:

1. Put loyalty to the highest moral principles and to country above loyalty to Government persons, party, or department.

2. Uphold the Constitution, laws, and legal regulations of the United States and of all governments therein and never be a party to their evasion.

3. Give a full day's labor for a full day's pay; giving to the performance of his duties his earnest effort and best thought.

4. Seek to find and employ more efficient and economical ways of getting tasks accomplished.

5. Never discriminate unfairly by the dispensing of special favors or privileges to anyone, whether for remuneration or not; and never accept for himself or his family, favors or benefits under circumstances which might be construed by reasonable persons as influencing the performance of his governmental duties.

6. Make no private promises of any kind binding upon the duties of office, since a Government employee has no private word, which can be binding on public duty.

7. Engage in no business with the Government, either directly or indirectly, which is inconsistent with the conscientious performance of his governmental duties.

8. Never use any information coming to him confidentially in the performance of governmental duties as a means for making private profit.

9. Expose corruption wherever discovered.

10. Uphold these principles, ever conscious that public office is a public trust.

Making ethical choices every day

You may have a code of ethics, but if you never behave ethically in your day-to-day business transactions and relationships, what's the purpose of having a code in the first place? Ethical challenges abound in business — some are spelled out in your company's code of ethics, or in its policies and procedures, and some aren't. For example, what would you do in these situations?

- One of your favorite employees gives you tickets to a baseball game.

- An employee asks you not to write her up for a moderate infraction of company policies.

- You sold a product to a client that you later found out to be faulty, but your boss wants you to forget about it.

- Your department's financial results are actually lower than what appears in your boss's presentation to the board of directors.

- You find out that your star employee actually didn't graduate from college, as he claimed in his job application.

- You know that a product you sell doesn't actually do everything your company claims it does.

We all make ethical choices on the job every day — how do you make yours? Consider this framework comprising six keys to making better ethical choices:

- **Evaluate** circumstances through the appropriate filters. (Filters include culture, laws, policies, circumstances, relationships, politics, perception, emotions, values, bias, and religion.)

- **Treat** people and issues fairly within the established boundaries. *Fair* doesn't always mean *equal*.

- **Hesitate** before making critical decisions.

- **Inform** those affected of the standard or decision that has been set.

- **Create** an environment of consistency for yourself and your working group.

- **Seek** counsel when you have any doubt (but from those who are honest and whom you respect).

Chapter 4

Managing with Technology

· ·

· ·

*Y*ou've gotta love technology. Unfortunately, like everything else in life, technology has its good and bad points. On the upside, computers make our work lives much easier and more efficient. As long as your computer doesn't crash, it remembers everything you've done forever and makes completing repetitive tasks (like merging a letter with a 1,000-person mailing list) a snap. On the downside, computers can be an enormous waste of time. Instead of working, some people spend a significant portion of their workdays checking their Facebook accounts, bidding on items on eBay, and keeping track of the latest celebrity gossip.

You may automatically assume that your employees are more productive because they have computers at their fingertips, but are you (and your organization) really getting the most out of innovative and expensive technology? Given how much money most companies invest in their information technology systems, hardware, and software, that can be a million-dollar question. Or more.

In this chapter, you find out how to harness information technology — technology used to create, store, exchange, and use information in its various forms. What you find here helps you examine the technology edge and consider how technology can help or hinder an organization. You consider how technology can improve efficiency and productivity, how to get the most out of it, and how to create a technology plan.

Weighing the Benefits and Drawbacks of Technology in the Workplace

Think for a moment about the incredible progress of information technology just in your lifetime. With so many tools at your fingertips, can you believe that only about three decades ago the personal computer hadn't yet been introduced commercially? Word processing used to mean a typewriter and a lot of correction fluid or sheets of messy carbon paper; computers have revolutionized the way businesspeople can manipulate text, graphics, and other elements in their reports and other documents. Mobile telephones, fax machines, the Internet, broadband wireless connections, and other business technology essentials are all fairly recent innovations.

You can't turn back the clock on technology. To keep up with the competition — and beat it — you must keep pace with technology and adopt tools that can make your employees more productive, while improving products and services, customer service, and the bottom line. You really have no other choice.

Making advances, thanks to automation

Information technology can have a positive impact on your business in two important ways, both related to the practice of automation:

- **By automating processes:** Not too many years ago, business processes were manual. For example, your organization's accounting and payroll departments may have calculated payroll entirely by hand with the assistance of only a ten-key adding machine. What used to take hours, days, or weeks can now be accomplished in minutes or even seconds. Other processes that are commonly automated are inventory tracking, customer service call analysis, and purchasing.
- **By automating personal management functions:** More managers than ever are moving their calendars and personal planners onto computers. Although paper-based planners aren't going to die completely, many managers are finding that computers are much more powerful management tools than their unautomated counterparts. Managers also use computers to schedule meetings, track projects, analyze numbers, manage business contact information, conduct employee performance evaluations, and more.

Before you run off and automate everything, keep this piece of information in mind: If your manual system is inefficient or ineffective, simply automating the system isn't necessarily going to make your system perform any better. In fact, automating it can make your system perform worse than the manual version. When you automate, review the process in detail. Cut out any unnecessary steps and make sure your system is optimized for the new, automated environment. The time you take now to improve your processes and functions is going to pay off when you automate.

Improving efficiency and productivity

The recent explosion of information technology accompanies the shift in industry from old-line standards, such as steel mills and petroleum refineries, to companies producing semiconductors, computers, and related products. The personal computer industry, which was still in its infancy three decades ago, has quickly grown into a market worth many billions of dollars in annual sales.

The idea that businesspeople who best manage information have a competitive advantage in the marketplace seems obvious enough. The sooner you receive information, the sooner you can act on it. The more effectively you handle information, the easier you can access that information when and where you need it. The more efficiently you deal with information, the fewer expenses you incur for managing and maintaining your information.

Management often cites the preceding reasons, and others like them, as justification for spending obscenely huge amounts of corporate resources to buy computers, install e-mail and voicemail systems, and train employees to use these tools of the Information Age. But have all these expenditures made your own workers more productive? If not, perhaps you aren't taking the right approach to implementing information technology within your business.

Before spending the money, a manager should take time to identify the questions that need an answer and to consider the following:

- ✔ Who needs the answer (customer, supplier, employee, management)?
- ✔ How fast do they need the answer (real time, one minute, one hour, one day)?
- ✔ How frequently do they need the answer (daily, weekly, monthly)?

When the answers to these questions become clear, you have a rational basis for evaluating alternate technologies based on how well they meet the criteria needed for your "answers." A lot of technology seems to be designed to provide a real-time answer to a question that needs to be asked only once a month.

When planned and implemented wisely, information technology can improve an organization's efficiency and productivity. Recent studies are beginning to show a relationship between the implementation of information technology and increased productivity. Examples like the following bear out this relationship:

- ✔ Implementing a computerized inventory-management system at Warren, Michigan–based Duramet Corporation — a manufacturer of powdered metal and part of the Cerametal Group — helped the company double sales over a three-year period without hiring a single new salesperson.

- ✔ By using information technology to provide employees with real-time information about orders and scheduling that cuts through the traditional walls within the organization, M.A. Hanna Company, a manufacturer of polymers that merged with Geon Company to form PolyOne Corporation, reduced its working capital needs by a third to achieve the same measure of sales.

- ✔ At Weirton Steel Corporation based in Weirton, West Virginia, which became part of Mittal Steel, the company found that it needed only 12 people to run the hot mill that once required 150 people to operate, all because of the efficiencies gained as a result of new technology installed in the production line.

Although evidence is beginning to swing toward productivity gains, studies indicate that merely installing computers and other information technology doesn't automatically lead to gains in employee efficiency. As a manager, you must take the time to improve your work processes before you automate them. If you don't, office automation can actually lead to decreases in employee efficiency and productivity. Instead of the usual lousy results that you get from your manual, unautomated system, you end up with something new: garbage at the speed of light. Don't let your organization make the same mistake!

Taking steps to neutralize the negatives

Just as information technology can help a business, it can also hinder it. Consider a few examples of the negative side of information technology:

- ✔ Widespread worker abuse of Internet access has reduced worker productivity by 10 to 15 percent. According to Forrester Research, 20 percent of employee time on the Internet at work doesn't involve their jobs. A study by Nucleus Research found that employee use of Facebook at work causes a 1.5 percent decrease in employee productivity all by itself.

✔ Hackers have sent periodic waves of computer viruses and malicious attacks through the business world, leaving billions of dollars of damage and lost productivity in their wake.

✔ E-mail messages can be unclear and confusing, forcing workers to waste time clarifying their intentions or covering themselves in case of problems.

✔ Employees are forced to wade through an ever-growing quantity of spam and junk e-mail messages.

✔ The slick, animated, and sound-laden computer-based full-color presentations so common today can take longer to prepare than the simple text and graphs that were prevalent a few years ago — especially if you're not technologically savvy.

You have to take the bad with the good. But don't take the bad lying down. You can maximize the positives of information technology while minimizing the negatives:

✔ **Stay current on the latest information innovations and news.** You don't need to become an expert on how to install a network server or configure your voicemail system, but you do need to become conversant in the technology behind your business systems.

✔ **Hire experts.** Although you must have a general knowledge of information technology, plan to hire experts to advise you in the design and implementation of critical information technology–based systems.

✔ **Manage by walking around.** Make a habit of dropping in on employees — wherever they're located — and observe how they use your organization's information technology. Solicit their feedback and suggestions for improvement. Research and implement changes as soon as you discover the need.

Using Technology to Your Advantage

Information technology touches every aspect of our lives — at home and at work. Computers and telecommunications technology are essential tools for any business. Even the most defiant, old-school CEOs are taking the plunge and becoming attached to their smartphones. Information technology can give you and your business tremendous advantages. As a manager, you must capitalize on them — before your competition does.

Before you act, you must become technology savvy. In the next sections, we recommend the four basic ways for doing just that.

Know your business

Before you can design and implement information technology in the most effective way, you have to completely understand how your business works. What work is being done? Who's doing it? What do employees need to get their work done?

One way to know your business is to approach it as an outsider. Pretend you're a customer and see how your company's people and systems handle you. Do the same with your competitors to see how their people and systems handle you. What are the differences? What are the similarities? How can you improve your own organization using information technology as a result of what you've discovered?

Create a technology-competitive advantage

Few managers understand how technology can become a competitive advantage for their businesses. They may have vague notions of potential efficiency gains or increased productivity, but they're clueless when dealing with specifics.

Information technology can create real and dramatic competitive advantages over other businesses in your markets, specifically by doing the following:

- ✔ Competing with large companies by marketing on a level playing field (the Internet)
- ✔ Helping to build ongoing, loyal relationships with customers
- ✔ Connecting with strategic partners to speed up vital processes, such as product development and manufacturing
- ✔ Linking everyone in the company, as well as with necessary sources of information both inside and outside the organization
- ✔ Providing real-time information on pricing, products, and so forth to vendors, customers, and original equipment manufacturers (OEMs)

Now is the time to create advantages over your competition. Keep in mind that the winner isn't the company that *has* the most data, but the company that *manages* that data best.

Develop a plan

If you're serious about using information technology as an edge, you must have a plan for its implementation. When it comes to the fast-changing area of technology, having a *technology plan* — a plan for acquiring and deploying information technology — is a definite must. Many businesses buy bits and pieces of computer hardware, software, and other technology without considering the technology that they already have in place and without looking very far into the future. Then when they try to hook everything together, they're surprised that their thrown-together system doesn't work.

Managers who take the time to develop and implement technology plans aren't faced with this problem, and they aren't forced to spend far more money and time fixing the problems with their systems.

Technology is no longer an optional expense; it's a strategic investment that can help push your company ahead of the competition. And every strategic investment requires a plan. In their book *eBusiness Technology Kit For Dummies* (Wiley), Kathleen Allen and Jon Weisner recommend that you take the following steps in developing your technology plan. (Find out more about general goal-setting in Chapter 2 of this Book.)

1. **Write down your organization's core values.**

   For example, some of your core values may be to provide customers with the very best customer service possible or to always act ethically and honestly.

2. **Picture where you see your business ten years from now. Don't limit yourself.**

   Will you be in the same industry or perhaps some new ones? What products and services will you offer, and to whom will you offer them? Will you be a small business or a large multinational corporation with global reach and influence? How many employees will you have? 1,000? 10,000? 100,000?

3. **Set a major one-year goal for the company that is guided by your vision.**

   This goal may be to create a system that tracks customer service complaints and gets them in front of the company's management team in real time.

4. **List some strategies for achieving the goal.**

   A strategy to achieve the preceding one-year goal might be to assign an employee team to work with your IT department to develop a set of recommended solutions within three months.

5. Brainstorm some tactics that can help you achieve your strategies.

Specific tactics to achieve the preceding strategy may include assigning responsibility for the project to a specific employee or manager and setting milestones and deadlines for completion and reporting of results.

6. Identify technologies that support your strategies and tactics.

Provide some guidance by defining the technologies to use in achieving the one-year goal, strategies, and tactics. For example, you may require that any new system work with existing systems or that the new system be web-based.

Gather your thoughts — and your employees' thoughts — and write them down. Create a concise document — perhaps no more than five to ten pages — that describes your information technology strategies as simply and exactly as possible. After you create your plan, screen and select vendors that can help you implement your plan. Close out the process by monitoring performance and adjusting the plan as needed to meet the needs of your organization and employees and to produce optimal performance.

Keep the following points in mind as you navigate the planning process:

✔ **Don't buy technology just because it's the latest and greatest thing.** It's always fun shopping for the latest whiz-bang gizmo. Unfortunately, just because an item is new, has lots of flashing lights, and makes cool noises doesn't mean that it's right for your business. It could be too big or too small, too fast or too slow, too expensive or too cheap. Or it may not even be compatible with the systems you've already got. Be sure that whatever technology you include in your plan makes sense for your business.

✔ **Check in with your IT department.** It's important to make sure your planned purchase will be compatible with existing systems. You also want to find out if your IT department is planning to change directions on how the company infrastructure is set up. You don't want to buy a program in your department that will be obsolete within a couple months.

✔ **Plan for the right period of time.** Different kinds of businesses require different planning *horizons,* the time periods covered by their plans. If you're in a highly volatile market such as wireless communications, your planning horizon may be only six months out. If you're in a more stable market such as a grocery chain, your planning horizon may extend three to five years into the future.

✔ **Consider the benefits of outsourcing.** You may be able to save significant amounts of money by outsourcing appropriate functions to further streamline systems and create efficiencies.

✔ **Make the planning process a team effort.** You're not the only one who's going to be impacted by all this new technology that you bring into your company. Make employees, customers, and vendors a part of your planning team. If you take time to involve them in the process and get their buy-in ahead of time, your technology rollout will go much more smoothly.

✔ **Weigh the costs of upgrading your old system versus going to a new system.** Every system eventually comes to the end of its useful life. Instead of continuing to patch a system that's becoming increasingly expensive to maintain, start fresh. Run the numbers and see what alternative makes the most sense for your organization before you finalize your plans.

Get some help

If you're a fan of technology and pretty knowledgeable about it, that's great — you have a head start on the process. But if you're not, get help from people who are experts in information technology. Does your company have knowledgeable people? Can you hire a technician or technology consultant to fill in the gaps? Whatever you do, don't try it alone. Even if you're a full-fledged techno-geek, recruit others for your cause.

Technology changes incredibly fast and on every front. No one person can be an expert in every aspect of the information technology necessary to run and grow your business.

Getting the Most Out of Company Networks

The personal computer began revolutionizing business a couple decades ago, shifting the power of computing away from huge mainframes and onto the desks of individual users. More recently, computer networks have brought about a new revolution in business. Although the personal computer is a self-sufficient island of information, when you link these islands in a network, individual computers have the added benefit of sharing with every computer on the network.

Does networking have any benefits? You bet it does! See what you think about these:

- ✔ **Networks improve communication.** Computer networks allow anyone in an organization to communicate with anyone else quickly and easily. With the click of a button, you can send messages to individuals or groups of employees. You can send replies just as easily. Furthermore, employees on computer networks can access financial, marketing, and product information to do their jobs from throughout the organization.

- ✔ **Networks save time and money.** In business, time is money. The faster you can get something done, the more tasks you can complete during the course of your business day. E-mail allows you to create messages, memos, and other internal communications; to attach work files; and then to transmit them instantaneously to as many coworkers as you want. Even better, these coworkers can be located across the hall or around the world.

- ✔ **Networks improve market vision.** Information communicated via computer networks is, by nature, timely and direct. In the old world of business communication, many layers of employees filtered, modified, and slowed the information as it traveled from one part of the organization to another. With direct communication over networks, no one filters, modifies, or slows the original message. What you see is what you get. The sooner you get the information that you need and the higher its quality is, the better your market vision can be.

Book II
Embracing Leadership

Five Key Roles That Leaders Play

- ✔ **The truth seeker:** Effective leaders seek the truth and adjust their sights according to what they learn. These leaders know to listen to the meanings of words rather than simply to the words themselves and to extract additional information from between the lines.

- ✔ **The direction setter:** The leader's job is to select and articulate the target in the future toward which the organization should direct its energies. To be a good direction setter you must set a course toward a destination that others will recognize as representing real progress for the organization.

- ✔ **The agent from C.H.A.N.G.E.:** For a leader merely to articulate a vision isn't enough. A good leader also is responsible for being the catalyst in making changes in an organization's internal environment. (Hence the acronym — the action you take Can Have A New Great Effect.) The changes make it possible for the organization to achieve its vision or reach its goals.

- ✔ **The spokesperson:** Being a spokesperson is often a necessary role for a leader of a new enterprise. A leader motivates people who are skeptical, which involves making the impossible seem merely difficult, and the very difficult seem to be just another day's work.

- ✔ **The coach or team builder:** To be an effective coach, you have to let your team know where you stand, what the vision means to you, and what you will do to make it happen. You must also be committed to the success of everyone in the organization, respecting them, helping them learn and grow, and teaching them how to improve constantly their ability to achieve the vision.

Are you ready to play these roles successfully? Assess your current leadership skills with the help of a free article at www.dummies.com/extras/managingaio.

Contents at a Glance

Chapter 1

Tapping into the Brain of a Leader

. . . .

In This Chapter

▶ Discovering the many ways to be intelligent

▶ Taking stock of your own emotional intelligence

▶ Calling on intuition and reason to make decisions

. . . .

A neuroscientist might tell you that your intelligence lies in the top layer of your brain, the *neocortex,* because judgment, decision making, and future planning all reside in this area. Albert Einstein may be the person you think of as the smartest person who ever lived. But his entire neocortex was not larger than average; rather, it was found to be thinner than others. Some specific areas of his brain showed marked differences that many people believe were the source of his genius.

Intelligence in Einstein's brain may be different from the intelligence that you possess. Scientific research suggests something unheard of even a couple decades ago — intelligence isn't fixed. In other words, you can increase your intelligence throughout your life.

This chapter introduces you to various definitions of intelligence and shows you that *how* you are smart may be more important than you think. It takes you through the very important emotional aspect of intelligence, showing you how to train and utilize that side of yourself — and your team members. The information you find here could affect your hiring practices, the makeup of your teams, how you delegate work, and how you make decisions.

Harnessing Multiple Intelligences

When it comes to discovering *how* you are intelligent, a psychologist named Howard Gardner came up with some great ideas. In 1972, Gardner was co-director of Project Zero, a research group at Harvard University that was established in 1967. Project Zero's mission is investigating how organizations, adults, and children develop learning processes. Gardner questioned the singularity of intelligence and searched for evidence that there was more than one way of being intelligent, of knowing.

Gardner proposed a theory of multiple intelligences in 1983. At that time, he anticipated seven intelligences. Later he added an eighth and finally a ninth. The following are the nine intelligences defined by Gardner that are addressed in this chapter:

- Verbal/linguistic
- Mathematical/logical
- Musical/rhythmic
- Visual/spatial
- Bodily kinesthetic
- Naturalist
- Interpersonal
- Intrapersonal
- Philosophical/moral/ethical

Understanding and using multiple intelligences in the workplace can help you see the gifts that your employees bring to the table and assist you in predicting how employees will work together well (and determining why they don't). This information can help you see your own intelligences and understand better how to complement those skills with those of the people you hire and work with.

The temporal intelligences

Language, mathematics, and music relate to either sequencing or timing. Each of these *temporal* ways of knowing relies on the ability to rapidly sequence digits, letters, or notes in a way that shows comprehension and the ability to manipulate these sequences.

Verbal/linguistic intelligence

She was in your leadership class. She took great notes. She wrote the most comprehensive business plan the professor had ever seen. Effortlessly, she took words and created beautiful pictures that everyone understood. You wanted to hate her, but you couldn't. She talked you right out of it. She listened to you, spoke poetically, and helped you write your business plan. Such are the qualities of the verbal/linguistically intelligent person. She could have been a he, by the way. Although females have a brain edge when it comes to language, many men have this intelligence.

People with a high level of linguistic ability succeed at most of the following:

- ✔ Writing reports
- ✔ Analyzing written and verbal information
- ✔ Understanding written and verbal language
- ✔ Telling stories
- ✔ Listening to stories and remembering them
- ✔ Adding humor when they speak
- ✔ Telling jokes
- ✔ Using language that suits the audience
- ✔ Organizing written and verbal information

Mathematical/logical intelligence

Mathematical/logical intelligence involves much more than math. Solving problems in a logical way and being able to communicate that logic, dealing with scientific and technical information, and fixing faulty machinery or products are talents of a person who has this gift. The ability to use logic to perform tasks in a sequential manner and unravel mysteries following a pattern of sequences is an additional trait of this temporal intelligence.

Mathematical/logical people may be political. Politics involves organizing people and laws in a logical manner. The mythical detective Sherlock Holmes had a logical intelligence. Clue-gathering and intuitive reasoning are characteristics of this brainpower.

People high in mathematical/logical intelligence do well with these tasks:

- ✔ Calculating
- ✔ Estimating
- ✔ Measuring
- ✔ Remaining unbiased
- ✔ Using logic
- ✔ Grouping
- ✔ Scientific reasoning
- ✔ Organizing or ordering

- Testing hypotheses
- Reasoning

Musical/rhythmic intelligence

The person with a talent for rhythm and music is an auditory learner. Musical/rhythmic people hear the sounds of your equipment and know when a machine isn't running right. They hear what you say and remember it.

People with musical/rhythmic intelligence often have these abilities or attributes:

- Interpreting changes in sound and pitch
- Working to a rhythm
- Remembering what they hear
- Picking out appropriate music for any audience
- Noticing changes in the buzz of conversation
- Becoming easily distracted
- Picking up foreign languages easily
- Hearing and repeating dialects
- Creating interesting multimedia presentations

If you have this intelligence, you may find that you need to have background music for meetings and for work. You may find yourself overhearing conversations without intending to do so. Distracting sounds may make you irritable because they interrupt your thought processes.

Unless your business is music-related, you're unlikely to have a specific job for the musical/rhythmic person. Not everyone can make a living from songwriting or becoming a disc jockey, and many people use intelligences other than their highest intelligence at work.

The spatial intelligences

Three of the nine intelligences are processed in the right brain hemisphere and deal with spaces and places. Visual/spatial, bodily kinesthetic, and naturalist intelligence are all spatially oriented. The ability to determine where you are in space and where you are going is part of what makes us human. A spatially intelligent brain can comprehend the dynamics of space (visual/spatial), successfully navigate within it (bodily kinesthetic), and differentiate among the objects that occupy space (naturalist).

Visual/spatial intelligence

He flies through the air with the greatest of ease. At least, you hope so. He has you 38,000 feet in the air, and you want him to land the plane safely. You want your pilot — and your surgeon, dentist, architect, and designer — to be high in visual/spatial intelligence. People expect artists, sculptors, and illustrators to have visual/spatial intelligence, but set designers, movie directors, and actors have it, too. Mountain climbers, skate boarders, and dancers all have a high degree of this talent, as well.

Characteristics of visual/spatial intelligence include the following:

- Sensitivity to color, form, and space
- Ability to understand and create visual representations
- Aptitude for reading graphs, charts, and so on
- Preference for things to be in place and pleasing to the eye
- Ability to rotate objects in the mind

Bodily kinesthetic intelligence

Michael Jordan would steal the ball, dribble down the floor, and in a movement that looked like flying, lift his body in the air and gracefully stuff the ball into the basket — an extreme example of bodily kinesthetic intelligence.

Jordan certainly worked hard to develop his body and his skill. Genetics play a part in having the height for basketball, but developing the body and skill requires opportunity, practice, and desire.

Bodily kinesthetic intelligence characteristics are not just about sports. They're about movement: fine motor and gross motor movement. They're about touch and feeling, and navigating your way through space — on a field, in a car, in design, and so on. The following list shows more characteristics of this kind of intelligence:

- Physical endurance
- Flexibility
- Muscle control
- Physical fitness and overall good health
- Fine and gross motor skills

- ✔ Agility and speed
- ✔ Excellence at physical demonstrations
- ✔ Ability to navigate through projects and processes

Naturalist intelligence

The naturalist is a must-have intelligence in any organization that is trying to make the world a greener place. Sensitivity to nature and an understanding of what is happening to the environment are qualities of an intelligence that is gaining respect and admiration. But the naturalist is more. She relates to her surroundings and knows how she fits in — a natural skill for a leader or a follower.

Classifying and categorizing things in nature have long been useful skills for working in museums, zoos, and state parks. Now major corporations are "going green" and need this talent to assist them in making many choices to preserve and serve the environment.

The naturalist may have the following gifts:

- ✔ Interest in nature
- ✔ Ability to classify and categorize things in nature
- ✔ Tendency to collect natural objects
- ✔ Enhanced alertness to the environment
- ✔ Affinity for animals
- ✔ Keen sensory skills
- ✔ Sensitivity to environmental changes
- ✔ Understanding of ecological systems

The naturalist at work is going to be most comfortable in a natural setting, probably outdoors. Short of that, a room with plants, windows, and natural sunlight may suit this person best. The naturalist can add a lot to your organization whether you're in the green movement or not. Perhaps you're the "natural" leader for your business. Or perhaps you need one.

The personal and social intelligences

The entire brain takes part in the personal and social intelligences. The frontal lobes in both the right and left hemispheres are particularly involved in building and maintaining relationships, understanding yourself, and knowing right from wrong.

Interpersonal intelligence

The people in the workplace with high levels of interpersonal intelligence have winning personalities. As part of a team, they usually are the team leaders. When you need someone with good social skills, an awareness of and concern for others, and an ability to relate to people in general, you call on someone with high interpersonal intelligence.

This people person reads others well. Recognizing others' moods, intentions, and motivations, interpersonal people are good negotiators and great friends. Among the characteristics they are known for are the following:

- Valuing relationships
- Collaborating easily
- Sharing their personal stories
- Demonstrating natural leadership ability

Having the ability to negotiate, persuade, and affect the working life of others is one way the interpersonally intelligent brain operates. Mediation skills make this person a good negotiator, counselor, and salesperson.

Intrapersonal intelligence

The person with intrapersonal intelligence knows his own strengths and weaknesses. Having the ability to recognize when to remain in a situation and when to leave reveals a level of intelligence and maturity that belongs in every organization.

Evaluating yourself in relation to your position at work and in life can be a valuable tool for redirecting or reinventing yourself or your career. Recognizing your own feelings and responding to them in a constructive way are attributes of intrapersonal intelligence.

Some characteristics of this intelligence include the following:

- Recognizing your own strengths and utilizing them
- Recognizing your own weaknesses and working on them
- Being able to work alone and enjoy it
- Understanding your own needs
- Knowing how to motivate yourself
- Accepting responsibility for your own successes and failures
- Using feedback to better yourself

To maintain a positive outlook as he deals with the introspection of his life, the intrapersonally intelligent person works on understanding his experiences and how they affect his life. You rarely find people who are guided more by their own values than by the values of others or of society, because so many people are taught to please others.

The ability to direct himself is one reason a person of this intelligence may be very important to your organization. The second reason may be even more important for the 21st century: With jobs changing rapidly, a person who knows a lot about himself can be more easily trained and change positions more easily. Therefore, this type of intelligence can be the most important to have in the global business world.

Philosophical/moral/ethical intelligence

Philosophical/moral/ethical intelligence is the heart of good leadership. Many seemingly strong businesses have fallen under the influence of leaders who lack moral and ethical intelligence. Having ethical leaders, managers, and employees is necessary for any business success.

A morally intelligent person has the following traits:

- Integrity
- Honesty
- Impartiality
- Fairness
- Adherence to ethical policies

Assessing and Applying Your Emotional Intelligence

When Descartes said that the emotions and the intellect were separate, he was wrong. Neuroscientists continually prove that we cannot separate the mind, the body, and emotions.

Emotional intelligence (often referred to as EQ) is the ability to recognize and use your emotions wisely. It's vital for working with others, and it can be learned, nurtured, and enhanced. Your emotional intelligence and that of your workforce can make the difference between success and failure. Working with other emotionally intelligent people is more motivating and fun than working with those with low EQs and high cognitive ability.

Grasping the role of emotions

Cognitive scientists sometimes refer to our emotions as *emotional states*. An emotional state is a combination of thoughts, feelings, and physiology. These states arise from responses to environmental cues. You respond to these cues emotionally, and doing so creates your thoughts. Every thought you think is in response to some level of emotion. Emotions cause you to change your behavior in order to survive. Whether to save yourself physically or socially, your emotions react to the environment you're in.

Reacting to your environment

The fly is buzzing around your picnic table and driving you crazy. You take the kung fu approach and try to catch the fly in your hand as it buzzes by. You fail. You roll up the nearest magazine and swat at the fly but miss. The fly returns, and he seems to be even quicker. That pesky fly has changed his behavior in order to survive. Why does he keep coming back if his life is in danger? Because he has to eat to survive. Instinctively, your fly reacts to the environment, darting and diving to get food and keep from getting squashed.

Book II

Embracing Leadership

It seems like a tough life, but you react in similar ways every day. On a purely survival level, you sprint across the street to keep from getting hit by a truck. On a more cognitive level, you respond in conversation depending on whom you are speaking to: With a close friend, you can throw in some expletives; with your mother-in-law, not so much; and with your superior, you may be very careful in your use of language, context, and tone.

Every action and reaction is the result of an emotional state. The emotional state you're in as you dart out of the truck's path is based on your physiology (your racing heart and blood being pumped to your legs), your thoughts ("Oh, crud, I can't believe I didn't see this coming."), and your feelings ("I don't want to die!").

Social survival

Emotions save your life. You look both ways before crossing the street because you fear death (or because you have your mother's voice inside your head). Social death is another motivator. If a teenager attends a party where alcohol is served and has a drink, she may think, "Please, don't let me get in a car accident tonight or my dad will find out and kill me." Her dad likely isn't a violent man; he isn't going to physically end her life. But she may be grounded if she's found out, and that means social death. Knowing that she shouldn't displease her dad keeps her very cautious — at least about getting caught.

Your emotions often lie at a subconscious level. In every environment, you learn the emotional and then cognitive responses that can help you survive and thrive under those particular circumstances. Some of these responses become so automatic that the reasons you react the way you do never enter your mind. Yet sometimes your purpose is clear, and you respond on a conscious level, using your emotional states as a basis for what is good for you at the time.

Becoming self-aware

Before you can identify and deal with emotions in others, you must begin to recognize and deal with your own emotions. Emotions are present in all relationships. Some emotions save lives, and others can destroy. Although many people think high IQs are the determining factor for success in the business world, some studies show that emotional intelligence is a stronger factor.

Noting your feelings

Can you choose how you feel? Some psychologists believe that you can. First, you must be able to differentiate among emotions. If you can identify your emotions and determine what you think about that mood, you're on your way to truly becoming self-aware. For instance, if you feel yourself becoming angry over a situation and think you may lose control of your actions or behaviors, you can choose your next action to create a better outcome.

Your sense of well-being relies on the emotional balance in your life. An extreme amount of emotion may lead you to poor decision making, poor relationships, and poor self-esteem. When asked to name their emotions, most people list the following in no particular order:

- Happiness
- Sadness
- Anger
- Frustration
- Disgust
- Fear

These six emotions are considered universal emotions. In other words, people around the world experience these emotions and show them with the same kinds of facial expressions. Consider how these emotions affect your performance, relationships, and reactions at work. Can you identify your own strengths and weaknesses? Doing so makes a difference in how you react to situations and to feedback from your employees and your customers.

Your brain's prefrontal cortex is in charge of many executive functions, including attention. Self-awareness involves attending to your feelings — and that includes your physical responses. The prefrontal cortex interacts with areas in the brain related to bodily senses: heart rate, respiration, digestive system, and temperature, to name a few. Awareness that your heart is racing provides information for the prefrontal cortex to determine what you're feeling and how you're reacting to it on a physical level. Armed with this information, you can make some choices as to how you respond to or control the situation.

Other emotional intelligence skills are based on your self-awareness. You are a self-aware leader if the statements that follow are true of you:

✔ I recognize my emotions.

✔ I am in touch with my body and its responses.

✔ I know my strengths and weaknesses.

✔ I understand my goals, dreams, and hopes.

✔ I trust my instincts and usually make good decisions.

✔ My work and my values match.

✔ I am inspired or energized by my work.

✔ I take time to reflect.

If you feel that you aren't good at recognizing your own emotions, try the following:

✔ Make the time to reflect upon your feelings throughout the day. How did you respond to them?

✔ Keep a journal of your feelings.

✔ When someone asks "How are you?" try to give a precise answer related to your current feelings. Instead of the automatic "fine" response, identify your feelings without boring people to death — "I'm curious about this meeting."

✔ Keep a scorecard of your feelings over several weeks. Average those feelings to determine which emotions are most prevalent and how they may affect your relationships.

Using your emotions productively

After you know how to recognize your emotions, you can then work on handling them. Emotional intelligence is not the ability to hide your feelings but rather to use your emotions wisely. Expressing your feelings in a productive way can be the difference between forming lasting relationships and destroying them. The prefrontal cortex of the brain plays a large part in regulating our emotions. However, the prefrontal cortex can also deregulate emotions.

After any instance wherein your emotions take over your focus, take some time to reflect on what was going on inside your head. That inner dialogue was saying something to you that changed your feelings and your mood. Recognizing the reactions helps you gain control over them in the future.

Lack of emotional control can hinder success. Learning to control your emotions in life-threatening situations is difficult, and controlling your emotions under perceived threat may be even more complicated. Some leaders respond to small hurdles as though their survival depended on it. Discovering what you need to do to handle your emotions and your impulses is sometimes a matter of trial and error.

What steps can you take to uncover and handle your emotions? Try the following:

1. **As you scan your work environment, be aware of the people, situations, spaces, and so on, that trigger emotional responses in you.**

   You may find that small meetings held in a cubicle affect your need for space, for example. Suggest the meetings be held elsewhere.

2. **Examine those triggers and learn to recognize them.**

   If you find yourself feeling angry every day at a certain time and you don't know why, take the time to go over any encounters you've had thus far and see whether you can pinpoint the problem.

3. **Determine the appropriate responses to each trigger.**

   As you become aware of repetitious responses, decide how you can control or change the emotional states that result from those environmental triggers.

4. **Make a list of any extraordinary challenges you face.**

   If you find it difficult to recognize and respond more appropriately to some triggers but are unable to avoid those triggers, write down the encounters and try to figure out another approach when you are away from work and no longer emotional about the situation.

5. **Experiment with coping strategies.**

   If you experience chronic stress from these challenges, choose some strategies that have helped you in the past and try each one until you discover what lowers your stress most. For example, exercise, meditation, or stopping by another colleague's office to chat may help you keep your stress levels low. Make time to institute your favorite strategy regularly.

Stress expert and neuroscientist Bruce McEwen refers to the body's adaptive responses to stress as *allostasis*. The body tries to adapt to the stress responses by maintaining balance or homeostasis. With just a little stress, the body produces hormones that improve your memory and help you store important information. Acute or chronic stress hinders these same processes.

If your allostatic load becomes too great, it affects your mood, emotions, and behaviors. For instance, perhaps someone in your personal or professional life suggests that you may be stressed. You don't believe him because you're so used to the load you're carrying that you aren't conscious of your stress level. You think this person is crazy, but then a second person suggests you may need a break. Even though you want to "shoot the messenger," you realize that doing so would just prove that person's point. You decide to give it a try.

High stress levels endanger your health, your relationships with others, and your ability to maintain your vision and reach long-term goals. Stress changes your outlook from long-term to short-term. Getting through the day or through a project is as far-sighted as you can be because stress keeps you in the moment.

Motivating yourself to move toward goals

Motivated people get things done. This emotional intelligence competency includes having both hope and optimism. In this section you find out how to motivate yourself and increase your hope and optimism so that you may model these competencies and teach them to your employees.

The prefrontal cortex, with the assistance of other brain structures, is in charge of self-motivation. Motivation comes from one of two sources: desire or need. If you or your brain feels you need something for your survival, you are motivated to do something about it. If what you're doing has no survival value, then you must desire it.

Your goals, your dreams, and your vision motivate you. With an optimistic outlook, you provide hope for your followers. As your organization works toward your goals, you find yourself hopeful. All of this provides pleasure that activates the reward system in your brain. The neurotransmitter dopamine is released, and it feels good. Because you want to maintain those good feelings, you are motivated to continue. Working toward a goal often is more pleasurable than attaining the goal. By the time you reach the goal, the brain has experienced enough of a reward for that particular accomplishment, and you're on to the next goal with equal determination, drive, and dopamine!

Cultivating hope

Hope influences inspiration and motivation, which in turn move you toward your goals. You have hope when you look forward to attaining your goals. It gives you energy to get the job done. Your hope inspires you, and you inspire those around you.

As an emotionally intelligent person, hope keeps you from backing down in the face of adversity. Hope keeps you from being overcome by depression because of circumstances that affect your goals and vision. Hope keeps you trying.

How do you become or remain hopeful? You *can* learn to motivate yourself. Follow these steps:

1. **Break your goals down into small chunks.**
2. **Focus on accomplishing one chunk until it's finished.**
3. **Celebrate when that chunk is accomplished.**

   Each accomplishment gives you hope that you can achieve more and accomplish not just the next chunk but the entire goal.

Think about how you inspire yourself with hope. Then reflect on whether you use that hope to inspire others. Leaders with goals, visions, and hope are willing to reshape those goals, especially in times of turmoil and change. If you find that you're unable to achieve any part of a goal, revisit the entire goal, rewrite it, and try again.

Moving from pessimism to optimism

If you've been accused of looking at the world through rose-colored glasses or of always seeing the glass as half full, you're optimistic. Hope and optimism are related. Optimists are usually hopeful, and those with hope are most often optimistic.

The good news is that optimism can be learned. According to optimism expert Martin Seligman, anyone can change pessimistic views to optimistic ones. Seligman explains that an optimist does the following:

- Views disappointments as temporary
- Sees adversity as situational and not personal or enduring
- Looks at external causes of problems rather than blaming herself entirely

Pessimists, on the other hand, look at their misfortunes as

- ✔ Permanent: "I never do anything right."
- ✔ Pervasive: "Things go wrong in every part of my life."
- ✔ Personal: "I am so stupid!"

If you're a pessimist who wants to become an optimist, turn negative thoughts into positive ones:

- ✔ Remind yourself that you will have other opportunities to get things right.

- ✔ Realize that adversity does not spread throughout all aspects of your life. Sometimes things go well!

- ✔ Although not blaming yourself is difficult if your background includes others telling you that you're an idiot, you can unlearn the habit. Look at the accomplishments in your life and realize that everyone makes mistakes.

Book II

Embracing Leadership

Recognizing emotions in others

When you become self-aware and can handle your own feelings and motivate yourself, you're ready to deal with the emotions of others. Timothy Leary famously advised people to "Turn on, tune in, drop out." When it comes to emotions, you need to turn on, tune in, and drop in: Turn on your emotional radar, tune in to others' feelings, and drop in to their world.

Tuning in — with a little help from the mirror neurons

You can tune into others' emotions after you have your own feelings under control. Because the brain cannot multitask, you can't focus on your own feelings and pay attention to someone else's. Tuning in to what someone may be feeling and thinking is usually called *empathy*.

Some levels of empathy make others feel listened to and understood. When an individual thinks you understand her, her brain releases important chemicals. Those chemicals — dopamine, serotonin, and endorphins — cause the brain to feel pleasure and feel close to you. When you listen as well as you speak, collaboration with employees or customers becomes much easier. You can persuade people to see your point of view through these healthy collaborations.

Many scientists believe that empathy is associated with *mirror neurons*. These groups of brain cells are located in the left hemisphere and connect when you watch someone perform a task. They connect to each other as though you're performing the task rather than watching. Mirror neurons may go beyond physical tasks and make connections through emotional observations. These neurons basically read minds, or at least intentions.

When you see someone walking toward a car, your mirror neurons tell you that he's going to open the door and get in. You would be shocked if the person smashed the window instead. In the same vein, if you observe someone upset over losing a loved one, you may get choked up; if you've been through a similar experience, you have a pattern for this kind of emotion stored in your brain. Those who have the most active mirror neuron systems tend to empathize more than those who do not.

Connecting empathy and influence

Empathy enables you to feel what others are feeling. Using your empathic skills to help others feel listened to and understood offers you an opportunity to wield your influence. Leadership expert John C. Maxwell points out, "People don't care how much you know until they know how much you care." Getting in touch with others' feelings is the pathway to understanding their values, interests, desires, and needs.

Empathy enables leaders to make better decisions based not just on facts but on intuitive reasoning. You may believe you know what is best for those you lead, but without using your influence from the strong emotional connections you have made, you may be the only believer.

Empathy begins early. Most babies respond to the cries in the nursery by crying themselves, an indication that they recognize emotions in others. Circuitry in the emotional brain combines information from facial expressions, voice recognition, and body movement to help keep you attuned to others' feelings.

Begin honing your empathy skills by observing facial expressions, tonality, and gestures or body language. Then make a comparison between those observations and what a person actually says to get an idea of what the person is feeling. This intense observation may cause you to have that same feeling or at least enable you to respond appropriately.

Leaders used to believe that they needed power and control, but they were wrong. Power comes from understanding relationships. Control belongs to every stakeholder. When you make others feel that they have some control over their lives and the power to make a difference, they follow your lead.

Modeling the emotion you want to see

Emotions are contagious. Catch up with someone whose emotions are stronger than yours, spend some time with her, and *voila!* You feel the same way. It's not voodoo; it's real.

Educators are experts at setting an emotional tone. Walk into a classroom in a neutral state and what do you get? Kids who don't care. Walk in excited about your content, and you get students who can't wait to learn. The same result occurs at a meeting. Team meetings, organizational meetings, and even client lunches need to be led by the emotionally attuned individual.

You can make an impact with your feelings both positively and negatively. Deep emotions tend to make the greatest impact, and negative emotions are more powerful than positive.

Studies have traced the flow of emotion from leader to subordinate. Researchers used vehicles such as movie clips to initiate positive or negative moods, and then they tracked leaders as they met with employees. The leader's mood usually prevailed and spread.

Before you step into your next meeting, check your crabbiness level. The consequences of spreading gloom or anger are easy to predict. Consider the following two scenarios.

- ✔ **The grinning leader:** You walk into your meeting with a smile from ear to ear. You greet others still flashing those pearly whites. What do your employees do? Smile right back at you. Viewing all those smiles looking at you makes the happiness escalate. The meeting is bound to be good with everyone in a positive mood.

- ✔ **The glum leader:** Doom and gloom have overcome you. You just lost an account and are very unhappy. Your meeting is scheduled, so you storm in. Your face shows anger or disgust. You look out at your audience. Of course, your subordinates react to the look on your face. They smile to try to change your emotional state. But their smiles infuriate you. After all, what are they smiling about? You just lost an account. You frown and their smiles fade. They're thinking, "What's wrong with him? What did I do? That son of a gun better not think I'm going to go out of my way for him." Getting your message across at the meeting becomes a steep uphill battle.

When you cannot spread good feelings, get someone else to do it for you. Intense emotions may lead to circumstances that produce only negativity, an emotional environment you want to avoid.

Book II

Embracing
Leadership

Dealing with out-of-control emotions

Even if you are able to recognize and deal with your emotions and the emotions in those you live and work with, and even if you're a pro at motivating yourself and others, you're going to have a few fluke moments. Sometimes, something happens and you discover that your emotions run away with you and from you.

The upcoming sections tell you about the way your brain reacts to these situations and what you can do to regain control.

When your emotional cool is hijacked

You're cool, calm, and collected. You know your working environment; you understand your emotional triggers. Life is good. But out of nowhere, it happens. When you least expect it, an emotional surge overwhelms your brain, and your frontal lobe has no chance of suppressing it. Daniel Goleman, author of many books on emotional intelligence, calls this surprising rush an *emotional hijacking*. Your primitive emotional center, the amygdala, is so inundated that it takes over your brain. It causes a loss of control so over the top that when you come down you usually don't remember what has happened. And you don't understand what came over you.

Emotional hijacking may occur under circumstances such as when you

- ✔ Have been treated unfairly
- ✔ Have been insulted or disgraced
- ✔ Suffer a blow to your dignity
- ✔ Feel that your self-esteem is threatened
- ✔ Experience frustration or difficulty reaching a goal

Watch out for the (emotional) flood

Although emotional hijacking is problematic, occasional outbursts might be forgiven. They may even be an avenue toward improving your emotional intelligence skills. Reflecting on the situation and creating more positive responses is certainly helpful.

However, sometimes hijacking leads to *flooding* — one hijack after another. Your allostatic load is so great that you are flooded with emotion. Ever hypervigilant, your body is ready for the worst. Your heart rate is up, your respiration accelerates, and you feel that you can't get out of the way of your emotions. Responses become inappropriate, working at all becomes difficult, and if another hijack situation doesn't arise, you simulate one of your own.

You anticipate a situation before it occurs. You make the worst happen; you damage relationships, say things you may regret, and lose the respect of your colleagues, coworkers, and employees.

Flooding is the worst-case scenario of not having a handle on your emotions. If you feel like you have been in control and things have been going smoothly, but suddenly you start to lose confidence, have difficulty being flexible, and feel stifled by indecision, examine what has happened in your life to cause these changes in you.

 Rather than missing solutions to problems, losing the confidence of your employees, and feeling lousy for hours, remove yourself from any situation that causes a hijacking or flooding. Step back and see what in your environment has changed that causes such inappropriate emotional responses. Answer the following:

✔ **Is your personal life under control?** Although you think you have left your home life at home, doing so is almost impossible. Check out what's wrong and fix it.

✔ **What changes have occurred at work?** Sometimes minor changes can put you on edge. Then when something goes wrong in a meeting or discussion, your already-stressed brain begins to overreact.

✔ **Is someone higher up on the leadership ladder putting pressure on you?** When your organization isn't producing to the satisfaction of your board or investors, you probably begin each day more stressed than usual. Create a plan to solve the problem and keep yourself focused on following it.

✔ **Are you eating well and getting enough sleep?** A lack of nutrients and/or sleep produces stress. Your emotions are harder to control when you don't properly care for your brain and body.

Thinking Your Way to the Top: Decision Making

Some days, decision making comes easily; on others, making up your mind isn't just an effort but a seeming impossibility. Successful leadership doesn't allow you the luxury of procrastination. Certain crucial decisions require you to make up your mind on the spot. Of course, what your brain determines is crucial may not be to others, which presents another dilemma: Do you decide right away or take the time to gather more information?

You may urge yourself or others to "look rationally" at a decision. Guess what? The brain doesn't work that way. You don't make rational decisions unless you look at data — the bottom line — and decide based solely on those numbers. The rest of your brain may be screaming for input, or quietly whispering something to you after you make the decision. Do you ignore that input and leave your decision as is? That may be the best way for a leader to present herself as a confident, no-nonsense, and goal-oriented person in charge. But will your brain leave you alone?

Making good choices is a matter of gathering input from all areas of your brain. Let the executive brain mull things over with the emotional brain and choose based on the perceptions of both.

Calling on your head and heart to make better decisions

Thinking about your thinking is called *metacognition,* and it's a uniquely human ability. Aristotle said that the rational and emotional minds can't be separated. Considering your emotions may be key in making decisions.

Acting when you don't know what to do

When you know what to do but don't do it, you're procrastinating. Doing nothing when you don't know what to do is different, but both of these situations end up with the same result. By not making a decision or not acting on one, you make a decision. Sometimes "deciding" by default can haunt you.

A good leader gathers great people around her to assist in decisions. It's okay to sit back, give others some power, and see what happens. But you must be ready to step in if you feel their decisions won't benefit your organization.

Thinking it through: Two types of decisions

Two kinds of decision-making strategies exist:

- ✔ **Veridical decision making** is based on fact and requires choosing the one correct answer.
- ✔ **Adaptive decision making** is based on facts plus prior experience or emotions because it relies on the decider's priorities.

Some of the knowledge you have stored in your long-term memory consists of veridical knowledge. When you decide whether to pay with cash or credit card, the decision may be made from a single answer as to how much money is in your wallet. Veridical decisions get you through some concrete problems that you deal with on a daily basis.

But most problems are somewhat ambiguous. Approaching fuzzy problems in a veridical fashion is difficult at best. Most leadership decisions are more adaptive in nature, and leaders must look at these problems from many different angles. When you decide whether to look for another employee for your accounting department, you have many angles to consider. Can you afford another salary? Can your current staff get the job done in a timely manner? Do you need specific expertise that you currently do not have?

As you run your organization, adaptive decision making affects your productivity and your success. When making this type of decision, you consider the following aspects:

- ✔ **Environment:** What are the expectations of your company; how can your decision affect its culture and climate?

- ✔ **Individuals:** Will others be directly affected and need some input?

- ✔ **Priorities:** Will this decision be beneficial based on your current priorities?

- ✔ **Consequences:** Brainstorm all possible consequences. If they occur, was the decision too risky? Or is the risk acceptable?

The brain's prefrontal cortex handles adaptive decision making and executive functions like judgment. The prefrontal cortex can consider various aspects of a decision, look at the options, and make a choice. Most of this work occurs in an area of the prefrontal cortex called the *orbito-frontal cortex,* which is right behind the eyes. This structure combines emotions from the amygdala with rational thoughts about the problem. It also takes into consideration the survival brain. Much of the adaptive decision-making process occurs without conscious knowledge.

Book II

**Embracing
Leadership**

The frontal lobe: CEO of your brain

Most people envision the CEO of a large company residing in the penthouse suite and working on the top floor of the building in an enormous office surrounded by windows that take in a beautiful view. The CEO of your brain, the frontal lobe, has a similar setting. It resides at the highest level of your brain, takes up quite a bit of brain geography, and has a view of the world like no other.

The frontal lobe is where decisions are made. Your rise to leadership depended on your frontal lobe abilities. But your frontal lobe didn't work alone. The interaction among many brain areas and the emotional center enabled you to work with others, handle relationships with clients and other employees, organize, plan, and make decisions.

Giving yourself time to decide

Whenever you face a decision, the problem or decision comes to the attention of the *reticular activating system* (RAS) in the brain stem. If you need to attend to the problem or are interested in solving it, the dilemma is transmitted up to your amygdala, the brain's emotional center, where you begin to feel uncertain, afraid, frustrated, or angry. If you don't act on these negative feelings right away, you have a chance to examine the issue at a higher brain level. The frontal lobe and the prefrontal cortex take over.

Give yourself ten seconds for the predicament to get up to the brain's executive areas and apply some logic to the issue. By doing so, you suppress those overwhelming negative emotions, and you don't act without some reflection. Instead, you take those feelings into account as you analyze, devise a plan, organize your resources, determine possible consequences, and then share your decision.

Becoming more aware of your body's responses to stress helps you control your emotions and take them into consideration along with your rational thoughts as you deal with an issue.

Deciding in the blink of an eye

When you're walking down the sidewalk and you see a piano falling from a window right above you, you don't stop to think about your options. You just move quickly. That snap decision works well for you.

Split-second decision-making, which doesn't happen often in the business world, follows a different pattern in the brain. Your RAS is alerted because your brain anticipates a survival situation. Information goes up to the limbic brain, where emotional reactions occur. Chemicals released as the fight-or-flight response begin to increase blood flow to your extremities. With less blood flow to your brain, your thinking may also be interrupted. Mild though the fight-or-flight response may be in such instances, it takes place when you face a novel challenge that has time constraints. Your heart beats a bit more rapidly and your head begins to swim. You decide to go with your gut and make a decision based on the emotions the current environment and conditions inspire.

Some studies suggest that making a decision over time using analytical strategies is not better than relying on your gut feelings to make quick choices based on those feelings. Your gut feelings come from years of experience at making decisions and using critical thinking skills. When your brain stores all the choices you've made and their consequences, you have a huge file of information from which to choose. What seems like a snap judgment is really based on your experiences and the wisdom you gained from them.

Maxing your working memory

Your brain lets you store your previous experiences, learn from your mistakes and successes, and learn from the mistakes of others. What enables you to juggle all those situations, including the results? Your wonderful working memory.

Making up your brain

Working memory — the process that enables you to hold information in your brain for a brief period of time — enables you to manage the activity of the outside world and the activity inside your brain.

Think of working memory as a sheet of paper. You are asked to make a decision regarding your business. You write the situation on the paper. Then you go through a typical decision-making process wherein you note the criteria for success, as well as all possible solutions and the consequences of each. All the information from your decision-making process goes onto that sheet of paper. Perhaps new information comes into the picture; onto the paper it goes. You begin to think about prior decisions you've made that apply to this issue; onto the paper they go. Then you think about what someone else might do in this situation: a famous executive like Bill Gates, your father, or a friend of yours. Those names and the thoughts you have about them go onto the paper as well.

Your working memory (sometimes called *scratch pad memory*) is like this sheet of paper, and it has a lot to hold. When you have the luxury of writing things down from your working memory (as you do when you have time to consider a decision), you empty your working memory to allow more information to enter.

But what about those rush decisions — the ones that don't allow you time to write anything down? Even when you're deciding on the fly, you still go through the decision-making process; you just have to do it all in your head. Working solely in your head requires more space in your working memory, or enough stored experiences in your brain to hook to the vital information that can help you make your decision. That scratch pad in your head has to be big enough to consider the information, your prior experiences, and what others might do. You start to juggle the information as though you are juggling balls:

- Ball 1 is the problem or situation.
- Ball 2 might be how the decision can affect you, your employees, the bottom line, and so on.
- Ball 3 is the way this situation compares to others you have been in.
- Oops, where were we? Ball 4 — what would Daddy do?

If your working memory is large enough, you can examine all these thoughts without losing any of the balls.

You increase your working memory by working your working memory! Practice the following memory-building strategies:

✔ **Play memory games.** For example, place a deck of cards face down, and then turn two at a time, looking for pairs. Try to remember each card you look at so that when you turn a card that has the same number on it, you easily find its match.

✔ **Do mental math.** Forget the calculator for a while.

✔ **Try to remember the names, occupations, and personal information of new people you meet.** This is a great skill for every manager to strengthen.

Living in the past

Your past situations and decisions stay with you. You rely on the results of some decisions to help you in the future. Much of the time those experiences enable you to make good or better decisions right now.

But you can't live in the past. The world has changed too much. Do you want your heart surgeon to use the methods and decisions he made 20 years ago on you today? Probably not.

People use the past to assist with the present and predict the future. But getting stuck in the past is disastrous for leaders. Living in the past can leave you stuck. Leadership is about change. For change, you have to look to the future.

Deciding for the future

Leaders who always focus on the present may stagnate. The leader who focuses on the future is able to stay on the cutting edge, take some risk, and make decisions based on possibilities. She has ideas that no one else has, and they may not necessarily be the most popular ideas. Leaders know that if they do something, if they make a decision, then something will happen. They count on that something to be positive, exciting, lucrative, and challenging.

Leaders make decisions based on wisdom from the past, knowledge from the present, and hope for the future. They use their gut feelings to guide their rational thoughts.

Chapter 2

Training and Developing Leadership Brains

*T*hat training matters is hardly a surprise to any manager anywhere. That you're most likely approaching it wrong probably is.

What works isn't necessarily intuitive, and what we now know about how brains collect and hold onto information opens up new possibilities and affords new techniques for conducting effective training.

Read on to find tips for bringing brain science into your training techniques. What you end up with is an arsenal for making trainings much more than the necessary evil that they're often regarded as. You end up with techniques for presenting new information, changing minds, and creating memories that last, all in service of making your team function more productively.

Holding Sticky Training Sessions

Training is time-consuming, costs money, and is the best investment that your company can ever make. Training your novices as well as your veterans pays off in the end — but only if you manage training so that the new information sticks in their minds.

Research that shows how malleable the brain is proves that you *can* teach old dogs new tricks. If you have a trainer or training company that understands how the brain learns and changes, how to emotionally charge the learning, and how to get people to have fun, real and permanent change can occur. That change is most likely to happen if you expect and encourage employees to learn.

Most trainings and presentations are built to teach information, but that doesn't mean anyone learns it. In an old cartoon, a young boy points to his dog and says to a friend, "Hey, I taught my dog to talk!" The friend says, "I don't hear him talking." The boy remarks, "I said I taught him; I didn't say he learned!"

Determining where you are and where you want to go

Good training answers these three questions:

- ✔ **Where are you now?** Getting a sense of participants' knowledge enables the training to find a starting point that includes everyone.
- ✔ **Where are you going?** Before embarking on training, determine exactly where you want it to take your employees. For example, a recent sales training at an insurance company focused on two goals, one for each day of the training. Day one's goal was finding new prospects. Day two's target goal was to sharpen communication skills to close the sale.
- ✔ **How can you get there?** Design strategies for reaching different types of learners, addressing multiple intelligences, and enabling participants to store information in various areas of the brain.

Organizing and presenting information

In order to present a training session with the brain in mind, consider several basic brain rules, outlined in the sections that follow.

Brains like chunks

Cognitive psychologists sometimes disagree on the amount of information that the brain can hold at one time. Researchers believe that the human brain can hang on to five, six, or seven bits of information for only about 30 seconds. The brain needs continual engagement with information to maintain it in working memory.

The best trainers understand how memory works and chunk information into memorable parts. The human brain remembers best what is presented first, and it remembers second best what is presented last. (This is called the *primacy-recency* effect or the *serial position effect.*) The middle of any training session is the least-remembered section.

Dr. David Sousa, author of several books on the brain, calls the first part of a training session, when retention is high, *prime time 1.* The second time for high retention — the information you hear last — is *prime time 2.* Researchers aren't sure how long prime time 1 may be. Most believe that ability to focus is age-dependent until the age of 22. After that point, focus time is about 20 minutes.

At the beginning of a training episode, most participants focus on the trainer with an interest in learning or finding out what this training is all about. During this time, the trainer needs to hook trainees with something novel or emotional and then begin teaching the new idea, skill, or concept. This prime time for retention may last no longer than 20 minutes, and so many trainers pause at the eight- to ten-minute mark for a minute or two to allow trainees to jot down information, share the information with another trainee, or compare notes with someone sitting close by. The training then resumes until the 20-minute mark, at which point another practice time, reflection time, or comparison of ideas may be shared.

Book II

Embracing Leadership

Down time gives the brain an opportunity to organize information and connect it to similar information already stored for later processing. This method is much different from the old training adage that allowed no processing time: "Tell them what you are going to tell them, tell them, and then tell them what you told them." The brain needs time to process if you want your employees to retain information. For maximum effectiveness, consider making prime time 2 a review or a different approach to the information that was presented during prime time 1.

In a 40-minute session, for example, you may want to schedule approximately 30 minutes of training and 10 minutes for processing. If the training is lengthy, fill it with segments of this kind. An all-day training, say from 8 a.m. until 4 p.m., would have roughly 10 to 12 of these training periods.

Brains don't attend to boring things

In this digital age — when information doubles every two years, anyone can find answers to important questions by typing a few words into Google, and people spend about two seconds on a website before moving on to the next — the brain has become accustomed to fast-paced, novel enticements. Trainings can offer no less.

In 1933, Hedwig von Restorff conducted memory experiments that focused on novelty. She gave groups of participants lists of items that were similar — except for one isolated item. The lists looked something like this:

Bird

Dog

Horse

Cat

Tiger

Lassie

Cow

Sheep

Goat

"Lassie" stands out because it is different — a proper noun in a list of common nouns. Participants more often remembered "Lassie" than any of the other items in the list.

The point of these experiments and others that followed is that people remember novelty — in this case, something different from the things around it. Advertisers use this concept when they try to convince you to remember their product over others. The drawback is that the novel or surprising element, though very memorable, makes you less likely to remember the other information in the list. The trick is to make the novel idea a trigger for the other information.

You can use this effect in a number of ways as you work to make trainings more interesting:

- **Change of state:** After a period of time, the brain begins to wander to thoughts other than the training. Here are some ideas for revving up the brain:

  - Have everyone stand for a few minutes as the training continues.

  - Ask everyone to take a deep breath.

  - Let the trainer and trainees change positions in the room.

  - Have the trainer change her tone or volume.

  - Ask trainees to stand, find a partner, and discuss the most-recently covered topic for two minutes.

  - Ask trainees to stand and find three people in the room they don't know, introduce themselves, and tell why they're attending the training.

- **Change of presentation:** Lecture works for short periods of time, but the areas of the brain used to learn and understand lecture lose energy. By changing the format of the content, you let that brain area rest and rejuvenate so it can work proficiently again at a later time. Some ways to change the presentation include the following:

  - Use small group activities to reinforce information.

  - Show video clips.

- Ask for suggestions to connect the new learning to what is currently known or being done at work.

- Have participants create questions that others might ask about the information.

✔ **Change of activities:** Different people learn in different ways, so vary activities according to learning preferences. Here are some ideas:

- Use hands-on activities for those who need to learn with their bodies.

- Use visuals to *show* those learners who need to see information to grasp it.

- Have participants teach each other the information that has been presented in whatever format they think is most effective.

Brains like breaks

There's a great Dale Carnegie story about two men chopping wood. One man rested only to eat quickly, while the other took frequent breaks. At the end of the day the man who worked continually was amazed to see that the other man had chopped more wood than he had. When he asked how this could be, the man who rested asked, "Didn't you see that while I was resting I was sharpening my ax?"

This is a wonderful metaphor for taking care of your brain and your memory. Breaks are necessary to rest and prime your brain for learning. The adult brain can focus for no more than 20 minutes. What happens when those 20 minutes are up can transform your effective training into one that is not only ineffective but an outright nightmare.

If the trainer is lucky, before the 20-minute mark (when he may lose all the participants to fuzzy thinking), someone in the session will be blatant about the need for change. Some trainers use a 1-2-3 rule. If one person gets up to use the restroom, keep on training. When a second person is having trouble keeping her eyes open, training can continue. (Maybe she just had a rough night.) But if a third person looks like he has mentally left the training or follows the first person into the restroom, it's time for a break.

Brain breaks do not have to be breaks from training. Brain breaks can be content-related. Consider the training format when fuzzy brain sets in:

✔ If it is a lecture and the participants are not climbing over each other in a desperate attempt to get away from the training, the break can be content-related. For example, the trainer may ask the participants to take a few minutes to think about where in their job description this content would fit. She could then ask trainees to share their thoughts.

✔ If it is shortly after lunch and members of the audience have glazed eyes, a state change may take care of the problem — maybe a 30-second stretch during which the trainer continues sharing information.

✔ If a small-group discussion is in progress and some trainees are frustrated with the discussion or with someone in their group, redirect the conversation.

Changes such as these add to rather than detract from the training content, and training goals don't change. If you're worried about loss of time, keep in mind that if you don't keep trainees' attention, they don't keep the information.

You may want to incorporate brain breaks directly into your training plan. Here are some ideas for brain breaks that work wonders:

✔ **Play Simon Says.** In addition to being fun, Simon Says wakes people up and emphasizes the importance of listening — all in just minutes.

✔ **Pair and share.** Trainees find a partner (preferably not one at their table) and share what they have learned thus far.

✔ **Review in groups.** Have trainees form groups of four. Ask each group to come up with a few key points that have been covered so far.

✔ **Get graphic.** Have employees form groups of four. Provide each group a piece of poster board and markers, and ask them to create a visual that depicts the main points of the training.

✔ **Conduct a mini-Q&A.** Instruct each participant to make up a quick question about the content and then ask the person next to him to answer it.

✔ **Connect the content.** Ask trainees to discuss in small groups one problem or concern with the information in the training as it relates to their job or their current approach to the topic.

The brain likes company

Some research suggests that putting trainees in pairs or small groups increases each trainee's retention of the material. Pairs may increase retention about 6 percent, and groups of three or four people may bump that up to 9 percent.

Put participants in groups with different people from the ones they chose to sit with at the beginning of the training. Splitting up friends and friendly coworkers lowers the risk of trainees losing focus on the task and instead catching up on personal conversations.

Any group activity that includes working with content feeds the memory process in two important ways:

- ✔ It provides an opportunity to rehearse the information. If the training is for new recruits or revolves around new product lines or concepts, the amount of rehearsal time needs to be very high when compared to a training that brushes up employees on sales or product information.

- ✔ Whether participants form relationships or not, their reactions to other trainees cause some of this information to be tagged as emotional memory, the most powerful memory system in the brain.

Moving from concrete to abstract information

Book II

Embracing Leadership

Trainers often develop their trainings according to their own learning style, but they're better off varying their methods so that their trainings address each kind of learning. Although there are many ways of looking at learning styles, the brain stores information both concretely and abstractly:

- ✔ **Concrete learners** are inclined to focus on immediate reality and prefer real-life examples, explicit directions, and using their five senses. They learn best when they move from the concrete to the abstract in a step-by-step sequence. They value practical knowledge and tend to be precise and accurate in their work. They tend to excel at memorizing facts.

- ✔ **Abstract learners** are comfortable creating theories about what they hear and observe. They tend to look at the big picture to get an overall impression of what's happening and often leap to a conceptual understanding of material. They may be inattentive during sessions that predominantly give factual information.

To meet the needs of both concrete and abstract learners, try the following:

- ✔ **Begin the training with the big picture.** For example, if you're teaching salespeople how to sell a new product, the big picture may be learning the three things this product can do to change the lives of customers. Abstract learners need the big picture.

- ✔ **Give real-life examples.** Show video clips, pictures, or charts that go along with stories of how this product changed lives. Concrete learners relate well to this step.

- ✔ **Use hands-on activities.** Enable the trainees to work with the product to see how it works and get a feel for how it may affect others. Concrete learners especially like the physical contact with the product; abstract learners may do more talking and throw out ideas about the product.

> ✓ **Step by step, show trainees how the product works and what the benefits are.** Have them work in groups or pairs to practice ways of sharing this information with customers. Together, abstract and concrete learners come up with big ideas and steps for selling the product.

Abstract and concrete learners make great teams. They cover ideas as well as facts, and they fill in any gaps for each other when they work together.

Creating Memories That Stick

Before it can begin the memory process, the brain filters incoming information for emotional content first. If you start a training session by reaching trainees on an emotional level, you lay a foundation that makes it easier to remember the important information to come.

For decades, researchers believed that information was stored in one area of the brain, and therefore how you learned or how you trained didn't seem to matter. Current research shows that memory is stored in multiple brain areas and that utilizing more of the brain's memory systems, or pathways, in training enables the brain to store more long-term memories.

If you want your trainings to truly stick, you want your trainer to access multiple memory systems. Two kinds of memory exist:

> ✓ **Declarative memories** are those that you can talk about. You are consciously aware of those memories. "My company has 50 employees" is an example. This is a fact, and you can tell others that fact.

> ✓ **Non-declarative memories** are not in your conscious awareness. This category includes things that you do almost automatically, like riding a bike and driving a car.

Declarative and non-declarative memory systems can be broken down into several more distinctive memory systems, each of which has unique characteristics and can be used effectively in trainings:

> ✓ **Semantic memory** is factual and conceptual. All the text in the training manual, the lectures in the training, and any audio or video information is considered semantic. In other words — all the words! Semantic information is the most difficult type of information for the brain to learn. It requires high motivation and must pass through several temporary memory systems before it can be stored in long-term memory.

> ✓ **Episodic memory** relates to events, locations, and people. Research shows that if you learn something in an airplane, you remember it better when you're in an airplane. If you learn something underwater, you remember it better underwater.

Episodic memory sometimes relies on location. The more unique a setting is, the more memorable it is. Transferring information from one location to another is easier if the locations are similar. If your employees are training in a technical skill that they will use in a specific location, have them practice these skills in the location where they will use them. Medical schools don't train surgical techniques in a classroom; they train future surgeons in an operating room.

✔ **Emotional memory** is a very strong memory system. If you learn something in an emotional way, your brain — which is always filtering incoming information for emotion — marks the memory and calls on many different brain areas to remember the information.

Emotional memory may be the most powerful way to make your training stick. If your trainees feel that the training will make a difference, they are more likely to remember it. If you have clearly established what's in it for them, they are more likely to remember. Your training must create excitement, passion, and drive. You establish these emotions through the environment, the passion of the trainer, and the modeling that you — the leader — provide.

✔ **Procedural memory** is sometimes called *muscle memory.* It involves movement and processes. This is skill learning, and it's vital to trainings in which participants need to learn how to use or repair a product or how to use a program. See the upcoming section "Going through the motions: Procedural memory" for a more detailed explanation of this type of memory.

Procedural memory may be a large part of any technical training. Just as location is important, learning the procedures in the correct location is also enormously important. This memory system can be associated with location as well. When trainees are learning how to run a computer program, physical practice places much of the memory of using the program in procedural memory.

✔ **Conditioned response memory** is sometimes best explained through antonyms: Someone says *hot,* and you automatically reply *cold.*

Conditioned response memory is often used for information that is difficult to remember. Flashcards help trainees commit vocabulary via conditioned response memory, and so do memory devices like putting information to music or creating rhymes.

Sticky trainings utilize most of these memory systems. The more places in the brain a memory is stored, the easier it is to retrieve.

Using movement to enhance learning

In recent years, staggering numbers of studies have shown convincingly that movement helps learning occur. In studies at schools, for example, physical activity led to improvement in grades and test scores, not to mention reading.

Book II

Embracing Leadership

Promoting movement in your trainings takes little time and offers employees' brains more oxygen and better blood flow throughout the body. It promotes the release of brain chemicals that enhance motivation. And movement also helps wake up sleep-deprived employees! Here are a few ideas for working movement into training sessions:

- At the beginning of the training, have participants stand and find someone they don't know well. Give them a few minutes to introduce themselves and find three things they have in common.

- Ask trainees to walk around the room and make three appointments with three different people at times you set. (For example, have them make 10 o'clock, 1 o'clock, and 3 o'clock appointments.) When those times arrive, trainees go to their appointments and discuss whatever aspects of the training you suggest.

- Instruct participants to stand up when they answer *yes* to a question.

- When you solicit opinions or agreement, send participants to one side of the room if they agree and the other side if they disagree.

- If weather allows, ask participants to take a walk with a partner and discuss points from the training.

- Give trainees time to physically demonstrate what they have learned. For example, role-play a sales pitch or repair a machine.

- Tell participants that the last person at their table who stands up must answer the question that you have posted on a slide or flip chart.

Going through the motions: Procedural memory

Procedural memory is formed by making movements repeatedly. Procedures help free up working memory — the temporary storage process that everyone uses constantly. Working memory is fragile and small; it can hold only about seven bits of information. As your employees are being trained, they hold information in working memory, and if their brains can connect this information to something they already know, they have a greater chance of working that information into long-term memory.

Remember that procedural memory is like a muscle memory. After the information is stored in the motor area of your brain, you don't have to consciously think about it anymore. Because you don't have to focus on it, it doesn't take up any space in working memory. For instance, in the retail clothing business, new merchandise is handled in a procedural manner:

1. **As soon as the delivery service drops off the boxes of clothing, the packing slips are removed and the merchandise on the slips is compared to the merchandise order.**

2. **If the packing slip and the order match, the merchandise is taken out of the boxes and hung on the appropriate hangers.**

3. Sales tags are printed out and placed on each garment.

4. Garments that need to be steamed are hung in the steaming room.

5. After the steaming is complete, the garments are checked in on the computer with the arrival date and the date they are displayed for customers.

6. The garments are then placed on the sales floor in an appropriate spot.

This procedure becomes second nature to the merchandise team. If Helen is receiving packages and one of the salespeople comes back to ask her a question about sizes in an order that has yet to arrive, Helen can answer the question as she continues to work. She does not have to consciously attend to every step in the procedure because it has become second nature to her.

Book II

Embracing Leadership

Procedures can save you time and money. Some managers ask trainees to watch for aspects of the training in which procedures can be set up. Employees more easily remember procedures that they create, and the procedures enable employees to be more receptive to the information they are learning.

Stressing the importance of exercise

You would be remiss as a leader if you did not understand the value of exercise for your trainees and all of your employees. Aerobic exercise can literally cut your risk of Alzheimer's by 50 percent, according to the research of Dr. John Medina, author of *Brain Rules: 12 Principles for Surviving and Thriving at Work, Home, and School* (Pear Press). Research also shows that if you take a 20-minute walk each day, you cut your risk of stroke by 50 percent. Those are just two of the health benefits.

Some studies show that the continual integration of oxygen to the brain aids cognition. Here are a few exercise options to help training stick:

- ✔ Rather than sitting in chairs, have trainees who are interested and capable walk on a treadmill during the training.

- ✔ Provide morning and afternoon exercise breaks of at least 20 minutes.

- ✔ Conduct part of the training on a walking track or outside where trainer and trainees can walk one to two miles per hour.

- ✔ Keep the hours of the training within reason so participants have time to exercise as well as get a good night's sleep.

Exercise releases stress. Trainings can be stressful for some employees. If the stress is not relieved, stress hormones build up in the brain and body and compromise focus and attention.

Calling on pictures to tell the story

If you're asked to picture the Eiffel Tower, what happens? The image pops right up in your mind; whether you've seen it in Paris or in a picture, the vision is stored in your brain.

Using visuals can make a difference in what trainees remember. The occipital lobe stores visual information and is attracted to certain types of information. What you see is sometimes what you get — as far as understanding information. The brain

✔ Pays attention to pictures

✔ Is drawn to color

✔ Notices different sizes

✔ Reacts to motion

Yes, a picture is worth a thousand words. You likely remember only 10 percent of information that you hear three days after the fact, but if you see a picture, the percentage of information that you remember goes up to 65!

Using visuals in trainings goes a long way toward making sure your employees "get the picture." Try some of the following tips for adding visuals to your training:

✔ Take a look at the PowerPoint presentations you currently use and redo them using more still pictures and animations.

✔ Look for opportunities to add visuals to your training manual. Think about adding color if your budget allows.

✔ Prime trainees' brains with pictures. Before the training, place pictures that relate to the training in the office or workspace. Prime their eyes and their brains for the new information or product. When they enter the training and see some of the same visuals, they may relax a bit because they feel somewhat familiar with it. This intentional priming may also wake up a few stored memories relating to the product, process, or idea.

Offering feedback

The brain loves to know how it's doing. Continual feedback throughout training is important for keeping trainees' focus on the road map. They need to think about where they're going and how they're getting there. Short conferences and conversations allow trainees to ask questions they may not ask in front of the group. Learning and feedback are ammunition for hitting the targets (goals). Rehearsal and review are the target practice.

Have a place for trainees to place sticky notes with questions and comments so that the trainer gets feedback from the trainees. Some trainers put a large piece of paper on the wall asking for concerns. Trainees write these notes anonymously, and the trainer reads them throughout the day and addresses their content.

Most trainings provide time at the end for participants to demonstrate their learning in some way — through demonstrations or role playing, for example. After such an exercise, a written assessment by the trainer can offer suggestions for improvement and positive reinforcement for their efforts. The assessment of their work may be as simple as this:

> *You did a great job at . . .*
>
> *Your technique could be improved by . . .*
>
> *I enjoyed having you in the training because . . .*

Some trainings have written assessments that ask trainees specific questions about the training. Other trainings have participants write papers describing the training strategies or techniques in relation to their jobs. Written assessments are fine, but actively engaging trainees in formats that demonstrate what they have learned is usually more fun and allows yet another rehearsal for those observing the performance.

When trainees leave the training on a positive note, their brains are more likely to retain the information, and they will be happier about returning for more training.

Evaluations at the end of the day are valuable to you as the leader and may help the trainer during a multiple-day training. However, if the training is one day only with follow-up at a later date, try asking employees for an evaluation of the training midday so that the trainer gets an idea of what trainees don't understand or don't like about the training. Perhaps hand out index cards with a 3-2-1 format:

> *Describe three things you have learned.*
>
> *Write two questions that you have.*
>
> *Share one idea or strategy you can use immediately.*

On the back of the card, trainees write suggestions for the training. The trainer has time to review or make changes for the second half of the day.

Book II

Embracing Leadership

Redesigning Brains: Helping Employees Train for Change

When organizations change, new job descriptions and new learning are part of the deal. The process of redesigning the adult brain brings with it the possibility of major changes. Change is not always easy. When current employees must change their ways of thinking in order to meet new goals and challenges, resistance may be part of the process.

Breaking habits, changing networks

Some habits are harder to break than others. Changing the brain's networks requires breaking up existing connections and building new ones. This process takes a lot of brain energy, as the following steps show:

1. **New information enters the brain and is held in working memory.**

   Working memory holds only a limited amount of information.

2. **The brain compares the new information with stored memories throughout the neocortex.**

   Because working memory is limited to five to seven bits of information, it makes the comparisons only in small chunks.

3. **The work of holding on to new information and comparing it to old information exhausts working memory and causes it to lose some of the information.**

   Because of the working memory's fatigue, new memories may not be committed to long-term memory.

In the brains of your current workers, this attempt at learning new information may be frustrating. People feel discomfort when given information that is contrary to what they already know and believe.

You know that 2 plus 2 equals 4, for example, and so when you're suddenly told to change that thinking to 2 plus 2 equals 5, your brain detects an error and experiences a stress response that causes it to respond without thinking.

Changing networks that employees have practiced repeatedly is a challenge. To change the 2+2=4 network, for example, the brain has to override the impulse to activate the old network and instead activate a newly formed 2+2=5 network. The process takes some time and is similar to changing a habit like smoking a cigarette after dinner. If you used to be a smoker and enjoyed a cigarette after a meal, when you quit, the desire or the routine thought remained for some time. You ate, you thought about lighting up, you tossed that thought aside, and you found something else to do. Slowly, you overcame the habit. After several weeks, your thoughts only occasionally turned to having a cigarette after dinner. You began to replace that procedure with other things to do.

Imagine that you're an employee who has worked for a firm for years. You have just been told that your job is changing. You need to be retrained in order to follow the correct procedures. As you begin to try out the new process, you find yourself going back to the old routine. Your brain is used to following specific steps, and now you have to stop yourself from following the old habit and refocus on the new one. Your thoughts and reactions likely mirror some or all of the following:

Book II

Embracing Leadership

- You feel that the old way was comfortable.
- You believe that the old process or program worked well — even better than the new one.
- You feel angry because you don't like the new system.
- You're afraid you won't be able to learn the system.
- Your stress levels rise as you try to learn the new information.
- Stress causes you to make more mistakes or forget some of the new information.
- You want to give up.
- You think you may lose your job.
- You think you may quit your job.
- You wonder why new employees caught on to the new system so easily.

As an employee's brain reshapes itself in response to new learning, he may experience all kinds of different emotions. The reshaping nonetheless can take place. But it may be slower for some of these previously trained workers whose old networks have to be disconnected as new ones are built.

Overriding old networks takes time and practice. The more emotional the new networks are, the stronger they are and the more easily they replace old ones. Motivation and commitment to the new networks also speed up the process.

Reinforcing changes

In order to reinforce the changes that have taken place from redesigning brains, you need to do the following:

- **Apply new learning.** Although some employees may be a little reluctant to implement what they have learned, doing so is a necessary step to rid them of the old habits and instill the new ones. The changes work best if employees apply their new learning immediately. Expect them to need coaching, which can be supplied by your trainer or by other employees who have had more training in the area.

✔ **Integrate the changes.** Make sure that employees at all levels in the department integrate the new way of doing things. The emotional message is "We're all in this together." Employees are more likely to help each other if everyone is at similar levels of performance and working on the same strategies, programs, or techniques.

✔ **Hold employees accountable.** After a few weeks of repetition, the new networks in employees' brains can make smooth connections. At that time, you can start holding employees accountable for utilizing their training. The method you use to measure the level of responsibility that the employees have achieved can vary according to the kind of training they received. It may be a change in profit, productivity, or proficiency. If you find that you aren't getting the results you expected, you and your employees and perhaps the trainer need to examine where the responsibility lies.

✔ **Celebrate change.** Whether you celebrate onsite or off, recognition and praise are part of keeping employees' emotional connection to the changes strong.

As you reinforce the new learning, follow the progress of your employees. Doing so assists with the steps described above. You may want to do these three things:

✔ Collect feedback from your newly retrained employees.

- Provide surveys.
- Have team meetings.
- Speak to team leaders.
- Examine data on productivity.

✔ Use this information to identify problems.

- Look for lack of motivation.
- Check stress levels.
- Identify employees resistant to changes.

✔ Fix the problems.

- Speak with anyone who may be resistant.
- Correct misconceptions.
- Recognize individual successes.

Dealing with minds that are difficult to change

Katy was a great salesperson. She loved working with customers and never had a problem making sales. When her company switched computer programs and every sale had to be entered in the computer at the time of the sale, Katy rebelled. After an onsite training, all the other employees caught on to the system right away. Katy still made sales, but she had to have another employee do her computer work.

Katy was confronted by her employer. She admitted that she was afraid of making mistakes. She needed practice and confidence, and so her employer set up some time for her to practice, and practice, and practice. Finally, she became confident enough to make the change.

Book II

Embracing Leadership

Resistance to change is a problem with some employees. While some employees look at change as an opportunity, others may see it as a punishment. For those who find that learning new skills or procedures is a problem, as their leader you must decide whether they still belong with your organization, whether you can do further training, or whether you can find another position for them that doesn't require the change.

When information has been ingrained in the brain for years and years, it is much harder to change. Sometimes employees feel totally stuck when they find themselves in a pattern that they can't get out of. In this situation some leaders would say, "My way or the highway." But a good leader takes a closer look at his employees. If what you see is loyalty, a strong work ethic, and talent that has contributed to more than just your bottom line, perhaps you need to offer this person a different opportunity.

You have probably put a lot of time and money into this employee. Training employees can become a huge expense. Loyalty is a hard commodity to find these days. You may try some of the following:

- Determine whether you're dealing with a real skill problem.
- If skills are there, check out the employee's attitude.
- Examine your expectations of this employee.
- Verify that the employee understands those expectations.
- Check out the employee's personnel file.
  - Find out what positions the employee has held.
  - Verify his productivity over the past several years.

✔ Look at other positions that are available within the company.

- Locate an open spot where this employee may fit in.

- Find another employee with whom this employee could switch positions.

Conducting Meetings That Matter

For meetings to matter, they have to appeal to those diverse brains in your organization. You can't differentiate a meeting to accommodate a lot of different intelligences and personalities, but you can address the universal needs that every brain has:

✔ The **survival brain** needs to be calm and open to new information.

✔ The **emotional brain** needs an emotional hook to hold onto the information and mark it for memory.

✔ The **thinking brain** needs challenge and choice to appeal to its ability to solve problems and make decisions.

The upcoming sections give you ideas for meeting these needs.

Creating continuity

Most meetings contain procedures that are followed to keep the agenda running smoothly. For example, meetings often begin with a welcome and a review of the minutes from the previous meeting. *Procedures* are established methods of getting things done. They are usually done at a specific time or in a particular order.

Rituals are acts that provide a sense of security and continuity. Whereas procedures don't elicit much feeling, rituals tend to bring forth warm feelings, such as a feeling of belonging. Adding rituals to meetings makes them more interesting, memorable, and fun.

You can weave rituals into meetings in various ways and make them much more pleasurable. The possibilities are endless, but here are some rituals to consider for your meetings:

✔ **Have music playing while people enter the meeting.** You might choose a theme song for the event. For instance, Queen's "We Will Rock You" may be a great tune for the sales team's meeting.

✔ **Address special occasions.** Acknowledge a birthday, for example, by playing The Beatles's "Birthday" song and presenting the team member with a gift — even something as simple as a pencil with the organization's name or logo.

✔ **Celebrate success.** When a goal has been met, have confetti and horns to blow, play a sound effect like a drum roll, or have a special treat.

✔ **Ask for the "story of the week."** Allow participants to share interesting or funny incidents that occurred since the last meeting.

✔ **Use novel ways of getting people interested in the agenda.** For example, sell the agenda. Like a carny who sells the acts at the carnival, ask participants to step right up and participate in the greatest show on earth as you hear from the most knowledgeable people in the company.

✔ **Conclude each meeting in the same way.** For example, you may do one of the following:

- Ask participants to pair up and review the meeting's important points.

- Ask participants who they feel contributed the most, and give that person a round of applause.

- Play music, like the theme from the movie *Rocky*.

 Rituals give meeting participants something to count on. Wouldn't it be nice for your employees to look forward to a meeting because they know it will be more than just another meeting — that it will be filled with fun, fanfare, and frivolity along with data, discussion, and decisions?

Sharing control

Employees may not get to choose whether they attend a meeting, but you can work choice into meetings so that they feel included and have some control over the meeting. Perhaps the group can discuss which agenda items are important and in what order they should be addressed. Sometimes not all team members agree, but you can work with a consensus.

As soon as the first employee arrives, the meeting has begun. Rather than having early arrivals sit around worrying about what other things they could be getting done, offer them a choice of what to do. It can be as simple as getting a refreshment to helping you distribute literature or writing information on the whiteboard or flip chart. They get a bit of a heads up on the meeting content and get some time to consider how they feel about it. When others enter and see their teammate helping, they may act as they did in grade school: They want to help the teacher, too! Soon everyone is coming early, anticipating what they can do to be part of the meeting.

You may add this idea as a ritual to your meetings: "Hit and Miss" is one way to attack the agenda as a team. What are the hits — the important or timely items you need to talk about? The misses are those items that should not be included in this particular meeting. If team members help redesign the agenda through a vote, you're sure to cover the points important to them within the allotted time.

At problem-solving or decision-making meetings, ask employees to choose how they want to attack the issue. Perhaps they want to get into smaller groups and discuss the issue on a more detailed level and then bring the ideas from each group together. Brainstorming may be a better way to attack the subject. Those who have few ideas to contribute initially may feel much better and become more knowledgeable through brainstorming.

Soliciting feedback

Exit cards — simple index cards on which the participants answer some pertinent questions about the meeting content — are an excellent feedback mechanism. (They're mentioned again in the next chapter.) You can use them just as easily at the beginning of a meeting. These cards provide valuable information that can be scanned quickly and easily if the meeting is not too large.

If you use these cards at the beginning of a meeting, you can get an idea of each person's feeling about the agenda you are about to cover. Use them after a meeting to find out how much employees understood and to get their feedback.

After employees have index cards in hand before a meeting, ask them to respond to the following statements, which you display on a flip chart, whiteboard, or PowerPoint slide:

The last meeting left the following problem unresolved:

I would like the following issue to be addressed at this meeting:

The most important item on the agenda to be covered is . . .

The most important item not included on the agenda is . . .

Two areas that need to be included on future agendas are . . .

Getting your message across

In order to get everyone on board, you need to find the best way to express your vision, your mission, or your dream. The brain likes stories, emotions, pictures, and facts. Using what the brain likes to remember makes getting your point across much easier.

Offering facts

According to some research, most individuals really like facts. People love television shows such as *Jeopardy!*, and Trivial Pursuit is still a popular game for people of all ages. Storing trivial information and sports facts is a popular hobby. Facts can be impressive to the general public. The public has been taught to respect data.

The facts that your employees and all your stakeholders want are the facts about what's happening in your company. The brain is curious, and especially in tough economic times, the brain needs to be reassured. When you present facts, you meet both these needs.

For instance, you may say to your employees, "A very productive business similar to ours in a city nearby had to close its doors because of high overhead."

That statement doesn't have the impact of the following: "Lancaster's in Bloomington had to close down because the overhead was up 45 percent over last year."

Details make the second statement more memorable.

Book II

Embracing Leadership

Adding emotion

Adding emotion gives the story a more personal feeling. A store closing is sad, even when a competitor is closing. In troubled times, no leader wants to see another business fold. When times are good, they are often good for everyone.

To make the story even more memorable, make it more personal:

> Thirty-three employees are out of work in Bloomington because Lancaster's went under. That's right, they closed their doors on Wednesday without even telling anyone, including their employees. When Bob Larson, the former president of the company, was finally reached, he broke down as he shared with me, 'I couldn't pay the bills. Our overhead was one of the main problems. We should have cut back last year; it's not like we didn't all see this coming. We were so far behind. I haven't taken a paycheck in four weeks. I can't even pay any severance to the great people who worked for me. I'm off to see an attorney about bankruptcy right now.' So, I'm just telling all of you right now, this could mean more business for us, or it could be some handwriting on the wall. We have to keep costs down if we want to make it in this economy. Turn off the lights when you leave a room. Don't make unnecessary road trips at the expense of the company. Meet your customers for coffee instead of lunch. Let's see if we can make it through this economic downturn.

The story calls up surprise, sadness, and fear — strong emotions that imprint a sturdy memory in the brain. Those employees are going to remember what their leader told them.

Humor is also a wonderful way to convey a message. When you express yourself using humor, you relieve stress in your audience.

Creating connections with symbols

To make your message more compelling, utilize symbols as well as emotions and facts. Concrete symbols create an instant connection between giver and receiver. Such is the case with the pink ribbon symbol for the Komen Foundation and its fight against breast cancer. Avon and Dr. Susan Love have their Army of Women who are going to beat breast cancer. Symbols and symbolic language are both shortcuts to the message.

Your symbol may be your logo, an anecdote, a metaphor, a song, or a story. Make your symbol or symbolic language a shortcut to a message. The previous story about the closing of Lancaster's becomes a symbol for your company. Whenever teams are thinking about spending money, the ritual statement is always made, "Remember Lancaster's." Doing so puts spending into perspective: Can the expenditure really help the company?

Leaders use their company symbols to keep the vision in sight. The logo is on the wall, the stationery, the uniforms, and the trucks. When the leader speaks using facts and emotions, the symbol is present. She shares it, shows it, and conveys it through her message.

Keeping the conversations going

Meetings end, but the work keeps going. You need to remind your team about the discussion, the decisions, and the camaraderie. You have a lot of options for communicating with employees, and how you choose to do so has a lot to do with the needs and styles of the people who work with you.

A newsletter or memo (printed or sent by e-mail) can be an effective vehicle for keeping up the team spirit. You may use such a communication for reporting meeting minutes, or you may want to produce a lively newsletter complete with team accomplishments and upcoming celebrations, holidays, or other events. Here are items you may want to include:

- Tips or suggestions for carrying out tasks discussed at the meeting
- An agenda for the next meeting
- Updates about how specific projects are going
- Personal information that may interest meeting participants (birthdays, accolades, and so on)
- Current goals and how they're being met

Putting together a newsletter can be time-consuming, but you can keep it simple and get your point across.

Chapter 3

Developing a Vision

● ●

In This Chapter

▶ What visions are, and where they come from

▶ Keeping a vision simple and doable

▶ Crafting your vision into a plan

▶ Applying vision to opportunity

▶ Making sure your vision is adaptable

● ●

*W*ith just a little training, people can learn to operate in a cooperative manner, without the imposition of leaders. A group can be trained to set its own goals, implement its own mission, and move to action just as if it had a leader, but with responsibilities shared among all members of the group. So why bother with leaders at all? Why not just train people in their tasks, integrate those tasks with other jobs and roles, and set a whole group in motion?

Invariably, situations arise that require something more than group thinking and collective action. A challenging problem may arise that requires a totally new direction, or a group may have been successful in its mission but reached a kind of dead end. In both cases, the group needs something that it can't always supply without guidance: *vision*.

Here you find out about the need for a vision, which is often the dream of a single individual who sees an opportunity to create change or sees a need for a product or service, an application of a technology, an opportunity to create a more effective organization, or a chance to right a wrong.

But the transformation of a vision into reality can often be a complex process. Many visions, though doable in theory, require tremendous technological or social changes in order to become reality. This chapter shows you how to create a vision that is doable in reality and how to shape that vision into a living, breathing plan for action.

The Origins and Benefits of Visions

Successful leaders provide vision to a group. Leaders communicate to their followers the overarching, doable dream that's somehow different from the present reality. That vision is what keeps everyone on track and is the touchstone against which the mission and goals of the group are judged.

As long as the circumstances facing a group remain constant, a group can operate pretty well without a leader. Even if circumstances change somewhat, if the change is gradual enough, the entire group can adjust to the change. But when people are confronted by the potential of radical or dramatic changes in their future, or when they feel that they need a dramatic change, they need the quality of vision that is offered by a strong leader. Vision is what defines a future and allows groups to seek continued growth and challenge.

Mapping where visions come from

A vision comes from three places:

- Experience
- Knowledge
- Imagination

All three are related, but each is different. The following sections explain how these factors combine to create a vision.

Experience: Visualizing from the way you live

If you're working on an assembly line in an uncomfortable position, a lot of formal education isn't necessary to figure out that standing rather than bending over all the time would reduce the pain in your back at the end of every work shift. That's exactly what workers at Volvo figured out on their own more than two decades ago. When they asked the company to improve the ergonomics of their jobs, the company complied by building a new factory in Uddevalla in Sweden. In the factory, the assembly line raised and lowered cars so that the part that was being worked on was always at mid-arm height, eliminating work fatigue. When women began working on the line a few years after the plant was opened, the company redesigned all its assembly tools so that they would fit into a woman's hands and multiplied a woman's mechanical advantage to equal a man's.

Knowledge: Visualizing from what you've learned

Knowledge is the reason you go to school. A large body of knowledge cannot be taught by experience alone. Sometimes, acquiring knowledge from books is the best way to do it. Reinventing the wheel isn't necessary when you can learn the process by which the wheel was first invented. After you have acquired knowledge, you see the world in a different light.

When Wilbur and Orville Wright were young, they were great kite flyers, and they were fascinated with the flight of birds and the rush of air currents. But it wasn't until they had some physics in school that they discovered Bernoulli's principle, which taught them that the differential between air flowing over a curved surface and air flowing over a flat surface would cause lift. It was Bernoulli's principle, not experience, that allowed them to design a wing that would support heavier-than-air flight.

Imagination: Turning randomness into a vision

Imagination springs from the randomness of life because it synthesizes knowledge and experience, but it's also connected to desire. By taking your life experience and factoring in all the possibilities and all the ways that you can see yourself and the world, your imagination allows you to grasp the possibility that waits just over the horizon. In a classic song called "Only in America" by Jay and the Americans, they sing, "Only in America can a kid without a cent/Get a break and maybe grow up to be president."

Luck and possibility are intertwined because a change in luck can determine your possibilities. And possibility is the stuff of visions. At the turn of the 20th century in the United States, Horatio Alger stories were popular. Young Horatio is a plucky lad who does everything right — he sells newspapers to support his poor mother, he studies hard and always looks for opportunity — but it isn't until he saves a rich man's daughter that his fortune turns.

Establishing a standard of excellence

Most people want to be thought of as doing a good job, to have the feeling that they are effectively advancing the organization's purposes, and to be recognized for their contributions. To do so, they have to be clear on what those purposes are and when an action is likely to advance those purposes. A vision spells out what the purposes of the organization are. It tells employees, suppliers, customers, and competitors what you stand for, as well as where you see yourself going now and in the future. A vision establishes a standard for everyone to live up to and lets people benchmark their own progress within an organization.

At salary review time within your company, write a memo that may loosely be titled, "What I Have Done for You Lately." In that memo, outline your achievements in helping the organization reach its current goals. This kind of memo will help your superiors see why you deserve a raise. But if you really want to be promoted, you should include a section in your memo addressing the ways in which you have helped the organization advance its vision even further.

Staying ahead of the game

A good leader, while managing in the present, is always looking ahead to see what threats are just over the horizon and what opportunities are there as well. Vision is a kind of distant, early-warning radar that is set two steps into the future, like a chess player anticipating his response to all the possible moves an opponent may make and knowing the outcome of the move after that as well. Good leaders train themselves to keep looking toward the horizon and beyond it, while maintaining a firm linkage to the present and to reality.

A vision requires a visionary, someone who can see what may become possible if only one or two things fall into place. The visionary, who is usually — but not always — the leader, has to look at existing events for her group and be able to say, "We can do a lot better and a lot different if X and Y can be made to happen."

Keeping ahead of the competition also entails keeping up with them. Don't be afraid to admit that someone else is doing something better than you are and to take advantage of that example.

As a leader, you're responsible for having a complete knowledge not only of your own group's resources but also of the widest possible resources available. Technology leaders, for example, build upon the work of thousands of others. So should you. If you're running a community group, you should make it your business to find out which other groups — anywhere — are running programs similar to yours, and you should learn from the best. If your Sunday school attendance is down, for example, and you have taken on the role of principal of the school, contact your synod or diocese or synagogue council and find out where Sunday school attendance is up, and then go off and learn what they're doing that you're not.

This process is called *benchmarking* because it comes from the idea that the best practices are a benchmark for everyone to emulate. But when you benchmark, don't confine your imagination just to Sunday schools. Think about other kinds of programs where attendance is vital and where people have worked hard to improve it. You may come up with something like a computer user group, or you may even want to take a look at a company whose sales have suddenly begun to improve by double-digit amounts. What are they doing right? Can you use their methods?

Linking the present to the future

Consider the old saying, "The future is now." Whoever first said it probably had vision in mind. A vision is a bridge between the present and the future. Because enterprises are increasingly complex, you can easily lose focus while you're caught up in the pressures of simply getting the job done. A vision moves an organization and its people beyond the status quo and keeps everyone sharply focused on why they are doing what they're doing in the first place. The vision sustains and constantly renews their commitment, keeping the organization moving toward the future, focused on new ideas and services. The vision also keeps everyone contributing not only to the operation of the organization but to its progress as well.

Building on the present

If you're going to tell a joke, you can't go over the head of the audience. People have to understand a joke's frame of reference before they can find a joke funny. The same thing is true for visions. If you're in the clothing business, and you assemble your workers and tell them you've decided to turn your company into an Internet Service Provider, they're going to look at you as though you've just gone bonkers. Nobody in the room knows how to do that. Your vision for a new enterprise probably means that they are all going to get fired so that you can hire an entirely new team.

Book II

Embracing Leadership

Visions are *doable* dreams; they have to be able to take advantage of the resources you have on hand or those you may logically be able to get. You can have the best idea and easy access to venture capital, but if you don't have the experience, persuading others to let you do what you think you want to do is going to be difficult. The best business plan in the world, and the ablest people, are not enough if no linkage exists between what those people are doing in the present and what they propose to do in the future.

Envisioning the future

Most people have difficulty seeing tomorrow, let alone next week or ten years from now. But successful leadership requires you to envision the future and persuade other people that your dream is both realizable and worth pursuing. This is a two-step process.

First, your vision must be realistic and doable. Many people have interesting visions that are immediately dismissed by their friends, family, or coworkers as pie-in-the-sky, or unrealistic, or beyond the scope of their resources. Listen carefully to what people are telling you, and see if you can connect the dots in your mind to create the vision that you see.

The second part of the process is convincing others that your vision is worth pursuing. Often, a person who has a vision isn't a leader at the time the vision appears. He has to articulate the vision and, by doing so, attract followers who believe in the vision strongly enough to help make it a reality. In articulating a vision, the person emerges as a leader. In other cases, group members have a goal that they can't reach and need someone to help get them there, and so a leader comes on board. Then the vision does not belong to the leader alone but to the group as a whole, and cooperation is generally easier to come by.

Developing a Doable Dream

Of all the elements that a leader must successfully execute, a clear vision is perhaps the most important. Remember *Man of La Mancha* and Don Quixote's "Impossible Dream," in which he is trying to right the unrightable wrong, beat the unbeatable foe? A vision is just the opposite. A vision is a doable dream based upon the realities of a group's strengths and resources. Far from being wide-eyed and dreamy, a leader's vision is sober and reflective.

What is doable? The physicist Isidor I. Rabi, who worked on the Manhattan Project and later won a Nobel Prize, once said, "With enough money, you can even suspend the laws of Nature. Temporarily!" What he meant was that if a thing could be imagined, it could be done. You have to figure out the cause, whether the price is too great to pay for the result, and whether the result is sufficiently permanent to justify the effort. These answers are often hard to know in the short term, but what makes certain leaders great is the persistence of their vision.

In addition, a vision should be simple and straightforward. People who are asked to help turn a vision into reality should be able to understand what the vision is, without a lot of additional explanation, and should have an innate sense that the vision is doable even before they begin to explore what's necessary to make it so. In a sense, a vision represents an interesting paradox: Visions are not obvious before they are articulated, or they would already exist. But after they are spoken, or put down on paper, they should inspire an "Aha!" or "But, of course!" from whomever is asked to help make the vision a reality. One obvious indicator of whether you want someone on your team to help make your vision a reality is how quickly she can grasp both the uniqueness and the obviousness of your vision.

Eliminating the luck factor

When it comes to making your vision reality, you can choose a slow, steady course (which has minimal risks) or a bold stroke (which has a higher risk but helps you reach your goal faster). You have to soberly assess what you know about the information you've been given. One of the easiest ways to do so is with a SWOT analysis.

SWOT stands for Strengths and Weaknesses, Opportunities and Threats. When you put them together, they give you a powerful tool for assessing your vision.

Suppose that you are assessing the competitive position of your division *vis à vis* competitors at other companies. You want to list all the factors that can contribute to the strength of your division — its people, manufacturing, distribution, marketing channels, customer base, product quality, innovation, and so on — and determine which factors are strengths and which are weaknesses. Next you do the same for each of your competitors.

By taking this approach, you can see where the opportunities and threats are. For example, you may not have as complete a product line as your competitors, but your product quality is better. If you increase product variety while maintaining quality, you have an opportunity to increase sales.

With your SWOT analysis in hand, you can devise a strategy that helps your team reach the goals expected of it. You may not do the unexpected, but you should have a clear picture of how to achieve your mission. Brilliance, if necessary, can wait until you are better prepared.

SWOTing your staff

Identifying the strengths, weaknesses, opportunities, and threats of the most important members of your team is a critical step in your leadership process as you develop your vision. Forget about job titles for a moment and look instead at the following:

- ✔ **What do previous leaders say about your team members?** Do they identify particular people as obstacles or say that your team is easy to work with? Do they identify people with important knowledge, or people who are especially effective? Ask about these things to get a fix on the capabilities of the group.

- ✔ **Do you see any discernible patterns?** Have several previous leaders told you the same things about the group? That could mean that there is an institutionalized pattern of behavior. It could make the group more effective and cohesive, or it could be the group's undoing.

- ✔ **Do any glaring weaknesses stand out?** Does the group consistently meet its goals, or are there constant struggles? If so, where are those struggles focused? Are particular individuals creating the issues, or is an entire department problematic?

- ✔ **Does the team member have particular strengths?** Skills such as written and oral presentation skills, analytical capabilities, decisiveness in action, and good judgment may indicate leadership potential, regardless of functional specialty.

- ✔ **Are there team members who are brilliant but don't fit in?** These may be team members to whom you want to delegate a special project in order to give them the encouragement to become a vital member of your team.

 Conduct a sober assessment of your own strengths and weaknesses, and be looking for people who can fill in for you where you are weak. If you've come this far as a leader, you probably know where you need improvement and what your skills are. Look around your group to find people who complement your strengths and who can help you overcome your weaknesses, and give them responsibility for doing those things you don't do particularly well.

Creating More than an Idea

Although many visions begin as ideas, a vision is different from an idea. Ideas are abundant; almost everybody has them at one time or another. An idea that becomes a vision begins with the desire to bring the idea to reality. Many people's ideas never get beyond the "What if . . ." or "I wish I could . . ." stage because they don't have the energy, the will, or the ability to carry their idea forward. To turn a vision into reality requires leadership: the willingness to embrace the responsibility for getting the job done.

Many more ideas are abandoned after a bit of research, when people discover that a reasonable approximation of what they want to do, or what they wish, already exists. But a few ideas become fully fledged visions when, with a little help from other people, a leader manages to translate an idea into reality. A vision depends on the ability to create a plan, create a team, and meld the two into an organization that can bring success to the marketplace. "Marketplace" doesn't mean only the world of business. It means a marketplace of ideas and a marketplace of social responsibility.

The following sections examine the components of vision.

Assembling a team

Most ideas come from the knowledge, experience, or imagination of a single individual. Edwin Land of Polaroid, Chester Carlson of Xerox, Fred Smith of FedEx, and many others are singular individuals who had a defining idea of a product or service. But shaping a vision from an idea is seldom the work of a single individual. Every single personal vision that has been translated into a successful and sustainable enterprise has been done by bringing together a group of forward-looking, knowledgeable people who understand the nature of the idea; its implications for the future; and the knowledge, resources, and leadership needed to make it work.

Perhaps the single best example of the kind of team it takes to turn a vision into a successful enterprise is the saga of Apple Computer. The idea for a cheap, affordable personal "computer for the rest of us" was not new. Companies such as Altair had been selling kit computers almost from the moment the microprocessor was invented in 1978, even though the kit computers didn't do very much and were lacking in the features people think of as typical of personal computers. But Steve Jobs and Steve Wozniak, two kit-computer builders, thought that they could mass-produce a low-cost computer that did more. Their early effort, the Apple I, was a hand-built machine, but their second device, the Apple II, incorporated major changes gleaned from a visit to Xerox's famed Palo Alto Research Center (PARC). Xerox had developed an advanced computer called the Star nearly a decade earlier that incorporated all the features you expect to see in a personal computer: a graphical user interface, a mouse, a large screen, WYSIWYG (what you see is what you get) word processing, and more.

When Jobs and Wozniak went out looking for money to finance their vision, their venture capitalists put together a team and really went to work. With Jobs in command of the vision, they teamed the new company with Regis McKenna, a public relations specialist, who designed the company's logo, and Mike Markkula, a savvy finance man who helped keep expenses under control. With additional team members handling software, and Frog Design providing hardware design integration, the first product, the Apple II, was a hit almost from the beginning. As the product was introduced, other members, such as Jay Chiat, who created the company's innovative advertising, were brought on to the team. Without the total team effort, the personal computer would have remained an artifact in a garage, and Silicon Valley would not be the driving force it is today.

Book II

Embracing Leadership

One of the best ways to learn about team building is to play Fantasy Baseball, in which you join a baseball league that exists on paper only. Each person in the league is a manager, and each person is given a certain amount of money to "spend" on personnel. Managers "buy" players until their roster is filled and their money exhausted. The players are actual major leaguers. As each day's major-league scores and batting averages are recorded, you get the production of the roster members of your team. The object of fantasy baseball is to force you to think about real players in real situations, and to force you to put those players together in optimal conditions.

When you're attempting to translate an idea into a vision, you have to do the same thing. You begin with a clean sheet of paper and a question: "If there were no restrictions on resources, where could I go and what could I do?" Such questions eliminate, for the moment, all the arguments from potential naysayers about why your idea can't possibly work and why your vision should be discarded or reduced in scope. By asking a no-limits question, you confront physicist Isidor I. Rabi's statement that there are no limits, except the laws of nature, and that even those can be overcome for a while if you want to spend the money.

After you put your idea down on paper, over weeks and months, if you investigate your idea, research it, and learn as much as possible about what it may take to bring it to fruition, a vision may emerge that has a chance of succeeding. As you're doing your research, you're beginning to know what types of knowledge you don't have and what knowledge and experience will be essential to making your vision into a reality. As the leader, it's your job to begin building a team.

You have to pencil in a name and responsibilities to fill in each gap in your knowledge. For example, if you're intent on providing shelter for the homeless, you have to get someone who knows about permits for homeless shelters, an architect, a banker or some type of money person, someone who has worked with the homeless and knows their needs, and someone who can be an advocate of your project to people who can help you. Each one of those people will be able to help you make your vision a reality, and each will help you shape your original vision and give it the limitations and scope that will make the project doable.

Because the process of building a vision generally involves the people who have to carry it out, team building helps you achieve a consensus and a common commitment at the early stages of a project that are needed to take a vision from a dream to a reality.

Moving from an idea to a plan

As you go from an idea or a dream to a vision, planning becomes your focus. The purpose of planning is to answer this question: "What should we be doing, and how should we do it?" Dr. William Ouchi, a consultant who wrote *Theory Z: How American Business Can Meet the Japanese Challenge* (Perseus Books), observed that Japanese firms spend about 80 percent of the time required to launch a new business in planning and only 20 percent in execution, whereas most American firms spend 20 percent of their time in planning and the rest of the time foundering around, struggling to execute properly.

To give any organization its best possible chance of success, you must develop an idea within the knowledge and experience of the team and within the context of its marketplace — where it is now and where it's likely to be five years from now. That plan will determine whether your vision is doable and whether it can become a reality.

To succeed, the idea that underlies a vision should be able to answer the following questions:

- ✔ **Why should customers buy your product or service?** What is the significant difference between your product and its competition? Why should customers buy from you rather than from someone else? A product or service does not have to be limited to a company. For example, if you're contemplating starting up a charter school, you will be offering a vision of the delivery of a service. Why is yours different from — and better than — what people can already get? Until you can answer that question convincingly — not to your satisfaction, but to the satisfaction of a potential customer or member — you haven't got an enterprise.

- ✔ **Will it last? Is it enduring or a fad?** You'd be surprised at how many things fit this phrase: "It seemed like a good idea at the time." Before you invest a lot of time and effort, take the trouble to investigate whether conditions are likely to change in the near future that will make your product or service obsolete.

✔ **Will competition let you survive?** What is the experience of others in your chosen competitive field? Who are the big players? Will they ignore you, try to force you out of business, or offer to buy you out? These questions are not ones to be answered lightly. Many excellent ideas never make it to the marketplace simply because their developers did not have the resources to see their ideas through to victory and were squeezed out by better-financed competition.

When you're contemplating starting a new enterprise, you have to ask yourself what the barriers to entry are. If they are low enough for you to enter, will they be low enough to attract additional competitors? And what about resources? If your major resource is people, your competitor may simply be able to outspend you and lure your best people away.

✔ **Can it be profitable?** Good enterprises require good profits. If you're starting a business, will it provide you with enough profit margin to allow you to maintain a steady pace of growth in the face of rising competition? If you're running a nonprofit, are you running it efficiently enough so that you can increase your levels of service without taxing the membership? Can you generate enough social profit to attract additional donations for your good work? That should be your goal, and if your enterprise is going to operate on a shoestring, you should rethink how you're doing your work.

✔ **Can it be implemented?** Are you using the right technology? Can you find the right people? Can you repeat what you're doing consistently? Can your enterprise be financed adequately? Turning a vision into reality requires resources. You should be able to design into your planning document a large margin for error, on the assumption that things are going to go wrong along the way. If you rely on a key person, what happens if a car hits him? Can you replace the person quickly? Make a depth chart so that you'll know whom to turn to in the event of the unforeseen.

Likewise, what happens when you're working furiously on a technology and a new technology turns out to work better than yours? Can you shift gears fast enough, or will you be dead in the water even before you start? You should make it your business not to be taken by surprise by events.

✔ **Can the enterprise grow?** Most enterprises, except specialty retail businesses and local social service agencies, ultimately fail if they don't grow. Does your enterprise have the potential to continue growing? Will your success lead to other products and to leadership in the field? Do you have a plan to move your enterprise from a local to a regional to a national level? You should be thinking of the next stage even while you're busy planning the current stage of your enterprise.

✔ **Will being in this enterprise satisfy your needs?** Start by asking yourself the question, "What would I do if I had no limits?" Then, after you've finished the planning process — but before you begin to implement your vision — ask yourself, "Do I really want to do this?" Implementing a vision

Book II

Embracing Leadership

takes time, energy, and commitment. It may require you to spend countless hours away from your family and friends. It may put you in contact with a lot of stubborn, tiresome people. If you're not prepared to "live the vision," think seriously about whether you should be leading the charge, or whether you need to find someone else to be the leader while you take on the role of *consigliere* — the behind-the-scenes adviser.

In turn, ask yourself whether your idea-turned-vision really inspires you to do your best. Does it fit your lifestyle? Will it meet your long-term goals? Is it worth the effort? Whatever you decide to undertake, remember that executing a vision takes maximum, unswerving commitment. Other people will be counting on you and pinning their hopes on your leadership. If you can't embrace that responsibility, rethink your position.

Planning requires the participation of every member of your team. If people don't participate, you'll never know whether they have wholly bought into the assumptions inherent in the vision. Spend time with all the team members so that you know their point of view going into the creation of an enterprise. You're likely to find, when you're turning a vision into a business, that there are many things you haven't anticipated. One of them should not be sudden and late opposition from members of your own team.

Proper planning involves finding out what your resources are and aligning those resources with your vision. However, proper planning can also involve the opposite: If you're bent on your vision, then you must make a list of the resources you're going to need to make your vision a reality and couple that with a list of where to find the resources you need. If you need money, you need to develop a comprehensive list of venture capitalists and bankers. If you need experts, you should be talking to the best and the brightest in your field, asking them for recommendations.

Staying realistic

Having a vision when you have little or no hope of bringing it to reality doesn't do you much good. All successful visions begin with a sober assessment of the strengths and resources of the group. These strengths are people, capital, location, intellectual property, desire, market share, and previous success, no matter what kind of enterprise you're leading.

A vision is not short-term. A vision is something that will carry you through the achievement of several short-term goals to achieve some sort of enduring greatness or distinction — something for which your group or enterprise will be known and remembered. It can be as simple as the desire to open and operate the best French restaurant in the neighborhood, the restaurant that everybody talks about and that will cause people to line up for reservations. Or it could be the goal of establishing an employment agency that helps large companies effectively recruit minorities. Every vision is different because it's based on the experiences, strengths, and resources of the person having the vision. But all visions should be the same in that they are a challenge — a call to action — to the people who will formulate a plan to execute the vision.

Thinking beyond available resources

In addition to recognizing the abilities of existing resources, a good leader thinks beyond the available resources. If you're running a company that makes toothpaste, you have to consider resources from all over the world. You have to consider your intellectual property to be your formula, but also the work that researchers may be doing elsewhere that may cause you to consider changing your formula.

You can't look only at what you have, but at what you may have if you were a little bigger or a little richer. A good leader is always a little covetous of what is just over the hill and wants to take his group there.

Responding to diminishing resources

The best vision in the world, coupled with the savviest knowledge and the deepest experience, can't help you if your resource base is cut or diminished. What happens, for example, when a rival company comes in and hires away your most knowledgeable workers? What happens when you own the best restaurant in town and decide to open another branch, but the community won't okay your zoning request?

Mocha Mike's is a drive-up espresso and cappuccino emporium located in Bethlehem Township, Pennsylvania. When it first opened in 1996, its single, tiny, drive-up booth was located in the parking lot of a local Italian restaurant along a moderately traveled road. As word of the quality of its coffee drinks spread, people began to come from miles around for coffee, bagels, and biscotti. But in late 1998, the owner of the Italian restaurant decided that he wanted to expand his parking lot and that he wanted to serve espresso and cappuccino also. So he told Mocha Mike's to vacate its premises. What to do? Mike took on a business partner, who invested enough capital so that Mike could open several new stands. Each one is in a less desirable location than the original, but with additional investment and good word-of-mouth, the business continues to thrive.

The lesson of Mocha Mike's is that any good leader has to respond to diminishing resources — or any new situation. Leaders have to be resourceful, which means that they have to find new ways to do the things they were doing before, or ways to do new things, if they want to put a vision into practice.

You should never be hindered by the word "no" if there is something that you really want to do — assuming, of course, that what you want to do is legal, moral, and ethical. (If not, then you should always be deterred by the word "no.") A way to turn a vision into a reality always exists.

Using Vision to Harness Opportunities

Don't think that opportunities are rare — they are abundant and have always been in every age. The magazine *Business Week,* for example, started in 1929, at the beginning of the Great Depression. The great failure of companies and individuals is not that they lack for ideas but that so few ideas are well thought out and planned. Ours is a society of abundance, but that abundance still rests on a product failure rate of greater than 90 percent.

Forget the phrase "Opportunity knocks only once." The reality is that opportunity is a steady hammer on your windows and doors, a constant noise that you spend most of your time attempting to block out by stuffing cotton in your ears. The reality is that opportunities abound. Opportunities are everywhere, if you can learn to recognize them for what they are.

Most opportunities arise in one of three ways, covered in the following sections.

Spotting an opportunity

In 1980, IBM was looking for a way to respond to the growing strength of Apple Computer, Inc., but did not want to invest the resources to invent a personal computer of its own. Bill Gates told IBM that he could do it on a very tight deadline at a very low cost. Gates bought the rights to QDOS (short for "Quick and Dirty Operating System") for $50,000 from Seattle programmer Tim Paterson, renamed it the Microsoft Disk Operating System (MS-DOS), and resold the rights to use it to IBM. Gates spotted an opportunity and created a giant company out of it.

Opportunities are out in the world all the time. All you need to do is open your eyes. Deborah Fields was walking through a mall with her husband and suddenly had a hankering for a chocolate chip cookie. She couldn't get one anywhere at the mall, so she said, "If I have a hankering, maybe other people will, too. And if I can fresh bake them, the smell will attract customers." Out of that idea came a vision for Mrs. Field's Cookies, one of the great franchise hits of the 1980s. It wasn't a giant leap for mankind, but it satisfied a genuine need.

If you want to get an idea of what kind of opportunity exists, take a trip to a big city and walk the streets for a couple of days. Look at the great number and variety of the shops, and every time you see a store that looks like nothing you've ever seen before in your own hometown or your local mall, go in and look at the merchandise. Take along a notebook and make notes. You'll come back home with at least a hundred ideas — guaranteed.

Searching out an opportunity

If a business is making money for one firm, it means that at least enough of a market exists for one, but it probably means that untapped market potential is available for a competitor. Never be deterred by someone else's success. In fact, that success ought to spur you to try to emulate it and then beat it. Some of the most successful businesses began as *me-too* operations that one-upped existing companies.

The same thing goes for social organizations. Just because a successful charity exists in town doesn't mean that it's immune from competition. If you don't like the way the organization goes about its work, join it and learn as much as you can about how the organization works (and doesn't work) and where and how the money is spent. You'll find the organization's weaknesses, and doing so will help you develop a plan for your own charity that will allow you to offer the same or better service at a lower cost, which ultimately will help you attract sponsorship. Your overhead and effectiveness will be your selling points.

Creating an atmosphere in which ideas flourish

In 1944, Minnesota Mining and Manufacturing Company chief executive William McKnight decided that the company could not rely solely on Scotch tape for its future. So he created a policy that encourages innovation, saying, "Management that is destructively critical when mistakes are made kills initiative, and it is essential that we have many people with initiative if we're to continue to grow." Today 3M expects its engineers and technical people to spend a portion of their time tinkering with new products. This time, called *bootleg time,* has been responsible for the creation of thousands of successful new products, such as Post-it notes and reflective, glow-in-the-dark tape.

Employees deep within every organization often have ideas about new products or services — and about possible new directions for your enterprise — but they simply haven't been asked to contribute. As a leader, your job is to ask them. You have to find a way — beyond the typical suggestion box — to get your people to come up with new ideas that move your enterprise's vision forward.

Many firms pay employees for money-saving or money-making suggestions. But firms should also get into the habit of developing vision quest competitions. If leadership can articulate its vision — and it should if it's effective leadership — then it should hold a competition every few years in which employees are encouraged to write about how they would extend the vision over a succeeding five- or ten-year period. Ask people what challenges they think the firm is going to face and how the firm may deal with those challenges. You'll get a lot of expected answers, but you may find a future leader deep in the pack. If you find such a visionary, put her in charge of developing the vision into a plan.

Keeping Your Vision Dynamic

In many organizations, because leaders know that their tenure is limited, a tendency to not want to make plans too far into the future is common. "After all," the leader reasons, "I'm not going to be here to see my plans carried out, and I don't want my vision to become a burden and an imposition on the person who succeeds me." This idea is wrong-headed. Because you don't know much about the quality of the people who may succeed you, giving your group or organization a very strong vision is always important so that they have a constant sense of mission and an expanding sense of possibility.

In fact, one of the jobs of a good leader is to spread a sense of vision throughout the organization. It's not enough for the leader alone to have a vision. That vision must be integral to everything that every member of the group does, so that when new challenges or opportunities arise, somebody — not necessarily the leader of the moment — will recognize that the time has arrived for an expansion or a change of vision.

Many leaders are reactive or hierarchical, which is to say that they are in the wrong place or are there at the wrong time. Such leaders often lack vision, but they can be effective nonetheless — if the situational leader before them provided a solid vision.

Because visions change, you should review the driving forces of your group on a regular basis. Say, for example, that you're trying to open the best daycare center in the area, and after a lot of hard work, you have done exactly that. Now what do you do? Do you improve the existing facilities to the point where they are "gold-plated" — that is, filled with expensive and unnecessary luxuries — or do you attempt to expand your daycare vision to new sites so that other parents can have access to the same high-quality facilities? Driving your enterprise successfully into the future requires continuously examining your vision and determining when and how it needs to change.

Chapter 4

Building Your Leadership Skill Set

*Y*ou may wonder why some people seem to become leaders naturally and effortlessly, whereas others don't. You've probably heard reverent whispers that so-and-so is a *natural leader,* but leadership is situational, not hereditary.

Although some people come naturally by personality traits common to leaders, personality traits can be developed, too — and so can the skills that turn so-so leaders into great ones. Think of it this way: Some people have to work hard to develop a good golf swing, while others seem to naturally have a knack for it. Similarly, with perseverance and work, anyone can develop his own leadership skills. (And people who work diligently to develop an ability often end up better than those who just get by on their natural abilities.)

Read on to find out about the ways that effective leaders dig in and make things happen.

Taking Stock As You Get Started

Retreat into your office and close the door while you read this section, or pick a quiet place in your house, because understanding why your superiors chose you to lead is vital to planning your course of action. The possibility that your selection to a leadership position isn't necessarily a reflection of total trust in your abilities to get the job done may deflate your ego, but assuming your new position with your eyes open can help you assess your situation realistically.

Your selection for a leadership position comes for one of three reasons:

✔ Your superiors expect you to succeed.

✔ Your superiors expect you to fail. (They're testing you.)

✔ Your superiors picked you by default.

All prospective leaders want to believe themselves to be the right person in the right circumstances at the right time, and management textbooks overflow with examples of chief executives who made their careers by being in place when good things were about to happen. Certainly, most companies expect that the leaders they choose are the right people for the circumstances and the time. But you have to consider the possibility that you may be a bad fit for the job, or that the new job may be a bad fit for you.

In this section, you get tips for taking stock of your situation objectively and completely so that you aren't completely surprised by what your future holds.

Assessing your situation

If you're accepting a leadership position, the first thing you need is information, and lots of it. Long before you meet your team, you need to make a quick but detailed examination of the group you're expected to lead. The questions to ask are these:

✔ **What has the group's past performance been?** In U.S. corporations, senior managers are often promoted every two or three years, and each new leader brings her own goals to the group. Often, a manager may move on before the group reaches a stated goal. When she is promoted or leaves, you have to ask, "Does the goal the group is working toward have the approval of the most senior current management?"

✔ **Does management care about my group?** Finding out whether the group's goals have remained constant or are constantly changing gives you a pretty good idea of where the group stands in the eyes of senior management. If each successive manager was given leeway to pick his own goals, that indicates that management probably doesn't know what to do with the department. In this situation, you're not exactly expected to fail, but there isn't much commitment to your success, either.

✔ **Has the group's success or failure been short-term or long-term?** Because managers move around so much, it's easy for them to evade blame for long-term failure and accept the accolades for short-term success. Have the division's accomplishments matched the accomplishments of the people who have been promoted out of it? Or is the department seen mainly as a training ground?

✔ **Have there been many personnel changes in the team, or is it stable?**
This question is another way of asking about the group's knowledge
base. Frequent personnel changes prohibit any kind of collective group
memory, which not only wastes time but can force mistakes. Is there
anyone in the group — in any position — with enough institutional
memory for you to rely upon in a pinch?

✔ **What are the group's goals?** Is there a pre-existing vision that you are
being asked to make good on, or are you being asked to supply a new
vision to the group? If you are new to leadership, taking on the responsibility of supplying a vision makes your task more difficult.

✔ **How does the group compare to similar groups in its ability to command resources?** You're going to be competing for resources when you
become a leader. If you're taking over a company division, you compete
with other division heads for personnel, resources, and attention. If
you're running a charitable organization, you compete with other charitable organizations for money and people willing to commit to your
cause. You have to make a sober assessment of your group's ability to
capture the resources it needs to achieve its goals.

✔ **What is the commitment of the larger organization to the group?**
Ultimately, how strongly and definitively does your group fit into the
organization's plans for the future? If you are expected to succeed, the
expectation and commitment may be high. But if you are getting your
new position by default or because nobody expects much from you, the
organization may not make much of a commitment to you in your new
position.

Book II

Embracing
Leadership

Doing a personal inventory

Presumably, if you are being selected for a leadership role, whoever does the
selecting is impressed by some component of your character or work history. Try to draw out this information during your conversation with senior
management about the new assignment. The answer to a question like "What
qualities do you think are most important for managing this group?" can tell
you both why you were selected and what's expected of you. Your seniors
owe it to you to tell you the problems and pitfalls that may arise. However,
there is no such thing as a perfectly honest person, so you're always at risk of
being blindsided by some bit of information you weren't privy to.

Before you accept a new position, match your skills against the job. What
areas are you good in, and where are you weak? Are your skills practical, or
are they based on using your intellectual abilities?

Examining your leadership skills

What goes into your personal inventory? First, you have to rate yourself on three main leadership skills:

- ✔ The ability to elicit cooperation
- ✔ The ability to listen
- ✔ The ability to place others above yourself

No one is equally good at all three. Rate yourself on a 1 to 5 basis for each, with 1 being the lowest and 5 being the highest. You are looking for your weaknesses as well as your strengths. If you are truthful and you rate low on your ability to place others above yourself, for example, then you will have to manage through a buffer — someone who can counsel you to go gently on team members who don't measure up to your high standards.

More than likely, on a scale of 0 to 15, your total score is about ten, with outstanding skills in at least one leadership component, and better than average skills in the other two. If you score above 10, you have strong potential as a leader. Scoring below ten indicates that you still have a way to go.

If you rate low on

- ✔ **Eliciting cooperation,** you probably got where you are by prodigious personal effort, but you may not be able to go much farther. Trying to make all decisions yourself just bogs you down and may lead to anything from the resentment of your subordinates to loss of your job. Work to correct this issue by picking a small task and surrendering control of it to a subordinate. After you see that the task can be done without failure, pick something else and keep enlarging the scope until you reach a level you are comfortable with.

- ✔ **Listening,** work to develop a more organized system for extracting information by having your group make regular presentations to you, in writing and orally. You should have people report to you on the status of the group's mission and how well it's on target toward achieving its goals.

- ✔ **Putting others' needs above your own,** keep this in mind: In some religions, the head priest will wash the feet of his acolytes as a symbol of humility. That may be a bit much in the business world, but you can do lots of little things as a leader to show that you are at least symbolically willing to put the needs of the group above your own. Bringing the morning donuts and making coffee for the meeting instead of asking your assistant to do it are examples of symbolic humility. Forming a committee to review personnel practices and figuring out better ways to compensate people for their work is another.

Assessing your functional skills

After you know where you stand on leadership skills, use your personal inventory to assess functional skills. For example, when Philip Smith was president and CEO of General Foods, he willingly told people that he wasn't good at details. "I knew this about myself a long time ago," he said. "In business school I took a lot of math and accounting, and it was nearly the death of me. The whole early part of my career was spent fighting to make sure I didn't screw up the details." When Smith was first made a brand manager and given his first leadership responsibility, he traded one of his assistant brand managers for a statistical clerk and let somebody else on his team worry about the details. By finding a way to compensate for this leadership deficiency, he was able to accept a promotion to chief financial officer of the company, despite his weak math background.

Just as you rated your leadership skills, rate your functional skills with an eye toward your weaknesses as well as your strengths. A smart leader fills a team with individuals who are strong where the leader is weak and delegates responsibility to those people.

Rating yourself on vision, creativity, and goal-setting

If you ask senior management the right questions about your new position, you ought to get a pretty good idea of their expectations for you in this role. Can you deliver? Can you come up with the new ideas that are required to make your position a success? What have you done in the past that counts as creative or visionary, or that showed an ability to reach a goal?

Whatever it was that management saw in you, you have to learn to see it also and then magnify that quality. So if you came up with a suggestion to streamline the operations of your last team, start by looking for ways to streamline your new group. If you had a great idea for boosting sales, see if something like it works in your new position.

Understanding your mission

A *mission* is the plan of action for reaching a goal. It sums up the tasks at hand and their expected outcomes. There are two components to your personal mission: The first involves your job, the second your career. Basically, you can break it down to the following questions:

✔ **What am I expected to accomplish?** If you want to be well thought of in your new position, you have to do the task you've been assigned, whether it's meeting a sales target as a brand manager, boosting your division's profitability, or finding new markets for your company. If you inherit a demoralized group, or one whose skill levels are low, it may be enough to turn the group around and bring them up to a standard equal to other groups.

Book II

Embracing Leadership

✔ **What can I accomplish that is unexpected?** You need to constantly think about what *more* you can do, how you can go beyond the expected. During World War II, General George S. Patton was given control of the center of the Allied Forces in their push against Germany. Instead of moving in lockstep with the rest of the armies, Patton pushed his troops — who were no different from other troops in terms of fighting experience — harder and faster into German territory, thereby changing the shape of the battlefield and preventing Russia from occupying even larger parts of Germany after the war. By exceeding expectations and doing the unexpected, Patton not only shortened the war in Europe, he affected the peace settlement afterward.

Anything unexpected that moves your group well beyond the minimums attracts attention. And because success follows success, it also attracts resources and talented new members to your team. Think of it this way: As a leader, your mission is to make your group a winner, not just a contender.

Getting to know your team

In American work life, most leadership situations are not organic. Before you say yes to a new leadership role, it's helpful to meet the group you're expected to lead, or at least some of its key players. At a minimum, try to meet with the heads of all the departments reporting to you. If you're a new brand manager, for example, meet all the assistant brand managers and the marketing people.

What do you want to accomplish in this initial meeting?

✔ Tell your assistants that you're up to (and up for) the responsibility of leading them.

✔ Ask for their cooperation.

✔ Listen to what they have to say.

✔ Promise to put the group's needs above your own.

Meeting with people before you actually accept the leadership mantle gives you a head start in recognizing trouble areas and identifying your probable allies and enemies. This first meeting also gives you the opportunity to assess the team's style and glean critical information that may not have been supplied when you were offered your new position.

If your promotion is to a lower- or mid-level position, you may simply be told when and where to show up to assume your new duties. In cases in which you don't have much time to prepare or to meet the people you'll be leading, you have to manage your own expectations. You may be very excited by the prospect of leading, but you have to hold back and allow situations to develop. You want to communicate enthusiasm, to be sure, but you don't want to be engulfed by the needs of your new group.

Strengthening Your Leadership Muscles

You *can* become an effective leader, even if you feel you're starting at ground zero, and even if you never expected to find yourself in a leadership position. As long as you're willing to put forth the effort to learn what makes an effective leader and to build those skills, you have everything you need to be successful.

This section outlines the most important traits common to great leaders. Developing these traits in your everyday life tells everyone you meet that you have the capability to lead.

Book II

Embracing Leadership

Using what you have

Many leaders are not highly schooled, but they are intelligent, and one of the most interesting things about their intelligence is that they can take a limited amount of information and translate it into a workable set of skills. Think of leaders as something like the classic TV character MacGyver. No matter what situation he got himself into, he was able to find a way to use little more than his handy Swiss Army knife and a roll of duct tape to improvise a solution. His skill was that he could imagine the things at hand to be other things.

Intelligence is critical to leadership because synthesizing information is often necessary in order to create a vision. When a group comes to you for leadership, their goals are often unformed or poorly formed.

The quarterback of a football team is usually the leader of the team. Some quarterbacks distinguish themselves with their improvisational skill. They can direct traffic on the field while linebackers are rushing at them, and set up a receiver for a critical play with nothing more than hand signals and eye movements even after the set play has fallen apart. They use the information at hand to create something new and move their teams forward toward the goal line.

A leader is required to have a vision — the subject of Chapter 3 in this Book. Creating that vision means recognizing what is possible for the group you are leading, which itself requires intelligence in the form of the ability to assess the skills of the group.

Responding to situations flexibly

Taking in new information and adjusting your response to a particular situation require intelligence. Instead of responding in a knee-jerk way, an intelligent person responds flexibly, based on circumstances and needs.

Here's a situation: You own a vacation house and you've been away from it for a while. Your brother-in-law, who is looking after the house, has turned down the heat in the wintertime to save you money, even though the area where your house is located is prone to short-term power outages. The power has gone off in your house, the pipes have frozen, and then the power has come back on. By the time you arrive, the frozen pipes have burst, and the furnace is merrily pumping hot water through all the leaks and flooding your house. What do you do?

If your first response is "I scream and curse the Fates," you are not responding to the situation very flexibly. If you threaten to divorce your spouse, who brought into your life the idiot who did this to you, you're not doing yourself any good, either. But if you open the door and a river pours out, along with a cloud of steam, and you run downstairs to the basement to shut off the furnace and then go out and find a couple of pails and mops and begin cleaning up, you are responding to the situation flexibly.

The goal is to prevent further damage. The effort requires that you elicit cooperation from your spouse, so you can't yell or make sarcastic remarks. And you need to listen to your spouse, who may know better than you do where the mops and towels are, and who may have some additional ideas to contribute to drying out the house.

Taking advantage of fortuitous circumstances

The Roman poet and playwright Virgil once said that fortune favors the brave. He didn't mean bravery in the heroic sense, but rather in the opportunistic sense. You not only have to be smart enough to adapt to new information with flexibility but also have to have the courage to seize opportunities when they present themselves. Often, the opportunity appears when you do nothing more than reshuffle existing information.

Take, for example, Sam Walton, the founder of Walmart. When he was working for the Ben Franklin stores, that chain served areas that were economically marginal, or what demographers call "C" counties. Walton noticed that a lot of the stores' customers were from out of the area, from towns and villages that were even more disadvantaged than the towns Ben Franklin stores served. So he asked permission to open a store in a "D" county — a place that is the bottom of the barrel economically. When the company denied Walton's request, he quit and opened his first Walmart. He reasoned, rightly, that no matter where people live, they have the same needs. They have to buy toothpaste and shaving cream and shoelaces and all the other little things that go into making life normal. If they could buy them without traveling a great distance or paying more money, they would become loyal customers.

Walton took advantage of a lack of flexibility on the part of his employer to create the largest retailing empire in history. He also listened to his customers and created a circumstance for them to cooperate with him: His store opened in their town in return for their patronage. And finally, he put his customers above himself by not charging a premium price even though it cost him more to get his goods to more remote locations. By opening several stores in an area at once, Walton was able to get manufacturers to absorb the extra costs through bulk-order discounts.

Making sense of ambiguous or contradictory messages

In Greek mythology, one of the great tests of leadership was a visit to the Delphic oracle. The oracle was a prophetess of the Temple of Apollo. This temple, at the foot of the steep slope of Mount Parnassus, was considered the center of the universe. When a leader or a warrior went to the oracle, she would descend into the basement of the temple and chew on the leaves of the laurel plant until she went into a trance. Her priests then translated her trance words into what was often highly ambiguous verse. How the hero or leader interpreted the riddle determined whether he succeeded or failed.

So it is with modern leaders. They get information from many sources. Much of that information is contradictory, hazy, or ambiguous at best. Modern leaders may hear many messages from a group waiting to be led, including the hostile "Who are you to think you can lead us?" message.

A good leader listens to all the information and then sorts through it. You test contradictory messages by asking for more information in order to find the truth. Martin Puris, the chairman of the advertising agency Ammirati Puris Lintas, calls this concept "piercing the fog" and believes that a leader's most important job is "the relentless search for the truth."

Often, in order to get at the truth, a leader has to elicit the cooperation of people who don't necessarily want to provide the answers. Working with uncooperative people may require leaders to restrain a natural tendency toward anger and place the need to solve the group's problems ahead of their own personal egos. Leaders use their intelligence to interpret riddles and to come up with the correct answers.

Ranking the importance of different elements

What happens when you are given all the information you need and all the information is truthful, but the problem itself is breathtakingly complex? Again, a trip back to mythology is in order. In 333 B.C.E., while Alexander the Great was marching through Anatolia — what is today the Asian part of Turkey — he reached the gates of Gordium, the ancient capital of Phrygia. There, he was shown the chariot of the city's founder, Gordius, with the chariot's yoke lashed to a pole of the city's gate by means of an intricate knot with its end hidden. According to local legend, this knot could be untied only by the future conqueror of Asia. Alexander drew his sword and sliced the knot in half. The phrase "cutting the Gordian knot" has come to mean a bold-stroke solution to a complicated problem.

The story of a quick cut to the Gordian knot is entertaining, but while quick thinking is often called for in real crises, bold strokes sometimes end in disaster. A true leader knows how to rapidly sort through the disparate elements of a problem and focus in on the most important component of a complex and interlocking set of facts.

Rather than slice through the Gordian knot, a strong leader often asks for yet more information. In the 1970s, when Louis V. Gerstner, Jr., joined American Express as executive vice president of its Travel Related Services (TRS) Division, he already knew a lot about the core of its business: credit cards. Yet according to Harvard Business School professor John P. Kotter, he "shocked the people running the card organization by bringing them together within a week of his appointment . . . and then proceeding to question all of the principles by which they conducted their business."

Gerstner used that same procedure when he became president of the TRS Division and later vice chairman of American Express, and again at RJR Nabisco, when he became chairman in 1989, and yet again at IBM, when he became CEO in 1993. Gerstner was insistent that senior management provide him with as much information as possible, and he frequently asked questions much farther down in the ranks of management in order to round out his knowledge of a problem. When Gerstner acted, he was much more likely to be decisive because he had listened to everything rather than just what was told to him.

Finding similarities in apparently different situations

One of the normal characteristics of intelligence is a talent for analogies. You may remember these exercises from when you were taking the SAT in high school. Analogies compare pairs of words, such as black::white as Evil::?. Analogous intelligence in leaders is the ability to draw on prior experience, no matter how tenuous the connection is, to find a similarity that can be used to solve a problem.

You are often a leader in your everyday life, even though you don't realize it. You can draw upon your everyday experiences and use analogies to lend insight into more complicated problems. People call this skill *common sense.* Here's an example: If you've planned a wedding and your boss asks you to plan a meeting, draw on the wedding experience to make the meeting successful. If you are asked to head a task force and you have been a Little League coach, remember that the members of your task force are looking to you for the same kind of coaching as your players did.

Drawing distinctions between seemingly similar situations

You can find differences among situations just as often as you can find similarities, and a good leader learns to recognize when A is not like B and emphasize the differences over what the two have in common. Humans and chimpanzees have more than 98 percent of their DNA in common, yet you wouldn't put a chimp in charge of getting a rocket to the moon. Conversely, human beings share more than 99.999 percent of their DNA with each other, yet the most minute differences give us our individuality and act as a yawning chasm between people. The same thing is true of situations: Every situation you encounter is the same, yet different.

As the great engineer and thinker Buckminster Fuller once said, "Unity is plural and, at minimum, is two." Situations are similar to people. You can do the same thing a hundred times, but the moment you begin to treat it as routine, something can change and gum up the works. For example, a physician who has done a thousand heart bypass operations may begin to work on automatic pilot. Maybe on the next chest, the doctor could face a heart that's in reversed position. Failing to recognize the difference could lead to disaster.

An effective leader recognizes that situations rarely repeat themselves exactly and will make minor adjustments and not always do whatever was done before. Find the minute differences that can give you an advantage, even a temporary one.

Putting concepts together in new ways

Along with analogies, one of the components of intelligence is the ability to synthesize new knowledge by putting together time-tested concepts in new ways. Take, for example, the *80-20 rule,* which says that 20 percent of your customers account for 80 percent of your business. In the 1990s, Mercer Management Consulting used that old idea to help its clients examine their retailing relationships, helping manufacturers realign their marketing channels to make them more efficient and more profitable.

The 80-20 idea is an old one, but when combined with a new idea — channel relationships — it takes on a whole new life. Out of Mercer's take on the 80-20 rule came the idea of selling into the channels where you sell the most. Many Mercer clients withdrew from small mom-and-pop retailers and cut more profitable deals with large "category-killer" retailers, trading per-item profit for much larger unit volumes.

Leaders are often expected to synthesize goals. In fact, much of what people who write about leadership call *vision* is really about the synthesis of ideas and information into a new direction.

Coming up with novel ideas

According to Ecclesiastes, "There is no new thing under the sun," yet sometimes leadership calls for *inspiration:* novel thinking that enables you to strike off in a new direction. When you are faced with a situation in which no existing solution will provide you with a clear advantage, you have to invent something entirely new. In 1988, with the Cold War more than 40 years old, "everything that could have been thought of had been thought of and tried," said one German diplomat with regard to the question of German reunification. But remember: Leadership is situational, and situations change.

In 1988, Helmut Kohl, West Germany's Chancellor, recognized that the Soviet Union was in serious danger of riots from food shortages because of a series of harsh winters and the economic hardship caused by Russia's prolonged war with Afghanistan. Kohl proposed a simple solution: He would deliver several hundred million dollars' worth of food, especially meat, to the Russians if they would allow reunification talks with East Germany to proceed without further hindrance. Mikhail Gorbachev, who needed peace in Russia more than he needed East Germany, took the opportunity, and the result was an almost overnight end to nearly 45 years of Soviet control of the eastern half of Germany. Kohl came up with a novel idea, and the world changed.

Communicating with skill

A leader has to keep her vision in the minds of her followers in every conversation, whether spoken or written. When a leader is speaking as a leader, and not as a friend or confidante, she needs to remind people in a simple and straightforward manner — without a lot of additional explanation — why they are being asked to turn the vision into reality.

In his book *Leadership IQ: A Personal Development Process Based on a Scientific Study of a New Generation of Leaders* (Wiley), Emmett C. Murphy says that the leaders he researched have mastered the art of conversation:

> As we eavesdropped on their conversations with the stakeholders in their organizations — a high-tech marketing manager talking with a recently hired sales associate, a cardiac care nurse conversing with her supervisor, a team of municipal council members discussing economic development with local businesspeople — we saw that they had followed well-crafted scripts in all their communications.

Murphy doesn't mean literal scripts. Instead, he means that there is a structure to communication between leaders and followers that tends to remain the same even when the circumstance or situation changes.

In other words, a leader has to find a kind of shorthand to remind the group of what the goal is. Often, such shorthand appears in our everyday lives as slogans. The problem with slogans is that they have been overused by advertising, so people tend to distrust them. Consumers may want to be sold on something, but they want to know the difference between a lofty goal and an impetus to purchase.

Leaders must not only explain but also motivate their followers. In ancient Greece, when Aeschines finished speaking, people said, "He spoke well." But after Demosthenes spoke to them, they cried, "Let us march (into battle against Philip of Macedon's army)!" In order to inspire people enthusiastically to do what is necessary to ensure success, a business leader must articulate the very reasons the people have gathered together to form an enterprise. A community leader must do the same thing, and you — no matter what kind of role you play — certainly need to motivate people in your everyday life.

How do you learn to speak to motivate? It all starts with our primary building blocks of leadership:

- ✔ **Eliciting the cooperation of others:** Eliciting the cooperation of others is the process of offering something for something. As a song from the 1960s says, "Nothing from nothing leaves nothing. You gotta have something if you want to be with me." Implicit in what a leader does is trading a goal or vision focused on the future for struggle and hard work in the present. The goal has to be real and attainable, and it must fit the needs of the people being led.

  For example, when a company is losing money and the rest of its industry is growing by 15 percent a year, it does no good for a CEO to set 20 percent growth as next year's goal. First, the executive has to find out why the company is losing money while its competitors are profiting. Then the chief has to set an attainable goal, which may be stopping the hemorrhaging of cash. Then and only then can the company think about moving forward, which becomes a next goal. Even then, the goal cannot be outlandish; it needs to be attainable.

Book II

Embracing Leadership

- ✔ **Listening:** A good speaker almost invariably is someone who can listen to or "read" the mood or tenor of an audience, even when the audience is not communicating verbally. Good speakers can sense nervousness, restlessness, or hostility among a group, and they learn to use the mood of the crowd to their own advantage. Listening also involves asking questions and paying attention to the answers.

- ✔ **Placing others above yourself:** As a speaker, how do you put the needs of others above your own? By speaking to the concerns and needs of the person you are talking to rather than your own. You have to acknowledge how hard a person is working toward a shared goal or vision early on. You must focus on the group's sacrifices and the importance of the mission, and you have to discover how to refrain from finding fault even while you are looking for the source of the roadblocks to completing the mission. This method sounds contradictory, but it isn't. Blaming people is distracting; finding the fault, correcting it, and moving on is not.

Modeling Great Leadership Behaviors

The best way to inspire your team toward the behaviors that support your (and your company's) mission is to walk the walk. No one expects you to be a model leader at every turn, but you'll go a lot farther toward your vision if you do model the behaviors that foster success — and so will your team. This section outlines key behaviors to put into practice.

Drive

The drive to succeed is composed of aggressiveness, self-confidence, and the ability to communicate. All these traits have to be present, balanced, and focused on the problem at hand, or the result can be a disaster. A leader who is only aggressive often substitutes short-term tactical advantage for a longer-term gain, to the company's disadvantage, whereas someone who lacks confidence is likely to reverse a decision or look for another course of action at the first sign of trouble.

In the 1960s, MCI was conceived as a microwave radio system that would allow truckers to communicate with each other while they were on the road. But making the system work required a connection to AT&T's lines, permission that the telephone company refused to give. Almost any other person would have given up in the face of AT&T's clear monopoly power, but William McGowan, a consultant to MCI, insisted that the fledgling company's headquarters be moved to Washington so that he could lobby MCI's case with the Federal Communications Commission (FCC) and Congress.

As a result, McGowan thought of MCI less as a phone company and more as "a law firm with an antenna on top." McGowan's drive to succeed not only made MCI successful, but it also completely changed the nature of telephone service in the United States.

A sense of urgency

Generally, business visions are born of a change in the marketplace that suddenly creates an opportunity. What separates a more successful company from a less successful one? The better leader has a sense of urgency about translating the vision into a business. A good leader doesn't wait for information but seeks it out. A great leader begins assembling a team and determining what resources are necessary to make the idea a success even while information is still coming in.

At Chrysler, in the early 1990s, the top leadership would meet for lunch nearly every day. The purpose of the lunch was not to talk about company problems but rather to shoot the breeze. However, within these informal conversations were often heated discussions about how people were using their cars and what types of vehicles people may want next.

Bob Lutz, then president and vice chairman of Chrysler, said that the give-and-take in these meetings was far more important than any formal market research study because it focused the best and brightest minds in the company on the future without putting anything at stake. "There's a lot you can do informally to move your company forward," says Lutz. "By the time an idea gets to the formal proposal stage, we ought to be able to say yes, because everybody already knows everything they need to know. Once a proposal is formally approved, then we move as rapidly as possible to getting the car into production."

Just because a leader has a sense of urgency does not mean that a good leader relies on hunches or intuition. Some leaders do, but the better leaders depend on systematic planning to guide them. Systematic planning is also required to start a business. Though businesses may be very different, starting any business requires most of the same steps: planning, determining needs, and raising or allocating money.

The best way to stay on top of information so that you can maintain your focus on goals and maintain your sense of urgency about reaching them is to form what President Andrew Jackson called a "kitchen cabinet" of advisors. These advisors are people who can not only act as a sounding board for ideas but can also form the nucleus of a team after all the information for making a go-ahead decision is available. This committee is not a clique or an elite palace guard, but a wide-ranging group of people who have ideas and knowledge in diverse areas. You can call upon them for advice and, when necessary, for help in making the connections that will help you reach your goal.

Book II

Embracing Leadership

Honesty

Leading well requires that people be honest when they look at information and resist their own biases, even when they think they already know the answer.

Intellectual honesty is perhaps the toughest trait for a leader to acquire. If you are at the top and truly believe Harry Truman's old maxim, "The buck stops here," you may well believe that you must have all the answers because you have the final say. Not so. A leader is allowed to say "I don't know" and ask for as many options as are needed to arrive at the best answer. After a decision is made and action is set in motion, it is too late for new information, so take the time to be rigorous in your search for the truth and discover how to recognize it when you see or hear it.

Good judgment

Leaders are generally pretty responsible people. One of the things that people look for in a leader is her willingness to accept responsibility from early on, and people tend to judge potential leaders by how well they meet their responsibilities. Continuing to rise as a leader means that you continually exercise prudent judgment and don't allow yourself to fall into extreme situations. It means that you always keep the needs of the group in mind and that you don't commit the group to a potentially disastrous course of action. If you gamble everything, you risk losing everything. But if you gamble a little and lose a little, you can figure out what you've done wrong and try again.

Good judgment goes out the window only in life-and-death circumstances, when failing to take a chance may result in the demise of the group. As a leader, even then you must communicate the options available to the group and persuade them that gambling everything is in their best interests.

Dependability

Woody Allen once opined, "Ninety percent of success is simply showing up." He meant that in order to reach a goal, you have to attack it consistently. A leader cannot be mercurial, whimsical, or wishy-washy. After a vision or goal has been selected and clearly articulated, you do not serve the needs of the group by altering course. Such indecision leads only to confusion and consternation among your followers.

Dependability is itself a form of good judgment. Of course, because a leader is dependable doesn't mean that a leader needs to be stubborn. Circumstances change constantly, and today's decision, made with the best information available, can mean tomorrow's disaster if external events change significantly. But consistency means that you follow the rules of leadership in a regular way. You are always searching for the truth, always listening, always working on the things necessary to keep your group cooperating toward its goal. You do not withdraw support from people on whom you depend.

Trust

Consistency and dependability, especially when they accompany the basic requirements of leadership, breed trust among followers. If you know that the leader of your group is always going to listen to what you have to say — he may not follow your advice, but you know you'll get a full and fair hearing — and that your leader is always going to find a way to elicit your cooperation, you are far more likely to trust that person than someone who doesn't communicate this way.

As parents are fond of telling their children, trust is earned. However, as parents often find out — to their chagrin — trust is a two-way street. The parents' actions must be consistent if a developing child is going to learn to trust them. A parent who constantly changes the rules regarding what is expected and what rewards and punishments are meted out is a parent who discourages a child's trust. Conversely, children have to turn the lessons their parents teach them into instinctive behavior before a parent can learn to fully trust them and extend privileges and responsibilities.

Encouraging a learning environment

Perhaps the most important thing a leader can do to ensure that a goal or vision is achieved over a long term is to promote group learning. *Group learning* is one of those terms that management consultants like to throw around, but it really means that as the whole group gets smarter, the leader makes better decisions.

When a leader makes the effort to keep everyone informed, to communicate new information rather than hoard it — in other words, when the leader places the needs of the group above her own — the entire group benefits in ways that can't be calculated. The leader benefits because with better information, members of the group are far more likely to come up with new ideas for solving problems that were thought to be intractable.

Grasping the Roles Leaders Play

Leaders always need to be grounded in reality and true to their own personalities. But most leaders also have the ability to adopt a new persona that gives the group the push it needs to move forward, playing the character the way an actor plays a role. You can think of adopting this persona as putting on a different hat that allows you to become a different person, doing a kind of leadership improvisational act.

A leader can play probably an infinite number of roles, but five are critical to effective leadership. At one time or another, a good leader will be all these things. Some leaders will be more of one than another, but you cannot be a good leader if you don't play some of these roles at least part of the time.

The truth seeker

A leader is like the head of a pilgrimage on a journey of discovery. As the head of the pilgrimage, the leader needs to know where the group is going and must have a general sense of how to get there. But just like the pioneers setting out into the American wilderness, much of the way is labeled Terra Incognito — unknown territory. Like Lewis and Clark searching for the Northwest Passage, a leader is constantly trading for information to illuminate the road ahead. Because much of the information is likely to come from unreliable sources, the good leader must be a diviner of the truth and have the ability to test the information that is given.

When journalists receive a piece of information, they attempt to verify it. Journalists call this verification process *triangulation,* a name borrowed from airplane pilots, who use it to mean the process of locating a radio beacon. Journalists use triangulation to corroborate the information from at least two, but preferably three, independent sources. An independent source is a source that does not know the first person who provided the information. For example, if someone tells a journalist that he has evidence of a crime, the journalist listens to the allegation. But before the story finds its way into circulation, a diligent, responsible journalist looks for a piece of information that proves a crime may actually have been committed.

Effective leaders seek the truth and adjust their sights according to what they learn. These leaders know to listen to the meanings of words rather than simply to the words themselves and to extract additional information from between the lines.

The direction setter

After you have the information you need to proceed along a route, you need to make certain that the destination you already have in mind is worth going to. That destination is a vision or a goal. The leader's job is to select and articulate the target in the future toward which the organization should direct its energies. Yitzhak Rabin's decision to make peace with the Palestine Liberation Organization in 1993 after decades of Arab-Israeli strife is one example of how a vision can set an entire nation on an entirely new course. In business, Lee Iacocca's decision to build the Chrysler minivan is a powerful example of how the selection of a vision can change the course of a company's destiny.

 To be a good direction setter you must be able to set a course toward a destination that others will recognize as representing real progress for the organization. Progress may mean

- ✔ Taking a clear step ahead in effectiveness or efficiency.
- ✔ Adding the ability to serve a new set of customers.
- ✔ Gaining recognition as the leader in a new technology or product area.

If you are successful as a direction setter, you will have established a vision so compelling that everyone in the organization will want to help make the vision a reality.

Book II

Embracing Leadership

The agent from C.H.A.N.G.E

For a leader merely to articulate a vision isn't enough. A good leader also is responsible for being the catalyst in making changes in an organization's internal environment. (Hence the acronym — the action you take Can Have A New Great Effect.) The changes make it possible for the organization to achieve its vision or reach its goals. Being an agent of change can mean taking on the responsibility for making adjustments in personnel, resources, or facilities to make the vision achievable. Often, being a change agent is the least glamorous part of being a leader because the efforts are trench work that has no clear payoff.

Articulating a goal is easy, but the process of achieving it is tough work for a leader. Your challenges can vary: forming a new team, pushing through a budgetary increase to buy new software that will raise the company's productivity, or persuading your firm to open a new office or marketing channel. The goal can be accomplished only if you can link the proposed change to an end benefit.

The spokesperson

Being a spokesperson is often a necessary role for a leader of a new enterprise. Consider Steve Jobs, cofounder of Apple. Jobs had the vision of a personal computer that everyone, even without any knowledge of computers, would be able to use to improve their work performance. Both internally, to his team, and externally, to the public, Jobs tirelessly promoted the vision of the personal computer, keeping his team focused when most people thought that creating such a device would be impossible.

Jobs wasn't talking through his hat. He had thought through the idea of the personal computer at every level so that he could sell the idea to anyone he needed to speak with. Jobs needed to persuade venture capitalists, as well as ranks of engineers, programmers, and chip designers who actually built the first machines. All these people had to be *evangelized* (to use a term common at Apple) to the belief that they could actually achieve Jobs's vision and that the effort was worthwhile.

How does a leader motivate people who are skeptical? Part of the task involves making the impossible seem merely difficult and making the very difficult seem to be just another day's work. This approach doesn't mean that a leader should lie or misstate the difficulty of achieving a goal. Rather, a good leader

- ✔ Is both frank and honest in describing the difficulties, but optimistic in his faith in the team's ability to overcome obstacles to reach the goal.

- ✔ Usually has a well-thought-through plan for moving from a vision to an implemented goal, and an unshakable determination to reach the desired goal.

The coach or team builder

Because every team has its problems maintaining focus in the face of internal conflicts and external pressures — especially the competitive pressures of the marketplace — a good leader needs to take on yet one more role to help the team along: the role of coach.

The most successful coaches live their jobs. George Siefert, who was the coach of the San Francisco 49ers and one of the winningest coaches in NFL history, spent countless hours in the film room watching tape of upcoming opponents, looking for any edge that he could turn into a winning play for the team. By game time, Siefert had reduced his entire game plan to a small series of set plays, which he unleashed on the opposition, as much in the hopes of demoralizing them as of scoring. Each play exploited a specific weakness and made the point that the 49ers could score at will.

To be an effective coach, you have to let your team know where you stand, what the vision means to you, and what you will do to make it happen. You must also be committed to the success of everyone in the organization, respecting them, helping them learn and grow, and teaching them how to improve constantly their ability to achieve the vision.

Chapter 5

The Process of Leadership

In This Chapter

▶ Recognizing the skills that make the leader

▶ Utilizing your strengths — and your weaknesses

▶ Navigating expectations from all sides

Coming into a leadership position means applying your knowledge and experience in ways you may not have before. It means that you're utilizing what you have and developing new skills along the way. How you go about that depends on some basic concepts of leadership and on thinking about what you're coming into the position with, how you can utilize those strengths (and make the most of the weaknesses), and how you can continue to develop as you meet the expectations of those around you — and yourself. This chapter gives you a basis for understanding what's coming, as well as some advice for moving forward with confidence.

Discovering the Skills of a Leader

Leaders are constantly asked to make choices, which generally fall into three categories: choosing among goals, choosing among missions, and choosing among people. The first two are fairly straightforward. But whenever people come into the equation, the choices you make automatically become more complex. Choosing among people not only means mediating the conflicting claims that people have on a leader's time, but it also means making a personal choice about how much involvement you want to have with your group.

Understanding how to apply the skills that enable you to make good choices can brace you for the real-life situations that define your role.

Making leadership decisions

Decision making is the most important day-to-day job of a leader. Decision making, in this instance, means something very specific: making decisions that focus on your resources, plans, missions, and goals. You create a plan and turn it into a mission: "This is how we are going to get to our goal...." You check it constantly, and you make small course corrections as new information comes in or as the unexpected pops up.

The only way you can make decisions well is if you have information — and lots of it. If you are the leader of a volunteer group, you may set a mission of raising 10 percent more money than in the previous year of fundraising. In this case, your goals may center around having one or two very successful fundraising events. To make decisions, you need to know the schedules not only of your volunteers but of the people whom you expect to contribute. You would want to be in constant contact with insiders of all the groups that you think would be potential donors and know their schedules. You would want to know about the most effective means of contacting potential donors so that you can decide how much of your budget needs to go to advertising your event. You need to know about the availability of hotel ballrooms, meeting rooms, and caterers at sites that would appeal to your potential donors. All this information is necessary for you to make effective decisions as to the right date, time, activity, and means of publicizing the events that will enable you to accomplish your mission.

 The 20th century Danish mathematician Piet Hein said "Knowing what thou knowest not is in a sense omniscience." In other words, concentrate on finding out what you don't know instead of showing off what you do know, and then make the effort to fill in those gaps in your knowledge. If you're going to be a leader, your decisions are always going to be called into question by someone, so the better informed you are every step of the way, the greater the likelihood that you will make the right choice.

Setting a direction

Direction setting means choosing among various goals. Perhaps direction setting really should be called destination *choosing* because the point of making the choice is to get somewhere, to reach a goal. You haven't been given your position of leadership because you are the most popular person. Your group has a strong expectation that you're going to take them someplace that they don't think they can go without your guidance.

If you know that your group can't reach a goal in the near term, or if attaining the goal costs too much in human terms (the amount of sacrifice is not worth the effort), it's your responsibility as a leader to explain your decision to your group and persuade them to accept a more practical near-term goal. Flip to Chapter 2 of Book I to find out more about setting goals.

In day-to-day terms, direction setting means making practical decisions about the goals the group wants to reach. You will always feel some pressure to reach for the stars — to go for the highest possible goal. But you need to consider a few factors as you make your decisions about the goals your team can reach without undo stress:

- ✔ The skills of your group
- ✔ Their ability to work together as a team
- ✔ The resources you have available
- ✔ The competition for those resources elsewhere

Conducting mediation

As a leader, you have to settle arguments within your group. Your job is to listen to team members before making decisions. If one person comes to you with a complaint about the performance of another team member, don't shrug it off. You need to gather information — about the conflict, and about how the conflict affects others. When you focus on the complaint of a single person, don't solicit input from other members of the group; instead, spend your time observing.

When you have enough information to make a decision, it's time for mediation. You look for a middle ground that satisfies both parties in the dispute, with the proviso that your decision doesn't take either party away from their mission, which is driving toward a goal. Try to avoid mediated solutions that involve changing the roles of team members by adding to one person's responsibilities and taking away from another's. Look instead for ways to get two people working on the same task so that they share the load.

Often, your attempts to mediate are going to be unsuccessful. Many decisions don't have a middle road. The situation could require you to choose between the needs of one person and another, or between the needs of a single person and the group. When you have to choose between the needs of an individual and the group, your choice should always be for the group. If you have to choose between one person and another, however, you will have to either find a new role for the person you did'nt choose or find yourself with a dissatisfied (and potentially subversive) subordinate.

When you make a discretionary decision, the person whom the decision affects deserves to know the exact reasons he or she is being targeted. A script helps you handle that conversation effectively. Here's an example:

> John, I'm taking you out of the role I've chosen you for. We had a goal, which we are not going to be able to reach within the allotted time, even though we have all agreed upon the mission. I have received information that we are not working effectively on the mission. As a group, we began looking into this problem last month, and the solution is not to change or increase resources or to make changes among the other roles being played by members of the team. You have not been able to meet your agreed-upon responsibilities, so I have to get a new person for that role.

This script shows that there's nothing arbitrary about your decision. You explain it in terms of goals and missions, and you show how you went about making your decision. You've given John the information he needs in order to accept your decision, and you have given him no grounds to question it.

You can apply the following dialogue structure to all sorts of situations where you have to explain a tough decision:

1. **State the action you are taking.**

2. **Explain how your action fits in with the goal you are trying to reach.**

3. **Explain how your action fits the mission.**

4. **Explain the agreed-upon tasks of the mission and each person's role.**

5. **Explain what is going wrong and why.**

6. **Explain how focusing on the individual is the solution.**

Whenever you make a discretionary decision, the two things you can't say are, "Because this is the way things have always been done" and "Because I said so." Such statements are arbitrary and contribute nothing to a person's understanding of what he's done wrong. Being arbitrary hinders a leader's ability to find a new way to help the team and engenders bad feelings if the person is removed from the team.

Facilitating

Facilitating is a fancy word for the things you do to make it possible for other people to do what they need to do. In a crisis, such as a flood, the facilitators may be the people who bring the sand, the sandbags, and the coffee to the front-line workers who are actually filling the bags to shore up the levee. Facilitating is another way of saying "providing support," and a good facilitator looks for ways to make other people's lives easier. (The word itself comes from the Latin *facile,* which means easy.)

Often, facilitating is the process of challenging, stimulating, and rewarding team members for doing the best for themselves. For example, when Carlo De Benedetti was CEO of Olivetti, an Italian office equipment company, he took the door off his office so that people at his headquarters knew they could always walk in on the boss. When that didn't work, De Benedetti invented what business author Tom Peters later termed "management by working around." De Benedetti would simply take himself into the office of a middle manager and ask him what he was doing at that moment. The two would then talk. De Benedetti would make some suggestions and offer encouragement, and then leave. People who worked at Olivetti in the early and mid 1980s, when De Benedetti was chief executive, reported feeling exhilarated, supercharged, but most of all, unthreatened, when their shirt-sleeved CEO stopped in to help them out. His words of encouragement and suggestions were facilitation at and from the highest level.

Book II

Embracing Leadership

 A good facilitator doesn't need to have all the skills required to solve a problem. You simply need to be able to remind your team members, in the most unthreatening way, about the goal toward which you're all striving and the mission by which you've agreed to reach the goal. Often, while in discussion, you discover things that are blocking your team members from accomplishing their tasks, and you can then focus together on finding appropriate solutions.

Cheerleading

A leader has to decide how involved she wants to become with a team. This decision is important because the higher up you go, the more indirect your leadership is likely to be in day-to-day events, and the more likely that you won't have contact with many of the people you lead. An army general rarely sees the men and women he leads into combat, except perhaps at a parade ground review. He doesn't look into the eyes of the people he is about to send into battle, perhaps to their deaths.

How, then, does a remote leader inspire a team to meet its goals and to find the mission worthwhile? Part of the answer is honesty, but a large part of the answer is cheerleading. Any leader has to be able to instill confidence in a group and do it in such a way that the group strongly wants to meet the goal, even though the risks are high. Leaders must not only explain; they must motivate their followers. A leader must articulate the very reasons people have gathered to form an enterprise, to inspire them enthusiastically to do what is necessary to make it a success.

Often, leaders motivate with the promise of rewards. In ancient times, the rewards of war were the spoils of battle, but finding appropriate rewards is still a task of motivational leadership. At many technology companies, leaders reward the efforts of their followers with special grants of stock to employees who create marked improvements in productivity or to teams who solve a particularly thorny problem in a timely manner. A rising stock price represents the efforts and productivity of everyone in the company.

REMEMBER

Your job as a leader is to make a fence-sitter want to follow you, through the right combination of stimulation and rewards. That's what cheerleading is.

Harnessing Your Strengths and Weaknesses

Not everyone has the same leadership skills or even the necessary skills in equal measure. That imbalance doesn't matter. If you have been chosen to lead, you have to figure out how to overcome the weaknesses in your leadership tools and how to turn them into strong points. In order to do this, you have to understand the difference between jujitsu and karate.

Both are Asian forms of martial arts, and both look good when you watch a Bruce Lee or Jackie Chan movie. But the two forms of combat couldn't be more different. *Jujitsu* takes its name from two Japanese words: *ju,* which means weakness, and *jitsu,* which means skill or art. Jujitsu emphasizes the exploitation of an opponent's strengths, which you are taught to turn into your own. *Karate,* another Japanese word, literally means empty hand, and it was meant to be an offensive method of fighting when a warrior was rendered weaponless on the battlefield. Karate is a method that relies upon your own strength to help you cripple or disable an opponent.

Karate depends on the forward thrust, jujitsu on using your opponent's strength as you retreat. Karate leaders push at problems. Jujitsu leaders let the problem come to them. Every leader needs to know when to be a karate leader and lead with strength, and when to use weakness to its best advantage. Not every problem can be solved with only one method or the other. The sections that follow help you determine how each form of leadership fits with your own needs and personality.

Cooperating

Cooperation is important to any enterprise because few things of size or consequence can be accomplished rapidly by a single individual. Leaders have to be able to get their followers to cooperate in order to accomplish the goals of the group and to realize the leader's vision. But cooperation is a skill that needs to be drawn out of individuals in order to turn them into groups.

Cooperation karate

If you have a natural talent at eliciting the cooperation of others and it's one of your major strengths, the reason can be that you have good selling skills. You are bold and unafraid to pick up the phone to ask someone to help you — or to do the same thing in person. You are concise in your thoughts, a natural conversationalist, someone who can articulate the goals and visions of a group in a direct, even obvious way. You instinctively put people at ease when you speak to them, and you have a quiet confidence that automatically elicits trust from people.

You are the first person to record the goals of the group on paper, the first to organize a discussion of how to develop a mission, and the first to take responsibility. If you were a soldier during World War I, you'd be the first over the trench wall, yelling, "Follow me," and everyone would follow, confident that you knew what you were doing and that you weren't about to be killed.

Book II

Embracing Leadership

Cooperation jujitsu

What does the soft, jujitsu version of getting people to cooperate with you look like? You are a quiet consensus builder. You ask others for their opinions and keep silent about your own. You gather information and intelligence and carefully put it together. Only then do you make your presentation, relying more on the facts to help you make your case than on an appeal to vision.

People trust you because they know that you aren't likely to lead them into a minefield; they know you will proceed cautiously, making certain that the way is clear before bringing your group along. In this, you are more like a platoon leader in the jungle, taking the point, map in one hand and radio in the other, eyes keenly focused on the underbrush ahead. When a surprise springs out of the undergrowth, you are prepared. Your people are properly deployed to deal with almost any threat because you have spent much of your free time teaching them how to respond and preparing them for the fact that there is no such thing as the unexpected, only the unanticipated.

Delineating the difference

The difference between the two styles is that the person who's strong at eliciting cooperation from others appeals to vision and goals and relies on trust, likability, self-confidence, and instinct to move the group forward. The person who is weak on eliciting cooperation appeals to the sense of mission and relies on preparation, information-gathering skills, consensus-building, and keeping the group informed of every move in order to maintain group cohesiveness, trust, and confidence.

Listening

If you don't make listening a critical skill, you can never be a leader. Leaders can only take people where they want to go, and if a leader can't hear the mood of his group, he can't take them anywhere. Listening provides advance warning about problems at all levels and helps a leader to become more effective at defining the possibilities of goals and missions. How you listen is as important as what you hear, as the examples in the following sections explain.

Karate listening

The karate listener says, "Tell me. I want to know." She actively hunts out information and intelligence and does not wait for bad news to find its way to her doorstep. The karate listener has people inside the organization or group whose primary responsibility is to keep the leader informed. The karate listener doesn't stop there but goes out and gets *more* information so that she doesn't become a victim of a staff that filters out information that they don't think the leader wants to hear.

Jujitsu listening

The jujitsu listener says, "I hear that . . . " or "People tell me that. . . ." The jujitsu listener listens by walking around, by taking in and monitoring the flow of memos and e-mail by which members of a group communicate, and by constantly evaluating situations and people within the group.

If you are a weak listener, you need to develop systems that allow you to hear more. The weak listener has to build the kind of listening organization that a strong listener probably already possesses.

Placing others above yourself

Whether you're facilitating or working on developing a plan that will take a group where it wants to go, to be effective as a leader requires that you be altruistic, placing the needs of the group above your own needs. The leader who concentrates on the trappings and perks of leadership rarely survives for long, while the leader who sees to the needs of the group in an effective manner will prevail whenever there is a crisis.

You can meet the challenges of altruism head on by going up to people and asking what they need and then getting it for them, or you can act as a facilitator, patiently listening to their complaints and easing their burdens when they are still small problems instead of larger, more complex problems. Both ways work, as you can see in the following sections.

Altruistic karate

The karate leader is the host at the party who grabs the tray of hors d'oeuvres and offers it up to new guests, taking their drink orders as he passes out canapés. He is the person who takes it upon himself to introduce strangers to each other — on the grounds that if they are at his party and friends of his, they ought to be friends of each other. He takes the initiative in saying, "Get together and do something."

Altruistic jujitsu

The jujitsu leader says, "How can I help? What can I do to make your life easier?" The jujitsu leader is the one who, while her programmers are writing code to meet a deadline on a major project or her accounting team is working late to untangle a thorny issue, does whatever she can to keep those employees happy and productive, from bringing in pizza at midnight to walking their dogs. In other words, this leader is the glue that holds an enterprise together, resolving conflicts and keeping everyone on track. No one can be strong in every skill that a company needs, but a jujitsu leader does what she can to facilitate the efforts of those whose strengths are called upon.

Book II

Embracing Leadership

Meeting Expectations from All Directions

When you find yourself in a leadership position, you have to manage several sets of expectations. Not only do *you* have expectations, but so do the people you're leading. Moreover, if you have been chosen to lead a group by people outside that group — a senior management team, for example — you have to deal with their expectations, as well.

Your job as a leader is to bring your expectations, the expectations of your superiors, and your team's expectations into line, creating trust among all parties and minimizing conflicts so that everyone remains focused on achieving the overall goals. If you fail to bring these expectations into line, you may get caught in that most unhappy of triangles, in which you, your group, and your superiors see things differently.

Your greatest enemy is unrealistic expectations. Your goals have to be realistic and doable, and they have to be communicated upward to senior management and downward to your team. This section shows you how to ensure that expectations are realistic and that everyone has a clear understanding of the goals. Managing expectations makes leading a joy rather than a chore.

Mapping out your expectations

Your expectations are the minimum items you expect your team to do in order to accomplish the mission, after you have defined the vision for them. (Book II, Chapter 3 tells you about developing and communicating a vision.) Your expectations are a kind of "Leader's Bill of Rights" — the things you consider reasonable about interactions between you and the people you're leading.

Your list of expectations is the mirror image of the responsibilities of leadership. For every responsibility, there is an expectation that goes along with it. For example, if it is your responsibility to have a vision, it is your expectation that, having communicated it well to your team members, they will go along with your vision.

Selling your vision

You have been made a leader because you were presumed by someone or by a group of people to have the ability to think on a larger scale than simply accomplishing a single task. You have been chosen to lead because you were able to articulate a vision that made sense, or at least demonstrate that you could achieve a desired end or goal. Now you have to go out and sell that vision or goal to the group you are actually leading.

Presenting your goals as realistic and doable

After your team accepts your vision in the largest sense, they have to accept that your goals are realistic and doable. No one wants to believe that he is being sent off to do an impossible job. In the Army, making goals realistic and doable is the heart of *doctrine*. An old story relates that soldiers, faced with a formidable foe, will flee rather than fight unless they believe that some combination of superiority in strength, weapons, generalship, or cause gives them a reason to stand and fight. The idea of doctrine is to persuade armies to stand and fight when it makes more sense, from a short-term survival perspective, to run away.

 A leader has to tell his team exactly what the problems in achieving a goal are, and what he is going to do to overcome those problems. Only then will a group accept that the goal they've been given is doable and realistic.

Touting your mission and collective goals

You have the right to assume that your team will accept your plan for accomplishing the mission that will get them to a goal — as long as you have taken the time to listen to them and answer their questions at the planning stage, and to collect the information that will allow you to pick the right method of getting everyone to a collective goal.

If you are a persuasive leader and can inspire trust in your new group, you can ask that the group accept your judgment of where the group needs to go and how they will get there. You will put your guide's hat on and, having carefully explained all phases of your mission and every team member's role, encourage them to get to work.

Providing leadership, motivation, and encouragement

After you've got the team going, you have to let them know that your role as leader is not just to give them marching orders. You have to tell them that they must come to you immediately if things are not going according to plan so that you and they together can figure out what needs to be done to get back on track. Also, you must parcel out work by establishing committees, and then work with and motivate your committees, encouraging them and helping them to solve their problems through your direct intervention.

In other words, you have to act like a leader in the most personal sense. If you want people to trust your judgment about where you are taking them, you have to remain highly visible to your team as you move toward a goal.

Book II

Embracing Leadership

Working as a team

Most teams are made up of people who are *not* all voluntarily in agreement about a vision, a goal, or how to accomplish a mission. Even after the team has reached general agreement, one or two people, or even whole factions, inevitably will continue to disagree with you. Those people go along with the process of achieving a particular goal because it suits their own ends, but not their own motivations. This situation is especially true in politics, where coalition building is a way of life and where people who ordinarily disagree can come together to achieve something useful once in a while. As a leader, you need to make sure that unhappy campers do not become disruptive.

Cooperating to accomplish the goal

Often, getting your team to cooperate to accomplish a goal is just the first step. If the goal is sufficiently difficult to attain, you also have to gain commitment: the team's willingness to work as hard for a goal as you will work to help them attain it. Just as you have the right to expect commitment to the goals and mission of the team, you have the right to expect that, after you have all gone to work on a problem, distractions will be minimal.

Commitment to reaching a goal is rarely complete. People have personal lives — spouses, children, bills to pay, health problems, and so on. They have issues about personal self esteem and whether they are more or less valuable to an organization than other team members. And they have personal aspirations and ambitions as well. None of these realities goes away when you are in the midst of accomplishing a task. Your responsibility, as the leader of the group, is to find ways to help your team members solve their external problems before they interfere with the team's ability to accomplish its mission. But you do have the right to ask team members to keep their minds on the mission and to focus on working through the mission in an orderly fashion.

Asking for team responsibility

You may be the leader of a group, and you may have the world's best tracking system, but you aren't a mind reader, and even the best-laid plans can develop unforeseen problems. You have the right to tell your team members that it is their responsibility to let you know about problems, and about the resources they need to fix those problems, before they become so serious that they derail the entire team. In other words, you have the right to ask your team members to be responsible — to the mission, and to each other. No leader can be expected to do everything.

Seeking accountability

Things do go wrong, even on the best team, and you have the right to hold people accountable for their mistakes. But accountability doesn't give you the right to single out people for blame or finger-pointing. These behaviors are useless and even counterproductive, and they take you away from accomplishing your mission and cause uncertainty among your team.

Accountability means finding out what is going wrong and figuring out a way to fix the problem. Accountability also entails asking that the person who created the problem either take responsibility for getting it fixed or explain to the team why that can't happen. Accountability does not mean assigning blame.

Understanding your team's expectations

As a leader, you have expectations for how your team is going to behave, but your group or team also has expectations about their new leader. Every team member will be a little nervous when you make your first appearance because each person has an unspoken or unwritten agenda for what she wants to accomplish personally and is unsure that you'll be able to provide her with that opportunity. As a leader, you are going to make the effort to listen to everyone to find out what those hidden goals are, whether they are personal or on behalf of the organization, but in the end you are either going to pick one of them or choose your own path.

The following are expectations that team members are entitled to have of you:

- **Intelligence:** Team members have the right to expect intelligence from their leaders. They don't want to put their fate in the hands of an idiot. But it's more than that; intelligence, combined with experience and resourcefulness, means that when things go wrong, the leader is far more likely to find a new path for the team to take that will still allow the team to reach the goal it has chosen for itself.

- **Effective communication:** Being smart and having good ideas isn't enough. Effective leadership depends on the maintenance of a bond between leaders and followers, and that bond is best served by communication. Your team has a right to expect that you will keep them in the loop, communicating not only the changes that need to take place but also the reasons behind those changes. Great leaders are often highly eloquent, but eloquence is required only when the task before the group is especially difficult. In most situations, a leader who communicates clearly, succinctly, and swiftly is doing a good job.

- **A drive to succeed:** Your group has the right to expect that your thirst to accomplish a goal is at least as large as theirs. You are counted upon to provide the motivation for the group, and the greatest motivator is success. You cannot appear to be lukewarm about the goals or the mission. If you are, rethink them before you take your team or group down a new path. Your team members will appreciate your foresight far more than if you realize that your goal needs to be changed suddenly, or too late.

- **A sense of urgency about the mission:** People respond to leaders who are constantly motivated. In the midst of a flood, the leader of the sand-bagging operation shouldn't suddenly call a two-hour lunch break as the water continues to rise. If the leader did that, everybody would jump in their cars and take off before the flood spilled over the levee, leaving the leader there with sandwich in hand. A leader is expected to communicate urgency even when the group feels like slacking off.

- **Intellectual honesty and a rigorous search for the truth:** Team members have a high expectation that you, their leader, will make every effort to find the truth in any situation rather than fix blame or make excuses for why things have gone wrong. You, in turn, have the right to expect them to cooperate in the search for the truth. You also have the right to expect them to bring problems to the attention of leadership early on, so that small problems don't become large ones, or large problems don't become insurmountable.

- **Good judgment:** What constitutes good judgment is anything but straightforward. You don't have to be a moral exemplar, but you are responsible for not putting your followers unnecessarily in harm's way or asking them to do anything that may cause the group as a whole to question the goal,

Book II

Embracing Leadership

the mission, or your commitment to either. Good judgment means doing the things that keep a team focused on its goals, but it also means not doing the things that distract the team from those goals.

✔ **Dependability and consistency:** Dependable behavior means doing the things that keep communication open between leaders and followers, and not behaving in an arbitrary or negative manner when things go wrong. Your team members have the right to expect that you won't act with arbitrary favoritism toward other members of the group or take action at their expense without an explanation that is consistent with the mission and goals of the group.

✔ **An atmosphere of trust:** Good judgment, consistency of behavior, and dependability lead to trust. Your team members expect that you will trust them, and that you will be worthy of their trust. For that to happen, you must be open and communicative.

✔ **A learning environment:** You and your team members are going to make mistakes. But instead of being punished for your mistakes or doing the same to your team members, you need to show them a better way to get your task accomplished. You also need to give them the opportunity to learn not only from your leadership but from the group as a whole. The best groups are learning environments, where new information is taken in, fit into a framework of existing knowledge, and then disseminated to the group as a whole.

✔ **Common ground and minimal conflict:** Your group has the right to expect that you will not become the group's major source of conflict, which is a polite way of saying that the group members expect you to reach out to them to find ways to create consensus. After you and your team have joined together, your team has the right to continue to expect that you will take the lead in resolving and minimizing conflicts. Chapter 5 of Book IV gives you the details for resolving conflict.

Living up to your superiors' expectations

The people who selected you to lead have expectations, too, and you are going to have to balance their expectations against your own and those of your group. Just as your group may be initially skeptical of you and your ability to lead, even the most enthusiastic and encouraging executive team will have you "on probation" until you prove yourself. The following sections outline common expectations of upper management.

Working toward goals and missions quickly

Most people who place individuals in positions of leadership, whether they are assigning someone to run a division of a company or to serve as the head coach of a team, have an expectation that you will do whatever it is you were hired to do, and do it quickly. Team owners don't like to hear about five-year rebuilding programs. Even if they know that it will take a full five years to reach championship level, they expect to see continual year-to-year improvement. If you are made the head of a division and you are given a three-year window to improve profits, your superiors still expect you to have some effect on profitability within a quarter or two of your arrival. If you don't at least appear to be making changes, you will be called in quickly and expected to give an accounting of what you've been doing with your time.

Marshaling your resources to the maximum benefit

Getting off the dime quickly means that you have to be expeditious about learning what resources are available and then getting the resources you need. As a business coach, that means making a quick but detailed assessment of your existing team, determining members' strengths and weaknesses, figuring out who can do the various tasks required, and then going out and getting additional resources if possible to fill any gaps.

Marshaling resources does not just mean throwing money or people at a problem. It means teaching people so that they are more capable of doing what you need them to do with the resources you have at your disposal.

Preventing surprises

Even more than quick positive results, senior managers are obsessed with not being blindsided by negative results. If you find that the division you've been appointed to head is in more serious trouble than you were led to believe, even if you made a detailed preliminary examination of the situation, do not hesitate to report this fact to senior management along with recommendations for fixing the problem. A little honesty early in the game goes a long way toward giving yourself the room you need to make effective changes.

Building a team that can operate without you

Leadership is always temporary, and nowhere is this more true than in situations where you have been appointed as a leader from outside the group. You know that, whether you succeed or fail, you are going to be replaced at some point, either because you are going to be rewarded with additional responsibility and more authority or because you were ineffective and are going to be looking for a new career somewhere else. Under the circumstances, senior management expects you not only to achieve your mission and goals but also to build an effective and cohesive team in the process so that your successor's job will be a little easier.

Building a cohesive team means delegating authority and responsibility early in your leadership tenure and teaching your team how to achieve its goals no matter who is leading them. It also means explaining the role of your group to the larger organization so that they think of your job as worthwhile (which, in turn, gives you a little job security in the future).

Book III

Mastering Key Management Duties

Five Key Reasons to Delegate

- ✔ **Your success as a manager depends on delegating.** Managers who can successfully manage team members — each of whom has specific responsibilities for a different aspect of the team's performance — prove that they're ready for bigger and better challenges.

- ✔ **You can't do it all.** No matter how great a manager you are, shouldering the entire burden of achieving your organization's goals isn't in your best interest.

- ✔ **You have to concentrate on the jobs that you can do and your staff can't.** They pay you the big bucks to be a manager — not a software programmer, truck driver, accounting clerk, or customer service representative. Do your job, and let your employees do theirs.

- ✔ **Delegation gets workers in the organization more involved.** When you give employees the responsibility and authority to carry out tasks — whether individually or in teams — they respond by becoming more involved in the day-to-day operations of the organization.

- ✔ **Delegation gives you the chance to develop your employees.** If you make all the decisions and come up with all the ideas, your employees never learn how to take initiative and see tasks through to successful completion. And if they don't learn, guess who's going to get stuck doing everything forever?

web extras

Delegating is a crucial management duty, and so is making meetings work. Find out eight keys to running efficient, effective, and maybe even enjoyable meetings by checking out the article at www.dummies.com/extras/managingaio.

Contents at a Glance

Chapter 1

Hiring: The Million-Dollar Decision

In This Chapter

▶ Determining your needs

▶ Recruiting new employees

▶ Following interviewing do's and don'ts

▶ Evaluating your candidates

▶ Making the big decision

*F*inding and hiring the best candidate for a job has never been easy. The good news about all the streamlining, downsizing, and rightsizing going on in business nowadays is that a lot of people are looking for work. The bad news, however, is that few of them have the exact qualifications you're looking for.

Added to that, the Baby Boom generation that has dominated most organizations for the past couple decades is beginning to retire. As the Baby Boomers continue to retire (and new jobs are created), a gap of about 23 million more jobs than available workers is expected by 2020. That shift is going to create a huge impact on recruiting, training, succession planning, transfer of knowledge, retaining, and leading.

Three conditions — an aging workforce, a shrinking labor pool, and a projected population peak — are converging to create one of the most competitive marketplaces ever. It's up to managers and other business leaders to address these issues soon or risk falling behind the competition.

Your challenge as a manager is to figure out how to not just find the best candidates for your job openings but also convince them that your company is the best place to work. This chapter guides you through both sides of that challenge. The lifetime earnings of the average U.S. worker are calculated at approximately $1 million, so hiring really is a million-dollar decision!

Starting with a Clear Job Description

Is the position new, or are you filling an existing one? In either case, before you start the recruiting process, you need to ask yourself some questions. Do you know exactly what standards you're going to use to measure your candidates? Does your company require department head approval? Do you have a designated pay range for this position? The clearer you are about what you need and the boundaries you need to work within, the easier and less arbitrary your selection process becomes.

If you're filling an existing position, you probably already have a detailed job description available. Review it closely and make changes where necessary. Ensure that the job description reflects exactly the tasks and requirements of the position.

When you hire someone new to fill an existing position, you start with a clean slate. For example, you may have had a difficult time getting a former employee to accept certain new tasks — say, taking minutes at staff meetings or filing travel vouchers. By adding these new duties to the job description before you open recruitment, you make the expectations clear and you don't have to struggle with your new hire to do the job.

If the job is new, now is your opportunity to design your ideal candidate. Draft a job description that fully describes all the tasks and responsibilities of the position and the minimum necessary qualifications and experience. If the job requires expertise in addition and subtraction, for example, say so. You're not going to fill the position with the right hire if you don't make certain qualifications a key part of the job description. The more work you put into the job description now, the less work you have to do after you bring in your new hire.

To ensure that your job description is on target, spend time observing employees and soliciting their input on the responsibilities the position requires.

Finally, before you start recruiting, use the latest-and-greatest job description to outline the most important qualities you're seeking in your new hire. Consult and compare notes with other managers on your team to get input on your descriptions, and ask employees for their feedback as well. Use this outline to guide you in the interview process. Keep in mind, however, that job descriptions may give you the skills you want, but they don't automatically give you the kind of employee you want — finding the right person is much more difficult (and the reason you spend so much time recruiting in the first place).

Making an interview outline carries an additional benefit: You can easily document why you didn't hire the candidates who didn't qualify for your positions. Pay close attention here. If a disgruntled job candidate ever sues you for not hiring him — and such lawsuits are more common than you may suspect —

you'll be eternally thankful that you did your homework in this area of the hiring process. One more thing: Don't make notes on the résumé — your comments could be used in a lawsuit.

Defining the Characteristics of Desirable Candidates

Employers look for many qualities in candidates. The following list gives you an idea of the qualities employers consider most important when hiring new employees. Other characteristics may be particularly important to you, your company, and the job you're looking to fill, and this list gives you a good start in identifying them.

- ✔ **Hard working:** Hard work can often overcome a lack of experience or training. You want to hire people who are willing to do whatever it takes to get the job done. Conversely, no amount of skill can make up for a lack of initiative or work ethic. Although you won't know for sure until you make your hire, carefully questioning candidates can give you some idea of their work ethic (or, at least, what they want you to believe about their work ethic). Of course, hard work alone isn't always the end-all, be-all of hiring. People can generate a lot of work, but if the work doesn't align with your company's strategies or isn't within the true scope of their role, then it's wasted effort. Be careful to note the difference as you assess your candidates.

- ✔ **Good attitude:** Although what constitutes a good attitude differs for each person, a positive, friendly, willing-to-help perspective makes life at the office much more enjoyable and makes everyone's job easier. When you interview candidates, consider what they'll be like to work with for the next five or ten years. Skills are important, but attitude is even more important. This is the mantra for the success of Southwest Airlines: "Hire for attitude, train for success."

- ✔ **Experienced:** A résumé may highlight an advanced degree from a highbrow college and a long list of impressive internships and volunteer work, but an interview gives you the opportunity to ask pointed questions that require your candidates to demonstrate that they can do the job.

- ✔ **Self-starter:** Candidates need to demonstrate an ability to take initiative to get work done. In an Internet survey conducted for the book *1001 Ways to Take Initiative at Work* by Bob Nelson, Ph.D. (Workman), initiative ranked as the top reason employees were able to get ahead where they work.

✔ **Team player:** Teamwork is critical to the success of today's organizations that must do far more with far fewer resources than their predecessors. The ability to work with others and to collaborate effectively is a definite must for employees today.

✔ **Smart:** Smart people can often find better and quicker solutions to the problems that confront them. In the business world, work smarts are more important than book smarts.

✔ **Responsible:** You want to hire people who are willing to take on the responsibilities of their positions. Questions about the kinds of projects your candidates have been responsible for and the exact roles those projects played in their success can help you determine this important quality. Finer points, like showing up for the interview on time and remembering the name of the person they're interviewing with, can also be key indicators of your candidates' sense of responsibility.

✔ **Flexible/resilient:** Employees who are able to multitask and switch direction if necessary in a seamless manner are real assets to any organization.

✔ **Cultural fit:** Every business has its own unique culture and set of values. The ability to fit into this culture and values is key to whether candidates can succeed within a particular company (assuming that they already have the technical skills).

✔ **Stable:** You don't want to hire someone today and then find out he's already looking for the next position tomorrow. No company can afford the expense of hiring and training a new employee, only to have that person leave six months later. You can get some indication of a person's potential stability (or lack thereof) by asking pointed questions about how long candidates worked with previous employers and why they left. Be especially thorough and methodical as you probe this particular area.

Hiring the right people is one of the most important tasks managers face. You can't have a great organization without great people. Unfortunately, managers traditionally give short shrift to this task, devoting as little time as possible to preparation and the actual interview process. As in much of the rest of your life, the results you get from the hiring process are usually in direct proportion to the amount of time you devote to it.

Finding Good People

People are the heart of every business. The better people you hire, the better business you have. Some people are just meant to be in their jobs. You may know such individuals — someone who thrives as a receptionist or someone who lives to sell. Think about how great your organization would be if you staffed every position with people who lived for their jobs.

Likewise, bad hires can make working for an organization an incredibly miserable experience. The negative impacts of hiring the wrong candidate can reverberate both inside and outside an organization for years. If you, as a manager, ignore the problem, you put yourself in danger of losing your good employees — and clients, business partners, and vendors. Hiring the right people is paramount. Do you want to spend a few extra hours up front to find the best candidates, or do you later want to devote countless hours trying to straighten out a problem employee?

Of course, as important as the interview process is to selecting the best candidates for your jobs, you won't have anyone to interview if you don't have a good system for finding good candidates. So where can you find the best candidates for your jobs? The simple answer is *everywhere.*

Most managers find they have better experiences with hiring when they take a long-term view of the hire: undertaking a broad search and long hiring cycle that involves other employees in the process. The short-term, "We've gotta have somebody right away" approach often results in selecting an applicant who is the lesser of a number of evils — and whose weaknesses soon become problems for the organization.

Going through traditional recruiting channels

Your job is to develop a recruitment campaign that helps you find the kinds of people you want to hire. Don't rely solely on your human resources department to develop the campaign for you; you probably have a better understanding of where to find the people you need than they do (no offense to you folks in HR!). Make sure your input is heeded.

The following list presents some of the best ways to find candidates:

- ✔ **Internal candidates:** In most organizations, the first place to look for candidates is within the organization. If you do your job training and developing employees, you probably have plenty of candidates to consider for your job openings. Only after you exhaust your internal candidates should you look outside your organization. Not only is hiring people this way less expensive and easier, but you also get happier employees, improved morale, and new hires who are already familiar with your organization.

✔ **Personal referrals:** Whether from coworkers, professional colleagues, friends, relatives, or neighbors, you can often find great candidates through referrals. Who better to present a candidate than someone whose opinion you already value and trust? You get far more insight about the candidates' strengths and weaknesses from the people who refer them than you ever get from résumés alone. Not only that, but research shows that people hired through current employees tend to work out better, stay with the company longer, and act happier. When you're getting ready to fill a position, make sure you let people know about it. Your employees and coworkers may well mount their own Twitter and Facebook campaigns for you, getting the word out to a wide audience.

✔ **Temporary agencies:** Hiring *temps,* or temporary employees, has become routine for many companies. When you simply have to fill a critical position for a short period of time, temporary agencies are the way to go — no muss, no fuss. And the best part is that when you hire temps, you get the opportunity to try out employees before you buy them. If you don't like the temps you get, no problem. Simply call the agency, and they send replacements before you know it. But if you like your temps, most agencies allow you to hire them at a nominal fee or after a minimum time commitment. Either way, you win. One more point: If you're using temps, you can complete your organization's necessary work while you continue looking for the right full-time employee. This buys you more time to find the best person for the job without feeling pressure to hire someone who doesn't really meet all your needs.

✔ **Professional associations:** Most professions have their accompanying associations that look out for their interests. Whether you're a doctor (and belong to the American Medical Association) or a truck driver (and belong to the Teamster's Union), you can likely find an affiliated association for whatever you do for a living. Associations even have their own associations. Association job fairs, newsletters, magazines, websites, blogs, and social networking sites are great places to advertise your openings when you're looking for specific expertise because your audience is already prescreened for you.

✔ **Employment agencies:** If you're filling a particularly specialized position, are recruiting in a small market, or simply prefer to have someone else take care of recruiting and screening your applicants, employment agencies are a good, albeit pricey (with a cost of up to a third of the employee's first-year salary, or more) alternative. Although employment agencies can usually locate qualified candidates in lower-level or administrative positions, you may need help from an executive search firm or *headhunter* (someone who specializes in recruiting key employees away from one firm to place in a client's firm) for your higher-level positions.

✔ **Recruiting at colleges:** If you're near a university that has a major program related to the job you're trying to fill, you're sitting on a goldmine. You find a number of ways to get your name out on a campus, and a recruitment office can clue you in to the exact opportunities, which likely include on-campus visits, job fairs, and advertising in university publications and on job-posting websites. To be most effective, campus recruiting entails efforts on your part to build your name recognition so that you get noticed by top students and give them reasons to want to find out more about your company and the opportunities within it. The pool of talent on a campus is vast, but so is the competition.

✔ **Want ads:** Want ads can be relatively expensive, but they're an easy way to get your message out to a large cross-section of potential candidates. You can choose to advertise in your local paper, in nationally distributed publications such as *The Wall Street Journal*, or on popular websites such as craigslist (`www.craigslist.com`). On the downside, you may find yourself sorting through hundreds or even thousands of unqualified candidates to find a few great ones.

As a manager, it is in your interest to work with your human resources team to develop an ongoing talent pipeline for key and hard-to-fill positions, or where there is high turnover such as in sales roles.

Leveraging the power of the Internet

Every day, more companies discover the benefits of using the Internet as a hiring tool. The proliferation of corporate web pages and online employment agencies and job banks has brought about an entirely new dimension in recruiting. Web pages let you present almost unlimited amounts and kinds of information about your firm and your job openings — in text, audio, graphic, and video formats. Your pages work for you 24 hours a day, 7 days a week.

Consider a few of the best ways to leverage the power of the Internet in your own hiring efforts:

✔ **Websites and blogs:** If you don't already have a great recruiting page on your company website, you should. In addition to this baseline item, also consider setting up company blogs where employees can describe what they do and how they do it. This gives prospective job candidates insight into your organization, helping them decide for themselves whether yours is the kind of organization they want to actively pursue. Be sure to include a function where people can supply their e-mail address or sign up for an RSS feed to be updated as new positions open. Prices to set up a website or blog vary from free to a few thousand dollars a year, depending on how many bells and whistles you require.

Book III

Mastering Key Management Duties

For an example of a particularly effective recruiting website, point your browser to www.qualcomm.com and click on the Careers tab.

✔ **E-mail campaigns:** If you set up the e-mail function on your website as just mentioned, you'll soon collect a large number of addresses from potential job candidates. Don't just sit there — use them! Be sure to e-mail an announcement to everyone on your list every time you have a job opening. Even if the people who receive your e-mail message aren't interested, they may know someone who is and may forward your announcement.

✔ **Social networking sites:** Although many social networking sites exist, a handful have risen to the top of the heap. Two, in particular, deserve your attention if you hope to broaden your search for good candidates: Facebook (www.facebook.com) and LinkedIn (www.linkedin.com). Millions of people have established accounts at both of these sites; however, LinkedIn was specifically designed to help job seekers network with one another to find new job opportunities. This makes it a particularly effective way for you to get the word out about your open positions. Although Facebook isn't specifically set up for job networking, you can set up a fan page there and use it as an effective recruiting platform. There's no charge to set up and use a Facebook or LinkedIn account.

✔ **Twitter:** Many organizations use Twitter (www.twitter.com) as a real-time platform for getting out information to anyone interested in getting it. This includes prospective job applicants. The variety of information you can send out to the world is limited only by your imagination — and by the 140-character limit for individual tweets. There's no charge to set up and use your Twitter account.

✔ **Traditional job-hunting sites:** A number of job-hunting sites have become popular with people looking for new positions. This makes them good platforms from which to pitch your own job openings. Some of the most popular include CareerBuilder.com (www.careerbuilder.com), Monster.com (www.monster.com), and Beyond.com (www.beyond.com). You'll likely have to pay to post your jobs on these sites; prices vary.

Becoming a Great Interviewer

After you narrow the field to the top three or five applicants, the next step is to start interviewing. What kind of interviewer are you? Do you spend several hours preparing for interviews — reviewing résumés, looking over job descriptions, writing and rewriting questions until each one is as finely honed as a razor blade? Or are you the kind of interviewer who, busy as you already are, starts preparing for the interview when you get the call from your receptionist that your candidate has arrived?

Here's a hint: The secret to becoming a great interviewer is to be thoroughly prepared for your interviews. Remember how much time you spent preparing to be interviewed for your current job? You didn't just walk in the door, sit down, and get offered the job, did you? You probably spent hours researching the company, its products and services, its financials, its market, and other business information. You probably brushed up on your interviewing skills and may have even done some role-playing with a friend or in front of a mirror. Don't you think you should spend at least as much time getting ready for the interview as the people you're going to interview?

Asking the right questions

More than anything else, the heart of the interview process is the questions you ask and the answers you get in response. You get the best answers when you ask the best questions. Lousy questions often result in lousy answers that don't really tell you whether the candidate is right for the job.

A great interviewer asks great questions. According to Richard Nelson Bolles, author of the perennially popular job-hunting guide *What Color Is Your Parachute?* (Ten Speed Press), you can categorize all interview questions under one of the following four headings:

- ✔ **Why are you here?** Why is the person sitting across from you going to the trouble of interviewing with you today? You have just one way to find out — ask. You may assume that the answer is because she wants a job with your firm, but what you find may surprise you.

   Consider the story of the interviewee who forgot that he was interviewing for a job with Hewlett-Packard. During the entire interview, the applicant referred to Hewlett-Packard by the name of one of its competitors. He didn't get the job.

- ✔ **What can you do for us?** Always an important consideration! Of course, your candidates are all going to dazzle you with their incredible personalities, experience, work ethic, and love of teamwork — that almost goes without saying. However, despite what many job seekers seem to believe, the question is not, "What can your firm do for me?" — at least, not from your perspective. The question that you want an answer to is, "What can you do for us?"

   One recruiter shares a story about the job applicant who slammed his hand on her desk and demanded a signing bonus. And this was before the interview had even started! We're not surprised that this particular candidate landed neither the job nor the bonus.

Book III

Mastering
Key
Management
Duties

✔ **What kind of person are you?** Few of your candidates will be absolute angels or demons, but don't forget that you'll spend a lot of time with the person you hire. You want to hire someone you'll enjoy being with during the many work hours, weeks, and years that stretch before you — and the holiday parties, company picnics, and countless other events you're expected to attend.

You also want to confirm a few other issues: Are your candidates honest and ethical? Do they share your views regarding work hours, responsibility, and so forth? Are they responsible and dependable employees? Would they work well in your company culture? Of course, all your candidates will answer in the affirmative to mom-and-apple-pie questions like these. So how do you find the real answers?

Some recruiters try to "project" applicants into a real-life scenario and see how they'd think it through. For example, you may ask the prospect what she would do if a client called at 5 p.m. with an emergency order that needed to be delivered by 9 a.m. the next morning. This way, there's no "right" answer, and candidates are forced to expose their thinking process: what questions they'd ask, what strategies they'd consider, which people they'd involve, and so forth. Ask open-ended questions and let your candidates do most of the talking!

✔ **Can we afford you?** It does you no good to find the perfect candidate but, at the end of the interview, discover that you're so far apart in pay range that you're nearly in a different state. Keep in mind that the actual wage you pay to workers is only part of an overall compensation package. You may not be able to pull together more money for wages for particularly good candidates, but you may be able to offer someone better benefits, a nicer office, a more impressive title, or a key to the executive sauna.

Following interviewing do's

So what can you do to prepare for your interviews? The following checklist gives you ideas on where to start:

✔ **Review the résumés of each interviewee the morning before interviews start.** Not only is it extremely poor form to wait to read your interviewees' résumés during the interview, but you miss out on the opportunity to tailor your questions to those little surprises you invariably discover in the résumés.

✔ **Become intimately familiar with the job description.** Are you familiar with all the duties and requirements of the job? Surprising new hires with duties that you didn't tell them about — especially when they're major duties — isn't a pathway to new-hire success.

✔ **Draft your questions before the interview.** Make a checklist of the key experience, skills, and qualities that you seek in your candidates, and use it to guide your questions. Of course, one of your questions may trigger other questions that you didn't anticipate. Go ahead with such questions, as long as they give you additional insights into your candidate and help illuminate the information you're seeking with your checklist.

✔ **Select a comfortable environment for both of you.** Your interviewee will likely be uncomfortable regardless of what you do. You don't need to be uncomfortable, too. Make sure that the interview environment is well-ventilated, private, and protected from interruptions. You definitely don't want your phone ringing off the hook or employees barging in during your interviews. You get the best performance from your interviewees when they aren't thrown off track by distractions.

✔ **Avoid playing power trips during the course of the interview.** Forget the old games of asking trick questions, turning up the heat, or cutting the legs off their chairs (yes, some managers still do this game playing!) to gain an artificial advantage over your candidates.

✔ **Take a lot of notes.** Don't rely on your memory when it comes to interviewing candidates for your job. If you interview more than a couple people, you can easily forget who said exactly what, as well as what your impressions were of their performances. Not only are your written notes a great way to remember who's who, but they're an important tool to have when you're evaluating your candidates.

Interviews are an imperfect method for determining who can best handle a job's responsibilities, but they're one of your best tools for determining whether a candidate is right for your company culture. Asking the right questions helps you get the most from the interviews you conduct. Although some amount of small talk is appropriate to help relax your candidates, the heart of your interviews should focus on answering the questions just listed. Above all, don't give up! Keep asking questions until you're satisfied that you have all the information you need to make your decision.

Don't forget to take lots of notes as you interview your candidates. Try to avoid the temptation to draw pictures of little smiley faces or that new car you've been lusting after. Write the key points of your candidates' responses and their reactions to your questions. For example, if you ask why your candidate left her previous job, and she starts getting really nervous, make a note about this reaction. Finally, note your own impressions of the candidates:

✔ Top-notch performer — the star of her class.

✔ Fantastic experience with developing applications in a client/server environment. The best candidate yet.

✔ Geez, was this one interviewing for the right job?

Book III

Mastering Key Management Duties

Avoiding interviewing don'ts

The topic of interviewing don'ts is probably worth a chapter of its own. If you've been a manager for any time at all, you know that you can run into tricky situations during an interview and that certain questions can land you in major hot water if you make the mistake of asking them.

Some interviewing don'ts are merely good business practice. For example, accepting an applicant's invitation for a date is probably not a good idea. Believe it or not, it happens. After a particularly drawn-out interview at a well-known high-tech manufacturer, a male candidate asked out a female interviewer. The interviewer considered her options and declined the date; she also declined to make Prince Charming a job offer.

Blunders of the major legal type can land you and your firm in court. Interviewing is one area of particular concern in the hiring process as it pertains to possible discrimination. For example, although you can ask applicants whether they are able to fulfill job functions, in the United States, you can't ask them whether they are disabled. Because of the critical nature of the interview process, you must know the questions that you absolutely should never ask a job candidate. Here is a brief summary of the kinds of topics that may get you and your firm into trouble, depending on the exact circumstances:

- Age
- Arrest and conviction record
- Debts
- Disability
- Height and weight
- Marital status
- National origin
- Race or skin color
- Religion (or lack thereof)
- Sex
- Sexual orientation

Legal or illegal, the point is that none of the preceding topics is necessary to determine applicants' ability to perform their jobs. Ask questions that directly relate to the candidates' ability to perform the tasks required. To do otherwise can put you at definite legal risk. In other words, what *does* count is job-related criteria — that is, information that's directly pertinent to the candidate's ability to do the job. (Clearly, you need to decide what this information is *prior* to interviewing!)

Five steps to better interviewing

Every interview consists of five key steps:

1. **Welcome the applicant.** Greet your candidates warmly and chat with them informally to help loosen them up. Questions about the weather, the difficulty of finding your offices, or how they found out about your position are old standbys.

2. **Summarize the position.** Briefly describe the job, the kind of person you're looking for, and the interview process you use.

3. **Ask your questions (and then listen!).** Questions should be relevant to the position and should cover the applicant's work experience, education, and other related topics. Limit the amount of talking you do as an interviewer. Many interviewers end up trying to sell the job to an applicant instead of probing whether a candidate is a good fit.

4. **Probe experience and discover the candidate's strengths and weaknesses.** The best predictor of future behavior is past behavior, which is why exploring applicants' past experience can be so helpful to see what they did and how they did it! And although asking your candidates to name their strengths and weaknesses may seem clichéd, the answers can be very revealing. Ask also about specific examples of behavior — how your candidate contributed to successful projects and what frustrated her about those that didn't go well.

5. **Conclude the interview.** Allow your candidates the opportunity to offer any further information that they feel is necessary for you to make a decision, and to ask questions about your firm or the job. Thank them for their interest and let them know when they can expect your firm to contact them.

Book III

Mastering Key Management Duties

Evaluating Your Candidates

Now comes the really fun part of the hiring process — evaluating your candidates. If you've done your homework, you already have an amazing selection of candidates to choose from, you've narrowed your search to the ones showing the best potential to excel in your position, and you've interviewed them to see whether they can live up to the promises they made in their résumés. Before you make your final decision, you need a bit more information.

Checking references

Wow! What a résumé! What an interview! What a candidate! Would you be surprised to find out that this shining employee-to-be didn't really go to Yale? Or that he really wasn't the account manager on that nationwide marketing campaign? Or that his last supervisor wasn't particularly impressed with his analytical skills?

A résumé and interview are great tools, but a reference check is probably the only chance you have to find out before you make a hiring decision whether your candidates are actually who they say they are. Depending on your organization, you may be expected to do reference checks. Or maybe your human resources department takes care of that task. Whichever the case, don't hire new employees without first doing an exhaustive check of their backgrounds.

The twin goals of checking references are to verify the information that your candidates have provided and to gain some candid insight into who your candidates really are and how they behave in the workplace. When you contact a candidate's references, limit your questions to topics related to the work to be done. As in the interview process, asking questions that can be considered discriminatory to your candidates isn't appropriate.

Here are some of the best ways to do your reference checking:

- **Check academic references.** A surprising number of people exaggerate or tell outright lies when reporting their educational experience. Start your reference check here.

- **Call current and former supervisors.** Getting information from employers is getting more difficult. Many businesspeople are rightfully concerned that they may be sued for libel or defamation of character if they say anything negative about current or former subordinates. Still, it doesn't hurt to try. You get a much better picture of your candidates if you speak directly to their current and former supervisors instead of to their firms' human resources department — especially if the supervisors you speak to have left their firms. The most you're likely to get from the human resources folks is a confirmation that the candidate worked at the firm during a specific period of time.

- **Check your network of associates.** If you belong to a professional association, union, or similar group of like-minded careerists, you have the opportunity to tap into the rest of the membership to get the word on your candidates. For example, if you're a certified public accountant (CPA) and want to find out about a few candidates for your open accounting position, you can check with the members of your professional accounting association to see whether anyone knows anything about them.

✔ **Do some surfing.** On the web, that is. Plug your candidate's name into a search engine such as Google, perhaps along with the name of the company where the person last worked or the city where she lives. Or do a search for your candidate on Facebook (www.facebook.com) or LinkedIn (www.linkedin.com). You may be surprised by how much information you can uncover about a job candidate — good and bad — doing just a few simple web searches.

Reviewing your notes

You did take interview notes, didn't you? Now's the time to drag them back out and look them over. Review the information package for each candidate — one by one — and compare your findings against your predetermined criteria. Take a look at the candidates' résumés, your notes, and the results of your reference checks. How do they stack up against the standards you set for the position? Do you see any clear winners at this point? Any clear losers? Organize your candidate packages into the following stacks:

✔ **Winners:** These candidates are clearly the best choices for the position. You have no hesitation in hiring any one of them.

✔ **Potential winners:** These candidates are questionable for some reason. Maybe their experience isn't as strong as that of other candidates, or perhaps you weren't impressed with their presentation skills. Neither clear winners nor clear losers, you hire these candidates only after further investigation or if you can't hire anyone from your pool of winners.

✔ **Losers:** These candidates are clearly unacceptable for the position. You simply don't consider hiring any of them.

Book III

Mastering
Key
Management
Duties

Conducting a second (or third) round

When you're a busy manager, you have pressure to get things done as quickly as possible, and you're tempted to take shortcuts to achieve your goals. It seems that everything has to be done yesterday — or maybe the day before. When do you really have the opportunity to spend as much time as you want to complete a task or project? Time is precious when you have ten other projects crying for your attention. Time is even more valuable when you're hiring for a vacant position that's critical to your organization and needs to be filled right now.

Hiring is one area of business where you must avoid taking shortcuts. Remember, hire slowly and fire quickly (but within the rules). Finding the best candidates for your vacancies requires an investment of time and resources. Your company's future depends on it. Great candidates don't stay on the market long, though, so don't allow the process to drag on too long. Make sure the candidates know your required timeframe, and stick to it!

Depending on your organization's policies or culture, or if you're undecided on the best candidate, you may decide to bring candidates in for several rounds of interviews. In this kind of system, lower-level supervisors, managers, or interview panels conduct initial screening interviews. Candidates who pass this round are invited back for another interview with a higher-level manager. Finally, the best two or three candidates interview with the organization's top manager.

But keep in mind that the timeline for an offer differs depending on the job you're interviewing for. Lower-level job hunters cannot afford to be unemployed (if they are) for long, and they often get and accept job offers quickly. A higher-level position — say, a general manager — gives you more time.

The ultimate decision on how many rounds and levels of interviews to conduct depends on the nature of the job itself, the size of your company, and your policies and procedures. If the job is simple or at a relatively low level in the company, a single phone interview may be sufficient to determine the best candidate. However, if the job is complex or at a relatively high level in the organization, you may need several rounds of testing and personal interviews to determine the best candidate.

Hiring the Best (And Leaving the Rest)

The first step in making a hiring decision is to rank your candidates within the groups of winners and potential winners that you established during the evaluation phase of the hiring process. You don't need to bother ranking the losers because you wouldn't hire them anyway — no matter what. The best candidate in your group of winners is first, the next best is second, and so on. If you've done your job thoroughly and well, the best candidates for the job are readily apparent at this point.

The next step is to get on the phone and offer your first choice the job. Don't waste any time — you never know whether your candidate has interviewed with other employers. It would be a shame to invest all this time in the hiring process only to find out that your top choice accepted a job with one of your competitors. If you can't come to terms with your first choice in a reasonable amount of time, go on to your second choice. Keep going through your pool of winners until you either make a hire or exhaust the list of candidates.

The following sections give you a few tips to keep in mind as you rank your candidates and make your final decision.

Being objective

In some cases, you may prefer certain candidates because of their personalities or personal charisma, regardless of their abilities or work experience. Sometimes the desire to like these candidates can obscure their shortcomings, while a better qualified, albeit less socially adept, candidate may fade in your estimation.

Be objective. Consider the job to be done, as well as the skills and qualifications that being successful requires. Do your candidates have these skills and qualifications? What would it take for your candidates to be considered fully qualified for the position?

Don't allow yourself to be unduly influenced by your candidates' looks, champagne-like personalities, high-priced hairstyles, or fashion-forward clothing ensembles. None of these characteristics can tell you how well your candidates will actually perform the job. The facts are present for you to see in your candidates' résumés, interview notes, and reference checks. If you stick to the facts, you can still go wrong, but the chances are diminished.

One more thing: Diversity in hiring is positive for any organization. Its benefits extend in ways that you might not expect. Studies show that a diverse workforce is more productive and has higher staff retention. Including employees from various generations, cultures, backgrounds, and experiences creates a more creative environment in which people are better able to respond to change, resolve conflict, and relate to customers and the community at large — all good reasons to check your bias at the door.

Book III

Mastering Key Management Duties

Trusting your gut

Sometimes you're faced with a decision between two equally qualified candidates, or with a decision about a candidate who is marginal but shows promise. In such cases, you have weighed all the objective data and given the analytical side of your being free rein, but you still have no clear winner. What do you do in this kind of situation?

Listen to yourself. What do you feel in your gut? Not nausea, we hope. Although two candidates may seem equal in skills and abilities, do you have a feeling that one is better suited to the job? If so, go with it. As much as you may want your hiring decision to be as objective as possible, whenever you introduce the human element into the decision-making process, a certain amount of subjectivity is naturally present.

In reality, rarely are two candidates equally qualified, although often one or more people seem to have more to bring to the job than anticipated (for example, industry focus, fresh ideas, previous contacts, and so forth). This is again where your pre-work can be so valuable in keeping you focused. Can they both do the job? If so, the bonus traits can tip the scale.

Other options:

✔ Give them each a nonpaid assignment and see how they do.

✔ Try them each on a paid project.

Keep in touch with other top candidates as additional needs arise or in case your first choice doesn't work out.

Revisiting the candidate pool

What do you do if, heaven forbid, you can't hire anyone from your group of winners? This unfortunate occurrence is a tough call, but no one said management is an easy task. Take a look at your stack of potential winners. What would it take to make your top potential winners into winners? If the answer is as simple as a training course or two, then give these candidates serious consideration — with the understanding that you can schedule the necessary training soon after hiring. Perhaps a candidate just needs a little more experience before moving into the ranks of the winners. You can make a judgment call on whether you feel that someone's current experience is sufficient until that person gains the experience you're looking for. If not, you may want to keep looking for the right candidate. After all, this person may be working with you for a long time — waiting for the best candidate only makes sense.

If you're forced to go to your group of almost-winners and no candidate really seems up to the task, don't hire someone simply to fill the position. If you do, you're probably making a big mistake. Hiring employees is far easier than unhiring them. The damage that an inappropriate hire can wreak — on coworkers, your customers, and your organization (not to mention the person you hired) — can take years and a considerable amount of money to undo. Not only that, but it can be a big pain in your neck! Other options are to redefine the job, reevaluate other current employees, or hire on a temporary basis to see whether a risky hire works out.

Chapter 2

Engaging Your Employees

*A*lmost every organization claims that its people are the most valued asset, but few companies systematically follow through on that belief in ways that can truly empower employees to make a difference. By being proactive, positive, focused, and forward-looking, managers can inspire employees — and employees can inspire themselves and their coworkers — in practical ways that obtain real results and allow their companies to become stronger, more profitable, and more competitive in even the most difficult marketplace.

Taking control of their circumstances helps employees take control of their jobs — and their lives — and makes positive things happen where only negatives existed before. Redefining circumstances in this way puts employees in the driver's seat.

This chapter shows you how to create a framework for managing employees in positive and practical ways to overcome negative times and circumstances. It offers a strategy, process, and critical success factors to focus on, all supported with examples, techniques, and case studies of how other managers have succeeded in fostering more engaged employees.

Understanding the Power of Employee Engagement

Most employees are motivated to do a good job where they work. (It's hard to imagine that many people get up in the morning hoping to make a mess of things at work.) They want to help the organization as best they can to be successful and to keep their jobs. But they can't do this in a vacuum. They need the leadership and support of management where they work to help create the context for their success.

The problem of employees who aren't engaged in their jobs has a devastating impact on many organizations. The Gallup Organization, which tracks more than 3.8 million workers around the world, looked into employee engagement, and the results weren't pretty. According to Gallup's survey of American companies, only 29 percent of workers — less than a third — are engaged in their jobs. These employees feel a profound connection to their company and are passionate about their work. However, most workers — 54 percent — aren't engaged in their jobs at all. These employees show up at work and punch the clock, but they pour neither energy nor passion into their work. Believe it or not, the statistics get worse. Fully 17 percent of American workers — almost one in five — are actively disengaged. These unhappy employees get little or no work done. Why? They are often fearful of change and of being accountable for their own futures.

Envision for a moment raising the engagement level of your workforce — transforming both the average 54 percent of workers who aren't engaged in their jobs and the 17 percent of workers who are actively disengaged at work. Imagine the power, energy, creativity, efficiency, innovation, and customer service you could unleash.

This is the power of employee engagement, and it's why you, as a manager, need to find ways to tap it.

Creating a Clear, Compelling Direction

The starting point of any effort to improve employee engagement is to give employees a clear and compelling vision. If employees don't know — or aren't inspired by — what the organization is trying to do, they'll find it more difficult to summon the motivation to succeed, especially in tough times. Frances Hesselbein, president of the Leader to Leader Institute, once put it this way: "No matter what business you're in, everyone in the organization needs to know why."

People who perform well feel good about themselves. When personal or company goals are being reached or surpassed, the level of engagement among employees is typically at its highest, which then affects other areas of performance as well. If this engagement spills over to better customer service or higher-quality products and services, it can have a direct impact on customer loyalty. Increased customer loyalty can positively impact sales and revenue as well.

Attaining or maintaining high levels of engagement and motivation among employees is decidedly more difficult in challenging economic times. If employees spend most of their time fretting over the financial state of the company (which has a direct impact on their personal financial state), they spend less time on their work, causing productivity as well as customer service to suffer. For advice on dealing with economic challenges and other hard times in your business, turn to the later section "Communicating bad news and dealing with rumors."

Assessing employees' understanding of mission and purpose

Do a reality check: Ask employees what the mission or purpose of the organization is and what their role is in reaching that purpose. If you get a different answer from each person you ask, it's a good indication that the message has drifted — or perhaps hasn't been clear for some time. Use this opportunity to revisit the purpose of your business group or function.

To gain clarity about the organization's mission, management guru Peter Drucker recommends that you ask five questions to get at the core of your business. These questions help connect what your organization is trying to achieve with your customers in the marketplace:

Book III

Mastering Key Management Duties

- ✔ What is our mission?
- ✔ Who is our customer?
- ✔ What does the customer value?
- ✔ What are our results?
- ✔ What is our plan?

Clarifying the vision is a useful starting point in deciding what is most important for the organization (or department) to focus on to be successful. The result needs to be a compelling purpose that can inspire everyone. "A vision is not just a picture of what could be — it is an appeal to our better selves, a call to become something more," says Harvard professor Rosabeth Moss Kanter. From that vision, you can shape your *unique competitive advantages* — that is, the aspects that you can offer your customers and that your competition cannot. These advantages represent your strengths in the marketplace that you most need to capitalize on to succeed. In changing times, the unique advantages you have to offer and the needs of your customers can shift drastically, so looking at them frequently makes sense.

Modifying strategies to meet goals

When you've clarified your vision for your group and started to reassess and revitalize your goals, analyze what's currently working — and what's not — for the business. For example, established customers may be cutting back on using the services of your firm, but what new clients have recently started to invest with you? What do those new clients have in common, and how can you approach similar clients in the marketplace? Changing times call for changing strategies to meet your company's goals. Engage employees to help with these changes by seeking their input and ideas for improving business operations, saving the company money, or better serving customers.

Opening Lines of Communication

The need to know what's going on is pervasive. People want to know not just the necessary information to do the work they're assigned, but also what their coworkers are doing and how successful the organization is. Management needs to communicate information to employees about the organization's mission and purpose, its products and services, its strategies for success in the marketplace, and even what's going on with the competition.

In our research, the highest-ranking variable that 65 percent of employees want most from their managers is ample information at work. This statistic has a degree of significance that places it in a category of its own. These research findings correlate with recent research from Accountemps that found communication to be the leading variable that 48 percent of executives reported could best impact low morale in their organization.

One of the most common errors many organizations and managers make is to not share adequate information with employees. In some instances, top management doesn't share information because managers themselves are uncertain about the constantly changing economic landscape. In other instances, managers feel that sharing information with employees decreases their power and status. Management also may try to "protect" employees from fears surrounding a potential job loss or the ability of senior management to effectively handle a pending crisis. More often, these well-intended actions backfire; closed-door meetings and hushed hallway conversations create a sense of unease among employees and lead to speculation, heightened fear, and worst-case-scenario rumors.

Employees want and need to know what's going on within the organization, even if the information isn't positive. Nothing is wrong with being honest with employees when the firm is struggling. Doing so can lead to an increase in teamwork and dedication, especially if you use the bad news as an opportunity to brainstorm and communicate with employees about ideas and plans for turning things around. Bringing employees into the loop during down times can instill a greater sense of involvement and responsibility, which ultimately leads to increased employee feelings of value and trust.

Employing direct, two-way communication

To maximize employee engagement, keeping employees abreast of management's goals and ensuing plans is imperative. Something as simple as a company-wide meeting that presents the state of the organization to all employees and clearly addresses goals (both financial and nonfinancial) can make a world of difference in easing employee tensions and fears.

When discussing major issues like organizational changes, communication should come in the form of a dialogue instead of a lecture, and management should encourage questions. Such key updates should also be shared in advance of information that is made public, as in a press release. Employees must be made to feel as though they have the freedom to express their fears and concerns, and receive honest and informative responses. Feedback sessions, departmental meetings, and company-wide gatherings should ideally serve two purposes: to gather feedback and to provide information.

Exploring communication techniques

Methods for communicating with employees depend on the situation. Group settings require different interaction than one-on-one communication. Following are suggestions for communicating with individuals and groups:

✓ **Individuals**

- Engage in periodic one-on-one meetings with each employee.

- Offer personal support and reassurances, especially for your most valued employees.

- Provide open-door accessibility to management.

- Invite employees to write anonymous letters to top management about their concerns.

✓ **Groups**

- Conduct town hall meetings. Allow questions and provide answers. Take questions in advance of the meeting or allow written questions to be submitted anonymously.

- Host CEO-led breakfasts or brown-bag lunches.

Book III

Mastering Key Management Duties

- Maintain a 24-hour "news desk" on the company intranet.

- Provide periodic "state-of-the-union" updates on the business.

- Be open and honest in explaining the situation and challenges going forward.

- Record meetings and distribute the proceedings to employees who are unable to attend.

You can communicate outside the structure of a meeting. Create a question-and-answer section in your internal newsletter or on your company website. Or set up a blog site for your CEO (especially if your company has satellite offices or employees who travel frequently) to gather immediate feedback concerning key issues and updates. Have key contacts from your human resources, public relations, and legal departments on hand to support the CEO in answering specific questions from those areas.

Communicating bad news and dealing with rumors

One of the most important points to remember is that employees aren't looking for a sugar-coated delivery of information. The best way to explain the state of an organization is in a clear, concise, and honest manner. If sales are declining at a rapid or steady pace, every member of the staff has to know. Sharing this information emphasizes to all employees the collective ownership of the organization's performance. From front-line staff to mid- and upper-level management, everyone shares a portion of the responsibility for an organization's revenue, performance, and future.

By including each employee in an honest, behind-the-scenes look at the fiscal landscape of an organization and the approach or plan to resolve the crisis, you send the underlying message that every single person is a critical part of the whole. That message, in turn, creates a greater sense of accountability. Feeling as though they're part of the solution instead of the problem gives employees the confidence they need to buckle down and do their part to pull the organization through a time of crisis.

Establishing open lines of communication across the company can put an end to one of the most detrimental viruses that spreads throughout an organization: rumors. Human nature dictates that it's easier to believe negative statements than positive ones. Because most rumors are clothed in a shroud of negativity, it's crucial to stop them at the source, if possible, even openly asking employees about rumors they've heard.

Withholding information is a great way to give birth to rumors that spread like wildfire. Merely talking to employees can ease uncertainty and let them know that you're there to provide information, not keep it from them.

Gathering the departments and giving each of them an opportunity to share brings the entire organization together. Most important, employees receive information based on fact, not fiction, and are better equipped to move forward and make well-informed decisions.

Encouraging Involvement and Initiative

Communicating better with employees is the first step in empowering them to act in the best interests of the organization. But that's just the beginning. When employees are armed with more frequent and relevant information, they're more likely to act on that information in ways that can best help the organization. The act of honest and open communication shows that managers have both trust and respect for their employees. Adding the explicit request and encouragement for employees to get involved in helping the company can lead to profound results, from improved daily operations to a better bottom line.

According to a survey conducted of employees in a variety of industries, 50 percent of employees want their managers to ask for their opinions and ideas at work, and more than 50 percent want their managers to involve them in decisions made at work. This section explores ways for you to become a more engaged manager, with engaged employees who share their ideas and have some input in decision making.

Book III

Mastering Key Management Duties

Guiding employee focus

Managers and workers are entering into a new kind of partnership in the workplace. Today's managers are discovering that they have to create an environment that encourages employees to *contribute* their best ideas and work, to help seek out new opportunities (such as new sources of revenue), and to overcome obstacles facing the company (such as rising costs) wherever possible. Workers are discovering that if they expect to survive the constant waves of change sweeping across the global business marketplace, as well as hold on to their current jobs, they have to join together with other employees to contribute to their organizations in ways they've never before been called upon to do. Managers need to discuss the following questions with their employees:

- ✔ **Employee impact:** Are employees aware of how they impact the company's bottom line — that is, how their jobs financially impact the organization?

- ✔ **Revenue-generating ideas:** How can the company generate additional income? Whether it's new fees, cross-selling, or up-selling, what new ideas can the company try?

- ✔ **Cost-saving suggestions:** How can the company trim, delay, or eliminate costs? Which expenses are critical, and which are optional or can temporarily be cut?

- ✔ **Process improvements:** What steps in the organization's processes can be streamlined to save time, resources, and money?

- ✔ **Customer needs and requests:** How can employees help others in the company who are focused on customer needs and requests? How can the company further explore customers' needs?

- ✔ **New products or services:** What ideas exist for new products or services? How can those ideas be better developed and implemented?

- ✔ **Morale and teambuilding:** Who's interested in helping to improve employee teamwork and morale? How can this be done at little cost?

- ✔ **Telecommuter integration:** How can the organization better use and integrate virtual employees?

Asking employees for their input and ideas

Almost every organization has an "open door" policy encouraging employees to speak to their managers about any concerns, ideas, or suggestions. But in practice, this policy doesn't work well. In the typical U.S. company, the average employee makes 1.1 suggestions per year at work. Contrast that employee with the typical Japanese worker, who offers an average of 167 suggestions a year, and you see the potential opportunity for improvement.

Soliciting ideas needs to be a constant strategy. Anonymous surveys and casual questions at the end of a meeting aren't enough to accomplish the task. After initial cost-saving measures are put into place, it's time to talk seriously about how best to move forward in an economical yet productive manner to make the changes stick. The company needs to revise policies and procedures, reinforcing its effort to do things smarter, cheaper, and better.

To maximize buy-in and motivation, challenge your employees to identify ways to improve. Employees must understand that you need their efforts now more than ever. After communicating this, you need to create new mechanisms that inspire ongoing employee involvement.

Do you want more ideas from your employees — ideas for saving money, improving customer service, streamlining processes, and so forth? What business manager or owner doesn't?

Most likely, every employee has at least one $50,000 idea just waiting to get out. The trick is to find a way to encourage it to emerge. Most companies do little, if anything, to get ideas from their employees. If they do decide to take action, it's in the form of a suggestion box placed in the lunchroom with (for some reason) a lock on it. The first dozen or so employees who submit suggestions, if they hear back at all, often get a form letter months later that more or less states, "Here's why we're not using your silly idea. . . ."

The result? The suggestion program grinds to a halt. One company even ended its suggestion program because, it announced, *the company had already gotten all the ideas.* How convenient.

Involving employees in decision making

Most decisions regarding reductions or changes come from the top down, but is that really the best direction? No one knows jobs or departments better than the people who live and breathe them every day, so it makes sense to start there.

For example, if a reporting process is ineffective or costly, talk to the individual responsible for managing the process. Consider the example of a receptionist at Champion Solutions Group in Florida who received expense reports from field sales representatives via overnight delivery. When her suggestion that the reports be faxed instead of shipped was implemented, the company saw a 40 percent reduction in postage costs. This led company leaders to seek employee advice for ways to realize cost savings.

When employees believe they have a hand in making decisions, company-wide buy-in and participation are much easier to obtain. If the general consensus among staff is that decisions will be made with or without their input, the likelihood of anyone providing open and honest feedback is quite small. Asking employees for their input shows that you respect and trust them and will likely increase the quality of the decisions being made. But ultimately, the responsibility for any decisions remains with the manager, so collecting input from employees doesn't mean you're obligated to use what's shared in every instance.

Employees who offer solutions that result in cost savings must not go unrecognized. Incentives such as bonuses, trips, or gift cards not only reward the employee but also inspire others to develop cost-saving ideas of their own. Make the process fun and rewarding. Hold contests, departmental competitions, or other organized events to increase employee involvement and interaction. Ask employees what type of incentives they value; they may want an extra vacation day or time to volunteer at a favorite charity.

Book III

Mastering Key Management Duties

You can't secure support for change without involving employees, so you need to ensure that employees have the opportunity to be involved in the decision-making process. Some simple ways to include employees follow:

- ✔ Ask for their opinions on matters important to the department.
- ✔ Invite them to actively participate in setting objectives and revising goals for the department.
- ✔ Establish task forces made up of employees whose objective is to identify better ways to work.

Increasing Employee Autonomy, Flexibility, and Support

All employees need to have a say in how they do their work, to make it more meaningful. When employees find their work meaningful, they become more engaged and effective. In tough times, the need for fully engaged employees is amplified. It's critical that they go beyond their job descriptions to do whatever they can to make a difference not only in their jobs, but also for the greater good of the company.

After employees have been enlisted to get involved and make suggestions and improvements, they need to be encouraged to run with their ideas, take responsibility, and champion those ideas through to closure and completion. Managers can encourage this increase in autonomy by doing the following:

- ✔ Allowing employees to approach anyone they need for help
- ✔ Giving them the authority to use resources
- ✔ Permitting them to take necessary actions to get the work done

In our research on employee preferences at work, "autonomy and authority" and "flexibility of working hours" were two of the top motivators for employees. Providing these motivators greatly increases employee morale and performance and prompts them to do their best work possible.

Giving employees a say in their own work

No one likes to be micromanaged, and most employees prefer to determine how they work best. In other words, they prefer to be assigned a task and given the freedom to develop a work plan that suits them.

Roles and responsibilities may already be defined, but they're customized based on the individual who occupies the position. Truly knowing your employees becomes important here: Understanding their strengths and weaknesses allows you to properly assign projects and tasks. Take it a step further by allowing employees to pick and choose the projects and responsibilities they can work on.

Allowing flexible work schedules

Most employees cite increased flexibility in employee work schedules as a top motivator. Furthermore, depending on the type of work, a flexible schedule can increase efficiency in getting the work done.

For example, when a work group experimented with having employees work from home on certain projects, everyone logged their hours and was available as needed to discuss work issues. Not counting the saved commute time, employees were twice as efficient in the work they could accomplish. With less socializing and fewer interruptions, employees were better able to focus on the work at hand.

Many employees struggle with how to effectively maintain a balance between their work and personal lives without compromising their success as employees, parents, or spouses. Research shows that involvement in activities outside of work can serve as a stress reducer and create better, well-rounded employees. Your company can help employees achieve a better balance in their lives by implementing policies that promote a life outside the workplace. Among many options for increasing flexibility are the following:

- Alternate hours (arriving early and leaving early or vice versa)
- Four-day work weeks, with longer hours worked on fewer days
- Telecommuting (a topic discussed in the next chapter)
- Job sharing
- Permission to leave work early, when necessary, or to take time off to compensate for extra hours worked

Flexibility shouldn't be limited to just the times when employees are struggling. Many companies have found that giving employees the options of a flexible schedule or telecommuting increases morale and productivity. Some employees appreciate the decreased amount of time they have to spend in the car each week and the money saved on gas or mileage. Other employees value limited childcare expenses or simply like the opportunity to spend more time with their children. Whatever the motivation, employees appreciate having some control over their own schedules and, as a result, feel as though the company has their best interests in mind.

Clearly determine and communicate your company's point of view regarding flexible schedules (as well as your department's viewpoint), and work with employees to make it happen where possible.

Making the most of technology for working remotely

Our lives have changed drastically over the decades, partly because of continuous technological advances. The way in which business is conducted has also changed. Operating on a global scale has become much easier and more streamlined, thanks to new methods of communication that have aided decision making, smoothed operations, and eased expansion. Fortunately, technology has also opened up new possibilities for how employees work.

Gone are the days of communication limited to phone lines or face-to-face meetings. These days, some businesses operate entirely on a virtual platform, with employees scattered throughout the country or even the world. Although not every company is able to operate this way, a large percentage of jobs can be done outside the typical 9-to-5 in the office. As a result, many companies have experimented with flexible schedules or telecommuting options in recent years.

Although it's tough for some managers or business owners to welcome the option of employees working remotely, remember that employees are adults and should be treated as though they're responsible. Most employees perform better if they feel empowered and trusted. Consider these statistics:

- ✔ Eighty-six percent of employees today wish they had more time to spend with their families.

- ✔ In the past five years, nearly 30 percent of workers have voluntarily made career changes that resulted in a salary reduction, in an effort to lead a more balanced life.

- ✔ Almost 50 percent of employees value the option of flexible or work-from-home hours.

- ✔ Fifty-four percent of employees appreciate the option to leave work early to tend to family or child issues.

- ✔ A large percentage of workers would take a reduction in pay if doing so gave them more time for personal interests or allowed them to spend more time with family.

- ✔ More than 60 percent of workers feel that their jobs are part of their identity instead of simply a means to a paycheck.

A sense of balance between the personal and work aspects of life tops the list of most employees when asked what they need to feel good about their work. Not to be mistaken with just a desire to "work from home," the definition of *balance* to employees is, for the most part, the ability to retain a sense of self-identity. Even though a large percentage of employees feel as though their jobs constitute their identity, that's not necessarily the way they want it to be. Encouraging employees to explore interests outside their daily roles or expressing interest in their lives outside the office can convey a dedication to ensuring a good balance.

Providing managerial access and support

When employees are encouraged to have more autonomy, independence, and flexibility in their jobs, management needs to support them in those roles. In one Gallup survey, 66 percent of respondents said their managers had asked them to get involved in decision making, but only 14 percent felt they'd been empowered to make those decisions. When changes occur within an organization as the result of a financial setback, employees are likely to feel a bit lost. Even with solid communication plans, an air of uncertainty and worry can permeate. Managers can set an example by involving employees in the transition process, providing recommendations for working with the changes, and providing adequate resources for problem solving.

 To help employees sustain necessary levels of motivation, work with them to identify potential barriers to their success. Don't simply assume that no obstacles exist or that all the obstacles are evident. Look to employees for guidance and input, and allow them to point out barriers to accomplishing a task, completing a project, or merely going about their daily duties.

Establishing effective lines of communication that involve and support *all* employees is especially imperative if managerial or other staff changes occur — for example, if new managers are put in place, project groups are reassigned, or departments are downsized. No matter how small the changes, employees will feel as though they've lost some control over their situation.

Consider some guidelines for building rapport with and supporting your employees:

- **Take time with employees.** Everything comes back to communication: Getting out and talking to employees, spending time with front-line staff, and making an effort to truly listen to employees can open your eyes to seemingly small accomplishments that may otherwise go unnoticed. No matter how small, the roles and responsibilities of every employee are a critical factor in the overall success of an organization.

- **Ask employees what they want and need.** Don't assume that you know automatically. And don't assume that employees who have been with you for several years want the same thing today that they did five years ago. Encourage open and honest dialogue.

✔ **Be available for questions from employees.** Best, Best & Krieger — a large law firm in Southern California — promotes an open-door policy in which anyone who has questions or concerns regarding personal or professional security is free to discuss those worries with the firm's managing partner. Employees are facing some very real fears, and ignoring them only makes them worse.

✔ **Show understanding and empathy.** All employees need to feel that their managers are on their side, rooting for their success and helping them succeed in any way possible. When employees face life changes, tragedies, or circumstances that demand more of their time than usual, employees need to feel comfortable discussing their situation with their managers or employers. If they're met with understanding and a willingness to help, they won't ever forget it. And the happier and more stable your employees are, the better your business will fare.

✔ **Support employees when they make mistakes.** Employees need their manager's support more than ever when they make a mistake. It's easy to find fault and openly criticize employees, perhaps even in front of their peers. But if you take that approach, your employees will lose a degree of self-esteem, as well as the willingness to act independently and use their best judgment — and may never get those qualities back.

To get the best of what employees have to offer the organization, managers must tap into their employees' talents, interests, and skills. Getting to know employees on a personal level and asking for their input, help, and ideas is a great starting point for any manager. In most cases, giving employees the autonomy and authority to act in the best interests of the organization and offering words of encouragement and praise along the way work wonders. Encouraging employees to pursue their ideas and supporting them in that process are also important for yielding positive results in the workplace.

Regardless of the approaches you ultimately decide to take in your efforts to increase employee engagement, remember these tips:

✔ **Encouraging initiative starts with taking initiative.** Everyone has an idea that can improve his job, department, or company. Find a way to get those ideas out. Do something different, and learn along the way.

✔ **The system is more important than any single idea.** Set up a system that is simple, doable, and fun. If the suggestion program becomes a boring burden, it isn't likely to continue for long.

✔ **Stick with it.** The best idea may not always be the first one, but the process of valuing your employees' ideas will lead to better ones.

Chapter 3

Managing Virtual Employees

. . . .

In This Chapter

▶ Managing a new flavor of employee

▶ Leveraging the Internet to manage virtual employees

▶ Leading different shifts

. . . .

A major shift has occurred in the attitudes of companies toward a more worker-friendly workplace. Today's managers are much more flexible and willing to work with the unique needs of their employees than ever. Why? Because savvy managers realize that they can get more from employees with a little consideration (and employees increasingly expect this). So whether employees need to drop off their kids at school in the morning, work only on certain days of the week, or take an extended leave of absence to care for an ill relative, managers are more likely to do whatever they can to accommodate workers' needs.

This shift in attitudes (as well as changes in the nature of work, the improvement of technology, and reduced levels of management in many organizations) has led to its eventual conclusion: virtual employees who spend most of their work hours away from established company offices and worksites, employees managed from a distance, employees who work a variety of shifts or have differing starting and ending times, and employees who telecommute to the office from the comfort of their homes.

Of course, these changes haven't been easy for the managers who are required to implement them. For managers who are used to having employees nearby and ready to instantly respond to the needs of customers and clients, managing off-site employees can be a bit disconcerting. But that doesn't have to be the case. Virtual employees can be just as good as the ones in the office with you. In fact, they can be more loyal, more effective, and more highly motivated . . . as long as you know how to manage them effectively.

In this chapter, we take a look at this new kind of work arrangement and how best to work with virtual employees. You find strategies for effectively managing far-away employees and employees who work differing shifts, and you get some insights into the future of telecommuting.

Making Room for a New Kind of Employee

A new kind of employee is out there — the *virtual* employee. A virtual employee is simply someone who regularly works somewhere outside of the regular bricks-and-mortar offices that house a company's business operations. Virtual employees join employees who have accepted (and often clamored for) a variety of alternative working arrangements, including alternate work schedules and flexible work schedules.

According to a U.S. Department of Labor report, approximately one in four employees today has an alternative work arrangement. These alternative work arrangements can range from something as simple as starting and ending the workday outside the standard (or core) business hours, all the way to working full-time from home.

But don't these kinds of arrangements cost a company more or result in less productive employees? At this time, the evidence says no. IBM found that it saves an average of 40 to 60 percent of its real estate expenses each year by eliminating offices for all employees except those who truly need them. The company recorded productivity gains of 15 to 40 percent after instituting a virtual workplace. Hewlett-Packard doubled revenues per salesperson after it created virtual workplace arrangements for its people. And Andersen Consulting discovered that its consultants spent 25 percent more time with clients when their regular physical offices were eliminated.

Managing people who aren't physically located near you can be particularly challenging, and you must approach it differently from managing employees who work in the same location. Perhaps your employees are located at a different facility or even in a different state (called *remote* employees), or maybe they're telecommuting from their homes. But regardless of the reason for the separation, these new distance-working relationships make it harder for managers to identify and acknowledge desired behavior and performance. You must be more systematic and intentional in determining whether employees are fully performing their duties to the same standard as employees housed in a regular office.

Preparing to get virtual

Is your company ready for virtual employees? Are you ready for virtual employees? The following checklist can help you determine whether your organization is ready and taking steps to make it so:

❑   Your company has established work standards to measure employee performance.

❑ Prospective virtual employees have the equipment they need to properly perform their work off-site.

❑ The work can be performed off-site.

❑ The work can be completed without ongoing interaction with other employees.

❑ Prospective virtual employees have demonstrated that they can work effectively without day-to-day supervision.

❑ Supervisors can manage and monitor employees by their results rather than by direct observation.

❑ Any state or local requirements for virtual workers (including overtime pay requirements) have been discussed with your legal and human resources departments.

❑ The company policy on flexible work arrangements is clear and has been well communicated.

❑ A standard agreement is in place to be used to document the terms of each customized work arrangement.

❑ Employee worksites have been examined to ensure that they're adequately equipped.

If you have lots of check marks, your organization is ready and able to initiate alternative work arrangements with your employees. If you have several empty boxes, you have your work cut out for you before you can expect virtual employees to be a viable option in your organization.

To make your organization more ready for virtual employees, take another look at the checklist. By addressing each box that doesn't have a check mark, you bring your company closer to making virtual employees a reality. For example, if your company doesn't have the equipment virtual employees need to do their work off-site — say, laptop computers, wireless modems, and smartphones — then you can budget for and buy them. Or if you don't have a clear company policy on flexible work arrangements, you can create one. As you address each unchecked box, you're one step closer to your goal.

Book III

Mastering Key Management Duties

Understanding changes to the office culture

One of the key concerns for managers when an increasing number of employees become virtual employees is this: What happens to the company's culture (and employee performance) as more workers work outside the office? After all, a company's culture is mostly defined by the day-to-day interactions of employees within a company's four walls. Employees who work outside these interactions may have no grounding in an organization's culture and have little attachment to other employees or to the organization's values and goals. The result? Employees who are potentially less productive than regular employees, with lowered teamwork and loyalty.

The good news is that you can take a number of steps to help your virtual workers plug into your company's culture, become team players, and gain a stake in the organization's goals in the process.

Consider the following ideas:

- ✔ **Schedule regular meetings that everyone attends — in person or by telephone conference call or Internet videoconferencing system.** Discuss current company events and set aside time for the group to tackle and solve at least one pressing organizational issue — or more, if time permits.

- ✔ **Create communication vehicles that everyone can be a part of.** One limousine company gave all its drivers a monthly audio recording that updated the company's employees — most of whom were out on the road doing their jobs — on current company happenings, policies, questions and answers, and more. You could do the same thing by sending employees digital recordings or podcasts to listen to when and where convenient.

- ✔ **Hire a facilitator and schedule periodic team-building sessions with all your employees — virtual and nonvirtual — to build working relationships and trust among employees.**

- ✔ **Initiate regular, inexpensive group events that draw out your virtual employees to mingle and get to know regular employees — and each other.** Going out to lunch on the company's tab, volunteering to help a local charity, having a potluck at a local park — the possibilities are endless.

As a manager, you need to consider the reality that virtual employees face issues and challenges that conventional in-house employees don't:

- ✔ Virtual employees may find that they're not fairly compensated by their employers for the home resources (office space, computers, electricity, furniture, and so forth) that they contribute to the job. Many employers feel that employees should contribute these items for nothing — as a *quid pro quo* for being allowed to work outside the office.

- ✔ Virtual employees may feel that their personal privacy is being violated management efforts are too intrusive. Remember that your employee is not available 24/7. Respect her work hours and use work phone numbers and e-mail addresses — not home contact information — when you want to communicate.

> ✔ Regular employees may become jealous of virtual employees' "special privileges."
>
> ✔ Family duties may intrude on work duties much more often for employees who work at home than for employees who work in traditional offices.

These issues don't mean that you should just forget about offering your employees alternative working arrangements. It just means that you need to be aware of them and work to ensure that they don't cause problems for your virtual — or your regular — employees.

Weighing pros and cons of telecommuting

With the proliferation of personal computers and the availability of fast and inexpensive broadband Internet hookups and communications software, telecommuting is becoming a common arrangement with many benefits. According to studies, employee productivity can increase by 30 percent, less time is lost as people sit in cars or mass transit to and from work, workers are more satisfied with their jobs, and society (and our lungs) benefits from having fewer cars on the road every rush hour.

When her fiancé accepted a job in New Mexico, Amy Arnott, an analyst at Chicago-based Morningstar, Inc., was faced with a tough decision. Should she quit her job and move to New Mexico with her husband-to-be, or should she try maintaining a long-distance romance? Fortunately for Arnott, she didn't have to make the choice. Morningstar allowed Arnott to telecommute each day from Los Alamos to Chicago — a journey of more than 1,000 miles each way. Arnott used her computer and modem to tap into the Morningstar mutual fund database. By using the database, along with off-the-shelf word processing, spreadsheet, and e-mail software, Arnott performed her job just as well as if she were at her old office in Chicago.

Although the idea of virtual employees seems to be catching on in the world of business, you, as a manager, need to consider some pros and cons when your thoughts turn to telecommuting.

Following are some advantages to telecommuting:

> ✔ Depending on the job, employees can set their own schedules.
>
> ✔ Employees can spend more time with customers.
>
> ✔ Distracting office politics are often reduced.
>
> ✔ Employees can conduct more work because everything is there where they need it. (And when they get bored on a Saturday afternoon, they just may do an hour or two of work.)

Book III

Mastering Key Management Duties

- ✔ You may be able to save money by downsizing your facilities.

- ✔ Costs of electricity, water, and other overhead are reduced.

- ✔ Employee morale is enhanced because employees have the opportunity to experience the freedom of working from their own homes or other locations of their choice.

And following are some of the disadvantages to telecommuting:

- ✔ Monitoring employee performance is more difficult.

- ✔ Scheduling meetings can be problematic.

- ✔ You may have to pay to set up your employees with the equipment they need to telecommute.

- ✔ Employees can lose their feelings of being connected to the organization.

- ✔ You must be more organized in making assignments.

For many employees, the prospect of being able to work out of their own homes is much more appealing than merging onto the freeway each morning. For example, Scott Bye still gets out of bed at about the same time he did when he worked at a large corporate publisher, but now his commute is a few steps down the hall instead of an hour and 15 minutes of bumper-to-bumper, smog-filled, Los Angeles stop-and-go traffic. By 9:30 a.m. (15 minutes before his old starting time), Bye has already made several calls to his East Coast clients, sent a message or two to publishing contacts overseas, and created a sales presentation on his computer.

However, telecommuting isn't just a plus for your current employees. It can be a powerful recruiting tool when you're on the hunt for new people to supplement your workforce.

As the Baby Boom generation retires and moves on to greener pastures, the younger generations have fewer people to replace them. Long story short, as the economy rebounds in coming years, a shortage of good workers is going to arise. Anything you can do to attract and retain good employees in the future will be not just a nicety, but a necessity.

Managing from a Distance

With the changing nature of work, managers have to adapt to new circumstances for managing employees. How can managers keep up with an employee's performance when that employee may not have physical contact with the manager for weeks or months at a time? It's hard enough for many managers to keep up with the employees who are in the office, much less a group of employees working outside it.

Increasing your interaction

Today's managers have to work harder to manage distant employees. If you value strong working relationships and clear communication (and you should), you need to reach out to your virtual employees to be sure adequate communication is taking place. Some of the answers to managing virtual employees effectively lie in a return to the basics of human interaction:

- ✔ **Make time for people.** Nothing beats face time when it comes to building trusting relationships. Managing is a people job — if you're a manager, you need to take time for people. It's a part of the job. And you need to do so not only when taking time is convenient, but also whenever employees are available and need to meet.

- ✔ **Increase communication as you increase distance.** The greater the distance from one's manager, the greater the effort both parties have to make to keep in touch. And although some employees want to be as autonomous as possible and want to minimize their day-to-day contact with you, other employees quickly feel neglected or ignored if you don't make a routine effort to communicate with them. Increase communication by sending regular updates and scheduling meetings and visits more frequently. Also encourage your employees to contact you (communication is a two-way street, after all), and go out of your way to provide the same types of communication meetings with each work shift or to arrange meetings that overlap work shifts.

- ✔ **Use technology.** Don't let technology use you. Use technology as a more effective way to communicate with your employees, not just to distribute data. Promote the exchange of information and encourage questions. Have problem discussion boards or host chat rooms with managers or executives, or create an electronic bulletin board to capture the exchange of individual employee and team progress, problems, and solutions. You can set these up on your company intranet or within a password-protected area of your company's website.

Providing long-distance recognition

Every employee needs to be recognized by a manager for a job well done. Just because an employee is out of sight doesn't mean that person should be out of mind. Consider some steps you can take to make sure your virtual employees feel just as appreciated as your regular employees:

- ✔ Ask virtual team members to keep the leader and other team members apprised of their accomplishments, because they can't be as readily seen.

- ✔ Keep a recognition log of remote team members so that they don't fall into the cracks — a particularly important consideration for mixed teams (with both traditional and virtual team members).

- ✔ Make sure that virtual team members are appropriately included in recognition programs by passing around recognition item catalogs and by ensuring that remote employees are kept fully in the loop.

- ✔ Provide a treat of some kind for virtual team members who can't join in face-to-face socials and celebrations.

- ✔ Utilize recognition activities and items that are appropriate for a mobile workforce, such as thank-you cards and gift certificates.

- ✔ Tap into the recognition capabilities of e-mail, such as virtual flowers or greeting cards.

- ✔ Involve executives in recognition activities by way of conference calls, videoconferencing, or periodic in-person awards programs.

- ✔ Make a point of employing a variety of team recognition items (such as coffee mugs, T-shirts, jackets, and so forth) when rewarding members of virtual teams. Such items help remind them of their team membership.

Using the Internet

It's hard to believe that just a couple decades ago, only a handful of academic researchers and government employees used the Internet. Today the Internet touches almost all of us, at work and at home. You can do so many things online, including managing your virtual employees.

Managing employees is a challenge when you've got them right there in front of you. However, when your employees are across town — or on the other side of the globe, nine time zones away — this challenge is multiplied. The good news is that the Internet can help bring your far-flung employee team closer together while making your job of managing easier. These tools can do just that:

- ✔ **Teleconferencing and videoconferencing:** The widespread proliferation of broadband Internet connections has provided most businesspeople with the bandwidth they need to make real-time phone teleconferencing and videoconferencing work on their computers. You can find a number of Internet-enabled teleconferencing websites, including www. freeconferencecall.com and www.accuconference.com.

Some of these sites provide service for free, but others require you to pay. All offer a variety of features, including instant conference calls, scheduled calls, recording, conversation transcription, and more. If you want to conduct videoconferences, many of the teleconferencing companies' sites can also do that. However, Skype (www.skype.com) allows you to set up videoconferences for free.

✔ **Virtual meetings:** If you've got a group larger than just a few people and you want to integrate your computer into the proceedings (to display documents, spreadsheets, graphics, and so forth), consider checking out some of the providers of virtual meeting services. Some of the most popular are Microsoft Office Live Meeting (included along with the Microsoft Office software product) and www.gotomeeting.com. Prices for these services vary, but most offer a free trial period, so be sure to try before you buy.

✔ **Project collaboration sites:** One of the most difficult challenges in managing virtual employees arises when you're working together on a project. Usually team members need to swap a lot of documents and files, plus occasional get-togethers are necessary to ensure that everyone is working from the same page.

Project collaboration websites such as Basecamp (www.basecamp.com) and Easy Projects (www.easyprojects.net) make the job much easier and more effective. Most offer a variety of online project-collaboration tools such as project milestone charts, project updates and check-ins, shared task lists, virtual brainstorm sessions, and much more. Again, prices and exact services vary, so be sure the system meets your needs before you make a long-term commitment.

Book III

Mastering Key Management Duties

Of course, you can still use your telephone as well as e-mail or text messages to conduct the majority of your interactions with your virtual employees. And don't forget to schedule an occasional in-person team meeting where everyone has an opportunity to spend some time together and put faces behind the voices. However, when you need to manage a project or pull together a meeting with more than an employee or two, these Internet-based tools give you a distinct advantage.

Managing Different Shifts

The challenge of managing today's employees is made harder by the fact that the nature of work is changing so dramatically and so quickly. Employers have increasingly supplemented traditional work schedules with more flexible scheduling options. Managing employees who work differing shifts is a special challenge.

Following are some strategies to consider when making the most of working with shift employees:

- ✓ **Take time to orient shift employees.** All employees need to get their bearings, and shift employees can often be at a disadvantage because they're working outside a company's normal hours. Be sure to let them know what they can expect about the job and the organization, including work policies you expect them to abide by. And create opportunities for them to personally meet all other individuals they need to know or work with.

- ✓ **Give them the resources to be productive.** Such resources can range from the right equipment to do the job, to access to others when they have a question. Other resources include the right instruction and training, especially about company products and services, work processes, internal procedures, and administrative requirements.

- ✓ **Make an ongoing effort to communicate.** The importance of communication is almost a cliché, but you can't underestimate its value. Many employees prefer to suffer silently through poor directions instead of running the risk that they'll seem slow to grasp an assignment — and possibly be labeled as difficult to work with. Constantly check with shift employees to see if they have questions or need help. Make every personal interaction count to find out how the employees are doing and how you can better help them.

Some managers schedule meetings at shift changes to get two shifts at once, or they host a dinner with later shifts for a question-and-answer session around key initiatives. Have key staff contacts from your human resources, finance, and legal departments come in occasionally to answer questions as well.

- ✓ **Appreciate employees for the jobs they do.** Even if an employee is at work only outside the standard work schedule, his need to be recognized for hard work and accomplishments is still as great as any other employee's, although his circumstances make it less convenient to thank him. Fortunately, a little appreciation can go a long way. Take the time to find out what may motivate extra performance and then deliver such rewards when you receive the desired performance.

- ✓ **Treat shift employees the way you want them to act.** If you want shift employees to have a long-term perspective, treat them with a long-term perspective. Make them feel a part of the team. Treating shift employees with courtesy and professionalism can help establish your reputation as a desirable employer to work for and thus attract additional talent when you need it.

Managing employees who work different shifts is an achievable task if done with the right effort at the right time. Make the time and the effort, and you'll reap the benefits.

Chapter 4

Conducting Meetings That Work

*W*hen you were a kid growing up, you learned some dirty words that were absolutely forbidden at home, right? Now that you're an adult and experienced in the world of work, you've encountered a dirty word that people say out loud in polite company. That word is *meeting*. Say *meeting* to employees at all levels and many cringe, grunt, and groan. Why do you think that is?

If you're like many people, you've attended many, many business meetings that just weren't productive. More than once, you've walked out of a meeting feeling worse than when you walked in. You recall that many meetings were a total waste of time. But now that you have a team to run, what's one of the key mechanisms that you need to use for pulling your team members together? Oh, no — *MEETINGS!*

The good news is that teams can find the right tools and techniques to turn the dreaded "M" word into a clean and positive word, even a way of life. And no religious conversions are necessary, either. Just make sure to pass along the meeting skills that you find in this chapter and apply them often.

Why You Should Toss the Old Meeting Model

People make up all kinds of excuses to miss meetings — just like kids who show up at school without their homework. (Anyone on your team have about six dead grandmothers?)

Take a survey at your organization, and you're likely to find some of the following reasons that meetings get such a terrible rap:

- ✔ Meetings never start on time.
- ✔ There was no agenda.
- ✔ The agenda wasn't followed.
- ✔ It was too long.
- ✔ It was too short — not worth it.
- ✔ A memo (e-mail, text message) would've been sufficient.
- ✔ Too much time was wasted talking about unimportant items.
- ✔ People talked during the whole meeting; I couldn't hear a thing.
- ✔ The room was too hot (cold, warm, dark, bright, crowded . . .).
- ✔ Not enough people were there.
- ✔ Too many people were there.
- ✔ The supervisors weren't there.
- ✔ Reports were read aloud; I know how to read.
- ✔ The refreshments were stale.
- ✔ There were no refreshments and I was starving.
- ✔ I couldn't concentrate because cell phones kept ringing.
- ✔ The content had nothing to do with my job.
- ✔ Nothing was accomplished.
- ✔ People could have been making sales instead of wasting time.

And the list goes on and on. The only solution to the problem is to reconstruct how meetings are held. Some organizations call them *non-meetings*, but that joke gets old. Grab the attention of the brains in your organization by making your meetings matter. Keep reading to find out how.

Developing Focused Agendas

Question: What's one of the million-dollar secrets for having a focused and productive team meeting?

Answer: A well-defined agenda.

An agenda is a written plan that guides the flow of a meeting toward accomplishing its purpose. That's right — a *written* plan for all to see. Not a verbal outline, not notes to yourself, and not a laundry list of topics with no order or purpose.

Developing a meaningful agenda for a team meeting takes planning. The team leader takes an active responsibility in helping to shape the agenda but also involves the team members so their input is included. Express to your team that everyone has a responsibility to help make a good agenda for the team meetings. You can even periodically delegate to a handful of team members the responsibility to take the lead in planning the agenda.

Planning the meeting agenda pays off well: Walking into a meeting with a well-organized agenda greatly increases the likelihood for a focused and productive meeting. This section offers you some tools, tips, and samples for showing your team members how to create a purposeful meeting agenda.

Starting with five essentials

A good agenda for a team meeting, and for most group meetings, answers five basic questions about the meeting. The first four are simple and obvious, but the last one can be complex. These are the five things you're looking for:

✔ **The group involved in the meeting:** Who are we? What's the name of our group or team? This point of reference needs to be prominently listed at the top of the agenda, much like a title. For example,

- Executive Staff Meeting

- Operations Team Meeting

- Policy Task Team

- The Make It Happen Team

- The Employee Fun Bunch Committee

The right title helps everyone know who's supposed to attend. If you're part of the named group, come; if you're not, don't bother. Knowing the team or group improves the odds that the right people are present and the wrong ones are not.

✔ **The day and time:** When is the meeting to take place? Identify not only the date but also a start time and (drum roll, please) an *end* time that you've projected. People have their own schedules. A meeting without an end time doesn't respect the fact that participants have other things that they'd like to plan for and do. Worst of all, it tends to encourage meetings to drag on and on. Meetings can end sooner than planned; however, without a stated ending time, they may never end at all.

✔ **The purpose or objective of the meeting:** Why are we meeting? What, overall, is to be accomplished at the meeting? A meeting can have more than one purpose, but without at least one good one, why meet?

✔ **The topics to be discussed:** What are the items or issues to be discussed at the meeting? List them on the agenda in the order that they're to be addressed. Consider including two standard agenda topics — an introduction and a close — that give you a kickoff point before you dive into the issues and a wrap-up point for making sure that closure is achieved.

✔ **The process for working through each topic.** The *process* represents $900,000 of the $1 million secret behind effective agendas. It's the element that's generally least found in group meeting agendas. The process defines how the group will work through each topic from start to conclusion. Its two main points are

- The steps to follow in working through each main issue or topic.

- The ways by which participation will be governed in working through each step.

To illustrate what a discussion process looks like, say that your team has been working on a customer service problem. Part of the team meeting today is devoted to developing a solution to the problem. Figure 4-1 shows how that part of the agenda can proceed.

As you can see in Figure 4-1, a problem-solving process answers the what, the how, and the who — *what* you're working on, *how* you're going to work through it, and *who's* going to participate in each step. Defining the process on the agenda makes keeping people focused and involved easy.

Other agenda parts to include as needed

Sometimes you may want a little more structure to the five agenda essentials. Items in the following list describe some options that may be useful in a longer or more involved meeting than normal, or when you sense a special need for discipline in keeping participants focused.

✔ **A special theme:** On occasion, meetings may have a special theme or focus. When that's the case, state the theme just below the group name at the top of the agenda so that it becomes part of the meeting title.

✔ **The location of the meeting:** When your team meets in different places, naming the site of the meeting is important.

✔ **The names of attendees:** Naming attendees is helpful when you're bringing together a relatively new team or one that is cross-functional, or when special guests or presenters are part of the agenda.

The Customer Service Problem

I. Review of Problem Issue
  A. Recap of previous work - Team leader presents
  B. Other comments - Group discussion

II. Developing the Solution
  A. Brainstorming ideas - Individuals give ideas going one at a time in turn
  B. Initial discussion of ideas
    1. Clarification - Individuals identify ideas needing clarification, group discusses
    2. Consolidation - Group discusses if any ideas can be combined
    3. Elimination - Group discusses if any ideas can be easily eliminated
    4. Categorization - Group discusses if main themes exist among ideas and, if so, places them in identified categories
  C. Evaluation of ideas
    1. Group discusses merits of each idea one at a time
    2. Group consensus on ideas most applicable to use

III. Moving Forward on Solution
  A. Define next steps to do - Individual inputs listed
  B. Finalize next steps - Group discussion and consensus

Figure 4-1:
An all-purpose process for working through a team problem or issue.

Illustration by Wiley, Composition Services Graphics

✔ **The amount of time allotted for each topic:** Estimating the time required for each topic on an agenda helps you and the team to stay focused. But remember, the time frame is an estimate. Don't become so rigid that you move forward just because the time for an item has expired. Use the time schedule as a reminder for how you're doing. As you get to know your team and team members get to know one another's styles, you'll be better able to plan the time with more accuracy. Best of all, this planning helps prevent you from loading the agenda with so many items that you simply have to quit before you're really finished.

✔ **Break times:** For the occasional meetings that run two hours or more, plan break times and list them on the agenda. Doing so minimizes the distraction of people running in and out of the meeting at any old time.

✔ **Desired outcomes:** This part of the agenda describes what work products are to be created during the meeting or what other results are expected. Stating the outcomes alerts participants to the work that they need to get done during the session.

✔ **Participant preparation:** Reminding attendees about their homework or about action items that were set at a previous meeting often is a worthwhile addition to the agenda.

Adding a *meeting evaluation* piece to the agenda is an especially good idea for teams that are in their early stages, discovering the discipline needed for productive meetings. You can add a checklist for meeting effectiveness to the agenda. At the end of the meeting, you run down the checklist with the team and see how well you as a team did in achieving each factor. Checklist factors may deal with the quality and level of people's participation, starting and ending the meeting on time, quality of facilitation, whether you stayed focused on the agenda, and so on. Have the feedback from the evaluation included in the meeting minutes. Taking a few minutes for this evaluation helps build in the discipline that you need for having effective meetings.

Formatting the agenda

The two best agenda formats are the *chart style* and the *outline style*. Figure 4-2 shows the chart form, and Figure 4-3 shows the outline form. What these two formats have in common is that they describe the topics to be covered in the meeting and the process for working through each topic. Which style you choose doesn't matter — use the one that you find most comfortable.

In most cases, a well-defined agenda, including all essential ingredients, can be written on one page. Remember, the agenda is a plan for guiding the meeting and not a detailed script.

A good agenda gives structure to a meeting. Don't be afraid that structure will inhibit free-flowing discussion. Just make sure that you include enough time for discussion on your agenda.

Facilitating a Productive Meeting: Tools and Outcomes

This section provides you with tools for facilitating meetings so that you have two overall outcomes:

✔ Attendees participate in the meeting.

✔ The meeting produces results.

These two outcomes together make for a productive meeting.

Chart-Style Agenda

Group/Meeting Name: _Special Project Team: Project Planning Meeting_

Date: _November 21, 2014_ **Time: from** _9:00_ **to** _11:00_

Location: _Building 1 Conference Room_

Facilitator: _John Doe_

Purpose: _Develop project plan for upcoming special ABC project_

Desired Outcomes: _Written project plan that outlines the following:_
- _Milestones_
- _Target dates_
- _Roles and assignments_

What	How	Who	Time
1. Overview of agenda	Present	Facilitator	9:00 - 9:05
2. Background & expectations for special ABC project	Present Discuss as needed	Team Leader All	9:05 - 9:15
3. Determine milestones	• List options • Discuss, evaluate • Reach agreement	All	9:15 - 10:00
4. Set time frames for milestones	• Discuss • Reach agreement	All	10:00 - 10:15
5. Determine roles & assignments	• List options • Discuss, evaluate • Reach agreement	All	10:15 - 10:45
6. Set deliverables for first phase	• Discuss • Reach agreement	Team Leader All	10:45 - 10:55
7. Close	• Recap	Facilitator	10:55 - 11:00

Figure 4-2: A chart-style agenda.

Illustration by Wiley, Composition Services Graphics

Book III

Mastering Key Management Duties

Creating the foundation of effective meeting facilitation are the interpersonal communication tools known as *active listening* and *assertive speaking*. *Facilitating* effectively means tuning in to what the participants are telling you verbally and nonverbally (active listening) and, at the same time, speaking positively and confidently so that the team moves forward through its agenda (assertive speaking).

Outline-Style Agenda

Operations Committee Meeting Evaluation

November 21, 2014
(10:45 - 12:30)
Main Objective: To define the role of the Operations
Committee and shape ways to enhance
effectiveness with its meetings.

I. Introduction: Overview of Meeting – Team leader presents   (10:45-10:50)

II. Current Meetings   (10:50-11:10)
    A. What's Working – Individual inputs
    B. What's Not Working or Needs Improvement – Individual inputs
    C. Main Conclusions – Group Discuss

III. Establishing The Purpose Of The Operations Committee   (11:10-11:50)
    A. Why Should This Committee Exist–People Write
       and Post Individually
    B. Group Discuss Views and Build off Common Themes
    C. Collaborate and Shape Into Purpose Statement

IV. Structuring The Meetings   (11:50-12:05)
    A. Frequency and Timing – Group Consensus
    B. Key Roles and Shaping The Agenda – Group Consensus
    C. Other Actions – Group Discuss

V. Issues To Tackle In Near Term   (12:05-12:25)
    A. Brainstorm – Group, going one person at a time
    B. Evaluate Ideas – Collective Discussion
    C. Set Near Term Priorities – Group Consensus

VI. Close: Next Steps   (12:25-12:30)

Figure 4-3:
An outline-
style
agenda.

Illustration by Wiley, Composition Services Graphics

The word *facilitate* means to make easy. That's the role of a facilitator at a meeting — helping to make a group's agenda easy to work through so that results are accomplished.

You can become an effective meeting facilitator by applying six important facilitation skills — planning, summarizing, recording, focusing, stimulating participation, and gatekeeping — that are described in the following sections.

Planning

Planning is what you do before the meeting. It means playing an active, if not primary, role in preparing the meeting agenda and, most important, defining the process that the team will use when working through each main issue. The process shows you how to guide the group through the meeting. Planning also includes having pre-meeting conversations with individuals to prepare them for the meeting and anticipating any possible challenges from participants and determining how you'll handle them if they should arise. For instance, if you know you have a controversial issue to work through with the team that some members have some strong feelings about, you can have pre-meeting discussions with these individuals so they come ready to be focused and constructive at the meeting.

Summarizing

Summarizing is the same thing as recapping, and it sometimes is used for capturing points that come out of a discussion. Summarizing is especially useful as a transitional tool from one topic to the next — recapping the key points or decisions made on one topic and then moving on to the next. Summarizing also is important to apply at the end of a meeting as a means of bringing closure to the session.

When summarizing, be brief. Generally a few sentences, at most, do the trick. After all, you're recapping the highlights, not all the details.

Recording

Recording means writing on a board or a flip chart the discussion inputs, group conclusions, ideas from brainstorming, and any other important information that comes up during a meeting. Recording is different from merely taking the meeting minutes. Recording happens live — in real time — and in front of everyone. It captures the activity and important points that emerge as the meeting rolls along, makes a discussion *visible,* and helps team members feel that their points are being heard.

When recording, capture what people are saying in their words. Don't interpret the messages and then record them in your own words. Not writing what people are saying *exactly* makes them feel that you're not really listening and, perhaps, that you're pushing your own agenda. However, if you paraphrase someone's point out loud and confirm with that person that you heard it right, then recording the point in your own words is fine. The confirmation indicates that you understood. (Many times, a participant will consider your paraphrase better than the original.)

Focusing

The facilitation skill known as *focusing* pushes you toward stepping in and asserting yourself in running the meeting. In focusing, you summon the group's attention so that you are accomplishing the following:

✔ Maintaining order in a meeting

✔ Extinguishing side conversations

✔ Moving a team to the next agenda item

✔ Moving a group past its seemingly endless discussion into taking some form of action

The emphasis of focusing is on guiding the attention of participants to the agenda and to the issue at hand.

When you focus, project your voice, sound firm, and keep the message short. Here are a few examples of what to say when focusing team members during a meeting:

✔ "We covered everything we need to in Item 2. Let's move ahead now to Item 3 on our agenda."

✔ "Let's please have everyone's attention back to the front and let Sue state her point now."

✔ "We've discussed different options for quite a while. It's time now for us to make a decision on what's best to do going forward."

Stimulating participation

Stimulating participation means taking an action that gets team members involved in the meeting. Organizing your agenda in advance and defining the process for working through the issues help you stimulate your team's thoughts and actions because they outline the flow of participation. In addition, this tool relies on other efforts for promoting active and positive participation, such as the following:

✔ **Calling on people individually, including quiet people, to express their thoughts and ideas:** Don't wait for people to raise their hands and speak up. Make it a regular practice to call on people, including everyone. Ask good open-ended questions and wait patiently, enabling the person to think and respond. Using this tool tells team members that they're expected to think and contribute and not just passively sit by and eat the donuts. (But do make sure that someone brings the goodies.)

✔ **Probing deeper when someone's message is vague or unclear:** Probing an issue deeper helps people to fully explain or clarify their thoughts. Sometimes it takes people below the surface level of their points. Probing gives team members enough space to truly speak their minds and be heard, which is encouraging for participation.

✔ **Paraphrasing when people make important points:** Paraphrase periodically so that you make sure what people are saying is what they really mean. You can ask and encourage participants to do the same with each other, too. Using this reflective feedback not only helps you check your understanding, but also helps other participants receive the right message. Likewise, it helps the speaker realize she is being properly heard, which encourages other people attending the meeting to speak up and participate.

✔ **Systematically problem-solving when differences of opinion arise:** When discussions become lively, sparked by differences of opinion or flat-out diatribes, moving the team into a problem-solving mode is sometimes a good idea. Guide team members through the steps, from defining a problem to creating its solution. If you must engage in problem-solving to deal with an unexpected difference of opinion or strong concern, take special care to involve the entire team and not just the few parties to the dispute. Getting everyone involved avoids a situation in which two people get stuck on opposing points of view.

Gatekeeping

Gatekeeping is a tool that helps you encourage full participation by gracefully seeing to it that no one dominates any discussion. Gatekeeping comes in two varieties — *gateopening* and *gateclosing*.

✔ **Gateopening** invites participation, giving people a chance to say something without having to speak the loudest. Sometimes, especially with the more reserved individuals, you notice a facial expression indicating that they're about to say something or that they're at least concerned. Because these team members can easily be drowned out by the others or ignored because of their soft-spoken manner, you have an opportunity to open the gate for them. By picking up on their nonverbal cues, you can invite participation by saying something like, "Angela, you were about to say something, right? Please go ahead."

✔ **Gateclosing** temporarily ends someone's participation and redirects attention to a different participant or different item on the agenda. Keep in mind, however, that the skill is gate*closing*, not gate*slamming*. You don't put people down for what they've said or how much they've been participating. ("Sharon, we've heard enough out of you for today!")

Book III

Mastering Key Management Duties

> When gateclosing a long-winded person tactfully yet assertively, you sometimes can first paraphrase to acknowledge that person's point. Upon confirmation, you can move ahead. At other times gateclosing can mean deferring what someone is saying because it more closely relates to another item later on the agenda: "Andy, please hold that thought, because it ties in with what we're going to discuss in Part 3 of the agenda."

Sometimes you close one gate and open another simultaneously: "Hold on, José (gateclosing), Amy had a thought she was about to express (gateopening). Please go ahead, Amy."

You may find that you use facilitation tools in rapid succession when guiding a team meeting. For example, when you call on people directly for their thoughts on an issue, you record their inputs on the flip chart, you gateclose to keep people from rambling, you gateopen to invite others to join in, and you summarize the key points of discussion. That's the idea — plug in the tools for gaining good participation and moving the team forward toward results with the agenda.

Dealing with a few familiar challenges

Some challenges can arise in team meetings that may test your skills as a facilitator. This section presents some common challenges and helps prepare you for what to do and what not to do.

Use the four situations described below as a learning activity with your team. As a facilitator, what do you do and say? Compare your responses with these don't-say and do-say suggestions.

A team member makes a point that doesn't make much sense.

Don't say (even though it would be fun if you did):

> "Bill, that idea you're offering makes no sense at all. You'll have to do better next time. Let's move ahead."

Do say:

> "Bill, I'm not fully clear on what your idea is about. Please explain more what your idea means and how it will help us on this issue." (Using questions to stimulate participation.)

A team member raises an issue that isn't relevant to the issue that you're discussing.

Don't say:

> "Julie, we can't discuss that. It's not relevant to what we're working on right now!"

Do say:

> *Situation 1: When the issue relates to a later part of the agenda, say, "Julie, we're going to get into that issue in Part 4 of today's agenda, so please hold the thought until we get there."* (Gateclosing.)

> *Situation 2: If the issue doesn't seem to have any relevance to the meeting, you have two useful and constructive options:*

> *You can post the point on a side board, which sometimes is referred to as parking an issue. Say you're doing this: "Julie, that issue sounds important yet different from our focus today. Let me post it over here so we park it for consideration in an upcoming meeting. Recorder please note this in our minutes." Parking the issue ensures that the thought is not lost so that it can be addressed at a future meeting.* (Recording and gateclosing.)

> *You can say: "Julie, I'm not clear how your issue relates to what we're working on today. Please briefly explain if there is relevance to it. Otherwise, we can move ahead and table it for a future meeting."* (Stimulating participation.)

The team has an issue that needs to be resolved

Don't say:

> *"Team, here's what we need to do to resolve this issue."*

Do say:

> *Ask for a brainstorming effort by calling on each team member one at a time, including yourself.* (Stimulating participation.) *Resist the temptation to lead first with your ideas for solving a problem. As team leader, your ideas may sound more like directives and thus may make people less likely to offer any opposing ideas.*

Two team members start an argument over what method to use to execute an assignment

Don't say:

> *"John and Maria, you two need to pipe down. We're going to do this assignment my way because you two can't stop arguing about it."* (This is another line that you should never use at home.)

Do say:

> *You can paraphrase, or ask the two people to paraphrase each other's points to make sure their respective messages are understood. Post the paraphrasings on the board.* (Summarizing, focusing, and recording tools.) *Then invite team members to offer ideas about how to resolve the differences and even plug in a conflict resolution model to guide this discussion.* (Stimulating participation.)

Juggling act: Facilitating and participating at the same time

Your biggest challenge in running meetings as the leader of the team is playing two roles simultaneously: facilitator and participant. That's a real balancing act! Whenever you get caught up in the content of the meeting, offering your many thoughts and ideas, you may end up dominating and not facilitating. On the other hand, whenever you remain a neutral facilitator, you're not providing the valuable input that your team needs as it works through issues.

In the truest sense of the role, a meeting facilitator is supposed to be neutral — the objective guide staying out of the content and helping to manage the process. But in teams, that neutrality usually doesn't work because your contributions are needed as a member of the team, especially as its leader. Here are some tips for handling the challenge of having dual roles:

✔ **Design your participation into the agenda.** As you plan how you want participation to flow through each main issue, factor in the places when you'll speak up, taking your turn with all others or as an identified speaker. Either way, just plan for it so that your participation doesn't disrupt the flow but rather fits in with everyone else.

✔ **Keep your self-awareness up and stay focused on the agenda.** Be conscious of what you're doing in the meeting at all times — self-awareness goes a long way in effective team leadership. Sometimes you can announce what role you're playing: "Let me put on my participant hat for a moment on this issue." Then step back into your facilitating role, following the agenda.

✔ **Finish speaking by directing a question to a participant.** This tip can work in tandem with the previous one. One technique to help prevent yourself from becoming an overzealous participant is developing the habit of finishing any comment that you make with a question to another participant: "Julio, what's your thought on this issue?" This enables you to spark the team's participation and to step back, guiding the flow of the meeting once again.

✔ **Delegate the facilitation to others on occasion.** Depending on the issues, you may want to ask someone else on the team to serve as facilitator. Ask the person in advance and indicate on the agenda what parts that individual will guide. Then that person can run the meeting, and you can participate to your heart's content without worrying how the discussion process is working. Bringing in an outside facilitator also can be helpful at special meetings, such as off-site retreats with your team. Make sure that you spend some planning time with the outside facilitator so that the issues and your objectives for the meeting are well known in advance.

Chapter 5

Delegating to Get Things Done

· ·

In This Chapter

▶ Managing through delegation

▶ Debunking the myths about delegation

▶ Putting delegation to work

▶ Choosing which tasks to delegate

▶ Keeping tabs on your employees

▶ Making things happen when you aren't in charge

· ·

The power of effective management comes not from your efforts alone (sorry to burst your bubble) but from the sum of all the efforts of each person within your work group. If you're responsible for only a few employees, with extraordinary effort you perhaps can do the work of your entire group if you so desire (and if you want to be a complete stranger to your friends and family).

However, when you're responsible for a larger organization, you simply can't be an effective manager by trying to do all of your group's work. In the best case, the group may view you as a *micromanager* who gets too involved in the petty details of running an organization, spending more time on other people's work than your own. In the worst case, your employees may take less responsibility for their work because you're always there to do it (or check it) for them. They will be less engaged in their work, and morale will plummet. Why should they bother trying to do their best job if you don't trust them enough to do it?

Managers assign responsibility for completing tasks through *delegation*. But simply assigning tasks and then walking away isn't enough. To delegate effectively, managers must also give employees authority and ensure that they have the resources necessary to complete tasks effectively. Finally, managers who delegate like experts can monitor the progress of their employees toward meeting their assigned goals.

Delegating: The Manager's Best Tool

Now that you're a manager, you're required to develop skills in many different areas. You need good technical, analytical, and organizational skills, but most important, you also must have good people skills. Of all the people skills, the one skill that can make the greatest difference in your effectiveness is the ability to delegate well. Delegating is a manager's number one management tool, and the inability to delegate well is the leading cause of management failure.

Why do managers have such a hard time delegating? A variety of possible reasons exist:

- ✔ You're too busy and just don't have enough time.

- ✔ You don't trust your employees to complete their assignments correctly or on time.

- ✔ You're afraid to let go.

- ✔ You're concerned that you'll no longer be the center of attention.

- ✔ You have no one to delegate to (lack of resources).

- ✔ You don't know how to delegate effectively.

Perhaps you're still not convinced that managers need to delegate at all. If you're a member of this particular group of reluctant managers, consider these reasons why you must let go of your preconceptions and inhibitions and start delegating today:

- ✔ **Your success as a manager depends on delegating.** Managers who can successfully manage team members — each of whom has specific responsibilities for a different aspect of the team's performance — prove that they're ready for bigger and better challenges. Nice perks often accompany these challenges, including bigger and better titles, fatter paychecks, and other niceties of business life, such as offices with windows and larger budgets to play with.

- ✔ **You can't do it all.** No matter how great a manager you are, shouldering the entire burden of achieving your organization's goals isn't in your best interest unless you want to work yourself into an early grave. Besides, wouldn't it be nice to see what life is like outside the four walls of your office?

- ✔ **You have to concentrate on the jobs that you can do and your staff can't.** They pay you the big bucks to be a manager — not a software programmer, truck driver, accounting clerk, or customer service representative. Do your job, and let your employees do theirs.

✔ **Delegation gets workers in the organization more involved.** When you give employees the responsibility and authority to carry out tasks — whether individually or in teams — they respond by becoming more involved in the day-to-day operations of the organization. Instead of acting like drones with no responsibility or authority, they become vital to the success of the work unit and the entire organization. And if your employees succeed, you succeed!

✔ **Delegation gives you the chance to develop your employees.** If you make all the decisions and come up with all the ideas, your employees never learn how to take initiative and see tasks through to successful completion. And if they don't learn, guess who's going to get stuck doing everything forever? (Hint: Take a look in the mirror.) In addition, doing everything yourself robs your employees of a golden opportunity to develop their work skills. Today's employees increasingly report learning and development opportunities as one of their top motivators.

As a manager, you're ultimately responsible for all your department's responsibilities. However, personally executing all the tasks necessary for your department to fulfill its responsibilities and for you to achieve your organizational goals is neither practical nor desirable.

Suppose, for example, that you're the manager of the accounting department for a healthcare consulting firm. When the firm had only a few employees and sales of $100,000 a year, it was no problem for you personally to bill all your customers, cut checks to vendors, run payroll, and take care of the company's taxes every April. However, now that employment has grown to 150 employees and sales are at $50 million a year, you can't even pretend to do it all — you don't have enough hours in the day. You now have specialized employees who take care of accounts payable, accounts receivable, and payroll, and you have farmed out the completion of income tax work to a CPA.

Each employee that you've assigned to a specific work function has specialized knowledge and skills in a certain area of expertise. If you've made the right hiring decisions (see Chapter 1 of this Book), each employee is a talented and specialized pro in a specific field. Sure, you could personally generate payroll if you had to, but you've hired someone to do that job for you. (By the way, your payroll clerk is probably a lot better and quicker at it than you are.)

On the other hand, you're uniquely qualified to perform numerous responsibilities in your organization. These responsibilities may include developing and monitoring your operations budget, conducting performance appraisals, and helping to plan the overall direction of your company's acquisitions. In the section "Sorting Out What to Delegate and What to Do Yourself" later in this chapter, you find info about which tasks to delegate to your employees and which ones to retain.

Book III

Mastering Key Management Duties

Seeing Past Myths about Delegation

Admit it, you may have many different rationalizations for why you can't delegate work to your employees. Unfortunately, these reasons have become part of the general folklore of being a manager. And they're guaranteed to get in the way of your ability to be an effective manager.

You can't trust your employees to be responsible

If you can't trust your employees, who can you trust? Assume that you're responsible for hiring at least a portion of your staff. Now, forgetting for a moment the ones you didn't personally hire, you likely went through quite an involved process to recruit your employees. Remember the mountain of résumés you had to sift through and then divide into winners, potential winners, and losers? After hours of sorting and then hours of interviews, you selected the best candidates — the ones with the best skills, qualifications, and experience for the job.

You selected your employees because you thought they were the most talented people available and deserved your trust. Now your job is to give them that trust without strings attached.

You usually reap what you sow. Your staff members are ready, willing, and able to be responsible employees; you just have to give them a chance. Sure, not every employee is going to be able to handle every task you assign. If that's the case, find out why. Does someone need more training? More time? More practice? Maybe you need to find a task that's better suited to an employee's experience or disposition. Or perhaps you simply hired the wrong person for the job. If that's the case, face up to the fact and fire or reassign the employee before you lose even more time and money. To get responsible employees, you have to give responsibility.

You'll lose control of a task and its outcome

If you delegate correctly, you don't lose control of the task or its outcome. You simply lose control of the way the outcome is achieved. Picture a map of the world. How many different ways can a person get from San Francisco to Paris? One? One million? Some ways are quicker than others. Some are more scenic, and others require a substantial resource commitment. Do the differences in these ways make any of them inherently wrong? No.

In business, getting a task done doesn't mean following only one path. Even for tasks that are spelled out in highly defined steps, you can always leave room for new ways to make a process better. Your job is to describe to your employees the outcomes that you want and then let them decide how to accomplish the tasks. Of course, you need to be available to coach and counsel them so that they can learn from your past experience, if they want, but you need to let go of controlling the *how* and instead focus on the *what* and the *when*.

You're the only one with all the answers

You're joking, right? If you think that you alone have all the answers, have you got another think coming! As talented as you may be, unless you're the company's only employee, you can't possibly have the only answer to every question in your organization.

On the other hand, certain people in your organization deal with an amazing array of situations every day. They talk to your customers, your suppliers, and each other — day in and day out. Many members of this group have been working for the company far longer than you, and many of them will be there long after you're gone. Who are these people? They are your employees.

Your employees have a wealth of experience and knowledge about your business contacts and the intimate, day-to-day workings of the organization. They are often closer to the customers and problems of the company than you are. To ignore their suggestions and advice is not only disrespectful but also short-sighted and foolish. Don't ignore this resource. You're already paying for it, so use it.

You can do the work faster by yourself

You may think that you're completing tasks faster when you do them than when you assign them to others, but this belief is merely an illusion. Yes, discussing a task and assigning it to one of your employees may require more of your time when you first delegate that task, but if you delegate well, you'll spend significantly less time the next time you delegate that same task.

What else happens when you do it yourself instead of delegating it? When you do the task yourself, you're forever doomed to doing the task — again and again and again. When you teach someone else to do the task and then assign that person the responsibility for completing it, you may never have to do it again. Your employee may even come to do it faster than you can. Who knows? That employee may actually improve the way that you've always done it, perhaps reducing costs or increasing customer satisfaction.

Book III

Mastering Key Management Duties

Delegation dilutes your authority

Delegation does the exact opposite of what this myth says — it actually extends your authority. You're only one person, and you can do only so much by yourself. Now imagine all 10, 20, or 100 members of your team working toward your common goals. You still set the goals and the timetables for reaching them, but each employee chooses his own way of getting there.

Do you have less authority because you delegate a task and transfer authority to an employee to carry out the task? Clearly, the answer is no. What do you lose in this transaction? Nothing. Your authority is extended, not diminished. The more authority you give to employees, the more authority your entire work unit has and the better able your employees are to do the jobs you hired them to do.

As you grant others authority, you gain an efficient and effective workforce — employees who are truly empowered, feel excited by their jobs, and work as team players. You also gain the ability to concentrate on the issues that deserve your undivided attention.

You relinquish the credit for doing a good job

Letting go of this belief is one of the biggest difficulties in the transition from being a doer to being a manager of doers. When you're a doer, you're rewarded for writing a great report, developing an incredible market analysis, or programming an amazing piece of computer code. When you're a manager, the focus of your job shifts to your performance in reaching an overall organizational or project goal through the efforts of others. You may have been the best darn marketing analyst in the world, but that talent doesn't matter anymore. Now you're expected to develop and lead a team of the best darn marketing analysts in the world. The skills required are quite different, and your success is a result of the indirect efforts of others and your behind-the-scenes support.

Wise managers know that when their employees shine, they shine, too. The more you delegate, the more opportunities you give your employees to shine. Give your workers the opportunity to do important work — and do it well. And when they do well, make sure you tell everyone about it. If you give your employees credit for their successes publicly and often, they'll more likely want to do a good job for you on future assignments. Don't forget that when you're a manager, you're primarily measured on your team's performance, not on what you're personally able to accomplish.

Delegation decreases your flexibility

When you do everything yourself, you have complete control over the progress and completion of tasks, right? Wrong! How can you, when you're balancing multiple priorities at the same time and dealing with the inevitable crisis (or two or three) of the day? Being flexible is pretty tough when you're doing everything yourself. Concentrating on more than one task at a time is impossible. While you're concentrating on that one task, you put all your other tasks on hold. Flexibility? Not!

The more people you delegate to, the more flexible you can be. As your employees take care of the day-to-day tasks necessary to keep your business running, you're free to deal with those surprise problems and opportunities that always seem to pop up at the last minute.

Taking the Six Steps to Delegate

Delegation can be scary — at least at first. But as with anything else, the more you do it, the less scary it gets. When you delegate, you're putting your trust in another individual. If that individual fails, you're ultimately responsible — regardless of whom you give the task to. A line like this isn't likely to go very far with your boss: "Yeah, I know that we were supposed to get that proposal to the customer today, but that employee of mine, Joe, dropped the ball." When you delegate tasks, you don't abdicate your responsibility for their successful completion.

As a part of this process, you need to understand your employees' strengths and weaknesses. For example, you probably aren't going to delegate a huge task to someone who has been on the job for only a few days. As with any other task that you perform as a manager, you have to work at delegating — and keep working at it. Ultimately, delegation benefits both workers and managers when you do it correctly. Follow these six steps in effectively delegating:

1. **Communicate the task.**

   Describe exactly what you want done, when you want it done, and what end results you expect. Ask for any questions your employee might have.

2. **Furnish context for the task.**

   Explain why the task needs to be done, its importance in the overall scheme of things, and possible complications that may arise during its performance.

3. **Determine standards.**

   Agree on the standards you plan to use to measure the success of a task's completion. Make these standards realistic and attainable.

4. **Grant authority.**

   You must grant employees the authority to complete the task without constant roadblocks or standoffs with other employees.

5. **Provide support.**

   Determine the resources necessary for your employee to complete the task, and then provide them. Successfully completing a task may require money, training, or the ability to check with you about progress or obstacles as they arise.

6. **Get commitment.**

   Make sure your employee has accepted the assignment. Confirm your expectations and your employee's understanding of and commitment to completing the task.

Sorting Out What to Delegate and What to Do Yourself

In theory, you can delegate anything you're responsible for to your employees. Of course, if you delegate all your duties, why is your company bothering to pay you? The point is, some things you, the manager, are better able to do, and some things your employees are better able to do. As a result, some tasks you make an effort to delegate to your employees and other tasks you retain for yourself.

When you delegate, begin with simple tasks that don't substantially impact the firm if they aren't completed on time or within budget. As your employees gain confidence and experience, delegate higher-level tasks. Carefully assess the level of your employees' expertise, and assign tasks that meet or slightly exceed that level. Set schedules for completion and then monitor your employees' performance against them. This is a good opportunity to see if an employee isn't being challenged or is bored. When you get the hang of it, you'll find that you have nothing to be afraid of when you delegate.

Pointing out appropriate tasks for delegation

Certain tasks naturally lend themselves to being delegated. Take every opportunity to delegate the following kinds of work to your employees.

Detail work

As a manager, you have no greater time-waster than getting caught up in details — you know, tasks such as double-checking pages, spending days troubleshooting a block of computer code, or personally auditing your employees' timesheets. You can no doubt run circles around almost anyone on those detailed technical tasks that you used to do all the time. But now that you're a manager, you're being paid to orchestrate the workings of an entire team of workers toward a common goal — not just to perform an individual task.

Leave the detail to your employees, but hold them accountable for the results. Concentrate your efforts on tasks that have the greatest payoff and that allow you to most effectively leverage the work of all your employees.

Information gathering

Browsing the web for information about your competitors, spending hours poring over issues of *Fortune* magazine, and moving into your local library's reference stacks for weeks on end isn't an effective use of your time. Still, most managers get sucked into the trap. Not only is reading newspapers, reports, books, magazines, and the like fun, but it also gives managers an easy way to postpone the more difficult tasks of management.

REMEMBER

You're being paid to look at the big picture, to gather a variety of inputs and make sense of them. You can work so much more efficiently when someone else gathers needed information, freeing you to take the time you need to analyze the inputs and devise solutions to your problems.

Repetitive assignments

What a great way to get routine tasks done: Assign them to your employees. Many of the jobs in your organization arise again and again, such as drafting your weekly production report, reviewing your biweekly report of expenditures versus budget, and approving your monthly phone bill. Your time is much too important to waste on routine tasks that you mastered years ago.

Book III

**Mastering
Key
Management
Duties**

If you find yourself involved in repetitive assignments, first take a close look at their particulars. How often do the assignments recur? Can you anticipate the assignments in sufficient time to allow an employee to successfully complete them? What do you have to do to train your employees in completing the tasks? When you figure all this out, develop a schedule and make assignments to your employees.

Surrogate roles

Do you feel that you have to be everywhere all the time? Well, you certainly can't be — and you shouldn't even try. Every day, your employees have numerous opportunities to fill in for you. Presentations, conference calls, client visits, and meetings are just a few examples. In some cases, such as in budget presentations to top management, you may be required to attend. However, in many other cases, whether you attend personally or send someone to take your place really doesn't matter.

The next time someone calls a meeting and requests your attendance, send one of your employees to attend in your place. This simple act benefits you in several different ways. Not only do you have an extra hour or two in your schedule, but also your employee can present you with only the important outcomes of the meeting. Plus, your employee has the opportunity to take on some new responsibilities, and you have the opportunity to spend the time you need on your most important tasks. Your employee may even discover something new in the process.

Future duties

As a manager, you must always be on the lookout for opportunities to train your staff in their future job responsibilities. For example, one of your key duties may be to develop your department's annual budget. By allowing one or more of your employees to assist you — perhaps in gathering basic market or research data, or analyzing trends in previous-year budgets — you can give your employees a taste of what goes into putting together a budget.

Don't fall into the trap of believing that the only way to train your employees is to sign them up for an expensive class taught by someone with a slick color brochure who knows nothing about your business. Opportunities to train your employees abound within your own business. An estimated 90 percent of all development occurs on the job. Not only is this training free, but also by assigning your employees to progressively more important tasks, you build their self-confidence and help pave their way to progress in the organization.

Knowing what tasks should stay with you

Some tasks are part and parcel of the job of being a manager. By delegating the following work, you would fail to perform your basic management duties.

Long-term vision and goals

As a manager, you're in a unique position. Your position at the top provides you with a unique perspective on the organization's needs — the higher up you are in an organization, the broader your perspective.

One of the key functions of management is vision. Although employees at any level of a company can give you input and make suggestions that help shape your perspectives, developing an organization's long-term vision and goals is up to you. (See Book Chapter II, Chapter 3, for an in-depth discussion of how to develop a vision.) An organization is much more effective when everyone moves together in the same direction, but employees can't collectively decide the direction in which the organization should move.

Positive performance feedback

Rewarding and recognizing employees when they do good work is an important job for every manager. If this task is delegated to lower-level employees, the workers who receive it won't value the recognition as much as if it came from their manager. The impact of the recognition is therefore significantly lessened.

Performance appraisals, discipline, and counseling

In the modern workplace, a strong relationship between manager and employee is often hard to come by. Most managers are probably lucky to get off a quick "Good morning" or "Good night" between the hustle and bustle of a typical workday. Given everyone's hectic schedules, you may have times when you don't talk to one or more of your employees for days at a time.

However, sometimes you absolutely must set time aside for your employees. When you discipline and counsel your employees, you're giving them the kind of input that only you can provide. You set the goals for your employees, and you set the standards by which you measure their progress. Inevitably, you decide whether your employees have reached the marks you've set or whether they've fallen short. You can't delegate away this task effectively — everyone loses as a result.

Book III

Mastering Key Management Duties

Politically sensitive situations

Some situations are just too politically sensitive to assign to your employees. Say, for example, that you're in charge of auditing the travel expenses for your organization. The results of your review show that a member of the corporation's executive team has made several personal trips on company funds. Do you assign a worker the responsibility of reporting this explosive situation? No! As a manager, you're in the best position to present this information, to defend it, and to absorb any repercussions.

Not only do such situations demand your utmost attention and expertise, but placing your employee in the middle of the line of fire in this potentially explosive situation is also unfair. Being a manager may be tough sometimes, but you're paid to make the difficult decisions and to take the political heat that your work generates.

Personal assignments

Occasionally, your boss may assign a specific task to you with the intention that you personally perform it. Your boss may have good reasons for doing so: You may have a unique perspective that no one else in your organization has, or you may have a unique skill required to complete the assignment quickly and accurately.

Whatever the situation, if a task is assigned to you with the expectation that you, and only you, carry it out, then you can't delegate it to your staff. You may decide to involve your staff in gathering input, but you must retain the ultimate responsibility for the final execution of the task.

Confidential or sensitive circumstances

As a manager, you're likely privy to information that your staff isn't, such as wage and salary figures, proprietary data, and personnel assessments. Releasing this information to the wrong individuals can be damaging to an organization.

For example, salary information should remain confidential. Similarly, if your competitors get their hands on some secret process that your company has spent countless hours and money to develop, the impact on your organization and employees can be devastating. Unless your staff has a compelling need to know, retain assignments involving these types of information.

Keeping delegation on track

Sometimes delegation goes wrong — way wrong. How can you identify the danger signs before it's too late, and what can you do to save the day? You can monitor the performance of your workers in several ways:

✔ **Personal follow-up:** Supplement your formal tracking system with an informal system of visiting your workers and checking their progress on a regular basis.

✔ **Sampling:** Take periodic samples of your employees' work and make sure that the work meets the standards you agreed to.

✔ **Progress reports:** Regular progress reporting from employees to you can give you advance notice of problems and successes.

✔ **A formalized tracking system:** Use a formal system to track assignments and due dates. The system can be manual (perhaps a big chart pinned to your wall) or computerized.

If you discover that your employees are in trouble, you have several options for getting everything back on track:

✔ **Increasing your monitoring:** Spend more time monitoring employees who are in trouble, keeping closer track of their performance.

✔ **Counseling:** Discuss the problems with your employees and agree on a plan to correct them.

✔ **Rescinding authority:** If problems continue despite your efforts to resolve them through counseling, you can rescind your employees' authority to complete the tasks independently. (They still work on the task but under your close guidance and authority.)

✔ **Reassigning activities:** As the ultimate solution when delegation goes wrong, if your employees can't do their assigned tasks, give the tasks to workers who are better able to perform them successfully.

Checking Up Instead of Checking Out

Assume that you've already worked through the initial hurdles of delegation: You assigned a task to your employee, and you're eagerly waiting to see how she performs. You defined the scope of the task and gave your employee the adequate training and resources to get it done. You also told her what results you expect and exactly when you expect to see them. What do you do next?

Here's one option: An hour or two after you make the assignment, you check on its progress. In a couple more hours, you check again. As the deadline rapidly approaches, you increase the frequency of your checking until, finally, your employee spends more time answering your questions about the progress she has made than she spends actually completing the task. Every time you press her for details about her progress, she gets a little more distracted from her task and a little more frustrated with your seeming lack of confidence in her abilities. When the appointed hour arrives, she submits the result on time, but the report is inaccurate and incomplete. The employee is also stewing because of your micromanagement.

Here's another option: After you make the assignment to your employee, you do nothing. Instead of checking on your employee's progress and offering your support, you assign the task and move on to other concerns. When the appointed hour arrives, you're surprised to discover that the task is not completed. When you ask your employee why she didn't meet the goal that you had mutually agreed upon, she tells you that she had trouble obtaining some information and, instead of bothering you with this problem, she decided to try to construct it for herself. Unfortunately, this diversion required an additional two days of research before she found the correct set of numbers.

Clearly, neither of these two extremes is a productive way to monitor the delegation process. In between lies the answer to how to approach this delicate but essential task. Depending on the situation, monitoring may mean daily or weekly progress updates from your employee.

Each employee is unique. One style of monitoring may work with one employee but not with another. New and inexperienced employees naturally require more attention and hand-holding than employees who are seasoned at their jobs. Veteran employees don't need the kind of day-to-day attention that less experienced employees need. In fact, they may resent your attempts to closely manage the way in which they carry out their duties.

Effective monitoring of delegation requires the following:

- ✔ **Tailor your approach to the employee.** If your employee performs his job with minimal supervision on your part, establish a system of monitoring with only a few critical checkpoints along the way. If your employee needs more attention, create a system (formal, in writing, or informal) that incorporates several checkpoints along the way to goal completion.

- ✔ **Diligently use a written or computer-based system for tracking the tasks that you assign to your employees.** Use a daily planner, a calendar, or project-management software to keep track of the what, who, and when of task assignments.

- ✔ **Keep the lines of communication open.** Make sure your employees understand that you want them to let you know if they can't surmount a problem. Of course, this means making time for your employees when they ask you for help. Find out whether they need more training or better resources. Finding out early — when you can still do something about it — is better than finding out too late.

- ✔ **Follow through on the agreements that you make with your employees.** If a report is late, hold your employees accountable. Despite the temptation to let these failures slip ("Gee, he's had a rough time at home lately"), ignoring them does both you and your employees a disservice. Make sure your employees understand the importance of taking personal responsibility for their work and that the ability of your group to achieve its goals depends on their meeting commitments.

Be compassionate if your employee has indeed gone through a tough personal challenge (a parent died, a spouse was diagnosed with cancer, and so on) — you may need to assign someone else to cover her duties for a short period of time. However, if an employee consistently misses goals and shows no hope of improvement, perhaps that person is in the wrong job.

✔ **Reward performance that meets or exceeds your expectations, and counsel performance that falls below your expectations.** If you don't let your employees know when they fail to meet your expectations, they may continue to fail to meet your expectations. Do your employees, your organization, and yourself a big favor and call attention to both the good and the bad that your employees do. Remember the old advice (which happens to be accurate advice) to praise in public and criticize privately.

Excelling at Leadership Tasks (Even When You Delegate Them to Yourself)

Book III

Mastering Key Management Duties

Lech Walesa — one of the founders of Poland's Solidarity movement, and its long-time leader — once said that "you become free by acting free." The same is true of leading. You become a leader by acting like a leader. You don't need the title or the authority. You only need to be willing to embrace responsibility and to be able to elicit cooperation from people, listen to their needs, and place those needs above your own.

Making yourself a leader when you aren't one does not mean running around (as General Alexander Haig reputedly did after the assassination attempt on President Reagan) yelling, "I'm in charge. I'm in charge." It does mean acting on the moment and helping to pull your team together.

The way to become a leader is to view every situation as a leadership situation.

Leading as a follower

Even if you don't have a specific leadership role within your company, you can take initiative to make the work environment better for everyone in it — to foster human dignity on the job. That's an incredibly valuable role to play, but it isn't without some particular challenges. This section offers ideas for how to perform that role well.

Improve even the simplest things

Often, the simplest thing you can do to add to the dignity of the workplace is to clean it up and make it more cheerful. Many people take the attitude that physical conditions in the workplace are solely the responsibility of top management, and that they should not be spending their own time and money for the benefit of the company. But putting together a work detail one weekend to paint the walls of your office a brighter color, instead of waiting for maintenance to do it three years from now, can brighten everyone's attitude, both through the doing and through the end result. It will also make an impression on your group's leader and make him more receptive to your next suggestion about ways to improve work flow or profits.

Use information to build team spirit

An effective leader is someone who pursues information so that she can make the best possible decisions. But often, information is valuable not for what it can do for you but for what it can do for others.

For example, every person in your office or plant has a birthday. Take the responsibility of acknowledging those milestones with a card and a brief ceremony. Everybody has important family moments; you should acknowledge these events also. If your company has a newsletter, take the responsibility for your group to supply it with information. If there isn't a newsletter, start one, even if it's just a photocopied single sheet of paper.

You can contribute to the cohesiveness of the group by showing coworkers how much they have in common, and you can also help to build team spirit.

Always ask on behalf of the group, never for yourself

Doing any of these things may ultimately improve your leverage with management when you want to ask for a bigger, more significant change. But when you do ask for a significant change, such as upgraded training, ask on behalf of the group, not yourself. If you couch your request in terms of how the group benefits, it may be taken more seriously.

In order to demonstrate leadership in these situations, it has to be clear to whomever you're speaking that you represent the goals or needs of a group, not yourself alone. Group aspirations are why the need for leadership exists, after all.

Get your group involved in the community

Companies and organizations exist within their larger communities, so take it upon yourself to improve your group's ties to the community as a whole. The public relations department or the head of the company may be making charitable grants, but that doesn't stop you from organizing a group to help in an area where you think you can do some good.

For example, a playground near your workplace may need some cleanup or improvement; you can organize it. If there is an accident or a local disaster, you can help with organizing a fundraising effort. Is there a mentoring program or a literacy program to which you can contribute? All of these are opportunities to demonstrate leadership and involvement.

Most companies and organizations are open to efforts that engage with the community and make a difference. Take advantage of that fact to gain volunteer time and access to company resources. Doing so may get you noticed by higher levels of management, and it certainly makes employees feel good about where they work.

Don't pick fights with your bosses

Workplace dignity provides fertile ground for leadership opportunities. This *doesn't* mean actively seeking out confrontations with management. It means looking for ways to add to the value of the worker in the workplace.

Leading when your position is honorary

Book III

Mastering Key Management Duties

Under any number of circumstances, someone may name you as a leader but you may have no real authority. With any honorary title goes a *grant of opportunity.* Think of a grant of opportunity as a gift of money. How will you spend your new position? What will you do with it? Will you simply enjoy it until it's gone, or will you attempt to use it to improve your life and the lives of people around you?

Any time you're given an honorary title, take it as a grant of opportunity to do something besides stand on the dais beaming. Whatever you choose to do may be unexpected, and it may be more than anyone did before. It may also reinforce the good feeling that led the group to make you its honorary leader in the first place.

Keep in mind, however, that you're not really the leader, and you have to suggest and offer rather than plan and command. You have to prepare yourself for the real leader to say no, and you have to make certain that you in no way threaten the real leader of your group.

Leading when you're not expected to succeed

Welcome to the Department of Lost Causes. Because of the nature of organizations, even failing and dying organizations need leadership, lest they sell the furniture, close the offices, and let their workers go. An organization in its death throes is a sorry sight, especially if the organization has a proud history.

If it should come to pass that you're chosen to lead such an organization or group, what do you do? You could refuse and allow the group to fail without you, or you can accept, even if you know that your chances of resurrecting the group are slim to none. If you choose to accept, you have to make sure that you won't get the blame for the group's failure, even if your turnaround efforts are unsuccessful.

Rally the troops

It is important for you to meet with your group as soon as you have taken on the leadership role. Let the group members know that you are aware that things are grim, but that if they give you their support, even temporarily, you can at least attempt to find a workable course of action, which may include an orderly shutdown. People who work for a company often freeze up at the possibility that they may lose their jobs, for example, so it's your job to explain to them that even if that happens, you will do all you can on their behalf.

In this situation, you're much like a doctor who is attending a dying patient. On the one hand, you want to do everything possible to save the patient; on the other hand, you want to know when it is time to cease heroic intervention in favor of making the patient's last moments as comfortable as possible.

Follow the money

Every organization depends on a flow of funds, so the very first thing you should do is have someone audit the books. This way you know how much money is really in the till and how it has been spent. Announce and publish your results to the entire membership. If you find that there has been no wrongdoing, your publication of the results may spur some members to increase their contributions. If there has been poor administration, you have given yourself and others valuable information about why things are going badly, and you can begin to correct them.

Pick a short-term goal

After you know the money and the people situations, develop a short-term goal. That goal will almost inevitably involve the funds of the organization. If there are problems that you can fix by spending money, spend it. If there are problems that you can fix by not spending, stop spending.

A second short-term goal is rebuilding trust. If you have a failing business, you have to rebuild trust with your customers. If you have an organization with dwindling membership, you have to rebuild trust with the community. They are your greatest allies in helping you to grow again.

Know when events are beyond your control

Say your business is dwindling because of a demographic shift in your neighborhood. It used to be populated mostly by young people, but now many retirees live in the community, and they don't need the particular service you provide. If you can, invite community members to take part in activities you sponsor, and consider ways to adjust your business model to meet their needs.

But what happens when events are beyond your control? The demographic and lifestyle shifts that change so many communities, and the "creative destruction" of market forces, almost inevitably mean that no group lasts forever. Under the circumstances, you have to be like the pilot of a plane that is crashing. Keep the wings level even as you crash so that when somebody does the postmortem, he will say that you acted diligently and prudently and that nobody could have done more.

REMEMBER

Failure can be a stepping stone to success at a later time — if you handle the failure well and learn from your mistakes.

Book III

Mastering Key Management Duties

Book IV
Communicating with Employees

Five Ways to Foster Productive Brainstorming

- ✔ **Follow an agenda.** Create a solid meeting agenda and ask participants to choose a topic from the list and focus their conversation on that point until they're ready to move on.

- ✔ **Remember that any idea is a good idea.** Brainstorming is about articulating any and all possibilities before deciding on anything.

- ✔ **Follow time limits.** Some of the best ideas come when people are pressed for time. Keep the brainstorming short, and then spend quality time refining the ideas.

- ✔ **Say, then weigh.** Generate as many ideas as possible before weighing and evaluating a single one. Don't let the brainstorming process derail by getting bogged down in the details.

- ✔ **Create a parking lot.** If one of the parties has an idea for a different agenda item, quickly jot it down next to that topic — park it — until you're ready to move to that point. If the employees think of something they need to check out or want to add another topic for discussion, into the parking lot it goes.

Managers must master communicating in many situations, including performance appraisals. Discover key words to include in your appraisal conversations at www.dummies.com/extras/managingaio.

Contents at a Glance

Chapter 1

Encouraging Commitment through Coaching and Mentoring

In This Chapter

▶ Casting yourself as a business coach

▶ Recognizing ways to stimulate employee commitment

▶ Setting a leadership tone for effective coaching

▶ Managing assertively and collaboratively

▶ Introducing a model for guiding efforts that build employee commitment

*T*ake any group of managers and ask them if they want employees with high levels of commitment. Except for the rare person (who probably needs to be committed — sorry, couldn't resist), the answer will come up a resounding "yes!"

Employees with high levels of commitment are the ones most dedicated to the job and the organization. They're the ones who show drive and initiative, who work hard, and who aren't satisfied until they deliver top results. They're also the ones most likely to stick around and not leave the company. Simply stated, employees with high levels of commitment make a manager's job much easier and much more effective.

Achieving this commitment is no small feat, and it starts with putting yourself in the role of coach and mentor. This chapter shows you how to communicate your expectations to your employees as a coach and how to model the behaviors you want to see in others.

Getting the Lowdown on Business Coaching

You probably relate the term *coaching* to the sports world, but you don't have to be a sports coach (or even a fan) to be a manager who coaches effectively in the business world, where the definition of coaching includes the following:

- ✔ Coaching is an approach to management — how you carry out the role of manager.

- ✔ Coaching is a set of skills for managing employee performance to deliver results.

Being a coach means that you see and approach the role of manager as a leader who challenges and develops your employees' skills and abilities to achieve the best performance results. If you manage as a coach, your staff members learn, grow, and work hard, too. As you seek to get the best out of their performance, you also have to work very hard.

As a coach, you develop and possess various skills and efforts that are aimed at guiding employees to achieve high productivity and positive results. The more you manage as a coach, the easier you'll find coaching as a manager because you'll be putting those skills into practice.

Managing as a coach versus as a doer

While different leadership or management styles exist, managers tend to approach their roles in one of two ways — as a coach or as a doer:

- ✔ **Coach approach:** Managers work to achieve the best operational performance results by developing and maximizing the talents and abilities of employees to their fullest.

  Those who manage as a coach still perform tasks; in fact, many work alongside their staffs doing some of the same duties. Yet those who approach management as a coach recognize they also need to lead and develop others to top performance because that is how the tasks best get done. Such managers live by the principle of *and:* They approach their jobs as a balance of managing both task issues *and* people issues. They see the two as connected. They see managing people as part of managing the work the people do.

✓ **Doer approach:** In this approach, managers tend to focus more on task issues of the job (and also the technical issues of their work), as well as on the group's performance. Their attention tends to go first to the things they themselves have to do and to the areas of greatest comfort — task and technical issues. Doers, as a result, tend to function as senior individual contributors.

While the style of doers varies from controlling to very hands-off to a combination of the two, the doer approach to management tends to live by the principle of *or*. Doers have task issues to handle *or* people issues to handle. These issues are often viewed as separate sides of the manager's role rather than interrelated ones. Doers therefore put much less emphasis on how people are performing, which is usually less comfortable to deal with, than on getting things done.

Mentoring and developing staff

Mentoring and developing involves making the effort and showing interest in helping your staff grow in their skills and capabilities. It involves teaching, encouraging, and challenging them to do their best. Consider how seeing yourself as a coach allows you to do a better job with mentoring and developing:

✓ **The coach approach to mentoring and developing staff:** Such managers thrive on working with their employees and helping them develop their skills and capabilities. They ask questions more than they give answers; they give their staff challenging opportunities and work; and frequently they exchange feedback to spur learning and growth. They regularly take an interest in employees' careers and job situations and encourage training and other learning experiences.

From the coach perspective, the more capable your employees, the more productive and self-sufficient they are. Developing strong people resources is a source of pride, not a source of insecurity.

✓ **The doer approach to mentoring and developing staff:** Quite often, the doer is too busy to spend time mentoring and stimulating employee development — or the comfort to do so is lacking. If employees are particularly observant, they can still learn from the doer because many doers are knowledgeable and skilled in their work. But employees tend not to learn *with* the doer. (And if employees watch carefully, sometimes they may learn what not to do.) Beyond good old-fashioned on-the-job training in which you learn on your own, any organized or focused efforts on employee development are infrequent occurrences.

From these descriptions, it should be pretty clear which approach is more likely to stimulate employee commitment. Keep reading to find out how else to create high levels of commitment in your organization.

Book IV

Communicating with Employees

Tuning In to Personal versus Positional Influence

Influence means to have an effect on other people and on outcomes. From a negative perspective, influence can mean the use of manipulation and coercion. But from a positive stance, it can mean using your influence to gain an added value or a good effect. And when managers exercise leadership, they influence — positively or negatively.

Although managers are seen as leaders in organizations, not all managers assert much leadership. Many managers are somewhat *laissez-faire* in their style of leadership; that is, they are hands-off and passive. Such managers tend not to have too much influence over their employees. On the contrary, managers who do exhibit influence tend to do so in one of two ways, by use of positional influence or personal influence.

In the next two sections, you take a look at how these two styles of influence usually work. In addition, Table 1-1 gives an overview of how managers tend to assert their leadership influence. It shows clearly that personal influence is far more effective for business coaching than positional influence.

Table 1-1	Management Influence
Management by Positional Influence	*Management by Personal Influence*
Exercise authority	Exercise personal qualities
Look to maintain the chain of command	Look to build working relationships
Seek control	Seek employee ownership and involvement
Likely result: compliance	Likely result: commitment

Managing by positional influence

Management roles are positions of authority in organizations, and managers who wield *positional influence* view their titles as important and expect employees to respect their authority. Managers who use positional influence view having authority — and pushing it as needed — as the path to best results. Those who exert their positional influence also seek to achieve the following:

✔ **Maintain the chain of command:** Private and public organizations historically have been patterned around hierarchy — the many levels of positions from the non-management ranks through the management ranks. In military terms, the hierarchy represents a chain of command to be followed and never circumvented. Positional-influence managers generally follow this thinking. For them, the flow of communication and decision making needs to adhere to this chain of command. The hierarchy of management is to be abided by and respected, starting with the authority of their own positions.

✔ **Gain control:** Management literature of the 1960s and 1970s touted four main functions of a manager: to plan, lead, organize, and control. Managers who exert positional influence tend to really like that control part. Things are working right when everything is under their control and running the way they want it. In the groups they manage, they grant the approval for most decisions and give the solutions for most problems. The extreme types here are what employees call *control freaks*.

Control isn't necessarily a negative factor. Managers certainly need to ensure that the company's goals are being met and work with their employees to make modifications as needed. Most employees want this kind of organization or control; they tend not to respond well to chaos. However, employees also don't respond well to managers who are stifling in their attempts to maintain control.

✔ **Promote compliance:** The result of this management influence is often employee compliance — people do what they're told, work does get done, and sometimes quality performance does occur.

Managing by personal influence

Now take a look at what happens on the other side of the coin. Managers who exhibit *personal influence* strive to earn respect from others rather than expecting it automatically because of their titles. They do so by demonstrating traits and behaviors such as honesty, respect for others, and all that leadership-by-example stuff. By exerting personal influence, they seek to achieve the following:

✔ **Build working relationships:** Personal-influence managers attempt to establish positive working relationships with their employees instead of worrying about who has what authority in the organization. They do so by getting to know their employees professionally and personally so that the qualities that make both the manager and the employees good people and good workers can come out. Ongoing two-way communication is the norm in these relationships.

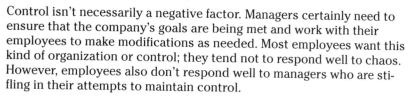

Book IV

Communicating with Employees

The emphasis here is on building working relationships as opposed to personal relationships. These managers know that understanding both the professional and personal facets of an individual is helpful in working with that person. These bosses are the ones who can be friendly with their staff members without trying to become friends with their employees. A friendly boss is far different from a boss who is trying to be your friend.

- ✔ **Seek employee ownership and involvement:** Managers who exert personal influence encourage employees to take ownership in their jobs — that is, they delegate responsibility, provide support and guidance as needed, and expect results to be delivered. Employee involvement and initiative are invited. Control for these managers doesn't come from telling employees how to do their jobs; it comes from having empowered employees follow through on the responsibilities they're given.

- ✔ **Develop commitment:** The likely result of management by personal influence is commitment. Managers who demonstrate positive personal qualities, build constructive working relationships, and drive employee autonomy with accountability increase the likelihood of getting commitment in return. Management of this kind creates situations in which employees respect their managers. Employees like working for someone who knows and cares for who they are and, at the same time, provides challenges and opportunities to grow. The roots of employee commitment come from this kind of environment.

Seeking commitment versus compliance

Positional influence and personal influence have radically different effects on employees and their performance. Commitment tends to yield greater productivity and employee retention than compliance does — especially in today's work world in which job security, and therefore loyalty to the company, has been eroded.

At the same time, from the 1970s until now, the U.S. workforce itself has been changing greatly. Beyond the changes in the demographic makeup of the workforce, changes like the following have been happening:

- ✔ Education levels have been rising.
- ✔ Technical skills and knowledge of computer use have been on the increase.
- ✔ Desire for challenge and meaning in one's work is on the upswing.

If the job situation isn't quite right, today's highly skilled workers are likely to look and go elsewhere — even out of state — for employment. Today, the norm for the workforce is to have multiple jobs in their lifetimes, if not multiple careers. The employers' concerns about so-called unstable *job-hoppers* (individuals who have held many jobs, with short life spans at those jobs) are shifting more to concerns about applicants who have spent many years at one job — because surely these applicants lack creativity and flexibility!

Are today's employees prepared to follow orders and revere authority? In subtle to more overt ways, employee responses come back with a resounding, "Don't tell me what to do!" The more managers attempt to push compliance and their positional influence, the more employees push back with various forms of resistance.

When compliance is encouraged, you find employees doing the minimum, taking little initiative, blaming you — the manager — for everything that goes wrong, and sitting back, taking little responsibility on their own. These employees still do what they're told, but their efforts are likely to be minimal and fall short of achieving the quality results you need and want.

Finding ways to build commitment offers the best hope for ensuring employee retention and productivity. When commitment occurs, you see employees with drive, creativity, positive morale, and willingness to make the extra effort and take responsibility. Ongoing research done on employee retention points out more and more that the major factor that keeps employees with an organization is the quality of the relationship they have with their managers. Pay alone is not enough. If people are working for a manager who cares about them and their careers and who provides them with challenges in their work, their reasons for staying far outweigh their reasons for moving elsewhere to work.

Personal influence, not positional influence, builds connections between employees and managers and commits employees to your company.

Maintaining your personal influence under pressure

While many managers want to build positive working relationships with their employees, the nature of the relationship often changes when pressure and stressful situations come into the picture. At those times, their mode of operation shifts to the compliance side.

For example, imagine that yesterday a manager was willing to be friendly and discuss ideas with you, but now stress has arrived, so today the manager demands the employees "do what I say!" Or yesterday a manager was willing to show interest in your work and career, but stress arrived, and that person is too busy to be bothered with you.

Managers who skip back and forth in their mode of operation limit their credibility for having much personal influence. If you always give orders and push authority, at least your manner is clear and consistent. If you shift back and forth, in which case your employees are always trying to figure out whether you're going to be open to listening and engaging in two-way discussions, you'll quickly lose credibility.

Your best bet is to find ways to build positive relationships with your employees, in spite of stressful situations.

Managing as a Tone Setter

Effective coaching is based on building positive working relationships and exercising personal influence with your employees. These efforts are what stimulate the development of mutual trust. One of the critical aspects of the leadership side of management is *tone setting,* in which managers understand that their own behavior often sets the tone for the behavior and overall performance for the group(s) they manage.

In other words, how your employees work and conduct themselves on the job is a reflection of how you, their manager, work and conduct yourself. And the higher you go up the organizational ladder, the greater the number of people you influence and affect.

A manager who, rather than face a problem, looks to find blame when problems occur produces defensive employees who often walk on eggshells. On the flip side, a manager who avoids dealing with problems so that she doesn't have to place blame is one who leads frustrated employees working in chaos. And another example: A manager who openly complains about management whenever he gets frustrated about something in his job is almost assuredly in charge of a group that frequently whines and complains, especially about its manager.

These examples illustrate how the tone-setter role can come back to haunt you as a manager. You need to stay aware that your own faults and weaknesses may be magnified within the staff you manage. Of course, if you lead by positive example, there's no guarantee that you will get positive behavior and performance in return, but doing so certainly increases the likelihood. Therefore, for managers to exert influence and coach effectively, maintaining awareness of their tone-setter roles is important.

When asked to identify the leadership-by-example behaviors that managers need to exhibit to set the right tone for their groups, here are the "Sweet 16" that managers and non-managers most often name:

✔ Listens to understand; isn't judgmental

✔ Follows through and meets commitments

✔ Takes an interest in employees as people

✔ Works productively and meets deadlines

✔ Is flexible and open-minded

✔ Treats others with respect

✔ Stays calm under pressure

✔ Addresses issues in timely and constructive ways

✔ Shares information and stays in touch

✔ Collaborates with others

✔ Is solutions-oriented and doesn't blame

✔ Recognizes good performance of others

✔ Displays honesty and integrity

✔ Shows interest and enthusiasm for the work of individuals and the group

✔ Shows up on time for meetings and other important events

✔ Takes a positive focus in interactions

When you make these behaviors regular practices, they earn you respect in return. Most importantly, they build your personal influence as a manager, which puts you on the road to ensuring the commitment of your employees. It's easier to ask your employees for high levels of performance and professional conduct when you demonstrate these efforts yourself.

So how are you doing as a manager at making these behaviors consistent practices? Evaluate yourself. On a scale of 1 to 5 — with 1 being seldom and 5 being frequent — with what frequency do you exhibit each of the Sweet 16 behaviors in your management practices? After this self-evaluation, if you're open to the feedback, ask your employees to rate how frequently they see you exhibiting each of these leadership-by-example behaviors. As a gauge of how you're doing (and don't shoot any of your employees if they give you a low frequency rating), consider an 80 percent level a competency level (80 percent is a total score of 64 out of 80). Anything above 80 percent is outstanding. Be honest with yourself! Your overall score is just a gauge; more important is the level of your awareness of whether and how frequently you demonstrate behaviors that build your personal influence as a manager.

The toughest person to manage in your group is none other than yourself. When you recognize this fact, you can work on you, and then you can apply the coaching practices that stimulate high levels of performance and employee commitment.

Coaching Assertively, through Collaboration

Coaching is carried out in an effort of collaboration: the act of working together. *Collaboration* is cooperating and willingly assisting others in some kind of effort.

Swinging to the other end of the manager's pendulum, what's not collaboration? Here are some examples of what managers often do that is *not* collaboration:

✔ Staying frequently uninvolved in the work that employees are doing.

✔ Telling people how to do their jobs.

✔ Correcting all the mistakes employees make and solving all the problems employees encounter — *for* them.

Collaboration is about working with someone else to set plans, solve problems, gain skills, and focus performance in the right direction.

The collaborative nature of coaching recognizes that managers and employees don't have the same level of responsibilities, and it doesn't seek consensus on all decisions. Managers practicing assertiveness and collaboration don't focus on making employees happy or on sitting with employees to help them get all their work done — *hand-holding,* as the expression goes. These approaches focus on communication, on taking action and responsibility, and on performance. Instead of coercion or acquiescence in stressful and challenging situations, assertive and collaborative coaches engage in dialogue with their employees. Even though these managers are decisive about getting an action done, they are willing to listen and are open to discussion. They are positive, firm, consultative, and understanding in the face of pressure.

Engaging in two-way conversations

The collaborative nature of coaching requires two-way conversations. Two-way conversations occur when people are willing to listen to each other's points of view and express their own points of view. Two-way conversations are discussions — not debates, dialogues, or lectures. They also convey that the employee and what she has to say are important and deserve to be heard with respect. You don't have to agree with each other, but you must be willing to understand one another and maintain dignity in your working relationship. The next chapter contains lots of tips for promoting these types of discussions.

Asserting yourself

For the two-way conversation and the collaborative nature of coaching to work, managers must be assertive in their manner and actions. In your role as manager, *assertiveness* is your ability to communicate and take action in a positive, sincere, and confident manner that maintains respect for others. Assertiveness translates into such actions as communicating directly, using language constructively, addressing problems with a focus on solutions, following through, taking initiative, and leading the way to bring issues to closure.

Coaching assertively involves flexibility tailored to the individual employee and the situation at hand. Sometimes this flexibility means being encouraging; other times it means being firm. Sometimes it means being persistent; other times it means being patient. Sometimes it means pushing a person to take action; other times it means backing off and seeing what the individual will do.

Coaching assertively encourages input and ideas but doesn't compromise high standards of performance. It encourages dialogue but not endless discussion with no closure.

Although many managers understand on an intellectual level that coaching is an assertive, collaborative effort that takes place through two-way conversation, they don't act upon it until this understanding reaches an emotional level. Only then are these concepts internalized and truly understood and practiced. The shift begins at times like the following:

✔ When a disagreement is recognized as an opportunity for listening and entering dialogue rather than as a time for arguing or just backing away.

✔ When a manager reacts to an employee's resistance by seeking to find out why the resistance occurred in the first place and how the issue can be settled, instead of using the resistance as an excuse to yell and order or to appease and do nothing at all.

✔ When problems in an employee's work are seen as opportunities to ask questions and challenge employees to come up with solutions — versus telling them how to fix their problems or letting problems linger.

When these kinds of shifts take place, you're starting to coach. Your focus shifts as well to be performance-based rather than personal-based, to working together rather than working against, to figuring out what works best to get a job done rather than seeing everything as either right or wrong.

Book IV

Communicating with Employees

Holding the pickles, onions, and aggressiveness!

Being assertive isn't the same as being aggressive. Although both approaches are action-oriented, they are quite different in their manner and behavior. An assertive manager allows dialogue; an aggressive one permits little listening and holds one-way conversations. An assertive manager addresses problems in a solutions-oriented manner; an aggressive one addresses problems in a shoot-first-and-then-blame manner. An assertive manager is direct; an aggressive one is blunt. Being assertive means being willing to take charge; being aggressive means being hard-charging — my way or the highway. In simple terms, assertiveness invites collaboration; aggressiveness seeks compliance.

The point is worth repeating: The collaborative nature of coaching requires assertive managers, not aggressive ones.

Choosing not to be passive

Passive and nonassertive approaches don't work when trying to achieve collaboration. Being meek, hesitant, indirect, and *laissez-faire* in manner and actions renders coaching useless. The give-and-take and constructive dialogue of coaching don't occur when managers are passive in their approach with employees.

Testing your collaboration skills

To help clarify the value of the assertive nature of coaching, check out the following responses made by managers who approach their roles in different ways.

Here's the scenario: One of your employees expresses an idea for the direction in which she would like to see a project go, and you, the manager, don't agree with her idea.

- ✔ **Aggressive response:** "That idea will never work. I disagree with it totally. I don't know what you were thinking, and who asked for your ideas anyway!"

  This approach creates a one-way conversation — end of discussion.

- ✔ **Passive response:** "Well that idea has possibilities. Maybe we could consider it. If you want to work on it, uh . . . maybe you don't have to. But I do appreciate that you have ideas. But if you want to explore it more, we could."

An indirect and hesitant response creates confusion and leaves
hanging.

✔ **Assertive response:** "I have some concerns about whether that idea
will help the project. Here they are (constructively expressed). Please
address my concerns or clarify any misunderstandings."

An assertive response sparks two-way conversation, collaborative problem solving, and an opportunity for closure on how to proceed with the
project.

The Five Pillars for Building Commitment

The five pillars for building commitment compose a model for your coaching
efforts to build commitment and achieve high levels of performance. The pillars serve as your guideposts. If you implement them, you impact employee
performance and increase commitment levels. Here they are:

✔ **Focus:** Employees know what they need to accomplish in their jobs, they
know what is expected of them, and they are aware of the values of the
group or organization. They know where the group is going and what its
priorities are. While the group's plans may change, chaos and mystery
are not frequent visitors.

✔ **Involvement:** Employees feel that they have some say over the matters
that affect their day-to-day work situations. They have input into the
planning, problem solving, and decision making that affect their level
of responsibility. They feel included. The adage that "people support
most what they help create" highlights what the pillar of involvement
emphasizes.

✔ **Development:** Opportunities for learning and growth are encouraged
and supported. These opportunities are both formal and informal in
nature, ranging from such activities as a training course to a mentoring
discussion between an employee and a senior manager. Helping people
continuously strengthen their knowledge, skills, and experience are
common practices.

✔ **Gratitude:** Efforts for and accomplishments of good performance are
noticed and acknowledged. As with the other pillars, how gratitude
is provided varies from formal to informal practices, but efforts to
recognize what employees do well occur regularly.

✔ **Accountability:** Employees are given responsibility along with the
authority to carry it out, which creates in them the desire to produce results with high standards. Lax performance is not tolerated,

Book IV

**Communicating
with
Employees**

> while measuring progress and reporting results are normal practices. People produce quality results not just because it is expected of them, but, more importantly, because they enjoy experiencing a sense of achievement.

These five pillars for building employee commitment hold influence only when you make them regular practices. Just a little effort now and then doesn't do the trick.

Analyzing an Instance of Poor Coaching

The following is a commonplace scenario of good intentions. As you read the story, you may want to analyze the manager's (Jack's) efforts by considering the following questions, each of which is addressed later in this section:

- What are Jack's efforts to coach Tim, his employee?
- What are Jack's efforts to encourage commitment from Tim?
- (Ah, now the tricky one.) Regarding Jack's decision on making the corrections for the project that Tim is assigned to handle, how would you as a manager deal with this situation?

Tim was quite eager when he started his new job. Early in the job, Tim's manager, Jack, met with Tim and assigned him an important project as his primary area of responsibility. Jack gave Tim a general description of what the project entailed and three directions — to do what it takes to get the job done, to come to him with questions, and to complete the project within three months.

As the weeks passed, Jack was pleased with Tim's progress. He noticed that Tim was meeting with the right people, was often working efficiently, and seemed self-sufficient. Jack held a brief review meeting with Tim a few weeks after the project started, and Tim appeared to be on the right track. Also, every now and then, Jack informally asked Tim how things were going and received an enthusiastic response of "really well."

Tim liked the freedom Jack gave him. He appreciated the fact that Jack was not a harsh or demanding boss and offered only an occasional reminder to stay on schedule with the project. On the other hand, Tim found that Jack was often tied up in meetings and burdened with his own projects, so Tim learned to get answers to questions elsewhere.

In a little less than three months, slightly ahead of the deadline that Jack had set, Tim informed Jack that the project was complete. When they met to go over the project, Jack's excitement about Tim's work soon turned to disappointment. Jack didn't like some of the decisions Tim had made — decisions that resulted in the project going in a somewhat different direction than Jack had envisioned.

Jack also didn't agree with some of the methods that Tim used to do his work. Jack wound up telling Tim that the project needed quite a bit of correction and that because of the tight deadline, he (Jack) would handle it and let Tim work on another, smaller assignment. Tim became deflated and frustrated.

Reviewing the manager's coaching efforts

Jack had good intentions at the beginning. He gave Tim a meaningful assignment, allowed him autonomy to run with the project, and gave clear directions about when the work needed to be completed. Early on, Jack met with Tim and did a brief progress review.

After that, however, any real coaching was nonexistent. The results expected were never spelled out nor were parameters set for Tim to work within. As for feedback of any substance and progress reviews along the way, well . . . *nada.*

So after the first few weeks, the two had little regular communication — and don't forget, Tim was a new employee. Jack didn't really take an interest in what was happening for Tim and the project until the deadline. Jack illustrates the classic "doer" who stays busy with his own affairs until something critical comes up.

Studying the manager's efforts to affect his employee's level of commitment

Jack gave Tim meaningful responsibility and initially a sense of autonomy in his work. So you could say that Jack made an initial effort to involve Tim. Jack also gave Tim a sense of focus at the beginning by letting Tim know the deadline within which he needed to complete the project.

These two early efforts did scratch the surface of two pillars for achieving employee commitment: involvement and focus. But Jack's lack of ongoing involvement and guidance fell short of building a working relationship and influencing high standards of performance in Tim's case. Jack failed to lay a foundation on which to build commitment. Jack then further undermined Tim's potential for commitment with the decision to leave him out of the correction phase of the project.

Ascertaining how to handle corrections for this project

You have a tight deadline and a project that needs fixing. The quickest course is to fix it yourself, as many managers do. While this decision may seem to be an easy solution (and many people have taken just this course when faced with similar circumstances), it actually has serious shortcomings and may create more difficulties than meet the eye. Here are some of the issues to consider in this example:

- ✔ When Tim is left out of the effort to correct the project, he can't learn from the experience. And, in a short period of time, trying to match Tim's knowledge of the project is no easy task, even if Jack has the technical expertise. (Also, if Jack had the time, why didn't he do the project himself in the first place?)

- ✔ In determining what went wrong with the project, Jack is focusing on the methods Tim used. From this perspective, you can say that Jack is placing methods over results — which is common with the kind of managers who worry more about how a job should be done than about the desired outcomes. In this case, it's possible that many of the results Tim produced are acceptable. But not involving Tim in evaluating the results and not focusing on results wastes time and a valuable resource.

- ✔ Even if Tim is invited to sit alongside and watch Jack make corrections, Tim will learn more from the experience than if he has no involvement in the effort at all. In most tough business decisions, two key factors must be considered: the business at hand and the impact on the people involved or affected by the decision. Jack's focus was on the first factor only, the business at hand (how to fix the project). As a result, Tim's potential for future commitment was shot down. The trust and working relationship between Tim and Jack were greatly damaged.

Jack needs the hands-on experience of fixing the project, but doing so with Tim's help is the most performance-effective course to take for this problem and any future problems.

Coaching focuses on performance but recognizes that people are connected to the work they do. Building employee commitment requires a focus on developing working relationships and on the growth of the individual doing the job.

Chapter 2

Communicating Effectively

. . . .

In This Chapter

▶ Grasping common ways of speaking — and the effectiveness of each

▶ Making listening much more than a passive pursuit

▶ Harnessing communication that doesn't come from words

▶ Communicating clearly via e-mail

. . . .

You'd be hard-pressed to find any job function or field of employment where communicating effectively with people isn't vital. Regardless of your job title or the type of organization or industry you work for, if you're like most people, the greatest challenges you face lean less toward the technical side of your job (your area of expertise) than they do toward interacting with other people.

Communication can feel like a tug of war, with a lot of tension as each side pulls but nothing gets accomplished. Nobody has to end up in the mud, however, and getting some basic knowledge about how speaking and listening work best can go a long way toward making all your communications more productive.

Understanding the Four Approaches to Speaking

People express themselves in four ways: aggressively, nonassertively, passive-aggressively, and assertively. This section discusses each of the four patterns of communication in detail so that you can recognize each pattern and begin to move your own way of speaking toward assertiveness.

If you're like most people, you've used all four speaking approaches at various times. But you may find that when you deal with certain people or encounter certain situations — especially challenging and stressful ones — you often fall into one of the less-productive patterns of expressing yourself (aggressive, nonassertive, or passive-aggressive). If you do, join the club known as the human race. You become a successful communicator by dealing with these situations assertively, the most positive and respectful way of resolving issues with others.

The aggressive approach

Aggressive speaking is a hard-charging approach that's often hostile and comes across as controlling or dominating. Here are some common messages you may hear when someone speaks aggressively:

- ✔ "You must. . . ."
- ✔ "Because I said so."
- ✔ "You idiot!"
- ✔ "You always/never. . . ."
- ✔ "Who screwed this up?"

There's nothing subtle to the aggressive approach. The following are common behaviors that an aggressive speaker displays:

- ✔ **Blaming, accusing:** In problem situations, an aggressive speaker is quick to find fault and focus on the wrongs that the other person supposedly committed.

- ✔ **Intimidating body language:** An aggressive speaker sometimes uses threatening or intimidating body language, such as demonstrative finger pointing, moving closer to you, getting in your face to argue a point, or pounding on a table with his fist.

- ✔ **Demanding, ordering:** The aggressive approach to getting something from another person is to demand it or give orders. An aggressive speaker tells you what you must do.

- ✔ **Raised voice:** As you may have guessed, when someone is making a point aggressively, her voice gets louder and the tone becomes sharper.

- ✔ **Harsh, personal language:** An aggressive speaker focuses more on the person than on the issue. The language is often filled with a lot of insults and, at times, with profanity. Tact or diplomacy is tossed aside.

✔ **Verbal browbeating:** When you have a difference of opinion with an aggressive speaker who feels strongly about a point, or when something isn't going the way that person desires, the conversation quickly turns into a competition — a battle to be won. The way to win is to interrupt, to talk louder, to argue, and to verbally attack the other person.

The nonassertive approach

Nonassertive speaking comes off as the softest of the four approaches. A non-assertive speaker is passive and allows others to dominate the conversation. Here are some common messages you hear when someone speaks in a nonassertive manner:

✔ "Uh . . . if that's the way you want to do it . . . um, that's fine with me."

✔ "I don't know if I could do that."

✔ "I'll talk to him soon about that problem; I've just been really busy."

✔ "I'm sorry to ask you."

✔ "I hate to bother you."

✔ "Maybe that's a good idea."

There's nothing strong or certain about the nonassertive approach. Instead, nonassertive speakers often display the following behaviors:

✔ **Soft voice:** In nonassertive speaking, the volume in the speaker's voice is often low and sometimes hard to hear, especially in group settings. The tone also may come across as meek.

✔ **Overly agreeable, no point of view expressed:** A nonassertive speaker agrees with you in order to go along and keep everything nice. A nonassertive speaker also seldom expresses her point of view and certainly doesn't express an opinion that's contrary to yours.

✔ **Avoidance:** The nonassertive way to deal with a concern is to avoid dealing with it: Avoid talking to the person, let the problem linger, and try to put off dealing with the situation for as long as possible. The more uncomfortable the matter is, the more effort a nonassertive person puts into avoiding it.

✔ **Withdrawn body language:** A nonassertive speaker doesn't make direct eye contact with other people, stays at a distance, and may slump or cower. Nothing confident comes across in the speaker's physical effort to communicate the message.

Book IV

Communicating with Employees

- ✔ **Sounding unsure:** When someone speaks nonassertively, he hesitates and sounds unsure. A nonassertive speaker may use qualifier language such as *perhaps, maybe,* or *hopefully,* or may start sentences with comments like, "I don't know if this idea will help."

- ✔ **Beating around the bush:** Nonassertive speakers express critical or sensitive points by talking around the issue and rambling, leaving the point — at best — implied. The speaker never states the point clearly and directly.

- ✔ **Sounding hopeless or helpless:** Another common nonassertive speaking characteristic is language of despair or inaction. A typically resigned or hopeless message, such as, "I tried that once, but it didn't work, so what can you do?" is common. You may hear a lot of *I can't*s and *I don't know*s such that no plan of action or possible solution is introduced.

The passive-aggressive approach

Passive-aggressive speaking is an approach in which a person comes off as subtle and indirect but with an underlying tone that may hurt or manipulate others. Take a look at some messages you hear when someone speaks in a passive-aggressive manner:

- ✔ "I knew that wouldn't work."

- ✔ "If that's the way you want it. . . ."

- ✔ "How could you even think that?"

- ✔ "When was the last time you helped me?"

- ✔ "The problem with Joe is. . . ."

The subtleties of the passive-aggressive approach aren't pleasant. Someone speaking passive-aggressively often displays the following behaviors:

- ✔ **Appears to agree but really does not:** One of the common behaviors of passive-aggressiveness is that the speaker sounds as though he is going along with or agreeing to something, but his actions that follow don't show support or commitment. Instead, the passive-aggressive speaker claims that any agreement was actually a misunderstanding, or the speaker carries out actions that are contrary to the supposed commitment.

- ✔ **Tells others but not the source of the concern:** A passive-aggressive person does not deal directly with concerns about others. Complaining about that person to other people — behind that person's back — is a common way to handle concerns. Generally, such behavior stirs up gossip and divisiveness.

✔ **Makes subtle digs and sarcastic remarks:** Heard the old line that many a truth is said in jest? This line summarizes one behavior of passive-aggressive speakers: Put-downs are concealed with sarcasm. When the speaker uses no sarcasm, her tone may be condescending and hurtful to the person hearing it. Sometimes a passive-aggressive speaker expresses displeasure not through words but through nonverbal means, such as rolling the eyes, shaking the head, or making sighs of disgust.

✔ **Keeps score, sets conditions:** In the passive-aggressive approach, cooperation comes with limitations or conditions. Ask a passive-aggressive speaker for support and you'll likely meet reluctance. Memories are long and forgiveness is short. Sometimes a passive-aggressive speaker comes off sounding like a martyr: "For all the work I've done for you, this is the appreciation I get!"

A passive-aggressive speaker also may try to settle the score by giving you the silent treatment, not showing up when help is needed, sabotaging your efforts behind the scenes, and sending harsh messages via e-mail and copying others on them.

✔ **Nonverbal message contradicts the verbal message:** In passive-aggressive behavior, stated words sound positive, but body language or tone of voice gives the words the opposite meaning. *Everything is fine* means that something *is* wrong, *Nothing is bothering me* means that something *is* bothering me. *That's a good idea* means that it *isn't,* and so on.

✔ **Holds back expressing concerns or providing assistance:** A passive-aggressive speaker may withhold information or other forms of support when others can use it to get a job done. In addition, he holds emotions in, although you may get a sense of them in the speaker's body language or from implied negative messages. Nothing is said directly, and when asked about a concern or issue, the passive-aggressive speaker often responds to the inquiry by saying "Never mind" or "No big deal."

✔ **Criticizes after the fact:** This behavior is sometimes referred to as *second-guessing* or *armchair quarterbacking.* After an event or action has taken place, a passive-aggressive communicator responds with what you should've done or what you did wrong — sometimes even when you requested input beforehand and she gave none. A passive-aggressive speaker is quick to pass judgment.

Book IV

Communicating with Employees

The assertive approach

The last of the four common speaking approaches that people use to express messages to others is assertiveness. *Assertive speaking* involves expressing yourself in a positive and confident way and allowing and encouraging others to do the same. This pattern of speaking requires the most skill and effort because, unlike the other three approaches, it requires you to think before you speak. Here are some common messages you hear from assertive speakers:

- ✔ "Yes, that was my mistake."
- ✔ "As I understand your point . . . "
- ✔ "Let me explain why I disagree with that point."
- ✔ "Let's define the issue and then explore some options to help resolve it."
- ✔ "Please hear me out and then work with me to resolve my concern."

The following are some of the behaviors that someone who speaks in an assertive fashion displays:

- ✔ **Takes responsibility:** The assertive approach says that each individual is responsible for his own actions — no excuses, no woe-is-me language, no blaming others for problems. The speaker accepts what has happened and focuses on what needs to be done next.

- ✔ **Takes initiative:** An assertive speaker doesn't play games. If something needs to happen, she takes the initiative to get the process rolling — no waiting for others to say what to do and when to act. The assertive approach is action oriented.

- ✔ **Listens actively:** Assertiveness allows for two-way conversation. Assertive speakers show a willingness to hear other people out and understand their points of view.

- ✔ **Speaks up, is direct and constructive:** If a point needs to be made or a thought needs to be expressed, an assertive communicator speaks up. He states the point directly without beating around the bush. Assertive speakers use language *constructively;* that is, they communicate the message in the best way possible and make the point clearly. The language focuses on the issue at hand.

- ✔ **Shows sincerity:** When you express yourself sincerely, you say what you mean and mean what you say — and do so with respect for others.

- ✔ **Is solutions focused:** In problem situations, an assertive speaker takes a problem-solving approach. She examines the problem, not to blame or find fault with anyone but to understand the issue and move toward developing a solution. Creating the solution becomes the main focus in working with others.

- ✔ **Assumes a confident voice and body language:** The voice of an assertive speaker sounds strong, certain, and firm when needed. The speaker's posture, gestures, and facial expressions support his message. He sounds and looks alive when speaking, coming across nonverbally as positive and enthusiastic to an appropriate degree.

✔ **Addresses concerns directly to the source:** An assertive speaker addresses issues directly to the source as opposed to telling others about the problems. At the same time, the speaker states the problem constructively and places the emphasis on collaborating with the other person to work out a resolution. No browbeating or blaming occurs.

✔ **Requests needs:** Whereas an aggressive speaker demands or orders to get what's needed, an assertive speakers asks for or requests what's needed. The message makes the sense of importance clear so that the request and any rationale for it are understood.

Recognizing the Impact of Listening

How do you feel when someone really listens to you? Here are the responses that people give the most:

✔ Respected

✔ Cared for

✔ That you've gained rapport

✔ Rewarded

✔ Satisfied

✔ A sense of achievement

What do these feelings have in common? They're all very positive. When someone listens well to you, the experience is definitely positive. The converse, of course, is that poor listening creates stress and resentment, decreases productivity, increases error-making, and generally detracts from the work environment.

Listening is a powerful means of communication that can increase your effectiveness on the job. People often overlook or take for granted the power (*power,* in this case, meaning "positive influence") of this tool. When you become aware of the power that active listening gives you, you're ready to develop and use listening tools and begin to have a positive impact on others.

Breaking down the listening process

Listening occurs in three stages:

✔ **Stage 1 — receiving:** In this first stage, you take in the speaker's message through your senses, most notably through hearing and seeing. In fact, you listen as much with your sense of sight as you do with your

Book IV

Communicating with Employees

sense of hearing. (The exception is when you're talking to someone over the telephone.) Your eyes help you read the nonverbal cues that play a part in how the speaker expresses her message.

✔ **Stage 2 — processing:** After you take in the speaker's message with your senses, the internal processing begins. This activity takes place in your mind and involves analyzing, evaluating, and synthesizing. It's done to make sense out of the speaker's message — to help you figure out the answer to the question, "What does the speaker mean?" Because all this processing is internal, the speaker doesn't yet see any visible reaction from you, the listener.

If problems occur in this stage of the listening process, they're most often caused by attention levels and stress levels. When you're distracted or not fully tuned into the speaker's message, you don't get the intended meaning. When your stress level is high, you may react emotionally to bits and pieces of the message instead of capturing the whole thing. The processing stage requires a great deal of concentration so that you get what the speaker is truly saying.

✔ **Stage 3 — responding:** At this stage, the speaker sees and hears what the listener does. The listener verbally and nonverbally acknowledges that he has received and understood the message.

When the speaker feels respected and understood by the listener, a strong connection is made — and productivity goes up. When the speaker encounters nonverbal or verbal barriers from the listener, the communication process breaks down; productivity goes down and stress increases.

Eradicating patterns that crush listening

One of the common ineffective patterns that occurs in conversations is that a speaker speaks to a speaker instead of a listener. Little true listening takes place. Table 2-1 illustrates this pattern, which makes for less-than-productive conversations. Check out this sample conversation between two coworkers related to a customer order.

Table 2-1	Heated Conversation with No Listening
Ann's Role and Message	*Sue's Role and Message*
Begins as speaker: "Sue, that new account you have, Alpha Inc.? I'm running into a problem trying to fill the order for it."	**Reacts as speaker:** "Oh, no! I worked so hard to finally get business from this new customer, turn it over to you to get the order fulfilled, and then the very next day you show up with a problem. Why can't I get support for the sales I bring in, Ann?"
Reacts as speaker: "If you knew how to qualify customer orders, we wouldn't run into this problem."	**Reacts as speaker:** "This is the support I get. Every problem is my fault. If you folks in customer fulfillment understood how we in sales keep you employed, you would be a lot more helpful."

As the conversation in Table 2-1 shows, Ann and Sue are talking *at* each other. Turn up the volume on what they have to say, and you have an argument. This is a conversation with two people talking and no one listening.

Table 2-2 shows another example of what people commonly do in this less-than-productive conversation pattern.

Table 2-2	Calm Conversation with No Listening
Joe's Role and Message	*Ramon's Role and Message*
Begins as speaker: "Ramon, we need to increase efficiency in our operation by creating some process improvements."	**Reacts as speaker:** "Joe, I think the answer lies in putting in some organized training for the staff."
Reacts as speaker: "I disagree. The inefficiencies that occur in our operation are all process related. If we find ways to streamline our processes, we can serve our customers better."	**Reacts as speaker:** "No, Joe. If you look at the kinds of errors that staff members make, most are because of not knowing how the processes work. We tend to throw people into their jobs as opposed to training them on how to do the job right."

The example in Table 2-2 again illustrates the pattern people often have in conversations: two people talking at each other and no one really listening. While the conversation between Joe and Ramon is less heated than the one between Ann and Sue in Table 2-1 — and they're talking on a related subject about making efficiency improvements — Joe and Ramon are still busy expressing opinions back and forth to each other. Neither is making the effort to understand the other's thinking.

Table 2-3 illustrates the pattern of more productive conversations. Take a look at Ann and Sue's conversation under this different pattern.

Table 2-3	Respectful Conversation with Active Listening
Ann's Role and Message	**Sue's Role and Message**
Begins as speaker: "Sue, that new account you have, Alpha Inc.? I'm running into a problem trying to fill the order for it."	**Responds as listener:** "A problem? Tell me about it."
Continues as speaker: "A couple of items. First, some of the prices quoted on the order form don't match what we have on our guide sheet in customer fulfillment. Second, a few of the part numbers listed on the order form don't match our listings."	**Responds as listener again:** "So what you're telling me is that you're running into some confusion in trying to fulfill the order here. Is that right?"
Confirms as speaker and then becomes listener: "Exactly. What can you do to help us out?"	**Becomes speaker:** "Let me take a look at the items in question on the order form. I can check to see whether they are just my clerical mistakes or whether I need to get back to the customer to clarify his needs for the order. I'll also check our guide sheets so that we're all on the same page. I should be able to get back to you with some answers by tomorrow."
Responds as listener: "Sounds like you've got a plan."	
Closes as speaker: "Thanks for your help. We'll talk tomorrow and get Alpha Inc. off to a good start."	

In productive conversations like this one, both people take turns being speaker and listener. They hold off on making assumptions and make every effort to find out more about each other's viewpoints. They are collaborative as opposed to adversarial in working out the issue.

Table 2-4 gives you a look at how Joe and Ramon's conversation can use this more productive pattern.

Table 2-4	Respectful Conversation with Active Listening
Joe's Role and Message	*Ramon's Role and Message*
Begins as speaker: "Ramon, we need to increase efficiency in our operation by creating some process improvements."	**Responds as listener:** "Help me understand more of your thinking behind this suggestion."
Continues as speaker: "From my thinking, Ramon, our current processes for order fulfillment can be quite cumbersome. They create a lot of work and often confusion, too. If we can find ways to streamline them, I think we can better serve our customers."	**Responds as listener again:** "So you're seeing the root of our operational problems as being centered around processes?"
Confirms as speaker and then becomes listener: "That's right. What do you see as the main factors for our operational problems, Ramon?"	**Becomes speaker:** "In my view, the area we need to tackle most is training. That's the quickest and best way to start to make the improvements we need."
Responds as listener: "Training, hmm? What's your reasoning?" (And the conversation continues from there.)	

Unlike in their previous conversation (refer to Table 2-2), Joe and Ramon are now talking *with* each other as opposed to speaking *at* each other. They are expressing opinions, but this time the opinions are explored and heard out. The conversation flows as a two-way interaction instead of two one-way interactions.

Book IV

Communicating with Employees

Discovering the ways people listen

As discussed earlier in the chapter (refer to "Understanding the Four Approaches to Speaking"), people express their messages to each other by using four common approaches. Likewise, there are four common approaches to listening:

- Passive listening
- Selective listening
- Attentive listening
- Active listening

Most people don't receive formal instruction in how to listen effectively and don't usually have standout role models for it, either. Of the four common patterns for listening to others, passive listening and selective listening occur the most often. As many people engage in listening, they tend to function in one pattern as a regular practice — whether in stressful or nonstressful situations. You may see yourself, plus others in your life, in the patterns described in the following sections.

Is anybody really home? The passive approach

In the passive listening approach, the listener is present nonverbally but verbally provides little feedback to the speaker. Here are some common behaviors exhibited by someone who is listening passively:

- Eye contact with the speaker
- Fairly expressionless look on the face
- Occasional nods of the head
- Occasional verbal acknowledgments, such as, "Uh huh," especially on the telephone

As you can see, the listener is with the speaker but adds little to stimulate the flow of conversation. As the speaker, you're on your own. Talking to a passive listener can be quite frustrating because you generally want more participation from the other person. You may begin to wonder whether that listener really cares or understands anything about the message you're expressing.

Getting what you want, not what you need: The selective approach

Selective listening is most commonly defined as hearing what you want to hear. When you hear the message you want to hear, you may function as a more engaged and understanding listener. But when you don't want to hear about the particular message being delivered, you tend to tune out or become reactive to the speaker. In other words, you're inconsistent in your listening efforts when you function as a selective listener.

Someone who is listening in a selective manner to a message that she doesn't want to hear displays these behaviors:

✔ Gives looks of disinterest

✔ Looks away at other things — a cell phone, papers, and so on

✔ Sits quietly

✔ Reacts with high degrees of emotion, such as being defensive or debating every point

✔ Jumps in before the speaker has finished and takes over the conversation as a speaker

✔ Changes the subject

✔ Asks a question about a point of self-interest, sometimes in an interrogating manner, that doesn't fit in the speaker's current message

Judgmental actions by a listener, from tuning out to reacting harshly, create barriers in conversation. They put up hurdles that cause the listener not to get the full message and add strain and tension to the working relationship.

Falling into the trap of being a selective listener is easy to do. Humans have emotions and biases, and sometimes a speaker says something that triggers them. In addition, people are selective not just based on what they hear — the subject matter — but also on who is speaking and how the message is presented. For example, your department vice president comes into your office to make a request of you. You're fully attentive and receive the message well. A few minutes later, a coworker stops by, one who turns you off because of his verbose nature. What do you do when he starts talking? Tune him right out. That's selective listening.

Grabbing the facts: The attentive approach

Functioning as an *attentive listener* is more productive than functioning as either a passive or a selective listener. When you function as an attentive listener, you're more engaged and less judgmental, both nonverbally and verbally. Attentive listeners display these behaviors:

✔ Give steady eye contact to the speaker

✔ Show interested looks and sincere facial expressions

✔ Nod to indicate understanding

✔ Provide simple verbal acknowledgments ("I see," "Okay," "Yes," and so on) to encourage the speaker to express his message

✔ Raise questions to begin to draw out the message

✔ Ask questions that seek greater detail out of the message

A speaker's message contains two parts: the facts or content and the feelings or emotions. Together, they create the meaning of the speaker's message. This concept is fundamental to results-oriented communication:

Facts + emotions = The meaning of the message

Attentive listening focuses on the facts being heard in the message. The facts are the more tangible part of the message. Emotions tend to be stated less in words than in nonverbal behavior — emotions are much less tangible. So when you function as an attentive listener, you take the *Dragnet* approach to listening; you become the Sergeant Joe Friday of communication, looking for "Just the facts."

As an attentive listener, you seek the facts and information that the speaker wants to relay to you in your conversation. When the message is mostly factual, you do well. When the message involves much emotion, you tend not to deal with it, or you neglect to acknowledge it directly. In essence, you say, "I can tell what you're talking about, I hear your words, but I may not be able to tell fully what you mean." This is where attentive listeners fall short. They don't capture the entire message to get the full meaning — both the facts *and* the feelings.

Capturing and confirming the message: The active approach

Active listening, sometimes referred to as *responsive* or *reflective* listening, is the most powerful way in which people engage in the effort of listening. An active listener receives a speaker's message with care and respect and then works to verify her understanding of that message — as the speaker meant it to be.

When you function as an active listener, you capture the speaker's whole message — the facts *and* the feelings. The speaker is able to get his message out and then walk away knowing that the listener has understood it.

Among the behaviors displayed by active listeners are the positive ones listed in the "Grabbing the facts: The attentive approach" section, plus the following:

✔ Showing patience

✔ Giving verbal feedback to summarize understanding of the message

✔ Acknowledging the emotions being expressed with the message to fully understand where the speaker is coming from

- ✔ Exploring the reasons for the emotions being expressed when they are significant to the overall message
- ✔ Speaking up when something is unclear or confusing

Active listeners talk. But what they talk about and where their attention goes is the speaker's message — not their own message or their commentary on the speaker's message.

Putting Active Listening Tools to Work

Active listening is about showing an understanding of the speaker's entire message, not agreeing with or having opinions about that message. Achieving understanding is the emphasis of active listening, but doing so in a nonjudgmental manner is critical to the listening behavior necessary to make it all work. This section provides you with tools that help you listen actively and effectively.

Drawing out the speaker's message

Active listeners rely on the four tools covered in this section to help draw out and focus a message. They aid and stimulate the speaker to express the message freely. By using these four tools, the listener is better equipped to help the speaker express the content of the message and, as needed, explain the basis of the feelings being heard in the message.

Letting the speaker in: Door openers

Door openers are signals listeners use to encourage speakers to express and elaborate upon their messages. Like red lights changing to green for motorists, door openers tell speakers to proceed without caution in presenting their messages.

Door openers can be nonverbal or verbal expressions by the listener; however, nonverbal door openers are especially helpful because they can be given while the speaker is talking without being interpreted as interruptions. The following list describes nonverbal door openers:

- ✔ Nodding your head to acknowledge that you're following the message
- ✔ Giving a sincere smile for an upbeat message
- ✔ Showing a look of interest

   ✔ Showing a look of concern for a serious message

   ✔ Turning and facing the speaker

   ✔ Leaning in slightly toward the speaker

   ✔ Offering steady eye contact

   ✔ Providing a patient look with silence

Providing a patient look with silence is one of the more powerful and sophisticated nonverbal door openers. Use it when someone is expressing what sounds like a serious message.

Sincerity is key to the effectiveness of nonverbal door openers. Facial expressions showing insincerity often close rather than open the door. If you're smiling when your speaker is saying something serious, the behavior may come off as a smirk, which is a major turnoff to the speaker.

Nonverbal door openers are only half of the green lights that stimulate a good flow of conversation. The other half are verbal door openers: one or two spoken words that have the same effect as their nonverbal counterparts. The following verbal door openers communicate to your speaker, "I'm following along — go ahead and tell me more."

   ✔ Uh-huh

   ✔ Um-hum

   ✔ Right

   ✔ I see

   ✔ Yeah

   ✔ Yes

   ✔ Really

   ✔ Neat

   ✔ Oh

   ✔ Okay

   ✔ Wow

The tone of your verbal door openers is critical. The tone needs to be non-judgmental — in a range that allows for curious, interested, and patient sounds. When the tone comes across as judgmental, you're creating a barrier to the conversation and are likely blocking the speaker from communicating the full message. For example, if you say "right" in a sarcastic tone as someone is talking to you, that door opener becomes a door closer.

Say again: Echoing

Echoing is repeating a key word or phrase of the speaker's message as a way to draw out more of the message and gain a clearer picture of it. Echoing works like little sparks, hardly noticed by the speaker, that help you ignite the vague and unknown elements of a message into fiery specifics and well-defined details. It involves two steps:

1. **Repeat the key word (or two) from the speaker's message (use the speaker's words, not your own), making your pitch go higher at the end of your remark so that it sounds like a question.**

   That's the echo.

2. **After making your echo response, wait patiently.**

   The inquisitive sound of the tool invites a response to come from the speaker without the listener having to ask a direct question.

To echo correctly, you need to know when to use the technique. Three such situations work best:

- ✔ **Vague, general statements:** Vague, general statements tell you little and may mean a variety of things. For example, the person says to you, "That was a really interesting meeting yesterday." Who knows what that means? It's unclear.

  You, as the listener, should echo, "Interesting meeting?"

- ✔ **Vague yet loaded statements:** Vague yet loaded statements give you little substance or clarity, but by the tone of voice or body language, you can tell emotionally that a strong message lies beneath the surface. For example, you ask a coworker how a meeting went, and you get a response with a very sharp tone: "Fine. Just fine!" What happened is vague, but the emotion is strong — in essence, loaded.

  You should echo, "Fine?"

- ✔ **Unfamiliar word or term:** In this case, you hear a word that isn't familiar to you or that is being used in a way that seems unusual or different to you. Often this happens when a speaker uses various forms of technical jargon: language that isn't familiar to people who aren't connected to the subject of the conversation. Sometimes the unfamiliar terms are *acronyms* (letters that stand for words) that not everyone knows. Here's an example:

  The speaker says an unfamiliar term: "We got a new MRP system that I'm not sure will help us."

  The listener uses echoing: "MRP system?"

Book IV

Communicating with Employees

In all three cases, echoing encourages the speaker to open up to you and explain her point. Using an inquisitive tone encourages the speaker to tell you more information about the message without your having to work hard to get it.

Digging deeper: Probing

Questions are phrased as either close-ended or open-ended. *Close-ended* questions solicit short, definitive answers that often can be said in a word or two. Here are a couple of examples:

- ✔ "Did you get that report done?" Answer: "Yes."
- ✔ "When is the meeting?" Answer: "2:00."

Although asking them can still result in verbose responses, close-ended questions nevertheless aim for brief and definitive answers. *Open-ended* questions, on the other hand, ask for information, explanation, expressions of thoughts and feelings — things that can't be said in a mere word or two. Here are a couple of examples:

- ✔ What are your ideas for solving this problem?
- ✔ How would you go about implementing that new program?

Exercise caution when asking *why* questions. Why? Although why is a good first word to shape open-ended questions, it often carries a judgmental tone. Here are a couple of examples:

- ✔ Why did you do that?
- ✔ Why would we ever want to try that way?

Why questions can have an accusatory or critical tone that can put a speaker on the defensive rather than inviting that person to speak freely. Therefore, either manage your tone carefully so as to sound inquisitive or rephrase the question. For example, instead of asking "Why did you do that?" you could say, "Please explain your thinking on the handling of this issue." Comments like "Tell me more" or "Help me understand" also are effective prompts.

Making sure you're following along: Checking the subject

Checking the subject is clarifying a detail of the speaker's topic or subject. Checking the subject enables you to follow the flow of the speaker's message without becoming sidetracked or confused. You can use the checking-the-subject tool when the topic of your speaker's message starts to become unclear or fuzzy, implicit instead of explicit, or off the stated subject.

Instead of sitting back passively when the topic becomes unclear, implement the following steps:

1. **As soon as the speaker takes a breath, jump in.**

   Don't let the speaker continue. Interject the moment that the subject becomes unclear.

2. **In an inquisitive tone, state the subject you think the speaker means.**

   Sometimes you can use starter phrases like the following:

   - "You're referring to . . . (then say what you think the subject is)?"
   - "You're talking about . . . ?"
   - "You mean . . . ?"

Checking the subject by this two-step process invites an immediate response before the speaker has a chance to proceed with more of the message. The response you get either verifies what you thought the topic was or clarifies what it means.

When checking the subject, your interjection is brief and focuses on the speaker's message, not away from it. As a result, many speakers don't even notice this little clarifying effort by you. Instead, they end up benefiting from it.

Verifying your understanding of the message

The active listening tools covered in the previous section draw out the speaker's message and help focus it. They stimulate the flow of the message and allow that message to be expressed. The active listening tools covered in this section go further. They have you checking whether what you heard the speaker say, nonverbally and verbally, is what the speaker really means. Checking understanding and not assuming you know what is being said are key here.

Using these tools as regular practice is what turns you into a full-fledged active listener. People often walk away from conversations *thinking* they understood what the other person meant. With these tools, you walk away *knowing* exactly what the other person meant and knowing that the person feels understood. That's how productivity increases and working relationships strengthen.

To use these tools you have to listen for the entire message. Recall this important formula as you discover each of the tools in this second set:

Facts + emotions = The meaning of the message

Book IV

Communicating with Employees

Capturing the emotions: Reflecting feelings

Reflecting feelings is checking your perception of the speaker's feelings in the message to understand the emotional meaning being expressed. You use this tool when the feelings being expressed represent a great deal of the message's meaning.

As the name of the tool says, you're acting like a mirror, reflecting the emotional meaning you're hearing from the speaker. Here are some tips:

- ✔ State the emotion you perceive is being expressed.
- ✔ Use the word "you" because the message is from the speaker, not from you.
- ✔ Because you're checking, your voice inflection should pick up at the end of your statement to make it sound like a question. If you can't do that clearly with your voice, you can add a question to your reflecting statement, such as: "Is that right?"

The following are a few examples of reflecting feelings, based on what has been heard from the speaker:

- ✔ "Sounds like you're excited by that opportunity. Is that right?"
- ✔ "Seems like that was a frustrating experience for you?"
- ✔ "I sense you're irritated with Don. Is that correct?"

In each case, the emotion being expressed — excitement, frustration, irritation — is the main emphasis of the speaker's statement. It reflects the significance in the speaker's message.

Capturing the content: Paraphrasing

Paraphrasing is restating the main idea of the speaker's message in live conversation to show and check — verify or clarify — your understanding of the facts or content of that message. It's a restatement in your own words but not a reiteration of the speaker's exact words. The latter tends to be mimicking, which usually turns people off. Paraphrasing is similar to reflecting feelings except that its purpose is to establish understanding of the content side of the message.

In most cases, you can paraphrase in one sentence. You're looking to capture the essence of the speaker's message, not all the details. Quite often, you can set up the paraphrase with starter phrases that cue the speaker that you want to check your understanding. Here are some common starter phrases to use:

- ✔ What you're saying is . . .
- ✔ In other words . . .
- ✔ What you mean is . . .

> ✔ What you're telling me is . . .
>
> ✔ If I understand your point correctly . . .
>
> ✔ What I'm hearing you say is . . .
>
> ✔ Sounds like you're saying . . .

Like reflecting feelings, with paraphrasing you're checking your understanding, not assuming that you know what the speaker means. You want to have that inquisitive inflection in your voice at the end of the paraphrase statement or add "Is that right?" so that you clearly sound like you're checking and asking for confirmation in return.

Utilizing the combo version: Reflective paraphrasing

Many times, messages you hear have meanings that take in facts and feelings. In these cases, call upon the reflective paraphrasing tool. *Reflective paraphrasing* is a combination of reflecting feelings and paraphrasing, capturing the emotion and content being expressed to show and check understanding of the speaker's meaning. In most cases, you can check the meaning with just one sentence.

You identify the emotion in the meaning of the message and summarize in your own words the content that serves as the explanation for the emotion. Sometimes it's done by saying, "You're feeling (emotion you hear) because of (content you heard that explains the situation behind the emotion)." For example: "You're feeling frustrated because your proposal has gotten little response so far from management. Is that right?"

Relating when it counts: Sharing a relevant example

At times, you may want to share an example of a situation that relates to the point the speaker is making to show an understanding of where that person is coming from. You use this tool in special circumstances; when done right, it can be powerful in a positive way.

You must meet a couple of prerequisites before you can use this tool:

> ✔ You've heard the whole story from the speaker.
>
> ✔ You have an example from your experience that you see as relevant and believe will help show the speaker that you understand her circumstance.

WARNING!

If those prerequisites have not been met, don't use this tool. You want to avoid giving your speaker a feeling of *one-upmanship* — "If you think that's bad, you ought to hear what happened to me!" Your role is to keep the focus with the speaker, not take it away. That's why you want to use this tool only under special circumstances.

Book IV

Communicating with Employees

When the prerequisites have been met, you follow one of two processes in applying the tool. In either case, you may paraphrase or reflective paraphrase first to check that you do understand your speaker's situation.

In one process, you give a brief (usually one-sentence) relevant example: "So the struggles you've encountered with this client are much like what Joe went through last year when he was assigned this client, right?"

The other process is good to use when you have an example from your own experience that you want to share. It follows three steps:

1. **Make a connecting statement from the speaker to you.**

   "Your situation sounds similar to something I went through."

2. **Tell your related story briefly, briefly, briefly.**

   Get to the point. Just because you heard a detailed story doesn't mean you offer one in return. Yours should be the concise highlights version that you're sharing only to show relevance to the speaker's situation.

   "I encountered this, that, and the other."

3. **Make a connecting statement back to the speaker.**

   "Much like you've experienced, right?"

Checking by asking, "Right?" at the end of the statement lets the speaker know that he still is the focus of the conversation. You merely shared something to add value to what you heard and to show that you understood where the speaker was coming from. Speakers greatly appreciate that.

What You Say and How You Say It

Your words alone — the verbal stuff — aren't the only component of speaking. Nonverbal tools can greatly impact how your message is expressed and received by others. Although what you say is important, how you say it often carries more weight.

Communicating with eye contact

In conversation, who provides more direct eye contact to the other person: the listener or the speaker? More often than not, it's the listener (as long as that individual is making the effort to listen).

What is the speaker doing with his eyes? At times, the speaker looks at the person with whom he's conversing, but quite often, his eyes are wandering around gathering thoughts about what to say next. Some speakers also do the following:

✔ Look skyward

✔ Look at the floor

✔ Look over the listener's shoulder

✔ Seem to be looking within themselves

The eye contact tool works differently: To be an assertive speaker, you provide steady and sincere eye contact with the other person while expressing your message. Here's how you use this tool:

✔ **Make steady eye contact.** The idea is to look at people when you're talking to them. Steady eye contact is the key. Steady does not, however, mean constant. Blinking and occasional glances away are expected and normal. Add a touch of sincerity to your looks, and you'll attract people's attention to you and your message.

✔ **Maintain eye contact.** People often ask how long you should continue eye contact. Certainly, no set time exists for maintaining eye contact and then momentarily glancing away. Life and interactions don't exist by formulas. Instead, the more familiar and comfortable a relationship you have with someone, the longer the eye contact can be maintained without discomfort for either party. In general, eye contact can range comfortably from 6 to 20 seconds in one-on-one interactions, while in group situations, the time is less per individual — three to six seconds — because you want to address everybody in the group.

✔ **Look in the right places.** Look directly at your listener's face, near the eyes. Looking above and below the face captures less of the listener's attention and can make the listener uncomfortable.

Making sure your body talk supports your message

Body language refers to everything you do with your body to express your message, including facial expressions, posture, and gestures. The idea behind assertive speaking is getting these myriad expressions and cues involved in your message — that is, coming alive when you speak. No one wants to listen to an uncertain, stiff, and uptight person for long.

Here's how you use the body language tool:

- **Posture:** Posture is how you carry and position yourself. Sit up and face your receiver as a means of expressing your message assertively. It is sometimes helpful to lean forward a bit as well.

- **Facial expressions:** Technically, you can't see your face when talking unless you carry a mirror and hold it up to yourself. Yet you can sense what your face is doing. You likely know when you're smiling, when you have a look of concern, or when you're showing a strong feeling about something. Your face communicates these emotions to others. The idea in expressing yourself assertively is to show positive life through your facial expressions.

  You've probably heard an expression about putting a smile in your voice, meaning to sound more upbeat by smiling as you speak. The muscles in your face change with a smile and help pick up the inflection in your voice. That's the idea here. Have your facial expressions match what you're saying in your message. Doing so gives your message confidence and sincerity — a double dose that positively engages people to want to listen to you.

- **Gestures:** Gestures are what you do with your hands when you're talking. Use gestures to come across assertively, to help your message flow properly, and, in essence, to punctuate or emphasize key points when you're talking. People often do just that in casual and social conversations. Just apply that same effort to your important messages at work. You may also notice that your gestures have connections to your facial expressions, helping you deliver your message in an animated way within your own style.

Putting oomph in your voice

Your voice is a powerful tool for delivering your message in an assertive manner. When not used wisely, it can cause you to come across as nonassertive, passive-aggressive, or aggressive. When used wisely, however, it makes others pay attention to what you have to say.

The emphasis on the vocal tool for assertive speaking is not about the physical quality of your voice. You have what you have. And like everyone else, you never sound like you think you will the first time you hear your voice recorded on tape. No, the emphasis is on utilizing the richness of your voice in terms of volume, inflection, and tone, so that your delivery commands positive attention. Here are some tips for using this tool:

- **Project your voice.** Are you audible enough when you speak? The idea is to be heard loud and clear. This effort becomes even more important when you're interacting in group situations such as meetings.

The tendency many people have, especially in group meetings, is that if they don't hear you well, they ignore what you're trying to say. They're less likely to ask you to speak up and repeat yourself.

Therefore, vary your volume for the situation. Go a little louder in group situations, and then turn it down slightly for one-on-one interactions. Always keep it at a volume that makes your voice easy to be heard.

Using the volume of your voice wisely can help you put a greater emphasis on an important point that you want to make. Increasing your volume at an important point commands attention, and sometimes softening your volume at a particular point of emphasis has the effect of drawing people's attention closer to you. In either case, the variation from your normal volume helps the point you're trying to make stand out — an effective and assertive way to get people to listen.

✔ **Show inflection in your voice.** Inflection deals with your pitch. If you're at a high pitch, your voice comes across as shrill, which nobody wants to hear. More common, if you stay at one pitch, and a rather flat one at that, you sound dull. Who likes to listen to dull-sounding people? The key to being assertive is to have variety — known as _modulation_ — in your pitch. Modulation makes your voice pleasant to listen to and conveys energy in your message.

Like volume, showing a greater variation in the inflection of your voice when you want to drive home a point helps you command positive attention. Exhibiting slightly higher or slightly lower levels of enthusiasm about the point you're trying to make draws your listener's attention to that point.

Knowing when you want something important to stand out, and then using variation in either volume or inflection to highlight that importance, comes across to the listener as confidence in your message — an assertive characteristic that tends to positively engage the attention of others. It's a good idea to know what's vital in your message so that you assertively apply your voice to help convey that importance.

✔ **Display sincerity in your tone.** Tone wraps up the volume and inflection in your voice. It conveys the feeling of your message and, therefore, plays a huge part in what your message means and how others receive it. You want your tone to communicate a sense of importance in your message, greatly affecting whether the message is clear.

You also want your tone to communicate sincerity. When you're sincere, your message is better received. Sincerity certainly is impacted by the words you say, but it is greatly affected by the tone of your voice. A tone of sincerity basically says to the other person, "I mean what I say, I say what I mean, and I do so with respect toward you." When your tone communicates this kind of message, you're in control. When you're in control, you can have a positive influence in your interactions and thus assertively get your point across as you want others to understand it — productivity at its best.

Managing your pace

Pace is the rate at which you speak. It determines how fast or slow the words come out of your mouth and how clearly those words are heard and understood.

Maintaining a steady pace of speaking so your words come out clearly and exhibiting a flexibility to relate to the people with whom you're talking are so important. This tool is about finding the happy medium with your rate of speaking somewhere between too fast and too slow. A steady pace can help you speak effectively with a wide variety of people. At the same time, this tool tells you to sometimes vary the rate a bit, especially based on the type of audience you're addressing.

Here are some tips for applying the pace tool:

✔ **Enunciate your words clearly.** Enunciation is about saying words as they are meant to sound. Are you goin' to the meetin', or are you going to the meeting? Do you have some-un importin' to say, or do you have something important to say? These subtle differences are often noticed by your receivers and at times create confusion — exactly what did you say? — or a sense that you're not certain or knowledgeable about your own message. When people start judging how you use vocabulary, they're less tuned in to what you mean, and you no longer have their attention.

Enunciating words clearly helps you manage your pace. It keeps you focused on saying your words well so they'll be clearly heard, as opposed to rushing your pace and slurring your words in the process. When you enunciate clearly, your words and the meaning of your entire message are more easily understood and captured by your listeners.

✔ **Insert pauses occasionally in your message.** What's your hurry? Thinking before you speak and allowing yourself the chance to breathe comfortably enhance your message. That's what pauses do for you. Instead of racing ahead or thinking out loud with all sorts of filler sounds, pauses help you smooth out your pace, gather your thoughts, and enunciate your words clearly. Simply give yourself permission to think and breathe as part of your speaking habits.

Showing a variation in your pace adds flavor and significance to key words. It also helps those words stand out more clearly to your listeners. Sometimes this means speeding up from your steady pace as you say a key phrase or sentence. Sometimes this means slowing down from your steady pace at these critical points. In either case, managing pace with this gas pedal and brake being applied adds an emphasis to your message that makes it more appealing to be heard.

✔ **Match your pace of speaking with your listener's pace of speaking.** This last aspect of pacing is close to but not quite the same as *mirroring*. The main idea with mirroring is that your communication matches what the other person in the conversation is doing — from body language to use of words and rate of speech.

The idea is to tune in to the other person in the conversation and show some flexibility based on that person's communication style. For example, if you're talking with someone who is highly expressive and speaks at a fast rate, pick up your pace a bit. If you're conversing with someone who has a low-key, reserved communication style, slow down a bit. Focus on being on a similar pace level with your listener. When your pace is the opposite of the person to whom you're talking, your message often becomes harder for that other person to listen to — and that has nothing to do with how fast she is able to listen. People generally receive and take in messages at rates faster than they're being said.

Pace helps build rapport. Having good rapport with someone else is having a working relationship with mutual trust and respect. We normally work best with people who have those qualities. When you manage your pace to be at a level similar to the level of the person with whom you're speaking, you show that you relate well to others. When people think you understand where they're coming from, the likelihood of their understanding where you're coming from with your message is much greater.

Navigating E-mail Communication

So far in this chapter, the discussion has focused on communication that occurs via speaking and listening, whether in person, on the phone, or in a video conference. What about written communication? This section touches on just one medium for written communication: e-mail. While people often receive class instruction for writing formal letters or reports, rarely do they learn how to construct shorter, less formal written messages that accomplish what's needed.

If your preferred form of electronic communication is texting or Tweeting or otherwise relying on short written messages, this section offers tips you can use as well. With so much business communication occurring via keyboard (or the keypad of a smartphone), you need to use skill and judgment to maximize your communication's value. This section shows you how to develop that skill and judgment.

Knowing when to use e-mail

Because of its speed and ease of use, e-mail can be a tool for many useful communication purposes, such as the following:

- **Sending interoffice memos:** You can send memos to other staff members sharing news and announcements about business, personnel, and policy matters via e-mail.

- **Making requests:** E-mail works well for making requests, such as asking for assistance on a project or setting up a meeting.

- **Making inquiries:** The quickest and easiest way to find an answer to a question often is to ask in an e-mail — as long as the inquiry isn't overly involved and doesn't require a great deal of explanation. (If that's the case, a conversation may be better.)

- **Keeping in touch:** Letters and cards aren't going away; they make for a nice personal touch in communications. On the other hand, e-mail enables you to drop quick notes to clients, staff in other departments, and other business associates. A simple *here's-what's-been-happening-with-me, how-goes-it-with-you* communication lets key businesspeople know that you care about how they're doing even if you haven't seen them for a while.

- **Conducting routine business transactions:** Some business relationships, such as customer–vendor ones, run under established processes. In such cases, e-mail helps transactions run efficiently. For example, you (the customer) need so many parts from your vendor. The vendor tells you the price and when he can ship them, you confirm, and away you both go. When transactions and negotiations require little discussion, e-mail helps you exchange information and get the deal done.

- **Providing status and news:** If you're a manager who, for example, has salespeople in different locations or who oversees the work of field-service technicians — employees you don't have the opportunity to see very often — you can use e-mail to find out the status of their work efforts. If you want to keep your boss in the loop on your latest project or on what happened with that important customer issue you tackled today, e-mail is a great option for passing on the news and highlights. These kinds of updates and status communications can usually be handled via e-mail.

✔ **Recapping agreements and discussions:** One of the best uses of e-mail is to reinforce verbal interactions, especially when decisions or agreements are made or when action items are established. Instead of leaving what you worked out in a meeting to your memory, you can recap these important points in an e-mail to team members. When minutes of meetings — the absolute essentials, such as decisions and agreements — need to be recorded, e-mail works well. By not leaving these important items to memory, you enhance productivity.

✔ **Seeking ideas:** E-mail can be useful for generating ideas. Maybe you're working on an assignment or planning an event for which you need assistance in brainstorming ideas. Using e-mail to solicit this input, which often doesn't require a thorough discussion or a meeting, enables you to save time.

✔ **Giving simple feedback on others' work:** *Simple feedback* means that the comments you write aren't long, aren't controversial, and have been requested. Many an occasion arises in which people want your feedback or thoughts on their plans, proposals, or other work. If that feedback doesn't require a great deal of explanation, e-mail can be a quick and easy way to pass along your comments.

Recognizing when not to use e-mail

Many of the problems connected with e-mail communication result from people using e-mail when they should be talking — and listening. E-mail is one-way communication and isn't usually live. You have less opportunity with written messages to be understood clearly than with live conversation because you can't use your tone of voice and body language to convey sincerity. In fact, on sensitive (or even some not-so-sensitive) matters, people often interpret your e-mail messages in a far worse light than you ever intended. Relying on e-mail, when engaging in live conversation is more appropriate, tends to increase the tug-of-war in working relationships.

To keep working relationships on a constructive level and to enhance productivity, following are some situations in which you should not use e-mail.

When you need to give constructive feedback on performance

There are two types of constructive feedback: positive feedback for good performance and negative feedback for performance that needs improvement. Although positive feedback given in an e-mail message may be well received, it has less impact and seems less sincere than feedback given in person. The less frequently that positive feedback is given in person, the less sincere any attempts at giving positive feedback seem.

Book IV

Communicating with Employees

The recipient of negative feedback given via e-mail message often interprets that feedback as far worse than was ever intended and may stew about what was written. When the feedback is given via e-mail, the receiver doesn't have the opportunity to discuss the matter and work out solutions. Verbal, face-to-face communication allows the giver of feedback to explain his messages and to help the other person understand them, as they were intended, and then to listen to and understand the recipient's perspective.

The nature of giving constructive feedback — positive and negative — is verbal and informal. It works best when it's part of a two-way conversation.

After your previous e-mail messages get little or no response

You may encounter situations in which your inquiries made by e-mail get no response or your questions are met with partial answers. When you send follow-up messages, you may still get little or no response. The reasons for this lack of response vary: Disinterest in your issue, confusion about what you've written, too many e-mails to pay attention to yours, or poor follow-through skills are some of the culprits. Just because you think that you write the message clearly doesn't guarantee that the receiver thoroughly reads and acts on it.

Continuing to send follow-up e-mail messages after a couple of tries may turn you into an irritating pest and give those who want to ignore your messages even more reason to do so. Instead, talk to the person to find out what has happened and determine when you can get an answer to your inquiry. Although reaching the person, either by phone or in person, may take a few attempts, it's well worth the effort. Only live conversation can get an unresponsive person to respond.

When you address sensitive issues

Suppose you have a coworker who wants to act on an idea that you know from experience will lead to problems, or you have reservations about your boss's proposal for a business change, or you've received a message from a customer who is unhappy about service. In these kinds of circumstances, attempting to share your feedback, thoughts, or feelings via e-mail often exacerbates an already touchy situation.

With e-mail, you don't have a chance to listen to what the other person is thinking. When you choose one-way communication to communicate about sensitive matters, you increase the risk of misunderstanding and tension, which is the opposite of what you're trying to achieve.

When you want to elicit support and understanding for important changes and initiatives

Organizations are going through so much change that, in many companies, change is the only constant you can count on. (The chapters in Book VI all focus on dealing with business change.) Written communications can help reinforce announcements and updates about changes or new initiatives, but as the sole communications for these matters, e-mail messages can create anxiety.

Only live and ongoing face-to-face communication about significant changes help get people on board. The chance to explain the company's rationale, answer employees' questions, seek input and involvement, and address concerns is lost when this kind of communication is handled by e-mail. Rumor and innuendo — key ingredients in resistance to change — often fill the voids that are created.

When you need to resolve concerns and conflicts

Want to aggravate a conflict? Attempt to address it in an e-mail message. Trying to resolve conflict via e-mail is one of the major abuses of e-mail communications.

If you voice concerns or express disagreements involving strong opinions through e-mail messages, your message tends to be interpreted as far worse than you ever meant it. Attempts to address conflicts in this way come across as hiding behind e-mail — a passive-aggressive form of communication. The only tried-and-true method for resolving concerns and conflicts is live, person-to-person interaction, either face-to-face or by telephone or video conference. E-mail just can't do it for you.

If you find yourself getting worked up or rewriting much of what you want to say when you're drafting an e-mail, you shouldn't send that message. If you have an important issue or problem that involves a high degree of emotion, go directly to the source to talk and listen.

Staying on the right track when writing e-mail

Use care when communicating your messages via e-mail. Here are a few tips that will enhance your electronic communication:

- **Go for short instead of long in your messages.** The same adage applies with e-mails as it does with office memos: If you write more than a page, nobody wants to read it. The shorter your message, the more likely people will read and comprehend it.

  If you find your e-mail exceeding a page in length and you can't edit it to be much shorter, paste the information into its own document, attach the document to your e-mail, and use your e-mail message to briefly introduce the information in the attachment.

✔ **Make your points directly and concisely.** Get to the point and say what you need to say as briefly as possible. Give the highlights (not all the details), and make the point relatively simple. Go with the main point first and give supporting information next as needed. Verbosity in writing creates more confusion and less interest than face-to-face conversation, where at least you have the chance to adjust your message and help your listener understand it.

✔ **Keep your language constructive.** Write your messages in the best way possible. Keep the words respectful rather than harsh. Avoid anything that sounds blaming or threatening, such as "You didn't do what you said you would do" or "If you don't do this, I won't do that for you." Also avoid words that can trigger negative reactions, such as *always, never,* and the not-words (*don't, won't,* and *can't*). Here are a few such examples:

- "You always forget to follow the procedure."

- "You never help out when I request your assistance."

- "That idea won't work."

- "We can't do that on such short notice."

In many cases, you can rephrase your message to be more constructive. And in some instances, you may be better off talking to the other person rather than sending an e-mail. The idea is to keep your language straightforward and to focus on the issue rather than the person. Say what you mean while sounding matter-of-fact and positive.

When people use all caps for some or all of an e-mail message, readers interpret it as shouting. Stick to the standard practice of using caps only at the start of your sentences.

✔ **Watch the humor.** Having a sense of humor is a great attribute, especially in the workplace. Displaying that humor is much harder to do in writing than it is in person-to-person interactions, where you can gauge how the other person is reacting to what you're saying. The receiver of an e-mail message may interpret your attempts at clever wit as biting sarcasm.

If you can add an occasional lighthearted touch to your e-mail messages, great. The key is to focus on the content rather than the delivery.

✔ **Write for your audience.** As you do when speaking, consider whom you're addressing when sending an e-mail message. Understand your audience. If they respond best to brief highlights, keep the message short and sweet. If they like detail, give them explanations. If they speak in technical terms, use the jargon they understand. If they don't speak in technical terms, skip the jargon. Keeping your audience in mind helps you keep your messages clear, concise, and respectful.

Chapter 3

Having Critical Conversations

*L*ook around and you see that people are talking everywhere and talking about everything. But a conversation where all the parties involved examine the facts, express each person's point of view, and allow others to do the same — and then come to an agreement about what to do next — is much harder to find. That's where critical conversations come in.

A *critical conversation* occurs when two or more parties discuss an issue, problem, or situation in which there are different points of view. Most critical conversations involve high emotions, and the goal of the conversation is for something to change after the conversation ends. For example:

✔ A manager needs to work with an employee to improve his performance at work.

✔ Employees aren't getting along, and the behavior is hurting the performance of the team. (The behaviors need to change so the focus can be on the project rather than on personality differences.)

✔ A customer is upset with a product and wants a resolution.

In all these examples, emotions are likely to be high because part of the discussion includes differing perspectives and opinions of what's happening. A manager may have examples of an employee's poor performance, and the employee may disagree if he fears his job is in danger. Or two employees may have different views on acceptable workplace behavior. Or a customer may be furious if she isn't getting precisely what she wants — and the customer may not be exactly right. A critical conversation's job is to get to the root of the problem and bring these differing perspectives to a common solution.

Another commonality in these situations is that if nothing is done, there could be negative consequences. If the performance of an employee doesn't improve, he could be fired. If employees can't work together on a project, the productivity of the entire team may be at risk. And if a customer is upset, she may stop being a customer. You want to avoid these situations. In mastering the methods of a critical conversation, you can become the hero by avoiding the negative consequences that unresolved issues bring.

Knowing When It's Time to Have a Critical Conversation

With a few exceptions, there really is no time like the present to have a critical conversation. In fact, if you turned to this section of the book, you probably know that you should address an issue. In an ideal world, critical conversations are just conversations that happen every day: managers continuously provide feedback to employees, employees speak freely to their leaders, and employees work out any differences with direct yet respectful dialogue. Because this ideal world usually exists only in corporate fairy tales, check out the following situations that demand a critical conversation:

✔ **Struggling workplace dynamics:** Workplace dynamics can make a good team perform at an extraordinary level or a great team fall to pieces. Look at the sports world as an example. When an underdog team wins a game, it's often because the team came together. The United States Olympic hockey team that beat Russia in 1980 did it because their workplace (the ice rink) dynamics flowed perfectly. Teams may not be going after an Olympic gold medal, but if a workplace seems to be stumbling more than striding, you may need to have a critical conversation.

✔ **Performance issues:** Performance issues are often the most common problems in the workplace. Unfortunately, many managers wait to address them until it's too late and the problem has become much bigger than when it started. For example, an individual may start acting indifferent about a project, and then begin to let others carry the load, and finally withdraw from the project entirely. It would be much easier to just address acting indifferent.

When is a good time to intervene with a critical conversation, without being a micromanager? The simple answer is before the behavior or action becomes a trend.

✔ **Inherited issues:** Past problems can come your way from a change in personnel — such as when you change roles and move to a new team, or when another manager sends an employee to your department so she doesn't have to deal with the issue. However the problem comes to you, deal with it quickly to get the team off and rolling on a positive note.

✔ **The elephant in the room:** Elephant issues are those things that most people in the organization are automatically thinking about but may not talk about because of legal or cultural reasons or simple politeness. Yes, everyone knows the issue is there. And everyone is looking away.

Avoiding Pitfalls through Preparation

The success of a critical conversation depends on the amount of planning that goes into the conversation. Often, critical conversation catastrophes link to four big pitfalls. The good news is that you can avoid these pitfalls with the right planning.

✔ **Pitfall #1: Unmanaged expectations of the conversation.** A critical conversation isn't just water cooler talk; you have reasons and expectations for the discussion. Critical conversations are complex; spell out the goals up front. Taking the time to write down your expectations of the conversation brings clarity to the conversation and helps you manage the outcome.

✔ **Pitfall #2: Badly defined scope of the conversation.** Trying to accomplish too much with a conversation can make the discussion seem overwhelming and unorganized. Doing the preparation work up front helps you identify the most important issues to address so that you can create a focused discussion that generates the desired results.

✔ **Pitfall #3: Unclear roles.** Knowing who does what in a conversation may seem like a no-brainer — one person talks, the other listens, right? Sometimes. But sometimes you may need to hire a mediation expert or bring in a facilitator. Other times, the initiator of the conversation may need to play two roles: a manager giving feedback and a facilitator keeping a discussion on track. Prep work helps clarify your role and the roles you expect of others.

✔ **Pitfall #4: Uncontrolled emotions.** This pitfall often results from a lack of the preparation work in Pitfalls 1, 2, and 3. When you have confusion about expectations, roles, and the purpose of the conversation, any of the parties involved may quickly feel that they're being attacked or blamed. Focusing on the facts and using the critical conversation process are the best remedies when high emotions take the conversation off track.

With so much at stake during a critical conversation, spending a little more time up front pays off by reducing the risk of these four specific problem areas and helping you to be physically and emotionally prepared for the conversation.

Book IV

Communicating with Employees

Heading off stress through preparation

Of course emotions are high. People aren't in agreement. Managing stress before and during a critical conversation is like having a golden ticket; it can help alleviate almost any emotional situation. Here are a few proven ways to manage the physical stress associated with a critical conversation.

Schedule so you're not rushed

Calendars are often filled with back-to-back meetings, but try not to bookend a critical conversation with nonstop meetings. Allow yourself to take a time-out before and after a critical conversation is scheduled. Moving from one meeting to the next and squeezing in a critical conversation can cause stress. If you happen to be scheduled back to back, and you don't have a minute to spare, even 30 seconds to positively focus on the conversation or to go get a glass of water can help you start the conversation calm and collected.

Plan to keep a critical conversation from going off track, but try also to remain flexible to manage the stress. For example, if someone voices a new concern, be flexible enough to leave the topic and address the concern. A conversation should keep a steady pace but not be rushed. If the conversation gets through only half of the agenda in the time allotted, either keep going or schedule a second meeting to complete the agenda. Bottom line: Don't veer off course in the discussion, but stay flexible to keep stress at bay.

Eat, rest, exercise

Try to maintain a healthy lifestyle. Although this book isn't about health and fitness, one of the most proven ways to reduce stress in the workplace is to get in shape and take care of your health. Long-term healthy practices are the key to lowering stress, but don't ignore how one day of taking care of your mind and body can positively impact the conversation. Reduce your stress before a big conversation by exercising or simply taking a walk around the block and eating a healthy meal. Relax as much as possible before the conversation; going without adequate sleep or failing to eat prior to a conversation can lead to more stress than the conversation would cause by itself.

Design the questions

Which questions are you going to ask? To make a conversation go smoothly, balance the presentation of your facts and opinions with listening to others' facts and opinions. Don't underestimate the power of planning to ask the right questions to help guide the discussion. You want a mix of questions that guide the conversation through simple yes-no responses and questions that encourage discussion and contemplation.

Have a clear plan

You don't need to follow a strict agenda, but having an outline of what you want to accomplish and the conversation process can keep the conversation focused. An agenda is also a great way to take notes during the conversation so that everyone remembers what the next steps are after the discussion. The plan and agenda can also put other parties at ease and reduce stress because they know they're following a process.

Being mentally prepared

Part of preparation is having a clear purpose in mind for the conversation. But preparation doesn't stop there. Remaining calm, open to discussion, and able to step back when emotions get strong increases cooperation and helps you be poised and capable during conversations.

Getting to know your motivations

Motivation and attitude before, during, and after the conversation show how different people are. When working with critical conversations, knowing your own motivation and attitude not only prepares you mentally but also allows the discussion time to focus on the motivations and attitudes of the other parties.

What motivates people? Money, respect, recognition, action, making a difference, building relationships . . . the list goes on and on. Sometimes it takes seconds to find out what motivates people; other times it can take years of working together to find out what makes another person tick. But before diving into knowing what motivates other people, take time to know what's motivating you to have the critical conversation. Think through the list of motivations in Table 3-1 and see which ones you identify with most closely.

Table 3-1	Motivations
Motivation	*Definition*
Action	Getting things done is your number one priority. Why handle it later when you can handle it now? You work quickly and take timelines and milestones seriously.
Money	Being paid fairly for the work done drives your work ethic.
Recognition	Being acknowledged for work done by your team and leadership is important to you. High praise and being admired as an expert drive work and actions.

(continued)

Book IV

Communicating with Employees

Table 3-1 *(continued)*

Motivation	*Definition*
Respect	You crave a professional work environment, where employees treat you (and one another) with genuine concern, listen to ideas with open ears, and value different opinions.
Teamwork	You value teams working together and can work quickly through conflict. You believe the whole team is much stronger than the sum of its parts.

None of these motivations is right or wrong. However, if you're honest about what motivates you, you can create an environment that's open, honest, and genuine.

Not sure what's motivating you? Work through this list to find the answers:

- **Think about what brings you the most satisfaction in life.** Do you love having time to spend with friends and family? If so, flexibility and balance between work and life may motivate you. Do you love being the go-to person for any problem? You may be most happy with recognition in your role.

- **Find out what energizes you.** What are you doing when you have the most energy? Do you love being part of a group that works together to achieve results? You most likely have a passion for teamwork and action. Do you get the most energy when you get to pore over data and reports or when you're reading a captivating book? You may just love knowledge and research.

- **Ask others for ideas.** If you have trouble finding out what motivates you, ask peers and close friends where they think your inner drive comes from. Sometimes an external point of view is the answer to discovering your internal drive.

Many people identify with multiple motivators. Knowing your own motivation and even sharing it with the parties involved in the conversation help to create a genuine and safe talking space. You don't have to come in and say, "If this work isn't done, I won't get my bonus!" (You can imagine how many eyes would roll with this comment.) A better option may be, "The work we need to get done impacts the team and me financially. I respect that this may not be what motivates everyone, but can we agree to work together to get this done?" Voicing your motivations in a positive way can help build trust and credibility during a critical conversation.

Meeting the needs of others

If you've studied psychology, you may remember something called Maslow's hierarchy of needs. If you fell asleep during Psychology 101, here's what you missed: Every human has basic needs that need to be met, including food, shelter, and safety. Humans need relationships and to be part of a group, and they need achievement and, ultimately, personal growth. (Some research has shown that these needs may not need to be met in an exact hierarchical order and that they aren't mutually exclusive, but the fact stands: People have needs that need to be met.)

These needs reveal some clear insights into why people act the way they do. During critical conversations, look at how needs are being met — or aren't being met — to understand different behaviors.

For example, the need for security and safety may cause a number of team and work relationship issues. If a team member doesn't feel safe expressing his views or ideas, thinking about how to be part of a team will be hard for him. If a person does not feel part of a team, he may not be doing much to achieve tough goals for the group. Unmet needs can and do impact the way people act.

Being aware of everyone's motivations and beliefs helps the conversation accomplish personal goals as well as meet the organization's needs. You don't need to go digging for those textbooks to realize that people say and do things for different reasons. People can waste lots of energy by trying to guess what others believe, their motivations, or their intentions. This time and energy can be better used to solve a critical issue during the conversation. Leave out the guesswork, and ask. This issue is touched on again in the section "Supporting others' needs" later in this chapter.

Knowing and controlling your hot buttons

Critical conversations are successful when you recognize and address the needs and motivations of others. Ideally, in a critical conversation, you examine the problem you're dealing with, decide on options to solve it, and then gain commitment on what to do next. But only robots would be able to have that type of conversation without emotions playing a role. Because robots haven't taken over the workplace just yet, address the emotional side of the conversation when you're communicating with individuals who have different motivations, needs, and beliefs. Knowing, controlling, and potentially adapting the emotional side is fundamental to a successful critical conversation.

Everyone has *hot buttons* — triggers of an emotional reaction. These things drive you crazy; examples may include drivers who don't use their turn signal, having meetings canceled at the last minute, and people who bring onions onto airplanes. Everyone's hot buttons are different, and knowing your own hot buttons helps keep a critical conversation in check.

By simply knowing your own workplace hot buttons, you're able to start controlling them during an emotional conversation, and you can stop your reaction from getting out of control. As part of the prep work for a critical conversation, think through your hot buttons. You probably know them by heart. (If not, ask your spouse, boss, or employees — they can probably tell you when you lose it!)

Although you have no easy way to stop these hot buttons, the best way to control your emotions is to physically slow down your reaction. When a cellphone goes off during a meeting and your blood pressure rises, you have two choices: You can stare at the phone, roll your eyes, and attack the other person with sarcasm, or you can count to five, smile, and ask for the behavior to stop in a calm and rational voice. The latter alternative is much more useful and productive, especially in a critical conversation.

Maintaining a positive attitude

It would be better *not* to have a critical conversation than to go into one with a poor attitude. Motivation and attitudes are closely linked, and both factor into how people behave. Attitudes that negatively impact a conversation can stem from personal self-interest, misunderstanding, or disagreement on the outcome. During the preparation phase of a critical conversation, take time to understand — and possibly change — your attitude and view of the situation.

You've probably seen a bad attitude in the workplace. It's easy to spot but tough to change. The following positive attitude adjustments are beneficial when you're having a critical conversation:

- ✔ **Think that change is possible.** If you think all the parties in the conversation can change their behavior or attitude, chances are good that they can. Studies have shown that merely thinking positively can make people more confident, and having positive expectations for someone can actually increase the likelihood of positive change.

- ✔ **Have patience.** You will always have a learning curve when you're trying to change behaviors, and that takes patience. Knowing that you won't accomplish your action plan in one day can help put everyone at ease with realistic expectations.

- ✔ **Check your ego at the door.** Yes, you may be the expert, but the person receiving the message probably could do without an ego. Having an answer to everything can lead to a know-it-all attitude. Remember to ask questions, listen to the answers, and be accepting of other ideas and opinions.

- ✔ **Be genuine.** This mantra bears repeating. Having concerns, building trust, and developing ongoing support create an environment and relationship where people see critical conversations as positive rather than negative events. Being genuine shows in what you say and do, so don't just say that you're concerned for someone else; show it by supporting all the parties in the conversation while they work to resolve issues and change behaviors.

In the end, a positive attitude comes down to making sure that you want to create open communication and understand the needs of all parties. Whether you're leading your first critical conversation or hundredth, coming to the table with this positive point of view sets the tone for a productive conversation.

Bad attitudes come in many shapes and sizes; complaining, arguing, and gossiping are a few of them. All bad attitudes are disruptive in a work environment and need to be addressed. A critical conversation probably can't end successfully, however, if it starts with, "You have a bad attitude!"

Starting with rapport and trust

The final step to preparing for a critical conversation is moving from thought to action. As you get ready to kick off the conversation, building rapport and trust to set the tone can get the conversation on the right track from the start. Everything you've done to this point in preparing for the conversation will give *you,* the deliverer of the message, confidence that the conversation will be successful. Rapport and trust give the recipient of the message confidence that the conversation will be successful. During the preparation work, your agenda helps you open the conversation with the right words, but the recipient is paying just as much attention to your tone and observing the environment.

Although not always easy to define, rapport and trust are usually quite easy to see. Most people have been part of a discussion with trust and a good rapport among all the parties in the room; sadly, most people have probably seen the opposite. When it comes to critical conversations, think of these terms as follows:

- ✔ **Rapport:** Rapport is a positive relationship among people that fosters effective communication. When you have good rapport during a critical conversation, the room is free from unnecessary emotions, yelling, and arguing, and it's full of respect and active listening.

- ✔ **Trust:** Trust means that everyone believes that all parties will do what they say. You can often gauge trust by noting how willing individuals are to talk about tough issues.

So how do you build trust and rapport? Mostly, be prepared, keep a handle on your emotions, and enter the room and relationship with a positive attitude. Outside of these elements, the two make-or-break elements to building trust and rapport are openness and honesty. Both of these behaviors are positive, and they set the stage for how you expect the other parties to act. If you're open with how you feel and what you see, others will follow. If you're honest and do what you say and say what you mean, you build instant credibility.

Book IV

Communicating with Employees

Trust, honesty, openness, a positive attitude, and being emotionally controlled take time, so while you're being patient with others in the conversation, also practice patience with yourself. You can't build these skills and relationship tools overnight.

How do you begin to build rapport? Here are a few ideas:

- ✔ **Let other people talk.** Building rapport is sometimes as easy as asking questions, actively listening, and then reflecting on what was said. In other words, be present in the conversation. When you come to the table with a genuine desire to help, others will see that their concerns and needs are your priority during the conversation. On the other hand, one of the quickest ways to destroy trust and rapport is to dominate the conversation.

- ✔ **Observe body and verbal language, and adapt yours accordingly.** People trust those they feel most comfortable with; try to adapt your style to match, or at least mix well with, other communication styles. If the other party is speaking calmly and making small gestures, observing these behaviors and then mirroring them creates common energy. That is not to suggest that you mock the other person — quite the opposite. The goal is to observe and match other styles to put others at ease.

- ✔ **Smile.** People usually like being around genuine, happy people. If smiling isn't natural for you, practice being authentic and content, and others will soon follow your lead.

- ✔ **Get moving.** You can smile all you want, use common language, and listen like a pro, but in the end, people will trust you if you do what you say you're going to do. Actions speak louder than words when you're trying to tell others you can be trusted.

The bottom line: When people feel comfortable with you, they will be more open and trusting.

Keeping Challenging Situations Productive

Imagine a workplace full of happy people who are well versed in critical conversations. The entire workforce gives feedback productively to one another in a timely fashion, no one ever loses her cool, and people sing around a campfire after work. Sounds nice, right? Now welcome back to reality. Because you probably don't live in this parallel universe, you have to work through demanding critical conversations. Yes, challenges will threaten the success of a critical conversation at times. Your mission when this threat happens: Keep the situation positive. You don't need to move an irate workforce to the dreamland just described, but you can create an encouraging and optimistic environment in the face of challenge.

Righting a wrong

Mistakes happen, managers lose their cool, and people say things they wish they could take back. Yes, conversations go wrong. The good news is that with a few essential words, you can turn even the most spoiled conversation into one with a positive outcome.

Okay, so you lost your cool

You went into the meeting with the best intentions, but you let go of your cool and you lost it. As soon as that happens, do these three things to turn the conversation around:

1. **Acknowledge the comments you made.** If you just keep going after losing your cool, you can be 100 percent certain that the focus will be on what just happened — not on the task at hand. As soon as you lose your cool, take a few deep breaths. And then, before doing anything else, be honest with the group. Here are a few key phrases that will accomplish just that:

    - "I realize I just yelled, and my emotions may be out of control, so do you mind if I take a few minutes to regroup so we can get back on track?"

    - "I realize I yelled/screamed/just let my head pop off. This conversation is important to me, and it's important for me to have a level head. Let me just take a few breaths so I can be more productive for the rest of the meeting."

2. **Summarize what happened.** This step takes attention off your head exploding and moves the attention to the process and what to do next. To demonstrate your commitment to resolving the issue, say, "This issue is important to me, and I felt we were going back on what we just agreed on," or, "We agreed on the ground rules for the discussion and it seems like we weren't following them." These statements let the others in the room know what set you off in the first place.

3. **Reflect on what to do next.** You may not need to call off the conversation, but take a moment to resolve the blowup and try to get back on track. Demonstrate your willingness to find a solution in a positive way.

Book IV

Communicating with Employees

When you need to take a moment to get the conversation back on track, you can try these methods:

- **Ask for ideas.** Reopen the conversation if you lose your cool by simply saying you want to create a win–win situation and discuss the other party's ideas on how to keep moving forward. Then use your active listening skills to find a good solution.

- **Say it.** Let the other party know you want to keep the conversation positive and productive by saying exactly that, after acknowledging you lost your cool. Then make a recommendation on what to do next.

- **Work together.** Sometimes both parties may be unsure of how to proceed after a blowup. In these cases, say, "I want to work together to find a good solution. Are you still willing to work together?" Then you may defer the meeting for a while to allow emotions to cool down, or you may be able to pick up right where you left off before you lost your cool. This approach also works when someone else loses her cool.

- **Take a timeout.** If a few breaths and an apology don't seem to be enough, take five to ten minutes to regroup. You aren't the first person who has gotten emotional during a conversation, and you won't be the last. Ask the group for a short break so you can regroup and refocus. You may be thinking, "I've never said something like that at work. Won't people think I'm weak?" Quite the opposite is true. Individuals who have a high level of self-awareness and are able to verbally communicate their feelings and their errors are seen as calm, flexible, and focused in the face of crisis and panic.

- **Ask for help.** After acknowledging your outburst, ask the other parties how to move forward. This step takes the pressure off you by giving the other parties input into whether they want to continue the discussion now or reschedule the conversation for later (if that's an option). You can also ask them whether focusing on the issue or concern that sparked the emotion in the first place would be helpful.

- **Reschedule the meeting.** If you lose your cool, you may feel your blood pressure rising even after you acknowledge your behavior. If this happens, be honest with the group members and let them know that you're obviously passionate about the issue but will need more than a few minutes to refocus. This technique works, but if you reschedule the meeting, you can't just pick up where you left off. You'll likely have to solidify the original agreements again, and you may even need to bring in a facilitator to help with the discussion.

If you make a mistake during a conversation, admit it and try to move on. Building trust during a critical conversation and creating a safe environment for the discussion rely heavily on honesty. Admit your faults, and others will be more likely to agree that they may have areas of improvement as well.

Time to ask for support

There's no shame in asking for help. If a critical conversation starts to take a turn for the worse, asking a coworker or manager to step in and help facilitate the meeting can be a smart move. You're still able to lead and participate in the discussion, but you have another resource to guide the decision-making process to take off some of the stress. Here are some more benefits to asking for help:

- ✔ **Power is distributed around the group.** Asking others to help can shift the balance of power from the leader running the show to a more collaborative effort.

- ✔ **Leaders can focus on content; facilitators can focus on process.** If you're able to ask others to help lead the conversation so that you can participate rather than facilitate, you're then free to contribute to the content of the meeting without having to worry about controlling the process. This refocusing takes a tremendous amount of stress off you as the initiator of the conversation.

- ✔ **The process keeps moving forward.** A facilitator or other neutral party can make process suggestions along the way when the parties in the conversation get stuck during the discussion.

- ✔ **The leader has time to listen.** You can't communicate without listening. Taking a step back and letting someone else run the meeting frees up your time to listen.

Not every critical conversation needs a facilitator to help get results, but having someone else guide the process can help the conversation bounce back quickly if it has already gone off track. Choosing wisely is key. Here are the two main steps to follow when you enroll others to help make the critical conversation a success:

- ✔ **Find a neutral party.** When a conversation goes south, people often begin to take sides. The best solution is to find a neutral party who can focus on the process of building agreements throughout the conversation, resolve conflicts and diffuse potential conflicts, and keep all parties on track. The facilitator is the chauffeur of the process, making sure the conversation gets from point A to point B safely and efficiently.

- ✔ **Solidify the roles.** One of the first things an outside facilitator should do is be clear about her role. The facilitator can say, "My role will be to serve as facilitator. That means I'm going to be your 'conversation chauffeur.' I'll let you talk about the content, but I'll occasionally intervene to make suggestions to keep the process moving at the right speed." Making sure everyone agrees to the facilitator's role is critical. If the initiator and the receiver in the conversations don't understand or accept the facilitator's role, the facilitator isn't able to function.

One often overlooked way to get help is to ask all the parties *in the conversation* for help. If the critical conversation involves a group of people rather than just two people talking, the group can be your biggest ally when trying to create a positive outcome. When the conversation goes south, ask the group members how they want to bounce back.

Get help from across the table

An option you can keep up your sleeve is to put the conversation on the other party's shoulders. If you're the initiator of the conversation and nothing is working, or if you have had a similar conversation multiple times, ask the other party what she hopes to achieve with her current behavior or performance.

Here's an example:

> I know this is the third time we've had this meeting to discuss not including teammates in the group decision-making process. I'm not sure what to do next, so I thought I'd ask you to help me better understand your perspective. Can you help me understand what you want to achieve by making these team decisions on your own? What do you recommend I do as the manager of the team to make sure we meet the goals of the company?

This statement and follow-up question aren't sarcastic. They allow the other party to express her perspective and goals. This tactic is never a first line of defense, but it does help a conversation move past the déjà vu stage and into the action stage.

What can you expect from this method? First, the other party may express her views on how the issue needs to be resolved, or whether the issue needs to be resolved at all. Second, if you can find out the process the other party wants to use to solve the issue, you have the opportunity to create a common goal of working toward a resolution of the problem.

What did you say?! Handling the unexpected

If you use the tools in this chapter to work through a tough situation in a positive way, you'll have a successful critical conversation. But sometimes someone says or does something that throws you completely off guard. Literally, you're speechless. If this happens, don't panic. Critical conversations are emotional, and when you hear something unexpected or receive personal attacks, the individual is probably speaking from emotion rather than logic.

What is the best course of action when you hear or see the unexpected during a critical conversation? Be honest, of course. If someone swears or gets unexpectedly upset, saying "I don't know what to do with that information" immediately diffuses and neutralizes the incident. At this point, the other party may back down when she realizes you're not reacting emotionally. But if the other party continues to react unexpectedly, call the conversation off and enlist a third party. Implement this step by restating, "I don't know what to do with this information/statement/behavior. I would like to ask for the help of another party, so let's stop the conversation now and regroup later. Are you okay with that approach?"

No matter the situation, being honest and open is always the best policy. Fighting back with fighting words only makes the situation worse. After you close the conversation, take a break and talk with another manager or mediation expert about the meeting and desired outcomes. When you do regroup, either you or the mediator can specify the consequences of the behavior that happened in the earlier meeting and then start working toward a common goal.

Making tough discussions encouraging

You can probably tell that many critical conversations involve delivering less-than-perfect news. Yes, some critical conversations start with wonderful news, but for the most part, a critical conversation deals with a highly emotional issue with a goal of turning the issue into a positive solution. That's a tall order. Tough conversations can be an emotional and physical drain. So how in the world do you keep a tough discussion encouraging?

Here are a few straightforward suggestions for keeping a level head and maintaining an encouraging and positive environment when the conversation gets tough:

- ✔ **Separate behaviors from the person.** No matter what has happened in the past, remember to separate the actions and behaviors from the person, and give the other parties the benefit of the doubt. If all else fails, remind yourself that the critical conversation's ultimate goal is to change a behavior or action, and change can be uncomfortable for everyone. Having empathy and understanding the needs and emotions of others will help you do this.

- ✔ **Stay positive, physically and mentally.** Sure, everyone knows that being positive is important, but knowing isn't enough. Your body will tell you a lot about how you feel, so listen to your own body language as a good indicator of your attitude. When asked about the person or the action at the center of the critical conversation, do you immediately cross your arms or do you lean in to discover more? When you're about to walk

Book IV

Communicating with Employees

into the critical conversation, do you feel more energized or just plain exhausted? If you're exhausted or closed off to the process or person, find ways to work through the stress.

✔ **Practice, practice, practice.** Critical conversations aren't easy! Find a peer or friend who can help you practice the conversation and practice how you may react to a negative comment or situation. All the practice will pay off because maintaining a positive environment and flexibility helps keep the conversation moving forward.

✔ **Focus on the purpose and process.** When a discussion starts to become challenging, and maintaining a positive attitude seems next to impossible, remember the message you're sending. If you get upset or even ignore the problem, you're indicating that you have better things to do or that you've potentially given up and thrown in the towel. The other party in the discussion will follow this behavior. But if the purpose is to find a mutually positive outcome, you dramatically change the tone of the meeting. If you come into the meeting working toward a positive outcome, the other party will likely put her best foot forward as well.

With these four ways to keep a tough discussion encouraging, your conversations have a leg up when it comes to positive results. Now you're ready to take a positive attitude and put it on turbo-charge.

Supporting others' needs

When you're having a critical conversation, you should know your own motivations and needs. If the conversation focuses on an employee issue, you're probably pretty clear on the needs and expectations of the organization. But what many people forget during a critical conversation is to be supportive of the other party's needs. This means having empathy for others by recognizing and accepting what other people need and feel.

Most likely, everyone in this conversation has at least one other thing on her mind outside of the critical conversation. Because very few people will tell you their needs right up front, your job as the initiator of the conversation is to help the other parties identify their needs and then find ways to be supportive of their needs.

How do you find out other people's needs? Ask. Think of how powerful this message is when asked with a genuine desire to help: "What do you need from me to make this change happen?" This conversation may be the first time any manager has asked the employee this question. After you ask the question, listen to the answer and come up with a game plan to help all the parties involved in the conversation reach the common goal.

You aren't trying to be a therapist; you're just allowing the other parties to voice what they need to help make the situation better for everyone.

Using power wisely

When a conversation gets tough — because individuals start to argue, raise their voices, or simply disagree — you may be tempted to play the power card. That is, you give up finding a collaborative approach to the solution and just say "because I said so" or "because I'm the boss."

At times, a leader can simply say, "You know this solution needs to get done, so we just need to get it done." Deciding on and announcing a solution to a problem is perfectly acceptable in situations where you may not need a long-term commitment, when you have little time to invest in a dialogue, or when the dialogue is merely for show and the boss will ultimately decide, regardless of the feedback. But here's an alternative to the power card.

Think of the different reactions a CEO would get to these two statements:

> **Option A:** "I am the CEO and this is what we are doing."

> **Option B:** "As the leader of this company, I have a vested interest in exceeding our sales forecast. Can you help me get there?"

In option B, the CEO is opening up discussion and asking people whether they can help. The CEO builds an agreement with the audience by asking this question, and now the environment is perfect for exploring options to meet the sales forecast and then deciding which approach to take. Explore, decide, get moving, and evaluate the impact. Seems like this CEO has the first parts down perfectly and is ready to get her sales force moving.

You have many other options to the power card when you need to use your position of influence to get the critical conversation moving. Here are some alternatives to simply saying, "Because I'm the boss!"

- ✔ **Use your skills and expertise.** Leaders in companies often bring some skill or technical expertise to the table. Acknowledge this skill and then ask for help in other areas. This approach is a no-nonsense tactic because you're not asking for information you may not use. For example, a manager may say, "I have the skill needed to bake the best cupcakes in the world. Now how do we get more customers?" The initiator of the conversation isn't asking for recipes he may later throw in the recycling bin; he's asking for help with getting customers. He's asking for specific information rather than opening up every problem for discussion.

- ✔ **Be informational.** Having important information is often associated with power or position in a company. So rather than tell someone what to do just because of your title, enlist the other party to help create solutions based on this knowledge. A manager may say, "Knowing that our goal is to be number one in our market share, how should we best accomplish this task?" That's a much better collaborative alternative than stating, "I need to get the job done."

✔ **Take a relationship-driven approach.** Power, position, and connections to influential people are often related. That doesn't mean it's time to name-drop! Relationship influence is most powerful when you can give insight into how someone else may think. Knowing how another person would respond in a given situation and sharing this information with the other party in the conversation is an example of relationship influence. Using relationship influence, a manager may say, "Last week I spoke with the senior manager in our western division, and she's looking for a new solution for a client. How should we address this need most efficiently and productively?" Notice how differently this discussion would be received if the manager said, "I know Bob, our Most Senior Vice President of the World, and he thinks we need to do something different."

Each of these different levers of influence related to power and position can help create a positive environment for a critical conversation. Avoid the punching power game in a critical conversation! Power is often met with power. Newton's laws of motion state that for every action, there is an equal and opposite reaction. If an initiator of a conversation speaks first about how powerful he is, the recipient of the information will most likely punch right back.

Dealing with resistance

Some people are just plain difficult to work with. These individuals put up resistance, disagree for fun, and basically just come into work to make your life challenging, to put it nicely. If you work with people who are a little more difficult than you'd like, or if you fear that your next critical conversation may be faced with resistance, this section is for you!

Stay flexible

Balancing focus and flexibility when you're faced with resistance is the name of the game. If you tell someone who's already being difficult that she has to do something or act a certain way, 999 times out of 1,000, she'll put her feet in the ground and do exactly the opposite. But just letting the meeting go astray isn't a good option either. Think of focus and flexibility as the out-of-bounds line in a soccer match. As long as they follow some general rules and stay within bounds, players have a lot of flexibility to move one way or the other. In a critical conversation, make the boundaries clear and then let the other parties know where they have flexibility in the discussion.

Here are two easy ways to show flexibility with boundaries:

✔ **State what is and isn't acceptable.** Being flexible doesn't mean you need to let someone walk all over you. If someone's behavior is unacceptable — like abusive language — you may say, "I ask that you treat me as a professional and stop using abusive language. I want to work with you, and I'm flexible with how we proceed, but first we need to talk to one another with respect."

✔ **Set ground rules.** If you think boundaries may need to be established during a conversation, set them now, and show flexibility when you set these rules. Before the conversation even starts, you may want to say, "I want to propose some ground rules for our conversation, but I would like to first ask if you have any ground rules you want us to follow." Some ground rules may be agreeing to stick with an agenda, speaking the truth, staying on time, or using a professional tone throughout the conversation.

Know when to push and when to stop

A broad range of problems can rear their ugly heads during critical conversations. If the behavior is interrupting the agenda or any progress forward, you have a couple paths to take. First, you may need to assess whether or not all the parties in the room are willing to work toward a common goal. If not, clarify the process and purpose of the conversation and check for agreement.

Here's a good way to approach a person who's starting to show signs of resistance:

> In the beginning of the meeting we agreed to work on finding a solution to why team members aren't comfortable with the language you use in the break room. Are you still willing to work on this issue together, or do you want to find a different way to resolve the issue?

If this calm and gentle approach doesn't work, be a little more direct in finding a solution. In the previous example, you give the other party the opportunity to decide what to do next. A more direct way of dealing with difficult behaviors is to give two options for what to do next. Acknowledge what the person is saying or doing, validate his opinions, and then either deal with the behavior or defer it until later. Here's how:

1. **Acknowledge:** Acknowledge the behavior by describing it neutrally. When Mr. Negative makes a comment that the problem isn't solely his problem but rather the team's problem, you may say, "You don't think you're part of this problem, is that right?"

2. **Validate:** Without casting judgment, let the other individual know that he can have a different opinion than you have. Continuing with the previous example, you could say, "You may be right. We may need to work on this problem from multiple perspectives." By simply validating opinions, the difficult behavior may stop.

3. **Defer or deal:** To defer the resistance, ask whether dealing with the other opinions later is okay. For example, you may say, "I'll commit to having the same discussion with other team members, if you can commit to working on this side of the problem now."

A last resort is to give even narrower options: stop the behavior or stop the conversation. Be careful not to use this option as a threat but as a way to move forward. Here you may say, "John, it seems to me that you're placing the blame on other team members, and this is making it difficult to make progress. I see two options. We can work on a solution together, or we can stop the conversation and I can formalize a performance improvement plan." Remember that this statement isn't a threat, but a statement with options.

A light push in the right direction often helps to direct resistance more positively or to cool down difficult behaviors. This approach works especially well when the parties in the conversation have worked together successfully in the past, and a particular issue has created a need for a critical conversation. If you need to take a more frank approach, however, remember the golden rule of coming to the conversation with a genuine desire to make the situation better.

Silence is an influential tool. Don't shy away from using silence when you're faced with resistance. Listening or simply choosing to be silent allows others to talk and process information.

During difficult critical conversations, sometimes the best option is agreeing to disagree. You don't live in a fantasy world where all critical conversations end up in utopia. Sometimes disagreements are just disagreements. This is okay, as long as the disagreement doesn't significantly impact the outcome of the conversation.

Take two steps forward and one step back

Taking one step back and then two steps forward isn't just a great way to square dance — it's also a necessary tool in critical conversations. One of the easiest ways to keep a critical conversation on track is to continue to build agreement on what to do next. If the conversation goes astray or begins to face resistance, go back to the last agreement and work from there.

Pretend that you're a mountain climber. Most mountain climbers (at least those who tend to make it back down the mountain alive) use anchors to protect them from falling completely down the mountain if they slip or fall. Agreements throughout the discussion are your anchors, preventing the conversation from falling back to square one. During a critical conversation, you may use these types of agreements. When you need to go backward to review a previous agreement, rephrasing or recapping the agreement can help clarify any uncertainties or vagueness.

When you kick off the conversation, ask whether all parties are willing to work on a solution. When exploring and examining what's happening, ask whether all parties agree on what the problem is and why the problem exists. When deciding on options to move forward, make sure all parties agree to the value in solving the issue and know which options everyone can agree to, do, and support.

Gaining focus when conversations go off track

If you work to develop an actionable consensus among all the parties during a critical conversation and use a positive facilitation approach, all your conversations will be perfect. Wait, back that up. *Many* of your conversations will go smoothly. But conversations can go off track for many reasons. When one does, refocus the conversation.

Refocusing the conversation can be done in three simple steps:

- ✔ **Clarify the focus.** When you sense that the discussion is going off track, you may not be the only one who's thinking the same way. Any party involved in the critical conversation can start this clarifying process by opening the dialogue to generate the information needed for discussion. Clarifying sounds like this: "In the beginning of the conversation, we agreed to work through a disagreement on how to productively ask questions during our team meeting. It seems we're now trying to solve the problem of why people are late to meetings."

- ✔ **Check for agreement.** After you clarify the focus of the conversation, develop agreement on the priority of the conversation. To check for agreement, the leader may ask, "Do we want to focus on solving the question of why people are late to meetings first, or should we finish the earlier discussion?"

- ✔ **Continue the conversation.** Finally, help all the parties in the conversation come to closure and move on with the discussion. When the group agrees on what to do next, write down the agreement and continue the conversation. The leader could say, "Great. I've put 'finding out why people are late to meetings' on the discussion board so we don't forget it. Now let's get back to the first concern we were addressing: how to productively ask questions during team meetings."

You may notice that during the agreement process, you're not throwing away the original purpose of the meeting. Sometimes, having flexibility in what the parties will discuss next creates a better environment for tougher discussions and will, most importantly, get the parties in the conversation working together.

Although boundaries and flexibility are important, be cognizant of and respect the hierarchical, cultural, and social norms, values, and rules between parties in the conversation. Ignoring organizational rules or cultural values can cause unnecessary anxiety or anger — neither of which is good for a positive critical conversation.

Book IV

Communicating with Employees

Closing the Conversation with Ease

The last part — and one of the most essential parts — of critical communication is what happens after the conversation is done. You're done talking, the meeting is over, and all the parties have committed to how to solve the problem. Now you want to make sure these solutions happen. Closing the conversation means finishing the actual discussion and being in agreement about what will happen next. By closing the conversation constructively, you support individuals on their paths to success. And by following up in a timely manner, you help create a positive outcome that lasts.

Creating powerful action plans

Thanks to your prep work, planning, and expert delivery, you aced the conversation. Now you want to make sure all the agreements, ideas, and feedback aren't lost in a post-conversation black hole. Time to create an action plan. Action plans provide goals and timelines that help all parties to be productive immediately and set a positive foundation for future feedback and conversations.

While the action plans may be most applicable in performance discussions, sometimes the action coming out of a conversation is not about performance. For example, if the critical conversation happens between peers who avoid conflict and just talk behind each other's backs, the action plan may simply be an agreement to continue to talk directly with one another when there is a concern or disagreement. In this case, the action plan would be an agreement of what to do if either one of the parties falls back into the old habit of avoiding tough discussions.

Agreeing on next steps

At the end of the discussion, you're ready to agree on clear goals and expectations for the action plan. These goals help all parties involved agree on what success looks like by giving you a clear, measurable way to evaluate, track, and reflect on progress. Gaining agreement is more than just writing down your own thoughts and directives; gaining agreement means all the parties involved in the conversation feel confident in what happens next and are willing and able to make the actions happen.

Gaining agreement is often as simple as asking, "Do I have your agreement that the next step should be to talk with one another immediately if we disagree on what is happening on the project?" By checking for agreement, you continue to build buy-in for how the situation or behaviors will change after the conversation is done.

Even in the most challenging conversations, you can find something that everyone can agree on, especially if you come to the table genuinely wanting to improve the situation.

Determining elements of an action plan

Although you may come across many types of action plans, the basic elements are consistent. This section outlines the basic elements: what will happen next, who will make it happen and who can help, and when it will be done.

Try to incorporate SMART goals in the action plan: Goals that are **s**pecific, **m**easurable, **a**ction-oriented (and agreed-on), **r**esults-oriented (and relevant), and **t**ime-bound. Try to keep the action plan limited to two or three key SMART goals with action steps to maintain focus on the most important desired results of the conversation:

- ✔ **What will happen:** Having clear goals and action steps will help all parties involved walk out of the room knowing what needs to happen next. An action plan divides work into achievable steps in the short term and should be aligned with longer-term goals.

  Drafting the action plan on a piece of paper while you're closing the conversation puts everything in black and white. After the conversation, ask the recipient to summarize the action plan and send it back to you; there is tremendous value in gaining ownership and clarifying the action plan if you do.

- ✔ **Who will make it happen:** Just as conversations aren't one-sided, neither is the action plan. Don't put the entire weight of the world on the shoulders of the other individuals. Instead, make recommendations on who can help make the plan work. Helpers may include a mentor, an expert in a particular field, or even you. Providing a network of support helps the situation move forward in a positive way.

- ✔ **When will things be done:** At the end of the conversation (whether it goes well or not), ideally everyone can agree on what's going to happen next and when these things will happen. If you're asking an employee to change behaviors that are negatively impacting the team, you'll probably want to see some type of change in the next few days to know he heard the message. If he doesn't show that he's working toward change, you may have to deliver the message again.

A finite timeline is the simplest way to judge whether the situation is going to change. For each step in the action plan, include a target date when the action will be complete.

Book IV

Communicating with Employees

Following through for success

After you prepare for the conversation, have the conversation, and write an action plan, you may be exhausted. Take a deep breath and remember that the last step toward closure is following up with the progress of the action plan. Follow-through usually includes the following steps:

- Writing a follow-up note to clarify the main points of the meeting
- Scheduling a follow-up meeting to discuss progress, obstacles, and feedback on the action plan
- Creating formal documentation when needed
- Responding to ignored action plans

Writing the perfect follow-up note

A simple note to the parties involved in the conversation reemphasizing the purpose of the initial meeting can do wonders to move forward positively. A follow-up note isn't a legal document; a follow-up note is a summary of the main points. Even if you delivered the message flawlessly, some emotion during the meeting will cause both small and large details to be forgotten. Documenting the main points helps alleviate the potential for confusion when the stakes are high.

The perfect follow-up note is simple, positive, and timely.

- **Simple:** You don't have to revisit every word that was spoken, especially when you have a powerful action plan to follow. Keep the note to the point, and always provide an opening for more discussion to happen.

- **Positive:** Thank the other party for discussing the issues with you, and reemphasize that the intent of this plan is to make things better (for example, to help the other party be successful in his job or improve his contribution to the department). Mentioning the consequences of performance or behaviors not changing is acceptable, but remember that the goal is to genuinely want to help the situation improve. At this point in the conversation, focus on an optimistic, productive future rather than everything that could go wrong.

- **Timely:** Write the follow-up note before the day is over. The note officially closes the conversation and launches the action plan, and waiting even a day to send the note drags the discussion out too long.

Scheduling follow-up meetings

The follow-up conversations don't need to be hours long or incredibly detailed; simply agreeing to have weekly check-ins over the next few weeks to make sure that everything is going according to plan will suffice.

You'll get a good reputation as a leader if you're fair with individuals and hold them accountable to delivering on their part of what you just discussed and agreed on. The follow-up will make your job much easier in the future by establishing clear guidelines for behaviors and performance. This check-in is perhaps one of the most beneficial things for employees receiving feedback or for teams that need intervention because it gives them extra time and space to process information (much more than any single meeting could give them). Additionally, checking in and making sure you see progress helps people see the importance of the conversation and your commitment to helping the situation change for the better.

Ongoing discussions drive accountability and lasting change. You will most likely need to have more than one follow-up meeting to check on the progress, especially if problems have been occurring for quite some time or are significant (and most issues that lead to critical conversations are!). During each of the check-ins, you can continue to summarize your commitment to making things change and ask what the other parties need and expect of you in the months ahead.

Creating more formal documentation

In some cases, an action plan, a follow-up note, and an ongoing discussion may be all you need to drive accountability and change. Other critical conversations — those that were emotionally heated, or those that are revisiting poor performance and behaviors — may need a little more documentation.

In addition to the action plan, these conversations may need a formal employee letter. In some cases, human resources or your boss may want to have a copy of the follow-up letter. Instead of copying everyone, ask these individuals whether they need a copy of the note and then forward it on as needed.

Formal documentation may include capturing the main points of the critical conversation, confirming what happened during the meeting, summarizing expectations of what happens next, and acknowledging that the summary is accurate.

When capturing what happened, stick to the facts, just like you did during the conversation. Be careful not to write down your opinions, like, "You had a really bad attitude in the meeting" or "I am sure you are depressed about the conversation." Instead, capture facts, timelines, and agreements.

Responding to ignored action plans

Even perfect conversations can be quickly forgotten when emotions are high. If action plans or agreements regarding changes in behavior aren't happening immediately, be more assertive before the situation gets out of control.

You send action plans and follow-up notes immediately to reinforce that changes need to happen immediately. But if those changes aren't happening, have a follow-up critical conversation.

Use the following model to make sure your employees are following action steps and agreements:

1. **Request the follow-up meeting.** "Hi, John. Can you please come to my office for five minutes?"

2. **Examine what happened.** "Two days ago we had a conversation about changing your tone when you communicate with team members. Yesterday afternoon I heard you tell Sally, our new intern, that she is just going to have to find out the answer to her problem on her own. We agreed that all future conversations would be positive and cooperative. Do you agree with what the expectations were?"

3. **Decide on next steps.** "I would like to ask the human resources team to join us in creating a formal plan for expectations to help this behavior change immediately."

4. **Gain commitment.** "Can we set up this meeting for tomorrow morning at 9 a.m.?"

5. **Evaluate the impact.** During the meeting with HR, examine how the behavior or performance has or hasn't changed.

If behaviors and conduct don't immediately change, the follow-up conversation is more direct than the first conversation. You're still genuine, wanting to turn the situation around, and you're still using facts rather than emotions during the conversation. The difference is that you're leaving no room for misunderstanding or forgetfulness by directing what commitment is made to move forward.

If you don't see an immediate change in behavior, leave no room for misinterpretation about what that change looks like and the consequences of not making the change happen. But keep in mind that mastering critical conversations isn't about being a legal expert or an auditor of company human resources policy. Mastering the art and science of critical conversations is about coming to the table with a genuine desire to help make situations better.

However, if everyone follows the action plan, it is appropriate to thank the other parties for their work. Changing behavior isn't easy, and recognizing the effort will help to reinforce behaviors and create an environment to build off the success of the action plan.

Chapter 4

Conducting Performance Appraisals

In This Chapter

▶ Getting together the data you need

▶ Checking your assumptions at the door

▶ Ensuring productivity within the appraisal session

▶ Helping employees develop and grow

*A*s the time to conduct performance appraisals approaches, many managers experience one or more of the following feelings: anxiety, nervousness, nausea, aggravation, frustration, confusion, fear, stress, or dread. Frankly, based on the way that many companies put together their performance appraisal programs, these reactions aren't surprising.

The good news is that most of today's performance appraisals are user-friendly, easily administered, and an essential component of effective management. Performance appraisal plays a central role in developing your employees and enhancing their performance and productivity. As such, the appraisal process plays a key role in adding value to your employees — and ultimately to your department and your company at large. This chapter walks you through how to create a performance appraisal program that is efficient and effective for everyone involved.

Gathering and Analyzing a Year's Worth of Information

One of the main determinants of the effectiveness of your appraisals is the quantity and quality of performance-based information that you gather. This information provides the foundation and support for the evaluations you create, as well as for the feedback that you provide. If the information is thin or flimsy, the same will be said of your appraisals.

In any company, numerous resources can provide you with important performance-based data. Your notes on your employees' performance are at the top of the list, but several resources beyond your notes provide additional insight into your employees' performance — and give your evaluations additional impact.

In order for your performance appraisals to be effective, you need to maintain regular communication, contact, and coaching with your employees throughout the entire evaluation period (typically, one year). Your employees shouldn't have any doubt about how they're doing. If they run into performance glitches, issues, or problems, they should feel confident that you'll identify and address these situations quickly.

Doing your homework

Before you can begin filling out a performance evaluation, you have to spend time reviewing key documents related to each employee's position. In doing so, you set the stage for a meaningful assessment of each individual's performance and opportunities for improvement.

Checking out job descriptions

Take a look at your employees' job descriptions. You need to be sure that the criteria you use to evaluate your employees' performance are actually part of their jobs today.

As the year goes by, any number of formal responsibilities can slip by the wayside, while other roles, expectations, and standards can slip in and take their place. Sometimes this happens so subtly that neither you nor the employees notice it, but by the end of the year, their jobs may bear only a slight resemblance to what they were when the year began.

Reading last year's appraisal

Assuming that your employees worked for you or for another manager in your company last year, another important early step is to take a look at last year's evaluation. Presumably, that evaluation contained areas in which the employees needed to demonstrate some improvement. Identify those areas, as well as possible sources of such deficiencies, and keep them in mind as you conduct this year's evaluation.

For example, if a particular performance issue is interfering with an employee's effectiveness, it would be very helpful to know whether this is a new development or a problem that was apparent last year. If this is a new development, you can address it in the performance evaluation and offer some strategies to correct it. If it's a problem that has lingered for a year or more, you need to discuss with your employee why last year's feedback hasn't changed the behavior and what needs to happen differently going forward.

Revisiting the objectives

Go back to last year's evaluation and look at the specific objectives that you (or another manager) established with your employees for the current evaluation period. At this point in the process, you aren't evaluating their performance. Instead, your goal is strictly to familiarize yourself with the objectives and the priorities that were attached to them.

Reviewing your notes

When you regularly spend time with your employees, you're in the perfect position to observe their work and provide them with the coaching, feedback, guidance, and support that they need to do their jobs well. Your face time with them also allows you to gather data regarding all aspects of their performance.

Your notes don't need to be a detailed treatise. They can be a list that includes the dates, a few words describing the incidents, and a few more words describing their impact. When the time for the annual evaluation arrives, these notes provide you with accurate firsthand information regarding your employees' performance during the evaluation period. If you rely on your memory for this information, you probably won't remember exactly what happened, when it happened, and who did what to whom, especially over the course of a year.

When you go back over the log that you've kept on your employees' performance over the year, you'll find several areas that are rich sources of data for their evaluations:

 ✔ **Getting the job done:** Upon initial review, your notes are going to provide you with the factual information you need in order to determine whether your employees actually carried out all their job responsibilities.

 The idea at this point is not so much to evaluate data as it is to gather it. Depending upon the job position, this is where you generate specific and measurable performance-related totals (such as sales calls made, number of designs completed, number of programs accepted or rejected, amount of errors, number of returns, number of projects completed on time, training programs attended, and the like). You can feed this information back to your employees, and it establishes a credible framework for the evaluative feedback that you'll also be providing.

Book IV

Communicating with Employees

✔ **Meeting objectives:** Your notes will tell you whether your employees met the agreed-upon objectives. Because you've already reviewed the objectives, you're also able to make an accurate judgment regarding the value of meeting one objective versus the value of meeting another.

✔ **Performing up to par:** Your notes will also show you how your employees handled the full spectrum of incidents that they encountered, all the way from carrying out the most important functions of their position down to their handling of the most basic chores. You can find clear and specific examples of your employees' key behaviors, actions, and interactions, as well as the results that your employees achieved in myriad situations.

✔ **Applying competencies:** Your notes will provide you with valuable insight into the full range of your employees' competencies in such areas as communication, technical knowledge, dealings with others, managing time, and so on. Although observing your employees' skills in these areas is important, it's even more critical for you to see how effectively your employees are able to apply these skills to their work. Your on-site observations will also provide you with firsthand data on your employees' commitment to upgrading their competencies, as well as their ability to impart their knowledge to others.

Checking employee files

As part of the process of accessing and gathering a full range of information about your employees' performance during the year, take a look at each employee's file. (If you haven't been keeping a file on each employee, consider this a good time to start.) A file can contain important pieces of performance-related data that enhance and round out the information you've already assembled.

If other managers have work-related contact and dealings with your employees, you can gather additional information for the evaluations by discussing your employees' performance with them. Don't forget to ask your own manager.

You need to consider the following types of information:

✔ **Complaints:** Whether from other managers, employees, or customers, and regardless of whether complaints impact an employee's ratings, you need to be aware of them, review them, and calibrate the role you believe they should play in the employee's appraisal.

✔ **Compliments:** As you look through your employee files, you may also find letters, e-mails, and other documentation praising your employees. Be sure to mention these compliments when you're conducting evaluation sessions. They'll motivate your employees to keep up the good work!

- ✔ **Reprimands:** When you find reprimands on file, consider the number of incidents, their severity, and any actions taken as a result, whether by the employee or by the company. If the problematic behaviors are continuing, make a note of that.

- ✔ **Honors and awards:** Companies provide awards for all sorts of behaviors, such as for volunteering, coming up with suggestions for safety or sustainability, or referring friends to come to work for the company. In addition, you may find honors that have been bestowed on your employees from outside organizations.

- ✔ **Milestones:** Look for information regarding classes, seminars, continuing education credits, certifications, degrees, and designations that your employees have pursued and achieved during the year.

Eyeing evaluations

If your company's appraisal process includes self-evaluations — the employee's own assessment of her progress and accomplishments — or if you've opted to include them in the process, this is the time to look them over.

When reviewing employees' self-evaluations, the first step is to take a look at how your employees approached this assignment. Employees who are careful, thorough, and detailed in their approach to work will demonstrate these characteristics in the way that they complete their self-evaluations. Employees who are lackadaisical or careless will reflect these attitudes in this assignment.

After you've looked over the appearance of the forms, it's time to look at the content. Look carefully at an employee's ratings and try to get an overall sense of how she sees her own performance. If the employee's ratings are in sync with the data that you've generated, you can make three strong suppositions:

- ✔ Your employee has a realistic view of how she's been performing.

- ✔ You've been providing the employee with effective feedback during the course of the year.

- ✔ The employee is being honest in completing her self-evaluation.

As a result of these suppositions, you shouldn't have any trouble discussing your ratings during the evaluation sessions.

If you find that an employee's self-ratings are totally different from what his performance data indicates, a couple things could be going on:

- ✔ Either your employee is living in dreamland, or you haven't been adequately monitoring his performance and providing feedback.

Book IV

Communicating with Employees

✔ If you have overwhelming performance data to substantiate your views of the employee's performance, and you've been actively managing him, then the employee is naïve, lying, manipulative, or uninvolved and uninterested in the evaluation process.

As a result of these two possibilities, you may face some difficulties when you and your employee sit down to discuss the performance appraisals. Make sure you're thoroughly prepared with clear, accurate, and specific performance data.

If your company includes 360-degree feedback (evaluations from others in an employee's immediate work circle) in the appraisal process, this is the time to review the findings. This data — gathered from an array of anonymous individuals, such as coworkers, managers, peers, customers, and others — can provide a good deal of additional insight regarding your employees' performance competencies and effectiveness.

If you've been provided with an overview of the 360-degree feedback findings, you should find significant overlap between this feedback and the data you've generated on your own. If major differences exist, stay with *your* assessments, because your data focuses more directly on your employees' specific job responsibilities and goal attainment.

Completing the evaluation form

After you've reviewed all the performance data from the various sources and resources that you were able to access, the next step is to complete the evaluation form. These forms vary from one company to another, but some overarching principles can help you handle this step more easily and effectively:

✔ **Start with your best employees.** As a result of your direct observations and analysis of the performance data, you're probably able to name the better employees in your department. These employees should be the first ones you evaluate.

By starting your evaluations with these individuals, you can clearly define, for yourself, the actual meaning of excellent performance. With this standard in place, you'll be able to interpret and evaluate the performance of the rest of your team more easily.

✔ **Write first, rate later.** Because many companies have evaluation forms that combine written comments with numerical ratings for each component that's being evaluated, it can be difficult to know which to do first — ratings or written comments.

The best approach is to go to a given item, write out your written comments, and then enter a numerical rating. When you write the numerical rating first, you may find yourself adjusting your writing in order to match the number.

✔ **Get specific while writing.** Whether you're writing a positive or negative comment, be sure that it's laced with examples and supported by times and dates as you deem necessary. As you create and review your written comments, adding appropriate descriptive phrases as needed, you'll be generating a clearer picture of each employee's performance and the rating that it merits.

✔ **Consider how it will be read.** Don't forget that whatever you write in the appraisals is going to be read by your employees. If your comments are vague, unsubstantiated, or focus on personality over performance, you're setting the stage for problematic sessions with your employees.

Describing strengths and weaknesses

When writing about your employees' strengths, your comments will be most effective if they focus on specific behaviors and competencies. For example, although it's nice for employees to hear that they "do excellent work," the focus is totally unclear and the employees can't anchor your comment to any particular action. So, although your employees would like to receive positive feedback in the future for their excellent work, they don't know which behaviors to repeat.

Your comments take on more meaning, have a greater motivational impact, and have a longer shelf life if you phrase them in behavioral terms. For example, instead of saying that your employees do excellent work, give them specific examples of such work, such as "Provides extremely high-quality work on time." With this type of comment, your employees clearly know the two components that generated this positive feedback — quality and timeliness. Strive for comments that are measurable: "Friendly" is hard to quantify, but "Greets customers within 30 seconds of walking into the store" is specific and measurable.

When writing about your employees' weaknesses, the same basic framework applies. You need to be specific and avoid phrases such as "attitude could use improvement." Your comments will be more effective and more motivational if you leave out the word *attitude* and focus specifically on behaviors that are indicative of a questionable attitude, such as complaining, arguing, or refusing to help others.

After the review, part of your job will be to work with each employee to help him become more effective in the areas currently needing improvement. The more specific you are in your description, the better able you'll be to focus your developmental efforts. And because your employees understand the specifics of the areas needing improvement, they're likely to be more receptive to your guidance.

Selecting a rating

After you enter your comments for each factor that you're appraising, you're ready to enter a numerical rating (assuming your form calls for one). The key to success with this step is to familiarize yourself fully with the rating scale.

With many numerical rating scales, a mini-description is associated with each number. For example, the rating form may list several behaviors associated with communication, accompanied by a rating scale that reads:

5 — **Exceptional:** Consistently exceeds expectations.

4 — **Excellent:** Frequently exceeds expectations.

3 — **Fully competent:** Meets expectations.

2 — **Marginal:** Occasionally fails to meet expectations.

1 — **Unsatisfactory:** Consistently fails to meet expectations.

Without the mini-description following each rating, it would be easy for each manager to have a different opinion on what *excellent* means. The descriptions result in far greater consistency in the process.

Determining an overall rating

As you work your way through the performance appraisal form, you'll start to get a sense of the overall rating of each of your employees. In some evaluation forms, the final rating is based on little more than this overall perception. In this case, you're asked to give your own overall rating of the employee based on all the comments and rankings that you've entered into the form. The best guideline in this case is to make sure that the overall rating you provide is consistent with the individual ratings that you've provided in each category.

The only time to stray from this strategy is if your employee has done extremely well or poorly in parts of the job that are truly the most important elements of the job itself. If you have full latitude in determining the final rating, you can add weightings to various areas that you evaluated in order to make sure that performance in those areas has a greater impact on the employee's final rating.

At the other end of the continuum, some performance evaluation forms include mathematical calculations and weightings for each of the ratings that you enter. In some cases, these forms are designed to take the ratings that you provide for each component, calculate an average score, and convert that into the overall rating.

When you've finished writing the appraisals and made your final evaluations, set them aside for a few days. Doing so gives you time to think about them and let any of your concerns incubate. When you revisit these evaluations, you'll do so with a fresh perspective. Give each evaluation a final look, make any needed adjustments, and then lock them in as final. You're guaranteed to be more certain about your ratings, and more comfortable with them, after this second visit.

Managing Your Misperceptions

One of the main errors that managers make in the performance appraisal process is failing to see employees as they truly are. When this happens, managers typically place too much emphasis on matters of minimal importance and too little emphasis on the stuff that matters most.

Managers who misperceive the realities of their employees' behaviors do so as a result of their own needs, biases, expectations, prior experiences, and memories. And no matter what the source of these misperceptions may be, the result is the same: The managers' thinking is distorted, and they end up with evaluations that are equally distorted. This section helps you anticipate these issues and work to overcome them in your own performance appraisal process.

Overpowering bias and stereotypes

Biases and stereotypes are really about prejudice, which literally means "to prejudge." Prejudging is particularly problematic in performance appraisals because one central managerial role in the process is to judge each employee's behavior. If the judging component is completed before the process even starts, there's no point in starting the process at all.

If the potential damage that bias and stereotyping heap on the performance appraisal process is not enough to convince you to dispel your prejudicial beliefs, something else just might grab your attention: a lawsuit. If you allow factors such as race, religion, gender, national origin, sexual orientation, age, or disability to affect your appraisal of your employees, you and your company are likely to face a claim of discrimination.

Beating bias

Managerial bias is a strong preconceived leaning or inclination about a person or situation. Such bias can be positive or negative, and it can cause managers to look at their employees' performance and see accomplishments where there are none and overlook failures where there are many.

Book IV

Communicating with Employees

The first step in eliminating bias is recognizing it. One of the most compelling ways to conduct a bias test on yourself is to take a sample of one of your employee's behaviors that you rated as "excellent" and ask yourself if all your other employees would have received the exact same ratings if they had performed at the exact same level. If you would've rated some of them lower, some bias has slipped into your thinking.

Stopping the stereotypes

When it comes to stereotyping, managers take the supposed characteristics of a group and apply them to all its members. Although some stereotypes are positive, most are unflattering, unfair, and inappropriate. When stereotypes enter any phase of the performance appraisal process, the information is instantly tainted, and the credibility of the appraisal drops to zero.

When you're aware of the stereotypes you hold, you'll have taken a gigantic step toward eradicating them. A quick way to see whether stereotyping is entering your own thinking is to pick any particular group of people, whether based on political affiliation, nationality, weight, age, or any other factor. With that group in mind, ask yourself whether you believe that there are any personality traits that are typical of all its members. If you think such characteristics exist, you're finding the stereotypes that exist in your mind. Whether these stereotypes are positive or negative, they're sure to interfere with your effectiveness in the appraisal process.

Rethinking "just like me"

When managers sense that they have a lot in common with certain employees, they tend to be extra lenient when appraising the performance of these employees.

If a manager and an employee share common backgrounds and experiences, the manager is likely to feel significantly greater levels of trust, understanding, and familiarity with this employee — which leads to more positive evaluations. For example, say you grew up on a farm in the Midwest, worked your way through college, and married your high school sweetheart. You're likely going to feel much closer to an employee who has a similar background than you will to an unmarried employee who grew up in a major city, partied through college, and spent his summers traveling around Europe. When it's time for the performance evaluation, that common bond between you and the first employee may generate higher ratings.

By letting the bonds of commonality overpower the facts of performance, you're overlooking three key and costly points:

- ✔ Although you may have an employee whose background is remarkably similar to yours, there is no reason to assume that her performance is going to be equally remarkable.

- ✔ Plenty of employees are just like you in many respects, but certainly not in *every* respect. And some of those dissimilar respects just may be their competence, work ethic, loyalty, or honesty.

- ✔ If an employee senses that you're somehow swayed by a commonality in your backgrounds, that employee may also sense that she has a wild card that will automatically condone marginal work, self-serving behaviors, and flaunting of company policies and standards.

When a manager has a lot in common with an employee and that sense of commonality leaks into the performance evaluations, the rest of the employees have a different term for this situation: They call it *favoritism*. If you're looking for a way to undercut teamwork, cooperation, loyalty, and productivity, favoritism is right at the top of the list.

Recognizing the halo effect

If you're looking for one of the most common errors in the performance appraisal process, you'll find it in the *halo effect* — the tendency to allow your employees' excellent performance in one area to impact the way you evaluate their performance in all other areas.

When your employees have performed extremely well in one key part of the job, you need to provide them with a very positive rating in that area. But after you've assigned that rating, you need to approach the next item with a clean slate and no lingering positive predispositions from the last item.

The halo effect comes into play when managers don't make a clean break from the rating on that previous item. Instead, their positive rating on one item leads to equally positive ratings on every other item, regardless of actual performance.

For example, say you're a real stickler for detail, and you just finished giving one of your employees an outstanding rating on his thoroughness, detail-mindedness, and accuracy. However, instead of moving to the next factor and making a merit-based rating, the halo that you just placed on your employee gets in your way, leading you to conclude that because he performed with distinction in one important area, surely he's deserving of equally high ratings in all other areas.

Book IV

Communicating with Employees

That one halo leads to halos in every category, and that leads to trouble. Here are some of the problems caused by the halo effect:

- ✔ **When employees figure out which category is the key source of all the positive ratings, they focus their behavior on only that category.** For example, if neatness and accuracy are the hot buttons that trigger a vast array of positive ratings, you'll end up with employees who devote all their energy to this area. Of course, this means that they're devoting less energy to other areas, such as productivity, communication, and quality of work, to name just a few.

- ✔ **When employees are provided with positive ratings across the board, they know that many of those ratings were undeserved.** Instead of feeling appreciative for such ratings, they're more likely to view the process as meaningless. If they're going to get a barrage of outstanding ratings that have nothing to do with their performance, sure, they'll accept the praise, but they won't accept the notion that performance appraisal is a valuable process.

- ✔ **A collection of equally positive ratings across the board actually sends a less flattering message about the manager's attitude — namely, that the manager didn't devote much time, energy, or effort to the appraisal process.** Instead, the manager simply hooked onto one piece of performance and used it as the litmus test for ratings in all other categories. Employees generally believe that their managers' lack of interest and concern in the appraisal process is indicative of a lack of interest and concern for them as individuals. Although recognition has consistently been found to be linked to motivation, that isn't the case for recognition that's perfunctory or undeserved. A string of undeserved positive ratings is likely to be perceived as insulting, degrading, and even embarrassing.

Dismissing the horns effect

The halo effect has an evil twin known as the *horns effect*. With the horns effect, when employees perform poorly in one key performance area, managers give them lower ratings in all areas.

As you may expect, the horns effect generates even more negative reactions than the halo effect. At least with the halo effect, the employees receive positive ratings. But with the widespread negative ratings associated with the horns effect, not only are the ratings inaccurate, but they can reduce possibilities for employees to receive raises, promotions, and other pluses that accompany positive ratings.

The horns effect results in some significant problems:

- ✔ **When employees know that they've at least been performing satisfactorily but they're given uniformly low ratings, they see the entire evaluation process as unbalanced and unfair.** When employees believe that a process that's at the heart of their tenure, earnings, and career is somehow inequitable, their attitude toward their job, their manager, and their work takes a major hit. And their performance and productivity soon do likewise.

- ✔ **If the employees can figure out which specific behavior contaminated their overall ratings, they'll place undue emphasis on that area, while putting less emphasis on all other areas.** This situation leads to further gaps in their performance, productivity, and overall satisfaction.

- ✔ **Most managers actively say they treat employees honestly, fairly, and respectfully, but when they let the horns effect horn in on their evaluations, all these pronouncements go down the drain — along with the managers' credibility.** And when you lose credibility with your employees, your potential effectiveness across the board is severely compromised.

- ✔ **When employees see that their evaluations are inexplicably and unacceptably low, they're disappointed and angry — which comes out in full force in the one-on-one sessions with their managers.** The likelihood of having an open discussion about the employees' performance and development is impossible when the horns effect has tainted the ratings.

Getting beyond first impressions

The shelf life of first impressions is remarkable. If you think back to the first time you met the significant others in your work life or personal life, you can probably remember, and in many cases picture, that first encounter. Not only does the image of that first encounter stay with you, but so do many of the initial feelings you had toward that person.

The problem is, when employees make a positive or negative first impression, it often stays with their managers and leads to an equally positive or negative impression of their work.

Even as early impressions are overshadowed by more recent events, they never totally disappear. And one of the times when they typically reveal themselves is during the performance evaluation process. As managers mull over the data that they've gathered, some of that first-impression data can still leak into the evaluative process.

Book IV

Communicating with Employees

Instead of ignoring first impressions, try to remember them. By drawing them out, considering them carefully, placing them in the context where they belong, and acknowledging that your employees have come a long way since then, you'll be far less likely to allow them to alter your thinking and ratings.

Setting the Stage for the Appraisal

The next step in the appraisal process is having a meeting with each employee to discuss your performance appraisal findings. A few days before each sit-down session, you can take several key steps that will greatly increase its effectiveness and improve your chances of succeeding.

Identifying your objectives

Regardless of the nature of the feedback that you'll be providing, take the time to note two or three major points that you definitely want your employees to hear and remember. For example, these points may focus on specific competencies that your employees need to upgrade, various behaviors that are interfering with individual or departmental performance, or opportunities for growth and development.

By identifying these major points before the sessions, and then emphasizing and reemphasizing them during the sessions, you'll greatly increase the likelihood that your employees will leave with a clear understanding of the most important components of your feedback.

Preparing an agenda

You don't need an iron-clad agenda for appraisal meetings because the dynamics of these sessions can draw the discussions into unplanned topics — and that's not necessarily a bad thing. After all, such topics can include unanticipated suggestions, complaints, and concerns that help identify existing problems or prevent new ones. However, when the discussion strays from what you had intended, you need to be able eventually to guide it back to the main points that you need to cover. An agenda can help you keep your discussions on target.

Your agenda should include

- The highlights of your opening remarks
- The step-by-step sequence of the performance-related feedback that you're planning to provide
- A list of the key points that you want your employee to remember
- The point in the session when you plan to discuss the employee's raise (or lack thereof)
- The key points you want to make when closing the session

Scripting your delicate comments

When you have to provide negative feedback to an employee, knowing exactly what to say can be difficult. If you fumble for words and then hedge around a problematic issue or behavior, your employee will sense your apprehension and confusion and either shrug off your comments or seize the opening and challenge you.

One of the best ways to prevent this problem is to look carefully at the areas in which you're going to give some negative feedback and write down exactly what you want to say. You don't have to give a lengthy diatribe — a well-crafted sentence or two can say it all. After you've scripted your comments, practice them aloud several times until you can say them easily and naturally.

Bringing the data

Before the evaluation session, decide which pieces of documentation you're going to bring. You don't need every piece of data that you touched in determining the ratings, but you should have some data at your side:

- **Evaluation forms:** Be sure to bring two hard copies of the completed evaluations. If your employee completed a self-evaluation, bring two copies of that as well.

- **The employee's file:** You aren't likely to need to thumb through the employee's file during the evaluation session, but if you do need to access some primary support data, having the file nearby is helpful.

- **Your notes:** If your employee raises questions about specific times and dates regarding the issues that you're discussing, having your log or notes nearby is helpful.

Setting positive expectations

Your expectations play a key role in many aspects of effective management, and they come into play again at this point in the performance appraisal process.

One of the most effective ways to increase the likelihood of a positive, open, and highly productive two-way conversation during an appraisal session is for you to set positive expectations. Visualize how you want each session to go — you'll have an easier time achieving your goals if you've visualized them.

Holding the Meeting

When the time for the evaluation sessions with your employees arrives, several strategies will help make these meetings more effective from start to finish. You've already put the foundation in place, and now you're ready to build some solid review sessions.

Make sure that you hold your meeting in an office or conference room that ensures privacy. Without privacy, both parties in the session feel awkward, distracted, and unable to be totally honest. And if these sessions lack honesty, there's no point in holding them.

Opening the discussion

Your opening comments will set the tone, tenor, and atmosphere for the entire discussion and need to accomplish the following:

1. **Greet the employee.**

   Start by making friendly and welcoming comments to break the ice. To help further relax your employee, you can even ask a question or two about some informal topics that interest both of you.

2. **Set the framework.**

   This is the "here's what we're going to do" section of your opening. The idea is to give your employee an understanding of the structure of the meeting, including an overview of the topics and timing.

3. Ask for questions.

If an employee asks questions that deal with your opening remarks or with matters that should be addressed on the spot, this is the time to answer them. However, if the questions pertain to matters that you plan on discussing later in the review, advise the employee of this fact and make a note to yourself so you don't forget to cover these topics later.

Leading the discussion

There is no single path for you to follow in order to conduct highly successful evaluation sessions. At the same time, when you're leading these discussions, the following steps will help make the meetings more interactive and productive:

1. Let your employee talk.

If your employee has completed a self-appraisal, your first step is to indicate that you'd like to hear his thoughts. Although you already have a copy of the appraisal and you've looked it over prior to this session, tell your employee that you'd like to know more, especially in terms of his performance and results that he believes are particularly important, as well as the way in which he arrived at his specific ratings.

If you or your company doesn't use self-evaluations, you can still encourage the employee's input at this point in the session by asking a question such as "How have things on the job been going during the past year?"

Giving your employees the chance to discuss their actions, achievements, and competencies is rewarding to them because it further emphasizes your respect and trust, while also reinforcing your partnership with them.

2. Give an overview of the session.

After you've heard your employee's thoughts regarding her performance, your next step is to give her a brief overview of topics that you'll be covering in the session.

3. Focus on objectives.

This part of the discussion focuses on the agreed-upon objectives and the extent to which your employee met them.

4. Focus on performance results.

The emphasis in this section is on the various additional performance-related outcomes that were the result of your employee's actions and efforts, even if such outcomes were not directly attached to the overall objectives.

5. **Focus on critical incidents.**

   Your comments here highlight particularly outstanding employee behaviors and/or especially questionable behaviors. Examine the way in which your employee handled noteworthy situations, whether positively or negatively.

6. **Focus on competencies.**

   This is where you discuss instances in which your employee applied his skills effectively to the job, shared his knowledge with others, or took specific steps to further build his competencies.

7. **Focus on points of agreement.**

   Whether based on your employee's self-evaluation or on her opening comments regarding her performance, your focus at this point in the session is on the areas in which your employee agrees with your ratings.

   These points are typically the more positive ratings in your evaluation. Many of your comments at this point are focused on encouraging your employees to continue to engage in the behaviors that generated these positive outcomes and ratings.

8. **Focus on points of disagreement.**

   This is the time to discuss the areas in which you rated your employee lower than he rated himself, whether based on his self-evaluation or his opening comments. Your objective is to learn more about your employee's rationale for giving himself ratings that are higher than yours and for him to understand the rationale behind the ratings that you gave.

   This is not a negotiation session, and you should not revise your ratings based on your employee's comments. Even after you provide an explanation of the rationale behind your ratings, your employee may still disagree. However, that isn't a major problem as long as he truly comprehends the reasons why his ratings were lower than what he expected or wanted.

9. **Focus on the overall rating.**

   At this point in the process, you and your employee have discussed all the key performance-related issues and concerns, and it's now time to discuss the overall rating. Your comments should focus on the steps you took to determine this rating.

   If part of this overall rating is based on additional weightings that you placed on any of the areas within the performance appraisal, make sure that your employee understands the rationale and methodology behind this adjustment.

10. **Focus on raises.**

There is a good deal of debate among managers as well as management theorists as to where to place raises in the performance appraisal session. Some managers don't even think that raises belong in the session at all. Here are your options:

- **Bring up raises in the beginning.** This approach is premised on the belief that employees don't pay much attention during appraisal sessions with raises at the end because they're fixated on what their raises will be. Letting them know at the outset is supposed to put an end to their wondering and allow them to pay attention to the feedback you're providing. However, if they expected a better raise, they may end up being consumed with their disappointment and not hear what you're saying anyway.

- **Bring up raises toward the end.** Here, the idea is to provide employees with a clearer understanding of the relationship between their performance and the raise they receive. After giving glowing reviews, you're ideally able to provide a direct reward for an employee's stellar behavior, demonstrating the clear link between better performance and better rewards. The same principle applies in reverse, when you're providing less of a reward (or no reward) for less-than-stellar performance. The primary concern with this approach is that employees won't hear what you're saying until you talk about raises.

- **Eliminate raises from the discussion.** The idea behind this approach is that raises don't belong in the performance appraisal session at all. Instead, these sessions should focus exclusively and extensively on the employees' past performance, while issues such as raises and objectives should be discussed in separate sessions.

Because there is no uniform agreement on this matter, be sure to have a clear understanding of the way in which your company's raise process is linked to the performance appraisal process. If you're given a choice, opt for separate sessions to discuss raises. Doing so will allow you to focus thoroughly and unequivocally on an employee's performance during the appraisal session, while focusing equally thoroughly on raises in a later session. With this approach, your employees will have a clearer understanding of the most important factors in both of these key areas.

If your company includes goal setting as part of the performance appraisal session, this would be the point in the evaluation when you and your employees discuss specific objectives and action plans for the coming year. Shifting gears can be difficult for you *and* your employees, so try to set up a separate time with your employees to carry out this very important function.

Providing negative feedback

Many managers have lingering fears about giving negative feedback to their employees during their evaluation sessions. But the negative comments that you provide in these sessions will be less stressful for you because this won't be the first time that you've made them to your employees. By spending a good deal of time with your employees, you've already provided them with negative feedback when their performance merited it. They already know where they're performing well and where they're performing poorly, and they could just as easily provide themselves with the same negative feedback that you provide in these sessions. Additionally, staying focused on the positive result — an opportunity to improve performance — can take some of the sting and stress out of providing negative feedback.

In addition, three strategies can make this process even easier for you:

- ✔ **Sit down.** People are far less likely to get heated up when they're sitting down. *Where* you're seated matters, too: A desk that separates you from your employee can be a psychological as well as physical barrier. In order to send a message to your employee that you want to partner with her in the appraisal process, try either sitting next to her or pulling your chair around your desk and sitting face-to-face with no barriers between the two of you.

- ✔ **Use *I*, not *you*.** When you're providing negative feedback to your employees, one surefire way to generate a harsh reaction is to lace your comments with the word *you*. Frequent use of the word *you* sounds like a combination of accusation and scolding, and employees are likely to become increasingly defensive with each additional *you*.

  Try using the word *I* instead of *you* when possible. For example, instead of saying "You didn't complete the project on time," try saying "I'm wondering why the project came in late." In this way, you've centered the issue on yourself and the project, which opens the door for a conversation instead of a confrontation.

- ✔ **Focus on behaviors.** The essence of performance appraisal is focused on behavior — and that's essential to keep in mind when providing negative feedback. The idea is for your employees to sense that you're concerned or upset with some aspect of their *behavior* but not with them as individuals.

  For example, if you asked an employee to give a particular report to certain employees, but she gave it to all the employees, you *could* say, "You made a mistake by giving this report to everyone." Your employee will probably perceive this statement as a direct attack, and she's likely to react in kind. With some minor tweaking of the wording, you can rephrase and refocus the feedback so that it's targeted on the behavior and perceived as less of an attack: "This report should have been distributed only to the managers in XYZ division."

Actively listening

As you lead appraisal sessions, your effectiveness will be enhanced if you display solid listening skills. By listening carefully to what your employees are saying, not only will you be able to learn more about their actions and their motivations for taking them, but also you'll be better able to determine whether your employees fully understand the reasons behind the ratings that you provided.

Regardless of ratings, employees feel better about the evaluation process if they truly sense that they're being heard. As part of the open exchange of ideas that is at the heart of appraisal sessions, you can take some steps to strengthen your listening skills.

- **Focus on what your employees are saying.** Some of the best ways to do this are to restate, rephrase, and summarize what they say — for example, you can say, "Let me make sure I understand," and then put their comments in your own words. Anytime you aren't sure what they mean, ask for clarification. Chapter 2 of this Book gives more detail about effective communication tools.

- **Focus on what they're *not* saying.** Pay extra attention to their body language, such as their facial expressions, whether they're slouched or sitting forward, whether their arms are crossed, and whether they maintain eye contact.

- **Show your employees that you're engaged in the discussion.** Your body language and comments should show your employees that you're interested in this dialogue with them. You can do this by sitting forward, nodding when appropriate, and adding occasional comments and interjections indicating that you're involved and listening (such as, "I see" and even "Uh-huh").

Wrapping up the discussion

If you've fully worked your way through the agenda that you created for a given session and you're satisfied that the objectives you established prior to the session have been met, it's time to bring the session to a close. As you do so, follow these key steps:

Book IV

Communicating with Employees

1. **Give your employee a recap of his performance, particularly the major areas of strength and success, along with the one or two areas where the most improvement is needed.**

2. **Tell your employee that you'll be meeting again soon to talk about objectives and plans for growth and development for the coming evaluation period.**

   Ask the employee to do some thinking in these areas and to write a draft of her objectives and development plan between now and that next meeting. If you can do so on the spot, set a specific date and time for that meeting. If you can't finalize a date at this time, let your employee know that you'll be setting a date to meet within two weeks.

3. **If you did not discuss a raise during the appraisal session, let your employee know that you'll soon be setting up a separate meeting to do so.**

4. **Ask your employee if he has any further questions or if there are any other matters that he wants to discuss in this session.**

5. **Sign and date the evaluation form and ask your employee to do likewise.**

   Be sure to mention that she can add her own comments to the form if she wants.

6. **Express your positive expectations as you bring the session to an end.**

   Let your employee know that you have confidence in him and his ability to succeed in making the improvements that were discussed during the appraisal session.

Setting Goals

There isn't much point in providing your employees with a stack of feedback if nothing happens with it. Simply turning the employees loose and telling them that you expect to see some improvement is tantamount to turning your back on your employees and on the appraisal process itself. When your employees see your lack of involvement and support, they're likely to take that stack of feedback and toss it aside.

If you want to raise an employee's performance to the next level, your most useful and compelling tool is your completed performance appraisal. That completed appraisal opens the door to goal setting, and the goals that you establish with each of your employees are at the heart of their motivation, development, and success.

Looking forward instead of backward

At this point in the process, you're turning around to face the future with your employees. And the notion of turning around is particularly appropriate because these goals can truly help stage a turnaround for any of your employees who may be struggling.

Your employees' futures are filled with opportunities to build their competencies, achieve outstanding results, and take their overall performance to new heights. By working with your employees to help establish their goals, and then providing them with coaching, guidance, and support along the way, you're creating the perfect climate for them to grow and for their performance and effectiveness to do likewise. And if this happens, it'll be reflected in every aspect of your employees' work, as well as in their appraisals at the end of the next evaluation period.

Managers who keep focusing on their employees' pasts instead of their futures tend to dwell on problems and failures, which sets the stage for repeat performances in the coming year.

Opting for goals over dreams

Say you have an employee who says that his goal is to do a better job in every area next year. That sounds great except for one little problem: It's not a goal.

Your employee has actually articulated a dream, essentially a general wish or desire for a particular outcome. Nothing is wrong with dreams, but just having a dream doesn't mean it'll come true. If your employees want to turn their dreams into reality, they need to formulate them as goals.

Real goals have several distinct characteristics in common:

- ✔ **Goals are specific.** When your employees have real goals, nothing about them is general. Their goals won't be just to improve performance; instead, their goals will focus directly on the precise aspect or aspects of performance that they're aiming to improve.

- ✔ **Goals are realistic.** Your employees' goals need to be appropriate for their positions, responsibilities, and training. Real goals don't impose expectations that are totally unrelated to the employees' knowledge, skills, abilities, or standards.

✔ **Goals are prioritized.** All goals are not the same. Some are clearly critical and high priority, while others are important but lower in priority. As a result, every goal should have a clear and identifiable priority associated with it. Whether it's a numerical or alphabetical ranking makes no difference. What does make a difference is that the employee understands the priority associated with each goal and takes care of the most important goals first.

✔ **Goals are measurable.** As an employee pursues her goals, she and you need to know exactly where she is in the process. And, even more important, you both need to know if and when she's met a particular goal. As a result, true goals have a quantitative quality that allows them to be clearly measured at every point along the way. Because goals are measurable, employees and managers know exactly how the employees are performing every step of the way. At the end of the day, or at the end of the evaluation period, neither you nor your employee has any questions about goal attainment.

✔ **Goals are reachable.** Goals should certainly be challenging, but they should also be attainable. Granted, they should stretch your employees, but people can only stretch so far. If a goal is truly out of an employee's reach, it isn't truly a goal.

✔ **Goals are supported by action plans.** In order for your employees to reach their goals, the goals need to encompass clear planning. Action plans should include dates and deadlines, along with expected levels of project completion or goal attainment associated with each benchmark date. These plans set the path for employees to follow as they pursue their goals. Without action plans, employees may see where they want to go, but they don't know how to get there.

As you work with your employees to establish action plans, think of yourself as a reporter and ask lots of questions that start with *who, what, where, when, why,* and *how.*

If even one of the preceding elements is missing, it's back to dreamland.

The preceding characteristics of goals apply whether you're talking about a performance goal or a personal goal. But when it comes to goal-setting in the workplace, performance goals need to meet the following guidelines, too:

✔ **Performance goals should be aligned with the organization's goals.** Performance goals should support the style, standards, ethics, vision, and mission of your company.

✔ **Performance goals should be linked to your goals.** The idea is that the employees' goals should support the goals of their manager. As a result, when your employees reach their goals, it should help you meet yours. In turn, the attainment of your goals should help your manager meet her goals. In this way, the employees' goals from level to level are linked together and aligned with the goals of the company's top leadership.

✔ **Both you and your employees should agree on their performance goals.** When you've finished helping your employees formulate their goals for the coming year, the process should end with total understanding and agreement. If there are questions, doubts, or concerns, you need to address and resolve them before anything is finalized.

Motivating employees to meet their goals

Just because you and your employees have been working on setting goals doesn't automatically mean that your employees will be motivated to reach them.

When goals are simply dumped on employees, without any employee involvement or input and without any consideration of the employees' needs, the goals are likely to be rejected and, thus, void of any motivational impact. One of the key steps in establishing goals that are truly motivational is to establish them *with* your employees, rather than *for* your employees.

The presence of goals doesn't necessarily mean that employees will be motivated, but the lack of goals undercuts the likelihood of *any* significant motivation. After all, motivation energizes employees to take action to move toward a particular goal. If there are no goals to meet down the road, the employees will have no particular drive to get there.

If your employees sense a link between fulfillment of their needs and the goals that you jointly establish with them, the goals are likely to have more of a motivational impact. For example, if the employees' needs are focused on receiving recognition for successful performance, and your policy is to provide recognition for excellent work, your employees are likely to be motivated to do a great job.

Challenging your employees enough but not too much

When establishing goals with your employees, you need to give some extra thought to the level of difficulty of the goals themselves.

Extremely challenging goals

Some managers believe that goals should be as challenging as possible. The hope is that, if goals are extremely difficult or maybe even impossible to reach, employees will be highly motivated to reach them. Such challenging goals will energize employees to push themselves to great lengths, well beyond their normal efforts. And by doing so, they'll have raised their performance and surpassed the milestones and standards associated with less-rigorous goals.

Managers who subscribe to this theory believe that, when faced with impossible goals, some employees will rise to the occasion. Plus, even if employees aren't able to reach these goals, they'll have the satisfaction of truly exerting themselves in the pursuit of goals that would've scared away less-hearty souls.

Here's the reality: When goals are nothing short of impossible, the employees may initially hit the ground running, but as they realize that the goals pose insurmountable barriers and their efforts to reach those goals lead to back-sliding, the outcome is a motivational meltdown. Most employees reason that if goals absolutely can't be met, there's no point in even trying.

Extremely easy goals

At the other end of the continuum, some managers believe that easily attainable goals are the most motivational. The idea is that when employees meet their goals, whatever the goals may be, they experience a strong sense of accomplishment, and that's a strong source of motivation.

Plus, when employees reach their goals, they get recognition from their managers, which is yet another motivator. And when employees meet their goals, they experience increases in self-confidence, self-esteem, and self-image, all obviously positive outcomes. Hence, the reasoning goes, because employees are motivated to receive these psychological rewards, it makes sense to provide them with numerous opportunities to do so, and this is just what easy goals will do.

Here's the reality: Easily attained goals don't even register on the motivation scale. When employees can exert little or no effort and reach their goals, the message is that such goals are insignificant and meaningless.

When employees meet too-easy goals, they don't experience feelings of achievement or accomplishment. Instead, the goals are so minor that the employees who reach them believe that they haven't achieved or accomplished much of anything.

When goals can be reached with minimal effort by anyone who strolls into the department, they're void of any of the feelings of success that accompany the attainment of serious and significant goals. In fact, some employees are actually embarrassed when granted recognition for meeting unchallenging goals.

When goals are viewed by the employees as frivolous, simple, insignificant, and meaningless, they contribute more to disinterest and dissatisfaction than they do to motivation. After all, if a basketball hoop is 1 foot high and the size of a swimming pool, there isn't much satisfaction associated with hitting a shot — and there isn't much fun in that either.

Challenging goals

Goals that have a positive motivational impact are challenging, but they must be realistically challenging. They aren't a walk in the park, nor do they call for your employees to walk on Mars. Instead, they require a good deal of work on projects that are demanding, significant, and meaningful.

There is no guarantee that your employees will meet challenging goals, but with serious effort, energy, drive, and focus — along with support, guidance, and feedback from you — there is a chance that your employees will experience a major success. And with that success will come meaningful recognition and a true sense of achievement and accomplishment, which is highly motivational.

Creating performance goals

When you create performance goals with your employees, place your emphasis on jointly establishing clear, specific, measurable, and meaningful objectives in three interrelated areas:

- ✔ **Output and results goals:** Goals in this area focus on quantitative measures of productivity, yield, and results that the employees are expected to achieve. For example, goals in this area can be targeted at numbers of units produced, hours billed, claims handled, or sales closed.

- ✔ **Competency goals:** These goals focus on the way in which your employees carry out their job responsibilities and strive to build their output and productivity. Goals in this arena focus on such measurables as quantity and quality of work, interpersonal skills, leadership effectiveness, job knowledge and expertise, communication skills, planning and administration, and problem solving.

- ✔ **Behavioral goals:** These goals focus on the specific behaviors that your employees demonstrate every day while carrying out their various job responsibilities. Goals deal with targeted improvements in such areas as attitude, friendliness, dedication, energy, handling pressure, and supporting the company's values and mission.

Book IV

Communicating with Employees

Establishing developmental goals

As you work with your employees to establish their performance goals, you also need to use this opportunity to establish additional goals that focus on your employees' growth, learning, and development.

In order to set developmental goals that actually enhance your employees' knowledge, skills, abilities, and effectiveness on the job, you need to keep in mind some key points all the way through the goal-setting process.

Identifying each employee's needs

Some of your employees will have individual areas in which their performance falls short. When working with them to create developmental goals, the first step is to identify the areas in which further development is actually needed — for example, in terms of leadership, communication, teamwork, or administrative and planning skills.

The best source of this type of information is each individual employee's evaluation. Take a close look at the areas in which you gave relatively low ratings, consider the significance of each area, and select those that are most critical for effective performance and success on the job.

A good deal of development is focused on areas in which employee performance needs some improvement, but don't forget to also take a look at the areas in which your employees performed particularly well. These areas may be significant strengths already, and with additional development, they can grow into major assets for the company as well as for the employees themselves.

Building your employees' motivation to learn

If you just take the findings from the evaluations and throw your employees into a training program, the outcome is likely to be underwhelming at best. In order for true learning to occur, the participants in any kind of educational program should be motivated to learn. Without motivation, any efforts to build their skills and upgrade their knowledge will be little more than background noise.

One of the best ways to increase your employees' motivation to learn is to make sure that their thoughts, ideas, and opinions are included in designing their developmental program. Have individual meetings and open discussions with each of your employees to make sure that they have input in their developmental program. As part of these discussions, be sure to let your employees see how they can benefit by meeting their developmental goals.

Defining developmental goals

With your employees' developmental needs clearly identified and the employees' inputs included in the process, you're ready to jointly establish developmental goals. Developmental goals clearly outline the performance areas where your employees will pursue development, as well as the specific outcomes they'll be seeking in each. These goals are held to the same standards of specificity, measurement, challenge, and prioritization as the employees' performance goals.

For example, assume that one of your employees is starting to take on some leadership responsibilities, and she clearly shows potential for advancement. However, she hasn't had any formal leadership training. One developmental goal would be focused on building her leadership skills by having her spend a specific number of hours in leadership training and guided leadership experiences. The action plan for this developmental goal would include specific benchmarks regarding classes and seminars to attend, articles and books to read, predetermined and closely monitored leadership opportunities, and predetermined formal feedback and coaching sessions to review her effectiveness in these leadership roles.

Setting the developmental plan

As soon as you and your employees have agreed on the developmental goals, the next step is to create a thorough plan to energize and guide the process throughout the evaluation period. This step-by-step plan includes developmental areas to be covered, resources required, programs to attend, training materials needed, commitments from other employees who will help, follow-up meetings, and clearly defined benchmarks and deadlines.

Devising a developmental training program

As you and your employees review the various developmental options and educational programs, pay attention to seven key factors that are the hallmarks of better programs:

- ✔ The program should emphasize learning by experience.
- ✔ Your employees should have numerous opportunities to practice their newly acquired knowledge and skills.
- ✔ Your employees should receive prompt, accurate, and supportive feedback every step of the way.
- ✔ The educational atmosphere should be open, communicative, and highly receptive to questions and discussions.
- ✔ The material being covered should be directly applicable to what your employees will be doing on the job.

Book IV

Communicating with Employees

✔ Varying educational techniques should be employed that identify and build on the individual learning styles of your employees.

✔ The program should be evaluated on the basis of the actual results that are achieved. For example, if the program is designed to help employees deal more effectively with customers, a decrease in customer complaints should result.

Some educational programs use questionnaires to evaluate their effectiveness, but the questions miss the mark because they either ask the employees if they enjoyed the program or test the employees on what they learned. The problem is, the employees may enjoy a program but learn absolutely nothing. Or they may learn a laundry list of information but have no idea how to apply any of it. One of the best ways to evaluate the effectiveness of these types of programs is to look at subsequent employee behaviors and performance results.

Employees generate much of their knowledge while on the job, and you're their primary trainer. They're learning not only from the formal sessions that you provide but also from the example that you set every day. You're their central role model, and that makes you their most compelling trainer.

Managing after the Evaluation

After you and your employees have jointly created and agreed upon performance and developmental goals for the current evaluation period, your role as a manager includes ongoing and regular communication, contact, and coaching.

This doesn't mean that you'll be sacrificing any of your core job responsibilities (for example, planning, organizing, problem solving, or dealing with customers or vendors). Instead, you'll be balancing your more traditional managerial responsibilities with responsibilities that focus on the most important assets in the company: your employees.

Wandering around

Wandering around is one of the best ways to monitor your employees' progress as they strive to reach their goals. If you observe your employees making great strides, you can easily provide some informal feedback that helps them understand how they're doing, while simultaneously encouraging them to continue the same successful behaviors.

At the same time, if you find your employees falling short for any reason, you're in an advantageous position to do something about it. Had you not been wandering around, you may have learned about the issue at a later date (when it turned into a crisis), or you may not have learned about it at all.

By wandering around, not only are you able to spot specific problems early, but you're also able to take proactive steps to control and correct them. Plus, your onsite observation gives you much greater insight into the cause or causes of the problems, and that insight helps you set the stage to prevent recurrences in the future.

 While you're wandering around, try also to treat the process as managing by *wondering* around: Do more than observe and gather data. Try to understand the reasons behind the behaviors and outcomes you're observing. With such knowledge, you're even better armed to prevent recurrences.

Coaching employees toward their goals

When you find your employees engaging in particularly productive behaviors, you can take some powerful steps to keep them on this positive track. Plus, when you find your employees engaging in behaviors and outcomes that aren't helping them advance toward their goals, you can take equally powerful steps to help them get back on track. In both cases, you can generate these positive outcomes by playing one of the most important roles in management today: the role of the coach.

Some managers regard coaching as occasional words of encouragement or casual suggestions. Coaches do engage in these behaviors, but there's more to coaching than this.

Coaching is actually an ongoing managerial function in which you work with your employees to build their strengths and competencies, draw out their most effective and productive behaviors, help them identify and surpass obstacles, provide them with counseling for counterproductive behaviors, and keep them on target as they follow their developmental plans and pursue their goals. (Chapter 1 of this Book offers a detailed look at what business coaching entails.)

When you see your employees engaging in particularly effective behaviors, give them some words of encouragement. This type of positive feedback increases the likelihood that they'll repeat these behaviors.

And if your employees are engaging in behaviors that appear to be counter-productive, how you respond depends on how serious the problems are. If the employees' actions aren't particularly serious, a few words to the wise, preferably not in front of others, are probably all that is necessary.

However, if a behavior is more problematic, meet with the employee to review the issue in more detail. When you do so, keep the following key points in mind:

- Meet with your employee as close to the problematic behavior as possible.

- Hold the meeting in private.

- Be specific in describing the questionable performance and the problems that emerged or can emerge as a result.

- Provide clear and specific guidance and modeling.

- Be sure your employee understands and agrees to change his behavior.

- Tell your employee what will happen if the questionable performance continues.

- Set a follow-up date, preferably within 30 days, to meet with your employee to discuss the status of the situation.

- Document the discussion and place a copy in your employee's file.

- In your wandering around, be sure to follow up on this specific aspect of your employee's performance.

If employees are surprised in a performance evaluation, you haven't been doing your job. Make sure that you respond to critical events — positive and negative — as they happen. Enter these conversations in the log that you use when formulating performance evaluations.

By acting as a coach, you're providing your employees with regular feedback, guidance, and direction, whether for problematic behaviors or productive behaviors. You're helping to build their performance, competencies, and behaviors, while simultaneously helping them advance toward their goals.

Chapter 5

Resolving Conflict

As a manager, you inevitably spend a considerable amount of time involved with employee conflicts. Although few managers look forward to stepping in to manage conflict, getting a jump on conflict resolution saves you time, money, and energy. Too many managers overlook the cost of conflict, or the cost of doing nothing about a conflict, when considering the impact of disagreements. As one executive wisely said, "I provide conflict resolution training for my employees so I can implement their ideas rather than solve their problems."

Read on to find out how you take action when the time is right. Find out about how to plan for and facilitate a negotiation that is most likely to lead to resolution, including the right questions to ask and even how to ask them, as well as engaging both parties, brainstorming, and reaching agreement.

Developing a Plan to Resolve Conflict

Managers often have to address the conflicts of the people on their team. You've probably worked with managers who've tried to rush headlong into a conversation with the people in conflict, without giving much thought to the process or the techniques that could maximize their chances of success. You may have taken such an approach yourself because it was quick — and possibly even necessary for a temporary answer. But rushing into a conversation doesn't usually yield good, long-term results.

People in your organization probably see you as a problem solver because you're one of the people the company wants on the front lines. And that's a good thing. But solving your employees' conflicts for them actually does more harm than good. Think about your own life for a moment: You're more likely to support an idea when you have a stake in creating the solution than you are when someone else arbitrarily decides the answer for you. The same thing is true for your employees. They want a say in how a conflict is resolved because they're the ones who have to live with the consequences.

Preparing the parties for a conversation

You may have had your eye on a conflict for a while and perhaps even chatted briefly about the problem with one or more of the people affected by it. Regardless, if your employees have reached the point where they need some help, it's time to intervene and facilitate a mediated conversation. Follow this strategic process that takes your employees from preparing, to sharing, to understanding, to brainstorming, to agreement:

1. **Invite your employees to a meeting.**

   The timing of this invitation may be as important as the invitation itself. Whether you choose to inform your employees that you're requesting their attendance in person or in writing, do so in a manner that allows them enough time to process their thoughts but not *so* much time that they dwell on it. And unless you feel like doling out cruel and unusual punishments, don't set the meeting for a Monday and send the invitation on a Friday afternoon — your employees' entire weekend will likely be ruined worrying about the meeting.

2. **Explain your role.**

   If your employees can see you as a facilitator and a guide rather than as an enforcer of policies or a disciplinarian, they'll be more likely to speak openly and thoughtfully. Seeing you in such a way frees them up to think creatively about possible solutions and allows them to speak more freely about information that may be essential to getting to the root of the problem.

3. **Help employees get into the right frame of mind.**

   When you invite the parties to the meeting, do a couple of things to prepare them and to help them create some opportunities that will make this conversation go well:

   • **Ask them to come prepared to discuss all the topics that are pertinent to their conflict.** It's important that they're willing to participate fully and give the meeting an honest-to-goodness effort.

- **Remind them to be aware of their language — which includes tone of voice and body language.** The best conversations are ones in which your employees, though they may disagree with each other, speak respectfully and without interruption. No one genuinely receives an apology that includes eyes rolling and ends with a *tsk!*

4. **Assure confidentiality.**

   Start by addressing the extent to which you'll be acting in a confidential manner. Specifically, clarify with your employees exactly what you will and won't share with others. If you'll be reporting to your manager the results of the discussion, be clear and upfront about it.

   Encourage employees to limit any conversation with others regarding your meeting or the person they're in conflict with. Although expecting them to remain completely silent on the matter may be unreasonable, at the very least you're planting the seed that other voices may only complicate matters rather than help and that this conflict, along with its resolution, is their responsibility.

5. **Define meeting parameters.**

   Let them know that you're expecting them to attend, participate fully, and give it a good-faith effort, but that they are not required to reach a solution at any cost during the session. Also, though the meeting may be mandatory, any offers they make or solutions they arrive at are entirely voluntary.

6. **Give pre-work/homework instructions.**

   Your invitation to the meeting should include assignments. Give the parties some specific tasks to work on in the days leading up to the conversation. Depending on the nature of the conflict, you can vary your approach and instructions, but consider asking them to spend time identifying their specific concerns and issues, possible solutions, and their own responsibility in the situation and its resolution.

Setting up the meeting

Before your employees are ready to sit down with you and get the conversation started, you have some work to do. By preparing the space for your meeting, you maximize your potential for a successful conversation.

Make sure that you choose a neutral location. You must maintain the appearance and substance of neutrality at all times throughout your conversation. Any suggestion — whether real or imagined — that you've compromised neutrality will derail your process. Here are a few things you can do to create a sense of safety and neutrality:

✔ **Consider the location of the room itself.** Make sure the room you choose doesn't hold more or less power for either party. Specifically, try not to schedule your meeting in any location that could be described as either employee's "turf." Work to balance the power early to avoid having to address a power struggle during the meeting.

You may think that your office is the ideal spot because, as a manager, you'll be calling the shots and your employees will be more likely to follow your lead. But the truth is, your office only reinforces the idea that this meeting is a disciplinary action — which is a message to avoid.

✔ **Choose a meeting room that's as private as possible.** Meeting someplace where other employees are wandering in and out or lurking (and listening) won't create the kind of environment you want. Find a place where the curious eyes of others won't affect your discussion.

Private should also mean minimal distractions. A room with a telephone constantly ringing or computer beeps announcing the arrival of new e-mail serves only to distract from the conversation. Listening well is hard when you have distractions competing for your attention.

Facilitating a comfortable environment

These kinds of conversations can be difficult and uncomfortable for employees. You can help create a more positive response to the conversation, however, by improving the comfort of your surroundings.

Holding the meeting on neutral ground is important, but location is only part of that equation. Both of your employees must have equal access to all the amenities that you provide.

Consider the quantity and quality of everything in the meeting. For example, if you provide three pieces of paper to one employee, make sure the other employee also has three pieces of paper. If you provide a black pen with a cap to one, make sure that the other person has the same. Any indication of partiality can disrupt your process.

Preparing yourself

With all the work you've done to prepare your employees, you also need to take a few minutes to focus on yourself. Getting caught up in the conflict is pretty easy to do. Don't allow yourself to get over-invested in the outcome, though. In fact, the less emotionally invested you are, the better.

This is your employees' conflict. They own the problems, so they own the solutions! If you allow yourself to become attached to the conflict, and you become invested enough to make suggestions or offer solutions, you've effectively become responsible for those outcomes and whether they succeed or fail. Your employees will be more likely to buy in and follow through on an agreement when they themselves propose and refine it.

Before your meeting begins, take about 30 minutes and prepare yourself for what's to come. Strong conflict creates strong emotions, not only on the part of the participants but for any observer as well. Expect to hear language that's affected by emotions, and prepare yourself accordingly.

Facilitating a Mediation Meeting

Mediating a discussion is a lot more than just positioning yourself between two people who aren't getting along and blocking verbal punches. There's an art to reading the situation in a way that puts you in the facilitator's seat but allows you enough involvement in the discussion to move the conversation forward. It's not refereeing; it's guiding. And it's guiding without the parties feeling manipulated. Stay on top of the conversation without getting too involved in it. For instance, don't talk too much or say things like, "Well, Vanessa made a good point there, Brent. It's hard to argue with that."

Reviewing the ground rules

Set the right tone for the meeting from the get-go. It's important that your participants are clear in your expectations of them and are as comfortable as is reasonably possible given that they may not have spoken to each other in quite a while or have been at each other's throats. Bring them in together, and begin by inviting both of them to take a moment to relax as you outline some of the housekeeping items that will make the meeting run smoother. Set up the parameters by using clear language in an organized and professional manner. With that said, don't freak everybody out by being so scripted that it sounds like they're on trial. Set boundaries, but let the employees know you're willing to be flexible.

If this is the first time the two have been able to talk, be aware that a lot of new information will be exchanged, and it's up to you to make sure they're really hearing what the other has to say. On the other hand, if they've tried talking to one another before, they've probably shared most of the details but can't agree on a solution. If the latter is the case, let them know you'll focus on helping them brainstorm solutions that work for both sides.

Also let them know that you'll spend most of the time together understanding from each person what keeps them in conflict and then working to find what each needs in order to limit further problems. For now they've probably prepared some pretty tough language about the other person (or even regarding their thoughts about this meeting) that may threaten to derail your process. But don't panic! Go over rules of common courtesy, and point out that you won't tolerate name-calling or disrespectful language.

Emphasize collaboration by stressing to your employees that this conversation is their opportunity to come together and work on a solution that's satisfactory to both of them. Include language that emphasizes the responsibility that each shares in brainstorming and implementing solutions.

Explaining roles and responsibilities

You're the manager, and your employees are used to you being in charge. This meeting is different, though, and it's vital that they understand your objective role as mediator. Explain that you aren't acting as a decision maker, an advocate, or even a counselor. You aren't influencing outcomes, offering advice, or determining liability. You're here to help them explore their issues and concerns, assist them in brainstorming options, and aid them in creating their own mutually agreeable outcomes and solutions.

This is *not* your conflict. Though you may have a stake in the outcome, it's important to remember that the conflict and its solution rest in the hands of your employees. If you become invested in the outcome, take sides, or offer solutions and ideas, you risk alienating one (or both) employees.

Additionally, you may find that if your ideas or suggestions don't meet their needs, in their eyes you've effectively become responsible for the failure of the process. By reinforcing that the responsibility for solution rests on their shoulders, you effectively reinforce ownership and buy-in for the process.

After you state your role, clearly stress the importance of the participants' roles. Specifically, outline the kinds of behavior you'd like to see from them during the course of the conversation. Discuss these key points:

- ✔ **Willingness to listen:** Asking employees to communicate respectfully means allowing time to finish sentences and thoughts and choosing not to interrupt when the other is speaking. It also means not monopolizing the floor when speaking.

- ✔ **Willingness to share:** Encourage them to speak from their own perspectives. Remind them that it's important to hear what each person has to say and that this meeting is a safe setting in which to do so.

- ✔ **Courteous treatment:** Most people are fairly courteous in their day-to-day interactions with others, but when in conflict it often becomes difficult to maintain the same manners. Acknowledge this fact, and then ask your employees to remember that courteous treatment of one another is a simple way to make your meeting go smoother.

- ✔ **Openness to new ideas:** Although each employee has likely come to this meeting with only one way of addressing the conflict, encourage them to remember that there are multiple ways to solve problems. There are no wrong answers while brainstorming; ideas they never imagined may come from the most innocuous comment.

Directing the flow of information

Encourage your participants to start out by speaking directly to you. They'll have an opportunity to speak to one another later, but for now, you want all their energy and attention focused on you. They likely have prepared scripts running in their heads, which include a laundry list of things that the other person has done, and they may use language that isn't terribly helpful. Rather than have them lob this language at one another, ask them to give it to *you*.

Stressing uninterrupted time

Uninterrupted time means that while one person is speaking, the other is listening. Seems pretty straightforward, right? They may have agreed not to interrupt, but face it: It's hard to sit and listen to someone say things you disagree with. Encourage your employees to honor the agreement, rather than calling them out. If you blurt out, "Don't interrupt!" you dismiss the fact that the topic is uncomfortable for the interrupter. You may have to be stern later if they continue to talk over one another, but the best first step is to ask them to jot down their thoughts for when it's their turn to speak.

Supply your participants with some paper and pens before you begin. When the inevitable interruption comes, simply gesture to the paper as a reminder for the interrupter to make note of his thoughts.

Giving the participants a chance to present their perspectives

Up until now, you've been outlining ground rules and maybe sounding to your employees a little like Charlie Brown's teacher droning on and on. The reason your employees have caught only about every third word you said is that they're likely concentrating on what they're going to say, what they're going to keep to themselves, and how they're really going to let the other person have it when it's their turn to talk. From the moment the first person opens his mouth, your job is to move them from blaming to eventually creating solutions. Do this by listening to both parties, pulling out pertinent information, acknowledging emotions, and neutralizing statements.

Deciding who speaks first

Ask the parties which of them would like to speak first, and allow them to make that choice on their own. No matter how tempting it may be, don't make the decision for them. You can inadvertently set the expectation that when things become difficult you'll step in to solve the problem (both in this meeting and in the future). Instead, be patient and allow them some time and space to work it out. If they still struggle, comment on the fact that there's no benefit to going first (or second, for that matter), and ask for a volunteer.

Although it's important for your parties to make the choice on their own, watch for power moves. An employee may bully his way into speaking first, or he could gallantly let his coworker go first because he feels certain he'll be able to rip her perspective to shreds. A quick check with the other person ("Is that okay with you?") lets him know it really is a joint decision.

Listening to the second participant

After the first employee has had a chance to express his thoughts, take the time to summarize what you heard. Then turn your attention to the second party. Start by thanking the first party for his statement and the other party for waiting and being patient (even if she really hasn't shown a lot of patience!). Reaffirm that this is the second party's chance to share her thoughts, and then put some additional parameters around your expectations.

Tell the second party that although she may be tempted to respond to what the first speaker has just said, you want her to speak as if she's sharing first. This mindset gives her an opportunity to present her story in a fuller way.

After the second employee has shared her point of view and you've reflected back to her, turn your attention back to the first party and say, "Is there anything you'd like to add that hasn't already been discussed or a particular point you'd like to respond to?" More than one response during opening statements just makes for a prolonged back-and-forth that looks more like a tennis match than a productive conversation.

You may find that your parties attempt to begin the negotiation process here by turning to one another and bypassing you as a facilitator. It's important to prevent this from happening because it can seriously derail the meeting, but bear in mind that this action is actually good news. It means that your parties are active and engaged and ready to get to work, so use their desire to talk to each other to your advantage. To guide the conversation and get it back on track, say, "I can see that the two of you are anxious to get started. Let's complete this part of the process and then we'll move forward."

Summarizing what you hear

After the first party shares his perspective, briefly summarize what you've heard before moving to the other person. Likewise, after you listen to the second person, summarize before giving the first person a chance to speak again. Summarizing not only allows the speaker to know that you've heard and understood what he had to say, but it also gives the other employee the opportunity to hear the concerns from a new source (you) and with new ears.

Think of it this way: There's probably not much chance your employees are going to hear anything new if the same old script keeps running. But when you skillfully craft your response to the speaker in the form of reflecting and reframing the information, you create the opportunity for the other person to hear something in a new way. Imagine that they each hear your perspective not as a list of all the things that were "wrong" with the way they handled things, but rather as a conversation about what's important to the speaker.

For more information about summarizing and using other tools to communicate effectively, turn to Chapter 2 of this Book.

Creating an agenda

You may be wondering why creating the agenda comes midway through your meeting process. Well, an agenda in mediation is *not* a pre-generated list of topics that you use to guide the discussion. Nor is it a schedule of events and activities for your dialogue. Instead, it's a list of topics the employees want to talk about that they collaboratively create after hearing each other's perspective. By generating the list together, they're much more likely to see each topic as belonging to both of them rather than feeling that you're forcing topics on them.

Start by standing up and moving to a whiteboard or easel. Tell the parties it's time to build a meeting agenda that will cover the topics and issues that are important to them. They talk; you write. (Manage what gets written down so you can ensure that inflammatory or hurtful language stays off the list.)

Use the agenda to make an important point: It's time to move from the past to the future. Set the stage for the conversation to come by saying, "Thank you for sharing your perspectives. As we begin to build an agenda, keep in mind that you'll discuss each of these items thoroughly, but you'll do so with a focus on the future rather than rehashing the past." Your statement should focus the employees to move them away from where the problems have been and toward where the solutions are.

Whatever you do, don't let go of the marker! Take responsibility for creating and editing the list so that one of your employees doesn't hijack the process by erasing all your hard work or adding language that derails the conversation.

Let the parties know that it's not necessary for them to agree on the topics listed on the agenda. In other words, if one wants to have a conversation about a topic, it goes on the list as a potential topic for discussion. This point is important because it creates ownership in the topics an employee suggests and in his coworker's suggestions as well.

Make sure all the topics you list are neutral and presented objectively. Creating neutral topics is an important part of generating buy-in to the process. But if you're relying on the parties to create the topics, how can you expect them to keep the list civil? The truth is, you may not be able to. What you can do, though, is reframe their language to make it more palatable.

Although every facilitated conversation is different depending on the participants and their concerns, a few themes tend to surface when dealing with work issues. Having some sample language at the ready helps you frame topics in an objective, constructive manner. The following agenda topics are quite common:

- **Roles and responsibilities:** This topic can describe a number of situations in which employees see their job responsibilities differently. Put this phrase on the board if you need to discuss disagreements about job descriptions and areas of influence.

- **Respect:** Another common theme in workplace scenarios is the hard-to-define yet all-important concept of what respect means to employees. Although each party is likely to describe it differently, they get an opportunity to speak about how they wish to be respected and what it means to show respect to others.

- **Communication:** This agenda topic is a simple way to discuss differences in how employees speak to one another. Many workplace conflicts boil down to either a lack of communication or different approaches to communication.

- **Confidentiality:** Confidentiality is huge in mediation, so even if your employees don't bring it up, you should. This is a great topic that covers other employees' interest or curiosity in what's happening in the meeting or when to share details about the conflict.

Negotiating Possible Solutions

Negotiating any sort of resolution to conflict is tricky. You may think that because employees have shared their perspectives about the impact of the problem a few times, you won't have to address the impact again. But not so fast! Get ready to twist, turn, and adapt to whatever your employees need to assess their unique situation while they shift into the negotiation phase.

Encouraging communication

The part of a mediation meeting in which participants try to negotiate a solution is notoriously complex, largely because each and every conversation of this sort is different depending on the people involved, the issues tackled, and the conflict's intensity.

Up to this point, your meeting has been clear and sequential, with some identifiable benchmarks and goals. Now, however, you need to be flexible and adapt to wherever your employees take you while keeping in mind some overarching guidelines that focus and organize the conversation. Get the parties to talk, talk, and talk some more, but direct their conversation and guide them to stay positive, think creatively, and move beyond their immediate problems. Talking in circles never gets anyone anywhere. This section helps you steer the conversation in the right direction.

Transitioning from past to future

When asked earlier to share their points of view, your employees probably spent a lot of time talking about the past. That makes sense, after all, because the problems they've experienced have already happened. They likely focused their attention on each other's actions that caused harm. They may have even given you a litany of dates, times, and specific moments when the conflict escalated or became especially troublesome.

But now it's time for them to begin moving forward. Make a statement about moving out of the past and into the present so you can set the stage for dialogue about solutions rather than problems. If you encourage them to speak to what they'd like to see in the future, or how they believe the issues can be solved, they're much more likely to find solutions than dwell on past difficulties.

To get employees to talk about the future, use the agenda they created as a visual tool by standing next to it or pointing to it. Then say something like, "Thank you for sharing your perspective on what's happened so far. What we're going to do now is take what we know about the past and apply it to the future. Looking at the list you've created, I'd like the two of you to choose a topic together and decide where you'd like to begin your conversation. Stay focused on what you'd like to see, and try not to rehash what's already taken place."

Motivating and encouraging your employees

Conversations about conflicts are hard work. Creating a dialogue in the midst of problems takes courage and energy, so validate and praise your employees for their efforts and find ways to acknowledge the good work they accomplish. In other words, encourage the behavior you want to see more than discourage the behavior you don't want to see.

Look for areas of common ground between your employees. Even if the two seem miles apart on everything, they still have one or two things in common — both are likely frustrated with the situation, and both are anxious to get some solutions on the table. You could note that each has a stake and a responsibility in creating a stable and comfortable workplace. And anytime that you detect values they have in common — like respect or autonomy — point them out. Allow them to talk about how they define those values differently and what actions need to be taken for those values to be fulfilled.

Book IV

Communicating with Employees

Don't treat this conversation as some sort of disciplinary action. Instead, emphasize that this discussion is an opportunity to create what they want their ongoing relationship to look like. Encourage them to see the conversation as a turning point in their interaction with each other rather than as a trial for you to judge who makes the better case.

Listening and interjecting

The negotiation process is about your employees working together to create their own answer to the conflict. If you consistently jump in with your insights and observations, you're apt to get in the way, so do more listening than speaking. And when you do interject, use these strategies:

- **Ask questions.** The majority of the speaking you do should come in the form of good questions. Focus on encouraging your employees to negotiate together rather than on drawing their attention to you. Think of yourself as a conversation starter, not an investigator.

- **Clarify and summarize.** Listen for any language that threatens to derail the process such as blaming, antagonizing, pushing hot buttons, or name-calling. Be aware, however, that because of the emotional state your employees are in, they may be more apt to misinterpret or misunderstand what the other person says. This is where your summarizing skills become so important. If you hear your employees struggling with language, summarize what you've heard with more neutral language and help them clarify their intent.

- **Capture proposals.** When you hear proposed solutions from either party, summarize the important points and frame them in language that's easy for the other party to digest. Ask the other party what she likes or doesn't like about the proposal, whether she accepts it as is, or if she'd like to make a counter proposal.

Focusing on values rather than issues

During the course of the meeting, you're likely to hear a lot from both people that describes how the conflict should be resolved. The language will likely come in the form of a position they've taken, also known as their *issues*.

It's important for you to hear and understand the issues because they give you a sense of the nature of the conflict. However, it's more crucial to understand *why* those issues are of importance to your employees. As such, you need to focus more on discovering their *values* — the things that drive them to act the way they do and make the decisions they choose.

Employees often come to a mediation meeting with a win-lose approach in mind, arguing about the merits of each other's position. By focusing the conversation on values, you can help them find common interests — or at least those that aren't in conflict — and develop a collaborative approach to negotiating.

Both your employees may feel, for instance, that they need to improve their communication, or that being a professional is important, even though they describe each of those values differently. At the very least, by encouraging them to concentrate on common values, you move them away from speaking about what they *don't like* and nudge them toward talking about what they *would like.*

Understanding and validating your employees' values help you identify and articulate appropriate responses to emotional outbursts. Acknowledging these values is the best intervention strategy in many conflict resolutions. Uncovering values takes a little work. The key is to listen for what lies beneath the statements your employees make. Tune your ear to strip away the things you hear them saying, and listen instead for what drives their positions.

Fostering brainstorming

Problem solving begins with brainstorming, and good brainstorming draws on the best that each of the employees has to offer. Still, you need to do a significant amount of coaching during the brainstorming process. Motivate your employees to think creatively about problem solving, let them know that this is their process, and remind them that there's no one right way to solve difficulties. The following sections give you some brainstorming guidelines and help you evaluate the results of your efforts.

The best brainstorming occurs without limits to creativity but focuses on one area at a time. Suggest a few ground rules, such as the following:

- ✔ **Use the agenda.** The agenda isn't just for show. Ask them to choose a topic from the list and focus their conversation on that point until they're ready to move on. This technique helps prevent them from jumping around from topic to topic.

- ✔ **Remember that any idea is a good idea.** Brainstorming is about articulating any and all possibilities before deciding on anything.

- ✔ **Follow time limits.** Some of the best ideas come when people are pressed for time. Keep the brainstorming short, and then spend quality time refining the ideas.

- ✔ **Say, then weigh.** Generate as many ideas as possible before weighing and evaluating a single one. Don't let the brainstorming process derail by getting bogged down in the details.

> ✔ **Create a parking lot.** If one of the parties has an idea for a different agenda item, quickly jot it down next to that topic — park it — until you're ready to move to that point. Similarly, if the employees think of something they need to check out or want to add another topic for discussion, into the parking lot it goes.

Because brainstorming favors extraverts, if you notice that an employee isn't participating, try asking both parties to write responses on paper instead of sharing aloud.

After the employees generate a number of ideas, start making some decisions. Help them establish evaluation criteria for their proposals, and determine how best to choose agreements that meet both of their needs. Such criteria are typically related to common values, or expectations and guidelines set forth by your workplace.

Ask questions that address the benefits and limitations of each proposed solution. Specifically:

> ✔ What do each of you like about this proposal? What don't you like about it?
>
> ✔ How might the idea be improved?
>
> ✔ Does it meet the needs you both stated as being important? If not, what can be changed for it to do so?

Asking great questions

Good questions are the primary tools of a skilled mediator. Throughout the negotiation part of the meeting and in any private meetings you have, good questions are an important way of encouraging your employees to find their own answers. Asking questions enables you to gather information, expand your employees' perspectives, generate options, and orient your process to the future. Additionally, good questions help you reinforce that this conversation is a dialogue, not a monologue (no lengthy speeches!).

Different types of questions accomplish different tasks. The trick is knowing which questions to ask and what kind of response each type generates:

> ✔ **Closed-ended questions** require a specific and direct answer to a specific and direct question. The answer is often implied by the question itself. You may think of closed-ended questions as those that elicit only a yes or no answer. Here's an example of a closed-ended question you would frame after hearing a few proposals: "If your options are to continue working on this program with William or begin a new program from scratch, which option best meets your needs and the needs of the company?"

Use these questions to clarify a situation with employees in order to develop a common understanding, or to call attention to a situation that you believe needs some action or further steps. For example: "Is this the kind of communication the two of you typically use together? Is it working for you? Would you be willing to try something different?"

✔ **Open-ended questions** are designed to widen your discussion and invite your employees to participate in a dialogue. For example: "What possibilities do you see? What solutions can you imagine that would work for both of you?"

These questions don't presume any answers. They open doors and expand the conversation in ways that you never expect because they invite listeners to provide more information and expand their thoughts. For instance, "How is this impacting you? How could you get that information? What else might work?"

Working through resistance

Employees may be resistant to your mediation skills and strategies regardless of how hard you work to keep an open, safe, and respectful environment. This is pretty normal. You'll likely experience resistance in a number of forms, and that's okay. In fact, to some extent, you should expect it.

No magic formula exists for moving through resistance. Every one of your employees is unique and carries his own experiences, personality, and core values. And because each person comes to this conversation with different needs, each one will likely respond differently to different techniques.

Your goal is not to bully your employees into working through resistance. As satisfying as it may initially be to headbutt your way through an impasse, that approach rarely gives you anything but a migraine. You have a lot of power in your role, and if you use it to force your employees to find a solution, they may not arrive at an appropriate or sustainable answer.

Book IV

Communicating with Employees

Identifying common causes of resistance

Before you address how (or whether) you want to work through resistance, have a sense of where it's coming from. Take a look at some of the common causes of resistance to discussions:

✔ **Strong emotion:** The parties involved are either stuck in the past, reacting to each other's actions or language, or unable to hear what each other is saying. Strong emotions tend to limit people's ability to think critically and can hamper progress.

- ✔ **Distrust:** Your employees may not trust each other to keep the conversation civil and on track, or they may not trust your process. This can be because of their work history, their relationship, bad experiences, or even threats, both real and perceived. They may not trust you, either, as a neutral facilitator. Don't take it personally — do your best to prove them wrong.

- ✔ **Failure to communicate/listen:** Lack of communication may happen because employees simply have different communication styles, or it may happen because they choose hostile or unproductive language. An employee may use specific body language to indicate that she can't (or won't) listen to what the other has to say, such as turning her back while the other is speaking, crossing her arms and refusing to make eye contact, or even putting her hands over her ears (yes, that has actually happened!).

- ✔ **Failure to see options:** An employee may come to the meeting with only one idea in mind, and it usually involves never having to see or work with the other person again. Mediation meetings work best when a plethora of ideas are on the table; a narrow view of solutions certainly slows down the progress.

- ✔ **Overconfidence/moral high ground:** If an employee believes, justly or not, that he's in the right and that he has been wronged, he may be overconfident in his position. He may think his position is stronger than it is because others in the workplace may have sided with him. You'll often hear an employee in this state of mind say that he "just wants to do what's right for the company." Parties who take this stance are reluctant to negotiate because they believe their power comes from being justified in their position.

- ✔ **Negative association:** Essentially, an employee may choose not to negotiate or accept offers simply because it's the other person who proposed the solution. A suggestion or offer that would be perfectly reasonable if proffered by anyone else is regarded as not good enough, based entirely on the messenger.

With all the things that can cause folks not to want to negotiate, you may be thinking, how on earth do people ever get past this part? It takes some work and some attention, but you can do a number of things when you reach an impasse. Read on for those ideas.

Exploring the impasse

To help your employees see the conflict that brought them to the table with a new set of eyes, start by asking each of them to describe the stalemate. They may find that they're stuck for very different reasons, and they may discover some workarounds for the areas where they can find commonality.

You may want to ask them to describe each other's position or concerns, which helps them see beyond their own view. Do this carefully, however, as you don't want them to mischaracterize the other's position or downplay the significance of the other's view.

Creating options

If your employees are stuck repeatedly talking about the details of the problems they face, encourage them to focus on potential solutions instead. This step seems like a no-brainer, doesn't it? But don't be surprised when the conversation turns into a rehashing of all the difficulties.

Help them brainstorm answers rather than dwell on problems. You can accomplish this by turning their attention away from the past and focusing instead on the future. Your questions should be future-focused, opening conversations around what *could be* rather than what *has been*. Ask things like:

- ✔ If the issues were solved today and it's three weeks down the road, can you describe how you see the project being completed?

- ✔ What new possibilities might come from working this out?

- ✔ How would each of you like to see the schedule assigned for the next month?

Encourage both people to attempt a form of detached brainstorming. In other words, get them thinking about what *others* might do in a similar situation, rather than what *they* are doing. This kind of brainstorming isn't limited by what they think they know about each other, so it's easier for them to respond. Ask the parties to share any ideas they'd give Joe in accounting if he were to describe this conflict to them. Or, when one says "I don't know" in response to questions about possible solutions, ask, "Well, if you did know, what would you say?" Works like a charm.

Testing the margins

Create clarity around the boundaries of the situation by asking the parties to give some thought to their other options. Ask if they've considered what happens next if they're unable to reach an agreement. Are they comfortable moving forward without a solution? Your questions should help your employees consider the impact and the implications of not moving forward. Similarly, encourage both parties to describe the best and worst solutions that *could* come out of their meeting. Perhaps they'll be able to find some daylight between the ideal and not-so-ideal agreements.

After they give descriptions of the best and worst outcomes, discuss what they see as the best and worst results of ending the meeting without agreements in

Book IV

Communicating with Employees

place. If they're unable to come up with a solution during the meeting and they choose to walk away, what's next for them? You may know the answer to that question already, but ask it anyway.

Refocusing on values

Mediations rely heavily on dialogue that's centered on the employees' core values and the positions they've taken. Your employees have likely gotten off track, or maybe they're having a difficult time articulating the points that are so important to them. Help by really focusing the conversation on the critical elements.

Ask them to describe what values their proposals address. Ask questions such as these:

- ✔ What does each of your proposals give you? How do they each meet your own needs? How do they meet the other person's needs?
- ✔ How do your proposals satisfy the values that each of you has identified as important?

If you've gone through this exercise and still find that they're struggling, ask them to mentally step away from the negotiation and to describe the qualities of a good agreement instead. Whatever their answers, ask if any of the ideas they've thrown out so far match the good agreement criteria. If the answer is no, encourage them to create new proposals that include the qualities that each of them just described.

Don't be afraid to address negative behavior. If it's affecting your conversation, it won't likely go away without assistance. And if you've noticed it, you can bet big money that the other party has noticed it as well.

Trying one last time to overcome resistance

A time may come when you realize that, no matter how hard you've tried, your employees are unable to resolve their problems with you as the facilitator. When this happens, your participants probably already know it and are prepared to move on to the next step, whatever that may be. But you may not be finished just yet. Many mediations find solutions and closure in the last few moments. Your employees may attempt to make a last-ditch effort to solve the problem if they know you've reached the end of your line. So as you're wrapping up, ask whether they have any last (or even best) offers before you end the discussion. This question gives them an opportunity to share any last-minute goodies they may have been holding onto, and it can be exactly what you need to finally get the breakthrough you've been looking for.

If, after you ask for any additional thoughts or offers, you hear crickets or stone-cold silence, it's okay to adjourn, regroup, and try something else.

Developing Solutions and Agreements

As your employees' proposals begin to turn into agreements, you may be tempted to think that it's all downhill from here. The truth is, even though you've spent a good amount of time and energy facilitating this conversation, and even though you and your employees are probably pretty exhausted because of the energy it takes to have this kind of meeting, you still have some work to do.

Recognizing the nonnegotiable elements of a good settlement

If you hear any proposed agreements, be sure to probe, prod, and tweak them to make sure they're the best they can be. Good, solid agreements that satisfy everyone's needs and hold up over time don't just fall out of the sky. They have specific qualities that are important for you to look for in each of the proposals you discuss. Think of this part of the mediated meeting as a litmus test to identify these particular attributes. If one of the following elements is missing, you increase the chances of the agreement falling apart and adding to the frustration of those involved. Give these elements proper consideration, and you'll send the parties away with the greatest chance for success.

Doable

Agreements have to actually fit with reality. This attribute may sound obvious, but it's surprising how quickly unrealistic agreements can become part of a plan that sounds good on the surface but inevitably falls apart. When your employees begin to make agreements on the heels of a lengthy or difficult conflict, a lot of good energy can be generated. This is a good thing, and you want to tap into that energy, but don't be surprised when employees begin to agree to things that aren't doable because the two are on a roll or they're ready to agree to anything. Agreeing to something because it feels right in the moment can cause additional problems.

Support the parties wherever you can, but don't set them up for failure by allowing a creative solution you know won't fly with the rest of the company.

Specific

Clearly outline what each employee is agreeing to do. Additionally, ensure that agreements describe the steps that each person will take in order to accomplish tasks, in a way that leaves no ambiguity as to the expectations each has of the other.

Imagine two employees who decide that the best way to make sure that all the tasks assigned to them are getting fulfilled is to meet once a month for half an hour to discuss the workload. You can write it like this: "Matt and Kate agree to meet once a month to discuss the workload."

At the moment, Matt and Kate may think they have the exact same understanding of this meeting. But do they know when they're meeting? Are there certain days or times that are better or worse for the discussion? For how long will they meet? And where will this meeting take place? How will they be sure that what needs to be discussed will get addressed? A better agreement looks more like this:

> Matt and Kate agree to meet at 10:30 a.m. on the first Wednesday of every month, beginning next month, for a half-hour discussion in Conference Room A. This conversation will focus on making sure all the goals assigned to the training team are being met. Kate will bring a copy of the team's goal statement and a calendar to make a note of project deadlines. Matt will use the information to update the online team calendar by close of business that same day.

Durable

Although some agreements may be intended to be only short term or even one-time actions, agreements relating to ongoing relationships, processes, and procedures should have a reasonably long shelf life.

Give both people permission to "be real" about what they can commit to, and ask them not to sign up for anything they feel they won't be able to sustain. Ask them to consider personal commitments, calendar commitments (like holidays), unpredictable factors (like traffic), and any possible organizational changes in the works.

Of course, you can't predict every unforeseen situation or event that could derail an agreement, but the more questions you ask — and have them answer — the more durable the agreement becomes. Give your staff permission to rework the agreement if it warrants a change down the road, and ask them to add language about any "what ifs" they can foresee.

Balanced

Balanced agreements are not necessarily ones in which employees split their resources 50/50 or agree to do exactly half the work on a project they're assigned. Instead, balanced agreements show that both parties are willing to give something and receive something.

Even where one of your employees has decided to take the lion's share of the responsibility for resolving the problems at hand, look for ways to include the other employee in the process. Doing so can be as simple as one employee agreeing to do a task and the other employee agreeing to acknowledge him for it.

Balance in agreements goes hand in hand with the quality of durability (see the preceding section). This fact becomes evident after you've reached a settlement and your parties have moved into implementing their agreements. If one employee looks back over the agreement down the road and feels as if there was imbalance in the outcome, she may be less likely to honor her end of the arrangement, or she may even revisit the conflict anew.

Complete

Has everything of importance to the conflict been addressed by the agreements? If something was important to either party, address it in the agreement — even if the arrangement is to discuss it at a later date. Cover all the agenda items. If it's on the agenda, make sure that you've addressed the issue in some way — either by documenting a solution or by coming to some verbal agreement regarding how the parties intend to deal with it. If you don't make it through the list, note in the agreement that the parties didn't have a chance to discuss the item or were unable to come to agreement on it. This item will be a good starting point for any follow-up meetings.

Dot the *i*'s and cross the *t*'s. If either party starts to resist pinning down exact details, coach him by letting him know they'll both have a better chance at success if they take care of these details with you as a facilitator instead of walking away with a new misunderstanding to an old conflict.

Satisfying

Often, in the midst of conflict, employees express a concern that their agreements be fair. We encourage you instead to support the idea that agreements be satisfying.

Look back on the rest of the meeting and note any values or interests that an employee shared with you, and ask him if the agreement meets those values. For example, if Curtis talked about his need for autonomy, and the agreement doesn't mention anything that delivers autonomy to him on some level, it isn't satisfying.

Troubleshooting problem areas

A number of factors can contribute to problems when you're facilitating the solution/agreement portion of your mediation. Be aware of these factors and pay attention to how they can affect the overall quality of your process.

Vague language

Although using open-ended language is a good idea, when it's time to write up agreements, be as clear and specific as you can. Avoid language that can be interpreted differently by the parties. Instead, be specific. Use language that almost feels like it's bordering on nitpicking, such as the following:

- ✔ By (date and time)
- ✔ No later than
- ✔ Completed on
- ✔ Via company e-mail

Settlement by attrition

Sometimes parties can begin to make agreements that they don't necessarily intend to live up to. They may feel as if their important issues haven't been addressed or that they lack the power or the authority to effect a change. Don't let this happen!

When you hear language like "I don't care — write down whatever you want" or "Let's just get it over with so we can move on," pay attention. Your employee is telling you something. Explore what's happening for him when you hear this kind of language.

No settlement is better than a *bad* settlement. If a settlement is going to fall apart, better that it happen in the meeting where you can address the situation than after the employees have left and returned to the workplace. Bad agreements can undermine trust in the process and adversely affect your employees.

Fatigue

Fatigue can greatly complicate a settlement. If employees are tired or worn down, they may be more likely to settle for an agreement that's incomplete or unrealistic, which places the likelihood of lasting satisfaction in jeopardy. Watch for signs that the participants are settling because they're exhausted and just want the process to come to an end. Don't let impatience move you too quickly through this part of the process. Take a break if necessary, but do make sure to take the time required to craft your agreements thoroughly.

You always have the option to schedule another meeting, so there's no need to continue this one if the energy level is so low that productivity has waned.

Uncooperative behavior

You're thinking that you're an amazing mediator because you've been able to guide your employees through a tough conversation that resulted in a list of agreements. Suddenly, one of your employees says she doesn't like the arrangements and starts talking in circles again. What just happened? Probably one of these issues:

- ✔ **The employee never intended to come to agreement.** It's not unusual for an employee to come to a mediated meeting because she thinks she has to "for the record." She went through the motions and did what she suspected you wanted her to do but didn't really negotiate in good faith. Try calling a private meeting to discuss the situation with her frankly and honestly. Create an atmosphere in which she feels comfortable telling you the truth.

- ✔ **The employee's needs haven't been met.** In one way or another, the agreement isn't meeting an employee's needs or delivering what's most important to him. Hear him out a bit more, ask open-ended questions, and see whether you can help identify what's missing or has yet to be discussed.

- ✔ **Another plan is in play.** Sometimes, one of the people you're meeting with has something else in the works and isn't ready to spill the beans just yet. Maybe she's leaving the company, looking for a transfer to another department, or seeking the advice of a third party. You may not be able to find out what's going on, but calling a private meeting for a candid conversation could help.

- ✔ **The employee just isn't ready.** Your employees will process conflict at different rates. Often, one of the employees isn't ready to let go of a grudge or doesn't yet trust that the future could be any different from the past. That's okay. Do what you can to let him talk, share his perspective with you, and identify the issues. Consider arranging another meeting after he's had time to process a bit more.

Incomplete contingency plans

Your employees may have the best of intentions and may have created a solid and complete agreement that they fully intend to live up to. However, even the best plans can fall apart if you don't address the "what if" questions. Pay attention to all the possible areas that may cause an agreement to become invalid or would cause it to be renegotiated.

Look for any assumptions or expectations on which your employees are resting their agreements, and test what may happen if those assumptions are incorrect. Having a backup plan may seem redundant, and they may think it's overkill, but it benefits them greatly if and when things don't go according to plan.

One of the most common "what ifs" that affects the success of agreements is the inclusion of third parties. If the person isn't in the room, he probably shouldn't be in the agreement. Agreements that are based on the actions of someone who hasn't had a chance to speak for himself often fall apart when that person is unwilling or unable to deliver on the agreement. Include language that takes the situation into account and makes room for adjustments.

Book IV

Communicating with Employees

Writing it down

Clearly spell out all the agreements in written form — not only to help your employees know that you expect them to honor the agreements they've made, but also to memorialize all the hard work they've done in the session. When writing the agreements, keep the following things in mind:

- ✔ **Use plain language.** Avoid using unnecessarily complex or legalistic-sounding jargon. Complex language only complicates your document and contributes to misunderstandings about content and context.

- ✔ **Address who, what, when, where, and how.** Make sure that your employees can identify all the details for each of the points of their agreements. Specifically, consider who will be undertaking actions. What actions will they be performing? When and where will they be performed? How will the actions take place?

- ✔ **Remember confidentiality.** The intent of mediation is for everything that happens in the room to stay in the room. If others in the workplace know that the mediation is occurring, they may approach you or your participants for information. Encourage your participants to come up with a strategy for handling those requests, and consider including that strategy in the agreement. It may mean agreeing to simple, stock language like, "Everything went well and we're happy with the outcome." Encourage your employees to keep the mediation confidential and not discuss any specifics with coworkers or associates.

Sometimes after covering everything on the agenda, no specific agreements need to be documented. That doesn't mean, however, that you should simply send your employees out the door with a pat on the back. You may still want to make sure that your employees are on the same page and have come to some understanding about their situation.

Typically, such agreements are formulated when your employees have had a conversation about something intangible, have cleared up a misunderstanding, or have a new way of approaching their work relationship. As long as you feel no details need to be captured to keep them on track, create a brief summary that they can take with them to remind them of their accomplishments.

Concluding the Meeting with Optimism

Congratulations! You've reached the end of your meeting. Your employees' relationship with one another has been transformed, and they're in awe of your mediation prowess. Now they can return to work with a new sense of purpose and an all but inexhaustible source of energy and enthusiasm. All is once again right with the world.

Sounds wonderful, doesn't it? It would be nice if all mediations ended on such a triumphant note. And in fact, sometimes they do! You can have a profound impact on your employees and workplace if you give your employees a chance to talk through their difficulties, provide an open atmosphere that encourages dialogue, and are interested in the continued stability and comfort of the work environment.

Not every mediated conversation ends with such pomp and revelry. This section helps you come up with a plan for dealing with all the possible outcomes.

Settlement

When things go smoothly, celebrate! And put your employees' efforts at the forefront. Let them know that you

- ✔ Appreciate their hard work
- ✔ Applaud their efforts
- ✔ Hope that their agreements will yield a stronger work dynamic for themselves and those they interact with on a daily basis

These conversations can dramatically change relationships. And when one relationship in your workplace changes for the better, it has the ability to radiate to the rest of the group.

Even when settlement doesn't produce a ticker-tape parade of good feelings, at the very least it can provide closure and a sense of relief. Capitalize on whatever goodwill the settlements generate, and let your employees hear your appreciation. Wherever you can, offer your sincere praise of their work, and remind each person of the value and benefit in following through with his agreements. Tell both people that you want to assist them in following through with their agreements and that if you can do anything to help them be more successful, you're available. Knowing they have you as a support in their ongoing work can help normalize and stabilize their commitment to making this agreement work.

Interim agreements

Not all agreements are fully realized and ready to become full-blown written settlements. In fact, sometimes writing a full agreement may be premature and can become a potential problem down the road. This situation is where interim agreements shine. Interim agreements are temporary in nature, such as trying out a new communication model for a period of time or adopting a new policy in the workplace and testing to see its effects.

When you help employees construct such an agreement, both people should understand that it's for a specific amount of time. Be sure that they're clear about how long this agreement will last, how they'll know it's time to reevaluate, and when they'll address the outcomes of the interim agreement.

Taking one step at a time with agreements is not a negative reflection of your abilities as a facilitator or manager. You want to set up your staff for success, so let them try things out for a while, discover what works and what doesn't work, and then retool the agreement. Let them know that it's better to have something that works for both parties than a promise neither of them can keep.

No settlement

No matter how hard they try, your employees may be unable to come to a solution. Impasse happens even when employees have the best of intentions and you're relying on a strong process and skill set. Your employees (and even you) may leave frustrated and disheartened.

As long as you've stuck to the process, asked good questions, and encouraged the coworkers to talk with one another, you've done all that you can. The process belongs to you, but the solution belongs to your employees. Yet it's frustrating to know that you've done everything in your power and still found a roadblock at the end of the trail.

As you bring your process to a close, try the following to help bring closure to the discussion:

- ✔ **End on a positive note.** Even though they may not have reached any agreements, look for anything that you can highlight as a positive outcome. Even something as simple as validating that each employee shared his perspective — and heard what the other had to say — can help them feel as if the meeting wasn't a waste.

- ✔ **Discuss next steps.** Clearly outline what their options are after they (or you) have decided that mediation isn't going to be a good solution for them. Helping your parties have a clear picture of other avenues for resolving this issue can help them leave with some sense of closure. This may be where you offer to bring in an outside mediator or talk about what other resources are available in the company. Feel free to ask them what they feel their next steps are. That question often brings out important details for both to consider and may bring them back to the table for another discussion.

- ✔ **Don't close the door.** While closing up shop, mention that this is not their one and only chance at a solution. Inform them that, although now may not be the best time for mediation, they're always welcome to return if they want to give it another shot. One of the employees may have a change of heart after he's had time to consider something that you or his coworker said in the meeting.

Book V
Managing Teams

Five Ways to Foster Accountability

- ✔ **Conduct status review meetings.** These meetings create positive peer-group pressure, keep you in the loop without having to micromanage, provide focus, and build accountability.

- ✔ **Report results outward and upward.** Monthly or quarterly, create a written progress review of your team's work that broadcasts your progress to people outside the team. Occasionally make presentations to management above you or to other groups that are interested in your team's work.

- ✔ **Conduct postmortems.** With your team, evaluate their performance after a project or special event has concluded. Learn lessons from the past and apply them to future performance.

- ✔ **Conduct a performance evaluation.** Guide your team in evaluating its overall performance at the end of a given cycle, generally at the end of a quarter or six-month period. The team evaluates results against established performance criteria that are selected in advance.

- ✔ **Use peer feedback.** For any team that's going to be together for an extended period, peer feedback is one of the stronger strategies for building accountability among individual team members.

As your team's leader, do you model accountability? Do your actions enhance or detract from your credibility? Find out by taking a quick team leadership inventory at www.dummies.com/extras/managingaio.

Contents at a Glance

Chapter 1

Putting Together a Strong Business Team

*E*veryone knows what a team is. You understood instantly as a school kid when you were chosen as captain and got to pick your team for the kickball game at recess. Maybe you also played soccer or were on the school basketball or baseball team.

Yes, you know what teams are — they're the heart and soul of sports. For many people, the whole idea of *team* is based on the sports model. More and more these days, you see another model of *team* that is associated with the way employees spend their time in the workplace. Many people work in some kind of team from 9 to 5; it's a growing trend in private- and public-sector organizations.

But when it comes to the workplace, you can throw away most of the sports analogies. For one thing, not everyone plays sports or is a fan. More to the point, asking people to work in teams isn't the same as choosing sides for kickball. The goals of work teams are usually more expansive than merely beating an opponent.

The sports analogy, in fact, breaks down very early when you transport it to the business scene. Think about it: In professional sports like the NFL or NBA, potential team members must compete against one another to make the team or win a starting position. And though they wear the same jerseys and cooperate on plays, the pros have to show in every game that they're worthy to remain on the team. That's competition.

Asking people to compete against other members of the same team in the workplace destroys the team concept. For a business team to succeed, team members must cooperate, and that's no easy feat to achieve. If you're going to succeed as a manager of a team, you need to understand first what a business team is all about. That's what this chapter does — it lays the foundation, defining common types of teams in business organizations and explaining why businesses are using teams more and more to get work done.

Giving "Team" a Business Meaning

The word *team* has a positive connotation and gets thrown around a lot in workplaces, usually with good intentions. But just because people have a good time at lunch or get along well at work doesn't make them a team, not even if some manager or executive calls them one.

For the purposes of this book, a *team* is a group of people organized to work together to accomplish a common purpose for which they share accountability. As you can see in this definition, three essential factors define a team:

- ✔ **Putting people together to do work:** The left hand and right hand are meant to work together. (For soccer fans, it can be the left foot and right foot — but enough sports references.)

- ✔ **Having an overall common purpose:** Team members all work to achieve the same end result.

- ✔ **Being mutually accountable:** Each team member is equally responsible with every other member for accomplishing the team's mission.

What distinguishes a team from another kind of work group is the way its members are organized to capitalize on the interdependence that exists among them when they're at work. In simple terms, they need to work together to get something done.

Sometimes you can see a bit of interdependence within a work group or even an entire department, yet the individual employees function in their specialized roles and focus on their own tasks and issues. Sorry, they aren't a team.

Telling the Difference between Work Groups and Teams

Teams definitely are forms of work groups, but not all work groups are teams. In fact, plain work groups are much more numerous than teams. Imagine that you are a contestant on a TV game show and the emcee is about to ask you the question that makes you rich forever (or for a few months, anyway). You're in the spotlight and the audience is hushed. Here's the question:

> Teams are a form of work group, but not all work groups are teams. What's the main difference between work groups that are teams and those that are not?

You think hard. You bite your lip. Your forehead glistens with sweat. Then you speak, slowly but with certainty: "Teams," you say, "have an interdependence among members . . . whereas other forms of work groups do not."

"That's right!" the emcee shouts as the audience thunders applause. When the house quiets down and you are chitchatting about your keen insights into team structure, you casually remark that work groups function on three levels:

- Dependent level
- Independent level
- Interdependent level

The TV host finds this so fascinating that he asks you to explain, and here's the gist of what you say.

Dependent-level work groups

Dependent-level work groups are the traditional work unit or department groups with a supervisor who plays a strong role as the boss. Almost everyone has had some experience with this work setup, especially in a first job.

Each person in a dependent-level work group has her own job and works under the close supervision of the boss. The boss is in charge and tells the employees the do's and don'ts in their jobs. Helping each other and covering for one another do not occur often and occur mostly under the direction of the supervisor. In fact, most problem-solving, work assignments, and other decisions affecting the group come from the supervisor.

A dependent-level work group can perform well in the short term. But for the long run, because group members operate separately and mostly at the direction of the supervisor, such work groups don't seem to go anywhere. Maintaining the status quo and keeping operations under control are what they do best. Creating improvements, increasing productivity, and leveraging resources to support one another are quite uncommon with dependent-level work groups.

Independent-level work groups

Independent-level work groups are the most common form of work groups on the business scene. As with a dependent-level work group, each person is responsible for his own main area. But unlike the dependent level, the supervisor or manager tends not to function like the controlling boss. Instead, staff members work on their own assignments with general direction and minimal supervision.

It's very common for sales representatives, research scientists, accountants, lawyers, police officers, librarians, and teachers to work like this, to name just a few examples. People in those occupations come together in one department because they serve a common overall function, but almost everyone in the group works fairly independently.

If members of an independent-level work group receive the managerial guidance and support they need on the job, such a work group can perform quite well.

Interdependent-level work groups

Members of an *interdependent-level* work group rely on each other to get the work done. Sometimes members have their own roles, and at other times they share responsibilities. In either case, they coordinate with one another to produce an overall product or set of outcomes. When this interdependence exists, you have a team. And by capitalizing on interdependence, the team demonstrates the truth of the old saying: The whole is greater than the sum of its parts.

An independent work group can often be brought up to speed faster than an interdependent group. It simply takes more time to get a group of individuals to work as a team than to set a group of individuals off on their independent assignments. Yet when teams move into a high-functioning and high-producing state where they capitalize on interdependence, they can outperform all other types of work groups. So if you want a quick fix, don't look to teams, but if you want to see strong results for the long term, do look to teams.

To call a group a *team* does not make them a team; wishing for them to function as a team doesn't work either. For a snapshot of the main differences between work groups and teams, take a look at Figure 1-1.

Differences between
Work Groups and Teams

Work Groups	Teams
• Individual accountability	• Individual and mutual accountability
• Come together to share information and perspectives	• Frequently come together for discussion, decision making, problem solving, planning
• Focus on individual goals	• Focus on team goals
• Produce individual work products	• Produce collective work products
• Define individual roles, responsibilities, tasks	• Define individual roles, responsibilities, tasks to help team do its work; often share and rotate them
• Concern with one's own outcomes and challenges	• Concern with outcomes of everyone and challenges the team faces
• Purpose, goals, approach to work shaped by manager	• Purpose, goals, approach to work shaped by team leader with team members

Figure 1-1:
Work
groups
versus
teams.

Illustration by Wiley, Composition Services Graphics

As you can see, work groups have a strong individual focus, and teams have a strong collective focus. The individual is not lost on a team, but that person's work is coordinated to fit in with the greater good. Team concerns are much more focused on the outcomes of the overall unit rather than an individual's accomplishments.

Figure 1-1 also indicates that teams meet more often than traditional work groups. Work groups may meet periodically, based on the manager's style, primarily to hear and share information. Teams, by comparison, do much more than communicate when they meet. Team meetings are forums for planning work, solving work problems, making decisions about work, and reviewing progress. In short, meetings are vital to a team's existence.

The last item in Figure 1-1 is crucial: Team leadership is participatory, in contrast to the primarily manager-driven nature of regular work groups. On a team, the manager or team leader frequently involves team members in helping shape the goals and plans for getting the group's work done. (May as well get them involved; they've got to do the work!) But in other kinds of work groups, managers more commonly work with staff individually to set goals and determine assignments. Of course, in many cases, managers just assign work with little discussion or collaboration with the staff members. The staff members are then left to figure out what's expected and how best to get it done.

How Teams Help Managers to Manage

More than just a fad or a nice word to throw around, real functioning *teams* are becoming a common way to get work done. That hasn't happened by accident. The turn-of-the-century idea (1900, that is — not 2000) that workers are little cogs inside big industrial wheels has been turned inside out. Now you see the "cogs" repositioned in team arrangements that vastly increase their influence and speed of action.

The increasing use of teams in private- and public-sector organizations has been done to adapt to a number of specific changes in the business climate, mainly the following:

✔ **Dealing with competitive pressures:** Your company may produce the world's best mousetrap today. But tomorrow, your competitor may roll out an even better trap — along with an A-plus customer service group. What's the team response when that happens? In a nutshell, it's the old proverb, updated: Two or more heads are better than one. When mousetrap makers need to think fast to answer a competitive threat, they understand that combining the talents of all their trap engineers just may get the job done faster than having members of your brain trust work separately, no matter how smart they are.

✔ **Responding to technological advances:** Advances in technology often change the way work gets done. Computer-driven manufacturing systems, for example, can reduce or totally eliminate the need for an individual to directly perform a piece of work. When that happens, the workplace needs more multi-specialists and fewer individual specialists. Teams are the natural gathering place of such multitalented generalists.

✔ **Meeting customer expectations:** Customers have high expectations and little tolerance for any delay. If your service is slow or sloppy, customers can take their business someplace else. If you say, "I'm sorry, the person who handles your problem is on vacation for two weeks," you're going to lose that customer. Teamwork is the natural way for colleagues to share responsibility for accomplishing Job One: serving customer needs.

✔ **Doing more with less:** This phrase has been the battle cry of management for quite some time: "Got to hold the line on costs. Can't just hire willy-nilly whenever the volume of work spikes up. Times are tough, so do more with less!" To get more work done without increasing the payroll, companies are asking employees to share responsibilities — fewer Lone Rangers, more teams. The logic is neat: Four people working together can provide more coverage and get more done than four people working independently.

✔ **Tackling complex problems:** Some of the thorniest problems are primarily internal, like improving the quality of an organization's products or services. Multidisciplinary task teams can do crucial work at times like these. Instead of each department dealing with a community problem from its own perspective, you can find a total, integrated solution faster by bringing staff together from all the departments that are affected.

✔ **Matching the pace of change:** In many companies the only constant is change — if you don't keep up with it, you'd better get out of the way! When they need to spark creative ideas and move people together quickly to keep up with the changing needs, more and more companies look to their teams for answers.

✔ **Turnover-proofing the company:** With staff turnover more common than ever before, even in some public-sector organizations, managers are chagrined when they flunk the *truck test:* "If one of your staff got hit by a truck tomorrow, can others in your group step in and do the job with minimal disruption in productivity?" Teams can fill the gaps because they are composed of people who — by team design — share responsibilities.

If you're like a lot of managers, when you hear that something works well for someone else, you want to try it yourself. Or if you have experienced success elsewhere, you may want to re-create it when you arrive someplace new. As teams grow in use, some experience significant success — greater productivity than any other form of work group. And as word of this success spreads, so have managers' and executives' initiatives to give teams a try.

Introducing the Most Common Types of Teams

Practically all teams can be classified as one of five types, which you see in the list below. Because of their objective, some teams work together indefinitely. Others have a short-term mission, and when their work is done the team disbands. It's common in many organizations for people to have job duties in a regular, old-fashioned work group that isn't a team, yet spend at least some time working in a genuine team setting to reach a short-term objective.

Here are the five most common types of teams that you find in organizations:

- **Work-unit teams:** They are the most common and usually are ongoing. Work-unit teams are part of departments and have skills related to the department or work group's main function. Think of the customer service team, the accounting team, or the technical support team, for example. A work-unit team may not always have *team* in its name, but you can tell by the way team members work together and share accountability for an overall outcome that they are a classic team.

- **Project teams:** This type of team often is *cross-functional,* meaning it brings together a few special talents — or quite a few, if necessary — to accomplish a project. Everyone has a role, and everyone needs to work with everyone else to reach the right outcome. Often time-limited, project teams can disband when they complete their assignments. But in some technical fields, like engineering, the nature of the work is one project after another; people spend whole careers in team assignments, moving to a new project when they finish the last.

- **Task teams:** Sometimes referred to as *task forces* (or even *committees*), task teams usually are time-limited and cross-functional. Team members have skills related to the task; they are brought together to study challenging issues or critical problems facing the organization or overall department and to recommend action. Task teams are growing in use in many organizations. Sometimes task teams implement their own recommendations, and sometimes they are kept on call to respond to whatever arises — kind of like a volunteer fire department. Some task teams operate over long periods with members rotating in and out; the membership changes, but the work of the team lives on.

- **Improvement teams:** As you can guess by the name, improvement teams work to make things better — usually work-related processes. For example, in municipal government organizations, improvement teams may streamline the registration processes for recreation programs and the application processes for obtaining building permits. *Quality circles* are a type of improvement team and became widely known as part of the total quality management movement in Japan and the United States. But you don't see them called by that name as much as you did a couple decades ago.

- ✔ **Management teams:** You can find so-called "management teams" all over the place, but seldom do you find one that functions like a real team. It's easy for a company to say it has a management team, but aside from coming together periodically, the members may seldom do any collective work in running the enterprise. Each manager has his or her primary area of responsibility and does little beyond that for the greater good. Yet there are some authentic management teams with leaders who involve the rest of the management group in working on issues and taking on responsibilities together for the greater organization.

Looking Before You Leap: Factors to Consider in Adopting Teams

Teams are a way to organize people to get work done, but they are not a cure-all. Just because you create a team doesn't guarantee you're going to see any benefits from it. Another person's success with teams does not mean you'll have the same experience.

On the other hand, if you see opportunities to capitalize on the interdependence of employees, creating teams may be just right for you. Before you announce, "Everyone, we're now a team!" take time to think and plan so that you can lead the transition into teams in an organized and purposeful fashion. (Don't worry, your employees will overcome the shock of seeing you look organized and leading with a purpose. Their shock may even turn into joy!)

This section provides you a list of factors to consider before moving into teams — factors to examine at the organizational level, the manager level, and the team member level. Generally, the higher you are in the organization, the more factors you need to consider and plan for to make the transition to teams successful.

Factors to consider at the organizational level

The first set of factors to consider are the so-called big picture items — organizational concerns that often reach beyond teams themselves, such as the following:

- ✔ The performance challenges your business faces
- ✔ The best structure for meeting those performance challenges — regular work groups or teams — and why
- ✔ If you go with teams, the types that are best
- ✔ Skill sets needed to perform the work, on both the team member and team leader level
- ✔ Other possible roles that may need to be filled, such as sponsor and management steering team, to help make teams happen and support their ongoing development
- ✔ The experience of teams elsewhere in the organization and the lessons you can learn from them
- ✔ Processes, practices, rewards, information systems, and related elements that need to be enhanced or put in place for teams to work
- ✔ The boundaries and level of authority that teams will have
- ✔ Resources that need to be invested, from people to money, to implement and develop teams
- ✔ The approach that will work best to start into teams — pilot program, transitional phase-in, or total immersion

The final item listed above focuses on how you begin. Sometimes, especially when fewer teams are involved, *total immersion* can work fine. This means that everyone who has anything to do with a team begins learning and working as a team right away — ready, set, go!

Sometimes you may want to take the *pilot program* approach: reconfigure one work group as a team and try them out for a while. Once they get rolling, then you form other teams.

If your objective is to create a number of teams, a *transitional phased-in* approach may be best. This means you start with a few teams and give them some time and support to get working, then add a few more, and so on from there. It's the old row-row-row-your-boat approach — move ahead in stages over time.

Factors to consider at the manager level

This next set of factors focuses on you as the manager responsible for leading one or more teams. You need to be concerned about the following:

- ✔ Understanding the purpose and overall goals of the team
- ✔ Providing guidance and direction as the team develops, and acquiring the skills you need to become effective as a coach and facilitator

- ✔ Acquiring the resources you need to train team members — and the tools they need to succeed

- ✔ Identifying the outside relationships your team needs to cultivate

- ✔ Identifying the obstacles your team must address

- ✔ Assessing your own willingness to share authority and decision making with the team

The last point above is one of the most crucial for a manager. If you are totally hands off in your leadership style, the team flounders. If you control everything, you stifle and demotivate the team. If you try to make every decision by consensus, it can lead to the analysis-by-paralysis syndrome, taking forever to decide anything.

Alternately, you can adopt a more participatory approach. You can share some level of responsibility and get your team members involved in helping shape the direction and operation of the team.

Factors to consider at the team member level

Team members are the lifeblood. Their performance and working relationships with one another make or break a team. So, from selecting the team members to developing them to work as a team, you want to consider these factors:

- ✔ The skills and talents, from technical to interpersonal, needed to perform the team's assignment

- ✔ The mix of members who potentially can work well together

- ✔ The development each team member needs to perform and fit well on the team

- ✔ The level of motivation you have to work with — or the degree of resistance you need to work through — among various team members

- ✔ The key roles required by the team and the individuals who can play them best

 You don't need to nail everything down before you launch a team. Don't let one or two free-floating concerns stop you in your tracks; some questions can be answered only as you move along. But do use the management factors above as your own personal team-management plan.

The Terrible Twenty: Why Teams Sometimes Struggle

Even when teams work hard, they sometimes founder and fail. Surveys of managers have revealed some common sources of issues — "The Terrible Twenty." You may recognize some of these problems:

- ✔ Team members shirking their responsibility, not pulling their weight
- ✔ Conflicts or personality clashes among team members
- ✔ Lack of cooperation among team members
- ✔ Cliques forming within a team
- ✔ Disruptive behavior by a team member that's left unaddressed
- ✔ Poor communication and withholding of information
- ✔ Disorganized team meetings that turn everybody off
- ✔ Little or no attention to the training and cross-training that a team needs to do its work
- ✔ Essential skill sets missing from a team
- ✔ Differing ideas among team members about what the team should focus on
- ✔ Apathy
- ✔ A dominating or controlling team leader
- ✔ A laissez faire or hands-off team leader
- ✔ Unclear team goals
- ✔ Unclear team purpose
- ✔ Constantly changing directions to the team from upper management
- ✔ Undefined roles of team members, sometimes leading to duplication of effort or tasks left undone
- ✔ Lack of resources — from tools to training
- ✔ Unrealistic expectations of the team by management outside the team
- ✔ Lack of cooperation or support from managers or others outside the team, throwing roadblocks in front of the team

As you look at this list of team problems, remember that any one can pop up unexpectedly, especially if your style of team management is merely to wave the magic wand and wish the members well. Sorting the problems by general type, you can see that they fit into three broad kinds of issues:

- ✔ **People issues,** brought about by things like poor interpersonal communication, poor leadership, and lack of cooperation

- ✔ **Structure issues,** stemming from missing skills or missing direction or poorly defined roles and goals

- ✔ **Support issues,** which can mean lack of training and essential team tools and lack of interest by management above the team — all factors that prevent teams from performing well

Concentrate on these three general issues as you develop and lead teams. Doing so is the hard work of managing teams.

Spotting — and Soothing — Resistance

Don't be alarmed when you see some employees resisting your teams program — they're only being human! They're also reflecting American culture, as this section shows. You may be surprised how much resistance is bred into people simply by their experience.

Cultural orientation — the rugged individualist

If you've grown up in the United States or been reared on U.S. cultural exports, you may be well conditioned as an *individualist,* someone who can stand on your own without team support. American literature romanticizes the rugged individualist: the cowboy, the sheriff, the wildcatter. TV and movies glamorize the solitary hero. In school, you're rewarded for individual achievements. You compete to get into a prestigious college and work hard for good grades and a degree. And that's only the beginning! You compete against others for the job you want and for career-advancement opportunities.

So, from an early age and well into your working career, you're prepared and even rewarded for taking care of yourself and competing for what you want.

And nothing is wrong with that! America is a great nation, in part, because of the wonderful achievements of many individuals. But you can see how this cultural orientation may make the transition into collective ventures — teams — hard for some people. Suddenly you have to change your focus. Rather than think only about your own needs, you need to think about the outcomes of an entire group of people, and working cooperatively becomes much more critical for success than functioning competitively.

Limited or poor experience with teams

For many people, their first significant experience working in teams occurs on the job, sometimes after years of working in other group situations that may look like teams but actually aren't or as members of genuine teams that struggled for one reason or another. (Or their prior experience may be limited to playing on a sports team, which is far different from a work team.) Other people may remember their team experiences in school; they worked on a project team in a class where they did most of the work and practically carried the team while others sat back and took equal credit. None of these experiences is motivating, especially when your livelihood is on the line.

Success as a solo

Some people are fiercely independent and enjoy working alone. That doesn't mean they don't like interacting with others, but what they like more is being responsible for their own work and seeing accomplishments from their own efforts. They like to do their own thing on the job and often are well trained to do so. They may work most of the time in independent work group situations, and when asked to double up by joining a task team or special project team, they may put less emphasis on the team. It isn't their main priority.

However, when the team becomes the biggest part of such individuals' job responsibilities, they may have the comfort level knocked right out from under them. The acts of coordinating work with others, problem-solving with others, and depending on others to do their parts of a job — all common features of team situations — render practically irrelevant the prized quality of working well on your own. No wonder some soloists have a hard time adjusting to teamwork!

Fear of change

Some people are happy with the status quo. They like their job situations and want nothing to change. For some, regardless of what the change is, fear and great discomfort set in as an initial reaction, affecting them for quite a while before they work through it. Think about how you, as manager, are viewed: You come along and announce that you're organizing everyone to work in a team. Say hello to resistance from the defenders of status quo.

Other people may outwardly support the team concept, yet they hold unrealistic expectations about how quickly the team will gel and perform well. When they feel some bumps along the road to effective teamwork, they grow restless and disenchanted. "Maybe this change to teams wasn't such a good idea after all," they think. Patience isn't a characteristic of many employees, let alone their managers.

Winning Them Over

Don't be alarmed if some of your employees show signs of great discomfort and resistance as you move into teams. In fact, you may have more reason to worry if they all seem overjoyed at the prospect of teams and think everything's going to be wonderful. Teams can and do deliver wondrous results but rarely before hard work and some frustration. So just roll with the punches and help your people to get on board. Here are some tips for moving people along and getting them adjusted to a team situation:

- ✔ **Set a tone of patience and persistence.** Team members need to see you set the right example. When they see you're in control and not upset at every little ripple, they calm down as well. When they see you stay the course and talk about where the team is going, they look ahead and work through each day.

- ✔ **Listen a great deal.** Sometimes the best way to help people adjust into teams is to spend more time listening to them than talking to them. That means *active* listening. Seek your team members out. Hear what's going on with them individually as they work in the team, find out their concerns, and acknowledge their feelings. When you understand what's going on with your team members, they know that you care. That knowledge can be a great boon in helping them adjust to the new team situation.

- ✔ **Provide ongoing communication.** Team members need updates from you, from one another, and from management above — news about the team's direction, progress, and performance, to name just a few of the issues for communication. Although e-mail is okay for passing on news, frequent, face-to-face communication in group and individual settings is far more effective. Make those sessions part of regular practice.

- ✔ **Get the team involved in planning its work.** Push as much as you have to on this one — otherwise, your inaction can spell disaster for the team. Get the members involved from the beginning in setting up the framework for performing their work. Meet with the team to develop goals and plans and to define roles and responsibilities. When you do all this, you relieve the team of waiting and wondering, the time when chaos and frustration can creep in and the resistance movement can declare victory.

✔ **Help the team to overcome obstacles.** If the team needs resources, get them. If the team needs information, create access to it. You're the team's advocate to others in the organization, from peers to higher levels of management. So push, push, push! Don't let anything distract you from helping solve the team's functional problems. The best news is that the team often can figure out ways of solving problems as long as you're there to facilitate the effort.

✔ **Train them and cross-train them.** From team-oriented work skills to technical job skills, team members often need training and cross-training. You may need to tap other internal resources or even external resources to teach your people. Whatever it takes, get rolling with training so that team members can grow while they work as a team rather than suffer through trial and error. The key team skills you want your members to master are highlighted in this chapter in the upcoming section "Training Your Team in Six Critical Skills."

✔ **Deal at once with performance issues.** Whenever you see any performance problems — for example, team members slacking off or becoming disruptive — consider them signs of resistance that must be addressed right away. If you do nothing, you may see these behaviors multiply, affect others, and drag down the entire team. In the early stages of a team's development, most members aren't ready or willing to address performance issues with other team members. That's where you as manager come in.

Coach to correct first. That means taking individuals aside and giving them feedback based on your observations about their performance and then clarifying your expectations and asking what steps they'll take to meet those expectations. In most cases, a one-on-one discussion like this refocuses people on the job and on conducting themselves professionally.

✔ **Focus on driving performance.** This tip sums up the previous seven tips. Performance is what teams are all about, and your main job is not to make everyone happy but to guide and lead the team to good performance, including everything from setting goals and assignments to monitoring progress and results.

Introducing the Three Cornerstones: Focus, Cohesiveness, and Accountability

If you want to show your team the road to success, pointing with your magic wand won't do any good. Neither will all your good wishes or days spent on retreat. What you must do is help the team set three main cornerstones in place as a solid foundation for all their teamwork (see Figure 1-2). The cornerstones are

✔ Focus

✔ Cohesiveness

✔ Accountability

In this section, you find out how each cornerstone supports a number of specific team strategies.

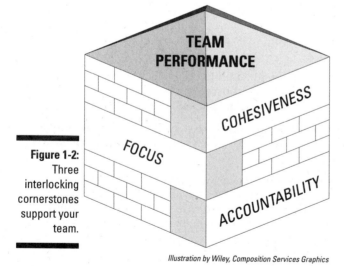

Figure 1-2:
Three interlocking cornerstones support your team.

Illustration by Wiley, Composition Services Graphics

Managing teams that are going to work well together for a while, from project teams to work-unit teams, is no easy feat. The key to success is heavily involving work groups in developing and utilizing strategies that build discipline for high productivity. Discipline is about continuous hard work and follow-through, not stop-and-start efforts.

What follows are definitions of each cornerstone and showcases of the strategies associated with the cornerstones that drive team performance.

Focus

The *focus* cornerstone supports the team's reason for being and helps define where it's going and what it needs to accomplish. Focus is about building the clarity and sense of direction that a team needs to perform well. Remember that strategies are developed with the team, not imposed on the team.

Here are some key strategies for developing a strong focus cornerstone:

- ✓ **Establishing a team vision statement:** The vision statement describes the long-term outlook — where the team is going and what it will be like when it's performing at a high level.

- ✓ **Defining core values:** Core values are guiding principles. They're the handful of beliefs that inspire team practices and guide team members as they do their work.

- ✓ **Developing a team-purpose statement:** The purpose statement explains why a team exists and what it's expected to do, defines the team's overall role, and gives members a common agenda for doing their work.

- ✓ **Creating team guidelines:** Guidelines are the behavioral expectations that define how team members work with one another and provide a focus on professionalism and excellence.

- ✓ **Setting team performance goals:** Performance goals are the *big* end results that the team needs to reach within a set period of time. Goals are updated periodically to stay current with new challenges while continuing to serve as the driving force in focusing the team on what it needs to accomplish.

- ✓ **Planning projects and assignments:** That means figuring out the key steps for the team to follow in accomplishing its goals. The idea is to plan the work and then work the plan.

- ✓ **Clarifying roles and responsibilities:** Figuring out who's going to do what is a strategy that often is devised at the same time the work is planned. Clarifying roles and responsibilities helps to avoid duplicating efforts and to prevent important obligations from slipping through any cracks — or any canyons — that may develop along the way.

✔ **Defining performance measurements:** With some teams, knowing what outcome areas to measure provides a strong focus. For example, when a team places a great emphasis on providing quality service to its customers, determining the areas of quality service to track or measure is important.

✔ **Setting team performance standards based on key factors:** If a team emphasizes customer service, for example, setting behavior or work standards based on good customer service practices gives the team a strong focus in that area.

Cohesiveness

The *cohesiveness* cornerstone helps the team to bond the various perspectives and talents of its members, creating a dynamic and positive work group. To repeat, these strategies are devised *with* the team, not imposed from its leader. Here are some key strategies for preparing and setting the cohesiveness cornerstone:

✔ **Developing backup coverage:** Backup means cross-training, preparing the team to pass the truck test so that if someone is run over by a truck, someone else can step up and keep the team moving ahead.

✔ **Creating shared responsibilities or joint assignments:** Managers need to employ this strategy whenever they can — getting people used to working with one another and accomplishing important things. In earthy terms, this is like working side by side to dig a ditch, making joint decisions about how deep and how far and coordinating the entire effort. Shared responsibilities and joint assignments are great for group dynamics, ending *I-do-everything-myself* kind of thinking.

✔ **Problem-solving with operational issues:** Cohesiveness develops as teams solve problems together. So as problems arise, managers must pull their teams together to work on developing solutions.

✔ **Employing team guidelines:** You want to post team guidelines on the wall, making them visible whenever the team meets, and periodically talk with the members about how they're following guidelines. Use the guidelines to direct discussion when the team is resolving problems and conflicts.

✔ **Addressing team functioning issues:** Sometimes conflicts come up, communication problems arise, or other group concerns become apparent. When such issues affect most team members, pull the team together to address these concerns and together find solutions. If the issues involve only one or two individuals, speaking with the individuals privately is okay.

✔ **Attending training sessions together:** From staging technical forums to receiving training on various team skills, having members learn together — and from one another — is a great strategy for building a cohesive team.

✔ **Redesigning a work process:** Improving a work process to increase efficiency, or creating a new process, is a team activity that can pull team members together. By pooling ideas and playing off one another's insights, teams find better ways to get the work done.

✔ **Involving the team in interviewing and selecting new team members:** Especially with teams that are working together for long periods of time, current members can help you interview candidates for open slots on the team. Making members part of the process adds credibility to your decision to hire (or not) and enhances team support of new team members when they come on board.

✔ **Conducting activities to build relationships and promote understanding:** Stepping away from the work at times to strengthen working relationships often aids overall team performance. This strategy, sometimes referred to as "the team-building stuff," may look like it's all about fun and games and getting to like your fellow team members. But it's really about enhancing group dynamics so that people pull together to get their work done.

Accountability

The *accountability* cornerstone reinforces high standards and the sense of shared responsibility that a team needs to produce top results. It is about collectively extending concern for a team's performance and outcomes from the manager alone to the group. As with the other cornerstones, accountability strategies are carried out with the team, not laid on the team by its manager. Here are some key strategies that surround the accountability cornerstone:

✔ **Delivering team presentations to management:** When a team reports its results or recommendations to management, it puts its work on display. The formal presentation to which all team members contribute gives everyone an opportunity to shine and to show how the team has delivered well on its responsibilities.

✔ **Conducting periodic status review meetings:** Important with project teams and useful with any type of team, this strategy requires each member to report progress on assignments. Status review sessions can build positive peer group pressure: Pete hears Mary deliver a strong progress report and thinks, "I can do that, too!"

✔ **Doing a team self-evaluation:** Best if done once a quarter or once every six months, a team self-evaluation poses questions like: How well has the team done in meeting its objectives? How well have team members worked together? What kind of progress has the team made in working toward its goals? The manager and team members assess the answers and suggest and implement corrections and improvements where needed.

✔ **Conducting post-mortems:** Post-mortems are evaluation meetings at the end of a project or major event. They're conducted to review what happened, from what went well to what can be done better next time. The idea is to learn from the past so that successes — and not mistakes — are repeated.

✔ **Recognizing and celebrating accomplishments:** Pausing to recognize and celebrate team successes is important. Don't take the team for granted! From big parties to simple gatherings, how you celebrate with your team doesn't matter as long as what you do is viewed as positive by the team.

✔ **Assessing the effectiveness of team meetings:** Because teams spend much of their time in meetings, assessing how team members run their meetings helps keep them on a productive track. Jointly determining criteria for productive meetings and taking time when meetings end to ask "How did we do today?" reinforces the idea that meetings shouldn't waste time.

✔ **Carrying out peer feedback sessions:** One of the best strategies for promoting team accountability is using peer feedback sessions so that team members exchange constructive feedback with one another about team member behavior and performance. Teams can use the guidelines they developed as a *focus* strategy to structure their feedback sessions. Such sessions challenge the maturity level of a team and its members and are useful for identifying problems as well as recognizing individuals making valuable contributions to the team. The feedback strategy can be introduced after a team has spent some time together and then used periodically, say once a quarter or every six months.

Make sure that you develop your team's skills by implementing strategies from all three cornerstones: focus, cohesiveness, and accountability. You need all three going strong together to maximize your team's performance.

Training Your Team in Six Critical Skills

Besides acquiring technical and job skills, teams need to discover the skills that are essential to working together. Your job as manager is to find the resources that you need to impart these critical skills, devote time to this training, and make the training action oriented — what team members discover in the classroom, they apply right away on the team.

Here are six critical tools that team members use when they work well together:

- ✔ **Interpersonal communication:** Communicating with one another is so much a part of life in teams that it greatly shapes the general quality of a team's work. Team members need to discover how to listen actively and to speak assertively (see Chapter 2 of Book IV).

- ✔ **Systematic problem solving:** People are not born with problem-solving skills, yet teams often deal with problems. Finding out how to attack problems instead of people and how to solve them instead of shooting from the hip is what systematic problem solving is all about.

- ✔ **Planning and goal setting:** To get ahead, you must plan ahead and set goals. Individual team members, not just managers, must master these skills — planning the work, and then working the plan.

- ✔ **Collaborative conflict resolution:** Conflicts are inevitable in team situations. Conflicts are rooted in differences — different opinions, different ideas. Working through these differences is key for teams to minimize interpersonal tension and perform productively. (See Chapter 5 of Book IV for a detailed discussion about conflict resolution.)

- ✔ **Group decision making:** Teams share decisions much more than other kinds of management groups do.

- ✔ **Meeting management:** People often dread going to meetings because of their many experiences in unfocused, chaotic, pointless meetings. But meetings are the backbone of a team's work, and discovering how to productively run your meetings is vital for team success. (See Chapter 4 of Book III for the lowdown on making meetings effective and efficient.)

Chapter 2

Strategies for Building Effective Teams

. . . .

In This Chapter

▶ Implementing strategies that set a foundation for a team

▶ Defining the work to be done and who does what

▶ Ensuring that each player knows his role and the plan ahead

▶ Getting all eyes on the prize and creating cohesiveness

▶ Reporting results and evaluating progress

▶ Encouraging efforts that bring success

. . . .

*T*he time for getting to work and making your team go is upon you. You need to plug in the strategies that are necessary for building focus, cohesiveness, and accountability within your team. (If you need to, flip back to the previous chapter for a refresher on the importance of these three cornerstones.)

Imagine, if you will, holding a camera. When you put it into focus, you get quality pictures (as long as you keep your hand away from the lens). Teams also need focus so they get quality performance. The focus cornerstone defines why a team exists, where it's going, and how it plans to get there. In this chapter, you find strategies for defining and sharpening your team's focus.

This chapter also contains strategies for building cohesiveness so that your team knows how to interact, handle problems, and learn together. Plus, you'll find in this chapter that accountability is a foundation for your team members to begin sharing in the team's overall results while remaining responsible as individuals. Distributing the burdens and successes of the team's work to everyone who is part of the team is your obligation as manager.

In nautical terms, although you may be the captain of the ship, every member of the crew shares responsibility for bringing the ship to its destination — and popping the cork to celebrate a successful voyage.

Laying a Solid Foundation

Every kind of team that plans to be around for a while needs to put together two critical pieces of its foundation: a team-purpose statement and team guidelines.

Even when the team has existed for a long time without these two elements, they're worth putting in place because they can sharpen a team's focus so that it continues to perform well.

Writing a team-purpose statement

A *team-purpose statement,* as the name implies, defines the purpose of a team and why it exists. It's not a lofty mission statement that you sometimes see for entire organizations. A team-purpose statement is simple and focuses on the team itself.

A team-purpose statement is best when it's boiled down to one sentence. Otherwise, nobody remembers it. The idea is to simplify the statement so that every member of the team can recite from memory why the team exists.

When creating a team-purpose statement, do so *with* your team, not *for* your team. Your team members must be a part of the process; people support most that which they help to create. Before you and your team start to work, briefly explain what a purpose statement is: "A one-sentence statement that defines why the team exists or what the purpose of the team is." Getting into more details, you then can explain that a clearly articulated team-purpose statement answers these questions:

✔ What's the team's role?

✔ What does the team do, or what's its overall function?

✔ How does the team want others outside of it to view the team?

When writing the purpose statement, your team needs to follow these steps:

1. **Using the three questions as a guide, have each member of the team write a one-sentence purpose statement.**

   You want everyone to write only one sentence that responds to all three questions, not one sentence for each of the questions.

2. **Ask team members to write their finished sentences on something large enough to post them on the wall for everyone to read.**

   A piece of flip chart paper will do.

3. **Begin a discussion by asking team members to point out the common themes or ideas they see in the various sentences.**

   List those themes as they're called out.

4. **Ask team members to suggest new sentences that incorporate those common themes.**

   Write the new sentences on a flip chart for all to see, and lead the discussion with your team toward deciding which statement does the best job of

   - Capturing the common themes

   - Answering the three defining questions

   - Expressing the ideas clearly and meaningfully

5. **Keep the discussion going until you've boiled your statement down to one (or two) sentence(s) that everyone can support.**

   Getting everyone to buy into the final statement is *consensus.*

Take a look at these sample team-purpose statements, which are based on real ones:

✔ Our marketing team is committed to functioning as a cohesive unit by developing and executing strategies and services that position, promote, and achieve high visibility, customer satisfaction, and profitability for our company's software products in the marketplace.

✔ Our administrative team is dedicated to providing our customers, the employees of this company, with top-quality facilities, purchasing, and office services in a courteous, responsive, accurate, and efficient manner.

✔ Fulfilling customer orders completely and accurately and shipping them on time is what our operations team makes happen.

✔ The policy task team's purpose is to create and implement key personnel and operational policies that provide the company and its employees with guidelines that are as useful and helpful in operating the business as they are in making it a great place to work.

Creating team guidelines

The second foundation-building focus strategy, which also is good to execute early in the process, is establishing team guidelines. Similar to the team-purpose statement, team guidelines are best established by creating them together *with* the members of your team, not merely *for* your team. That's how you can garner everyone's support.

Team guidelines spell out expectations. They are like codes of conduct or commitments, and they define the important behaviors expected of team members as they work together in and outside of team meetings.

As team members gather for one of your team's early meetings, you can explain what team guidelines are and how to write them. Tell your team that a good set of team guidelines spells out what each member can expect from other members while building and sustaining a cohesive and productive team. Try not to exceed ten guidelines; you want to create a working tool, not a rulebook.

Each written guideline should be

- ✔ Stated as one clear sentence.

- ✔ Stated in a positive way — telling what to do versus what not to do. For example, say, "Treat each other with courtesy and respect" rather than "Don't be inconsiderate, malicious, and rude."

- ✔ Defined as an observable behavior — something another person can see.

Guidelines describe how people act, not necessarily how they think. Observable behavior is key. Sometimes people come up with a guideline like, "Display a positive attitude." A positive attitude is great, but attitude is more about what goes on inside someone's head than how that person is acting. You can observe people's actions or behaviors, but you can only make assumptions about their attitudes or dispositions. Whenever you try to get inside people's heads and tell them how to think or feel, watch out — you're stepping into a minefield, and it will blow up on you.

Follow these steps to create guidelines with your team:

1. **Ask each of your team's members to write three or four guideline sentences using the criteria provided in this section.**

2. **Have them write their guideline sentences on flip chart paper and post them on a wall for all to see.**

3. **Together with your team, identify common themes or ideas that emerge from the various examples.**

   Look for similarities. List common themes that you see.

4. **Collectively craft each common theme into its own guideline sentence.**

Sometimes someone may have stated the guideline well from the individual inputs that were posted. If it works in capturing the point, use it.

5. **After you identify and apply all the common points, if any potential guideline statements remain that team members believe are important, discuss them and, as long as team members agree, add them to the list.**

But remember, limit the list to ten or fewer items.

6. **Check for consensus to ensure that everyone on the team supports all the guidelines.**

The following sections represent a few samples of team guidelines based on what real teams have done.

The Public Relations Management Team Guidelines

The management team members will

1. Communicate openly, honestly, and directly with each other.

2. Actively listen to show understanding and respect to what other members have to say.

3. Support one another and the decisions made by the team.

4. Challenge the status quo and show openness to new ideas.

5. Provide and be receptive to constructive feedback.

6. Focus on generating and implementing solutions.

7. Demonstrate that managing and developing people are priorities.

The Team Guidelines of the Policy Task Team

The policy task team members will

1. Come to all team meetings on time and prepared.

2. Follow through and meet commitments with assignments.

3. Actively and constructively participate at team meetings to help the task team get its work done.

4. Support all decisions made by the team.

5. Listen to each other with attentiveness and openness.

6. Maintain and respect confidentiality.

Communications Dispatch Team Guidelines

The communications dispatch team will follow these guidelines:

1. RESPECT. Accept team members for who they are as well as what role they have, and treat one another in a courteous, considerate, and understanding manner.

2. SUPPORT. Actively reinforce individuals' ideas and the decisions the team makes.

3. PATIENCE. Exercise self-control over your actions, and realize that some things take time.

4. TEAMWORK. Demonstrate collective effort, cooperation, and active involvement to help the team reach its common goals.

5. JOB FOCUS. Provide high quality to all internal and external customers.

6. ACCOUNTABILITY. Take responsibility for your actions and meet your commitments.

The common thread running through these examples is that each is stated in a positive way, is describing an observable behavior that's important for team members to follow, is action-oriented, and is written in one concise sentence. That's what makes the team guidelines concrete and meaningful.

Setting Goals, Not Activities

Goals define what a team needs to achieve. Their focus is on results, not on activities. Knowing the difference between goals and activities is important.

People are often activity-focused in their jobs. Ask them what they do and they can tell you all the things they're working on right now. When they're organized, they can show you a long to-do list. But when you ask them about the important results they need to accomplish with all that activity, you're likely to come face to face with the trout look — a mouth open, glazed expression. They simply don't know how to respond. "Just get stuff done" is a common reply.

Ask people, including team members, to state their goals and they'll write:

Complete Project X by July 1, 2015.

That isn't a goal; it's an activity. A goal defines a result to be accomplished, like this:

Complete Project X, resulting in a 10 percent reduction in material waste from current levels, by July 1, 2015.

A goal defines a meaningful outcome. It answers an important question: Why is the team working on this effort or assignment?

You want to establish just a handful of goals that all members share in and contribute to in one way or another. Establishing more than a handful of goals will probably result in a laundry list of activities, or more work than you can reasonably accomplish. The goals that you develop also must cover a set period of time, such as the next six months and certainly not longer than a year.

Making sure that your team's goals are results-focused means applying the *SMART* criteria:

- ✔ *S* **is for Specific.** A good goal statement is one sentence. It's so specific and clear that even people outside your team can read and understand it.

- ✔ *M* **is for Measurable.** The goal that you establish can be measured in one or more ways by quantifiable means (numbers) or by qualitative means such as surveys to gather feedback, testing, documentation, or by inspecting the finished product. You may have to create the measuring instrument when nothing suitable exists.

- ✔ *A* **is for Action-oriented.** Goal statements begin with action verbs. Among words that work well are *create, design, develop, implement, produce,* and *achieve.*

- ✔ *R* **is for Results-focused.** The goal statement answers the question, "What is the important result that needs to be accomplished?" It doesn't explain *how* but rather *what,* which gives meaningful purpose to the goal.

- ✔ *T* **is for Time-bound.** The goal has a target date, a time of completion. It's an estimate — no one's going to be shot if the date is not reached. But without a target date, work may never end. Target dates help teams focus on accomplishing results.

An easy way to write an effective, one-sentence goal statement is to write it with these four parts in sequence:

Action verb + Topic of goal + Result to be achieved + Target date

Here are a few examples that follow this structure of establishing team goals:

- ✔ Achieve through all spring and summer recreation programs and events an average customer satisfaction rating of 90 percent through the current cycle of March 1 through September 1.

✔ Implement communication, training, and other problem-solving strategies that result in a turnover rate in the department of less than 15 percent by the end of the year, December 31.

✔ Develop and implement a project-management process for the capital-improvement program that results in the completion of the 25 outstanding projects — according to defined budgets, quality standards, and set schedules — by December 31.

✔ Create and implement marketing strategies that result in a monthly hit rate on the company website of 2,500 and a revenue stream of $10,000 per month by October 1.

Making Plans and Assigning Roles

After the team knows the important results it needs to accomplish, you can help team members establish the work plan for getting the job done. By determining with your team how goals will be achieved, you're defining the main steps (not all the little tasks) that need to be completed along the way. Here are two useful planning strategies:

✔ **Going-forward approach:** When planning your strategy, start with today and outline each major step needed to reach the goal. You arrange these steps in sequential order, each with a target date that takes you from today until the date by which the overall goal is to be achieved. This approach helps you and your team set reasonable target dates for goals because everyone sees what's involved from start to finish. Even when the target date is prescribed, using this approach helps you figure out what efforts are needed to meet that deadline.

✔ **Backward-planning approach:** Using this approach, you start with the end date by which your goal is to be accomplished and work backward to the present day. Working in reverse, you outline each main step that you need to take all the way back to the present day.

The going-forward approach is the more common of the two planning strategies. But when faced with a hard deadline, a team sometimes finds that working backward in planning what must be done is easier. For example, if a show is set for April 1, the team needs to have

✔ Programs ready by March 24

✔ Stage sets completed by March 21

✔ Ushers lined up by March 17

✔ Flyers and promotional materials sent out by February 15

✔ And so on

Be sure to check out the next chapter for additional examples of what these two planning approaches may look like.

Go with the approach that works best for the work at hand and with what your team finds most useful for the situation. Be sure to document the agreed-upon work plans and make copies available for each team member as a reference and reminder. People who are more visually inclined may like seeing the plans outlined in the form of flowcharts or graphs.

Don't assume that your team members automatically know what part they play in the process just because they've had a look at the work plan. Even when certain assignments seem an obvious fit with the skill sets of only one or two team members, don't assume that everyone understands and will act accordingly. When you don't define roles, you can expect to see some tasks unnecessarily duplicated and others falling through the cracks. And when those things happen, say hello to the notorious three Cs — *chaos, confusion,* and *calamity.*

Talk with the members of your team so that their roles are clearly defined. In many cases, assignments may involve two or more team members working together. Talking about specific roles for each goal also helps you sort out and balance workload issues. Don't forget that documenting these assignments lets everyone know who's doing what in each work plan.

Not every team member aligns with every team goal. Because of varying responsibilities, some people may align with only three of the five team goals. That's fine; not everyone has to do the same things for a team. Just make sure that every team goal has one or more team members assigned to make it happen.

You may want to establish certain administrative roles that help your team manage its business better. Here are a few to consider:

- ✔ **Organizer:** Ensures that arrangements are made for every team meeting or special event, from advance agendas to materials distributed at the meeting.

- ✔ **Recordkeeper:** Keeps the official files and records of important work and information that the team produces, including meeting agendas and minutes, status reports, purpose statements, guidelines, and team work products.

- ✔ **Communications liaison:** Ensures that important news and information about the team's work is passed along to the right sources inside and outside the team.

- ✔ **Librarian:** Maintains important research materials and educational resources that team members need from time to time. The librarian may also be someone who retrieves these resources for the team.

You can give these roles any name that you like, and you can certainly add others as needed. You can assign one person permanently or the job can rotate. The key, however, is discussing these needs upfront with the team and settling on who will handle them.

Establishing Team Vision and Values

Next you need to consider two more strategies that help strengthen the focus cornerstone. They include developing a team vision statement and defining the team's core values.

Writing a team vision statement

Crafting a team vision statement is like drawing a picture of a team when it's successful in the future. The statement describes the team's long-term outlook — what the team will look like when it's at a high level of performance. Vision statements generally are broad and meant to last a long time, so they're best used with ongoing teams. A vision statement doesn't have to be unique or special, just a clear and meaningful description of the team in a positive future state.

Start by defining what a team vision statement is and why the team needs one, and then describe your view of the future. Write an *umbrella statement* first: an introductory sentence or two that sketches the broad vision. Then add the key features: items that support the umbrella statement, which often guide the development of team goals and strategies.

Here is an adaptation of an actual team vision statement created by a management team:

> This team seeks to become a financially self-sustaining city department, one that doesn't rely on general funds, intent on delivering recreational programs and services that meet the needs of its customers. To do so, the team will be characterized by:
>
> • Managers who are key drivers who develop staff and execute business strategies that achieve self-sustaining results.
>
> • High customer satisfaction with all the programs and services supported by the team.
>
> • Teamwork at all levels of the department.

- Staff who continuously look for ways of improving operations and services and take responsibility for delivering results.

- A work environment that promotes and supports learning and professional development.

The opening sentence of this example is an umbrella statement that defines the broader view. Beneath are five supporting key features that provide a more vivid description of how this future state will appear and how it will be accomplished.

Defining core values

Core values are guiding principles that govern behavior and reinforce the organizational culture or climate that you want to maintain within a group. Core values are not wishes but rather are shared beliefs or behaviors that people truly and strongly hold. Core values answer the question, "What do we stand for as a team?" Because they're *core* values, they are few in number, and yet they characterize what your team is all about.

Some organizations determine core values at the executive level as a means of guiding the entire enterprise. Although core values are seen in practice less often at the team level, they can be useful at that level in pulling a team together and enhancing its sense of purpose and organization.

As with the strategy of writing a vision statement, the strategy of defining core values applies more often to a team that's going to be around for a while. You apply the strategy *with* your team, not *for* its members. (This *with-them-not-for-them* dance step is one of the million-dollar secrets that can lead your team to a higher level of performance.)

Remind team members that core values define how your team functions, not what you want to become one day. You must be honest; they aren't values when you're not living by them. For that reason, it's best to employ this strategy after a team has been together for a while and has had a chance to develop some character or identity how it operates. By defining the values at that point, you not only reinforce them, but also you make them serve as a focus for the team in accomplishing the following:

- **Setting goals and work plans:** Do those goals and plans coincide with the team's core values?

- **Recruiting, hiring, and orienting new team members:** Will new members fit in with the team's values and therefore be positive assets to the team?

- **Evaluating team performance:** As the team produces results, has it kept its values alive and well so the team maintains its positive character?

A good question that can stimulate people's thinking about core values is this:

> *What beliefs, practices, and principles do we share and consider important on this team?*

Because you're probing for the team's core values, the statements that you develop need to stand up to this test question:

> *If the nature of some of our work or much of our work changes, or if new demands are made upon us, will these values continue to apply to us as guiding principles?*

Working off the common themes or ideas generated by individual team members, you can shape the final list of core values by paring it down to five at most. Then distribute the list of core values for everyone to live by.

Developing Standards and Measurements

This section addresses more strategies that support the focus cornerstone that you can use to drive team performance. These strategies of establishing standards and measurements tell you, among other things, what to track and focus on as the team seeks top performance results.

Setting team performance standards

A *performance standard* is a level of performance or a work practice to maintain to produce consistent, high-level results. Standards can be set at the policy or guideline level and at the operating-procedure level.

Avoid using the term *minimum standard.* That's an oxymoron. When a standard isn't meant to guide achievement at *high* levels of performance, it isn't a useful standard. Setting a minimum standard is like establishing an Olympic qualifying time so slow that even the slowest of runners can join in the action. Stick to high standards in what you establish with your team.

Standards established at the policy or guideline level usually address important areas of performance that many, if not all, of the team members share, such as customer service, quality, documentation, and even teamwork. When you draft these kinds of standards with your team, follow the short-and-sweet approach. Make them as clear and concise as possible. For example:

✔ Maintain a turnaround time of 30 days or less for processing all vendor invoices.

✔ Maintain past-due collections of more than 60 days as 5 percent or less of your total accounts.

✔ Maintain an accuracy rate of 95 percent on all coding work.

✔ Maintain all project documentation so that it is complete, organized, and 100 percent accurate by the end of each project assignment.

Developing standard operating procedures

Sometimes teams need to establish *standard operating procedures* (SOPs). That kind of performance standard often applies to teams that deal with business operations, such as processing, order fulfillment, financial management, and production.

SOPs define how certain functions are performed, often outlining a step-by-step routine or establishing consistent practices that ensure accuracy, thoroughness, and high quality. In other words, SOPs are supposed to prevent sloppiness.

When you want to develop SOPs with your team, try this process:

1. **Collectively (that means everyone!) determine what areas of your work can benefit from having written procedures.**

2. **Ask team members to select the SOPs that they want to write. They can work individually or in pairs.**

3. **At a follow-up meeting with the entire team, review drafts for clarity and completeness.**

Because SOPs guide the performance of key tasks, they contain some detail. But no one's going to read them when they're multiple pages long. So make them as short and sweet as possible — logical and concise, with minimal jargon.

Avoid letting your SOPs turn into staunch rules. That can happen when team members forget that procedures *guide* performance toward good results. Results are paramount; arguments about methods for method's sake usually are a waste of time.

People carry out tasks in different but equally valid ways, so enable your team members to work in their own styles while following SOPs. Keep the focus on consistent results; if a team member comes up with a better way of carrying out a function, by all means have that member share the new insights and then update SOPs as needed. And certainly, as work progresses, whenever anyone spots a function that can benefit the team by becoming an SOP, let the good times roll — create that new SOP on the fly.

Deciding what to measure and how to measure it

Another focus cornerstone strategy that you may want to use with your team involves defining *performance measurements,* sometimes referred to as *performance indicators.* This strategy determines what to measure and how to measure it — what progress in a team's performance is important to track. The idea with this strategy is a familiar one: If you can't measure something important, you can't achieve it. Put another way, for a team to focus on and achieve good results, it needs to measure key factors of performance that are important for achieving good results. As you may have guessed, this strategy supports the focus strategies of establishing team goals and team-performance standards.

By looking at what you do for your customers and deciding what things you can measure, you can establish performance measurements. A team's list of customers includes the obvious outsiders who buy things from you, as well as your inside customers: other work groups and individuals elsewhere in the organization you support.

For instance, assume that you run a fulfillment team with overall responsibility for packaging and shipping every order that your business receives from its external customers. With your team, you may decide that the following performance indicators are important to measure:

- ✔ Daily volume of orders shipped by type of order
- ✔ Number of orders returned for correction
- ✔ Number of orders shipped on time and to the right location
- ✔ Number and type of customer complaints
- ✔ Number and type of customer compliments

When you figure out what's important to measure, determine with your team how to measure it. Here are the most common and useful ways of measuring performance factors:

- ✔ Document, on an activity log, the volume and kind of transactions that occur.
- ✔ Utilize surveys to gather customer feedback.

Software usually enters the picture as the easiest and fastest way of compiling and analyzing data. Whatever it takes, performance measurements help a team achieve the following:

✔ Know what's most important to concentrate on for delivering good results.

✔ Provide timely information on performance.

✔ Spotlight problems while they're still easy to correct.

Building Connections, Creating Cohesiveness

In building the cohesiveness necessary for a team to perform productively, you must have strategies that connect people. Even when team members usually work on their own, something that binds each individual member to the rest of the team is needed. The following sections present a few important strategies for building these vital connections.

Teams need to meet on some kind of regular basis to build strong connections among all members. For some teams, *regular* may mean a few minutes every day, an hour once a week, or a couple of hours every few weeks. The idea is communicating and working together but not meeting simply for the sake of meeting — and for goodness' sake, not just because it's that time of the week.

Sharing responsibilities

A useful strategy for pulling team members together involves how assignments are made. As much as you can, make assignments in a manner that enables people to work with one another to get the job done — joint efforts. When working on projects, making these assignments often means mixing different disciplines so that each person's expertise is brought into play.

Joint assignments are great for breaking down tensions and I-work-solo styles. People neither have to like each other nor have the same work styles just to work together. When they depend on one another for achieving a shared outcome, they often find a way of putting aside or resolving their differences so they can get the job done well.

When you see an opportunity for using the joint efforts of a team to get work done, use these tactics to create good combinations among members of the team:

✔ Explain to your team what work needs to be done and how many people are needed to do it.

✔ When asking who wants to do what, suggest (but don't direct) that certain individuals take on certain assignments. "John and Sue, how about you two handle the market research aspects of this project?"

> ✔ Recruit people individually by talking with them privately before the team meeting, designating with whom you want them to work on a given job.
>
> ✔ Coach team members individually by preparing them for the upcoming work needed. But first, solicit any concerns or reservations they may have. Then you can focus on helping them move forward.
>
> ✔ Positively reinforce the individuals who perform well with shared responsibilities.

Putting team guidelines into action

Setting guidelines or expectations sharpens a team's focus. (That's the *focus cornerstone*.) Here are three strategies for using team guidelines to influence a strong sense of cohesiveness. (That's right — the *cohesiveness cornerstone*.)

Publishing and talking about guidelines

Team guidelines have to be visible if you want them to influence how people work with one another in getting the job done. As you establish the guidelines with your team members, be sure to talk about ideas for making them visible. Here are three common ways:

> ✔ Creating a poster for the team's common work area
>
> ✔ Giving all team members a copy of the guidelines to keep at their work stations
>
> ✔ Making sure a copy of the guidelines is available at every team meeting

Periodically, you can also end a meeting by having team members evaluate how they applied the guidelines during the meeting. The same tactic works well even when only a few individual members meet to work on an issue or to address a problem.

Also, encourage team members to speak up when they witness another person carrying out the team's guidelines. Positive reinforcement enhances team cohesiveness.

Guidelines aren't excuses for publicly scolding members of your team. When someone isn't living up to the team's expectations, you want to address the issue, but avoid encouraging team members to use the guidelines as "gotchas" on each other.

Solving an operational issue

Operational issues are any matters that have to do with getting work done. These issues pop up all the time in every kind of work situation. When team members solve operational issues together, they're applying basic team guidelines and shoring up the cohesiveness cornerstone. Here are the basic steps to problem solving:

1. **Define the problem.**

   If you need to analyze the problem to better understand its circumstances and causes, do that as well.

2. **Get some proposed solutions out on the floor.**

3. **Evaluate the ideas.**

4. **Decide what will work best, and implement it.**

Take care that everyone understands the problem before you go looking for solutions — no need to have solutions flying around in search of problems!

Remember at each step to ask individual team members for their input first so that everyone has a chance to contribute. When you begin general discussion, look for common themes before sorting out any differences.

Addressing a team function issue

Sometimes teams just don't work right because of a problem with an issue such as the following:

- ✔ Information sharing
- ✔ Coordination of tasks
- ✔ Interpersonal clashes and tensions

Group functioning issues like these, if left unaddressed, can become big impediments to team performance and can lead to the formation of factions and plenty of griping in the hallways. You don't need any of that.

Addressing these issues tests a team's mettle. If you shy away from these kinds of issues, a team never matures and comes together. Accept the fact that some team members may feel uncomfortable at first in addressing these group dynamics issues. Don't let the comfort level, yours or theirs, guide your judgment. If the issue is affecting the way the team functions, it's important to address.

When a matter involves only a few certain individuals on a team, address it only with those individuals. When the matter concerns all team members, address it with them collectively. Your role is to facilitate or support the conflict resolution meeting. (See Book IV, Chapter 5 for a detailed discussion of how to resolve conflicts.)

In addressing a team function issue, take the following steps:

1. **Prepare for your role by having a conflict resolution model in mind.**

2. **Make sure team guidelines are visible and identified as the ground rules for the discussion.**

3. **Start the discussion by inviting individual expressions — everyone contributes — without comment or judgment by others.**

4. **Steer the discussion toward resolutions that will make the situation better.**

5. **Close by recapping what action will be taken and by whom. Set a follow-up time for meeting again and reviewing progress.** (That's the *accountability cornerstone* coming into play.)

Training and learning together

Skill development is one key aspect of increased performance that often is overlooked. When you show people more about how to do their jobs and how to work effectively with one another, you increase the likelihood that they'll perform better. When team members go through training efforts together and, through that process, learn from one another, you add to the cohesiveness of your team. To enhance this process of development and cohesiveness, consider conducting the following:

✔ **Technical forums:** At these gatherings, team members explore and discover more about the technical issues related to performing their jobs. Sometimes such a forum may mean bringing in an outside speaker or a speaker from elsewhere in the organization. Often, a team member or two make presentations about areas of expertise.

✔ **Team skills workshops:** In these sessions, team members learn about working together. The skills covered may include the following:

- Interpersonal communications

- Systematic problem-solving

- Conducting productive meetings

- Planning and goal setting

- Conflict resolution

- Group decision-making

Who leads a workshop is less important than the fact that you're periodically spending time learning skills as a team.

✔ **Customer service sessions:** For teams with work that has a strong service emphasis, a workshop may be devoted to reviewing articles or books about customer service. It may also involve analyzing how customer problems were handled in the past and drawing lessons from those situations — examples of good service and bad.

✔ **Cross-training:** A useful strategy for building connections among team members for assuring coverage of important functions of a team's work, the idea of cross-training is that people who know particular job functions show others who don't know those jobs so that the learners can help perform those functions.

✔ **Sharing from outside education:** Team members are selected to attend outside training activities and then share what they learned when they return so that the whole team benefits. This process is routine in many organizations because of travel and budget limitations. It means that the week one team member spends in Hawaii for a special conference is something the whole team can benefit from (excluding the sand and surf).

Training and learning together as a team must become commonplace if you intend to gain the most cohesive effect. Remember the benefits of involving team members in scheduling, organizing, and delivering these learning events on a regular basis. Ensuring that they happen is your role as manager.

Working the process so you can process the work

Work process is the way that tasks or job functions are done. Ideally, you want to use the people who do the work to create better and more efficient ways of doing it. Redesigning a work process enhances a team's cohesiveness and applies best to work-unit teams that share an overall job function. Sometimes, task or improvement teams are formed specifically to redesign work processes, such as order fulfillment or manufacturing, that routinely cut across various departments.

You may want to apply a work process strategy in these situations:

✔ You see a need for greater efficiency in how a team does its work.

✔ A team has a hard time keeping up with the demands of its internal or external customers.

✔ You anticipate future demands that will make today's processes obsolete.

✔ Current processes limit cooperation and mutual help — too many single-task specialists and not enough multitask specialists.

To keep your team's redesign or process-improvement efforts simple and productive, follow these steps:

1. **Outline what happens today.** Account for every step of a work process from start to finish. Put it on paper for all to see. Everyone must understand what you're doing today before you can take steps to improve the process.

2. **Identify bottlenecks, confusing factors, and problems.** Analyze them from the perspectives of your internal and external customers. When something comes between your customers and your team's good products or services, that's usually an area that needs improvement.

3. **Explore ideas for process improvements.** You may have many choices. Sometimes, only small adjustments or additional cross-training do the job. Other times, however, you may need to forget old ways and start over from scratch, making even wholesale changes. Encourage team members to be creative and think outside the box.

4. **Evaluate ideas for implementation by set criteria.** The criteria may be:

   • Helping to serve customers

   • Creating better coverage and teamwork

   • Saving time

   • Reducing redundancy

   • Simplifying

   • Accomplishing some or all of the above

Following this routine helps the team not only to devise better work-process ideas but also to implement them, and that's the whole idea behind the cohesiveness strategy.

You may want to test an idea for improvement before officially implementing it. Conducting a trial run for a set period of time sometimes is safer than full-scale immersion, especially with a major change. Similarly, when a transition from old to new ways is necessary, plan it out with your team and determine whether you need to bring anyone outside the team into the loop.

With your team, periodically review the work-process changes that you make to ensure those changes are in place and that projected efficiency gains are occurring. Make adjustments as needed.

Fostering Accountability

Teams don't perform as well as they can when most of the responsibility for the outcome of their work rests on your shoulders as manager. So, as manager, you need to instill a shared sense of accountability by including the team when assessing its progress and evaluating its results.

Conducting status review meetings

The name says it all: At a status review meeting, the team reviews the status of its work. You see how each team member is doing by checking off action items on the list of assignments given to her. Another key objective of the meeting is planning ahead for the next set of work assignments.

You may have participated in a good old-fashioned staff meeting typical of so many regular work groups, where all the members take turns talking for a few minutes about what they're doing. Because most of what's said doesn't pertain to others in the group, heads drop from drowsiness as people drone on. Occasional sparks may fly when someone tells about something that actually affects someone else, but those are rare occurrences. In regular work groups, people tend to do their own things in their jobs, so not much of what concerns them pertains to the other members.

In contrast, when working in teams, each team member's part of the work affects the greater good of the team. Therefore, hearing what others have achieved is relevant to everyone else on the team. In addition, a good status review meeting focuses on what people are getting done, not merely on what they're working on. The spotlight is on results, not activities.

For status review meetings to be useful, they need to happen on a regular basis — say once every week or two, depending on what the work dictates and what team members need.

The status review meeting is one of the most important strategies that you can use in driving team performance and accountability. The significant benefits of the status review meeting are these:

> ✔ **It influences positive peer-group pressure.** Everyone commits to getting work done and reporting their results at the next meeting. No one can run and hide in the background. As a result, peers know who is contributing and pulling his weight and who isn't. Team members often talk informally with one another between meetings, a type of exchange

that helps everyone follow through and meet their commitments. At the same time, the status review helps you recognize who the reliable people are.

✓ **It keeps you in the loop without having to micromanage.** Status review meetings enable you to watch team and individual members' progress without chasing people around and bugging them to find out. In addition, you can find out which people need your individual attention to keep them on track.

✓ **It develops planning skills.** The status review meeting teaches team members how to plan and how to make realistic commitments about what they can get done between meetings. After a few meetings, newcomers to this process usually become better at estimating so that they can present a more accurate picture of what they can truly get done. At the same time, they discover how to plan ahead and not just live day-by-day in their work — a valuable skill to develop that drives team performance.

✓ **It provides focus.** You remember the focus cornerstone, don't you? Everyone knows who's responsible for what work because everyone has a copy of the team's tracking sheet. Everyone knows the priorities because they helped establish them.

✓ **It identifies issues for resolution.** When difficulties arise, the status review meeting becomes a forum for identifying them. The meeting helps you avoid situations in which team members struggle on their own in isolation. You hear what the issues are, and you involve the team in addressing them. No one is shot down for bringing a problem forward that affects the way an assignment gets done. And because problems are flushed out, the team makes progress.

✓ **It builds accountability.** Better accountability is, of course, the bottom line.

Your role in the status review meeting is to ask questions, clarifying what has or has not been done related to the team's action items. No public flogging is necessary when something doesn't get done. Team members know the situation and often are back on track by the next status review meeting. You can deal individually and privately with people who continually do not pull their weight.

Reporting results outward and upward

People outside the team, like management above you and groups affected by what your team does, may sometimes wonder, "Just what are you folks accomplishing?" You can answer that question with two strategies that add to the accountability cornerstone and help meet the needs of interested parties outside your team: publishing a summary report and making a team presentation.

Publishing a summary report

A *summary report* is a written progress review of your team's work. The report isn't only for the team's use; it also broadcasts the team's progress and results to those outside the team who want or need to know. Generally, you want to publish the team's summary reports at reasonable intervals — once a month to once a quarter often works best.

A good summary report gives those outside the team a picture of its progress, so stick to the highlights and avoid gobs of detail. Keep the length reasonably brief. Here's the sort of content you can include:

- ✔ Status reviews of important work issues
- ✔ Progress reports against key performance measures or indicators, if relevant
- ✔ Overview of any significant results
- ✔ Plans for the next period of time
- ✔ Other relevant news, business- and personnel-related

Because a summary report displays the team's performance, everyone on the team needs to play a role in putting the report together. Don't fall into the trap of being the only one who prepares and compiles the report every time. Your role as manager is best accomplished when you review the final draft. Make the report part of the team's work and ask team members how they want to do the work. Depending on how involved your report needs to be, each member can contribute in part to the report while one or two people are responsible for tying it all together.

Making a team presentation

The second useful strategy for "spreading the wealth" about your team's progress is making presentations to management above you or to other groups that are interested in your team's work. These are live, face-to-face events — teleconferencing is fine, too — where the entire team gets involved. A presentation is most useful when you want to do the following:

- ✔ Provide recommendations
- ✔ Explain plans for upcoming special events
- ✔ Share important research findings
- ✔ Report results from significant work

Presentations help other people, especially those in management, understand what your team is doing. They build support for the team. Presentations also serve as forums where your team receives feedback for revising or fine-tuning its work, which sometimes is a way of testing the waters before plunging forward with a plan.

Evaluating team performance

Your journey toward strong team performance and a sense of shared accountability continues. Two checkpoints lie ahead, and both relate to evaluating overall team performance. (Evaluating *individual* performance most likely is your job exclusively as manager; refer to Chapter 4 in Part IV for a discussion of conducting performance appraisals.) Buckle up for the tour.

Conducting postmortems (without a body)

In medical jargon, a *postmortem* is an examination of a body after the person has died. For teams, death isn't involved (at least you hope not). A team postmortem is an evaluation of performance after a project or special event has concluded. The idea is to learn lessons from the past (using hindsight), the pluses and minuses, and then to apply them to future performance. A project postmortem is most relevant when your team knows it will take on similar projects in the future.

When you don't stop long enough to evaluate what's going right and what's going wrong, you're doomed to repeat your mistakes and squander your successes.

A postmortem is best conducted as a team meeting. Reviewing the past and then planning for the future is a good method to use.

- ✔ **Reviewing the past:** Ask team members for individual comments on two questions:

    - What went well in the team's performance?

    - What didn't go as well?

    Record individual comments on a board or flip chart as they're offered by team members, but hold off on discussion until everyone has contributed. Then discuss and draw conclusions. You can highlight all the good outcomes as guidance for future performance and all the bad outcomes as opportunities for improvement.

- ✔ **Planning the future:** Ask the team members to brainstorm ideas that will be most useful to apply in the future.

Make sure that you document the postmortem so the team has some history (or basis) to apply when the next performance evaluation comes around. That's how an evaluation tool becomes a tool for planning and improving the quality of team performance — accountability at its best.

Conducting a performance evaluation

A team performance evaluation is similar to a postmortem. It's an evaluation of the team's overall performance at the end of a given cycle, generally at the end of a quarter or six-month period. It's a scheduled event, and the team is responsible for making it happen, evaluating results against established performance criteria that are selected in advance. This isn't you (the manager) evaluating the team but rather the team evaluating itself, including your input.

You have two jobs here as manager:

- ✔ Making sure the team selects criteria for evaluating its performance and knows where data is coming from
- ✔ Gathering any relevant data, such as computer-generated statistics or surveys of external and internal customers, that can help in evaluating the team's performance in delivering its services

With data in hand, your team is ready to start the evaluation meeting. Remember that focusing on total performance, instead of the work of particular team members, is important. As you facilitate the meeting, do the following:

- ✔ **Compare results to performance criteria.** With team members, go through each performance factor, such as goals or standards, that's being evaluated and have them report the data that describes the results. Enable team members to include their own observations, but keep the focus on measurable results. Remember to have someone taking notes.

- ✔ **Solve problems and plan for the future.** This second part of the meeting needs to be as long as, or longer than, the first. When critical issues or problems affecting the team's past performance arise, use this time for generating ideas for solutions and establishing performance plans that help you move forward. You may have to set new goals, update performance standards, or modify other performance criteria. As always, take notes so that the team's plans aren't left to memory.

Using peer feedback

For any team that's going to be together for an extended period, peer feedback is one of the stronger strategies for building accountability among individual team members. Don't be surprised, however, if some team members are scared to death of the idea because they may be used to complaining about others behind their backs (and even enjoying it, maybe). That means they're not used to talking openly and directly about matters of behavior and performance when everyone is present. So be careful. Avoid plunking everyone down around a table and declaring open season on personal assessment. That's a formula for disaster. You can, however, set the stage for a productive peer feedback session in which everyone is comfortable and from which everyone profits simply by educating your team, using a good feedback questionnaire, and following certain ground rules during discussion.

Educating the team

The key to educating your team is making sure everyone understands that *constructive feedback* means describing what you observe about another person's behavior — what you see that person doing — as opposed to voicing an opinion or an assumption about what he is doing or why he is acting a certain way. In short, constructive feedback focuses on observations, not interpretations, and it is far more factual and objective than an employee opinion survey.

You can show your team members the meaning of constructive feedback and familiarize them with the process of a peer feedback session by doing the following:

✔ **Perform a written assessment.** Team members fill out a feedback questionnaire about each of their fellow team members, including you (when you're an active part of their day-to-day interactions).

✔ **Summarize the findings.** Data gathered from the questionnaires is summarized into individual composite reports for each team member. This step needs to be done by a neutral party, such as the company human resources staff, a department administrative staff member, or an outside consultant.

✔ **Openly discuss the findings.** In a team meeting, each team member, speaking one at a time, shares her feedback results from the summary reports. You encourage other team members to offer comments to help provide insight to the individual team member, who then establishes goals for moving forward based on the feedback.

 For guidance when designing the content of a good feedback questionnaire, take a look at your team guidelines. Team guidelines are expectations and commitments developed *by* everyone on the team *for* everyone on the team. They define behaviors — how team members perform and work with others, helping the team achieve its targets.

Running the feedback session

The peer feedback session is a special meeting that may take up to half a day. At this meeting, you want to enforce ground rules that assure constructive participation and respectful listening. Remind team members that the focus is on the content of observations rather than on the person who made the observations — on *what's* being said rather than *who* is saying it. Here's a good agenda to follow for facilitating the meeting:

✔ Have team members silently read their own feedback reports, asking them to note two important factors as they read:

• Points that need clarification

• Key messages they're getting from the feedback, both positive and negative

✔ After providing everyone with copies of the composite reports so they can follow along, take turns — one person at a time in the discussion phase — having each person present her own feedback summary. Everyone starts by asking for clarification on points where needed and then offers her own take on key messages she observes in her own report. Encourage other team members to reinforce or add to those messages. Open and honest dialogue is what it's all about.

✔ Ask the person who's in the spotlight to develop and work on at least one personal goal that improves teamwork, having other team members assist in this effort. Then move on to the next person and the next. How long does this all take? Feedback discussion can run from 20 minutes to an hour per person.

✔ When everyone has finished, including you, do a quick debriefing. Ask members of your team:

- How did peer feedback go?

- When will you do it again?

Some team members may find the initial peer feedback session quite a challenge. It's important for you to set and enforce ground rules that support active listening and constructive dialogue. You don't want team members reacting defensively to their feedback reports.

Conducting peer feedback sessions on a quarterly or half-yearly basis provides the full benefit of this accountability strategy. Conducting these sessions right after a team evaluation sometimes is a good idea. Ideally, as peer feedback becomes a normal practice for the team, you can skip the part about compiling composite reports. When you reach the stage where team members openly give feedback to one another on the criteria, you have a mature team.

Reinforcing Good Performance

Behavior that's rewarded is repeated. This maxim applies both to individuals and teams. Here are a few more strategies that reinforce good team performance:

✔ **Assess team success.** Sometimes in the midst of working hard to achieve good results, the reasons for your success are overlooked. Take time to assess why you and your team are successful, recognizing good team and individual performances.

✔ **Celebrate with an outing.** You can plan to go off-site for a celebration marking the team's success: dinner, a movie, a ballgame, a trip to an amusement park, a night at the theater — whatever the team finds rewarding. The company foots the bill, of course.

✔ **Get some ink in the company newsletter.** Without gloating too much, highlight your team's achievements with an article in the company's newsletter. An article in the newsletter also lets others (who may not have a clue) know exactly what your team does and can lead to further informal recognition via conversations with other employees.

✔ **Send letters upward.** Writing a letter to your boss about the team's accomplishments can work even better than your routine reports of progress and results. The idea is to tell management above you about the good things your team is achieving. And if the boss doesn't get the hint, encourage her to drop by to express a little of that good old-fashioned appreciation.

A little clapping of hands by you at the right moment goes a long way in motivating and reinforcing high standards of performance. Your team will catch on and join the applause. Your bosses will, too.

Of course, teams are made up of individuals, and you want to recognize individual good work — without creating resentment among others. A key strategy is to offer this positive reinforcement one-on-one, not in a public forum. Here are a few ways to do it:

✔ **Give positive feedback.** When you notice and acknowledge what individual team members do on an ongoing basis (their own work and their contributions that enhance teamwork), you reinforce that behavior. One of the simplest and most powerful ways of reinforcing good performance is giving *positive feedback,* verbally acknowledging an incident of good performance with specific observations, not general statements — which is the difference between positive feedback and praise. So you say, "What I noticed you did well on that assignment was (fill in the specifics)." That's a lot better than simply saying, "Great job!"

✔ **Pass feedback to the individual's manager.** When you're leading a project team or a task team, you're usually managing people who aren't your direct reports or regular staff. But reinforcing accountability with them doesn't mean that they have to be your direct reports. So tell them periodically that you'll pass on significant news about their performance to their managers — and you hope most of it is *good* news. Remember to copy team members on whatever you pass on about them electronically.

✔ **Encourage team members to acknowledge one another's performance.** You're not the only one responsible for providing recognition; team members are, too. They're in the trenches every day, and they know what's happening. Let them know it isn't only okay but it's expected that they pat each other on the back. Tell them to let you know, too, when it's an exceptionally good performance they're recognizing.

Chapter 3

Developing Tools for Productive Team Players

....

In This Chapter

▶ Recognizing what active listening is all about

▶ Polishing speaking styles

▶ Looking at skills for more effective planning

▶ Examining behaviors to avoid and models to use for problem-solving

▶ Using brainstorming techniques to develop solutions

....

*T*he skills that team members need to work together effectively begin at a simple level: listening and speaking. Interpersonal communication is the core of a team's ability to function and perform and usually makes the difference between success and failure.

Being able to communicate well is an important element of moving past problems and planning for the future. You don't have to be a genius to make good plans or solve tough problems. But you do need to pay attention and think — think before acting, not the other way around. When teams are reactive to problem situations or just jump into work with nothing organized first, chaos and inefficiency reign.

This chapter provides you with the insights and tools you need in order to empower your team members to communicate well with one another — listening well and speaking to be heard and understood. This material largely mirrors what you find in Chapter 2 of Book IV, where you work on become an effective communicator yourself, but here the focus is on coaching your team members to adopt key communication practices. This chapter also gives you problem-solving approaches to share with team members and tips for planning so that your team stands the best chance of reaching its goals.

Making Active Listening a Part of Your Team Process

People learn to listen in four different ways. The default mode for many people is *passive listening* or *selective listening,* and neither one works well. When your team members really make an effort to listen, they can ratchet up and become *attentive listeners.*

But the highest and best level of listening is called *active listening.* And wouldn't you know, it's also the least used method. Coaching your team members to become active listeners is your goal. Look at these definitions to find out what kind of listeners are on your team right now:

- ✔ **The passive listener:** This team member shows up for a conversation, but you'd hardly know it. He sits there quietly but does little more. If the conversation is on the phone, you may hear a few *uh-huhs* but that's about it. Maybe you can blame passive listening on a person's upbringing — some kids never forget a scolding about being seen but not heard. As adults they continue to sit quietly in a conversation, passively listening, and frustrating a speaker who wonders if anything is getting through.

- ✔ **The selective listener:** This team member hears what she wants to hear. When what you're saying doesn't interest her, a selective listener almost ignores you — glancing away, looking down at her watch, or focusing her attention elsewhere. You may get a perfunctory, "That's nice," out of her but nothing to suggest that she's actually listening. On the other hand, when something you say doesn't please her — and it can be almost anything, she isn't that particular — a selective listener may become quite hostile, interrupting you with critical remarks and turning judgmental. In both patterns of selective listening, the listener isn't hearing the full message. The result places stress and strain on a conversation, promoting divisiveness rather than the cohesiveness that a team needs.

- ✔ **The attentive listener:** In a team meeting, this person maintains eye contact with the speaker and asks questions to draw out the speaker's message. His actions probably help the speaker feel free to express the message. But an attentive listener often doesn't go all the way. He deals with the tangible part of the speaker's message — the content — which is expressed verbally. But he may overlook the nonverbal components of the message, failing to acknowledge or explore the emotional side of the message. So an attentive listener can tell you what the speaker is talking about but may fail to capture fully what the person means.

✔ **The active listener.** This team member captures the speaker's full message — the facts and the feelings, the verbal and the nonverbal components. Active listening is about listening with care and respect and verbally acknowledging what the speaker is saying. Sometimes called *responsive listening* or *reflective listening,* active listening is the only form of listening that checks out what the speaker's message means from the speaker's point of view and without passing judgment on it. That's *empathy.* An active listener provides verbal feedback to the speaker, clarifying and confirming that the message expressed is understood — the opposite of passive listening. Active listening helps speakers because they know they are being heard and understood.

Book V

Managing
Teams

At first, active listening may be really challenging because team members don't necessarily know and trust each other from day one. In a meeting setting, it can be tough to tune into emotions and provide the kind of verbal feedback that helps clarify the speaker's meaning. However, active listening is a skill that you and your team members can perfect and use every day for better interpersonal communication. Your job is to coach your team members to use the five tools of active listening, which are explained next:

✔ Door openers

✔ Probes

✔ Reflections on feelings

✔ Paraphrasing

✔ Reflective paraphrasing

Opening the door to a good conversation

Door openers are verbal and nonverbal signals your team members give to a speaker that let her know they're paying attention. Here are examples of nonverbal door openers:

✔ Stopping whatever you're doing, turning, and facing the speaker

✔ Maintaining steady eye contact

✔ Looking interested or concerned as appropriate

✔ Nodding your head

✔ Looking patient

✔ Leaning forward slightly in your chair

✔ Maintaining a relaxed but alert posture

Here are examples of verbal door openers:

- "Uh huh" and "Um hum"
- "I see"
- "Okay"
- "Right"
- "Really?"
- "Sure!"
- "Yeah"
- "Yes!"
- "Wow!"

Door openers indicate that you're showing interest, following along, and wanting to hear more. In a team meeting setting, nonverbal door openers are usually your best bet. With verbal door openers, your tone of voice needs to be sincere and nonjudgmental; otherwise, they may be door closers!

Drawing out a speaker with probing questions

Probing with questions is a listening tool your team members can use to draw out and add depth to the speaker's message. By asking open-ended questions, they can move a speaker beyond short answers and help him reveal more details about his topic.

Open-ended questions often begin with words like *what, how, tell me, describe,* and *explain.* Here are examples:

- What are the key findings of your report?
- How did you come to the conclusions mentioned in the report?
- Tell me more about the idea that you think will help the team.
- Please describe an example to illustrate your point.
- Please explain your thinking behind this recommendation.

When asking a speaker for these responses, a team member shouldn't lead the speaker toward answering in a prescribed way but rather toward communicating freely. In other words, open-ended questions have no right or wrong answers.

When someone probes, they're being inquisitive. They're *not* conducting an inquisition or interrogation!

Reflecting a speaker's feelings

When you *reflect feelings* that you are picking up in a message (they're usually nonverbal cues), you're acting like a mirror. You reflect back the emotions that you think you sense, which carry significant weight to the meaning of the message.

You can coach your team members to use this technique by saying things like this:

- ✔ You're feeling excited about what happened?
- ✔ Sounds like that was a frustrating situation. Is that right?
- ✔ I sense you've become worried. Is that so?
- ✔ Seems like you had a fun time, correct?

The reflection is phrased in a question-like manner because the idea is to invite a response from the speaker, confirming or clarifying what was heard. That's understanding gained right on the spot! The wording should be soft and easy so the speaker doesn't feel that he's being cross-examined.

Paraphrasing to capture the content

Paraphrasing means summarizing the main idea of the speaker's message, not all the details, so you can check whether you understand its content. Similar to reflecting feelings, a paraphrase is one sentence to which you sometimes tag on an ending like "Is that right?" to show that you're seeking confirmation.

Coach your team members to paraphrase using their own words, not the exact words that the speaker used. Doing so shows that they're truly paying attention. Often a paraphrase begins with starter phrases like, "What you're saying is that (such and such) is important to you. Is that right?" Here are some variations:

- ✔ So what you mean is . . .
- ✔ In other words . . .
- ✔ As I understand your point, it's . . .

Combining reflection with paraphrasing

Reflective paraphrasing is a combo version (but please hold the pickles and lettuce). As the name implies, it combines the tools of reflecting feelings and paraphrasing when both carry important weight in the overall meaning of a message. Here are a couple of examples:

✔ You appear to be feeling frustrated because none of your proposals has received any comment from management so far. Is that so?

✔ Because you were able to find out so much, that experience turned out to be rewarding for you. Is that right?

Dodging pitfalls

As your team members begin applying the tools of active listening, check their verbal responses, making sure that, in their enthusiasm for gaining an understanding of the speaker's message, they're not, in fact, creating barriers for the speaker. That can happen oh-so-easily when team members slip into bad habits like this:

✔ **Criticizing:** The rule is don't become a critic until you thoroughly understand what the speaker is saying. It's amazing how a solid understanding sweeps away hasty criticism. Remind team members to hold off passing judgment and, instead, go for understanding first and foremost.

✔ **Reacting defensively:** You don't have to like or agree with everything someone else says to be an active listener — not at all. But when you react with verbal counterattacks or agitated responses, you show only that you can't listen and understand anything at all.

✔ **Debating:** Some people get a kick out of sparring with the speaker, challenging and debating nearly every point the speaker makes. But when a speaker thinks he must defend his message, he may be inhibited from getting the full message across, and that blocks understanding.

✔ **Giving advice:** Although many people like to give advice, it is best received only when it is requested. Not every concern expressed by a speaker is a problem looking for a solution. Active listeners do far better when they show understanding first, which is also the first step for good problem solving when a problem truly does exist.

✔ **Shifting the focus to yourself:** When responses to someone else's message concern mostly *me, myself,* and *I,* you're no longer listening. You're dominating the conversation. No, thank you!

As your team members get into the swing of active listening, you may see them begin to kid one another when they spot a listening tool being applied — or ignored — on the job. Don't be alarmed when they joke around this way; they're mastering a new skill, and humor helps them get through their initial discomfort. It's okay for you to join in the kidding and share in the laughter.

Speaking So That People Listen — and Get Your Point

Just like training for active listening, training for becoming an effective speaker mostly is ignored in school. People seldom are taught how to convey important messages positively and work through issues and differences constructively with others, which are keys for team functioning and success. In this section, you find out how to coach your team members toward better speaking habits so they can get their points across.

Changing old speaking habits

Three speaking approaches — aggressive, nonassertive, and passive-aggressive — seem to pop out in times of great challenge and stress. Teams certainly can be a Mecca for challenge and stress, so building awareness of these habits is a good way to introduce new and better habits. Here's the low-down on each approach:

- ✔ **The aggressive approach:** Aggressive communication is a hard-charging approach with a manner that often comes across as harsh, controlling, and dominating. Here are some common behaviors you see when people express themselves with the aggressive approach:

  - Demanding and ordering

  - Raising the voice to a loud volume to push a point of view

  - Being blunt with words and sharp with tone in expressing a message

  - Taking the my-way-or-the-highway stance for dealing with a disagreement

  - Blaming the other person when a problem occurs

- ✔ **The nonassertive approach:** Nonassertive communication comes across as passive. Because the speaker makes little effort to state a point of view, others are likely to take control. These behaviors are what you see when people express themselves in a nonassertive way:

- Beating around the bush while trying to make an important point

- Avoiding dealing with tough problems or issues of concern to others

- Sounding helpless and remarking that nothing can be done about a problem

- Devaluing their own contributions with words like, "I'm not sure this is a good idea"

- Showing withdrawal in body language and making little direct eye contact

✔ **The passive-aggressive approach:** Passive-aggressive communication is negative in effect but subtle in manner. Look for these kinds of behaviors:

- Appearing to agree with and accept a commitment yet not following through or doing something entirely different

- Using sarcasm or subtle put-downs concerning ideas or people

- Talking behind a person's back

- Sending venting-type messages — "flaming e-mails" — to other team members (and copying third parties) rather than speaking directly to the other person

- Second-guessing, saying in effect, "I knew that wouldn't work" or "I told you so," after the fact

- Expressing a message in words that sound positive yet displaying a facial expression or a tone of voice that gives the opposite impression

Stressful and challenging situations bring out the worst in all of us from time to time. Keep in mind that unproductive communication is about *patterns of behavior* and not about people. The idea is for every team member to be aware of his or her own behavior in exceptional circumstances. That's how you know where to begin making improvements.

Adopting an assertive speaking approach

Assertive speaking means expressing yourself in a positive and confident manner and allowing others to do the same. This manner of speaking promotes a two-way conversation and a collaborative effort to communicate. Coach your team members to work on speaking assertively, which means:

✔ **Being direct:** Get to the point of your message, clearly and tactfully.

✔ **Listening actively:** Hear and understand what others have to say.

✔ **Making the sense of importance clear:** Leave the listener in no doubt about how important the topic is to you.

✔ **Taking initiative and responsibility:** If a call needs to be made, make it. If dialogue needs to begin, begin it. Accept responsibility, neither making excuses nor blaming others.

✔ **Expressing confident nonverbal behavior:** Look people in the eye, speak to be heard easily with energy in your voice, gesture appropriately to emphasize a point, and have a sincere tone.

✔ **Collaborating to address concerns and problems:** When you have an issue to resolve with someone else, go to that person first and express the issue, listen to the other person, and work out a solution together. Avoid the issue? No. Attack the other person? No. Complain to others but not to the person? No. Go to the other person no matter how uncomfortable you may feel, and discuss the issue to work out a solution? A great big YES.

Every team member can become an assertive speaker — no special communication style is required. Someone can be low key or high energy; it makes no difference. What matters is dealing with situations and people in a positive, straightforward, and action-oriented manner.

Using nonverbal tools of assertive speaking

The nonverbal tools of assertive speaking help someone deliver messages in a positive and confident manner and make others want to listen. Here are some of the more important nonverbal tools to share with your team:

✔ **Looking at the audience:** Your eyes are like a magnet, attracting attention and interest. They also give you credibility and your message believability.

✔ **Projecting your voice and varying its inflection:** Speak to be heard easily. Especially in group situations, if you're too soft, people tend to ignore what you say. Also, put some variety in your voice. Don't squeak like a church mouse or drone in a monotone; people will tune you out.

✔ **Being sincere:** A tone that blends honesty and consideration of the audience commands attention in positive ways. Guard against sounding frustrated, angry, or sarcastic.

✔ **Looking animated:** People prefer to listen to others who appear confident and full of life. So forget that blank look, rigid posture, and hands jammed in the pockets. Smile, stand alert like you're ready for action, and use gestures to make your points.

✔ **Adopting a good pace:** Not too fast, not too slow, but *just right*. How do you know what's right? One trick is adjusting your pace to your listener's normal pace. But avoid speaking so fast that you slur words or so slow that your listeners lose patience with you. And don't forget to pause now and then. Pauses help refocus the listener's attention on what you're saying. Pauses help you minimize the overuse of boring, empty words like *uh, um, like,* and *you know.* Pauses also help you think before you speak, and that's much better than the other way around.

Speaking in the positive

How someone speaks involves one set of tools for assertive speaking. *What they say* — word choice — is the other set of tools. The objective when speaking assertively is to phrase the message in the best way possible, meaning honestly, directly, and constructively. The following tips can help keep your team members on track.

Say what you can do

Part of everyone's work is responding to other people's requests and inquiries. When someone asks you to do something, focus on what *can* be done. De-emphasize what *can't* be done. No one says you must act at once on every request or do things you aren't able to do. But most of the time, *something* can be done, so make that fact the focus of your response.

Compare these two different responses to the same request:

✔ Based on the requirements involved, I can have that request fulfilled in three days.

✔ With all that you're asking for, I can't possibly fulfill your request in any less than three days.

The first example says what can be done. The second example says what can't be done and even leaves some doubt about whether it will be done in the allotted time. Can-do language shows that you can act and plan to act. It shows that you're prepared to get work done and to provide service — a focus that helps teams perform well.

Say what you will do

For example, when someone suggests Friday as a deadline for certain work, and you say, "I'll try to get it done by Friday" or "Maybe I'll get it done by Friday," the other person walks away with little confidence the job will be done by Friday. Compare that to the firm commitment, "I will have it done by

Friday." Of course, if you have grave doubts that you can deliver, you need to negotiate the deadline. Will-do language communicates commitment and certainty.

Remember: Less is more

Everyone's busy, so remember to give the main idea and the important points, but don't overload people with all the details. You can always add more when an interest is expressed, but you can't go back and delete what you've already said when you've bored your listeners with too much information. Enough said.

Speak in language that your listeners understand

Avoid jargon and abbreviations when you talk with people who may not speak your language. Translate your technical terms and acronyms whenever they are vital to your message. Otherwise, use lay terms or common language.

When dealing with problems, use the language of solutions

To acknowledge "we have a problem" isn't a terrible thing; problems are business as usual for teams. But be sure to pay attention to the words that follow. When your language focuses on defining problems so that you understand them and then developing solutions for those problems, you engage others to work with you in the effort. Certain words can help you focus other people on working with you to develop solutions. Those words include the following:

✔ Recommendation

✔ Option

✔ Idea

✔ Suggestion

✔ Alternative

These are positive words that point toward solutions. They are not negative words that dwell on finding blame and putting people on the defensive.

Bring issues to closure

A big part of assertive speaking is bringing discussions to a clear end — to closure. You don't want people walking away from a conversation wondering what happens next or who's doing what. Make sure that important points stand out, agreements are confirmed, and action items are clear to everyone. Language like this can help:

✔ To recap, what I'm stressing that is important for us to do is . . .

✔ Just to make sure, we've agreed that you'll do such and such and I'll do this and that. Is that correct?

✔ Let's set some action items for what needs to be done before our next meeting.

Reviewing your team's written communications, both inside the organization and with outsiders, reinforces the importance of choosing the right words and helps you determine how well the team is following the good practices outlined in this section.

Avoid the negative

When you're equipping your team with language tools for assertive speaking, don't forget to warn them away from language that switches people onto the negative track, such as the following:

✔ **Trigger words:** They aren't negative by definition but often trigger a negative response in the recipient. Here are some examples:

- *Not, can't, won't, don't* — the language of being unable and not helpful

- *Should, need to, must* — the language of demands and directives

- *Policy, code, rule* — the language of inflexibility and mindlessness

- *Always, never* — the language of absolutes

- *Try, maybe, perhaps* — the language of doubt and uncertainty

✔ **Loaded language:** These are comments that others find instantly upsetting or offensive. Profanity; slurs aimed at someone's personal background such as race, religion, gender, or age; and labels like "stupid" and "idiot" are examples of loaded language.

✔ **Mixed messages:** These are *yes, but* messages. A mixed message may begin with what sounds like a sweet comment, but it turns sour after the "but" or the "however" in the middle of the sentence: "That's a good idea, *but* I don't see how it will help this team or why we'd want to do it." The real point is expressed at the end of the sentence, and it reduces to nearly zero the sincerity of whatever was said before. Being direct and sincere tends to work far better than saying nice things that you don't really mean.

✔ **Statements that negate your message:** Look for them in the opening phrase of what you say — and get rid of them. Statements like these tune listeners out; that's the opposite of what you want.

- Now don't take this personally . . .
- I hate to have to tell you this . . .
- You may not want to hear this . . .
- I don't know if you'll understand this . . .
- This may not be a good idea . . .

Coach your team to enable their listeners to evaluate the messages for themselves. If team members work on being direct and sincere, getting to the point, and speaking with a sense of importance, they will be using the verbal and nonverbal tools of assertive speaking for maximum effectiveness with the team.

Planning for Success — and Working Your Plan

Teams are all about getting work done and dealing with problems as a normal part of doing the work. This section gives you tools and tips for guiding your team toward using planning as a function of everyday work, for helping you recognize what you need to plan for and what benefits you can expect, and for developing strategies for creating plans.

Teams also need their leaders or managers — that's you — to model the behaviors that make for effective planning. When you want your team to perform efficiently and not chaotically and to have a sense of direction and not be lost, applying the tactics in this section is well worth your while. Just *plan* to do so.

Don't rely on memory for your plans — write them down. Until a plan is committed to writing, it doesn't exist.

Understanding what you need to plan

A team needs plans to support many important activities, such as the following:

- ✔ **Setting goals:** Goals define the outcomes or results that the team seeks to accomplish. Taking time for determining what those goals are is crucial for developing a team's proper focus.

✔ **Defining actions:** Work or action plans often support goals. They define what needs to be done to achieve the desired outcomes of the team's work.

✔ **Managing projects:** When you manage a project team, developing a project plan with the team is one of the first steps you want to take before launching into the work of the project. The project plan becomes the team's road map for guiding the work and the people doing the work from start to finish.

✔ **Defining priorities:** Deciding what issues or activities come first helps move team members in the same direction.

✔ **Solving problems:** Planning helps define how solutions are implemented and evaluated.

✔ **Mapping out work schedules:** Planning helps teams determine who's going to work when so that coverage is maintained even when people take time off.

✔ **Organizing short-term work assignments:** Planning can help determine what work each team member does from day to day and week to week. That, in turn, helps the team achieve its longer-term goals.

✔ **Addressing training needs:** Planning helps determine what skills need to be mastered and when time can be taken for learning them — especially important when cross-training is needed.

✔ **Guiding individual performance:** Planning in the form of time management helps individual team members outline their tasks and stay on top of them.

People support most that which they help create. Your job as manager is working with the team members to ensure that everyone affected by the team's plans is involved in developing them.

Making plans, step by step

Planning is a skill that you learn best by doing, but you don't need to reinvent the process every time you plan something. One all-purpose outline and set of questions can successfully lead you through the planning for practically any work assignment. Use the following outline and questions as your step-by-step guide:

✔ **Objective**

- What do we need to accomplish?

- What are the outcomes we need to achieve?

✔ **Milestones or key steps**

- How do we get from where we are today to the conclusion of our plan?

- What are the main actions that need to be taken to reach our destination?

✔ **Schedule**

- When does the objective of this plan need to be accomplished?

- When do we need to accomplish the key steps that must be taken along the way?

✔ **Resources**

- Who's going to serve in what roles for the team to achieve this plan's objective successfully?

- What materials do we need to do the work?

- Who outside of the team might we need to call on for assistance or support?

✔ **Contingencies**

- What obstacles or challenges might we face along the way?

- How will we deal with obstacles?

✔ **Checkpoints**

- When will the team meet along the way to review progress on its plan?

Your team can use this checklist as a guide for developing work plans, taking care to establish the steps sequentially in one of two approaches:

✔ **Going-forward approach:** You start with where you are today, mapping each key step and point in time as you move toward the target.

✔ **Backward-planning approach:** You start at the future end point and work in reverse, setting down each step your team needs to accomplish until you work your way back to the present. This planning strategy is particularly useful when your team faces a hard and fast deadline because the one thing you know for certain is the final date you must meet.

The length of time that a plan covers depends on the nature of the work. Major projects may go on for months, requiring months-long plans. A week-to-week plan may be more helpful in accomplishing ongoing work. The idea in either case is to apply issues and questions from the checklist as a guide to the development and redevelopment of the team's ongoing plans.

Going-forward approach

Figure 3-1 shows how a work-unit team, responsible for an ongoing function, plans its weekly output flow. This plan reflects a six-member team that handles customer order fulfillment.

Figure 3-1:
Weekly
work plan
for an order
fulfillment
team.

**Order Fulfillment Team Work Plan
Week of May 1–5, 2014**

1. Monday — Estimated 90 orders to fulfill for week.

ASSIGNMENTS:

- Picking orders — Jim and Sue.

- Packaging orders — Jose and Lou.

- Handling customer issues — Maria, Jose backup.

- Vacation — Sam.

2. Wednesday — Progress review and adjustments. meeting

3. Friday — Prepare report of results for the week. meeting

Illustration by Wiley, Composition Services Graphics

As you can see in Figure 3-1, the order fulfillment team has established a process for planning work and getting it done. On Monday, team members estimate how many orders they're going to fulfill that week and assign two-person teams to the three main functions. They also plan to cover for a team member who's on vacation, to meet midweek to review progress and make any needed adjustments, and to meet Friday to prepare the week's report. Come Monday, they're ready to plan for the new week of production.

Because of the ongoing nature of their work, the order fulfillment team finds it useful to plan weekly and keep the plan simple. Each week, using the going-forward strategy, they factor in contingencies such as vacations, training, and the volume of work they expect to handle. No need to make the plan any more complicated than that.

Backward-planning approach

Figure 3-2 illustrates the backward-planning approach. In this case, Team Y has been asked to make a 30-minute presentation on its key accomplishments for the past year and its goals for the coming year. The team has one month to get ready.

Team Y
Special Presentation to Management

Objective: Deliver a presentation within 30 minutes for the special July 1 management meetings that positively highlights Team Y's past year accomplishments and projected goals for the next fiscal year.

MILESTONES	DATES
• Presentation to upper management.	July 1
• Rehearsal of presentation.*	June 28
• Slides and materials for presentation set.* Presentation organized.	June 24
• Projected goals for next year set.*	June 20
• Data finalized on past year's accomplishments.*	June 15
• Assignments set for execution of plan.	June 1

    * Checkpoint meetings for whole team.

ASSIGNMENTS

- Data gathering — Rosie, Kevin, and Arlene

- Presentation materials — Don and Rachel

- Taking issues to management, setting outline for presentation — You (the manager)

- Delivering presentation — Whole team

Figure 3-2: Planning backward from a target date of July 1.

Illustration by Wiley, Composition Services Graphics

Figure 3-2 shows how Team Y plans to meet the drop-dead, no-excuses date when it must be prepared to stand up and deliver its report before a management group. The team starts with the delivery date, July 1, and steps backward, noting in reverse order everything that must be done, all the way back to the present. Note also that people are assigned specific responsibilities.

Figures 3-1 and 3-2 illustrate that a good team plan is simple and clear; it hits the important stuff but skips little details. You don't need to go into fine detail in the plan. Doing so confuses people and creates a document that no one uses. Details can be worked out at each step along the way.

For longer-term plans, you may want individual team members to keep track of their own details in a to-do list that's perpetually revised as tasks are completed and new ones come up.

Living the plan

Planning with a team involves more than merely setting up the plan. Planning also means living the plan: using it as a guide for doing the work. You can help make that happen for your team by doing the following:

- ✔ **Make the plan visible.** Everyone on the team receives a copy of the plan, either a paper or electronic version.

- ✔ **Review progress regularly.** Individual team members come to the review meeting ready to report on what they've done to help the team achieve its plan.

- ✔ **Update the plan.** No plan is carved in stone. Teams cannot afford to be that rigid. The farther a plan reaches into the future, the more you need to expect it to change as you move forward.

Solving Problems (Rather than Making Them Worse)

Problems are not the problem. They're a routine, normal part of any team's work. But the way a team goes about solving problems — ah, that's sometimes a problem.

In this section, you find out about team member behavior that only makes problems worse, including a few pitfalls to avoid. You also get a look at a couple of problem-solving models that your team can use in an organized or systematic approach to finding real solutions to work problems.

Avoiding the pitfalls

When a problem surfaces, certain kinds of team member behavior may pop up, making the problem worse. Stay alert for bad behavior like these five classic examples:

- **Finger-pointing and blaming:** Finding fault with other people is one of the all-time great aggravators of problem situations. The verbal barrage of accusations may sound like this: "Why do you always mess things up?" or "Why did you do you that?" Although problems sometimes can be upsetting, blaming others for them doesn't solve a thing and only builds resentment and anger in others.

- **Dwelling on the problem:** This behavior wins first prize in the *woe-is-me* category. It means constantly talking about how things are wrong, wrong, wrong. After a while, the doom and gloom begins creating a really bad stink.

- **Getting defensive:** Reacting in sharp tones, attacking others, and taking everything personally are characteristics of someone who's on the defensive. Defensive reactions to a problem situation shut down dialogue at a time when what's needed most is for dialogue to increase.

- **Avoiding the problem:** Problems can't be wished away. Yet people sometimes try to wave the magic wand and do just that. What usually happens? Chaos and frustration occur among team members, and you can say goodbye to positive morale and high productivity.

- **Developing a solution without understanding the problem:** Rushing in with a solution before you have a thorough understanding of a problem often simply compounds that problem. This kind of bad behavior may be based on good intentions — a team member's eagerness to be helpful, for example — but that doesn't excuse it. Sometimes a quick fix is, in fact, a solution to a problem that doesn't exist, making a complicated situation even harder to untangle.

Demand that your team's behavior generate positive energy and creativity, the kind of behavior that helps to solve problems. Encourage your team to do the following:

- Be patient and stay in control.
- Follow a systematic approach.
- Listen actively to one another.
- Understand the problem first and then focus on developing a solution.
- Solicit everyone's input.
- Be persistent, sticking with the work until you resolve the matter.

Revving up your problem-solving machine

This section walks you through two problem-solving models for the team to use as it works through issues. Like all good problem-solving models, these two ask you to understand the problem first before you work on developing a solution.

The S-T-P Model

In this three-step model, the *S* stands for Situation, the *T* for Target, and the *P* for Proposals. If the initials remind you of a certain well-known engine additive, that's a great way to remember this problem-solving model.

Here's what happens at each step of the S-T-P Problem-solving Model:

✔ **S = Situation:** The team defines the current situation concerning the problem or issue:

- What's working well? What isn't working well?

- What are the facts as we know them today, and how do people feel about the situation?

Ask each team member to answer these questions, and write what they say on a flipchart for all to see. Discuss the issues until everyone has answered.

Everyone seeing the current situation exactly the same way isn't as important as the team seeking the common sense of present conditions so that it can pinpoint the problem areas that are most in need of correction.

✔ **T = Target:** The target is the situation that you want in the future. When the present problem is resolved and everything is working well, what will the team's future look like? The target serves as the goal.

Have your team develop a target statement by following these steps:

- Ask each team member to write a one-sentence statement that defines the desired future state.

- Post the sentences for everyone to see.

- Using common themes from the posted sentences, collectively craft a target statement for the issue at hand. Try saying everything in only one sentence — make it a big-picture statement, skipping the details (they come next).

✔ **P = Proposals:** The gap between your situation today and your target for the future is what the P step is designed to fill — how you get from here to there. The proposals are the ideas for the solution to reach the desired target.

You can illustrate your words with an appropriate gesture. Try thi
Hold your left hand at waist level, palm facing upward, fingers out, to
indicate "where the team is today." Holding your right hand at the top
of your head as if you're blocking the sun out of your eyes, show that
you're looking toward "how high the team wants to go." The right
gesture adds a nice bit of visual reinforcement to the idea that you
want to communicate.

Follow the same routine that you use whenever you want the entire
team to engage in problem-solving: Ask team members for ideas that
they think can help solve the problem. Take enough time for everyone
to contribute before you begin discussing the issue, evaluating it,
eventually reaching consensus on the proposals that will help most, and
talking about the plans you need to make to implement the proposals.

The S-T-P Model often works best when a team has a fairly good understanding of the current situation and a well-defined and desirable target in mind.
It's usually the quicker of the two problem-solving models presented in this
chapter. But some issues are more complex or require more analysis to get a
good handle on them. In such cases, the second model is good to use.

The Six-Step Model

This is no dance lesson; it's a problem-solving model that works well when
the issues are complex or require more analysis than usual. Here's how it
works.

Step 1: Identifying the problem

Reach *consensus* with the team about what the problem is and describe it
briefly — in one sentence, if possible. Consensus is important because
reaching it ensures that you're all tackling the same problem.

Aim to define the problem in *problem* terms: for example, "Many customers'
orders are currently being shipped with errors and are going out past their
scheduled ship dates." *That's* a problem statement and much more precise
than, "The team needs to do a better job at fulfilling customer orders accurately and on time." The problem with the second sentence is that it looks
more toward the solution and doesn't zero in on what's going wrong in the
present.

Step 2: Analyzing the problem

You want to gain a clearer understanding of the circumstances surrounding
a problem, so answering these questions will facilitate this analysis:

- How long have we had the problem?
- What factors caused the problem?

✔ How often does it occur?

✔ What's the difference in performance between now and before the problem began?

Team members may find it necessary to research these questions so they can gather the data they need to answer them adequately. You're looking for root causes and patterns that explain recurring circumstances. People who like to use charts and graphs in problem analysis have an opportunity to put their talents to use.

Step 3: Exploring alternative solutions

The third step, searching for alternative solutions, has two sub-steps:

✔ **Brainstorming:** Team members generate all the ideas they can think of for solving the problem.

✔ **Evaluating potential solutions:** Team members discuss various possible solutions that have bubbled up during brainstorming, selecting a few that probably will work best. Sometimes more study and fact-finding are required for an improved understanding of how potential solutions actually can help.

In a later section of this chapter, "Brainstorming — Developing Ideas and Getting to Solutions," you find tips on facilitating the brainstorming and evaluating potential solutions with your team.

Step 4: Discussing how to implement a potential solution and forecasting the results

Sometimes team members hit on a solution that looks great, but when they examine what is needed to implement it and what probably can be expected to happen over the long term, they realize that the idea isn't feasible. Other times the opposite occurs: What looked like a lame idea at first, upon further review, turns out to be the one that works well.

Certainly you want your team members to remain creative and open to new options. They may have to run a possible solution through some trials to determine whether it's feasible.

Beware of the quick fix. Remind your team to be patient, following a systematic approach. Establishing good problem-solving habits is your objective, not repeating the slipshod ones that other people indulge in.

Step 5: Agreeing on a solution and presenting your recommendations

Agreeing on a solution may be the easiest step in the six-step model. A good solution often is a combination of several alternative solutions rather than one original idea. Remember, you're seeking consensus: Everyone on the team must agree to support the solution. So take your time in getting everyone on board.

The other part of Step 5, presenting a recommendation, comes into play when the designated solution requires support from people outside the team, including other groups or management above you. When you do need to make a recommendation, try this routine:

✔ **Get the entire team involved.** Members of your team are the knowledge experts just as much as you are. In addition, when a team presents together on a problem the members have worked hard to solve, you usually add a powerful punch to the presentation — strength in numbers.

✔ **Find out how much time you have for the presentation.** Key members of your audience may tell you how much time you have, but you may also be able to negotiate the time. Either way works as long as you touch all the bases while presenting your recommendation.

Less is generally more in formal presentations. Plan to cover all the main points, but skip the little details. Leaving your audience interested and eager to ask questions is better than boring them out of their minds.

✔ **Use the problem-solving model as your agenda.** Using the model as your made-to-order presentation guide, or agenda, shows your audience the thought process and work that was done before arriving at the recommended solution and demonstrates how thorough and organized your team is — traits that can really woo the crowd.

✔ **Define everyone's role.** Decide who will deliver what parts of the presentation. Everyone needs to participate, including team members who'd rather go to the dentist than make a public presentation. You can pair up your reluctant presenters with more eager participants — not everyone has to present equally in time. Just avoid bringing a team member along who sits there like a mummy. That looks bad.

Remember to assign someone to prepare and distribute any printed materials that the audience needs. Again, rely on people's strengths. If a team member or two are good at creating graphics and making PowerPoint slides, set them loose on those tasks.

Consider making your role the master of ceremonies. You can kick off the presentation, wrap it up at the end, and handle transitions from one presenter to the next. Working as an emcee gives you freedom to jump in and help a team member if an unexpected challenge comes from the audience.

✔ **Rehearse.** *Practice makes perfect* definitely applies when your team must make a formal presentation. Don't forget to set aside time to rehearse.

Above all, don't lose sight of your main focus: making a recommendation that others will support.

Step 6: Finalizing and executing the implementation plan

Take care to communicate with everyone who needs to know about the solution that you're rolling out. When a solution affects other people and they're not included in the loop, you often create a brand-new problem, one characterized by confusion, resentment, and even resistance. So make sure that you decide how to spread the word — in writing, face to face, or a combination. When the solution doesn't affect anyone outside the team, implementation is simpler: Just clarify who's doing what, and away you go.

Brainstorming — Developing Ideas and Getting to Solutions

Brainstorming is a group activity aimed at producing ideas — ideas about solving problems, for example. In some problem-solving situations, a few main ideas or options for solutions are obvious from the beginning, and you don't need to brainstorm. But in many other cases, quite the opposite is true: Your team is short on ideas and needs to be creative.

Making space for ideas

The goal in brainstorming is simply generating ideas, as many ideas as possible, but not yet evaluating them. (Evaluation takes place after brainstorming ends.) Here's how to get the best out of your team's brainstorming efforts:

- **Set ground rules.** You want an uninterrupted flow of ideas coming in at a good pace, so remind everyone that no comments or judgments are allowed until you reach the discussion stage. Only when someone's brainstorm is truly unclear can you permit a quick question for clarification, but try limiting even those instances. Otherwise, permit no discussion whatsoever as ideas are volunteered.

  On the other hand, you can encourage team members to take a *what if* approach in their thinking — if anything were possible and no limitations existed, what would you suggest? This kind of thinking opens people's minds and truly enables them to be creative. Remind team members that bad ideas don't exist when they're brainstorming.

- **Decide how long to brainstorm.** If you're under time constraints, set a time limit for brainstorming of, say, 10 minutes or so. But when time is not an issue, brainstorm until the team runs out of ideas. In either case, state up front whether you're watching the clock.

✔ **Select a brainstorming process.** You have two choices: *free-for-all* and *go-in-turn*.

  • In the free-for-all process, people shout out ideas as they think of them. This fast-paced approach often generates a great deal of creative energy.

  • In the go-in-turn process, the team follows a set order, like a batting order in baseball. The first person in line states an idea, then the next, and so on. If a person has no idea when his turn comes up, he just says "pass" so the process keeps moving at a good pace.

    Using the go-in-turn approach, you can give an idea only when it's your turn. No skipping turns, either — and one idea per turn, not five at once.

Unless a team has been together for a long time and is therefore skilled in the art of brainstorming, use the go-in-turn process. It equalizes participation and involves everyone on the team in generating ideas. Go-in-turn works better with less-developed teams where the free-for-all process tends to push quiet members to the sidelines while more vocal types dominate.

✔ **Warm up if necessary.** It may be useful for team members to think about ideas silently for a few minutes and write them down into notes before brainstorming begins. Doing so can prepare them to participate more easily when brainstorming begins, and it's especially useful for a team that includes introverts.

✔ **Record ideas for all to see.** A flip chart works well. Whoever is responsible for recording the ideas must be careful to capture the exact words without editing them. Rephrasing ideas may be well meaning, but it can be a drag on the process and irritating to brainstormers. Be sure, however, to permit the recorder to participate by adding her own ideas to the list in turn with the rest of the team.

✔ **Limit long-winded statements.** As team leader you serve as its Doppler radar. Remind team members when their brainstorming suggestions have been on the scope for too long. Keep the thoughts short and sweet. Go for the big idea. Save the details and explanations for the discussion stage.

✔ **Let people add on to ideas.** In the language of brainstorming, this is called *piggybacking* — adding on to ideas that already are on the list. Nothing is wrong with enhancing a brainstorm with a bolt of related lightning.

Brainstorming can be used for situations other than problem-solving. Think about using this technique whenever you're seeking ideas. For example, when you're leading a task team to develop key personnel and operational policies in a company where few exist, one of the first meetings with your team can be a brainstorming session to generate a list of issues for policy development. Or when you're leading a discussion about ways to recognize outstanding team and individual performances, brainstorming can jumpstart the conversation.

Guiding discussions

Brainstorming is a great process for helping people see new and different possibilities but also is frustrating when you produce a number of worthy ideas but can't possibly act on all of them. Getting down to the workable few is important.

Here's a five-step process to follow as you guide your team through the discussion phase after brainstorming:

1. **Clarification:** Go down the list with the team, asking if any of the ideas need clarification. For those that do, let the idea-givers provide an explanation, but avoid discussing the merits of ideas.

2. **Quick elimination:** Look at the list and ask whether any ideas can be eliminated right away. Prime candidates for the brush-off are ideas that sound interesting or creative but that everybody knows aren't feasible, as well as platitudes lacking any specific action to them. You may be talking a handful of expendable items at most. Be sure to get consensus agreement before you cross them off.

3. **Consolidation:** Combine similar ideas. This step, plus the first two steps above, shouldn't take more than a few minutes.

4. **Theme identification:** Look for common themes represented by the ideas, and label and group them by those themes. Doing so helps streamline the final step — evaluation.

5. **Evaluation:** Discuss the merits of each idea. How will the idea help the team get to where it's going? What will the team need to implement the idea? Use questions like these to stimulate the evaluation effort and push the team to scrutinize each idea thoroughly. *Remember:* You can't implement all the ideas at once — even when you like them all.

Allow enough time for discussion of the merits of each idea, but don't get into discussions of personalities. Who proposed an idea is of no consequence. When an idea seems to gain favor among team members, check with each one to see whether he supports the idea before you discuss the next idea.

Some ideas that fall off the list during evaluation still may be worthy of discussion at a later time. Make sure those ideas are documented so they can be reconsidered.

Voting for winners

If, after discussion, the team still has too many ideas and can't narrow the list down to a workable few alternatives, you can get the job done by employing a technique that's called *multivoting*. This technique is no more complicated than casting a ballot on Election Day, except it's done in the open. Here's how:

1. **Set the number of votes.** Decide how many votes each person can cast. Obviously, the number has to be much smaller than the number of candidate ideas you're voting on. Three to five votes per person can be just about right when you're looking at a list of 20 or more ideas.

2. **Hand out markers and let the voting begin.** Team members put a check mark by the ideas that they favor most. But don't permit *gang-voting* — one person casting all five votes for one idea. If the agreed upon number of votes per person is five, then each person casts a single vote for five different ideas she sees as most important to act on.

3. **Select the top vote getters.** When voting is finished, circle the ideas that received multiple votes. The top few vote getters are the ideas or priorities for the team to implement.

   If, after one round of multivoting, you still have too many ideas, conduct a second round of voting. For the second round, reduce the number of votes each person has in proportion to a shortened list of ideas.

Multivoting is used only after adequately discussing your team's ideas. Don't cut short the discussion simply to start voting and get the problem-solving effort over with. When multivoting is used at the right time, team members often find it helpful for setting priorities.

Chapter 4

Working Productively with Teams

....

In This Chapter

▶ Examining five group decision-making methods

▶ Sorting out a team conflict

▶ Making team meetings efficient and effective

....

*W*henever you're asking team members to pull together to get work done, having them help you make decisions about day-to-day work is part of the plan. In fact, leading your team effectively as a coach involves utilizing some form of shared decision making on a regular basis. In this chapter, you discover some techniques for ensuring that shared decision making is effective and relatively painless.

At times, a team is going to experience conflict; that's only natural. This chapter walks you through resolving team conflicts as well.

Of course, a team can't reach consensus without getting together from time to time. *Meeting*, though, is a dirty word in the work vocabulary, and breaking free from that perception isn't easy. You can apply techniques to make the dreaded but essential meeting a productive part of your team's process, and this chapter tackles that topic as well.

Making Decisions as a Team

People support most what they help create. Getting your people involved in making decisions about issues that affect the team gives them a sense of ownership. In addition, teaching them the decision-making process makes your team less dependent on you for every single decision. That's good!

Furthermore, if you're the leader of a group of people who do not report directly to you, such as a cross-functional task team or a project team, making all the decisions for the team by yourself is certain to cause rebellion.

Sometimes you may need to fly solo, but whenever possible, you should strive to include others in the decision-making process. How do you do so? For ideas, keep reading.

The five ways that decisions are made

Decisions are made in groups by one of five main methods:

- Unilaterally by the boss
- Unilaterally with some input from others
- By simple majority vote
- By consensus — everyone agreeing to support the conclusion
- By the consultative process — one primary decider with help from members of the group

No one method fits best for all situations. This section weighs the pros and cons of each.

The unilateral mode

In unilateral decision making, one person takes responsibility for making the decision for the whole group. Usually that person is the boss. As boss, you decide and announce your decision, and the others are expected to carry it out. Here are the pros and cons of the unilateral mode.

Pros

- **Enables you to move fast:** If you're willing to assert yourself and not be wishy-washy, unilateral decisions are quick — the fastest of the five main decision-making methods. Just make a decision and roll. Next issue, please!

- **Takes care of the small stuff:** Not every issue that you face in a workday requires a group to meet for discussion. Many such issues only require someone to act.

- **Works well in emergencies:** When the patient is in grave condition, everyone on the medical team wants the lead doctor to direct the surgery. When the building is on fire, everyone on the fire crew wants the fire captain to decide how to get water on the blaze. You simply don't have time to organize a meeting and have a group discussion.

Cons

- **Leaves some people scratching their heads:** When you're the only one doing the thinking, others may not understand your decision and thus may fail to implement it well.

✔ **Leaves you short of vital information:** No one person is all-seeing and all-knowing — not even you. When you make unilateral decisions, you shut the door on vital information that affects the way you make the final call. Because you don't ask around for input, you don't know what you're missing. At the same time, members of the group *know* what you're missing and may remark on your lack of common sense as they complain about you behind your back.

✔ **Generates less support:** People support most what they help create. If they're not present at the creation — well, you get the point. This point is especially true with issues that have a deep and broad impact on the group; the less they're involved in making the decision, the more they're inclined to resist the decision. You may have the greatest idea since the wheel, but when others who are affected by it are not consulted in any way, they have little motivation to buy in and support you.

The unilateral mode with individual inputs

Similar to the unilateral mode, one person, usually the person in charge, makes the call — but only after talking individually with others on the team, bouncing ideas off of them, and getting their thoughts. Here are the pros and cons.

Pros

✔ **Moves fast:** As decision maker, you can consult with as few or as many people as you desire. You get the input you need, and you act.

✔ **Gives you more information and insight:** The advantage is obvious: When you're speaking clearly to your team members about an issue and listening well to what they say, you're bound to be better equipped to make a decision than you are unilaterally without their input.

✔ **Creates more support and understanding:** The people with whom you consult usually understand your decision better and go along with it more readily than in the unilateral approach without input.

Cons

✔ **Gets little support from those who are left out of the process:** Individual consultation takes time, and some people may be left out. You can't count on support from people who are left out.

✔ **Short-circuits true discussion:** When it's just you and the other guy talking, neither of you reaps the rich benefit of a good group discussion, where differing perspectives can mix, creative sparks can fly, and new ideas can germinate and grow.

✔ **Can make explaining your decision difficult:** Because you consult with individuals individually, you alone hear a variety of views. No one else has the complete transcript, so to speak. If the things that you hear cause you to make quite a different decision than what seemed apparent in your first one-on-one, or if you just change your mind along the way, others may not understand why you did what you did and may initially oppose your decision. Explaining your decision after all that can be quite a challenge.

The simple majority mode

Making a decision by simple majority means half of the group plus one agrees with an option, and that becomes the group's decision. For example, five members of a nine-member group choose option A, and the other four choose option B. Option A is the group's decision. Here are the pros and cons.

Pros

✔ **Easy to administer:** People know how to vote — it's the democratic process. You can do it by raising hands, by shouting out choices, or by secret ballot.

✔ **Promotes group participation:** Unlike the two unilateral approaches, decision making by majority vote usually includes group discussion. Options are presented and discussed, and a selection process takes place. Everyone is present and can participate in making the final decision.

✔ **Helps in managing large groups:** When dozens or hundreds of people are in a common work situation, a majority vote on decisions works well. The process is efficient and familiar.

Cons

✔ **Breeds a winners/losers climate:** Quite often, people on the minority side feel like losers. Even when those in the majority don't gloat, the losers often turn into the opposition and don't support the decision. (See the U.S. Congress for examples of this gridlock.) This con tends to be the biggest problem with simple majority decisions in work group situations.

✔ **Lessens creativity and flexibility:** The first objective in majority decision making is deciding what choices to present to the group for a vote. If too many options are put on the proverbial table, a simple majority becomes much more difficult to reach. (See the Italian Parliament for examples.) Consequently, groups often try to artificially limit the number of choices by dumping them into categories. That process, in the name of efficiency, tends to turn off discussion and the possible discovery of even better options through the creative process of combining factors — for example, concluding that the best decision for the team is neither Option A nor Option B but a combination of the two as Option C.

The consensus mode

The word *consensus* is often misused. It doesn't mean a majority or a large majority agreeing to the terms of a decision. It doesn't mean that all agree — that's being *unanimous*. A decision made by consensus is one that everyone agrees to support. *Support* is the key word. Some group members individually may not agree with the group's conclusion, but they're willing to support it. Consensus is reached through collective participation. Here are the pros and cons.

Pros

✔ **Builds the strongest buy-in:** Decision by consensus requires more participation than any of the three modes described so far. The group is not finished with its work until every member expresses loudly and clearly her willingness to support the outcome the group reaches. That's buy-in.

✔ **Makes for the quickest implementation:** Unilateral decisions usually are the quickest to make but the slowest to implement. By comparison, decisions made by consensus usually are the slowest to make but the quickest to implement. Because everyone in the group participates in making the decision, everyone is on board and understands what needs to be done to implement the decision.

✔ **Develops a group's problem-solving skill:** Reaching consensus involves sorting out differences and resolving concerns — problem solving at its best. The more that groups, and especially teams, make decisions by consensus, the more their problem-solving skills develop.

Cons

✔ **Takes the longest:** Decisions made through consensus often involve a great deal of back-and-forth, give-and-take collective discussion. Reaching outcomes doesn't happen quickly. All it takes is one person not supporting the decision everyone else does, and the work for achieving a decision is not done yet.

✔ **Requires the highest level of communication skill:** You may wonder why this one isn't in the *pro* column. The reason is that people in group situations often don't bring communication skills to the table — the ability to actively listen and to speak up and express themselves constructively. They can get stuck arguing positions and never offer ideas to resolve the differences. These kinds of behaviors can swamp the consensus process.

✔ **Doesn't work for large groups:** The more people involved in the group, the harder reaching a consensus is. This especially tends to happen when a group size grows to ten or more. In groups of that size, it's hard for everyone's ideas to get a good hearing, and the likelihood of opposing points of view can often rise as well.

The consultative mode

In the consultative mode, one person — the primary decider — makes the decision but does so with the help of the group. In a collective forum, group members provide input helping to shape the decision to be made by the primary decider. This process happens in four stages:

1. **The primary decider establishes a starting position or clarifies an issue to be decided.**

2. **Team members provide input individually.**

3. **Team members discuss the options with the primary decider and among themselves.**

4. **The primary decider states the final decision and its supporting rationale.**

Here are the pros and cons.

Pros

✓ **Builds strong understanding about the decision:** Because group members are part of the collective work helping to shape the decision, they definitely understand what the decision is when it's reached. They're present to hear what the final outcome is and the rationale for it, and they know how it evolved during the discussion to which they contributed. You'll find no better way of gaining a strong understanding. In fact, the depth of understanding usually leads to group member support for the decision.

✓ **Mines rich input for the decision maker:** One big value of the consultative route, more so than the unilateral approach with individual consultations, is that the decision maker has the entire group together. Discussing the issue as a group generally produces a richer variety of points of view as the participants bounce thoughts off one another and the primary decider. In essence, more ingredients are thrown into the mix than typically are in one-on-one discussions.

✓ **Provides a structure for maximizing group participation:** The consultative mode follows a four-step process in reaching a decision. This organized process helps you gain full group participation in the decision and makes it clear who in the end makes the call. No one is left out, nor does the group have to keep going until consensus is reached. The structured process enables you to have good discussion and a relatively efficient way of reaching a decision.

Cons

✓ **Requires good listening and facilitation skills from the primary decider:** When you're the decision maker and your mind is fully made up on an issue, don't try using the consultative mode simply to gain the blessing of your group. It won't work. People see through this tactic. They can usually tell when you aren't genuinely open to differing points of view. You can save everybody's time by using the unilateral mode (described at the beginning of this section).

✔ **Requires recognition of someone as a primary decider:** In some team situations, such as task teams, project teams, and self-directed teams, no one person has the recognized authority to serve as a primary decider. Team leaders usually exist, but their roles generally are as coordinator or facilitator but not as manager. Unless the team designates someone as the primary decider of an issue, the consultative mode of decision making can't be used.

Because teams need collective efforts to succeed, they periodically need to employ collective forms of decision making — in particular, the consensus and consultative modes. But the key in showing team members the decision-making process is acquainting them with all five main methods so they're aware of possible approaches when an issue requires a decision.

Reaching a true consensus

Reaching a consensus may sound like the most natural thing in the world, but it isn't. Teams get derailed on their way to a consensus. But that doesn't have to happen when your team understands the steps that make the consensus tool work. That's the topic of this section.

Following the Yellow Brick Road to consensus

Your team can reach a decision by consensus in five steps. Show them all the details so that the next time you want to settle an issue by consensus, they'll know exactly what to do.

1. **Identify all options or views.**

   Get all the options and viewpoints out in the open. Write them on a board or flip chart, but hold off on any discussion until all points of view have been discovered. Groups sometimes derail their own efforts by jumping on the first idea or point raised, and doing so tends to cut off further input.

   When your team has more than one issue to decide, take issues one at a time through all five steps.

2. **Build on common ideas.**

   Look over your list of options or views to find out what thinking is in common. By piecing together commonalties before sorting out differences, teams build support for agreement easier and faster.

3. **Discuss the differences.**

   By identifying the commonalities first, you often begin narrowing the number of differences anyway. But before evaluating individual options, let people explain their thinking. You want team members to actively listen to various perspectives so that everyone truly understands the choices. Achieving this understanding makes the next step in the process so much easier.

4. **Propose alternatives or compromises to settle differences.**

The best way of settling differing points of view is first to listen and gain an understanding, and then to ask team members for ideas to resolve the differences among various points of view. Make sure that everyone feels free to be creative. Sometimes a good alternative is a compromise crafted from elements of two different viewpoints.

Sometimes the best question to ask team members when they wrestle with differences is "What would you suggest?" Doing so pushes everyone to think in terms of solutions instead of getting stuck on positions.

5. **Test consensus when you seem to have a conclusion.**

As a team works through the first four steps of the consensus process, a potential outcome and a potential decision may appear on the horizon. But appearances can be deceiving because group dynamics can fool you. Sometimes in group situations more vocal people actually reach an agreement on an issue while quieter folks just sit there, smiling at best. That's when you must test consensus with each individual not by asking "Do you agree?" but by asking "Will you support this decision?"

Consensus doesn't mean that you're seeking everyone's agreement with the decision or conclusion. You're seeking everyone's *support*. People sometimes may not personally agree with an outcome because it wouldn't have been their individual choice, but by being part of the discussion, they're willing to go along with or support the conclusion that the group has reached. Asking for someone's support is far different from asking for agreement. When you have every team member's support, you also have his or her commitment — that's true consensus.

Dodging the potholes that throw you off Consensus Road

Sometimes when teams try to reach consensus on issues, they take shortcuts that stymie the formation of a true consensus and undermine the decision. Here are some pitfalls you want to avoid:

✔ **Jumping to a majority vote:** When a team is getting stuck in its discussion to reach consensus, abandoning the path and settling the differences by taking a vote doesn't help at all. Team members in the minority often walk out in opposition to the decision. Informal voting can be useful as an interim step to determine how people are thinking about an issue, but you need to immediately return to discussion to sort out differences in a true consensus mode.

✔ **Striking a deal:** Making a deal sounds like this: "If you support me on this issue, I'll support you on some future issue that's important to you." Sorry folks, trading favors doesn't build support for a decision needed now, and it may create animosity later when the favor isn't returned. Don't make political bargains when you're working to reach consensus.

✔ **Using tie-breaking methods to end a stalemate:** Tossing a coin or drawing straws is okay for settling kids' disputes, but those tactics have no place in the consensus process. The problem is that you wind up with winners and losers and not a decision that everyone can support.

✔ **Browbeating a lone dissenter:** When one team member doesn't support a decision that everyone else favors, avoid launching a verbal barrage at the dissenter just to make consensus happen. Doing so intimidates some dissenters and causes others to argue even more. Neither outcome builds support but rather only stirs resentment. Differing views need to be welcomed and their proponents made to feel safe if a team ever is going to develop the skill of consensus decision making.

✔ **Accepting appeasement in place of affirmation:** As discussion drags on, some team members may conclude that they agree with a decision just to get the session over. Or they may say they agree simply to avoid expressing a difference and causing a conflict. You can hear it in their half-hearted "That's fine with me" or "Whatever you folks want." Don't let appeasement substitute for affirming support behind a decision; if you do, the appeasing team members sometimes walk out after the meeting is over and immediately criticize the decision — a surefire way to produce a false consensus and a decision that eventually is undermined.

Differences of opinion are natural and expected. Seek them out and involve everyone in exploring alternatives to settle the differences. Stick with it. That's how you work through discussions to reach consensus.

Selecting the right decision-making tool

After weighing the pros and cons of the consensus decision-making approach and the consultative approach, how do you decide which one to use in a given situation? Equally important, how do you know when an issue requires a shared decision-making process for resolution as opposed to a unilateral decision? If you use shared decision-making approaches for every little issue, your team won't have much time left for work!

This section provides you with answers and guidance so that your team makes the best use of its time.

Taking a moment to plan

Before deciding whether team participation is needed in decision making, you need to figure out a few basics. Here's your to-do list:

✔ **Define the issue first.** Clarify for yourself what the issue that needs a decision is. When you do that first, you begin discovering whether you need team involvement.

✔ **Clarify the role of the team.** When you have an issue for which team involvement can be beneficial, clarify the role that you want the team to play. Sometimes that means a decision-making role with you using the consensus or consultative modes. Other times you may want the team playing only an advisory role. You can avoid confusion and misunderstanding by making sure that team members understand what role you want them to perform.

✔ **Set parameters for the team's involvement.** Parameters are boundaries. They determine how far a team can go in deciding an issue, measured by factors such as these:

- Budget

- Time

- Responsibility or authority

- The objectives of management above you

Avoid misunderstanding and havoc: Let your team know this pertinent information as you involve them in the decision-making process.

✔ **Determine the decision-making mode.** The choice is totally yours, and that's the way it should be. Acting decisively and independently is appropriate for you as coach of the team. No hard-and-fast rules exist to help you with deciding when to involve the team in making a decision — the consensus and consultative approaches — or when to handle the issue yourself — the unilateral and unilateral-with-consultation approaches. (Wouldn't life be so much easier if there were rules?) But a few factors may influence your judgment one way or the other, such as these:

- The extent to which an issue directly affects your team's day-to-day work

- The scope of an issue beyond the team's direct work level

- The importance to you of garnering team member support behind an issue

Even when the factors above are present, *don't* involve the team in making the decision if your mind is strongly made up on what you want to do concerning an issue. You're better off explaining what you want to do and selling the team on why you think it's the best way to go rather than asking them to "share" in making a decision that you've already made.

If you seek consensus on every little matter, your team can be bogged down in a *paralysis by analysis*. Small issues that involve primarily you and management above you or other persons outside the team often are best decided by you alone. Sometimes you can get the team to agree to let a small subgroup handle an issue for them. In these cases, you (or the subgroup) need to report back to the team so that everyone is in the loop.

Resolving Conflicts on the Team

When you want to build a high-performing team, you want conflicts. That's right — conflicts are good for the team. How come? Because you don't want everyone thinking the same way all the time, and you certainly don't want people agreeing just for the sake of peace and what appears to be harmony.

As your team searches for better ways of handling the work or resolving business issues, you want different perspectives to come out. When they do, conflicts sometimes arise. But that's good because of what can be gained. Conflicts can spark creativity, promote richer exploration of an issue, build more meaningful solutions, and strengthen teamwork.

This section shows you how to steer conflicts in a constructive direction, including the communication and problem-solving tools that you need for resolving conflicts.

Using five steps to resolve conflict

Sometimes team members have conflicts over work procedures, or ideas for solving a work problem, or strategies for executing a work plan. Differences of opinion about work issues can pop up unexpectedly — even when you're meeting on a totally unrelated topic. But you can deal with them by applying the following five-step, needs-based model.

Step 1: Defining the problem

First, develop a one-sentence statement that defines the problem or issue. Limit it to only one sentence so that the central issue is clear to everyone.

Second, clarify what the differences are. What are the perspectives of the parties involved? Are the differences based on methods, ideas, goals, styles, or some other factor? Use questions like these to analyze where the differences are, but don't spend too much time at this point or you may fall into the pit of overanalysis and possibly more conflict.

Step 2: Identifying the needs of stakeholders

Moving away from people's positions — your way versus my way — and looking instead at people's needs is a critical step. Consider needs extremely important because they explain why you want what you want.

For instance, when you go car shopping, you can easily haggle with the sales representative about the price that you want to pay — that's your *position*. But a good sales representative seeks out what's important to you in buying a car — whether it's gas mileage, style, how you'll use the car, or your budget — before attempting to talk price with you. Meeting all your needs so that your purchase gives you value is key.

The same idea applies in this second step of the conflict-resolution model. Identifying needs moves everyone to a higher level, where seeing what is truly important is easier.

Stakeholders are parties affected by the issue and the outcomes. Certainly the list of stakeholders includes the team members involved and quite often the team as a whole. Stakeholders also can be people outside the team who are affected by what the team does, including other departments, management above you, and customers. What you do in this discussion is identify each stakeholder and then list the critical needs each one has. What you often find is that stakeholders have some needs in common or at least complementary needs.

Step 3: Developing options for resolution

Brainstorm to generate ideas for meeting the needs of the various stakeholders — without passing judgment on any idea they have. As people volunteer ideas, write them down for all to see, together with the needs that they address.

Step 4: Evaluating options against needs

Evaluating is the step where conflicts really get worked out, so spend the most time with it. You want to focus discussions on ideas or options that work best to meet stakeholders' needs. Avoid backsliding into the problem. Drill the ideas down into specific actions so what's to happen going forward is clear and concrete.

The key in conflict resolution is spending more time working on the solution than dwelling on the problem.

Step 5: Confirming and implementing the agreement

Recap the agreement you reach, making sure that it's clear and understood by everyone. After that, discuss how to move forward — who's going to do what and when — in the implementation phase. Set a date to review progress, and don't forget to put everything in writing.

Coaching a team to settle conflicts on its own

Your ultimate goal when conflicts arise in your team is for team members to settle the issues themselves. You want them to take responsibility for their behavior and for developing their own solutions.

When the team depends on you to resolve all its conflicts, here are some outcomes you can expect:

- ✔ You become complaint central, the place where team members constantly come to complain about one another.

- ✔ You become the almighty monarch, making all the decisions and preventing your loyal subjects from thinking and doing for themselves.

- ✔ You become the *source* of many conflicts. Team members who don't like what you decide criticize you, often behind your back.

- ✔ You have little time to focus on the important issues that you need to attend to as the team manager or leader.

To avoid creating a dependent team and, instead, facilitate the growth of a self-sufficient and responsible team, remember these tips:

- ✔ **Lead by example.** Never complain about other managers or other groups in front of your team. When you have issues with other people, go talk to them directly (don't use e-mail). When team members know that you address concerns and conflicts timely and directly, they have a role model to follow.

- ✔ **Teach.** One reason many team members dodge dealing with conflicts is they don't know how. Most have not had role models for conflict resolution (have you?). That's why you show your team how to use the communication and problem-solving tools outlined in this chapter. The sooner they learn, the better.

- ✔ **Coach with questions.** Questions are good coaching tools because they prod staff members into thinking issues through and working them out for themselves. When you provide answers instead of asking questions, you deny that benefit to team members.

When one team member comes complaining to you about another team member, use questions like these to lead the complainer to take responsibility for himself:

- ✔ What have you done so far to address your concern with (the other person)?
- ✔ What would be your objective if you talked to (the other person)?
- ✔ How would you express your concerns constructively — what would you say?
- ✔ What would you propose as a solution to this conflict for each of you?
- ✔ What did you learn in the training that can help you deal with this situation?

When team members understand that you turn their complaints into queries about what *they* intend to do in resolving their own problems and concerns, they'll get the idea and start figuring things out for themselves, sparing you the trouble. But you can take full credit for that breakthrough.

Asking for commitments and follow-up

When team members figure out how to constructively address a conflict, you want to hear a firm commitment. Ask "When will you address that issue with (the other person)?" Then say, "Check back with me after you've had the meeting and let me know how it works out." These statements ensure accountability, and the best part is that the team member is addressing the conflict without your intervention. Your good coaching pays off.

When a team member doesn't want to take any action himself, you can still ask him what he's going to do to remain respectful and cooperative with the other team member. Addressing the situation that way tells him that you expect him to remain a professional and a helpful team member. Telling you about his issues with another team member changes nothing as far as what's expected in his behavior with the other party and everyone else on the team.

Addressing performance problems

A performance problem is not the same as a conflict. Team members have their clashes and differences sometimes — those are the conflicts that you coach them to handle themselves. But when you see a team member whose behavior has become disruptive in the team, who isn't pulling her weight, or who remains uncooperative after good-faith efforts by other team members to address concerns, then you have a performance problem, and stepping in as coach to work things out with the problem team member is your responsibility as manager.

When team members know that you expect them to handle their own conflicts but that you're always there for performance problems, you're building a high-performance team.

Serving as the third-party facilitator

Occasionally, a third party must step in to help the first and second parties settle their differences. Observing when a third party is needed is easy: The other team members continue their clash; the tension between them grows so thick you can cut it with a knife. Clearly, they can't constructively resolve the conflict themselves and your intervention is needed. This section contains tips for working as a third-party facilitator.

✔ **Decide which players come to the table.** When the conflict involves only a couple of team members, the meeting is between them. When a number of team members are involved, then everybody comes to the table. Don't use a group setting to address a conflict that involves only two players — unless you prefer fighting fires with gasoline.

✔ **Select a problem-solving model.** Decide what you're dealing with: a personality clash, a dispute over a work-process matter, or a little bit of both.

✔ **Write an agenda and set ground rules.** You need an agenda so that you can hand it to participants in advance of the meeting. The agenda doesn't have to be any more elaborate than the numbered steps of the problem-solving model you want to use. When the meeting begins, set a few ground rules to govern the professional conduct that you expect. Stick to the agenda; insist on professional conduct. When the meeting involves the whole team, you may want to appoint a team member who understands the conflict-resolution models to serve as facilitator. You attend to provide guidance and support as needed.

✔ **When the clash is interpersonal, prepare the individuals separately.** Common sense tells you not to throw the combatants together without giving them a chance in advance to sort out their thoughts and emotions. While you prepare the team members separately, ask them to write out their concerns and their ideas about what each person should do to reach a solution. Doing so helps to move them from simply venting anger to focusing on being constructive and gives everyone a script, increasing the likelihood that the meeting will stay on track.

✔ **Put the agreement in writing.** Don't leave an agreed-upon resolution to memory. The written working agreement defines the solution, and everyone gets a copy.

✔ **Meet later to review progress.** Set a time for everyone to return to the table and review progress — perhaps a few weeks or a month out. At the follow-up meeting, use the working agreement as the agenda. Ask the parties to talk about how things are going with respect to the agreement. Don't forget to provide your observations, too. If the agreement needs to be modified, do so. If the team members are making progress, let them run the next follow-up session themselves and just keep you informed about their progress. But if things are not progressing, stay directly involved. If you don't see progress at follow-up meetings, set consequences such as disciplinary action and carry them out.

If you observe at the first follow-up meeting that both parties are sticking to the agreement, don't hold back on positive feedback. Your reinforcement of their good efforts to resolve differences encourages them to do even more of the same.

Giving Your Meetings New Life

Meetings are at the root of a lot of what happens in the workplace, and yet you'd be hard-pressed to find anyone who looks upon them favorably. Meetings have a reputation for being boring, frustrating, and a waste of time. But they don't have to be — and shouldn't be, especially considering the important purpose they serve. They're the place where individual efforts are brought together and coordinated into a collective effort.

To make team meetings run effectively, help your team members discover the basic elements of structure that meetings need to have, and then put those principles into practice. This section covers the fundamentals of productive meetings, and Chapter 4 of Book III provides more great information to consider.

Noting the three stages of a meeting

A good meeting has three stages: the organizational period, the meeting itself, and post-meeting work. Here's what should occur in each period.

Stage 1: The organizational period

Organization takes place before the meeting, encompassing all the planning and preparation that precedes the meeting, including any or all of the following:

- Defining the purpose of the meeting
- Inviting the appropriate people
- Writing and distributing the agenda to participants
- Making advance preparations with individuals when necessary
- Taking care of logistics — meeting room and materials — and food if you're lucky

Stage 2: The meeting itself

The group comes together to conduct its business and execute th
You get the details in Chapter 4 of Book III.

Stage 3: Post-meeting work

The final stage includes everything essential to following through on agreements made during the meeting, such as:

- ✔ Participants performing the action items they have agreed upon
- ✔ Communicating with other interested parties who did not attend the meeting
- ✔ Preparing the meeting minutes and distributing them to all participants and any other interested parties

Many meetings flop because of the lack of attention paid to the before and
after stages. Building in the discipline for top team performance includes
following through on all three important stages of a meeting.

Taking a minute for the minutes

Minutes are the written record of a meeting. You're going to want them for
nearly every team meeting because they document what the team did at the
meeting — much better than relying on memory.

A good set of minutes needn't be lengthy. You want the highlights of the
meeting, not a transcription of every word each person spoke. Structure
the minutes around the flow of the agenda and capture highlights by doing
the following:

- ✔ Covering the main topics
- ✔ Noting the decisions made and agreements reached
- ✔ Describing action items given, to whom, and when they're to be done
- ✔ Listing work products that were created
- ✔ Discussing issues that are in the works for next time

Have the minutes typed up and distributed as soon as possible after the
meeting. Retain a copy of them and the meeting agenda in the team's central file. This routine ensures that the team has a record of work completed
during meetings and helps members to stay on track and see their progress.

Performing meeting roles

For a team meeting to be a good one, three roles must be performed every time the team meets and a fourth role is performed as needed. Here's a look at each role:

- ✔ The **facilitator** guides the flow of the meeting by helping the group work through its agenda so that it accomplishes the purposes of its meeting. As manager or team leader, you certainly need to be able to facilitate your team's meetings, but you don't have to do it every time. Coach other team members to use the skills of the facilitator so that they're better able to take on this role and so that meetings can proceed in your absence. The last section of this chapter covers the skills of effective facilitation.

- ✔ The **scribe,** sometimes known as the *recorder,* takes the minutes, types them, and distributes them. This role can rotate among team members. The scribe needs to take good notes, but the focus of the minutes is on the highlights or key points of the meeting — a job that almost every team member needs to be able to handle.

- ✔ **Participants** contribute to the work of the meeting and are expected to come to the meeting prepared to be active and positive. They play the most important role for a meeting to be a success. Team guidelines can help to cover expectations of meeting participants, so make sure that you include those expectations in your guidelines (a topic covered in Chapter 2 of this Book).

- ✔ **Presenters** appear at team meetings as needed. They are people who report findings, share expertise, or relay other pertinent information that the team needs to have for its work. Sometimes a team member plays the role of presenter; sometimes the presenter is someone from outside the team.

Make certain that the presenter, especially when it's someone from outside your team, knows what to talk about and for how long. Also, don't forget to factor in some time for questions from the team.

Holding team meetings for meaningful purposes

Purpose tells everyone why the meeting is taking place. It indicates what you're trying to accomplish when your team comes together at the meeting table. The lack of a clearly defined purpose is a major meeting-killer. So, what are some of the good purposes for team meetings? That's easy:

- ✔ Planning
- ✔ Making decisions
- ✔ Solving problems
- ✔ Resolving group conflict
- ✔ Evaluating results
- ✔ Setting goals
- ✔ Setting assignments and schedules
- ✔ Training
- ✔ Recognizing and celebrating success
- ✔ Building working relationships
- ✔ Creating policies, procedures, and other work products
- ✔ Generating or testing ideas
- ✔ Reviewing status
- ✔ Making recommendations
- ✔ Conducting a postmortem

Good purposes lead to *working meetings.* A team coming together to get work done helps all its members perform better when they go back on their jobs — that's a working meeting.

Notice that *communicating news* and *sharing information* are not on the list of good purposes for meeting. Teams need news and information, of course, and some of that sharing occurs during all purposeful meetings. But making communication the primary purpose of a team meeting means that you don't need to meet very often. Communicating information frequently can be done just as well by e-mail and printed memos. For teams to perform successfully, they need to have regular working meetings.

Creating agendas

An agenda is a written plan that guides the flow of a meeting toward accomplishing its purpose. A well-written agenda is crucial to a meeting's success. Not surprisingly, developing a meaningful agenda for a team meeting takes planning, but often no one gives the agenda much thought until the last minute.

Your challenge is to coach your team toward taking an active responsibility in shaping the agendas for team meetings. You may want to have the final say about what's included, but each team member should have input so a meeting addresses the team's true needs.

Chapter 4 of Book III provides a detailed look at what needs to be included on a meeting agenda, as well as how to format it. Definitely flip back to that chapter to get the scoop on creating agendas. Keep in mind that in addition to the basic information you're used to seeing on agendas (such as the date and time of the meeting and the topics to be discussed), you should strive always to include the purpose of the meeting and the process for working through each topic. The process outlines *what* the team is working on, *how* team members are going to work through it, and *who* will participate in each step. Defining the process on the agenda is essential for keeping meeting discussions focused and fruitful.

Getting maximum participation

Also in Chapter 4 of Book III, you find tips for stimulating participation in meetings. You likely have some team members who always share their ideas freely in meetings and others who sit back and observe. Your goal should be to hear from every one of your team members in every meeting. After all, the loudest people in the room aren't the only ones who generate great ideas.

Organizing and distributing your agenda in advance of each meeting can promote greater participation. When team members know in advance not only the topics of discussion but the process for working through them in the meeting, they can walk in the door prepared for what's expected of them.

In addition to crafting and sharing a great agenda, here are tips for making sure that all team members participate in a positive way:

- **In every meeting, call on every person in the room to share ideas.** Ask good open-ended questions — those that can't be answered in just one or two words — and wait patiently. Give team members time to think and respond thoughtfully.

- **If a team member's ideas are unclear, ask follow-up questions.** Probing an issue can help team members think ideas through more completely and explain themselves more effectively.

- **When someone makes an important point, paraphrase it to make sure you understand it.** Encourage team members to do the same with each other. In addition to clarifying meaning, this tool lets the speaker know she's really being heard.

- **When differences of opinion crop up, systematically problem-solve.** Guide your team through the steps of solving a problem, involving the entire team and not just the people who are expressing disagreement. Getting everyone involved is your best bet for working through the issue creatively and positively.

Chapter 5

Managing Advanced Team Matters

Self-directed may be the opposite of your very definition of *team,* but a lot of advantages exist for turning ownership over to a team and its members. Doing so isn't without some challenges, however. Nor is arranging and managing a project or task team — those temporary affiliations brought together to complete a project or suggest solutions to an issue. How you reward teams or individual employees for jobs well done brings up another complicated set of questions to address.

But, hey — this is what you signed up for, right? As a manager, you have to be ready for handling details of all kinds, all while keeping your teams moving productively toward their goals.

Don't worry. Within this chapter you get advice for dealing with some of the more advanced (and interesting!) matters that you may face.

Managing without Supervisors: Self-Directed Teams

The idea of self-directed teams is to tap into employee potential and enable workers to take ownership of their jobs in reaching higher levels of productivity entirely on their own initiative. That idea certainly catches attention among management folks. Who's going to argue with increased productivity, cost savings, and greater employee job satisfaction and commitment? But no magic wand exists for tapping into the employee potential of self-managed teams.

Self-managed teams aren't the same as *unmanaged* teams. You can't just one day decide to ditch an old supervisor-to-subordinate relationship; doing so is an invitation for disaster.

Making these special teams work takes a lot of energy. Here you find tools to get through the transition, overcome challenges, and develop a self-directed team to its full potential so that it flourishes.

Defining and dissecting a self-directed team

You won't find *self-directed team* in the dictionary, but here's a commonly accepted definition:

> A group of employees organized around an operation or a process of work who are responsible for managing themselves and the day-to-day functions of the work that they do with little, if any, direct supervision.

Self-directed teams — sometimes called *empowered work units* or *autonomous work teams* — function in their truest sense without supervisory authority. Team members are interdependent, but the role of supervisor usually is missing. A self-directed team is as much a team as any other, but it has a unique management structure: no supervisor.

By comparison, a regular work group reports to a supervisor who is part of the group. In many such cases, the supervisor does much of the same work that the group members do, or he performs a higher level of the overall work that the group must accomplish. Self-directed teams report to a manager, but generally no management personnel are part of the team's ongoing and daily operations.

The role of manager or supervisor, in the case of a self-directed team, is replaced by all the members of the team. Together, they plan and execute the work, day in and day out, carrying out the directions set by management above them. It isn't unusual for only one manager to oversee several self-directed teams.

In most cases, self-directed teams are work-unit teams that are ongoing in nature. By comparison, project teams and task teams often have qualities of self-management, but their time-limited nature generally doesn't enable them to fully develop as a self-directed team. On occasion, you may see a management team functioning as a self-directed team trying to run a department or division within an organization. Such a team has no designated department head and no top dog — only a group of unit managers trying to run the entire operation together.

The premise behind the concept of self-directed teams is summarized in this formula:

Empowerment + Employee Involvement = Very Good Results

Empowerment means making people accountable for results by giving them timely and accurate information in addition to the authority, autonomy, and support they need to do their jobs. In essence, management above says, "I'm giving you the freedom and resources to do the job as you see fit, within certain parameters, and you're then expected to produce good results and will be held responsible for doing so."

Employee involvement is about enabling people to participate in the management of their own work and to have a voice in planning, shaping, and making decisions that affect the work they do.

The core idea about self-managed teams is permitting the people closest to the work to organize, coordinate, and manage the work so that it gets done. They're all capable adults; why not let them think and act as adults by providing them with the guidance, support, and direction they need and then setting them loose to do the job?

The flip side, of course, is that if you permit a group of employees to manage their own work without close supervision, they're likely to do little of it. You're putting the inmates in charge of the asylum . . . so to speak.

 If you like talking about *empowerment* but your actions don't match your words, avoid talking about your interest in self-directed teams. Why damage your credibility? Managers who want to make every decision run into difficulties helping self-directed teams get up and running, and they probably won't make regular work-unit teams thrive well, either. Dictating and controlling can stimulate compliance among workers, but they also tend to kill off commitment.

From a manager's point of view, the idea behind self-directed teams is extending control without limiting responsibility or completely letting go. People need to know the boundaries within which to operate. Instead of the supervisor having primary responsibility for the group's performance, the team members together have it.

There's no doubt that not every employee wants this level of involvement and responsibility. Keep reading to find out about the challenges and rewards of working with self-directed teams.

Casting the roles in a self-directed team

The biggest part of what every self-directed team does is identical to any team or regular work group: getting the work done. Whether that means making widgets, processing insurance claims, servicing customer calls, coding software, maintaining parks, producing books, or leaping tall buildings in a single bound, the work of the group needs to be done.

In addition, self-directed teams also handle many of the personnel, administrative, and operational responsibilities that a supervisor or manager otherwise handles. That includes things like

- ✔ Setting group direction and goals
- ✔ Managing the group's budget, from forecasting to monitoring expenses
- ✔ Purchasing supplies and materials
- ✔ Exercising sign-off authority on timesheets and other personnel matters
- ✔ Writing and conducting performance reviews
- ✔ Making work assignments
- ✔ Scheduling when work is to be done and deploying resources to do it
- ✔ Monitoring and reviewing work progress
- ✔ Reporting group progress, issues, and results to management
- ✔ Enforcing policies
- ✔ Setting standards and developing work procedures
- ✔ Counseling employees on performance issues
- ✔ Carrying out discipline
- ✔ Hiring new members into the group
- ✔ Organizing and implementing staff training
- ✔ Tackling major customer problems
- ✔ Responding to management inquiries and requests
- ✔ Representing the group to management above and externally as needed

This list isn't exhaustive, but you get the point. Where self-directed teams are concerned, many of these supervisory responsibilities are handled directly by the team. Generally, the longer a self-directed team exists and the more mature it becomes, the greater the number of supervisory responsibilities it tends to handle. The team owns these areas and is accountable for them — in addition to doing its work.

Common roles in the day-to-day operation of a self-directed team include the following:

- ✔ **Team member:** The team members are the worker bees on the team, and they share in the management responsibilities of the team. That doesn't mean everyone does exactly the same job. Technical skills vary, and certain duties may be delegated to certain team members because they bring specific skills to the table.

- ✔ **Team leader:** The team leader is first a team member who contributes to the work that all team members do but also serves as coordinator, facilitator, and the team's representative to management. As the point person with management, the team leader receives directions from management and facilitates their implementation by the team.

  However, the team leader doesn't exert supervisory authority and isn't the boss. The boss of a self-directed team is the manager to whom all team members report, including the team leader. Whenever a team leader tries to order team members around, a revolt usually occurs.

- ✔ **Coach:** The third role that impacts self-directed teams is sometimes referred to as *coach,* meaning the manager to whom the team reports. The coach's job is giving direction, setting parameters, obtaining resources, helping remove obstacles, and mentoring. Although coaches aren't part of the daily workings of the team, they're the ones who oversee what happens, and, most important, they hold the team accountable for its results.

Now featuring: The features of self-directed teams

Self-directed teams generally have seven common features:

- ✔ **Horizontal structure:** The organizational levels of most self-managed teams are flat; there is no hierarchy or vertical structure. Almost everyone is a team member. Although skills and responsibilities may vary among team members, scales of titles and authorities are eliminated. Self-directed teams are egalitarian: All members are equal.

- ✔ **Discretion over daily work:** No supervisor or manager tells people what their assignments or schedules are. Team members handle all the day-to-day responsibilities. In fact, much of their time together is spent planning and deciding who's going to do what in getting the work done.

- ✔ **Frequent meetings:** All teams meet frequently, but self-directed teams often meet *more* frequently, for reasons noted in the previous point: They must plan and make decisions about getting the daily work done. Meetings may last only a few minutes but can occur almost daily. Longer meetings that go into greater depth on team management and performance-related issues generally occur less frequently but, nevertheless, happen with some regularity.

✔ **Shared management responsibility:** Team members share responsibility for getting work done and managing the team. Specific management tasks include budgeting, scheduling, and other similar administrative issues. The team often works together on management matters. This approach requires greater transparency so that self-managed teams have the tools they need to make sound decisions.

✔ **Much cross-training and training:** Training is a continuous part of the life of a self-directed team. Training topics range from honing business administration skills to running meetings and solving problems. In addition, team members commonly teach one another their job functions to create more shared responsibilities (otherwise known as cross-training). Because of all their training, members of self-managed teams broaden and deepen their job skills, which contributes to their professional growth.

✔ **Shared concern about quality:** Self-directed teams with production-oriented functions have a quality control function built into the work process that often becomes a routine part of the job. That's different from the typical manufacturing or production work scene, where the quality assurance or quality control functions can be separate. Quality control is everyone's job on a self-managed team. It isn't the lone concern of a separate group of specialists in a different department.

✔ **Collective-based evaluation and pay systems:** This feature of self-directed teams occurs more often when teams have grown and matured over time, not with teams in earlier stages. Mature teams may spend considerable time collectively evaluating their overall performances and reporting the results upward to management. Team members employ peer review techniques for holding one another accountable.

Incentive pay also figures into the design of some self-directed teams. Traditionally in most business organizations, bonuses and commissions for hitting performance targets apply only to management and sales positions. In self-managed teams that have incentive systems set up, all team members share in a financial reward for the positive results of the team.

Making the transition to self-directed teams

Getting started and moving forward with a self-directed team structure represents a major change in your organization. You're asking people to cast off roles and responsibilities that are comfortable to them, and you need to prepare yourself for the work required to transition successfully. The first step is articulating why the self-directed team structure is what you need.

Determining why you're implementing self-directed teams

If you want people to support a change, they need to understand what's driving it. Here are a few questions for you to answer first so that you're better prepared for communicating coherently to others when rolling out the teams:

- ✔ What are the business and organizational reasons for making the move to self-managed teams?
- ✔ What are we seeking to accomplish through this team structure?
- ✔ What will the future look like when the teams are running well?

Your main reason for change must connect with better productivity and efficiency. Otherwise, why go this route? Maybe you run a large department and see a considerable amount of employee potential that's been left untapped. Maybe your department has a structure that promotes separation and turf issues and you want to break that down. Maybe you're spread too thin and have a large number of people reporting to you. Maybe you've had a few supervisors leave your group and you see an opportunity to replace them with a team structure. Regardless of what is prompting your line of thinking, make sure that you can articulate it clearly and persuasively to other people who will be affected.

Laying the groundwork

Before going forward into self-directed teams, you may need to build support for a change among people outside of your department, including peer managers, management above you, the information technology group, human resources — likely all of them. You definitely want to have conversations with all the stakeholders, telling them where you're going with the self-directed team concept and what support you're going to need. A big part of this advance work is defining what investment is needed to make the teams work — investment in terms of money, resources, training and equipment, and modifications that may be needed in personnel and information systems along the way. When the employees are union members, having early conversations with union representatives to build their awareness and understanding is a crucial step.

At the same time, laying the groundwork often means improving your grasp of the concept of self-directed teams — and doing the same for other key individuals who are involved in making the team structure work. Reading all the literature you can lay your hands on and visiting other organizations that have adopted self-directed teams also are good steps.

Thinking long term

For self-directed teams to work, you need to think about the future. Where do you want to see the teams six months from now, a year from now, and a few years from now? Answering these questions helps you with defining your vision so that you can communicate it to your team members, giving them a sense of direction and a positive outlook toward the team's future.

Making a hit-and-run change in management is a bad idea. Don't announce any change in structure and then immediately remove yourself from active involvement. All that does is invite anxiety and chaos. Moving to self-directed teams takes time and never is a quick fix.

Thinking long term, you must understand how much time is needed for the teams to develop and perform effectively. You need to be able to plan *your* time, too. For this effort to work, plan on being actively involved for a good, long time before you're able to step back and provide mostly direction and oversight.

When you initially move into self-directed teams, you won't save time for yourself. New teams need much guidance. Making a good return on your investment must be your objective, especially with your investment of time, because you want the time you expend in the early stages to pay off down the road when your teams are more self-sufficient.

Creating a steering team to help

Depending on the scope of your transition into self-directed teams, forming a steering team can be one of the best things you do. Your steering team can be made up of managers who will oversee the teams in a big-scale transition. The initial team leaders are probably involved in a medium-scale deal. And, when the transition is limited in scope, only a few key team members are involved.

A steering team plays two roles: planning and problem-solving. You want these people helping you plan the move into the teams and addressing issues and concerns that are likely to arise with that implementation. You may need to address a host of issues in a new self-managed team structure, such as evaluating customer or vendor relations, defining the size and shape of the teams, and redesigning the work processes.

Your steering team needs to remain in place for as long as you need it. Think months rather than weeks so that you have help with leadership issues.

Drafting the implementation plan

With help from your steering team, outline the following factors (as they relate to your particular situation) that are essential for moving into self-directed teams:

✔ Key events and when they will occur

✔ Roles, responsibilities, and makeup of teams

✔ Short-term — three to six months — goals for the teams

✔ Training needs

✔ Any other issues to work on as you move forward

✔ Communication strategies for initial implementation and ongoing efforts

You don't have to figure out every last detail, but you need an implementation plan so that you're guiding your team members with care and focus into a self-directed mode. And, of course, you must plan how often you'll review progress on the total performance of the teams — usually at least quarterly for starters.

Deciding what to do with the supervisors

Dealing with supervisor issues often is the biggest challenge that you face when creating a self-directed team, and it's one that you want to plan for and address earlier in the process rather than later. The whole idea of self-direction is that you don't have supervisors monitoring and controlling day-to-day activities of the work group. But when you leave former supervisors floundering without defined roles, you add to their already high level of anxiety and may turn them into leaders of the resistance movement against self-directed teams. So what do you do?

You have two choices concerning what to do with a supervisor. One is integrating the supervisor within the team structure; the other is moving the supervisor out of the group. In neither case should the supervisor's pay be reduced.

✔ **Integration:** Former supervisors can play many important roles on self-managed teams. Some supervisors can be a big help on your steering team because they know the operations well. Following are some other possible roles:

- *Team leader,* assuming that the former supervisor is able to lead through positive behavior rather than brute force

- *Trainer/mentor* based on the ex-supervisor's technical expertise and experience

- *Regular team member,* a good fit for former supervisors who are happy not dealing with the headaches and responsibilities of their former role

- *Manager overseeing one or more teams,* a possible role for a select few ex-supervisors if they have good coaching skills

> Discuss these options with your supervisors and determine what roles best suit them and the team.
>
> ✔ **Reassignment:** When a supervisor shows little interest or aptitude for playing a role on the team, talk to human resources and other managers in the organization to see whether a transfer to another group can be worked out.

In the end, if you can find no good fit for an ex-supervisor within your teams or elsewhere in the organization, consider providing an exit package with a safety net, meaning a reasonable severance package, some kind of outplacement support, and a transitional period rather than immediate departure. A transitional period of a few weeks to a couple of months is reasonable. During this interval, the person can undertake special projects for you, such as documenting current work procedures. You can be flexible and allow him to take time off for job interviews. Your objective is fair treatment for the affected supervisor, thus alleviating concerns among other employees that someone is being pushed out the door abruptly and harshly.

Responding to concerns about job security

People worry when they see reorganization in the works because restructuring often means workforce reduction. So it's understandable that moving into self-directed teams can create worker anxiety over a fear of layoffs. When anxieties flare up for too long, you know the detrimental effect they can have on employee morale. What do you do?

Don't use a change into self-directed teams as a mechanism for eliminating jobs. Doing so nullifies the value that you can gain with teams and damages your credibility.

Whenever you hear that people are worried about job security, address their concerns directly through face-to-face communication, both one-on-one and in groups. Certainly you need to mention that layoffs are not part of the plan, but don't spend a great deal of time dwelling on that point. Sometimes, the more you say that something *isn't* going to happen, the more people think that it *will*. Inviting people to talk about their concerns is a good strategy, but be sure to listen carefully and talk with them about the vision that you have for the teams and the plans that you have going forward to make your vision a reality. Emphasize that team members are actively involved in making these plans come to fruition. Listening with concern and focusing on the future can help your people work through their anxieties about the unknown.

When someone's role no longer is essential in the new team structure, do your best in helping that person find another job within the organization.

Getting a team rolling and working

At the beginning of the transition, team members won't know what the self-directed thing is all about. They may speculate that it's just another one of management's flavors of the month that soon will pass. And when work remains undone from the previous structure, team members may be wondering how it ever will be handled under the new structure. If you neglect these concerns, your teams sputter rather than roll, and your team members grumble rather than perform. What do you do?

Have your team develop a team-purpose statement and team guidelines, as discussed in Chapter 2 of this Book, so that team members understand their overall roles and what specifically is expected of them. As teams begin doing the work, make sure that team members understand the parameters of their decision making. Parameters define boundaries, and members of self-managed teams need to know how far their authority extends and where they need to bring their team manager into the decision-making loop. When you delegate assignments, make sure that you spell out these parameters.

When team members experience significant changes by becoming self-directed, they often need some structure that helps them adapt to and make sense of the chaos. Figure 5-1 shows a simple daily planning sheet that self-managed teams can use for organizing their work and monitoring progress.

Figure 5-1:
Daily
planning
sheet for a
self-
directing
team.

Daily Planning Sheet

Date _____

Assignment To Be Done	Team Member(s) Responsible

Training Schedule:

Progress Made From Yesterday:

Issues/Problems To Address:

Illustration by Wiley, Composition Services Graphics

Meeting for a few minutes every day to plan that day's work is a good practice in the early stages of a self-directed team. Some teams like using this routine so much that they continue daily meetings indefinitely because doing so helps them build their own structure instead of living in constant chaos. At the same time, reviewing planning sheets every day reveals progress and issues the team must resolve.

Notice that a planning sheet like the one in Figure 5-1 contains a "Training Schedule" line. Setting goals for the next three to six months also is a worthwhile exercise early in the implementation stage. Doing so gives team members a look at the big picture that their daily planning supports.

Building teams to self-manage and grow

Getting started is one big challenge with a self-directed team, but keeping the team moving forward is another. You can do it by remembering to focus on the important elements of the early stages of implementation that are covered in the following sections.

Communicating

Don't abandon all those great communication programs that you put in place for liftoff. Teams meet frequently to plan and carry out their work, and you want to use those face-to-face occasions to provide leadership and direction and not have to rely so much on e-mail messages. Keep in closer contact by being present at occasions like these:

- Regular team meetings with your core group of team leaders who pass on information to the teams
- Periodic all-hands meetings at which you bring together all the team members
- Occasional drop-in visits with team meetings to stay in touch
- Regular *MBWA,* or management by walking around

MBWA is an effective form of informal communications. You walk around to people's work areas for a few minutes of social chatter. You have the rest of the day to handle business issues, so have a little fun. MBWA is a communication strategy that makes you a visible leader and enables you to gain a better knowledge of your team members as people and not just as employees.

Establishing training as a regular business practice

Stating your expectations about training and helping your team find the resources it needs to meet those expectations are vital parts of your job. You can evaluate their success when you evaluate team performance.

Members of a self-directed team have much to discover. Pursuing ongoing professional development has at least two valuable results for your teams: It spurs individual motivation and builds skills that lead to higher levels of performance.

Expanding team responsibilities a step at a time

Ultimately, a truly self-directed team handles all responsibilities that a work group supervisor would. But a team can't assume all those responsibilities at once. Team members need time to discover and absorb various supervisory routines into their daily functions, especially administrative matters. When asking a self-directed team to take on new responsibilities, follow these steps to effectively delegate responsibilities:

- ✔ Spell out the results that you expect.
- ✔ Define the parameters that team members need to work within, especially limitations on time and authority.
- ✔ Provide the training and other forms of support that team members need to take on new duties.
- ✔ Set up checkpoints for reviewing progress.
- ✔ Evaluate the results.
- ✔ Set new goals.

Maintain ongoing accountability and focus with your self-directed teams by setting the frequency — quarterly, perhaps, but no less than once every six months — with which you plan to evaluate team results versus performance targets. Requiring the team to make presentations to you as part of this evaluation process really pushes the responsibility level for achieving results to everyone on the team. You may also want the team to produce an interim report of its performance — say, monthly — much as a supervisor is often required to do.

After a team evaluates its progress, with business direction provided by you, have team members reset their performance goals for the next time period and the plans for how they'll achieve those goals. That, after all, is why they're self-managed teams. Hold them accountable for achieving results.

Developing systems to fit the team structure

When venturing into self-directed teams, you often discover that the systems and policies of your organization don't always make a good match with the new team structure. For example, when company policy says that only some-one in supervisory authority can sign off on vacations, employee timesheets, and purchase requisitions, you need to work within your company structure to modify these systems. Administrative areas that may require change include quality assurance practices, vendor relations, compensation, staff administration, work schedules, employee recognition, and performance reviews. You don't want your self-managed teams constantly colliding with internal obstacles when they are charged with managing those same functions. You need to serve as a barrier buster, helping your teams grow in managing their own performances.

Be sure to take a look at your performance rewards. If they're encouraging competition rather than supporting collaboration, your system is undermining your team.

Continuously addressing issues and making improvements

When observing how your self-managed teams are progressing — from what's working well to what isn't — you have an opportunity to help them get better at developing solutions.

As much as you possibly can, delegate the development of solutions and periodic review of progress as a means of helping them maintain their accountability. Whenever people don't know what to do, show them and coach them, but seldom volunteer solutions yourself. When you want a team to become self-managing, you want team members taking responsibility for addressing issues and making their solutions work.

Managing Project Teams and Task Teams to Success

A *project team,* as the name suggests, is a group of interdependent people who come together to complete a project or a special assignment. A *task team* or *task force* is a group of interdependent people who commonly come together to study an issue and recommend solutions or courses of action. Project teams and task teams have several things in common:

- ✔ They work under deadlines, sometimes tight ones, and exist only long enough to do their work and then disband. They're not ongoing like regular work-unit teams.

- ✔ They often are *cross-functional,* meaning they are composed of people from different disciplines and departments whose expertise needs to be melded together for the project or the task.

- ✔ The members often have regular jobs that they do on a daily basis. Being assigned to the project or task team is an add-on to their regular duties. However, in some companies, people work solely in project teams, rotating from team to team as they are assigned.

  ✔ Management above sets the directions and objectives for the team, and everyone must live with those factors regardless of whether they agree with them.

Common factors between project teams and task teams also represent challenges to team managers. Whether you're called the project manager or task team leader, you're usually managing people who on an organizational chart don't actually report to you. You're not their direct supervisor. In addition, because they have other job demands on their time, this project or task team may not be as high a priority for them as it is for you. Add in occasional resentment for having to accomplish something they didn't ask for, and no wonder managing such teams is quite a challenge.

Beginning with the essentials for effective project management

The neat thing about projects is that they have a beginning and an end. The bad thing about projects is that when you don't get started on the right track, you may not end up where you want. Two keys that are particularly important as you begin are the team charter and the team project plan, which are the focus of this section.

Getting your charter set

Ships don't sail and planes don't fly without first determining in what direction they're headed and what destination they intend to reach. When you take on the leadership of a project team, you want to do the same thing by developing your project charter.

You create the project charter with your sponsor, who usually is the person in senior management who endorses the work your project team is about to do. In many cases, the sponsor approaches and asks you to become the project manager (as in, "Boy, do I have a project for you!"). At times, you may initiate a project, but in any case you routinely seek out a sponsor so that you have upper management support for the initiative.

Work out and document the following issues for your project charter:

  ✔ **Project objectives:** What do you need to accomplish with this project? What results are expected? Work with your sponsor to answer these questions. In most cases, you're looking at one or two main objectives for a project — any more than that may mean the scope of the project is too big for one team to handle.

✔ **Staff resources:** In some cases, you instantly know who should serve on a project, based on what is needed for it. In other cases, your resources already have been selected for you. You can often help determine who the right people are for the project by discussing staffing with your sponsor. When staffing a project, look for people with these three main qualities:

- The right technical skill sets for the project

- A record of good performance — plus enough time available to lend to your team's project

- The ability to coordinate and work well with others

✔ **Budget and material resources:** How much money can you spend on this project? What other limitations are in place? Asking these questions tells you upfront what constraints you face and enables you to remove any such obstacles whenever possible. You also need to determine what material resources you need: equipment, technology, tools, and so on. And don't forget to discuss any support services you may need from other groups. Work out all these issues with your sponsor.

✔ **Timeframes:** Most projects have deadlines. Knowing what those deadlines are and what to expect from them upfront is best because you can tell members of your team what you're working with, time wise. By exploring the deadline issue with your sponsor before you start, you may be able to negotiate a more advantageous schedule for the project.

✔ **Progress reporting:** You want to know when updates are expected, what's most important to report, and how it should be reported — in writing or orally. Take the initiative by recommending how you want to handle these issues and considering what your sponsor prefers. Keeping your sponsor in the loop and away from the need (or urge) to nag or micromanage is the idea here. Also, if any other key people or stakeholders have an interest in how your project progresses, find out who they are and how to keep them in the loop, too.

Document all the areas and issues that you discuss and resolve with your sponsor, and send her a copy. Voilà! — you have your project charter. You also have accurate directions for your new team.

Remembering to plan

The first piece of work that a project team needs to do isn't the actual project work but rather the plans it needs to make for the project. Many project teams operate without a documented project plan; at best, they may have a schedule. The project plan is one of your essential tools for managing projects and the teams that work on them.

Various project management software packages exist for developing and updating project plans. You can keep it simple by making your own form that addresses the following:

- ✔ **Project name or subject:** When giving your project a name or subject, choose your words carefully so that they incorporate the outcome you're expecting, such as "The Building Remodel Project." Doing so goes a long way toward avoiding the "Huh?" response from others outside the team who want to know what you're doing.

- ✔ **Project objective(s):** Listing your project objective (or objectives) fully defines the end results that you expect from the project. Project objectives connect the project charter to the project plan.

- ✔ **Deliverables:** Deliverables are products of work that the team creates to achieve its objectives. Describing what deliverables you're expecting explains to everyone on the team exactly what must be produced.

- ✔ **Schedule with milestones:** A schedule that highlights specific events is a major piece of the project plan because it outlines key steps of the project and timeframes for each step.

- ✔ **Assignments:** This piece of the project plan explains what roles and responsibilities team members are going to play, like actors in a movie script. You can share responsibilities, but make sure that every team member plays a role in doing the project.

- ✔ **Checkpoints:** Checkpoints are times when the team reviews its progress and works, as needed, on other project-related issues. Don't leave these meetings to chance. Scheduling them upfront (often around project milestones) tells everyone that your project is organized and that ongoing communication and accountability are expected.

Developing and using a project plan

The following tips describe the things you can do to help develop and implement a good project plan:

- ✔ **Involve team members in drafting a project plan.** Explain the objectives and the boundaries, but then have your team members help you map out the plan. Participating in that way helps them buy into the plan. A more important reason for having team members help you with planning is that they have much of the knowledge about the particular work that's needed to do the project.

- ✔ **Give a copy of the plan to every team member.** A plan is fairly useless when you're the only person with a copy. Everyone involved in a project needs a copy of the plan so they too can live by it.

✔ **Coordinate task lists with the plan's milestones.** The project plan contains essentials for guiding the project, but it doesn't need to be refined down to the detailed task level. On the other hand, individual team members need to prepare their own detailed task lists that coincide with the milestones of the project plan so they can provide copies for their team members. Their lists and descriptions of where the project is going compliment each other, helping team members stay on track together.

✔ **Revise the plan as needed.** A project plan is a guide, but it isn't carved in stone. The longer the term of a project runs, the more likely that changes will occur along the way. When changes occur, simply make sure you update the master project plan and distribute new copies to your team members.

✔ **Manage by plan.** This last tip summarizes the previous four and serves as a reminder that the project plan is one of your most important project and team management tools. The plan helps in everything you do in leading your team through the project. Details matter less and diversions are less of a distraction because you have a strong focus on the direction in which you're headed and the results that your team needs to achieve.

Set team guidelines with the members of your team. Guidelines serve as standards of excellence for the kinds of behaviors that members of your team can expect from one another when working together.

Starting a task team on the same page

Task teams offer challenges that sometimes are greater than even project teams. Generally, the work that people do as part of a project team is part of their job, and they're performing many of the functions that are required of them in their regular jobs. However, with most task team members, you're asking them to work with you on something that is in addition to their regular jobs. Often task team members are not even applying skills they use on their regular jobs but are working on issues quite different from what they normally do.

With these challenges in mind, establishing the right focus with your task team members is crucial from the beginning.

Doing some preliminary work

Much of the preliminary work that you do with project teams also applies to task teams. Two main areas of emphasis are establishing focus and forming the team.

Generally, task teams tend to have fewer sponsors than project teams do and are treated more like extra credit projects that are nice to do than like the important work that project teams are charged with doing. Nonetheless, when you initiate an idea for a task team, establishing an overall focus is a good thing to do.

Building the support you need when forming a task team means finding a sponsor — or turning to the manager who suggested the task to serve as your sponsor — so that you reach an understanding about the following topics before you start to work:

✔ What issue is to be studied and why it's important

✔ What outcomes are expected, such as recommendations for a solution, a design of a program, or the implementation of a new policy

✔ What resources you need, from staff to finances

Finding the right team members often is your biggest task. People who show little interest can't be counted on to show up regularly for team meetings or tend not to follow through on assignments. They are not individuals that you want on your task team. (They'll do just fine, however, if *you* want to do all the work.)

When organizing your team, be sure to steer clear of these two problematic approaches:

✔ **Allowing management to select team members for you:** Whether the idea to select your team for you is coming from your sponsor or from others in management, push back and don't let anyone who isn't a direct part of your task team tell you who should be on the team. You can certainly listen to suggestions from anyone, but strongly reserve the right to select team members you think will work best.

✔ **Accepting anyone who volunteers:** Volunteers are good because they usually already are interested in what your task team is going to do. On the other hand, volunteers may not have the kind of work ethic or teamwork abilities that you need for your team to succeed. Whenever that's true of a particular volunteer, say, "No thanks," and then go after the people you think will work best.

You may not be aware of everyone who's talented and available for task team service. So, define the main team-member criteria that you're seeking and ask managers from other groups for recommendations.

When recruiting an individual you want for your team, cover these points in your conversation:

- The purpose of the task team
- Why you're so interested in having that person on the team — tie it to your criteria
- The projected time and work commitments

After discussing these points, you then can address any questions or concerns the potential team member may raise before closing the deal with the simple but direct question: "Will you join the team?"

Getting the task team rolling

Use initial task team meetings for making sure that everyone on the team is on the same page. Remember to do as many things with (and not for) your team as possible. Here's your checklist for those sessions:

- **Determine the length and frequency of team meetings.** Task teams need some kind of regular meeting schedule to do their work. Although you must factor in people's regular work schedules when considering the needs of the team with respect to its task, you also must keep this general rule in mind: The longer the interval between meetings, the slower the progress the task team makes.

- **Develop a team-purpose statement.** This statement clarifies the overall role of the task team and sorts out differing points of view that people may have about the team's emphasis. Sorting out these differences upfront is better than running into obstacles later on.

- **Set team guidelines.** What handful of expectations do team members have of one another when they're working together? Consider these team guidelines as a staple on your team's diet that builds a healthy coexistence.

- **Develop a work plan.** At the beginning of a task, nobody knows the exact outcomes or recommendations that you'll reach at the end, but you nevertheless want to make a plan for dealing with your issue. By outlining key steps or milestones that you believe will occur, and including target dates for reaching them, your team has a direction in which to go. The plan can (and undoubtedly will) be revised as you go.

- **Define special roles.** Members of some task teams have special expertise or interests. Maybe one team member handles external relations well, another is best at handling policy research issues, and so on. Identify the expertise and special interests that exist among members of your team so that you can tap into them.

Keeping a team on the productive track

This section provides tips and strategies that you can use with project teams and task teams for managing their journeys successfully to their final destinations. It also gives you tips for helping task teams with their fact-finding and recommendation-generating efforts.

Maintaining focus and pushing accountability

A laissez faire or hands-off approach ensures two outcomes that you don't want when you're leading a project team or a task team: The team never really coordinates its efforts, and the results that you want never see the light of day. But that won't be true in your case because you understand that after your team becomes organized, the hard work of keeping team members on track and producing really begins. How do you do that?

Here are a few key tips:

- ✔ **Meet regularly and maintain discipline.** Project teams and task teams need to meet on a regular basis — no less than once every two weeks and often much more frequently, depending on the work. You don't want to wait for a crisis to develop before pulling your team together. From planning to problem solving, from status review to creating work products, these kinds of teams have plenty of good reasons to meet.

- ✔ **Address problems in a timely manner.** Encountering problems in team situations is inevitable, but whenever such a problem concerns the entire team, be sure to use the team meeting as a forum for addressing it. Problems with getting the work done well are the ones that you particularly want to put in front of the whole team. Problems with individuals, on the other hand, probably need to be addressed privately with the individual.

- ✔ **Conduct regular status reviews with your team.** Reviewing team status is one of the key tactics that drives your team's accountability and results. A status review is a follow-up progress check on how team members are doing with their assignments as well as a tool for planning the assignments for the next short-term period.

- ✔ **Recognize achievements.** When you're reviewing progress and addressing issues that crop up with your teams, remember to stop long enough to offer recognition to successes as they occur. Hitting a milestone definitely is one such success and so is on-time delivery of quality work. Celebrate successes like these. From making announcements on the floor to taking the team out for lunch, *how* you recognize good performance matters less than actually recognizing it. Positive reinforcement goes a long way toward melding a team together and building a successful collective experience.

Incentives and Other Rewards for Teams

Behavior that's rewarded is repeated. When you positively acknowledge good performance that you see occurring, you're likely to see it happening again. That's the principle of positive reinforcement.

But it works both ways: Wrong behaviors that are rewarded end up being repeated, too. Whether you're managing individuals or teams, recognizing and rewarding the right behaviors is the point. Taking good performance for granted never has been much of a motivator.

You can recognize good performance in many ways. Historically, in business organizations, *incentive pay* — that is, pay beyond a person's regular base salary, usually in the form of bonuses or commissions — was limited to people in management and sales positions. In recent years, however, incentive pay has been extended to many levels of employees. But money alone is not enough. To complement pay-based rewards for good performance, this section also shows you how to recognize good work in ways that cost little or nothing but richly express your appreciation.

Investing in team incentive pay

Incentive pay is a form of variable compensation. Sometimes called a bonus, it's a component of wages that varies by performance and is proffered in addition to your base salary. Incentive pay is a way of rewarding good performance with money rather than with promotion and without adding costs to base salary structures.

Incentive pay for teams can be a strong management tool that drives teamwork and performance. It's also a tool that can be helpful when you're working with work-unit teams and project teams.

Respecting the rationale

When you consider developing a team incentive plan, first ask yourself: Why do I want such a plan? What do I hope to accomplish with it? You want to be able to communicate answers to these questions to your team members so they understand where you're headed with an incentive plan.

Here are some objectives to aim for with a team incentive plan:

✓ **Stimulating increases in productivity:** Increased productivity is the number-one reason for establishing an incentive plan. You're pushing performance so that you gain good results — even better results than before. You want to create a link between performance and reward. When you do, you have a mechanism in place that helps you achieve the productivity you're after.

✓ **Rewarding key behaviors that you need for good productivity:** Remember, behavior that's rewarded is repeated. A team incentive plan is a tool that helps you reward the right behaviors for stimulating strong performance. In most cases, these behaviors deal with teamwork, output of work, and quality of work and service. These positive behaviors are what you need team members to exhibit so they produce the work results that are in demand. A team incentive plan serves as a tangible reward for such behaviors.

✓ **Increasing an understanding of business needs and the kind of performance required for meeting those needs:** A good incentive plan paints pictures for team members of the business targets that need to be achieved and the progress they must make in meeting those targets. Information gives people the power to make decisions and act. A good incentive plan helps your team achieve that objective.

✓ **Aiding in the retention of good performers:** Labor markets often are quite competitive, especially for good employees. You can't afford to give people more money just to stick around. However, you can be creative with your salary systems so that you remain competitive in the job market, giving employees reasons to stay with the organization because you reward them for helping deliver the results that the business needs.

Money is not the be-all and end-all for team member motivation and retention; in some cases, it can even be demotivating. Many factors other than pay come into play, such as the challenge of the work, the chance to grow, and the quality of your management. So think of a team incentive plan as just one tool among many.

Before you design and implement a team incentive plan, talk with your team members about your main objectives and ask for their feedback. When your team thinks incentives are unappealing, you don't need to bother with designing such a pay plan. More often than not, introducing the idea creates excitement, but check it out first.

Designing the incentive plan

A good team incentive plan rewards team members equally for the collective results of their work. When designing an incentive plan so that you reap the benefits you seek, make certain you accomplish the following:

- **Offer rewards that attract attention.** Incentive pay has to be big enough to be interesting. Otherwise, you'll hear comments like, "When you give us peanuts to do everything you're asking of us, why even bother?"

- **Budget for the rewards.** A team incentive plan is more than a reward system. When used wisely, it also serves as a financial planning tool. By determining the monetary level that team members find worthwhile, you can budget for that amount. Thus, you have the incentive pool in place and don't need to figure it out after the fact. One caveat: Cover yourself in case a major downturn occurs by making sure everyone understands that incentive payouts are based on economic and business conditions.

- **Define performance criteria.** Team members must understand the goals or targets that form the basis for the incentive plan. Quite often, you want to involve team members in defining what those targets are. Including them in the design of the incentives builds their willingness to buy in to the process, of course, but it also recognizes that they're the ones who are doing the work and ought to know what the unit needs to accomplish.

   How many goals or targets do you need? Three to five, at most, because you don't want a cumbersome plan. You want to include the areas that are most relevant to the collective performance of your team.

- **Measure the results.** Every goal you set for the incentive plan needs to be measured in a reasonable way; otherwise, it isn't a goal that will work. You may need to create new mechanisms for measuring results — from survey forms to software applications. Provide performance information that is generated to the team so the team members can see what's happening.

- **Connect performance and payout.** In compensation lingo, the connection between performance and payout is called *line of sight.* In other words, the plan offers team members a clear understanding of the relationship between what they need to achieve in their performance and the financial reward they receive for it. If team members do *x* in their performance, they each will earn *y* in dollars for their efforts. Connecting performance and payout gives team members a sense of control over their destinies.

✔ **Include a beginning payout level and a top end.** Does payout of incentive begin when the team reaches 50 percent of the target, 80 percent, or 100 percent? There's no right or wrong answer. Generally, you want teams to receive some incentive for going a good part of the way toward the intended target — definitely more than halfway before receiving any cash reward. When the team hits the 100 percent level, it should receive 100 percent of the incentive pool. When a team *exceeds* its target, the incentive payout also should be proportionally higher up to a predefined level. The idea is to define payout levels so team members know where rewards begin and realize that they can be rewarded for going above and beyond the 100 percent target.

✔ **Pay out frequently.** Longer intervals between payouts mean a lesser impact by incentives on performance. For instance, incentives paid only once a year occur too seldom to have much of a driving effect on performance. Six months may be the maximum interval for incentives to have at least some effect. Designing your incentive program to pay every three to four months can have a much greater impact on team performance.

✔ **Produce positive outcomes.** Incentive plans focus on improvements in productivity, such as increases in output per person. But when the agenda includes the elimination of jobs, an incentive plan is seen as a punitive rather than positive tool. A good incentive plan achieves outcomes that benefit the business and team members.

✔ **Keep your plan simple to understand and administer.** A good team incentive plan sticks to the keep-it-simple approach. Although numbers and formulas usually are involved, nobody needs a PhD in calculus to figure out the plan. When people can't understand how a plan works, it has little effect on performance. Furthermore, whenever tracking results and administering the plan are cumbersome, it won't last long. Those things said, you're nevertheless likely to experience a few kinks and more work when first implementing your new incentive pay plan. That's normal.

Rewarding individual team members: Skill-based pay

This section explores a pay structure that can be used with some work-unit teams. The structure works best where team members have the opportunity to gain and apply multiple levels of skills in helping their team achieve top performance. Known as *skill-based* or *competency-based* pay, this structure rewards individual team members rather than the entire team.

Counting the pluses of skill-based pay

The main idea of a skill-based pay structure within a team is rewarding individual team members for the skills that they possess, acquire, and apply toward helping the team achieve its goals. When team members develop new skills and put them to work, they earn increases in their base salaries. A skill-based pay plan is worth exploring with teams that have operations featuring many different functions that people can discover how to perform over time. Here are some benefits of skill-based pay:

- ✔ **It focuses the acquisition of skills on supporting business needs.** A good skill-based pay program identifies the skill areas that you want team members to develop — skills that are known to help the business run more effectively.

- ✔ **It increases workforce flexibility.** Because a skill-based pay structure encourages team members to broaden their skills, you gain more team members who can do more kinds of work, making it easier to shift team members around to meet work demands.

- ✔ **It allows for pay increases without creating a hierarchy.** For their accomplishments, team members are rewarded with pay rather than new titles. No one rises to a higher level than anyone else. You avoid building a hierarchy, and the equality concept of a team remains intact.

- ✔ **It recognizes individuals without reducing the team structure.** The idea that "we're all in this together" is important for team success. That's why team incentive plans reward all team members equally. Skill-based pay is a way of rewarding individuals for their contributions without affecting the collective sense of a team.

- ✔ **It provides for job enrichment.** The entire concept of skill-based pay focuses on building competencies — greater knowledge, skills, and abilities. Training and cross-training are key elements in the execution of this kind of pay program. When people are encouraged to acquire and apply new skills, their jobs become fuller and more challenging — factors that stimulate employee motivation, teamwork, and performance.

Designing a skill-based pay plan

Work with the help of your manager and human resources department when you design a plan that replaces the traditional salary system with a system that pays for personal growth and teamwork — skills-based pay. Such a plan usually means introducing broader salary ranges so that growth from skill acquisition can be rewarded. Prepare to introduce a skills-based pay structure for your teams by spending some time on five main elements of the framework:

✔ **Identify the skill set areas.** What sets or blocks of skills are needed to perform the tasks and duties on the team? You can identify skill blocks from two angles: depth and breadth. *Depth of skill* means the extent of specialization in an area of work. *Breadth of skill* describes the variety and number of skill functions. Depending on what your team does, you may have skill blocks for both depth and breadth.

✔ **Define the levels of skill or competency within each set.** Subdividing a skill block helps you determine where a person needs development. For example, in the block called *computer applications,* you have data entry, word processing, spreadsheets, database development and administration, graphics, and programming, to name a few.

✔ **Determine the pay value.** Determining the pay for acquiring new skills may mean grouping skills within a block instead of considering only a single skill. Although budget considerations need to come into play, you want to make mastering and applying a valued skill financially worth something to team members. Pay value doesn't have to be the same amount for each new skill developed. You can vary dollar amounts based respectively on the complexity of skills and the amount of performance value they add to the team.

✔ **Develop an evaluation mechanism.** How do you determine whether a team member has mastered a skill? Do you use a performance or demonstration test? A written test? Do you gather feedback from team members who provided the training? Or do you use a combination of evaluation methods? The *how* is less important than the fact that some sort of mechanism is in place to assess and certify that a team member has acquired a new skill.

✔ **Set the application time period.** The monetary reward kicks in when the new skill has been demonstrated on the job in a good skill-based pay plan, and setting a time period for that to occur is important. Don't make the time period long between when a skill is gained and when it's used on the job — three months can work. You may want to set longer or shorter time frames based on the complexity of the newly acquired skill.

Document your plan as a permanent record. The plan becomes your tool for educating your team members and for administering the pay program going forward.

Make sure that you distribute opportunities to develop skills fairly. You're thwarting yourself and your team if the very structure you put in place to encourage your team instead increases competition among team members.

Showing you love them in other ways

Money doesn't motivate everyone and generally isn't the sole motivator for anyone. You need to think about other forms of rewarding team performance as well. Sometimes nonmonetary rewards may be necessary. Perhaps, despite your good plans, you don't have the financial means or management support for implementing variations on traditional pay practices. This section provides you with ideas for showing your appreciation without cash-in-the-pocket rewards.

Gratitude at a cost

Often you can budget for the cost of suggestions like the ones that follow. But even when you sometimes have to cover the expense yourself, the cost is well worth it for celebrating success with your team.

- ✔ **Entertainment outings:** Examples include going to a ballgame, a movie, or the theater. The whole team comes together — sometimes with their families — for fun and entertainment at no expense to team members.

- ✔ **Social play outings:** A boat ride, a golf outing, bowling, an afternoon at the amusement park or video game arcade — choose something that your team members like to do.

- ✔ **Eating events and parties:** You never go wrong when food is involved. Whether it means taking the team out for lunch or a fancy dinner, or throwing a party, the idea is celebrating your success through the dependable eat-drink-and-be-merry approach.

- ✔ **Gift certificates:** Adding a little something to your words of thanks for a job well done never hurts. Gift certificates can be for shopping or dining or just cash, and the amounts don't need to be high.

- ✔ **Time off:** Leisure time is a valuable commodity. The idea: For the good results that you've recently delivered, take a little time off at company expense. This time off doesn't count against vacation time or sick leave. You handle it discreetly and probably don't have every team member take the time off all at once.

Appreciation at little or no expense

The following ideas for showing appreciation for team performance generally cost little or nothing in terms of dollars and require only a bit of time and attention; however, they sometimes are the best investment you can make in motivating team members.

✓ **Team outings:** Getting the team out of the office on company time that has some job-related value is a great idea. You can try attending a speech at a public gathering, visiting another company to witness its workings, or touring some place of interest that the team can gain knowledge from — probably with company-paid lunch as part of the deal. The idea: "We as a team go explore and discover together, and we don't have to use our own personal time to do so." Using this time on volunteer efforts also can go a long way toward encouraging cohesion and increasing effectiveness.

✓ **Letters giving credit:** You show your appreciation for the team's good performance by writing letters to the team and to individual members for the record. The letters can go in each team member's official personnel file. For team members who don't report directly to you, a copy goes to their manager. Sometimes you can even ghostwrite letters for management above you to sign and send to your team members. Recognition from above can mean a great boost for team morale.

✓ **Little gifts:** Small tokens of appreciation costing no more than a few dollars take advantage of the adage that "it's the thought that counts." Inscribed trophies and plaques fall into this category, and so do medals and ribbons — like the ones they hand out at 10K runs and marathons. You can even make your little gifts in the form of edible treats — always welcome.

✓ **Recognition meetings:** A team gathering to express appreciation for a job well done also is an opportunity to recognize individual team members in front of their peers in a positive way. Recognizing something good about each person is a good idea so that nobody is left out. Be specific: Identify and acknowledge particular contributions instead of just saying thanks for good work. Recognizing specifics shows that you have noticed and that you care, which goes a long way toward boosting motivation.

Sometimes, you can invite management from above to attend and show its appreciation, too. Make sure you prepare management guests well so that they can comment briefly but knowledgeably about what the team has been doing and why recognition is in order. A few words of appreciation from above often provide a big boost for team morale.

✓ **Articles in the newsletter:** A little publicity outlining your team's accomplishments is another idea that often triggers a positive spark of recognition and appreciation. Spreading the word publicly about what your team has done usually leads to informal expressions of appreciation by others in the organization — a sort of two-for-one burst of gratitude.

✓ **Positive feedback:** A few words of positive feedback through informal conversation is the cheapest and yet one of the most powerful ways of showing your appreciation for good performance. Positive feedback is far more than general praise. You state specifically what you've seen in performance that was good. This tactic works well for a team as a whole, in the form of public recognition, and for individual team members as they perform good deeds.

Recognizing accomplishments the same way every time gets pretty stale; everyone likes variety. So periodically ask team members, "Money aside, when the team performs well, what should we do so that people know that they are appreciated?" Keep a few notes on what team members tell you, and remember: What motivates one person may not be the same for everyone else.

Book VI
Managing Business Change

Five Ways to Build Trust during Change

- **Actively listen.** Open your ears, make eye contact, and have empathy. As a change leader, you build trust by first listening to understand the other person's perspectives and opinions, and then focusing on leading change, not the other way around.

- **Be credible.** Change leaders back up their vision for change with resources and action. This means setting targets that the organization can achieve and being genuine when talking about the vision. Then walk the talk and make sure resources are dedicated to the change to make it happen. Don't exaggerate the scope of change or the expected results.

- **Be open and honest.** Be cooperative with information. When employees ask questions about the future of the change, don't misrepresent the facts to make things sound better. Instead, be compassionate and offer what information you can.

- **Create an environment of mutual respect through solutions that suit both you and your employees.** Leaders often make the mistake of believing everyone has or should have the same motives as they do. Find out what your employees' motives are and tell them that you want the change to meet their goals, too.

- **Help employees resolve conflict.** One of the best ways to build trust is through effectively resolving conflict among group or team members.

Leading change is definitely challenging, but you can make change sustainable and impactful by adhering to leadership principles outlined in a free article at www.dummies.com/extras/managingaio.

Contents at a Glance

Chapter 1

Laying a Foundation for Change

- -

In This Chapter

▶ Comprehending the cycle of change in business

▶ Recognizing change early in the game

▶ Evaluating your company's readiness for change

▶ Defining and modeling the change that needs to happen

▶ Preparing to lead and to fulfill specific roles

▶ Working within your organization's structure

- -

*W*hether your company is changing technology to increase performance, merging with another organization to gain a competitive advantage, or facing strong economic pressures that are forcing things to be different, change is one of the few constants in business. Change can come from all directions and be driven by multiple reasons, but the core building block of successful change is always the same: *Successful change means creating a strategy that links the people, the process, and the technology to create a better future state.*

And although the motivation or desire for change may come from inside or outside the organization, one element of change is always required: *Leaders must inspire and engage employees in change efforts.* So even though leaders are in charge of change, they need to involve and motivate the people around them to make the change last in the long term.

 In today's business environment, change is constant. Because change isn't going away anytime soon, forward-thinking leaders should *want* to address the change before they *need* to. Instead of dreading change or hoping it won't ever happen to you (which is highly unlikely), assessing and addressing the need for change prepares you and your organization to remain competitive.

Understanding the Cycle of Change

Businesses can face a variety of changes: Companies merge or acquire other companies, new leadership comes in at the top, new technology is adopted, products and services evolve, and customers grow globally. The list could go on and on. Every change is different, but luckily you can expect and plan for a few commonalities during any organizational transformation.

Change can be compared to a journey: You and the organization will be moving from point A to point B. However, unless you have superpowers or are a genie on a 1950s sitcom, you can't just blink your eyes and be transported there instantly. Change takes work, planning, and effort, but in the end the change creates a better future for the organization (if done correctly).

Here are the states you move through during the change process while transforming the organization from A (current state) to B (desired state):

- ✔ **Current state:** The status quo, "the way things are done around here"
- ✔ **Transition:** The process of how you get to B, including but not limited to roles, emotions, measures, politics, and technology
- ✔ **Desired state:** Where you want to be

The process of moving through these states is called the *change cycle*. Companies often repeat the change cycle many times in response to competition, changing customer needs, economic conditions, and new technology.

In leading change, consider its two different aspects: the "what" and the "how" of change:

- ✔ **What: The content of the change at the desired state.** Identify what's changing in your organization. The change could be a new CEO being hired, a new product being introduced, expanding into global markets, implementing a new product-distribution system, or merging two complementary companies. The *what* of the change is simply the thing, person, or process that will be different.

- ✔ **How: The process of the transition phase.** Determine how you will reach the desired state and include the specific steps you will take during the transition phase to successfully lead the change. The process of how change happens is (almost) the entire focus of this Book. It involves how you set the vision and purpose of the change, how you communicate the change (and deal with resistance when people don't like what they hear!), and how you can include the people who are impacted by the change throughout the process.

How the change is implemented is almost as important as what the change is.

Moving out of the current state: Using SWOT to recognize a need to change

A *SWOT analysis* looks at an organization's *strengths, weaknesses, opportunities,* and *threats.* It's a good tool to help leadership identify what areas need to change in order for the organization to thrive in the future and to help executives begin to frame the need for change. Comparing your SWOT analysis with your strategic plan can also help your team align its vision and goals with the costs and benefits of making the change happen. See Book II, Chapter 3 for information about conducting this type of analysis.

Take a look at a quick SWOT analysis for a small consulting firm looking to expand its market share:

Book VI

Managing Business Change

- ✔ **Strengths:** The company's strengths include knowledge of its offering, strong leadership, and a great product design.

- ✔ **Weaknesses:** The big weakness it needs to overcome is a small customer base and being the "best-kept secret" rather than the best-known firm.

- ✔ **Opportunities:** After considering strengths and weaknesses, leaders recognize a few opportunities: The company could partner with other firms, focus on specific niche marketing, or perhaps work to build its local market.

- ✔ **Threats:** Threats come in the form of large competing firms that may have more recognizable names.

The company now needs to decide what is going to change. In this case, the change involves building the customer base. To convey to employees why things need to change, management should start by explaining that although being the best-kept secret in the industry sounds neat, not being known means not being in business. The company sees the need for change as becoming a recognized name to build a bigger business (more customers) while maintaining its expertise in the field (its strengths).

Defining the desired state: Deciding where you're headed

After identifying the threats and opportunities, the leaders are faced with a deceptively simple but critical step: identifying what changes they want to make to maximize their opportunities and minimize their threats. Before you can know how to make the change happen, you need to know where to go, and that direction depends on the kind of change you're talking about. Most changes address at least one of the six key change areas:

- ✔ Markets and customers
- ✔ Products and services
- ✔ Technology
- ✔ Productivity and business processes
- ✔ Reward systems and performance management
- ✔ Organizational structures

Although changing any one of these six areas can result in significant change, most likely any change your organization undertakes will not occur in isolation. For example, if a company is undergoing a significant technology change, the productivity gains will not fully be realized if processes that manage how work is done don't change as well. The leadership team may decide how to build a larger customer base, but don't neglect thinking about how new products and services may help expand your current customer base.

Checking out the change formula

Wouldn't it be nice if a formula could guarantee successful change? Unfortunately, whenever people are involved, change can be difficult and complicated. But the following formula will get you on the right track to success:

$$\text{Focus} \times \text{Drive} \times \text{Time and Resources} = \text{Change}$$

You have already begun to tackle both focus and drive: *Focus* comes from knowing where you are headed, and *drive* comes from an understanding of why the organization needs to go there rather than continuing to accept the status quo. The last part of the equation is time and resources devoted appropriately, and that factor is where planning comes in — the topic of the next chapter.

Spotting Change Indicators

How do you know if you need to change? Wouldn't it be nice if you had a big alarm that went off to let you know you need to change? Although that may seem like wishful thinking, you probably already have that big alarm button.

Unfortunately, it may be lost in a swarm of e-mails, reports, and meetings. To dig out the big alarm button, ask yourself whether your company is going through or has been through any of these big change events:

- ✔ **Are you losing market share? Are profits suffering?** If other companies are taking over your market share by offering a product or service that's more appealing to your best customers, start thinking about changing the way your company differentiates itself in the marketplace and brings value to your customers. If someone else is luring your ideal customers (even if they aren't yours yet), the time is right to start changing.

- ✔ **Are your best employees leaving to work for your competitors?** If competitors have a better work culture or more progressive employment practices (such as flextime or work-from-home options) or are growing and offer more opportunities for advancement, start thinking about how you can change to attract and keep the best and brightest brains in your company.

- ✔ **Has new technology made your products or services obsolete? Or is your company's image simply outdated?** Things change, and they change fast. A good indicator of the need for change is having products and services that are stuck back in 1999. For example, if you're still trying to sell dial-up Internet service, you could use a change.

- ✔ **Has the company been sold to another one or merged with another company?** If so, your company may have a perfect opportunity to implement change. When two companies come together as one, you can't just change the logo on the business cards and expect business to continue as usual. If no one steps up to manage the merge, issues will crop up in how people communicate, how teams work together, how performance is evaluated, and hundreds of other people and process issues.

- ✔ **Is the company expanding — either geographically or into new product and market categories? Has globalization resulted in shifts in labor and materials costs?** As your company grows, you have to identify what you need to change as well as what you should keep the same. Growth is a great thing in business, but growing without recognizing the need to change how the company operates is about as rational as trying to put an elephant on a kid's scooter: It's not going to happen, and the scooter will probably be damaged in the attempt.

- ✔ **Do you have a new CEO or leadership team?** High-level personnel changes merit a change plan because they're bound to cause shifts in organizational direction, business goals, and even how individual and team performance are addressed. The change plan should include a strategy to address concerns and ideas of the employees working for the new leadership team.

Book VI

Managing Business Change

✔ **Are you implementing a new technology platform in your company?**
New technology is exciting, but with new technology comes new processes for work and new ways employees will do the work. If you just
implement a new technology without addressing the people and process
side of change, you will most likely end up paying for a wonderful tool
that nobody can use or plans on using.

Don't sit back and assess whether you need to change how you do business
only once a year. Refer back to your business plan frequently to track growth,
market direction, and accountability within the organization.

On the flip side, a big mistake many executives make is changing too often just
because everyone else is changing. When you think about your change, make
sure you really need to shake things up for long-term success.

Assessing Your Organizational Change Readiness

Assessing your organizational change readiness is simply a way of finding
out the substantial common ideas that will either enable the change or stifle
it. Stakeholder mapping and stakeholder readiness assessment let you know
where you stand and how to proceed.

Mapping your stakeholders

When you start considering change (or if change suddenly happens), your
next questions should be "Who is it happening to?" and "What are they going
to think about it?" Answering these questions is where your stakeholder
analysis comes into play.

A *stakeholder* is any individual or group who has a significant interest in
the organization and, when it comes to change, one who will be affected by
the change or can influence the change. (Yes, that may be a very big list.)
Stakeholder mapping is a three-step technique you can use to categorize the
influence that key people, groups of people, or departments have on the
success of your change. By anticipating the kind of influence — positive,
negative, or indifferent — that these groups have on your initiative, you can
leverage their power proactively across the organization. Then, with a keen
eye on what people think and feel about the change, you can prepare strategies to enlist the support of the people who can help the change happen and
find ways to reduce obstacles put up by people who don't want it to happen.
What you're really getting down to is their attitude about the change.

Following are the three steps of stakeholder mapping:

1. **List all the change stakeholders (either groups of stakeholders, like the accounting department, or individuals, such as the VP of operations) and their roles in the organization on the stakeholder analysis.** See the first two columns in Table 1-1 for examples.

Table 1-1   Sample Stakeholder Mapping for New Finance System

Stakeholder	Role in Organization	Influence on Change Project	Influence within the Company
Annie Brown	CEO	Medium	High
Raajeev Smith	Finance department head	High	High
Stan Black	HR manager	Medium	Medium
Joe Bing	Team leader	High	Low
Finance Reporting Group	Finance	Medium	Low

2. **Identify whether each stakeholder's influence on the change is high, medium, or low.** Does a certain stakeholder sign the check to pay for the change? If so, the influence is pretty high. Is a particular person in the department the unspoken leader who basically can make anyone agree to anything just by voicing her opinion? Yep, that person is high up there, too. You don't need a fancy title to have a good amount of influence. On the flip side, although the office gossipers may talk a lot about the change and *think* they have influence, their influence over the project may be very low in reality. (This step is represented in the third column in Table 1-1.)

3. **Identify whether their influence within the company is high, medium, or low.** This ranking differs from Step 2 because this time you're looking at how much weight the stakeholder's opinion has from an organizational perspective. Stakeholders' organizational influence has a big influence on making changes stick after they're implemented. See the fourth column of Table 1-1 for examples of Step 3.

When identifying influence, make sure you differentiate the influence on the change and the influence in the company. These rankings can often be related to one another, but they're not always the same.

Your stakeholder mapping will look something like Table 1-1 when it's complete.

Assessing stakeholder readiness

Now that you have identified the key players and assessed their importance, you can find out who is going to help you and who is going to try their best to stop anything from changing. The readiness assessment is all about evaluation.

Don't overcomplicate the matter when it comes to change readiness. Using individual or group interviews, sit down with the stakeholders with high influence over the project and ask these power questions to help identify what you need to do to lead change in your organization:

- **What has been done to date to build commitment around the change?** Even in the beginning of the change, change leaders can start building commitment to the vision for the change or even the need to change.

- **What do you think or know about the forthcoming benefits of this change?** As the change gets moving into full gear, change leaders can start talking about the good things that will come from the change. Will jobs be easier to do when the change happens? Will there be more advancement opportunities in the new company?

- **What will you have to give up as a result of the change? What do you think other people will have to give up?** Although most of the change will be for the better, people may be sad about losing some things, like no longer working side by side with colleagues they have been working with for years or having to take the time to learn a new system or process while continuing to do their jobs.

- **What skills and resources do you believe are necessary? Do you have the right number of people and the correct skill sets on your team?** No one likes to admit that his team may need to upgrade its skills, but a change is a perfect opportunity to teach employees new technologies and processes. Understanding what additional skills may be needed to complete the change early on in the change cycle is always helpful.

- **Are you excited about the change?** The answer to this question speaks a thousand words. If the answer is "Uh, sure," then change leaders know they have some work to do on creating an inspiring vision. If the answer is "YES! We need this change," you know the change is off to a good start.

- **What specific employee issues may affect the success of the implementation in the organization? What other obstacles and barriers may impact the success of the project?**

- **Do you believe this implementation will disrupt business? What will the disruptions be? How can we minimize their impact on the business?**

When you have a wealth of knowledge about how your stakeholders feel about the change, you can make an assessment of how ready they are to embark on change. Some of your stakeholders will be excellent change adopters, others will be good change adopters, and some will be failing a little in the change department.

Are some of your stakeholders doing an excellent job at change and ready to quickly adopt the proposed change within their group or department? You can use these powerhouses of change to push this next change through. Your job will be to help partner these stakeholders with people in your organization who are not as "change ready." You can also use these change rock stars to help you communicate messages about the change and be your eyes, ears, and feet when it comes to making change happen.

Most likely, many of your stakeholders will be feeling neutral or somewhat supportive about the change. Your next step is to keep in touch with these stakeholders on a regular basis. You want to make sure these stakeholders have every opportunity to ask questions and be heard as well as get any support they need to help make lasting change in their part of the organization. Maybe their group is great at communication but needs help with planning. Plan on leveraging their strengths and beefing up on their weaknesses, and you'll be well on your way to change success.

The best way to beef up weaknesses is to find individuals who can teach and mentor and whose strengths complement the weaknesses. For example, if someone is great at strategy but not great at marketing your ideas, you can partner her with someone who is great at the communication and marketing side. Change leaders may find employees in other parts of the company or bring in a consultant to help coach employees on change skills. To make sure weaknesses do not hold you back, find a way to teach employees how to improve in the long run. When it comes to strengthening your weaknesses, live by this saying: *Give a man a fish, he eats for a day. Teach a man to fish, he eats for a lifetime.* Look for ways to teach and mentor weaknesses during change.

And, yes, you will have some skeptics (or *laggards*) who need a big push when it comes to change. If people who have a large amount of influence on the change are also laggards, remember that change takes time. If it was easy, well, you wouldn't be reading this chapter. Categorize what the laggards' biggest barriers are to supporting the change, and start brainstorming how to address those issues. Most of the time, simply listening and responding to concerns of those stakeholders who are doubters will move them from pessimists to supporters of the change.

Laggards can become an energy drain. Don't invest too much time with these stakeholders if nothing is happening. If you do, you may end up spending 80 percent of your time on them with very slow or little return, versus 80 percent on those who can champion or help lead the change.

Book VI

Managing Business Change

In some cases, laggards do require attention. Those who have a lot of influence can derail your progress if you don't work to get them on board. Identify the people who will have the most influence on whether the change will happen and how well it'll happen in the future. Keep these people within arm's reach. They say to keep your friends close and your enemies closer; in this case you want to keep everyone close and your high-influencers (both positive and negative) closer.

Deciding What Type of Change You Need

Deciding what kind of change you need is the pre-work to change in many aspects, because change leaders in the organization need to decide what they are doing before doing it. You find out about creating a vision of the change in Chapter 2 of this Book, but in this section you find ways to determine what change road you want to embark on before you and your organization get moving.

When you're making important judgment calls on exactly what kinds of changes your organization needs, you want to consider two things: the content of the change and the process of the change (the "what" and the "how," as discussed in this chapter's first section). If you go with the right type of change, employees will respond more positively, processes will function more smoothly, and your life will be easier.

As you consider possible changes you may make, assess and prioritize them by comparing their respective impact. Ask yourself these questions about each:

✔ **Goals and results:** If this action is taken, will the organization's goals be met? Will results be clearly positive?

✔ **Mission and vision:** Does the proposed change support the mission and vision of the organization? If the change is aligned with the bigger picture of where your organization wants to go, the change will have a higher chance of success.

Prioritizing possible changes allows you to evaluate each change against one another and choose the most important ones to dedicate resources. With your highest change priorities in mind, you can move on to determining the content and process of the change:

✔ **Content:** Are you dealing with transactional or transformational change?

• *Transactional change* is primarily task-focused. These changes usually focus on strategic realignment of structures, processes, and systems. Implementing a new customer service program or reorganizing a department is often a transactional change.

- *Transformational* or *transformative change* is inspirational change that occurs through radical strategic repositioning and leadership changes, or through turnarounds that enable organizational survival or skyrocket growth. New CEOs and boards of directors being appointed, culture changes, and many mergers and acquisitions are transformational.

✔ **Process:** A key consideration here is whether change will occur incrementally or immediately:

- *Incremental* change occurs in small steps. Have you ever felt that everything is constantly changing? That's true when it comes to incremental change, like slowly evolving a product line but still supporting earlier products for customers.

- *Immediate* change occurs rapidly and only for a short period of time. For example, your organization may switch from an old technology to a new one overnight, sometimes referred to as *flipping the switch.*

Implementing a Tried-and-True Change Model

The model you use to implement change has a big effect on what kind of change you get. There are probably as many change models in existence as there are changes, but at its core, all change follows a simple process. The hard part is applying the process to your change and applying it consistently.

You don't need to re-create the wheel of change. These four steps can get you where you need to be. The wheel that works, no matter what you call it, rolls like this:

1. **Create a vision for change.** Leaders identify the change that is needed and create a picture of what the future will look like after the change happens.

2. **Plan the change.** Planning the change includes creating a team that will make the change happen, developing measurable goals, and identifying ways to include employees.

3. **Communicate the change.** Communication is a big part of change, but not just the communication that comes from the top of the organization. Change lasts when employees understand the reasons for the change, are empowered to make changes, and see that their feedback is used throughout the change.

4. **Implement and revisit the change.** After you implement the change, everyone may be tempted to go back to what they were doing beforehand, but change needs constant attention. After the change happens, remember to check back in with employees to see how the change is working and find out if any modifications are needed to make it last.

Here's the change model you want to avoid: *announce, consult, surface,* and *move on.* It goes like this: An executive announces a great idea he read about in his favorite business magazine or overheard on the golf course. He hires a bunch of consultants to recommend options for implementing the change. The organization begins to discover the real issue for change (which isn't half as exciting), and the executive moves on to the next big thing. This "announce and go do it now" model almost always ends up as a big old binder and fancy presentations that gather dust on the shelf — not exactly the result you're hoping for with your change.

Even though every effective change uses a similar process, it can be extraordinarily difficult for some companies to do it alone, without a business partner guiding them. Going it alone may cost a company more money than if they had sought guidance in the first place, so give serious thought up front to whether you need assistance to accomplish the desired change.

Recognizing the Call for Leadership

When your business is changing, you can respond in one of three ways:

- ✔ Do nothing and let it look after itself.
- ✔ Manage it by sending out e-mails, creating a project plan, and having lots of meetings and a great internal website about the project.
- ✔ Lead the change by creating a vision, communicating change with passion, and inspiring employees by empowering them to make the change happen.

Did you guess that the last option is the best approach? Brilliant!

In this section, you find out how leadership differs from management and how to lead by example.

You can think of change like going on a trip. Your current state is where you are today, and your desired state is where you want to go. You have to do a few things first: Find a place to stay, pack your suitcase, decide who is coming with you, get delayed in airport security, and so on. Details like these are important aspects of the transition from one location to another. Your goal when leading change is to make sure such details are handled so the road from here to there is as smooth as possible.

Distinguishing managing and leading

How often have you committed to something 100 percent just because you read an e-mail or went to a meeting? Probably not often — or ever. People don't change because they are told to; otherwise, everyone would eat perfectly because the doctor said to and children would always listen politely and use proper manners.

Writing e-mails, making a beautiful project website and project plan, and having lots of meetings will get you only so far during a business change. These activities are simply the management of change.

Managing change is defined by making sure that steps are checked off. *Leading change* is making sure the change is giving employees the tools and information they need to make the change happen (and last). Communicating change is critical, but communication while leading change focuses on interactive dialogue, not just messages.

Sometimes simply managing a change works fine. For example, if you're just planning to change the mailroom hours at your company, go ahead and communicate the message and then switch over to those new times. But if the strategy of the business is changing, if the change impacts people (jobs, pay, roles, management structure), or if the change will alter the way you do business, leading change will make you and your change a success.

Business change involves working with human behavior. To generate lasting results, you need to align people around a common goal that everyone has committed to. And you need to strive for efficiency while achieving that goal. If you embark on business change by leading it, your change will result in an organization-wide commitment to making change happen that can be seen, heard, and felt by the business.

What does it take to lead change?

- ✔ **Set an example for others to follow.** Commitment is not just about saying the right thing; it's about doing the right thing. This topic is the subject of the next section.

- ✔ **Involve employees and get buy-in.** Nothing gets people invested like the leader asking for their opinion and then listening to it. Good change leaders know that listening to employees' ideas and engaging them in business decisions is one of the main ingredients to developing a motivated and innovative workforce. Employees need to be engaged in the process so they gain ownership of the change and want to make the change last.

✔ **Make procedural and structural changes, but don't stop there — make things look different.** If you desire a culture that rewards results, make sure people see results on the walls, in meeting rooms, and when they walk into the office in the morning. If you want people to focus on team behavior, tear down the large walls that separate teams (literally!). A small change like rearranging workspaces to help tear down the walls of "silo" departments can do a tremendous amount to boost conversations and interaction.

Don't get too caught up in physical changes and neglect real procedural change. Creating more open work environments with colorful and modern chairs is great, but if you still need to get 26 approvals on 14 different forms to buy a pencil, change will just occur on the surface.

As a change leader, you can take the first steps by personally making the change happen in your own team or department. Take the first step by walking the talk and making things look different by asking employees what the change means to them and then acting on it.

Leading by example

When a leader leads by example, maintains interest, and holds the pedal to the metal to keep intensity and commitment at their highest levels, the rest of the organization usually picks up on it, and people increase their own belief in the change. Regardless of your role, you have a great opportunity to make change happen by modeling that change with your own leadership style. Whether you have a team of 100 employees or just manage your own work, think about what you can personally change to be more aligned with the vision of the future for the organization.

The best leaders make change an organizational value by expressing, modeling, and reinforcing the principles in day-to-day operations. Have you ever had a manager who wouldn't walk the talk and who gave only face time to important issues rather than really working on them? Chances are it was a pretty miserable experience. While implementing change, leaders must demonstrate integrity and act consistently with what they're asking of the organization's members. Following are the four key actions that a leader should take to effectively lead by example:

✔ Express the desired behavior.

✔ Model the desired behavior through decision making and day-to-day activities.

✔ Reinforce the desired behavior through forms of recognition and rewards.

✔ Endure to the end.

Suppose that during a large technology change at your company, a new reporting system is implemented, but most of your team still is using spreadsheets to do work. Leading by example means you toss those formulas and worksheets and embrace and use the new tool. If you are asking someone else to do something, make sure you are willing to do it, too.

Here's another example. Many companies are trying to change to better support a culture of work–life balance, but if you're replying to e-mails at midnight, your own balance is pretty out of whack. You can say to employees, "Take time for yourself," but if you're not doing it, your employees will have a hard time doing it.

Leading by example is not always as black and white as those examples, but it's the foundation for respect from others in your organization. If you want people to show up to meetings but you're frequently leaving the room to answer phone calls, your employees and peers will think you're insincere. If you want to implement a new performance measurement system that rewards results, but you constantly reschedule performance discussion meetings with your employees, the change will be seen as superficial.

When leaders' actions are inconsistent with their words, they can destroy the trust needed for an organization to effectively implement change. Even the most intricate and well-orchestrated plans will fall on deaf ears when the trust and credibility of the change leader is lost.

Doing a changing-by-example audit

Leading by example seems easy enough at first, but in reality it takes practice. Because leading by example is so far-reaching, you may want to take a personal audit of the example you want to set for the change. The two areas you want to address in your personal "changing by example" audit are what you physically and mentally give attention to and what new skills you're mastering in the new environment.

✔ **Attention:** Where do you spend your time and energy? Are these items aligned with the goals of change? If not, what needs to change to make sure your calendar reflects the new way you want others to work?

✔ **Capabilities:** Have you taken the time to learn the skills you need as a change sponsor, change agent, or change advocate (see the upcoming section "Role Playing: Assuming Different Roles during Change" for details)? If you take the time to learn how to become a better change expert, everyone around you will follow your example. Do the same for the new capabilities you'll need in order to operate in your new business environment.

Sneaking in examples

When it comes to changing by example, the rubber really hits the road when new skills are ready to be put into action. Until things are really done differently, you can say one thing but do something else. When the time for action comes, everyone can see who isn't walking the talk.

Do any of these situations sound like your organization?

- ✔ Skills and knowledge are assumed, not taught or developed. People learn on the job or through water-cooler conversations.

- ✔ Quality issues are dealt with after the fact, rather than eliminated earlier in the product development process. Employees may be rewarded for being the hero and saving the day for a customer when a product breaks rather than being rewarded for stopping the problem before it happens.

- ✔ Individuals complain about not having information, clearly defined roles, or straightforward responsibilities, but they then run as fast as they can (the other way) when asked to adhere to new standards.

If you're nodding your head, here's some great news: All these situations can easily be turned into opportunities to lead by example. If skills and knowledge are assumed in your organization, have other employees (often your change agents and advocates) step up and teach classes. If you praise teams who get up at midnight to go fix something, start turning your attention to the teams that actually got to sleep through the night because they did things right the first time. If individuals complain about not having clarity, allow them to create the clarity for the new change.

Leading by example doesn't have to be a huge shift in the way things are done — small changes can add up to a big change in total.

Role Playing: Assuming Different Roles during Change

For each change leader, the authority and responsibility to remove barriers and provide adequate resources must be within reach. But the change leader must also have the softer skills necessary to get everyone on board with the change. Regardless of the leadership badge you may wear during change, these softer skills are common and essential for all roles. Beyond anything else, change leaders are individuals who

- ✔ Influence people
- ✔ Facilitate and drive discussions for answers
- ✔ Make decisions

Multiple levels of leadership commitment, resource support, and hands-on involvement are critical for successful change. Because each leader within your organization has different formal leadership capabilities (spans of control and authority) as well as informal competencies (political influence, leadership style), they take on distinct leadership roles during the change.

The three main roles to be filled by you and other leaders within your organization are change sponsors, change agents, and change advocates. Each role is pivotal to the success of the project in its own special way. Here, you discover the tasks associated with each role. Table 1-2 shows you a quick overview of what each change role is responsible for during sequential stages of the change. The following sections explain each role in more detail.

Book VI

Managing Business Change

Table 1-2	Responsibilities of Change Leaders		
Change-Cycle Step	*Role of Change Sponsor*	*Role of Change Agent*	*Role of Change Advocate*
Seeing a need for change	Encouraging organization to take risks and change direction	Taking the risk to make change happen; owning the change	Challenging the status quo; encouraging peers to do the same
Deciding where you're headed	Building change into the organizational strategy	Making sure the real change is part of the organization strategy	Making the strategy work
Developing the road map for change	Involving others to build the plan for how change will happen	Accepting and owning the road map; making the road map happen	Voicing concerns with the plan; recommending ideas

(continued)

Table 1-2 *(continued)*

Change-Cycle Step	Role of Change Sponsor	Role of Change Agent	Role of Change Advocate
Setting it into motion	Providing resources to support the change	Aligning the resources to make change happen	Enacting the plan
Communicating the progress	Sharing ownership of the communication plan; acting as a spokesperson for change	Relating communication to employees' day-to-day work	Informing peers of the change
Dealing with negative reactions	Working with senior leaders to resolve conflicts	Networking within their area to resolve conflicts	Raising issues with the change
Motivating to move forward	Giving recognition for the change; monitoring results	Getting recognition for the change; measuring results	Getting recognition from peers and leaders for making change happen
Making the change durable	Working with the team to design the new structure to support lasting change	Making the new structure real	Operating in the new way of doing business

All leaders involved in the change process must share the same view of the change and what it's intended to accomplish; you see how to come up with a shared vision and measures in Chapter 2 of this Book.

Sponsoring success

Many of the change activities discussed in this Book come under the banner of sponsoring change. *Sponsoring* a change means that you have the responsibility for the processes that are being affected by the change and the formal authority to make the change happen. Needless to say, sponsoring change is a pretty big deal.

Sponsors usually come in two varieties:

- ✔ **Initiating sponsor:** Typically a high-level executive who has both the vision and authority to launch the change effort
- ✔ **Sustaining sponsor:** Picks up the responsibility for his part of the organization

That being said, you may very well be or work with someone who is the perfect blend of both these roles. During most large changes, only one or two people are the official sponsors of change.

If you are sponsoring a change, what exactly have you signed up to do? Following is a rundown of what you'll be doing as you sponsor successful change:

Book VI

Managing Business Change

- ✔ Describing the compelling need for the change and communicating its benefits to others within your organization
- ✔ Providing resources such as people, money, space, and tools for the change to happen
- ✔ Making time available in the organization to allow the change to move forward
- ✔ Being available to the other change leaders, project leaders, and change-team members to resolve issues and set direction
- ✔ Personally demonstrating the desired behaviors wanted from the change
- ✔ Communicating to your organization the key messages and ideas in the communication plan

Did you fall over in your chair? Are you running the other way? Although this list may seem like a lot of things to take care of, remember you aren't going to do it alone. Not only do you have this trusty book at your side, but you also have a team of leaders within your organization to help you. This is where the change agents and change advocates come into play, so don't sweat it, and keep reading the next two sections.

The need for change is often seen first by people who aren't in a position of authority or power. Therefore, engaging employees in the change through two-way communication and cross-functional teams is very important. Change happens when leaders can bridge strategy and vision to real problems and opportunities in the organization.

Being a change agent

Sponsors are the ones building the plan and providing resources; *change agents* are the ones who get the plan off the ground. Change agents are embedded within the organization at the department or regional level, so they're always within arm's reach of the people doing the work that is changing. Think of change agents as field agents who find out what's really being said about the change, help to correct any discrepancies in the change, and make sure everything runs like clockwork throughout the change plan.

Change agents fill both a formal and informal leadership role during business transformations. Change agents possess a broad understanding of the business, especially in their functional area. Because of their close communication with the project team, they're one of the best sources of information for what's happening on the project.

So what exactly does a change agent do? You get a good overview of what change agents do in each stage of change in Table 1-2, and the following list addresses change agents' overall responsibilities and roles:

✔ Being the single contact source for specific change in their areas

✔ Ensuring that whatever changes happen meet the needs of people doing the work

✔ Actively working to demonstrate the desired behaviors

✔ Assisting in the training assessment process

✔ Helping with the transfer of knowledge for new roles and processes

✔ Gaining knowledge of the new change before it happens

✔ Assisting in the identification of area-specific communication needs

✔ Communicating key messages and ideas in the communication plan

When identifying a change agent for a project, ask yourself two questions. Is this person fully committed and passionate about the future of the company and making the future real? Is this person genuinely in a position, either formally or informally, to influence others, or would the role be better filled by someone with more credibility or authority?

Serving as an advocate

Change agents and change sponsors are formal positions within change projects, but one informal role — the change advocate — is what makes change happen successfully and efficiently. Change advocates can either be self-elected or be a standing, cross-functional team of front-line resources in non-supervisor and non-management positions. Either way, they're responsible for providing guidance and feedback to the change agents, change sponsor, and project team on critical decisions and approaches during and after the life of the program.

Change advocates understand the business needs and are passionate about facilitating positive change. With this in mind, following are the four most important qualities of change advocates:

- ✔ Living in the future, but understanding the past and present of the company

- ✔ Being fueled by passion, and inspiring passion in others

- ✔ Possessing a strong ability to self-motivate

- ✔ Understanding the people and processes around them (how things really work)

Anyone can be a change advocate as long as he or she is willing and able to facilitate change and be personally accountable for making change happen in an area of work.

Change advocates fill informal roles within change projects, but that doesn't mean they are an optional part of the process. Some of the most compelling changes happen when change advocates simply live and breathe the change and share this experience for change with others. Nothing supports change more than telling a story of how the change is helping you to do more or create better results. You don't always need to speak of some grand vision of the future to inspire people to do things differently. Sometimes the best change is driven by peers advocating the new way of doing things.

Change advocates can make a world of difference by being wonderful story-tellers. Change advocates, because of their hands-on, non-management role, can put the problem and solution in black and white, in a less threatening manner than more formal or senior roles can often do.

Create a front-line council to make sure the views of employees throughout the organization are heard. A *front-line council* is a formal group of change advocates who get the inside scoop on information and actively campaign for the change.

Facilitating Change across Leadership Structures

As a leader, you're challenged to align the needs of various individuals and teams with the strategy and changes happening in your organization to drive results. Understanding the leadership structure as it functions within your business gives you insight into the best ways to facilitate change.

Glimpsing two common leadership structures

Although every organization is unique, two basic leadership approaches drive decisions and results in most organizations (and at times can limit any results from happening): hierarchical leadership and shared leadership.

Hierarchical leadership

In hierarchical organizations, the flow of information is like a pyramid. It has a clear order and defined levels of leadership, and who has authority is obvious. This increased administration often delays the change, but the roles and responsibilities are crystal clear.

Are you in a hierarchical organization? The benefit of this organizational structure is consistency. The downside is, well, consistency. Although a change may happen like clockwork after it's put in motion, the initial impetus for change tends to get caught up in paperwork.

If you find yourself working with a hierarchical boss, use the structure to your advantage to create change. Ask your boss to push the idea up the chain of command and focus changes on how they will improve the processes and procedures within the organization. You also want to get a strong group of change agents who can translate the decision to real action on the front lines.

Some hierarchical leaders are also *top-imposing leaders,* who tend to have the hardest time implementing lasting, meaningful change because they decide what's going to happen and then hand it over to employees to make it work. In a hierarchical environment, the change flows in something of a stepladder fashion, but top-imposing leaders look more like an ivory tower in the sky with peasants down below. If you work with this type of leader, don't despair. With the right coaching, top-imposing leaders can reduce the emphasis on controlling people and conditions by listening more to employee ideas and being more accepting of those suggestions. Coach these leaders to recruit change agents and advocates to tell it like it is, and then make sure they don't throw the messengers out on the street when they tell the truth. Show these leaders that by listening with patience they may just find answers to the problems the organization is facing right on the other side of their desk.

Top-driven leadership can dictate the vision but then rely on employees to make their own decisions about how to make the vision come alive. This system creates a greater sense of shared ownership from the bottom up.

Shared leadership

Collective organizational styles and change leaders who focus on doing things together tend to see change happen the quickest and with the most acceptance. Although the change sponsor is still in charge of the change, sponsors work closely with change agents and the recipients of change to make sure the *right* change is put in place, even if it doesn't come from the top. In this type of environment, the emphasis is more on involvement in the decision-making process rather than who is making the decision. It sounds like a pie-in-the-sky ideal change environment, and, frankly, it can be.

Book VI

Managing Business Change

Keep in mind the downside to these shared organizational change structures during change: Without a specific boss to call the shots, your organization may experience confusion and even power struggles between leaders to show who's in charge. But when managed well, a shared ownership change style possesses a speed of communication and adaptability that other groups envy, in which employees are encouraged to make changes that are right for the organization.

Are you in a shared organization? Lucky you. You probably have been told you have a voice in change, and you actually do. If you find yourself in this type of a structure and love change, stand up and let your ideas be heard — and then get ready to get to work, because you may find yourself being responsible for making those great ideas happen.

Working with — and adapting — the established leadership structure

There's no absolutely right way to get change to happen and stick. No single mode of communication or leadership suits every operation's needs. Being able to adapt is what sets change leaders apart from those only capable of managing change.

However, change, innovation, and ownership come when people are involved in the process, not just told what to do. If command-and-control leadership works for your organization, that's perfectly fine, but change is about challenging the status quo. The more that change agents, change sponsors, and change advocates can have equal but different voices during the change process, the more likely change will stick long into the future.

If a sudden crisis situation hits an organization, leaders may need to make decisions that aren't shared or inclusive. If this happens, stepping up the communication and being open about why a decision was made by a select few rather than a larger population is the best alternative. And don't forget, even though a change decision may have been made quickly, all the work to make the change last still needs to happen, which is where you can include multiple opinions and ideas from employees.

Most organizations use both leadership structures in one form or another. For example, although your company may have a very clear pecking order, responsibility and ideas may be shared equally within a department. The following adaptability options help you navigate whatever leadership structure applies in the company or group you're working with:

- ✔ **Blend communications from the top bosses with those of advocates on the field to beef up your communication and make it a conversation.** Ongoing change needs robust, dialogue-based communication. The trickle-down method of communication rarely works at the speed change needs, so balance a shared-ownership change style with clear messages from the top. Target at least 50 percent of communications to be dialogue based, not top-down presentations.

- ✔ **Create a clear line of sight to strategic initiatives for all employees.** *Line of sight* means all employees know how their actions impact the bigger picture. Although shared leadership is great for ownership, it sometimes falls short in listing out how what one person does impacts another aspect of the business downstream. (Hierarchical organizations and leaders tend to excel at providing line of sight.)

- ✔ **Prominently reward new behaviors and accomplishments.** By acknowledging people and teams that change, you can help propel others to make changes. People do what they are rewarded for, so look for the new behaviors and let people know you appreciate the change.

When you make changes to the way leadership happens within your organization, people will notice. First, the murmurs may sound like, "Maybe this is different." Then they'll move to, "This *is* different." By the end of the process, people who may have been critical at first may be transformed into change advocates, saying, "What can I do to make it happen?"

Chapter 2

Putting Your Plan for Change into Motion

In This Chapter

▶ Getting ready for change with vision . . . and a road map

▶ Creating a plan that puts change on the right path

▶ Keeping an eye on measurement as you progress

▶ Ensuring effective communication through change

Starting right here and now, you need to begin filling your change toolbox. With what, you ask? With the right mechanisms for aligning your strategy, values, goals, and processes from top to bottom throughout the change project. You also need to assemble your core team who will help you cross the finish line. This task isn't easy, and you may feel somewhat overwhelmed. But here's help.

In this chapter, you come to an understanding of the steps you take to guide the process of change, and you find out how to use these steps to bring about the desired results. You find out how to measure progress and communicate the change your company needs to best ensure that it happens — and lasts. With all the new tools you receive in this chapter, you'll be able to get your change team up to speed quickly and get that change rolling.

Assembling Your Change Toolbox

As you fill your change toolbox, focusing on three core steps helps you move your organization from the current state (today) to the future state (where you want to be):

1. Building an inspiring vision

2. Creating a change road map

3. Factoring in what's helping or hindering change

Think of these steps as your hammer, glue, and saw. With them in place, you can do just about anything. Check out the how-to info on each step in this section.

Building an inspiring vision

What will the future look like when the change has happened? This vision is important because it keeps you moving forward and gets you through the transitional bumps in the road. It's a clear, compelling statement that gives everyone a picture of where you're headed. A vision usually considers the elements of products, services, customers, relationships, employees, technology, and culture and has supporting details that describe how the vision will be achieved. And you must make sure that the vision is inspiring, too.

Your vision should set expectations and help you continue moving toward the end goal even if obstacles are in your way. Having that clear vision of the future state of the organization is a powerful tool in creating stability when chaos is all around you, and it will help you create an accurate image in people's minds of what they can and can't expect.

What makes a good vision? For one thing, it is driven by senior leadership but created by many people at different levels and supported by the change leaders in the organization. Many great changes have come from grassroots efforts, but the vision of large-scale, lasting change must be defined by someone who can control and inspire the change. The vision is a statement of the organization you want to be, and therefore it must speak to everyone in your organization — not just those in the corporate office.

Great visions are also specific and clear. Don't spend time creating a vision of the future that's as clear as mud. A vision must address what the future looks like, when it will happen, and how people can get involved. The vision must state the capabilities the organization will have in the future.

As discussed in Chapter 1 of this Book, change needs a catalyst. Look for the *change driver* — the business need for the change. The change driver is either a problem that people need to address or an opportunity that will further the strategic value of the organization. The change driver (or drivers) must offer a reason to change that is more compelling than people's natural attachment to the status quo or comfort zone.

When you've pinpointed the change driver, make sure you don't muddy it up in your communications about the vision. Think about how different these two visions are:

- ✔ We will stop having issues with quality next year.

- ✔ Working together, we will improve the quality of our products next year so that all our customers are delighted with their experience.

You may have meant the same thing in both statements, but only the second one will impress employees with an inspiring shared need.

Keep your vision genuine. If a vision is out of touch with where the organization is today, employees may find it unbelievable and not act on it.

After you inspire people to change, you need to inspire them to want to change *now.* A sense of urgency may be incredibly obvious if your organization is faced with economic or market-driven challenges, but it's not always that clear cut. The easiest way to create a sense of urgency is to describe how a behavior is causing an undesirable consequence.

When you change, you are either addressing a problem people need to fix or an opportunity that will further the strategic value of the organization. You do not (or at least should not) change for the fun of it. If you find it hard to create shared urgency, go back and look at why you are changing in the first place.

Above all, be authentic in your vision. To get your change project done, a vision must be real — not just smoke and mirrors. An inspiring vision and shared sense of urgency don't mean you need to sugarcoat the outcomes of the project, just balance them. If the major end goal is to reduce expenses or reduce headcount, say so, but also discuss the importance of the other elements of change.

Book VI

Managing Business Change

Creating a change road map

Your inspiring vision gets people moving, and the change road map tells them how to get where they need to go. Too often, desperately needed changes fall short of their desired results because change leaders don't really understand how to lead change or have a clear map of how to get there.

Making a strategic road map

Your strategic road map, indicating where you're beginning and where you want to end up, should cover the following areas:

- ✔ **Why do we need to change?** In order to answer this question, you need to know what's happening now. Figure out where you're starting from so that you can define what changes are needed to get to the future.

- ✔ **What are the two or three key changes that are taking place?** When you keep uncovering new information or new changes that are needed, even the best-scoped project can get out of hand. So identify when and how the changes will be assessed and prioritized. Some changes may be strategic; others may be driven by economic concerns. The important piece is knowing how the organization will prioritize changes. Not all processes and changes are created equal, and the road map helps decipher which changes are absolutely critical and which ones will support those critical changes.

✓ **Where do you want to go?** Visions are needed to inspire change, but goals and measurements will eventually show that the change did what it set out to do. Measuring success in the road map addresses how benefits will be measured and tracked. These measurements will include how the company is doing from financial, customer, process, and employee perspectives, as well as key milestones that will happen during the change.

✓ **How will the change last?** Even if the action you're undertaking is not focused on changing the culture, the change road map should specify how ready the organization is for change and how the change will last. Actions may include creating a powerful, two-way communication strategy or changing reward systems to make sure individuals and teams are rewarded for doing what the change wants to accomplish.

To really define the starting point, change teams usually conduct a current-state analysis to understand the current capability of processes, organization structure, data, and technology. A comprehensive current-state assessment combines measurements of how key functions and processes are performing with honest, objective answers from leaders on their *perspective* of how things are working. This assessment can help identify, prioritize, and evaluate change recommendations as well as provide valuable suggestions to help solidify the vision and urgency of the change. Consider asking change leaders the following questions to identify the effort that moving from the current state to the future state will take.

✓ **What is happening today that is driving the need for change?** The answer to this question gives you good insight into the barriers and opportunities the change may face.

✓ **What do you have to do to make sure the change happens?** You want leaders to feel responsible for the change by communicating the vision, offering resources to help, and removing barriers that could stop the change.

✓ **Do we have the time, people, and financial resources to make the change happen?** Remember, change can't happen without resources.

Creating a 30-60-90-day road map

At this point in the change cycle, you won't have the full project plan developed, but putting together a plan for what will happen by 30 days, 60 days, and 90 days (and so on) will keep your team on track with the short-term goals. Check out Table 2-1 as an example. (Use the 30-60-90-day outlook as a guideline, and build out the schedule further when these initial milestones are met.)

Table 2-1	30-60-90-Day Road Map Example		
Aspect	*30 Days*	*60 Days*	*90 Days*
Why do we need to change?	Conduct a current state assessment. Integrate current state assessment into vision and reason for the change.	Share results of current state with leadership team. Share vision, actions, and goals with employees.	Create a front-line council to help communicate the need for change to employees.
What are the 2–3 key changes that are taking place?	Meet with leaders and employees in the organization to decide what types of changes are needed.	Decide on 2–3 critical initiatives for the change based on current state assessment; develop teams to create the tactical plans for those initiatives.	Communicate to employees what changes are happening and when.
Where do you want to go?	Define goals for the change.	Create a scorecard with metrics and goals for the change; edit based on the current-state assessment.	Communicate how teams will be measured against the change goals and metrics.
How will the change last?	Review current performance targets; conduct SWOT analysis. Create two-way communication forums to help support change in the long run.	Identify what organizational culture norms, behaviors, and individual skills may need to change to make the change last. Create a plan to make the changes to skills, norms, and behavior happen.	Share the plan and new rewards structure with the company.

Book VI

Managing Business Change

The purpose of your 30-60-90-day road map is to guide your next steps as you keep moving toward the future vision. It provides an accurate view of what needs to change in order to reach your goals.

Putting together your change team

If you have the right team, you will gain buy-in to the project more efficiently, communicate the project's vision and goals more clearly, help institutionalize the change, and get the change done. Consider these personnel aspects when picking your team:

✔ **Who:** When creating your team, make sure front-line staff and supervisors are involved. Change teams need to look and feel like the population you're changing, so they should include workers affected by the change as well as committed leaders. Involve people who can be advocates for issues that may be impacted by the project.

✔ **How many:** Depending on the size of your organization, the ideal team size for large change projects is a core team of 8 to 12 people. If you're undergoing a major change that impacts multiple parts of the business, you will need this number of people to help represent the various functions and ideas within the business. Any number more than 12 gets a bit chaotic; any fewer than 6 fails to represent everyone affected. Your job is to find the happy medium.

✔ **Skills needed:** Although you may really like someone and want her on your team, make sure the team has the right mix of skills to get the job done. The right mix of skills blends leadership skills that encourage open communication and idea sharing; strong technical skills applicable for the position; and strong talents in facilitation, conflict resolution, and team building. Yes, skills can be taught, but if they aren't taught quickly, anxiety will start to fester and people will wonder if the change can really be implemented.

Committing leadership

You probably have spoken with some leaders in your company, and many of them are likely on board with the changes. These people are your change agents and change sponsors (defined in Chapter 1 of this Book). But don't relax yet; you need to make sure the actions of these leaders are in line with their verbal commitments. While getting your ducks in a row, ask yourself the following questions:

✔ **Are the leaders communicating the vision and goals of the project?** Committed leaders don't just send e-mails; they hold meetings, participate in change-team events, and provide resources when asked.

✔ **Are the leaders recognizing that employees have a voice in the change, and are they helping employees reflect on what needs to happen?** If leaders are holding one-on-one meetings and team discussions about the change, you know they're on board with the vision.

✔ **Are the leaders responding to the needs of their employees?** The icing on the cake is when leaders ask for feedback from employees, reflect on it, and then respond openly to any concerns or ideas.

If you cannot answer "yes" to all these questions, take a step back and assess whether or not the change will last in the long term. Some leaders may need a coach or training on what's required to lead change. Try to work with these leaders to understand why they are not raising their hands and cheering. If coaching and training do not work, it may be time to recruit new leaders who are more fully on board with the change.

Book VI

Managing Business Change

Creating the change-team charter

The *change-team charter* is a document that defines the goal of the change, who will be working on the change, and the big milestones for the change. Just as planning the change leads to a more probable outcome of success, planning out the team's purpose and way of working increases the probability of a successful change.

In addition to listing the goals of the project and team, the processes for how the team will operate, the roles of team members, and how the interpersonal communication will work on the team, a charter should also include a list of resources available to the team. In addition to listing the financial resources (which are important), make sure your team charter also addresses how team members will secure additional human resources, management resources, and physical resources as well.

Aligning the team with a common goal

The common goal for the team is often the goal of the project, but just as you spend time developing and communicating the vision and shared urgency of the project, make sure you spend time ensuring that everyone in the change team has the same picture of the common goal in mind. The goal of the project and the vision for change are related but not the same thing. The vision sets the inspiring picture of the future, but the common goal simply describes what progress and events will happen when.

After the goals for the project are developed, put them in the 30-60-90-day strategic plan to help the team frequently review the progress it's making. If the team members can't describe the goal in one or two crisp sentences, they may be unclear about their task. Teams who lose focus of the goal will have trouble seeing the change through to the end.

Creating a Winning Project Plan: What's Going to Happen

Although your overall goal is to lead lasting change in your organization, your *project plan* is a short-term design to help create change. A winning project plan specifies how you're going to get to your desired future state.

Project planning is part science and part art. Established tools and frameworks provide a method for delivering results. Following step-by-step instructions to map out the time, budget, and resources you'll need is often the easier side of project planning. The art side of project planning, the part you have to feel out as you go, is sometimes more difficult, especially when it comes to working with the emotional reactions of the people involved in and impacted by the change.

Think of project planning not just as a piece of paper but as a mindset of how you do business. It is a disciplined approach to leading change and perhaps even managing the chaos during the transition period.

Checking your readiness to launch

Most project management methods have common fundamental areas: scoping, planning, managing, and closing. Before you can begin writing a project plan, you need to spend some time thinking about these areas of the project. If you can answer the following eight readiness questions, you're well on your way to creating a winning project plan:

✓ **Scope**

- What are we trying to do?

✓ **Planning**

- When will we start?

- Who will do the work and make decisions?

- How long will the project take?

- How much will the project cost?

✓ **Managing**

- What work needs to get done?

- How will we make sure the work gets done?

✓ **Closing**

- How will we know we have been successful?

53?

Planning to succeed

Even if people are ready to get changing now, you still have time for planning — if you make time for it. If you don't do it, you most likely will be playing catch-up later. Wouldn't you rather plan to succeed instead of pulling a few all-nighters dealing with risks you should have known about and tried to mitigate before they happened? Doing the following things will make your life easier during the planning phase:

✔ **Identify the types of project management in your organization that you have used in the past.** Don't start from scratch if you don't have to. You may be surprised to find that your organization has a project-planning method or template you may be able to modify to meet the needs of your change.

✔ **Piggyback onto existing project management tools.** Some organizations already have program offices in place or perhaps even project managers. If your organization has this resource, use it! If not, the Association for Project Management (www.apm.org.uk) and the Project Management Institute (www.pmi.org) have wonderful resources available on their websites for new and experienced project managers. You may want to consider joining these organizations to access a wealth of tools and information.

Book VI

Managing Business Change

Project management is about creating an environment conducive to getting critical goals accomplished during your change plan.

Looking at the elements of a project plan

Although having a project schedule is absolutely critical, the schedule is just one piece of the project-planning puzzle. This section covers the elements of a project plan to get you on the right path to successful change.

Focus on making the project plan comprehensive but easy to read. Try writing a one-page project plan for executives to review and a longer version for the change team to utilize.

Writing a project problem statement

The problem statement is a one- or two-sentence description of the symptoms arising from the problem to be addressed. It often parallels a business case for change quite closely, but the problem statement is more specific and focused than the business case. For example, "Turnover in our research department has increased from last year's level for three quarters in a row, reducing our knowledge base and limiting new product development." A problem statement then focuses on a key element of that larger issue:

"Experienced engineers have left the company three times as often as last year, contributing to a significant reduction in new product introduction." Problem statements usually answer these questions:

- ✔ What's wrong?
- ✔ Where is the problem appearing?
- ✔ When did the problem happen (time frame)?
- ✔ How big is the problem?
- ✔ What's the impact of the problem on the business?

Defining the goal of the project

Making a great project plan is a waste of time if you aren't certain of where you want to go. Defining your destination, the goal of the project, should be pretty easy because all you have to do is state what you expect to get out of the project. If this step sounds familiar, it's because it ties straight back to the vision of the change discussed earlier in this chapter.

Be specific about what the project is aiming to accomplish and make sure to define measurements around how you'll know the goal has been met.

Setting quality standards

When it comes to getting a project done, the two ends of the quality spectrum are using the quick-and-dirty method (which often lacks quality) and following previously established standards. Here is where doing a little research on best practices in your industry can really help, so that you can set goals that are competitive. Of course, not every project needs to pass the white glove test, but as a change leader you need to define what standards of quality are required. Will a review council be established to look at the milestones, or will a quality audit make sure deliverables for your change are acceptable?

The important thing is not necessarily which standard you pick but how well you communicate that quality standard to the rest of the organization. All the key players need to clearly understand what is required and how success will be measured each step of the way.

Allocating financial, human, and physical resources

Nothing gets done without resources. Whether these resources are financial, physical, or human, identifying the necessary resources (or lack of them) up front alleviates a tremendous amount of pain in the future. If you need a project manager, identify the person to fill that role. If you need financial resources to make a technology change, let senior leaders know how much money you need and how you came up with that number.

Outlining governance structure

You may have the best plan in place and have all the project resources you could possibly desire, but you still need to know who's running the show. The governance structure puts down on paper who is making each decision.

By identifying resources, you determine who will do the work, whereas the governance structure shows who oversees the project and makes key decisions on what will get done in what time frame with what level of investment. Please refer to the "Roles and responsibilities" section later in the chapter for more about these assignments.

Noting critical milestones

Critical milestones, also referred to as *critical-path items,* is just a fancy term for things that must happen before going any farther. You find out more about these action items in the later section "Identifying critical successes and critical paths."

Identifying dependencies and risks

Risk management is one of the most bypassed areas of project planning for large changes. When you're just starting, who wants to stand up and talk about the risks of the project not being an overwhelming success?

Change teams also sometimes avoid talking about the project's *dependencies:* the factors they're counting on in order for the project to succeed. For example, a team may require the support of the IT department to make necessary changes to information systems in order to track the progress of the change. This need may require the IT manager to shift priorities and workloads to accommodate this request. Dependencies are simply risks that you want to have happen.

But dependencies and risks don't need to be intimidating because every large change (and small change) holds potential risks and dependencies that can cause problems or delays. Your goal is to highlight them so they can be avoided or reduced through advance planning (sounds much better than failure, right?).

Risks and dependencies usually fall into a range of categories like financial, technical, legal, safety, personnel, and public relations. When you identify risks and dependencies, you should ask yourself the following questions:

- ✔ What risks and dependencies do we know of?
- ✔ What is their potential level of impact on the project timeline and cost?
- ✔ How likely is each risk to cause problems? How likely are we to have something we depend on not happen? *Very likely, somewhat,* and *not at all* are just fine as categories. You don't need to put too fine a point on this.

Book VI

Managing Business Change

Identify ways of reducing the risks or their impact if they do happen. Create a plan for if the risks happen or if the dependencies fail to happen. See the section "Assessing and Managing Risk" later in this chapter for more discussion on this topic.

Scheduling

A great project schedule identifies the major tasks or deliverables that need to be completed and then groups subtasks together according to how you can make these major tasks happen. The tasks should always imply action. For example, if your major task in the project plan of getting to work in the morning is making coffee, your subtasks may be as follows: grind the beans, fill the water in the coffee maker, push the *On* button, warm the milk, pour the coffee, and stir in the sugar. Your subtask may instead be getting in the car and getting your local barista to make your cup of joe, but that's where the art of project planning comes into play. There are many possible ways to make a great cup of coffee. The subtasks nail down the specific approach you plan to use in your project.

Many, many tools are available to create project schedules, from the simplest plans created in Microsoft Excel and Numbers to more advanced Gantt charting and Project Tools. DotProject (www.dotproject.net) is an open-source project-management tool.

The GRPI Model: Getting a grip on how change will happen

The GRPI model for project and team management is one of the most user-friendly, can-be-done-anywhere models out there. The GRPI model is simply a way of organizing your team around the project plan in a way that makes sense. *GRPI* stands for

- ✓ **Goals:** Clearly define the team's mission and establish objectives that conform to the SMART approach (that is, goals that are specific, measurable, action oriented and agreed on, realistic, and time bound).

- ✓ **Roles and responsibilities:** Clearly define each team member's function and the interrelationships between individual and team roles, objectives, and processes.

- ✓ **Processes and actions:** Identify and define processes inherent in and essential to the project's success (such as problem solving, decision making, and so on).

- ✓ **Interpersonal relationships:** Ensure open communication between team members, encourage creative and diverse contributions from all members, and discourage *groupthink* (quickly coming to consensus without critical reflection).

By enhancing your project plan with the GRPI model, you get a one-two punch for project success: a solid plan to make sure everyone knows what is going to happen (the project plan) and a structure of how it will happen (the GRPI model). Additionally, using the straightforward GRPI acronym is something most people in organizations can relate to, remember, and grasp with little or no project-management or team training. Use the GRPI acronym as your checklist to make sure you have everything accounted for in your project.

Create both a project plan and a GRPI model for your change project. Although most elements of a project plan fit perfectly into the GRPI model, the project plan gives you a very detailed listing of what's going to happen when, and the GRPI model details how it is going to happen.

You may feel like you're reiterating what you already completed, but each part of your change plan serves a different purpose. The vision is used to communicate and motivate others, the project plan describes in detail what you're accomplishing, and the GRPI checklist makes sure your change team knows how to get the project done.

Book VI

Managing Business Change

Goals

The first part of your project plan covers the goals of the project and the problem statement. Make sure to include the vision of the project, the goals and deliverables of the project (from your project plan), and the scope of the project.

Roles and responsibilities

The *R* in GRPI stands for both roles and responsibilities. This information pulls heavily from the governance structure part of your project plan. A RACI chart is a simple yet effective tool for assessing roles and responsibilities, ensuring the right people are involved (that is, you have the right management or governance structure). *RACI* is an acronym for

- ✔ **Responsible:** Who is responsible? List the individual or individuals (limit this role to one or two people) in charge of getting the job done.

- ✔ **Accountable:** To whom is the responsible person accountable? Make note of the individual or individuals (again, limit this role to one or two people) who have ultimate decision-making and approval authority. It is typically the owner of the budget or resources.

- ✔ **Consulted:** Who do the responsible and accountable parties need to get input from? The consulted group is the individuals or teams who should provide input into a decision or action before it occurs.

- ✔ **Informed:** Who needs to know about the change/project? This group includes the individuals or teams who must be informed that a decision or action has taken place. Be sure to include people who will be most impacted by the change.

Processes and actions

The processes-and-actions section of the GRPI model focuses on how the work will get done rather than on what is getting done, which you covered in your project schedule. In this section of your GRPI model, cover four big "hows" of getting the plan done:

- ✔ **Decision making:** How will decision making take place? Will decision making be in the hands of the project owner (the accountable person), or will the team make decisions and then propose the final solution to the boss?

- ✔ **Problem solving:** You may also want to discuss how you will work through problem solving. Will problem solving be done individually or as a team? Neither method is better than the other, but you can see how conflict will quickly arise if one person expects to handle all the problem solving on her own and the rest of the team thinks group discussions are needed for anything that happens.

- ✔ **Conflicting opinions:** What will you do in the face of conflicting opinions? Conflict happens on teams. Laying out the groundwork to make sure people know how to de-escalate conflicting opinions will put the team in control of resolving tough situations.

- ✔ **Communication:** How will the change team stay connected through communication? Communication is one of the most, if not *the* most, important aspects of making the change happen and getting the change team to work together. Focus on communication processes within the change team itself.

Interpersonal relationships

The interpersonal relationships part of the GRPI model can best be described as how the team is going to work together to get the project plan done. This part of the plan focuses on the team that's driving the change. Include how your change agents, change sponsors, and change advocates will work with one another and what is acceptable and expected behavior on the team. You may consider addressing some of these key interpersonal areas:

- ✔ Are openness and outspokenness valued and rewarded on the team, or should differences be handled in a less direct manner?

- ✔ What level of flexibility does the team have in working with one another? Can team members revisit ideas already decided on?

- ✔ How will the team value emotions and feelings about what is happening versus rewarding data and facts?

Staying focused on what matters most

Organizations, no matter how productive, can focus on only so many things at once. Furthermore, too many simultaneous changes are impossible to track and manage. When you have too many changes happening at once, the problem is usually that the change isn't aligned with the strategic plan and goals of the organization.

The solution is to make sure you're focusing your project plan on what matters most. You can do so by identifying the specific actions you need to take and focusing the change team on actions they need to accomplish.

Identifying critical successes and critical paths

Critical path items are milestones that are forks in the road — you can't just keep moving forward without making a decision. They impact downstream milestones and the overall timeline of a project. If you miss a critical path, the entire project will most likely be delayed (or you'll have to dash around to make up ground).

Here are two aspects of critical paths you may want to consider:

- ✔ Assigning a resource to them
- ✔ Identifying what depends on them in case they don't happen according to plan

You don't have to think of the worst possible thing that could happen, but be realistic about the potential for the project to be delayed or not adopted fully if critical milestones are not met.

Cutting the work that doesn't add value

If your team or you start feeling overwhelmed by action items, you may be focusing on parts of the project plan that have little or no impact on the final goal. To overcome this barrier, have your team list how their part of the project plan fits into these three categories:

- ✔ **Strategic:** These tasks may involve keeping the organization focused on the vision of the future state or continually aligning the change strategy with market forecasts and challenges.

- ✔ **Day-to-day operations:** These actions usually are tasks on your project plan, and if they're not done they'll lead to missing one of your critical-path milestones.

- ✔ **Firefighting/nonvalue:** This no-value-added work drains your energy and time. It's most likely work that should have been done correctly the first time but wasn't.

Now look at how these three categories balance out. If you're not focusing on what matters most, you're probably spending quite a bit of time in the firefighting/nonvalue category and not enough time in the operations and strategic roles. There's no magic number or formula, but a general rule is that no one on your change team should spend more than 10 percent of his time on no-value-added work.

Avoiding scope creep

Scope creep is a very real concern for even the best change projects and the most robust change plans. You know scope creep when you see it: A project's goal is meant to solve one problem, and then another problem arises and seems to work its way into the original project, and then another problem comes up and is added to what the original project was meant to solve as well.

The projects that get done successfully are meaningful (tied to the change vision and the desired future state) and focused (solving one or two problems, not the entire organization's problems that have been around for years).

How do you limit the project scope effectively and make sure you avoid scope creep?

- ✔ **Be clear on where the project stops and starts.** This step gets back to the project goal. If the goal is SMART, you'll have a much easier time acknowledging when additional work isn't part of the change.

- ✔ **Communicate what is inside the project scope and what is outside the project scope.** This advice may seem obvious, but many people assume your change project is going to solve everything in the entire world — and why wouldn't it, with such a great vision of the future? Do not overpromise what the change will do. Be open about what it will and will not do.

Leading unexpected change

A number of challenges happen when you don't have time to plan for change. The biggest of them is trying to plan and change direction when you're also trying to keep the business running. This challenge is real but not insurmountable.

Don't start changing everything at once in response to the challenge. You need to plan first and *then* act. Although you may feel pressure to move forward as quickly as possible, planning what to do next can be the difference between strategic steps and chaos. Just doing a bunch of things with no plan in place will most likely get you into a worse place than you are by doing nothing.

Clarify goals and objectives

If an organization faces unforeseen change, one of the first areas you want to address is clarifying the goals and objectives of the company and revisiting roles and specific performance standards. If a big external or internal change happens, you want to be crystal clear on what the business will continue to deliver and who is going to deliver it.

Decide how to shift resources

Lack of resources or changing resources is the outcome of many sudden changes. A fall in market demand, an increase in competition, or instability in the market after disasters can have a significant effect on businesses. When sudden change happens, identify how money, time, technology, and people will be allocated to address the change while the business continues running.

Book VI

Managing Business Change

Increase communication

If communication is important during a planned change (and it is!), you can imagine how critical communication is when the change is abrupt. Although communicating bad news to employees may be uncomfortable, communicating as much as you can immediately after the change fosters a responsive atmosphere, with employees willing and able to adjust to change. Always address the change and what you plan to do (even if you're still figuring it out) internally with employees and management. If appropriate for the type of change and challenge you face, communicate externally with your suppliers and customers as well.

Show strong leadership

Visible leadership is essential when reacting to change. Leaders can provide clear direction and positive motivation to help employees remain optimistic about the future. During times of unanticipated change, people crave the security that confident, straightforward leaders provide.

Having clear and visible senior management support for your action plan is the first way you can calm the rocky waters left by sudden change. Quickly pull together a map of your stakeholders showing their roles, interests, and authority, and assess who can influence the company to move in the right direction. Ask key stakeholders for their input and support as you conquer sudden change. Bringing these individuals together to discuss common issues helps them to develop a shared understanding of what's happening in the business concerning business continuity, strategic direction, performance, communication, and change management.

Assessing and Managing Risk

Change risk is any possible event that can negatively affect the success of the project. The list of change risks can be long, but your job involves much more than simply thinking about risks or listing them out. You also have to assess the risks, decide whether you're willing to take them, and then manage the risks to the success of change the best you can. As you identify the risks that may obstruct your change, you first review the existing risks and then plan how to respond to them.

Knowing your risks

You and your change team can hold brainstorming meetings or do an assessment to identify risks, you can ask experts on the subject what their opinion is regarding the risks (with data to back it up), or you may look at the past history of when something stopped a change before.

If you are still having trouble identifying risks or are not sure whether you have a complete list, here are the usual suspects of risks to your change plan:

- **Financial risks:** Financial risks with your change may include business or service interruption due to the change, or loss of customers if change is not properly executed.

- **Technical risks:** Technical risks can range from not having the right platform to support a large system change to losing data if information systems are replaced.

- **Legal risks:** Legal risks are the factors that could break the law if not handled correctly. These risks range from not having sufficient controls in place to catch insider trading when implementing a new financial-reporting system to not doing due diligence on financial reports during a merger and acquisition. By risking legal requirements, the result may be damaged reputation, loss of customers, or even imprisonment.

- **Safety risks:** Safety risks are the factors that could cause harm to employees, the environment, or customers.

- **Human resources risks:** Resignations, employees asked to take on additional work, unavailable skills, ineffective training, absenteeism, and poor quality/execution are just some of the many risks that come from the human element in change.

- **Public relations risks:** Public relations deals with risks to the reputation of your company and your brand. This area includes how the change is perceived in the court of public opinion and the press.

How big? How likely? Analyzing your risks' probability and consequences

After you have your list of risks, you need to analyze those risks. Ask your change team how big and how likely each risk is. Most organizations assign numbers to the size and probability of risk to make the equation more meaningful and action oriented, with higher numbers representing larger or likelier risks. The more likely an event is to happen and the greater the consequence, the more attention you should pay to it.

Limiting your risks

After you've defined your risks, the next step is deciding how to respond to them. In general, you can do three things with your risks:

- ✔ **Risk avoidance:** Take steps to avoid them or significantly lower the probability of them happening. This process means building a change plan that eliminates the causes of the risks. For example, if knowledge on how to do things differently is an issue, then offer training and mentoring to bridge the skill gap.

- ✔ **Risk mitigation:** Acknowledge that some risks cannot be avoided, and take steps to lessen the impact/consequence if the risks do occur. Risk mitigation is kind of like buying insurance for the change: You acknowledge that it could happen, but you want to lessen the blow to your change if it does. This step is where contingency plans frequently come into play. Contingency plans may be financial, task-focused, or management/people-focused.

  Often, losing key human resources is a risk during a change project. If your risk is losing top management or key employees, make sure you have a plan in place to backfill that talent.

- ✔ **Risk acceptance:** Accept that the risk may happen, and proceed as planned. This response is what you will probably do with your C-priority risks. You acknowledge they may happen and are willing to work with the consequences if they do. When you accept risks, you may be willing to work them into the project plan and then get on with the change.

Measuring and Evaluating

Measuring change isn't easy, but change that's left unmeasured gets you nowhere. Consider the measurement of change and the tracking of change to be like the gauges on your car's dashboard. Although the change may be running just fine, without indicators to tell you how much fuel you have left in the tank, how many miles you have traveled, and where the GPS says you should turn next, eventually you end up in the middle of nowhere, unsure of which direction to go and with your resources depleted.

Don't get left lost and alone. Read on to find out how and what to track during times of change.

Developing benchmarks

Benchmarking is the process of defining standards of performance by comparing yourself with others. In many change processes, when the time comes to set targets for where you want to go and how you will measure progress, you may have difficultly knowing what's good enough for the change. When it comes to moving toward the shared vision of the future, knowing who else is moving and how they're doing it helps catapult your change while maintaining a realistic eye on what's possible.

In order for change leaders to have benchmarks for assessing the change progress, you need to start with a clear assessment of how you're doing. Many leaders make the mistake of seeing a great idea out there and then directing a project team to implement it without having a clue about how the company is performing today.

 When creating benchmarks, you're not trying to define all the benchmarks that could determine success, just a few important ones. But articulating and gaining agreement on the vital few metrics can be your most challenging task in the integration process.

Establishing milestones

Change projects sometimes seem like they can last forever, so establishing big and small milestones to track progress is critical. The word *milestone* originated from the stones that were set up next to roads to indicate to travelers the distance in miles to a particular destination, and in your case milestones are events or actions that mark progress in your change project. You use them to communicate when your project has reached certain stages and to indicate what is coming up next.

Bigger milestones are, of course, more important and more visible, but luckily they're often easier to set and should be aligned to the steps of implementing change discussed in Chapter 1 and throughout this Book. Here are five big milestones that mark the end of these key implementation steps:

✔ **Building a vision and shared need:** As soon as the vision for the change is set and is beginning to be communicated to the larger audience, you can measure and evaluate whether you're on the right track early in the project. Setting and communicating the vision is the first big milestone.

✔ **Creating the change road map and planning the change:** Although a project plan doesn't make the change happen, the change plan is one of the first tangible outputs of the change, and getting it done right should be recognized as a major milestone.

✔ **Committing leadership:** Leadership is often a subjective area that people find hard to measure. The next section focuses on how to measure the leaders' commitment to change, but after your sponsor, change agents, and change team are aligned, you will have surpassed a big milestone worthy of celebration.

✔ **Implementing the change:** Throughout the implementation, you will want to communicate and measure larger milestones such as your critical path events.

✔ **Finalizing the change and recognizing results:** This milestone is the no-brainer. After the change happens, you will surely want to celebrate, recognize, and learn from everything that happened during the change. This milestone marks the conclusion of the project.

Within any change process lie small milestones, as well. They do two things: help generate momentum with small successes along the way to the bigger goal, and help you gauge how the change is moving. Creating milestones to identify early wins is one way of building momentum. Just like the bigger project goal, smaller milestones must be clear, tangible, and directly tied to the project. Small milestones may include getting the change team trained, finalizing the vision, completing benchmarking of better ways of doing things, and establishing communication channels for the change.

Keeping an eye on progress

You probably know by now how important it is to measure by fact, not feeling. So how do you know a change is an improvement? You measure it. The best way to keep an eye on progress is to keep an eye on your data.

When setting up change measures, find out where you are before the change so you can later prove that the benefits of the project have been delivered.

Your first priority for measurement is called your *key performance indicators* and should be linked to the strategy and vision of the change, the processes that are going to change, the impact to the people, and any legal or compliance issues that must be tracked during the change.

Book VI

Managing Business Change

To keep an eye on progress, just make sure you cover two main parts of data:

- ✔ **Measures to evaluate implementation, or whether the change was executed as planned:** These measurements may be tracking of project plans, critical milestones, and budgets. This type of measure is often objective: Did it happen or not? Did we meet our target dates? Did we meet the budget targets for the change project?

- ✔ **Measures to gauge effectiveness of the change, or how well the change accomplished the future-state goal:** These measures should be linked to benchmarks you identified for your change and to goals for the change. Although some of these measures may be objective (are management structures flatter rather than hierarchical?), other parts of the effectiveness assessment may be more subjective (does the organization operate with fewer boundaries, and has teamwork improved across functions and departments?).

You want change to be large and engaging, but you want the measurement of your change's success to be as simple as possible. Note that *easy* and *simple* are not the same thing — doing a little extra legwork to keep your measures simple can give your change team confidence when they're asked to review the measurements frequently.

Communicating the Change

When people start feeling the stress associated with major change, they develop an almost insatiable hunger for information. You will hear these questions: What is happening? When is it happening? Why is it happening? Is it happening to me? If you leave a gap in answering these questions, the gap is inevitably filled with rumor, and the rumor mill is the nemesis of change. On the other hand, successfully communicated changes result in project-management utopia: shorter timelines, widespread ownership in the new environment, lower costs due to speed of the change and/or increased efficiencies, and an organization ready to take on future changes.

Answering the three big change questions

As soon as your employees hear that change is coming, you can bet that three major questions will surface even before you have a chance to develop your full-fledged communication plan. Having well-thought-out answers to these questions sets up the change for success, starting day one. Change succeeds when a powerful case for the change is communicated relentlessly to generate understanding and consensus for that change. By planning for these questions in advance, you can present a case that's strong enough to win over your employees and keep them on your side.

Question 1: Where are we headed, and why?

er to the question of where you're . You need first to find out where you se; otherwise, you may be packing a you don't decide where you're going, few people will want to come along

ypewriting Company, a manual change. The company's leaders e for manual typewriters has y're moving to producing the next s. This change will impact the

/here are we headed? If Top-Notch's that hits the following points:

g its products, service, and culture oducts to writers across the globe —

s been focused on supporting those ual typewriter, and now it's going to e want to buy and use.

pany is going to be shutting down replacing them with the latest tech- entirely new skill set and will get ld to create and support the new on.

been a traditional and bureau- d now it's going to be innovative, chnology.

ehind! The answer is specific and writing tablets), customers (lots (state of the art). If you want to n of what's changing is one of your ere the change is headed.

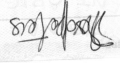

Question 2: WIIFM, or what's in it for me?

People tend to get comfortable in the current state and, after they hear that change is coming, they want to know how this change is going to affect them personally. It makes sense; work is where they spend much of their time, where they make their money, and where they have developed important professional and personal relationships. You, as the leader, must answer the big WIIFM question (What's in it for me?) in a way that resonates with them and encourages them to jump on board.

WIIFM drives home how the change affects someone personally. Your answer lets employees know what they need to do when the change is happening and after it happens. And when your answer is a good one, it will get people out from behind their desks and saying, "I am ready to change!"

To give employees the best WIIFM answer possible and start using this critical change tool, follow these four steps:

1. **Explain** WIIFM to the employees involved in change, letting everyone understand what you're asking them and why it's important to the company so the entire team understands the direction of the change. Providing initial thoughts about what's in it for them kicks off the dialogue about the change.

2. **Ask** about individual and team WIIFMs. Start with these two discussion questions: "Why are you here today? What do you want to get out of being part of this change?" Answers to these questions may range from being promoted in the next six months to learning new skills to getting a good recommendation at the end of the project. Everyone has different WIIFM goals; your job is to gather them. This step engages employees in exploring how the change will benefit them individually and as a team.

3. **Identify** ways that the project can motivate and reward employees according to their WIIFM goals while still meeting the project's overall goals. Although you can't promise employees that their WIIFM dreams will *all* be achieved, understanding and acknowledging different goals and helping employees achieve their personal goals goes a long way to motivating them to focus and commit to the project.

4. **Assess** whether the WIIFM goals you settled on are being achieved on a regular basis. This check-in may be in individual team-leader meetings or in casual one-on-one discussions. Your goal and role are to track the progress toward the WIIFM solution and make changes to the overall communication messaging as necessary.

Question 3: How are we going to get there?

Going from the current state to the future state (also known as the *transition state*) takes effort, so you can help the cause by having a transparent and easily understood forecast of how the change will take place. Crafting this message helps you answer the third question employees have about the change: "How are we going to get there?"

Most change efforts have a project plan. Project plans are great to keep project teams on task and are especially wonderful for the people who made them and people who love to have lots of information, but the general population can be overwhelmed by detailed project plans. That's where you come in: Communicate the basic outline of the plan and provide enough information to keep everyone informed of what is happening in the short term.

A high-level project plan may look something like this:

- ✔ Stage 1: Creating the change team happens in Month 1.
- ✔ Stage 2: Providing training for the change happens in Month 2.
- ✔ Stage 3: Change happens in Month 3.
- ✔ Stage 4: Following up on the change success happens in Month 4.

Simple. To the point. Just enough detail to help people understand what's going on during the entire change project.

Book VI

**Managing
Business
Change**

Developing an ideal communication style during change

Communicating during change is all about getting the message out in order to alleviate as much ambiguity and uncertainty as possible. Your job as a communicator of change is to encourage exploration and learning while maintaining productivity. It's a big task — but not an impossible one.

As a change leader, you have a choice about *how* you will communicate during change. Being inaccessible, telling only the partial truth, or ordering rather than seeking solutions may be effective in getting things checked off in the short term, but such actions taken together and repeated will *not* lead to a sustainable change (and most likely your change will backfire on you fairly quickly). Providing a compelling reason to change, listening to concerns (really listening to them), and making sure people have the right level of information *will* lead to sustainable change. Which one do you want to choose to do?

Keeping it fresh, frequent, and flowing

While you're communicating with your employees, use the acronym KIF — keep it fresh, keep it frequent, and keep it flowing — to make your communication successful.

✔ **Keep it fresh.** Give new information often to prevent broken-record syndrome.

✔ **Keep it frequent and diverse.** Make your communication more than just a checkmark on the project plan. Do it on a regular basis using a variety of communication tools to get the attention of employees. If you keep using the same two tools to communicate, people will eventually tune out.

✔ **Keep it flowing.** Nothing is worse than going out with a stellar communication plan, getting everyone excited about the change, and then hiding in a cave until the project is done. Employees must see, hear, and feel updated messages throughout the project. Otherwise, they'll assume the change has fizzled out.

Motivating and encouraging: Saying no to the status quo

The status quo is never a catalyst to change. Now is the time to remind your employees to leave the status quo and move to this wonderful new future. Here are some ways you can start challenging the existing situation and communicating why it's so important to "say no to the status quo":

✔ **Be the devil's advocate with a purpose.** Know the worst that could happen if you don't change, and be the spokesperson of those fears. What is the worst that can happen if you stay where you are? Could the market for your product or service go away? Could another company take over greater market share? These possibilities are compelling reasons to move away from where you are today and can motivate your employees.

✔ **Know what everyone else is doing.** Be able to tell your employees why your company is changing to align with the competition or differentiate from the competition. Has the rest of your competition begun moving away from the same-old-same-old? You don't need to jump off a bridge because everyone else is doing it, but if you notice you're diverging from the pack, it may be a good time to reevaluate where you're going and why.

✔ **Keep up with customers who want something new.** Communicate to your employees that having customers isn't the same thing as keeping them. Even if your customers love you and your product, at some point in time, they will want to try something new. Wouldn't it be nice if you could give that new something to them?

✔ **Deal with other external factors.** Explain how regulatory change, pricing pressures driven by the market, or other external factors are driving you to change. Some changes are thrust upon us by the government or the global economy.

Many people can't bear to give up the status quo because they think the fact that it worked in the past means it shouldn't change. Even if a process or product did *not* work in the past, you'll come into contact with a handful of people who won't admit it. By communicating the need to abandon the status quo and telling employees what's in it for them, you can offer a reason to change that's more compelling than their natural attachment to the status quo.

Listening

Listening is an important aspect of leading change successfully. Two-way communication implies opportunities for people to give feedback, share ideas, voice their concerns, make suggestions, identify problems, and surface rumors. Effective communication plans build in those opportunities, so lend an ear and start listening by

- ✔ **Creating buy-in:** Let employees (not just you or upper management) share why this change is important, in their words.

- ✔ **Gleaning ideas you may not have thought of:** Ask employees what other ideas may move the change along.

- ✔ **Making course corrections:** Let an employee steering committee gather feedback from peers during the change; peers are more likely to talk with peers than squeal to management.

- ✔ **Letting concerns surface instead of suppressing them:** Let employees discuss their concerns without responding immediately. Ask for feedback, listen to it, and then go research the correct answer (not a talking point or canned answer)!

Remember: The most effective tool in communication is the ear.

Communicating across differences

When team members or people in an organization have differences of opinion, they usually stem from the receiver of the information not getting the same message as the sender of the information. As a change leader, your goal is to make sure that what you are sending is the same as what is received. In this section you find out how to get a firm handle on what you want to accomplish, mediate differences of opinion, come to agreement on specific points, and implement the agreement. Book V, Chapter 4 goes into further detail about resolving conflict.

Knowing what you're trying to accomplish

When you're going to have a conversation with a dissenter, make a plan and know what you're trying to communicate to him. What is your objective when you are trying to overcome differences in opinion? Are you trying to gain agreement, change someone's point of view, or just make sure everyone can live with the outcome? Write down what your purpose is for working through differences of opinion before you open your mouth. A little planning avoids a lot of disagreements.

When communicating with people of different viewpoints, consider why you *think* there is a difference of opinion (it may not really be as big as you may think), why it is important to understand the difference of opinions and work through them, when you need to communicate, and where you will do it. Most people don't like being taken by surprise when you ask for their opinion or ask why they disagree with yours, so think about when and where you can get your message across without barriers or disruptions.

Exploring differences of opinion and agreeing on facts

No one likes being accused of disagreeing or not playing nice with others. When using communication tools to address differences, start by exploring what's going on from the receiver's point of view. Inquire about the individual's perspective without accusing, by stating something like, "When you walked out of the project team meeting, it seemed like you may disagree with our decision. Can I do anything to answer any questions you may have?" After you have asked for reasons for the receiver's opinion, you can then advocate your position and priorities (and the project's) and make the thoughts and facts behind your point of view clear (this is where planning the message is really important).

The point of exploring differences of opinions is not to argue; it's to get everything out in the open and have a rational discussion about the facts.

Deciding on specific commitments

After opinions have been given and you have been able to come up with a few facts everyone agrees with, now is the time to decide on specific commitments. Don't worry about getting everything agreed on upfront; some people and teams just need more time to adjust to the change than others. Your role is to get specific commitments from the dissenter so the change project doesn't come to a complete halt.

Although getting the commitments may not be easy, how you ask for them is. Try these questions for starters:

✔ What are you going to do?

✔ When are you going to do it?

✔ What may stop you from doing it?

✔ What support do you need from me?

✔ On a scale of one to ten, how likely are you to follow through on your commitment?

Now you and your disagreeing team or individual can work together to come up with an action plan that specifically lists what you both have agreed to do and when you are going to do it.

When you are coming up with agreements, think of the agreements as anchors in mountain climbing. When you make an agreement, you are putting an anchor in place so you don't fall back to square one again. This process helps prevent many repeat disagreements and keeps your change project on track.

Remember that at this point you aren't trying to get people with differences of opinion to agree on everything, just on some things.

Implementing your agreement and following up

At this point, everyone is in agreement and happy! Well, something like that. With your action plan in place, after you are absolutely sure you have agreements (no matter how small) in place, make sure you let your supporter of the project know you would like to follow up with him and how and when you will do so. This meeting isn't to check up on him or spy; it is merely to make sure everyone continues to agree on what's happening. This type of follow up helps the entire team address any problems that may have come up or further questions about the change or change communication.

Book VI

Managing Business Change

Chapter 3

Making Change Stick

. . . .

. . . .

*W*elcome to the reality of change: getting through the change when obstacles are in the way and making the change last long after the project is complete. When you know where you want to go and how to make the change process happen, you need to know how to break through resistance from employees, manage stress levels, and make midcourse corrections if necessary. Not to get too far ahead here, but you also need to know how to make sure the change everyone worked so hard for stays in place after it happens.

Sounds like a lot, right? Yes, but it's manageable, and you're just the person to make it happen. Read on to find out how.

Getting Employees on Board and Keeping Them Motivated

All the work you have done to this point in your change project has set a perfect stage for change success: You have a vision, a need, a plan with appropriate measures, and a great communication approach to getting the entire change moving in the right direction. In this section, you examine the importance of stepping away from planning so you can cultivate relationships with your employees to motivate them and make change last. You can't have change without cooperation, and no one likes to cooperate with people they disagree with or don't trust!

Building trust

Trust is one of those words everyone uses but rarely defines. *Trust* means belief and confidence in another person that he is presenting facts and circumstances entirely and being open and honest with emotions and feelings. It is your job as a change leader to build trust with your employees, peers, and team as well as throughout the entire organization. Without trust, you cannot cooperate, and without cooperation, no change can happen.

Cultivating relationships through trust is the building block for change that many leaders forget. Trust propels your vision of two-way communication into a reality because people will want to talk with you about the project, not feel that they are forced to speak with you. Although cultivating relationships and building trust take time, here are some things you can do to make them happen:

- ✔ **Actively listen.** Open your ears, make eye contact, and have empathy. If as change leader you want to build trust, first listen to understand the other person's perspectives and opinions, and then focus on leading change, not the other way around. You can practice being all ears with help from the upcoming section "Listening."

- ✔ **Be credible.** Change leaders back up the vision for change with resources and action. This means setting targets that the organization can achieve and being genuine when talking about the vision. Then walk the talk and make sure resources are dedicated to the change to make it happen. Don't exaggerate the scope of change or the expected results.

- ✔ **Be open and honest.** Be cooperative with information. When employees ask questions about the future of the change, don't misrepresent the facts to make things sound better. Instead, be compassionate and offer what information you can. If you don't have the information an employee is asking for or can't share it with her for regulatory, financial, or other reasons, say so.

- ✔ **Create an environment of mutual respect through solutions that suit both you and your employees.** Leaders often make the mistake of believing everyone has or should have the same motives as they do. Find out what your employees' motives are and tell them that you want the change to meet their goals, too. Your employees will trust you more readily if they know you respect them and you're on their side. Check your ego at the door unless you want to go it alone.

- ✔ **Help employees resolve conflict.** One of the best ways to build trust is through effectively resolving conflict, which you find out about in Chapter 5 of Book IV.

Building trust is not just a one-time deal. You have to prove yourself worthy of your employees' trust over and over again. But the upshot of having motivated, hardworking employees is worth the effort.

Over the course of the change, you need to build trust not only between yourself and your employees but also among members of the change team. Building trust on the team is a significant hurdle to overcome, and when you do, you will see the payoff in the form of an aligned and energized team.

Overcoming the negative impact of past change efforts

Book VI

Managing
Business
Change

Sometimes change projects face extra resistance due to past change failures. For example, perhaps the company attempted a big systems change that didn't deliver the expected results. Employees tried to make the change work, but their workload just got bigger, and now they're reluctant to commit to another large scale "improvement." Or if a company has something of a revolving door for senior leaders (they come in for a few years and then leave), some employees may have change baggage around accepting any new initiative or "this time is different" speech from a new leader, because their experience tells them the leader will be out the door as soon as the change is done.

Letting go of past baggage is not a quick fix that instantly turns around old and sometimes reinforced behaviors. Letting go of past behaviors is like resolving conflict and building trust: It takes time and follow-up. It requires the change leader to provide ongoing support, observe the teams in action when they're trying to move to a new type of behavior, debrief the teams, reinforce the desired/modified behavior, and push for continuous improvement in areas that still need it.

Getting over change baggage is important. Really important. Following are six steps to collaboration — key tools and techniques that leaders can use to facilitate a group through collaboration:

1. **Raise the change-baggage issue.** This step may seem obvious: The first move is to own up to the fact that a disagreement is happening. If you haven't already clearly done so, surface and name the issue now. You're then able to move to the next step.

2. **Get curious.** Holding an attitude of curiosity enables you to move away from defending your own position to explore other people's perspectives with an open mind. Balance advocacy (presenting your own views) with inquiry (seeking to understand others' views through questioning).

3. **Identify underlying concerns.** One of the biggest challenges with conflict is a lack of understanding or appreciation of others' perspectives. Although you may think that you understand the root of the issue, you may be incorrect or have only partial understanding.

Getting to the root cause of the problem helps people toss that old baggage that makes them reluctant to change and move to the bright future. A few questions to ask to get to the root cause may be:

- Why did these past changes not deliver the results you were expecting?

- What would you recommend doing differently with this change?

- How can this change avoid the same mistakes as the past changes in the organization?

- What was successful about the changes in the past? (There are probably a few things that worked well.) How can this change duplicate these successes?

4. **Develop a shared-purpose statement.** This step is the essence of collaboration: The group moves from having *my* concerns and *your* concerns to *our* concerns. In developing a shared purpose, include the concerns, interests, and needs of all parties. Look for and document areas of common ground. Deeper values are often a rich source of commonality. Creating common goals to rally around sets the stage for creative brainstorming.

5. **Generate solutions.** Now you get to the fun part. All parties work together to brainstorm solutions that can meet all the needs, address the concerns, and reach the goals defined in the shared-purpose statement. Be sure to use brainstorming rules to avoid premature judgment of ideas. You have the potential to create a holistic solution that's greater than the sum of the parts. By collaborating, you can develop novel and creative proposals that go beyond the original positions that created the conflict.

6. **Devise a plan for implementation and evaluation.** This step is where project management takes over. The hard work of collaboration can really pay off at this step because you have strong alignment and support for the plan of action. Take advantage of the momentum from the collaborative exercise to quickly develop an implementation plan to see the fruit of your labor!

Dealing with cynicism toward future change

One of the not-so-pretty outcomes of having past changes fail is the amount of cynicism that develops toward any future change. If you are staring cynicism in the face every day, you can do a couple things to improve the situation.

First of all, don't take it personally. What may seem like the best idea for the future for you may be really hard for others.

Allow employees to express some doubts. Go back to the conflict-resolution skills you find in Chapter 5 of Book IV and gain acceptance in baby steps. This process may take more time, but it will be worth it if you want everyone to move forward together.

You may find complete resistance to change or encounter someone who, no matter how well you cultivate relationships or resolve conflict, goes along with the process but doesn't actually participate in the change (or actively tries to derail it). This person says, "Oh yes, I'm so happy with the new change," but then he either tries to sabotage it or just does nothing to help the process. The problematic behaviors may take the form of being really late for meetings, canceling or ignoring any formal or informal activities that are part of the change plan, or participating by simply saying "yes" and "no" with absolutely no added value to the process.

After going through the conflict-resolution process and digging into root causes, prepare a script to deal with situations of complete resistance and be prepared to call out the nonparticipation either over the phone or face to face. An example of what you can say is, "I sense a reluctance to continue with this change process. Can we set aside some time to resolve your concerns, or should we try to pull in other leaders to help move this forward?" Be careful to be genuine and respectful with this type of statement. You want to convey not a thinly veiled threat but an opportunity for the person to get on board on his own or to ask a more senior leader to help resolve differences. This point is really your last straw, but when all else fails, getting back to honest, straightforward communication is your best bet.

Sometimes, just making reluctant or unhelpful employees aware of how their attitude and behavior impacts others is enough to prompt them to let go of past beliefs and behaviors and become more cooperative. Your job as a change leader and change coach is to get them there.

A stressed-out person looking for a place to vent will look everywhere for the perfect target, and change baggage is a great venting platform for these individuals. Someone may have significant frustrations at home, on other projects, and in life, and because the change is an easy target, you get to be the punching bag (lucky you). The best solution is to listen and ask how you can support the person most effectively. But some people are never happy, and setting limits on the number of punches you're willing to take is perfectly acceptable. Bottom line: Be empathetic, but don't let one person's issues put the brakes on your change.

Empowering employees to change

The advice in this section helps you empower your employees so they'll be inspired to perpetuate the change in their own ways. By delegating authority, offering feedback, problem solving together, listening, and rewarding positive behavior, you'll end up with employees who are on board with your ideas and are motivated to work hard to help you.

Delegating authority

So many leaders have a fear of delegating work to their employees. They either don't know how to do it or are afraid of being seen as handing off work to their already-busy teams. However, if delegation is done correctly, it can be both empowering to employees and engaging. Here are three different ways of delegating:

- **One-way:** Delegation down the pecking order is largely one-way. The leader chooses the change project, identifies the way to make the change project work, and then tells employees to go and do it. Forcing someone to sit, listen, and then go and do something rarely gets any results unless you're managing a group of well-behaved dogs. Sadly, this type of delegating is what most leaders do. The leader does all the planning, makes all the decisions, and just needs people to go and implement. Use this type of delegation only when employees have no idea what to do next and are asking for specific steps to follow.

- **Coaching and cooperation:** When leaders coach and cooperate with employees in delegation, two-way communication takes place, and often employees are the ones who come up with the best ideas on how to move forward with a plan. As a leader, you can ask questions, listen, share ideas, and guide the task at hand. Although this method of delegation does take a good amount of prep work, if it's done correctly employees feel a good balance of support and freedom to take on tasks throughout the change project. After the team identifies how to solve the problem and next steps (with reasonable explanation), a leader can then delegate tasks that the entire team agrees are important.

- **Independent delegation:** When a change leader chooses to delegate the problem and all decision making, the leader briefly establishes any guidelines or boundaries and lets employees get to work. This type of delegation requires the most trust in employees to do the right thing, but if it's done correctly, employees have tremendous potential to build confidence in their own ability by doing the work.

If you hand over the task, take care not to check up on it frequently. Independent work must be just that, so give employees the flexibility and freedom to get the job done. If you need frequent updates on the project, try the coaching-and-cooperation mode instead.

Delegation is rarely successful if a change leader holds on to the most important and glamorous aspects of change and delegates the seemingly trivial items to employees.

Offering feedback

By offering honest feedback, leaders can give employees the opportunity to change and learn on their own. This is empowering for many employees because feedback is really just an opportunity to give an opinion or idea so employees can make more informed choices. When dealing with conflict, the intent of feedback is not to criticize but to widen the repertoire of choices the other person has available in her toolbox.

To give effective feedback, you must do the following things:

- ✔ Listen, observe the specific behaviors that the person displayed, and document everything.

- ✔ Check to see whether the person or group wants feedback. You may also want to ask what kind of feedback the other person wants. Providing unsolicited feedback — positive or negative — is a risk you should take only when you absolutely need to.

- ✔ Offer a few suggestions of how the other person can improve his performance or continue to give a positive performance. Check for understanding and ask whether the feedback was useful.

Problem solving

Problem solving together with your employees helps them recognize their important role in seeing the change through. If they're able to help you solve whatever issues arise, they're more likely to stay engaged with the change. How you think about the process of problem solving and how you relate to others can have a dramatic effect on the outcome. At the risk of stating the obvious, problem solving, planning, conflict resolution, and even coaching change are all based on your ability to work with others.

A number of problem-solving techniques and methods are out there, but this section presents a unique way to think about problem solving to engage and empower employees. These steps focus on uniting everyone before any solution is proposed:

1. **Agree together that a problem exists, define what the problem is, and agree that the problem needs to be solved.** This beginning may seem unusual, but leaders often jump into action too quickly. Rarely are people asked if everyone agrees that a problem really exists. By making this small adjustment to the problem-solving method, you get the team to its first milestone — the definition of the problem and everyone being on board with working on the problem.

Book VI

Managing Business Change

2. **Ask the team to identify what is causing the problem.** This step may take five minutes or five weeks, depending on how easy pinning down the cause is. Until the source of the problem is uncovered, the team may be chasing after something that is not going to solve the problem at hand.

3. **Identify solutions to solve the real problem.** Have the group brainstorm ideas for fixing the problem.

4. **Decide and agree on the solution to the problem and steps to take.** Be sure to include the timing, milestones, roles, and what the solution looks like.

5. **Consider how the team will work together and what you'll do if the solution doesn't work.** After such hard work at getting to the solution, admitting that the solution may not work is hard sometimes. As a change leader, make sure the team knows that problem solving doesn't end when the meeting is over. Get agreement from your change team to work together until the problem is solved.

Listening

When people say they have trouble communicating, they're really talking about not feeling that their voice, motivations, or point of view is heard. Because people often don't say what they really mean the first time around, an expert change coach like yourself has to listen, understand, and then utilize the message. Here are some ways you can try to listen a little better. Engage the speaker this way:

✔ **Use open-ended questions rather than those that require a one- or two-word answer.** Don't ask "Do you think we are measuring the right thing in our change project?" Instead, ask "What are your ideas for measuring our change?"

✔ **Have appropriate body language.** Whether you're conducting an employee meeting, speaking in front of a crowd, or delivering bad news, focus on your hands first. Unless you are a cheerleader or a personal trainer trying to get everyone up and running, make sure your hands are either placed lightly on the desk in front of you or in your lap. This little trick automatically helps you avoid flapping bird arms and hands and allows you to center your thoughts on what is being said. Your eyes and the rest of your body language will follow.

✔ **Clarify perceptions, rather than parroting.** If you have ever been to a communication class, you have probably been told to paraphrase what you hear to make you listen better. Although checking for clarity and understanding is important, paraphrasing isn't always the best way to encourage a conversation. Sometimes, you can add depth to the conversation by listening to what the person has to say and then using your own words to confirm and clarify. Here is a way to look at paraphrasing to add depth to the conversation by clarifying perceptions:

Speaker: "I think the best raisins come from Fresno."

Listener: "It sounds like you really like Fresno raisins. Why do you think they taste so good?"

Speaker: "Well, I am so glad you asked. See, my family grew up on a raisin farm in California and . . ."

By adding inquiry, you keep the conversation going, learn more about the topic, and allow the speaker's true feelings to surface.

Rewarding and recognizing positive behavior

Focusing on results and execution rather than activities and effort ensures that you reach your business objectives as a company, challenges you to constantly improve performance, and provides employees with the latitude to innovate and develop dramatically improved solutions. Yet because swinging and missing is okay sometimes, you can also find and acknowledge value in employees' calculated efforts that don't achieve expected results but still lead to significant learning.

One common mistake is tying rewards and recognition only to money. Yes, money is a very nice reward, but it is not the only reward. Especially in an environment where money and promotions may have slowed down due to economic or market conditions, change leaders need to be a little more creative in recognizing and rewarding their team.

Here are some great examples of rewards for teams and individuals that don't break the bank and still keep employees motivated throughout the change project (and most likely jumping up and down to be part of the next one):

✓ **Financial or flex-time rewards:** Financial rewards are great and can do a good amount to maintain motivation, but they don't have to be huge. Some change leaders hand out $5 coffee-shop gift cards when someone goes above and beyond the call of duty. Other "financial" rewards can be a few extra days off or flexible hours during slower times on the project. Time is one of the most valuable rewards out there.

✓ **Informal rewards and recognition:** Even in our world of nonstop e-mail, texting, and cellphones, nothing conveys appreciation like slowing down, walking over to an employee's desk, and giving a sincere thanks. Informal rewards are spontaneous. You could even write handwritten thank you cards (no typing — pick up the pen and paper!) to employees when you feel a job was done incredibly well.

✓ **Formal company-wide awards:** A formal recognition during an all-employees meeting may be a wonderful motivator for some team members. Others may want to have the opportunity to be part of a leadership group within the company (status) or be asked to present the results of the project to senior leaders (recognition).

Money is a great motivator for some people (okay, a lot of people). But it isn't the only motivator, and you need to be sure to tie it to the behavior you are rewarding. A $10 gift card is probably not a great reward for someone who led a change that saved millions of dollars for the company, but neither is a 10 percent raise for someone who simply did his job. Don't throw those gift cards to the coffee shop in the trash just yet: Small rewards are appropriate for attaining smaller goals (like finishing a project plan), saying thanks for a particular unexpected effort (catching typos on a corporate message before it was sent out or helping another team member), or just to keep the motivation going when the change seems a bit overwhelming.

Regardless of the type of recognition you choose, make sure the reward for good work is seen as valuable to the individual and is specific. Just handing out certificates to everyone at the end of the project isn't personal. Put some time and effort into finding out what motivates your employees, and use that information to recognize them throughout the change project.

Dealing with the Challenges of Change

Too often, wonderfully planned and needed changes fall short because change leaders don't recognize and deal with common challenges and reactions during the transition period. This time is exciting, but it can also be filled with ambiguity and uncertainty. Your goal as a change leader is to help move ambiguity and uncertainty to a place of exploration and learning.

Addressing common people problems

People resist change for a number of reasons. They may feel a loss of control; a fear for their own job security; or confusion about their career path, status, or future workload. Some of these fears are rational; others may simply be based on habit, skepticism, or a short-term focus rather than focus on what is best for the organization (and jobs) in the long term. Some people have negative reactions to change because doing things the old way was wildly successful for them and they're not sure if the new way will generate the same results.

Just because you're encountering some less-than-favorable reactions doesn't mean your change is doomed. If you take care of your people by paying attention to how they're adjusting to the change, establish open two-way communication, and treat them with dignity and respect, you will very likely have a successful transition process.

Countering depression and withdrawal

People have to give up the old way of doing things in order to accept and perform new processes, new methods and procedures, and new skills. But letting go can be tough. Great change leaders acknowledge the positives of the past while communicating the great things the future holds. If a coworker seems depressed because of the change, encourage him to talk about his concerns and feelings. You may want to set up office hours so that people can talk to you one-on-one and ask any questions or express any concerns they may have.

For employees who still don't open up, perhaps your company can offer employee assistance programs as part of the benefits package. These programs can come in the form of individual counseling by a professional or facilitated workshops that give employees a chance to work through the emotional aspects of transition. You may want to set up these sessions during working hours to encourage employees to attend.

Book VI

Managing Business Change

Approaching apathy

You may encounter employees who seem just not to care about the change. Their apathy may manifest as a general lack of interest or by their pretending that the change just doesn't affect them in any significant way. Apathy can be a psychological defense mechanism that employees use to avoid having to directly deal with their own emotional reactions to change.

Try to test whether an employee truly doesn't care or is using apathy as a cover for something else, which is typically fear. One way to do so is to ask probing questions such as, "How do you see this change impacting your job?" If the employee says, "Not at all," you may want to help him more clearly understand how the change will directly impact him. If, on the other hand, employees are able to articulate their concerns about the change, you have likely discovered that fear is the root issue — not apathy.

Facing fear

Even people who believe in change can become scared of the personal cost of having to learn how to do things differently. This fear shows up in a number of ways, represented by the handy acronym SCARED. SCARED people engage in sabotage, conflict, absenteeism, rumors, exasperation, and distraction. If someone's really acting malevolently, you may have to state the obvious: "You have not attended the past four meetings," or "I feel you may be sharing incorrect information about the project." When these challenges surface, some change leaders may be tempted just to tell employees to get over it and move on. This approach does little to engage the workforce or bring about lasting change. Instead of telling fearful employees to get over it, a savvy change leader helps employees move from fear to confidence.

Talk to employees to understand what is driving their fear. Often fear is created by a lack of information, and you can address that problem through better communication. Another cause of fear may be a lack of confidence in one's ability to learn the required skills to be effective. Managers and supervisors should work with each employee to create a personal development plan to outline the steps to gain the required skills.

Fielding a general vibe of negativity

The people who think the change will negatively impact them are usually the ones who move more slowly or back away. These individuals may be confused about the purpose of the change and its implications for them, no matter how well planned the vision may be.

How do you balance getting the work done while acknowledging and helping people move out of this stage of change? First, know that each person will see the effect of change differently, and therefore employees will move to the acceptance of change at different speeds. Here are a few tips to help you field the negative responses to change related to denial or resistance:

- **Communicate once again.** Although you probably have discussed the value and expectations of the change until you're blue in the face, you should make sure you also talk specifically about what is changing and what is not changing. Make sure you are communicating in many different ways so that employees are hit from all sides and are informed in at least one way that's meaningful to them. Putting this structure around uncertainty can help people realize that their world is not going to turn upside down overnight.

- **Give people time to absorb the change.** Take a step back to listen, and then be as patient as possible. Be realistic about what absolutely needs to happen right now and what can move a little slower until more people get on board with the future state. You may want to ask your team not to react to the change immediately. Instead, ask them to think about it and then come back in one week with a list of what challenges and opportunities the change is presenting. This request moves the reaction away from a gut instinct to a more thoughtful inquiry.

- **Look in the mirror (and ask other leaders to do the same).** The way people respond to change has a lot to do with how people around them are acting. Sometimes people who are not willing or able to jump on board with change are doing so because they perceive senior management's attitude toward the change to be less than stellar. When you see a number of people reacting negatively to change, do a change assessment of your own leadership attitude and the attitudes of others. Are you feeling overwhelmed with the change, and is it visibly showing? Do you or other leaders seem to be on a short fuse because of the workload?

✔ **Encourage constructive discussion.** Although asking people what they fear or don't like about the change may feel natural, this type of discussion can turn ugly very quickly. Instead, ask people to express what they think should be done to achieve the future and make change happen.

✔ **Stay calm and carry on.** Take a lesson from the Brits — when you feel in the line of fire from employees who are upset, keep a stiff upper lip and don't take it personally. They may appear mad at you, but they are probably just using you as the outlet for fear or frustration. Don't overreact. If an employee needs to vent, cry, or express his anger, let him do it, but then ask him what he would recommend doing differently. Move the negative conversation to the positive.

Book VI

Managing Business Change

Becoming a change facilitator

Most of the industry terminology out there is focused on how to manage change. As a change leader, why not try to look at the change process as one you can facilitate, not manage? By being a facilitator, you share change ownership with your employees, which better prepares them to work under the new conditions. Your goal then is to provide the opportunity to change but not necessarily make the change happen.

The most straightforward approach you can take is to move from asking employees to do something else to asking them to *recommend* something else. If people feel that their ideas are heard, they're more likely to accept them.

To really facilitate self-direction, stop talking. Change leaders get excited about change, but a time comes when leaders need to let employees do the talking. Now is the time to step back a little bit and slow down. Make sure the project plan includes time to allow people who resist change the opportunity to work it out themselves.

Working through disruption problems

Workflow disruptions happen for a number of reasons. You may face technical problems, political issues, or cultural norms that prevent the change from moving full speed ahead. Even in the most change-excited and change-ready organizations, the road to change will have a few bumps.

Managing technical ills

Whether the technology failure is a sad little face on your computer screen or your payroll system crashing just as paychecks are ready to go out the door, technology can create a number of issues in the change journey. In order to manage technology ills, you need to pinpoint where they are coming from in the business. Following are the four primary suspects:

- **Has insufficient end-user input been received?** The best way to run change is to educate and communicate that a change is happening and involve the people who do the work in creating the solution. If you were handed a change midstream and didn't have the chance to communicate from the beginning, don't go back to the drawing board. Instead, ask end users what can be done better and where the gap between what they need and what they have exists with the new system. Most likely, the technology can do what they need it to (otherwise the change wouldn't have been implemented); it just looks different or needs a few different keystrokes. Giving end users a voice in the creation of the new system (the earlier the better) helps you manage technology change issues.

- **Was the system designed using incomplete or changing requirements and specifications?** During technology changes (or any changes, for that matter), deciding what is needed and designing the system both occur early in the process. But business happens, and change happens even when you're already undergoing change. Therefore, requirements and specifications may change along the way, too. If you have problems in this area, revisit what was planned and designed and compare that info with what is needed today. If something doesn't fit, change it. Technology is only as good as how it is used.

- **Does the team expect world peace from technology?** Unrealistic expectations are one of the top reasons for technology not being used to its full potential because when the technology goes live and fails to solve everything in the world, people become resistant to the change and tend to toss out the baby with the bath water. Manage expectations throughout the change process.

- **Do technology users have an unspoken (or spoken) lack of technical skill?** In our world of touch screens, smartphones, and every other gadget out there, admitting that you don't have the skills to work with changing technology can be really hard. Individuals create all sorts of work-around solutions to technology ills. Don't let this problem happen to you! Provide education and support for learning everything employees need to know about the technology in question.

Getting through political problems

Office politics usually boil down to people being afraid that their status/pay/team/responsibilities are threatened. Although this view tends to ignore the future of the business, it is real and you do need to deal with it if the politician in the office has the power to make the change come to a halt.

As a change leader, you can negotiate how to work together, give the politico an opportunity to save face, or go through the conflict resolution and trust-building process.

Negotiation usually doesn't bring about the fastest or best change, but it sometimes is your only option to move forward. If office politicians have the power to stop change, allowing them to have control over parts of the change may be a great incentive for them to give their support.

Saving face is a big change tool (if used wisely and sparingly) when it comes to politics. If you can agree to the end goal and the most critical aspects of the change, go ahead and allow political powerhouses in your company to make other visible, meaningful decisions that still keep the change on track. A possible strategy for you may be offering the political resister the opportunity to co-create a new organizational chart or have co-signing power on any major milestones (as long as you have the time to negotiate each one). Be careful not to use this method just to give the impression of having power, though, because it will cause leaders who are beginning to resist to move even farther away from the change.

Book VI

Managing Business Change

Sometimes a lack of information and communication issues can lead to a misunderstanding of why the change needs to happen. This issue can spiral into political problems quickly. State your opinion of the situation, and then ask for agreement and ideas. Start by stating a fact. For example, "Hey Mr. Misunderstanding, I see that you have been pulling your resources off the project. Do you agree?" Because this first statement is factual and therefore hard to disagree with, after Mr. Misunderstanding answers, you can follow up with, "How can I help clarify the importance of this project?" Now you have the perfect opportunity to clear up any misunderstanding about the project while allowing Mr. Misunderstanding to save face and lead part of the change.

Facing up to cultural issues

Like it or not, in addition to your organizational culture's wonderful aspects that have made it successful, it also has some not-too-wonderful aspects that need to, well, change. Some organizations are very determined to maintain security and stability. Things may have been done a certain way for decades, and that seems to be just fine with everyone. If you are facing a resistant organization, try these cues to get the group moving:

✔ **Introduce ways to take alternate opinions into consideration in group meetings.** Don't stop at "Are there any other ideas?" Instead, tell employees that ten minutes of every meeting will be devoted to brainstorming alternatives or asking specifically for arguments against doing things the same way.

✔ **Ask the change team members how they learned from mistakes and disappointments when they did not change quickly, and then seek out examples.** You may also ask what the advantages are for changing proactively rather than just learning from mistakes.

✔ **Provide an opportunity for teams to jump into the unknown.** Taking risks can be a learned skill. If a culture is resisting change, let employees practice change by participating in a competitive activity in a safe environment (such as paintball, trust exercises, or beating each other up in those sumo-wrestling suits) that can help teach people the value of unpredictability and quick thinking.

Managing stress levels

If change leaders don't feel some sort of stress during the change process, they probably aren't really leading change. When stress hits, projects often start moving a little more slowly, and decisions are made out of exhaustion. By managing your own stress and helping your MVPs deal with their stresses during the change, you are able to get projects moving back on track and get anxieties back to workable levels.

Dealing with your own stress

Stress can come in all forms, but it frequently ends up with late nights at the office, a poor diet, and your family and friends not recognizing you anymore. Try a combination of these strategies to reduce your stress level:

✔ **Schedule time for family and relaxation.** Setting some personal boundaries around your work schedule to spend time with family or friends will enable you to maintain your support network. By taking a little time for relaxation and recreation, you maintain your mental sharpness and are more ready to handle the stress that is inevitable in leading change.

✔ **Slow down to consider all the options rather than making snap decisions.** Take time to consider the impact of the change on others. Although slowing down seems like a bad way to get you through change more quickly, if you take the time to think how others will react before acting and you listen to what people have to say before commenting, change happens more quickly because you're allowing people the time they need to get on board with the change. In the long run, that time will reduce your workload and stress.

✔ **Let go of being a perfectionist.** This goal won't happen overnight, but you can try to release your perfectionist impulses one project at a time.

✔ **Cut back on multitasking and prioritize instead.** If stress comes from multitasking too much, take time to prioritize your list of jobs and tasks. If you find yourself spending time on things that don't add value, reevaluate how you can align your time to the change goals of the project. By spending time on things that make a difference, your energy (and stress) focuses on the positive.

✔ **Try a two-minute relaxation exercise.** Take one minute to get comfortable and allow your body to relax. Close the door to your office or room, turn off your phone and computer monitor, and then for the next minute pay attention to your breathing. Close your eyes and breathe slowly and deeply. Let the day's worries escape you for just two minutes.

✔ **Exercise, even if it's just walking up and down the stairs at the office.** A regular exercise routine, two to three times a week, produces endorphins in the body that maintain not only physical health but also mental agility. If you can't get to the gym, try walking up and down the stairs in the office or walking a few laps around the building. Consider having walking meetings with colleagues to get some exercise and get some work done at the same time.

✔ **If overtime is necessary, get to work early in the morning.** Your brain works better when it's refreshed in the morning instead of when it's fried after a full day of work. If you're not a morning person, at least schedule the complex activities that require a lot of concentration during the time of day when you are at your best, and schedule less-complex tasks when you tend to have less energy.

✔ **Take short visual breaks from the computer screen every hour.** Eyestrain can contribute to feelings of tiredness. Getting up and walking around to give your eyes a break from the computer screen, as well as your body a chance to stretch and move, will keep you more refreshed throughout the day.

Book VI

Managing Business Change

Helping your employees cope with stress

One of the best ways to help your MVPs cope with stress is to be a great leader. Most of the leadership techniques to help others cope with stress come down to these simple principles:

✔ **Clearly communicate directions but allow people to do their own work.** Having someone looking over their shoulder is really stressful for employees, so get the team going with a great vision and mission (have you heard that before?) and then let people do their work.

✔ **Delegate effectively.** Delegation is tough, but not doing it and taking everything on yourself is tougher. You'll get stressed, your employees will feel you don't trust them to do the work, and things will begin to spiral out of control. Ask others to take on work, give them the support they need, and share the workload associated with change.

✔ **Provide a motivating atmosphere that encourages everyone to perform successfully.** Your role as a change leader is to make sure the culture of change is supported by encouraging and rewarding positive behavior and helping to get rid of any negative behavior.

✔ **Don't avoid necessary unpleasant discussions and actions.** Everyone makes mistakes, even your MVPs. Your MVPs are probably smart enough to realize this — so don't let mistakes, misunderstandings, or bad situations fester. Talk about them and then move on.

Assessing Your Progress and Acting Accordingly

Your change project is well underway. However, you can't just get the ball rolling and take a break. You have work to do while the change is happening and your organization is in transition. Your role as a change leader now moves out of the "planning and envisioning the change" stage to overseeing the changes and supporting the team and organization while the change is in motion.

Using the transition model checklist

The *transition model checklist* is a simple tool to make sure your project is set to deliver the results you want. The list is broken up into five categories of accomplishments that you and your team will reach as you successfully complete the change project. You'll probably want to review the checklist on your own (something of a self-assessment) and with your core team.

Most likely, you probably are already delivering on some of your critical milestones. Even though your change project may be moving at full speed, run through the checklist to make sure you aren't forgetting anything.

Vision:

✔ You've created an energizing and bold sense of the future and articulated this vision to others in the company.

✔ Other people are asking lots of questions and beginning to embrace the idea of change.

✔ You know your key allies and you've reached out to them, building vital networks to launch and support your change initiative.

Road map:

✔ You have a plan in place to get you from the current to the future state.

✔ You're comfortable with what's coming up next (for both you and your team) to move the change forward.

✔ You've created a training plan to give people the skills they need in the new environment. (You may not have the training content in place just yet, but making sure this step is on your plan ensures they know that they will learn everything they need to about the change.)

Team:

✔ You have a team of at least three to five energized change agents with clear roles and responsibilities — plus all the skills needed to make the change happen.

✔ Your team has a strong connection to the executive level to help drive the change.

✔ Leaders are walking the talk and modeling the new behaviors within the organization.

✔ The core team has minimal conflicts of interests. If your core team is beginning to fight and disagree early on, you need to resolve these conflicts before moving forward with the change.

✔ Your team leads by example and challenges the status quo.

✔ You've instilled a sense of cooperation on the team, giving everyone a chance to solve problems instead of merely following orders.

Measurements:

✔ You have visible, practical ways of tracking progress, and you know your objectives.

✔ You hold people accountable for these milestones.

✔ You've scheduled frequent ways to track results of the change effort and have communicated the results as the change progresses.

Communication:

✔ You regularly update your team, organization, and leadership on the change journey.

✔ You engage in frequent feedback sessions with the organization, key employees, and leaders in the company to make sure the pulse of the organization is heard loud and clear.

Book VI

Managing Business Change

Keep in mind that this checklist is not a pass or fail list; it is simply a guide to keep you on track.

Celebrating milestones

Celebrating milestones is something you have been doing since you had your first birthday. Celebrating milestones during a change effort is really no different; unfortunately, noticing the milestones isn't as easy as putting a date on the calendar.

Even when you hit a marker of success, retain your focus and energy. The markers of success are *indicators*, not guarantees, that you're moving in the right direction. Just because you hit one marker doesn't mean all the others will fall perfectly into line — you have to keep your eye on the end goal until the change is complete.

Everyone likes to be thanked and rewarded for hard work and commitment. Celebrating and rewarding success improves morale and acknowledges the behaviors or actions that help drive the success forward. Recognizing individuals and groups is a terrific way to maintain positive momentum for the change. Flip back to the earlier section "Rewarding and recognizing positive behavior" to find ideas for recognition and reward.

Maintaining mid-change interest

A mid-change drop in interest often occurs just because people have no idea what is happening and begin to assume that *nothing* is happening. While the core change team may be working along very smoothly, employees may wonder what is happening behind the scenes. Communication with everyone in the organization is critical to keep the change effort in the front of everyone's mind.

The best way to maintain mid-change energy is to walk the talk — you need to keep your energy up. The general mid-change attitude is kind of how marathoners feel around mile 22 of the 26.2-mile run (that would be kilometer 35 out of 42 for those of you on the metric system). *Hitting the wall* is runner speak for the feeling that you can go no further, and change projects can hit a wall, too. One of the biggest reasons for failure in change is that leaders declare victory too early or assume that when the change is 80 percent done it will continue on without the leader's dedication and interest. Don't fall into this trap! When you see interest fading or feel like you have hit your own change wall, take a deep breath, gather the team together, and push through to the finish line.

If you have done a good job celebrating your successes and recognizing and rewarding key personnel and teams, you should already be in a good position to maintain the organization's interests in your change project.

Bouncing back from failure

You did everything you could do. You planned, you communicated, you created a great team. But when you assess your progress with the transition model checklist, you realize the project has gone splat! Even though you may be tempted to bang your head against the desk, don't. Now is a great chance for you and your organization to learn from the change and maybe even get the project back on the right track.

Figuring out how to start over

A "what now" session can help teams brainstorm new ideas to get a failed or stalled change back on track. Before the meeting, ask team members to think about what happened to stop the change and why. Remind the team not to place blame. This preparation before the meeting will give the team time to think about what they learned from the change and start to diffuse any emotions that may be out there because of the failure. A great way to phrase this pre-work is, "What do we need to start doing (something different), what does the team need to stop (what didn't go well or was not necessary), and what does the team need to continue (what went well)?"

At the meeting, ask team members to think through the following five key steps for each area of the project that either stalled or didn't work out as planned:

- **What area failed?** In other words, what didn't work as planned? This area of failure can be anything from the project plan not being followed (time delay) to the supplier of a new information system not being able to deliver software that worked.

- **Why did this happen, and what are the implications?** Now you can get down to the root cause of the failure. For example, if the information system wasn't delivered on time or it wasn't the quality you expected, was it because the project plan wasn't clear, or were these expectations not communicated? Often, the root causes of failure can be boiled down to resources (not having the right skills, not having enough money), expectations not being clear, or the scope of the project changing.

✔ **What are the lessons learned?** A failure does not need to stop the project cold. If team members didn't have the knowledge on how to hold meetings, then teach them, and make sure the lesson learned is captured as something like, "Did not provide adequate training" or "Assumed individuals already had skills needed." Again, you're not placing blame; you're just trying to make sure the problem doesn't reoccur.

✔ **What's next?** This "fork in the road" question covers several questions: What is the next step, who is going to do what to fix this area, and does it need to be fixed or can we just move on?

✔ **Who needs to know?** After a failure happens, you need to go back and communicate what happened and what is happening next to fix the problem.

When you kick off the meeting, make sure you lay some ground rules. Here are four critical ones to get the after-action discussion going:

✔ Trust that your colleagues want(ed) to do the best job.

✔ Avoid blaming anyone. Focus on what the team can do differently next time.

✔ Avoid "shoulda, woulda, coulda" language. Instead, talk about impact and learning.

✔ Identify areas where the organization still needs change or improvement, but focus on learning right now and not on inventing new solutions.

Increasing the probability of success going forward

The best way to increase the probability of success after you begin fresh or make a mid-change evaluation is to make sure you have a plan in place for things outside your control, have clear and realistic expectations, and maintain confidence when challenging times arise. This advice applies to any stage in the change game but especially after you've noticed problems and tried to fix them.

You also want to set expectations with your team and within the organization that more challenges may need to be dealt with along the journey. Even the best-planned journeys run into issues. Set expectations with employees that these surprises should be expected and not feared, and just because you've solved a few problems now doesn't mean that more, different problems won't arise.

Finally, maintain confidence in your own ability both to get things back on track and to encourage your team. Don't be discouraged when faced with obstacles. Babe Ruth struck out 1,330 times in his career and 30 times in the World Series, and the man didn't give up. See challenges as mere obstacles to overcome as opposed to roadblocks that cause you to give up and go home. This attitude gives your team the confidence to make necessary course corrections along the way.

Building the Structures to Make Change Last

In many cases of business changes, the change takes place and everyone is happy, and a new report may come out with metrics that show the change happened. But little if any change to the structure of the organization occurs to establish the change for years to come. As a result, things sometimes come unraveled rather quickly; other times the change remains on the surface of the organization, ready to be blown away in the winds of the next big thing.

To avoid this problem, you can develop organizational structures to make change last. This sustainability is not really that hard to tackle, as long as you know what you want to achieve.

Book VI

Managing Business Change

Creating useful performance measures

The most long-lasting changes within a business are accompanied by changes in how the organization measures the new desired performance or behavior and how individuals are rewarded for their performance. Both of these transitions require two things:

- ✔ **Ongoing evaluation and measurement:** You cannot stop at measuring how successful the initial change is. By helping your team evaluate and design how the new way of doing business is assessed — on a continuing basis — you can keep the change implementation rolling long after the change has happened.

- ✔ **Clear policies and guidelines:** At this point, even you may be overwhelmed by the volume of your own communications about organizational change. Well, to make sure change sticks, assure everyone that the new way of business is official by establishing — and clearly explaining — policies and guidelines. This step ensures that the new way of doing business is locked into daily operations.

With these steps in mind, you're ready to identify what the new organization should be measuring and how to tie these metrics to individual employee performance.

Measuring team and organizational processes

The first step in developing (or redesigning) new measurements for your organization is aligning them to the new way of doing business. You may be able to continue using the same measurements you used throughout the change, but some may need minor tweaks. If you're struggling to develop meaningful metrics for the organization — or if you need some creative juice to take a few metrics to the next level — you may want to ask your project team for new ideas.

For instance, you can ask the team, "What are you learning from the metrics we're using?" Often, measurements have been in place for as long as the company has been around. Use the change as an opportunity to refine measurements to best track current operations and how the company is meeting its future goals. If the measurements the team or organization had in the past are still the right measurements in the future state, the targets for these measurements may simply have to change. For example, if the change is focused on improving customer satisfaction, and the organization was measuring customer satisfaction before, you probably want to keep measuring it, but the target may move from 80 percent of the customers being satisfied to 95 percent. If the team seems happy with the current metrics and the old targets, something may be amiss, and you may want to revisit the purpose of the change.

The second step in developing (or redesigning) new measurements for the organization is identifying the target or goal for the measurement. If your measurements are staying the same, your targets probably have to change to show that you changed for a reason (not just for the fun of change!). Targets can be set based on industry performance, best practices in other departments, or company goals. In the end, your new performance measurements will be aligned to strategic goals and have clear targets like the ones shown in Table 3-1.

Table 3-1	Example Performance-Measurements Chart	
Strategic Goal	*Measurement(s)*	*Target*
Improve use of technology	Percentage of clients using web customer service	70% of sales
Stay on top of industry knowledge	Number of hours of professional development for employees	12 hours a year

Evaluating individual performance

After you refine your organizational metrics to support the change, you can adapt them to monitor the performance of individual employees. Organizational metrics are great at keeping the company on track, but the people make the metrics move. The closer you tie organizational metrics to individual metrics, the better your chances of individuals working to make the change last.

For example, say your change focuses on creating an organizational culture that runs the business more efficiently, resulting in higher profits. You may have a metric like profit growth to gauge this goal for the entire organization. Executives and investors will love this metric — it looks great on a spreadsheet — but the average employee may have a hard time tying it to his day-to-day work. So make that metric more meaningful at the individual level by asking an individual to make an improvement that maximizes company profit, such as finding three areas to cut costs in your daily job or identifying one process improvement to impact product quality. The key is to make metrics meaningful and actionable to individuals. When employees can tie what they're doing to the new way the business is operating, they often become more invested in the change.

When creating individual metrics, use these guidelines:

- ✔ **Focus on the critical few:** Don't try to accommodate every goal or performance metric that could possibly influence the survival of the change. In addition to being cumbersome and time consuming for managers, overly ambitious measurement systems for individuals lead to resentment of the new way of doing business. Instead, focus on initiatives that are most strategic to the business. Try to keep individual assessments to three or five metrics.

- ✔ **Include details:** Include both what needs to get done (the results you expect) and how it needs to happen (living up to the new company culture) in individual metrics to reinforce that you can't just get something done for the sake of accomplishing it; you have to get it done right.

Performance measurements and momentum are closely related, so track the progress of change regularly (at least each month or quarter) to make sure the change continues to reach organizational and individual goals.

Monitoring change over time

With measurements in place, the project team can implement a plan for collecting data. In some circles, this plan is known as a *control plan*. The purpose of a control plan is to make sure that the impact of the change is trending as expected and desired. A practical control plan includes the following information:

- ✔ **Goal:** Simply state the objective in a way that can be measured. What do you want to accomplish? Some examples of goals may be to reduce caller wait time to less than three minutes or to increase the online help-desk support by 50 percent.

- ✔ **Metric:** Describe the measurement with a straightforward two- to four-word definition of what you are measuring. Think: cost of goods sold, new jobs created, customer-satisfaction ratings, and so forth.

✔ **Data source:** Create a clear guideline on where the data comes from to ensure consistency and accuracy of findings. Asking people to tell others where the data comes from helps make collecting the data a little easier. If someone can explain where the data came from in less than a few words, it most likely is easily accessible. If someone has to write a novel on how to collect the data or where it comes from and who has to do what to it before it is used, the data may be a bit difficult to collect (and may slow down the process).

✔ **Review frequency:** Make sure the frequency of data collection is suitable for your information needs and not overused. If your objective is to create 25 new jobs over five years, for example, then a daily count of new positions is not likely to be helpful. A quarterly collection may be more suitable. There is no sense in collecting lots of daily data points if they will just sit alone in a database somewhere. Create a plan for communicating and responding to data so that you're utilizing the findings.

If your change potentially has daily results, then you may want to display daily reports in the early stages of implementation to encourage employees to embrace the change; after the change is securely in place, your reports may be more effective as weekly accounts. Bottom line: Make sure your control plan works for the project team and other stakeholders.

Just as the change plan focused on different stakeholders at different times in the process, the measurement system must address the information needs of people on different levels of the organization.

Aligning resources to the new way

With the change in place and the project team disbanded, sufficient resource support for the new way of doing business is critical. To support resources most effectively, make sure the change is reinforced through training, documenting info, integrating changes into daily operations, and clearly assigning process owners to champion the change for the long term.

Training

One of the most important aspects of implementing change that sticks is relevant and ongoing training to individuals and teams. Employees with the skill set and ability to perform according to the change are the best resources. Use this training opportunity to ensure that people know what to do and how to do it the right way to support the change for years to come. Flip on over to Book II, Chapter 2 to find out more about training.

Be on the lookout for unspoken confusion. People don't always know what they don't know. If people have been doing a particular process before the change, they may have trouble recognizing — let alone communicating — that they don't know or understand how to behave or perform a task differently in the new environment. Make sure you provide ample training and mentoring for everyone; don't assume people know what to do or how to do it.

Documenting the details of change

You, the change team, and perhaps the entire organization may think the change is obvious, but that doesn't mean it shouldn't be documented somewhere. The change should become part of the knowledge-management process in the organization so that as time passes and memories blur, people in the business can refer to it for reminders of who is supposed to do what. Following are a few aspects to document:

- ✔ New organizational charts
- ✔ Job roles and responsibilities
- ✔ Process maps and instructional guides
- ✔ Budgets and strategic-planning tools
- ✔ Action plan for what to do if the change reverts back to the old way it was done

Integrating change

Incorporating changes into daily operations takes much more than writing up procedures and policies (although you need to make sure that is done, too). An organization implementing change benefits tremendously by leveraging *formal and informal influencers* in daily operations. Here's what these terms mean:

- ✔ **Formal influencers** include the organization's top leadership, who must advocate the change and be role models for it. But formal influencers are more than people; they include clear responsibilities, new job descriptions, updated reward systems, and perhaps even new technology to support the change.

  New procedures are great, but if the team follows the procedures only when you're looking over people's shoulders, the changes aren't sustainable. That is where informal influencers can make a big impact.

- ✔ **Informal influencers** are people in the organization who may not have a leadership title but are trusted sources of information. These people often have been around the organization for a long time, have political savvy, and have a strong commitment to the success of the organization.

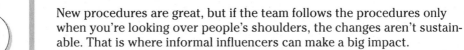

Book VI

Managing Business Change

A great example of an informal influencer was a long-term mechanic at a manufacturing company going through significant cost-cutting changes. The manager at the facility was the official change leader, but nothing got done until the mechanic said it was the right thing to do. People trusted his opinion, even though he had no direct management responsibility. Informal influencers can make things happen if you give them access to senior leadership and allow them the opportunity to voice their opinions.

Designating process owners

Until now, you (or a team member) may have been driving the change and owning (or co-owning) the improvements. But now you need to designate a clear owner for the change in the long term, and that person may or may not be you. If you have been in charge of revamping how new employees are recruited and oriented in the company, you have probably been working with the human resources, recruiting, and training teams. You may also have been working with hiring managers and new employees to get their feedback and buy-in for the change. As a change leader, it is time to make sure someone owns the new process. Ideally, the process owner has been part of the change all along and has authority to make modifications to the process as necessary to meet the organization's new challenges.

Top leadership can make this choice, but sometimes the process owner will step up and take ownership because it is a natural fit. If you are still looking for someone to own the process in the long term, consider finding someone who has these traits:

- **Making the change stick is her priority.** The process owner must be accountable for continued results, so now is not the time to drop the ball.

- **She has enough influence to make adjustments to the change if necessary.** Influence often means strong leadership skills in the areas of continuous process improvement and coaching others.

- **She understands metrics.** The process owner will need to explain and review how the process is going, so she should be comfortable and perhaps even excited by numbers and metrics.

You can't give someone a process without power. Process owners should have access to senior leaders, be involved (perhaps even lead) review meetings, have control of the budget, and be rewarded for making the results stick.

Leading the after-change review

Before you ride off into the sunset, be sure to deliver a meaningful after-change review. Great changes provide ample ideas to leverage during future changes; changes that hit a few potholes along the way can show you what to do differently in later projects. The process of the after-change review is much more than a one-hour meeting to say "thanks and good-bye." Here are the steps you can use to make the change review a part of integrating all the lessons learned into the new way of doing business:

1. **Conduct the after-change review.** Invite people who had direct experience with the change successes and failures to an after-change review session. At this meeting, lead the team in discovering what worked and what did not during the process of developing and implementing the change, plan out what to do with this information, and then decide how and when the change may need to be adapted.

   It's a good idea to use an experienced facilitator to manage the meeting. Otherwise, if politics come into play or if naysayers are in the room, an after-change review can morph into a complaining session or finger-pointing activity.

2. **Discover, plan, and decide.** During the after-change review, analyze where you've been and where you're going with your team of stakeholders. Use that time to

   - *Discover:* Document what parts of the change process worked and what parts didn't.

   - *Plan:* Focus on how to solve the project's problems and how to leverage its strengths. Many kinds of business change apply to more than one area of the organization, so identify small modifications that can help the change benefit the larger organization.

   - *Decide:* Figure out what to do with the recommendations to make the change even better. Some ideas may need to be postponed; others need to happen right away. Break down your list of modifications into time-based categories: short term (under 90 days), long term (over 90 days), and future (not applicable to current change but helpful for how change happens in the future).

3. **Revise, focus, and identify future change goals.** After the change review is complete, the ongoing process owners have an opportunity to step up and revise the changes as needed to keep the change alive. This part can be difficult for the change team because many team members have moved on from implementing the change and are busy with exciting new projects.

4. **Identify additional/new team members.** Selecting new team members is all about aligning resources to make the change sustainable. While you and your project team may always be living and breathing the change (and moving on to new projects), new individuals can help make practical modifications with new energy and perspective.

5. **Integrate learning into the way of doing business.** The real benefit of the after-change review is sharing it with others in the organization. Don't keep those lessons locked up! Communicate what you learned from the process and share information openly and honestly. A change leader never really stops communicating, but you knew that already, right?

Change takes time, so be sure not to skip over some of the more important parts of change: reflecting on the results (through an after-change review) and then integrating these results as the organization continually refines strategic objectives, metrics, and initiatives. Successful change projects can help an organization grow into a more adaptable organization if they end by reflecting on what went well and where they need to focus more energy.

Chapter 4

Applying Change Strategies in Specialized Circumstances

● ●

In This Chapter

▶ Tapping the power of technology updates

▶ Working (well) with restructuring changes

▶ Making mergers and acquisitions happen smoothly

▶ Shifting your workplace culture

● ●

*T*he advice you find in the earlier chapters of this Book, which enables you to lead through change, can be applied across whatever change you're dealing with. The techniques for assessing and addressing change-related challenges that you find throughout this Book are the foundation for making effective change happen. In this chapter, you see these ideas applied to specific situations common to businesses today.

This chapter gives you greater detail about working through technology changes, which seem to fly at businesses faster and faster each year. It shows you how to keep steady through restructuring changes and through the intricacies of change during mergers and acquisitions. And you discover ways to maintain your sanity while managing cultural change.

Aligning Technology Change with Results

Technology is changing the nature of jobs, customer demands, product markets, and organizations. Organizations have technology coming at them from two sides:

✔ On one side, state-of-the-art technology enables companies to respond better and faster to customer needs.

> ✔ On the other, continuously changing technology can propel organizations to always be on the lookout for the next great thing to increase productivity and become more adaptable to change as new technologies emerge.

You need vision and strategy when dealing with technology because you can't treat it as an afterthought; it should be integrated into the overall strategy and objectives.

Matching technology with people, processes, and strategy

When preparing for a new technology, most executives and project managers thoroughly examine, plan, and plan again for all aspects of the technical integration; some of the better ones even include redesigning business processes. Many executives have also begun to slow down and make sure technology fits into an overall strategy and isn't just something to implement to keep up with the Joneses. To ensure success in adopting new technology throughout the organization, a fourth piece of the change needs to be addressed: the people. The people factor is what makes the technology last.

Your people determine whether the technology gets used in a way that supports your strategy. To help people adopt new technology, include key users in designing the process and technology solution, and communicate how the technology change will enable them to better do their jobs and reach new levels of productivity and service.

As you begin to implement your change, pay careful attention to your training plan to ensure that the users will feel confident in their ability to successfully maneuver the new system.

 Ask stakeholders for their experience and insight into how the technology can support better business operations, and then make the technology fit the needs of the user, not the other way around. Although sleek technology demos can show businesses how wonderfully a process can flow, remember that the business need and the business process should be supported by technology and that the technology should not (in most cases) run the business.

Joining the online e-business revolution

At this point, if your organization isn't online with an e-business strategy, you're missing out on loads of customers! For traditional brick-and-mortar companies, e-business change has often meant a complete overhaul of how the business connects with customers, or at least a reengineering of the sales processes. Start-ups sometimes find they have to slow down the dot-com speed and make sure a product is sellable by fully integrating e-business.

What makes a company an *e-business* company? If you're doing part of your business on the web, you are using e-business. This includes advertising, providing customer support, selling products and services, and anything in between. Because e-business spans a pretty wide domain, achieving clarity around why, how, and when the organization will use online technology helps eliminate confusion and bring focus to the e-strategy.

Before picking a change strategy, identify how your organization may want to use (or is already using) e-business:

- **Traditional online presence:** Since the 1990s, companies have offered a listing of products, services, and company information online — no bells and whistles, just sharing basic information with customers. Say you're running a local flower shop, Blooming Blossoms. You put pictures of beautiful blossoms online, testimonials from clients who loved your designs, and a phone number to call to order flowers for Mother's Day.

- **E-commerce:** The next level is e-commerce, or selling products or services directly over the Internet. For example, Blooming Blossoms may put an Order button by its flower photos online, so anyone with an Internet connection can order flowers the day before Mother's Day and have the flowers delivered right to Mom's door the next morning.

- **Web 2.0:** At this level, an organization implements online customer service; does business with other businesses online; provides services directly online; and cultivates and maintains an online, often user-driven community using social media for marketing purposes. Your flower shop orders flowers just in time from the flower supplier. Your customers create arrangements themselves by choosing and dragging flowers around the screen, and they enter their card messages directly into a text box. Your website has a blog where you share helpful hints and updates about your company. You have a Twitter feed and maintain a Facebook page, engage directly with your customers there, promote special offers, and monitor both accounts to handle customer service questions and keep your reputation spotless. You may even create a smartphone app to make it even easier and more fun for your customers to order flowers.

If an organization is moving from one e-strategy to the next, a change plan is a good idea. Your change plan should include training on how new technologies integrate with all the systems your employees may already be using and a clear vision of what the technology will achieve for the employees and the company.

E-business is not just about putting a checkout cart on the home page. In order to make e-business change successful, the organization must be ready to do business differently, and processes should be revamped to support how e-business will be used.

Just because everyone seems to be doing e-business doesn't mean everyone in your organization is going to be happy when you start doing it too, and it definitely doesn't mean the endeavor will be easy. In the flower shop example, the person who used to take the orders on the phone now needs to fulfill orders processed online. It could be as complex as aligning the forecast for how many flowers are needed every day with the supplier's order system.

You can imagine how much more complicated things get when your organization does business around the globe. The same change principles presented in this Book apply to e-business, but you need to pay close attention to a few special considerations: integrating old technologies with new and aligning processes to the new technology.

Integrating old, new, and emerging technologies

Most likely, by the time an organization gets to the e-commerce level, it probably has some type of these technologies:

- ✔ CRM (customer-relationship management)
- ✔ SCM (supply-chain management)
- ✔ ERP (enterprise resource planning)

E-commerce is not as simple as just layering on a website that does a bunch of stuff. Not only do the systems need to talk to one another to make it work, but the people who work with the multiple systems also need to talk with one another.

Technology can have all the capabilities in the world, but if the people who use it don't support and know the value of it, it is useless.

When e-business is in full swing, how customers and businesses interact will be dramatically different than it was before the new strategy was created. Changing how the work gets done behind the scenes is commonly called *business-process reengineering.* Most of it happens in the *back office systems,* the systems that support business operations like finance, HR, inventory management, and so on.

These processes will, at a minimum, include almost anything employees do before, during, and after working with the customer:

- ✔ How customers can provide feedback on products
- ✔ How feedback is reviewed and responded to
- ✔ How customers can receive updates on orders, returns, and shipping
- ✔ How customers pay for their service

Using CRM to maximum effect

Customer-relationship management (CRM) is about building ongoing connections with your clients. CRM systems provide a place to collect information about who is buying products or services so a company can market, up-sell, cross-sell, and provide a more in-depth customer experience. The big kicker with CRM systems is making sure the data is used, not just stored on a big server or cloud somewhere. Imagine how happy Blooming Blossoms customers would be if they picked up the phone or went online to order birthday flowers for Mom and were able to hear or see exactly what they bought in the past and look at recommendations for flowers she might like.

The big organizational change piece of CRM is identifying how the data is used (process), who is going to use it (people and job roles), and how the information can be accessed (training).

Improving SCM processes

In a true e-commerce company, SCM processes change as well. Gone are the days of the purchasing department sitting in a cube in the back of the building; now SCM is in real time and online, feeding just-in-time information to suppliers on an organization's raw-material needs. This change dramatically impacts how people do their jobs (especially everyone in the purchasing department).

Whether you are a one-person shop or a Fortune 500 company, e-business really does touch and change every aspect of the business.

Including ERP and integrated systems

ERP (enterprise resource planning) was made popular in the 1990s when companies realized that spreadsheets and home-grown information systems weren't sufficient to compete within the emerging global Internet economy. ERPs and integrated information systems were set up to create a powerful tool for knowledge (data) to be shared quickly among lots of employees. For anyone who hasn't had the chance to work with such a massive technology system, here is the basic premise: Finance people link to the human resources system so they can better understand the costs in specific organizational cost centers. Manufacturing professionals link to the supply chain system so they know when and where to expect raw materials and can plan their production schedule accordingly.

Although ERPs and integrated systems have the power to truly transform a company, they are basically just big and very expensive databases sitting alone in a cold, dark room if they aren't integrated with the culture, policies, goals, communication channels, and infrastructure of the organizations using them. In other words, technology can't just be thrown at users; it must be part of how business is done, and this means . . . drumroll please . . . change.

Being smart about process redesign

During an ERP implementation, you can easily get caught up in how wonderful the technology looked during the sales demo. But the technology can only go so far to enhance productivity without substantial process change. You need to do more than provide a fancy user interface; ERP implementations should help facilitate changes in how work is done. If the process is not changed, you may risk just automating an inefficient process.

Process redesign can be broken down into five steps:

1. **Define what the future process should accomplish.** This step is where you benchmark other organizations and processes as well as use strategic tools like a *SWOT analysis,* an acronym that stands for identifying the strengths, weaknesses, opportunities, and threats to the organization. Here's an opportunity to set customer-focused goals and critical success factors for the process, as well as create service-level agreements between departments and with suppliers. When the future goal is defined, check back to make sure customer, cultural, financial, business, and technical considerations are all accounted for and voiced.

2. **Define the as-is state.** The as-is state should include what is happening today: the good, the bad, and the ugly. Process mapping is a powerful tool frequently used in improvement initiatives, but keep it to one or two pages and tackle the big steps each function does in the department.

3. **Create the future state process.** Have the team decide how it wants the process to work.

4. **Tie technology to the new process.** Remember that technology should support a process and make it easier; processes should not be built to make technology work the way it should.

5. **Identify the differences in the current- and future-state maps.** This step is often called a gap analysis. Focus your energy and resources on the areas with the biggest gaps.

Analyzing job roles

When new systems replace old ones and automation and knowledge transfer are better leveraged, job roles will change. A job-description analysis is basically a "who-does-what" chart and can be used to help retrain employees on new processes. It follows these steps:

1. **Identify who is impacted.** It may be a team, a person, or a function within a department. Let's return to Blooming Blossoms, your flower shop, because you're now implementing a finance system to better report the skyrocketing profits from the e-business implementation. One of the roles that will change is the financial analyst.

2. **List out what major tasks are changing or may be new for the role.** Now think of how work will be different for the people impacted. For the financial analyst over at Blooming Blossoms, the changes may include how reports are run, how quarterly information is reported back to executives, and how forecasting models are created.

3. **Identify what skill is required to do the new task.** Using the information above, start thinking of what skills may be needed. If someone has been running spreadsheets or manually entering data for years, he may need to be trained on how to check the accuracy of data feeds in the new system or how to make the data flow from one area to another using the new technology.

4. **Identify how to close the gaps between skills needed and the current state.** Find out which skills can be taught and which need to come from other resources. Remember that technical training is not a good fit for theory and lecture! Just-in-time training and practical examples are often the best ways to make sure employees know how and why they need to do something different.

The new trend in technology is to move away from the massive hosting servers and hardware at a client site to cloud ERPs. *Cloud ERP* basically means all the information and applications are hosted on the Internet (up in the invisible cloud, hence the name), taking away the hassle of handling data storage locally, often resulting in a faster implementation. But the general concept of change associated with ERP implementations is still the same: Companies that transfer organizational knowledge from one part of the company to another will be able to serve customers more efficiently.

ERP implementations are notorious for causing turf battles in organizations and facing tremendous resistance. Yes, to most people, doing away with physically entering in data eight times throughout a process may seem like a brilliant solution. Yes, eliminating the need to photocopy everything and then walk some type of data over to another person who is sitting on the other side of the building may seem like a really good idea. However, when the person

Book VI

Managing Business Change

who enters in the data or walks it over hears that he isn't needed anymore, well, he may fear for his job and resist change.

Change, especially when it relates to gaining efficiencies and changing job roles, is a very real threat to individual status, position, and power. A great way to avoid this turf battle is to bring the people who are going to be impacted into the decision-making and design process. It may take more time, but the solution will be more widely used, and involvement and participation are some of the best ways to create lasting change.

Effectively using social media and the next "it" thing

An organization's success (or failure) is often based on what employees do or don't do. Change is all about giving employees, customers, and other stakeholders the ability, flexibility, and power to adapt and share knowledge. Social media is often an easy tool to promote this behavior.

Some organizations treat social media as a random, over-caffeinated typing fest that is haphazardly thrown together because all the cool businesses are doing it. That's not a great approach. Social media — Facebook, YouTube, Twitter, LinkedIn, or whatever the next great social channel may be — is best used when your organization has an intentional, goal-oriented plan and a change plan to go with it!

You can utilize the major social networks in a number of ways. Companies use these opportunities for everything from customer service and product training to customer research, marketing, and PR. For example, Google uses YouTube training videos to attract and inform millions of potential viewers using or potentially using Google applications. These simple and short videos are geared to ordinary people, not just programming-savvy web developers.

Large companies, such as GEICO and Comcast, use Twitter to communicate in real time with customers. Rather than wait in the online phone queue, users can Tweet their issue and see a resolution in 140 characters or less. This system can also help companies create an online repository of issues and solutions to proactively manage.

Internally, Yammer can make companies more productive by allowing employees to privately exchange short answers to simple questions with one another. Tools like Basecamp help employees on projects organize to-dos, manage calendars, and keep every piece of project information in one central repository.

All these social-enterprise tools are part of the bigger communication picture when it comes to using technology to build awareness of what is happening in the organization, create understanding within the organization, and gain commitment and action from employees.

Companies are using social media not just to mass market their products and services but also to help support customers and encourage problem-solving employee behavior. These are perfect examples of how innovative behavior and social-media technology can go hand in hand.

Leveraging Restructuring Changes

Few words in corporate-speak can compare to *restructuring,* which means to change the way an organization looks and operates. In some executives' minds, restructuring is the solution to all evils in the world and the only thing that is holding them back from making huge profits. This section gives you the truth about restructuring — the good, the bad, and the ugly.

Restructuring an organization immediately brings the three Ps to most leaders' minds (people, pay, and job position), but these details are really the last part of the change, the results of more significant changes. The restructuring process should follow four guiding principles:

- **Focusing on the customer:** Restructuring changes should always start by addressing change that will improve the customer experience. Don't forget that the definition of *customers* can include stakeholders, the community in which the company operates, and employees, as well as the people who buy your product.

- **Putting strategy before structure:** What strategy and goals are needed to deliver a better product or service to your customers? The company may need to revamp a product line or introduce a new one. Other strategies may include having a broader reach in new markets, reducing the cost of services for customers, making the organization a great place to work, decreasing its global environmental footprint, or increasing profits for shareholders. Strategy before structure simply means making sure leadership is clear about the goals of the organizational change before the change happens.

- **Changing processes to improve performance:** Restructuring should not be done just to mask poor performance issues or hand them off to another group in the company. Often, greater profits, lower costs, or higher quality can be achieved by making process changes and increasing skill sets within the organization. After you look at improving the processes that can impact your strategy and customers, then you can look at aligning resources to the new processes or strategy.

✔ **Building an enabling structure:** When restructuring does happen, make sure the structure is flexible enough to last in the long term. If restructuring is just a short-term fix, the company can get in the cycle of moving people around and never really getting work done. People need time to adjust to change, and the amount of time it takes is significant. And, as with all change, the work does not stop when change happens, so being strategic about how employees' jobs are impacted will help decrease any "Here we go again" change attitudes down the road.

Saying that restructuring requires communication is kind of like saying Mount Everest is a big mountain. Yes, you need communication. Yes, you need a lot of it. And yes, you will need to plan for it in substantial detail. Chapter 2 of Book IV gives you the lowdown on effective communication.

Developing your restructuring plan

If you decide that a new structure for the organization is the best way to achieve your strategy and improve performance to deliver amazing results to your customers, you can get to work on a plan to make sure you identify and retain key employees and increase your competitive advantage after the change. Follow these steps:

1. **Define the goals and strategy the organization wants to achieve.** Refer to Chapter 1 of this Book for help developing your future state plan. Your goals and strategy will include starting to inspire a shared need, building a vision, creating a change road map, committing leadership to the change, and factoring in what will help or hinder change.

2. **Create the plan.** Your plan should include communication and how the restructuring will take place. You will use the plan to guarantee that all members of the organization (at the suitable time) have the information they need to do their jobs in the future.

3. **Identify the critical functions necessary to support your core strategy.** By starting with the core positions, you're able to focus the organization around these critical elements. All the other positions support these critical functions during the change and long into the future. If you are having trouble identifying which roles are critical, look back at the vision for the change and ask, "What three things absolutely need to happen in the future to help us reach our goals? Who will (or should) do them?" If you find that you don't currently have an employee who can do this job, don't worry; adding positions can come later in the process.

4. **Fill out the rest of the organizational chart to support these core functions.** This step prioritizes the focus of the organization. It's not the same as creating hierarchy in the organization; you simply define

what roles are aligned with the core competencies needed in the future and what roles will support that core group as it works to achieve these goals.

5. **Identify any changes in reporting relationships, consolidation of job responsibilities, or increased spans of control.** These changes will become key talking points in your change communication plan.

6. **Create a high-level job description for the core positions.** Determining the core functions is the first step. Second, describe what the role will be doing and what core competencies the person in the job should have, both now and in the future. A good job description should include the job title; purpose; responsibilities/duties; and required knowledge, skills, and abilities. You can find excellent templates on the Internet along with sample job descriptions for many jobs.

7. **Fill in the names.** Finally! After you know the positions that will be needed to reach the strategic goals and what each position will do, fill in the names of people who can do the job. You may have some blanks, which means you will have to train or hire individuals for the positions. You may also find you have some names left over, which means you may have to do job eliminations.

8. **If you haven't already done so, work with your HR department to review why new positions are needed or why a job is being eliminated.** HR conducts any appropriate review from a legal, compensation, and compliance perspective and can help in posting positions as necessary.

9. **Finalize any new or changing job descriptions or compensation changes.** Again, work with HR on this one.

10. **Finalize your communication plan.** Be sure to include in the plan what is changing, what work is moving, what work will be reassigned, and the new job descriptions.

11. **Go out there and change.** A new structure goes through the same change principles as any other large change. Some employees will be thrilled with the new opportunity; others will be upset by the change.

Identifying the necessary process changes and their impacts

To identify what needs to change during a restructuring, first take a moment to review what is happening today — your *process portfolio*. A company should never just invent a bunch of products and not look at how they are doing. The same principle is true for processes. Processes in many organizations have been created with years of toil, tears, and sweat, and taking a step back to make sure they are working and still make sense is the main goal of the process portfolio review.

Here are some questions you may want to ask during this review:

✔ **What is the most important goal for each process?** Many processes have multiple outputs, but when it comes down to it, a process should have an overarching goal; otherwise you may want to question why the process is happening in the first place. Is the goal of a report to provide information to executives? Is the goal of maintenance on a machine to ensure manufacturing doesn't come to a halt? If you can't think of a goal relatively easily, mark that process as one that potentially needs to change or be eliminated.

✔ **How can these goals be met more effectively?** Even in the most auto-mated process, some person needs to do something along the way. Make sure that responsibilities are clear, the right training is provided, and you have the right staff with the right competencies to make the process work. New technologies may be able to streamline a process to help improve quality and efficiency as well.

Another way to meet the goals of the process more effectively is to look at areas of duplication; sometimes processes are created because another process was not operating effectively, but the old process is still being done because it has always been done that way. Restructuring is a great opportunity to change any process that isn't meeting its goal or is delivering an output that no one uses.

✔ **Are there any changes in the organization that have affected or will affect the process in the foreseeable future?** You may look at processes that have been added, stopped, or significantly changed over the past few years to see if they've impacted the process you are reviewing. Processes are all connected! You may also identify new (or not-so-new) technology that may have changed the process. Finally, you may want to take a peek at customer demand. If customer demand has gone up or down recently, has the process adjusted to these needs?

Structuring performance metrics

A great place to start structuring your metrics is linking your process port-folio review and the guiding principles for successful restructuring. With these two activities complete, you will already have identified essential goals for the organization, customer requirements aligned to these goals, and your key processes (which by now all have clear goals attached to them too). The last step in the puzzle is to establish the means to measure these vital processes. Performance metrics are your key indicator of how well a change has been done and how well the change is being sustained in the future.

The key to making performance metrics tie back to the restructuring process is to align the strategy and goal of the change to the metric. If the goal of the restructuring is to improve customer satisfaction by adding more quality experts into key teams, you should measure product quality and customer service complaints (compliments, too). If the goal is to increase speed in delivery of products by restructuring the engineering and manufacturing teams into cross-functional pods, you should measure timely delivery of a product.

Consider an example of performance metrics that can help judge the success of restructuring, in both the short and the long term. In this case, the vision of the restructuring is to inspire innovation by removing extra approval layers in the organization. The vision to inspire innovation is being driven by the customer requirements, which are new software applications that are significantly updated and innovated at least once a month. This vision and requirements led to the restructuring goal of improving the quality, frequency, and speed of application research, creation, and development.

Book VI

Managing Business Change

Here are three possible metrics to measure the achievement of the restructuring goal:

- ✔ **Frequency:** The number of innovative ideas adopted across the company or number of best practices shared in the knowledge-management system (which now doesn't need as many approvals!)

- ✔ **Speed:** The new product introduction timeline (the time from when research has an idea to when it is ready to launch)

- ✔ **Quality:** The number of updates to fix "bugs" within 60 days of the new application launch

The measures help the organization determine if the vision, which is tied to a customer need for innovation, is being realized through the restructuring.

Organizing Change during Mergers and Acquisitions

Surprise, surprise: When two companies merge, change is going to happen! Mergers and acquisitions are increasingly common today. Look in any business magazine and you'll read about some company buying some other company. But what you see in that article is just the tip of the iceberg, because a company negotiating a great deal is just one part of the M&A puzzle. Other pieces of the puzzle include getting employees on board with how the goals of the company and their responsibilities will change (or not change) in the future, who will be part of the new company and who may not be, who is leading the new company, and what will be expected from employees in the short term and long term. And that's just the beginning of the change list during M&A activities: Throw in new benefit structures, different organizational charts, contrasting cultures, and new ways of working with customers, and you start to realize how extensive change can be during a merger or acquisition.

Taking change to a new level: Combining companies

The entire purpose of mergers and acquisitions is to change and grow stronger, bigger, or more efficient, all of which take a considerable amount of effort. As with all large-scale changes, especially something as large as combining companies, in order to be successful, employees must accept the change and be willing and able to work in the new environment. In this section, you're introduced to all the M&A jargon and possible reasons an organization may consider M&A.

What makes the M&A process successful? Although mergers and acquisitions have been happening for almost as long as organizations have been in business, companies still don't have a perfect formula for how to succeed with a business combination. However, two critical areas tend to lead to the companies meeting their strategic goals:

- ✔ **The process:** One of the most important areas successfully combined companies undertake is an organization-wide change process. This process starts with a clear strategy and specific goals, not only for the new company but for the integration process as well.

- ✔ **The fit:** The second area that helps to determine success is how complementary the products, services, and culture of the two organizations are before the change. The fit of companies often comes down to whether or not the other company's strengths complement your company's weaknesses and how much risk each company is willing to take.

Although each situation is different and each change and integration plan is different, these two areas are the make-or-break aspects of change during a merger or acquisition.

Following the M&A process

The M&A process has three fundamental steps:

1. **One or more executives have some motivation to merge with or acquire another company and start the process.** The motives are important because they determine the strategic goals of the entire process.

2. **The merger begins to happen.** Companies perform their due diligence as they move from wanting to combine to getting ready to integrate as a new company.

3. **The companies combine and the real change happens.**

Recognizing the need for enterprise-wide change and being realistic about how the two companies will work together in the long run, both operationally and culturally, should be continually addressed in the basic steps of mergers and acquisitions: during the decision to merge, during the due diligence and negotiation process, and as the new organization becomes one after the merger is official.

Book VI

Managing
Business
Change

Making the decision to merge or acquire

Before any of the benefits of mergers or acquisitions can happen, a company's leaders need to know why they want to combine forces and what they hope to get out of the endeavor. Many organizations pinpoint their reasons by identifying their *core competencies:* the capabilities they have that create a competitive advantage for that company in the long run, are hard for another company to copy, are part of the company's culture, and are meaningful to their customers. These capabilities can be managerial, people driven, or technical. Some companies' greatest competencies are their people, especially for service companies or for heavily R&D-focused companies where innovation and brainpower are at the core of the company's identity.

Performing due diligence and integration

Due diligence and integration can be seen as an in-depth data-gathering and decision-making process before the deal closes. Organizations start by creating clear objectives and goals for the merger, and then they evaluate whether the objectives can be met both strategically and financially. This part also includes negotiation and working through any regulatory or compliance issues that may arise. The goal of the due-diligence phase is to have a plan and agreement on how the companies will operate together after the combination is complete, which includes everything from which functions will combine and which will stay the same to what name the new company will have and how much the entire deal will cost.

During the integration and due-diligence phase, a number of steps are taken, departments are combined, and management decisions are made. Most problems in the post-integration phases come from lack of clarity about how decisions are made and who is making them. With so much happening in the integration and so much information being passed back and forth, M&A change leaders can help alleviate some of the pain by identifying differences and similarities in management style and facilitating how decisions will be made — both during and after the merger closes.

Supporting employees during the M&A process

During a merger or acquisition, you have to deal with the tangible aspects of change (better financial statements, new technology, and improved distribution networks) and the intangible aspects (organizational culture and employee morale). Although economics drive the overwhelming majority of reasons to merge, employees bring significant value to the combined entity. Even if the reason for merging is to combine manufacturing facilities, if employees aren't on board and supported during the process, the company won't obtain the full value of the integration because many employees will continue to do what they know — with a different company.

Combining two balance sheets is relatively easy; merging two cultures is not so easy. People are not like machines, and integrating teams of employees is much harder than changing the logo on their business cards. The goal of change leaders during the M&A process is to engage the people side of the business so the full financial value of the endeavor can be realized.

Assessing and assisting the employee transition

Following are the three benchmarks that successful M&A teams go through as they involve their employees in the process. By observing whether employees are acting in line with these goals, you can gauge your progress and increase assimilation efforts where needed.

✔ **Assimilating the new and old organizational culture:** Keeping employees in the dark about the future company is a surefire way to derail even the highest-value merger or acquisition. As soon as possible, employees in the acquired company should have the opportunity to work with leaders and employees on both ends to learn more about the history, culture, and values of the new company. Employees need this opportunity to learn what has worked in the firm doing the buying, why the bought firm is attractive to the acquirer, and how they may be able to best contribute to the new organization.

Assimilation goes both ways: Acquiring companies also need to know more about the culture that their new peers operated in before being acquired because, after all, the acquired company must have been doing something right to make it an attractive acquisition candidate.

✔ **Being ready to work together:** Acquired employees may feel they're being forced into doing things another way. You can't just throw together two companies (or people) and expect them to coexist perfectly without some help. When one company is bought, those employees may feel like their company is losing out and the other company is winning. If leaders encourage employees to work with one another and reward them for doing so, old routines on both sides of the deal are likely to come together to create better ways of doing business in the new company.

✔ **Sharing capabilities and knowledge:** Value creation is the main reason for mergers and acquisitions, and sustainable value is created only when information is shared and capabilities are continually developed. Thus the merger or acquisition is not a once-and-done activity but a long-term focus that ensures the new firm has the resources (technical and human) to operate in the new way and also makes sure that employees are encouraged and rewarded for sharing knowledge.

Considering what the "bought" company is thinking

Change required by a merger or acquisition can be jarring for employees, who may have been thinking that everything was going along just fine. Even if their view isn't a realistic picture of what was really happening, it could be the perspective of many employees in an acquired firm. How can leaders avoid this pitfall? While leaders "sell" the reasons for the merger or acquisition, often on a strategic and financial level, leaders on both sides should take the time to get individuals and small teams to identify advantages that will impact the employees on a day-to-day basis. Value creation must take place for the employees as well as for the firm. Value for the employees may be more job security, greater benefits, or career advancement.

Although employees in both organizations need to understand the purpose of the acquisition and their role in the new organization, the needs in the acquired company are different from those in the acquiring company. Taking these needs into consideration and knowing when to allow employees the time to assimilate and when to push for results helps speed the change process in the long term.

Handling staffing considerations during a merger or acquisition

The goal of M&A activities is to create greater value for both companies through more financial power, increased market share, or streamlined operating efficiencies. Before any of these benefits can happen, productivity and employee engagement need to be taken into consideration.

As with most changes, upfront and frequent communication partnered with proactive and sincere involvement in the process improves the business outcome. Mergers and acquisitions are a bit different from other organizational changes because of the rapid pace of change often associated with the process. Additionally, both companies experience quite a bit of uncertainty because even though plenty of planning, data collection, and strategic visioning for the future takes place, until the deal is signed nothing is 100 percent accurate due to the limitations of what can and cannot be shared before the deal closes.

During the M&A process, employees may become especially distracted by this uncertainty. The best thing leaders can do to decrease and shorten the productivity dip is to be upfront and honest about the changes ahead and clearly communicate what can and cannot be shared during the due diligence. Employees realize that before the deal is done there are regulatory, financial, and competitive reasons why everything cannot be disclosed. However, telling employees merely that much helps to create two-way communication that will benefit the company in the days to come. Besides communication, leaders want to focus on three staffing concerns common during the M&A process: minimizing employee attrition, retaining key staff, and maintaining employee morale.

Some companies try to keep acquisitions behind closed doors, leading to something of the white elephant in the room. Everyone knows something is happening, but rather than talk about it openly, employees take cues from water-cooler talk, become wary of company leaders and their messages, and may even hold back any extra effort because they have no real idea about what is down the road. These behaviors can destroy leadership credibility and have a negative impact on the overall acquisition. The best thing leaders can do is to be upfront and honest about the changes ahead and clearly communicate what can and cannot be shared during the due diligence.

Within the first 90 days of closing the deal, the change team should revisit the organizational and knowledge assumptions made during the due diligence and pre-close process and create a realistic plan regarding what needs to happen now that information between the two companies can flow openly.

Minimizing employee attrition

Employees throughout the organization provide continuity that customers are craving during a merger. Customers look for cues from the new company about what is ahead and how their needs will be supported. If all the employees that customers know within the company say *sayonara* (by their own choice or the company's), customers may soon leave for competitors.

Keep an eye out for stress in the organization. Allow employees time to deal with the added stress of the change, learn about the new company, and do their jobs. If the number of sick days starts creeping up or if productivity is dipping significantly, do a gut check and ask employees what else can be done to help people work through the changes the merger has created. Remember that change does not happen overnight!

As you work on minimizing employee attrition, include these key incentives:

✔ **A bright and believable future:** Employees want to know that the company's best days are ahead of it, and they want to know how they will play a role in this future. Be realistic and share as much detail as you possibly can.

✔ **A positive work environment:** If employees are supported and feel they're making a difference, you have a higher chance of retaining them. A positive work environment includes trusting and rewarding employees for doing the right thing and thanking managers who retain employees.

✔ **Opportunities for involvement, feedback, and personal development:** No one likes being told what to do. By involving groups of employees throughout the process, the leadership team can gain valuable feedback, and individuals have a chance to voice ideas and concerns. Additionally, as part of the integration, be sure to identify the new ways employees will be able to grow with the company through expanded roles and responsibilities. A defined schedule for training and professional development sends a strong message to employees that they are valued.

✔ **Money:** Keep in mind that each employee has financial needs and goals. Most likely, at least one of the companies in the deal will be changing its total compensation package (benefits, salary, bonuses), so as soon as you can, communicate the potential changes or additions. If employees don't hear anything about their pay, they may begin making career choices based on assumptions and fear rather than facts.

Employees will want to stay with a company if they feel they have room to grow, are encouraged to try new things, and feel valued for their work. Although money is a great motivator, so are two words: thank you. If you can tell employees how their work efforts are helping the team and the company, they will feel valued. And employees who feel valued rarely pack their bags and walk out the door.

Book VI

Managing Business Change

Maintaining employee morale

When employee confidence is high, employees usually are more likely to work harder to make the change happen and maintain a positive view of the changes and challenges that lie ahead. You can imagine what may happen when morale is low: This negativity can filter through everything from lunchroom gossip to damaging discussions with customers.

The most important way to maintain and increase morale is quite simple: Ask employees what you can do. By engaging your employees, you can find out what the organization and its leaders can do better. Not only does this conversation create a dialogue between management and employees, but as long as leadership acts on the recommendations (or at least some of the recommendations), it also shows employees that their opinions matter.

Here is what you can do to maintain morale during M&A:

- **Be honest with employees.** Really honest. A high trust environment creates productivity and innovation. It is great to be optimistic, but leaders also need to be realistic.

- **Focus on the future culture.** The culture of an organization includes a wide array of elements, from what people wear to work to the way people address problem solving. When the deal is signed, the two separate and different cultures still exist and can exist for quite some time.

  The best way to address cultural issues is head on and with completely open and honest communication. Don't tiptoe around how the culture will look, feel, and breathe — tell employees what is expected of them, what is expected to go, and what is expected to stay. Involve employees in making these expectations happen.

- **Talk about the process.** As soon as federal regulations allow it, clear communication helps keep at bay cynicism about the motives behind the merger or acquisition. Few employees have been through enough corporate combinations to understand the process, so explaining the process helps to build trust within the organization. Here are a few questions you need to answer:

  - How will the new leadership team be created? When will employees know about the new executive team?

  - How will processes and technology be integrated? Who is leading the integration effort? How can employees provide feedback about the integration?

  - What can employees tell customers or other individuals who may ask about the merger?

  - Where can employees go for more information?

Retaining key staff

Key staff members are people in your organization whose sudden absence would create difficulty in delivering on customer requirements. They may have a skill that is hard to replace or train. They may be your most amazing star performers, have a strong relationship with important clients, or be the ones that hold considerable institutional knowledge.

Key staff retention strategies should target roughly about 10 percent of the organization. If you find you need to retain more than 10 percent of your organization through targeted packages, you may consider offering a general retention for all staff. General retention may come in forms of a modest bonus (about 5 to 10 percent of annual salary) or restricted stock.

Your company may have individuals or teams who aren't necessarily key staff for long-term results but are needed to complete high-priority projects in the short-term. Offering these employees or teams some type of project-completion bonus helps make sure these employees wrap things up before they consider moving to another position or company.

Don't limit your key staff to the highest levels of leadership. Yes, having consistent and strong leadership will help dramatically in the days ahead, but so will your sales team and R&D team. Sales teams have relationships with customers that are next to impossible to rebuild overnight. R&D teams have institutional knowledge that spreads much farther than any documented procedure or process could ever account for in the company, and they may hold the secret to your next dominant product.

After you have identified your key staff, you can work on how to keep them from jumping ship. A retention package is simply a way of formally (and usually financially) letting employees know that although they do have the option of leaving, it's worthwhile to stick around and see how wonderful the new company will be in the future.

Keeping key staff on board is all about timing. Retention bonuses often include some type of obligation or delayed payout, timed with how long you believe it may take to iron out any kinks in the new organization and timed with how long it will take to help the employee see the value of the merger. Other retention packages may be focused on the short term. You may have a group of employees who must stick around long enough to get the new organization launched. Often this group is in support functions like finance, technology, and human resources. Although you may be able to replace these positions if needed, knowing that the lights will stay on without much thought in the immediate months after the merger is a safety net worth creating.

Most retention comes in the form of a lump sum payment or additional performance bonus, but other parts of the stay bonus may be stock or stock options or additional benefits like vacation time, future paid sabbatical, or the option of flextime. You may not want to promise anything, but when you begin to communicate to key staff about how their retention is important for the success of the merger and the future of the company, you have a great opportunity to ask what they would consider an ideal retention package.

Proceeding successfully after the deal is done

The deal is done, retention offers are signed, the communication plan is in full swing, and employees are beginning to explore the new environment with a positive attitude. Now your job as a change leader is to keep the momentum rolling so that all the value expected as part of the merger or acquisition can become a reality.

Here are a couple of things change leaders and executives can do to make sure the future is as bright as you expect it to be:

- ✔ **Keep your eyes and ears out there.** Conducting a 90-day post-merger assessment is a great checkpoint to ask what is going well, what still needs work, and what change lessons can be learned from the successes and challenges of the M&A process.

- ✔ **Retain, focus, and engage — in that order.** After employees feel secure in the new company (that is, they have a job and they may even have a retention package), you can begin to refocus teams on the work at hand. Having objectives and projects to work on reminds employees that even though they probably still have a number of unanswered questions, work still needs to get done and should get done. Finally, when employees are back doing the work that needs to get done, managers can work on reengaging employees around a common goal and mission. Trying to motivate employees and engage them in the new culture may seem artificial until employees have some experience working in it.

- ✔ **Give managers and supervisors the tools they need.** Give front-line managers the information and necessary training to address questions and concerns raised before, during, and after the integration. Executives are great at communicating the vision and direction of the company, but managers and supervisors are the ones who work on the details long after the deal is done.

- ✔ **Train staff to integrate them into the new organization.** The many changes that were identified during the integration and due-diligence phase must now be implemented. Inform staff of all the decisions that have been made regarding changes in processes, organization structure, and organizational culture. Provide training on how things will be done going forward in the combined company. Everyone needs to understand what is expected of them and gain the skills to be able to perform in the new organization.

✔ **Regularly check in with employees about what is happening.** Often, communication efforts are quite significant during the early stages of the integration. However, stopping or dramatically decreasing communication a few months after the deal is done can make employees feel either that they're being left in the dark or that all the ideals about the value the merger would create never came true. Formally providing employees with the continued results of the merger every three to six months until all the expected value is attained helps to build a change-ready culture — one that knows leaders have the capability to set a vision for change and follow it through to completion. Conduct an employee-engagement survey before, during, and after the merger or acquisition to keep a pulse on what employees are thinking and feeling.

✔ **Recognize that the work is just beginning for some people.** Even though the job of the executives and M&A team is coming to an end after the integration winds down, lower-level employees will just be starting to pick up all the work that needs to happen to make the merger a success. Continue to provide support to these employees and managers, because some gaps in information or organizational assumptions may surface long after the deal closes.

Book VI

Managing Business Change

Managing Cultural Change

Organizational culture tends to have a life of its own. Even though you may have spent a great deal of time focusing on communicating and implementing a new strategy or carefully maneuvering through a merger or acquisition, you may still find that old beliefs and assumptions about "how things are done around here" remain. These beliefs and behaviors can be like an anchor to a previous time that no longer works for the organization. It may well be time to take a serious look at shifting the culture.

Defining the current culture

Whether the old company culture was something that evolved naturally or was purposefully put into place years ago, changing culture is something that must be handled proactively. Clearly defining mission, vision, and values is the first place to begin to define the organizational culture.

Taking a deeper look at company values

Values serve as an ethical foundation on which to build an organization's culture. They are driven by the core shared beliefs regarding what is important as you go about conducting business. Values set the tone for acceptable and desirable interactions between co-workers, customers, and suppliers.

Here are some examples of common values for organizations:

- ✔ Trusting people and having the highest ethical standards
- ✔ Respecting decisions and choices of other employees
- ✔ Innovating to propel the company forward
- ✔ Using teamwork to drive results
- ✔ Putting the customer first

Many organizations tie their standards of business conduct to their core values. Training on core values supports employees to make ethical decisions in their daily work routines.

One best practice is to have dialogue sessions that discuss examples of what the values look like in real life. Examine ways to live these values as well as examples of what missing the mark looks like. For example, trust and respect may look like talking to a co-worker directly when you have a conflict. Lack of respect in this case would be to talk about that co-worker behind his back to his boss without first talking to him about the conflict. Even worse would be spreading rumors about him.

Another best practice is to tie your performance-management process and rewards system to your company values. Some organizations have specific sections on employee annual performance reviews that address each of their company-wide values. Pay for results for executives can also be tied to goals that support the company values. For example, valuing diversity may be one of the corporate values, which can be measured by the percent of minorities and women hired and promoted in a given year.

Examining your current organizational culture

As a change leader, one of the first things you need to do to understand organizational culture is to get a clear picture of what your employees believe. To gather this information, you need to do a variety of cultural assessments to dig at the hidden assumptions. You can choose from a number of methods to examine a company's culture, including the following approaches:

- ✔ **Interviews and focus groups:** Interviews and focus groups are powerful tools to get firsthand information regarding how employees view your organizational culture. You may also want to include customers, suppliers, and vendors in your evaluation to get an external perspective of your organization's culture.

Carefully craft your questionnaires and interview protocols in such a way that you drive a positive change in the organization. For example, a good question to ask would be, "What do you like the best about working at this company"? Another best practice question could be, "What changes would result in you being able to provide higher customer satisfaction?" Avoid negative questions such as "What bothers you the most about working here?" which can open the floodgates to faultfinding and finger-pointing. This purposely positive approach is commonly known as *appreciative inquiry* in academic circles.

You may be saying, "But I want to hear about the bad stuff, too!" Of course you want to understand what is not working. A best practice to get at this information is to ask employees what changes going forward would make the organization even better.

✔ **Quantitative assessments:** A number of commercially available instruments can be used to quickly capture a snapshot of an organization's shared assumptions and behaviors. These instruments go by a number of different names, such as employee satisfaction surveys, employee engagement surveys, and organizational culture indicators. Most of them are administered by third-party companies that provide online access to employees to complete the typical questionnaire in less than 30 minutes. One of the advantages of using an independent third party is ensuring confidentiality and the anonymity of the employees providing feedback on the survey. Another advantage is that most of these instruments are well researched and verified to measure key indicators of organizational health.

Assessing the leadership culture

The leadership styles and behaviors that dominate in your organization can impact organizational performance and employee morale. A favorite cultural assessment tool is the Leadership Culture Survey, published by The Leadership Circle (www.theleadershipcircle.com/assessment-tools/survey). Decades of research went into the tool and its 31 dimensions of culture. The Leadership Culture Survey provides a powerful examination of your leadership culture. Used for your entire organization or for just a leadership team, the survey tells you how your people view their current leadership culture and compares that reality to the optimal culture they desire. The gap between the current culture and desired culture reveals key opportunities for leadership development. The Leadership Culture Survey also measures how your leadership culture compares to that of other organizations.

To access the Leadership Culture Survey, you can obtain certification training through The Leadership Circle or hire a consultant who is certified to administer and interpret the survey. The assessment is administered via a confidential online questionnaire completed by employees and management. Respondents are asked to rate not only the current state of the organizational culture but also what they want as the desired future state. This tool can be a quick and cost-effective method to understand some of the deeper underlying assumptions driving an organization's behavior.

Commercially available cultural assessment instruments and tools can save you both time and money in the long run by leveraging best practices based on years of industry research by these survey companies.

Creating successful cultural change

The process of defining the desired future state is best done by engaging thought leadership from all levels, including executives, middle management, and individual contributors. Culture doesn't simply rest in the formal statements issued by managers; it's in the hearts and minds of all employees. You need to engage everyone in the organization to create the new culture.

Uniting executive support

One of the most common reasons for cultural change is new leadership at the top. New CEOs, especially when hired from the outside, come into organizations with strong beliefs and assumptions about how an organization needs to operate to be successful. Savvy change leaders quickly recognize instances where the new leadership's beliefs clash with the long-standing culture of the organization and take steps to bring everyone together.

One of the most powerful ways to create a new culture is to create stories and images that symbolize the new way of doing things. For millennia, people have maintained their cultural heritage through storytelling. This technique also works in the business setting. Spend significant time with your executive team to create a new story of what it means to work at your organization. Leaders need to develop and emphasize stories that demonstrate in vivid detail the desired future behaviors and beliefs in the organization, which may include specific stories about employees who have gone the extra mile to exemplify the desired behaviors. You can also have these stories tie back to the vision of where the company is going and its core mission.

Stories can be captured in writing and used by people throughout the organization to retell in speeches, small group meetings, and more. They should also be woven into your new-hire orientation or onboarding. You can develop ways to continue to elicit new stories. One idea is to request submissions through the company intranet, if you have one.

Frequently, the changing culture is associated with a change in brand strategy and external communications — a best practice that enables you to align your internal culture with how customers and others see you in the world.

Another technique for reigniting employees' commitments to core values is to dust off some of the older stories from company founders that exemplify the desired culture. Storytelling is a powerful way to communicate culture, because stories connect with employees at an emotional level.

Successful executives do everything they can to walk the talk of espoused values. Employees can be naturally skeptical of any changes to the company's core values. They watch vigilantly to see whether management is serious about these changes or just giving lip service to them. Communications as well as actions, including the reward system, need to reinforce the desired behaviors.

Aligning all work systems

As you ensure that your work systems align, and that they reward desired behaviors, think about how you can recognize and reward employees' behavior that supports the new culture and at the same time eliminate old reward systems that emphasize the old culture. Too often, organizations leave in place outdated systems that result in a mixed message to employees.

For example, imagine you have announced to your company that you want everyone to spend more effort on quality. However, your primary measures for calculating the annual employee bonus consist only of on-time delivery and cost-reduction goals. Can you realistically expect employees to focus on quality given that their pay is tied only to cost and delivery? Of course not! You need to add a new quality measure as part of the bonus calculation to drive new behaviors toward quality products and services. This change will no doubt create dialogue among employees on the relative importance of quality versus on-time delivery and cost. How you address these questions around priorities determines the fate of the new culture you wish to create.

Public recognition for employees who exemplify the desired future culture is another powerful technique to encourage the new culture to take root. You may want to create new monthly or quarterly rewards that symbolize each of the core values you wish to emphasize.

Corporate citizenship may be another value you wish to promote in your company culture. Giving employees the opportunity to volunteer their time at local nonprofit organizations one day a year is a way to show your company's commitment to local communities.

Safeguarding against failure

Culture change can be uncertain. But with the right tools, methods, and vision for the future, it can be done. A couple key tools help leaders safeguard against failure. If used correctly, they serve as a safety net that catches you and the organization if you veer off course.

Book VI

Managing Business Change

✔ **360-degree assessments:** A 360-degree assessment allows peers, managers, and employees to rate leaders on a number of areas. A cultural 360-assessment can give leaders in-depth information regarding how employees view the leaders' embodiment of the values of the new culture.

✔ **Employee-engagement reviews:** Many companies use employee-engagement surveys to determine the pulse of the organization. A one-time survey provides valuable insights into how content employees are with a wide range of people issues (compensation, management, ease of getting work done); annual surveys can show employers trends in the overall workforce attitude and satisfaction.

Working with the new culture

Whether you are changing a culture or just tweaking the current one, a bad fit with a hire is a big waste of money and time. And the problem is probably not that the hire doesn't have the skill set to do a job or overstated past experience significantly; the misfit usually involves personality clashes with the culture.

The best way to find the perfect employee is to look beyond the job description and the skills required. You have to look at the personality and make sure that the role you are filling fits this person's personality. When you hire someone purely for their skill, you miss out on an opportunity to enhance your team and your company's culture. Sometimes you can't uncover this fit with typical interview questions, so you need to plan out the interview to get what you want and what that new employee wants.

Too often, recruiters provide a stack of resumes to hiring managers and simply check off whether or not key words match the resume. On the other hand, when hiring to fit candidates to the organization, magic happens. Employees and employers go through a rigorous process to understand not only the strengths and capabilities they both offer but also what each potential employee wants to do next.

Many hiring managers look at bright, eager recruits and just think, "Wow, they could really change things around here!" This goal is lofty and worthwhile, but try not to put all the success or failure on the new person's shoulders. One person can come in and ask questions and stir things up in the company, but he can't single-handedly change the culture. Many of these great prospective employees leave within two to three years because they don't feel that they can make dramatic changes alone.

Cultural fit is not just for new employees. Every employee at the company is impacted by a new culture. Although it's tough, the best thing for an educated change leader like you to do when an employee doesn't fit in with company culture is to look at performance. You need to look at both what employees do and how they do it. Many top-talent organizations use the *how-and-what* model for performance management:

> ✔ *How* refers to how the work gets done, often referred to as the softer skills like collaboration, respect, and communication.

> ✔ *What* accounts for the hard results from an individual's performance.

Putting the two concepts together, for example: Does the individual respect others' opinions and make a fair judgment about what to do next (the how) and then go out and get the work done in a collaborative style (the what)? Or does the individual ignore everyone's opinions, yell at co-workers, and run over anyone in her way (the how) in order to meet the monthly sales targets (the what)? In both situations, the individual may be meeting her numbers, but most people would prefer to work with the former example.

Table 4-1 summarizes the performance reviews for a group of leaders and notes what the boss may consider doing next using the how-and-what model for performance. For this exercise, keep in mind that the company wants to create a collaborative and creative environment for all employees.

Book VI

Managing Business Change

Table 4-1	The How-and-What Performance Review		
Employee	*How the Work Gets Done*	*What Gets Done*	*What to Do Next?*
Albert	He doesn't build relationships, and he follows a command-and-control model that leaves employees in tears.	Meets numbers 100% of the time	Coach Albert on how aligning with a collaborative culture at times will make everyone work better. If coaching doesn't work, Albert may need to be let go.
Tobin	He spends most of the day gathering opinions from others; people go to Tobin when they have concerns or ideas.	Has not met a single target in six months.	Train Tobin on time management and balancing discussion with action.
Sally	She makes great relationships and treats employees with respect.	Always makes her numbers and gets things done on time.	Make Sally CEO!

The lessons learned through culture assessments and leadership discussions can be used to determine what type of "how" the organization should hire for in the future. These results should also be a primary feed into the development of all the current employees and should be the basis for who gets promoted, who is given the sought-after training opportunities, and who gets the best assignments.

Chapter 5

When Everything Changes: Working with Complex Change

Sometimes it hits you unexpectedly; other times it seems like a good idea at first but then you begin to have second thoughts. What is *it,* exactly? Complex change. Chaos. When everything, absolutely everything, is changing at once. Customers, technology, company culture, economic conditions, leadership teams — you name it, it's changing. This amount of change is not impossible to handle; it just takes a fine balance among assertive leadership, aggressive goals, realistic project timelines, near-perfect communication, fully staffed change teams, and a little luck. Not much, right?

You can't depend on luck, but you can prepare to deal with complex change, whether it is planned or unexpectedly winds up on your to-do list one Monday morning. In this chapter, you find real-world examples of complex changes to use as reference for your own situation. You get the tools you need to create simple, immediate changes during complex change and discover the fine art of balancing cooperation and creativity with necessary bureaucracy and structure.

If you want complex change to stick, you need to avoid the dreaded "flavor of the month" club, which can happen when everything is changing at once. In this chapter, you find out how to set your change apart. And finally, you learn how to tie everything together to make change easier in the future by integrating a change mentality into the organizational culture. It's a lot of ground to cover, but if you're in the midst of complex change, you've got no time to lose.

Getting a Handle on Chaos: When Everything Is Changing at Once

What does managing multiple changes look like? In 2010, the merger of United Airlines and Continental Airlines was seen by some as a matter of survival for the U.S.-based airlines. In the post-9/11 world, with the economy slowly coming out of the worst recession in decades, economic factors required companies to go big or go home. Call those economic factors Change #1.

The merger meant a new name and logo. Former United employees said that it would be odd not to see the big United "U" on the back of planes. Continental employees would adopt a new name. These changes just touch the surface of all the changes that go into creating a new company from two different cultures, which is Change #2: forming a new company.

The former CEO of Continental, Jeffery A. Smisek, took over as the new CEO of the new United. (There's Change #3: new leadership.) Updating planes, upgrading services, and changing routes meant the company was creating a new product for its customers (Change #4: new product offering). When you factor in dealing with two customer bases, multiple labor unions, and other airlines declaring bankruptcy, you have multifaceted change.

Changing everything at once can work out well for all the stakeholders involved. It can also be a complete failure that takes years, if not decades, to recover from. Even if everything really is *not* changing at once, when there are multiple initiatives, priorities, messages, and leaders talking about change, employees, customers, and shareowners may feel like they are in the middle of complete chaos, and this perspective doesn't easily go away. But you can manage the chaos to make the change more palatable to customers, less disruptive to employees, and more profitable to shareowners.

Managing what seems like chaos comes down to executing change variables perfectly from the perspective of shareholders, customers, and employees. Here are the key elements to keep in mind:

- ✔ **Structure:** Make the change effort cohesive. Even though a number of changes may be occurring, try to show external and internal stakeholders how they all relate to one another.

- ✔ **Communication:** Create two-way communication methods for customers and employees being impacted by the changes.

- ✔ **Leadership:** Get leadership out there talking and walking the change.

- ✔ **Shareholders:** Make sure the change makes sense to external parties, like shareholders who want the company to make a profit.

Whenever large-scale change takes place, you can safely assume there are going to be a few opinions (an understatement) about how well the change went. Some customers, employees, and shareholders will love the change; others will hate it. But if you keep those points as your main focus, the likelihood of successful change will rise exponentially.

Creating a Snowball Effect with Small Wins

Creating simple and immediate changes, or "wins," helps reduce the uncertainty of an environment in which everything feels like it is shifting. This snowball-effect strategy — making one simple change, followed by a slightly bigger change, and so on — reduces resistance by making discussions tangible and results-oriented early on during the change.

Creating a list of early wins, no matter how small, gets that snowball moving. As you plan the changes, rather than waiting to celebrate and communicate when everything is done, take a phased approach with clearly stated milestones for quick wins. Quick wins are low-hanging fruit because they are relatively simple to tackle, raise team confidence, and provide a sense of accomplishment along the long journey toward change. You may be able to measure these early wins with quantifiable returns on investment or through increased employee morale and productivity.

Quick wins are out there — you just need to make sure people know about them! Here are three questions that can help you find some quick wins with all the changes going on:

- ✔ **Can people see progress?** Getting executives together in a room to create a vision is not a quick win. You need to make real progress at the employee or customer level. The program may also be seen from a structure point of view. Did you train a core team of front-line employees and were they immediately able to go back and apply the training? That is a quick win. Employees can see it for themselves.

- ✔ **Are things getting easier, faster, or better?** Olympic athletes don't gauge their performance only once every four years. When you're facing organization-wide change, find ways to test success and progress. Ask a client to pilot a few of the changes being made in the organization. Test these changes out and see if jobs are getting easier and processes are becoming more productive. Offer employees the opportunity to trade jobs with each other or with another department for a day to get another perspective on whether the changes have made things easy to do. Having an "outsider" point of view will also give valuable feedback on other opportunities to make the changes even better.

Book VI

Managing Business Change

✔ **Is the early win influential?** Early wins don't have to be enormous, but they do need to be meaningful. Just checking an item off a project plan will hardly get doubters to jump on board the change train. Find something significant that makes you take a step back and say, "Wow, we're doing it." If a company is going through a merger in a challenging industry, this first wow may be a sales team that landed the first client for the newly created company or a production team that shipped the first product for the merged organization out the door.

Communicate early wins to gain momentum for change. Treat early wins as a winning sports team's fans do. People like success, and when they see it they want to be part of it.

Structuring and Organizing Complex Change

The word *bureaucracy* may conjure images of an outdated workplace with workers getting approvals for even the most repetitive, meaningless tasks, but a certain amount of bureaucracy is a fact of life in organizations. You need to balance the bureaucracy of management with the creativity needed for successful change.

Using project management to establish structure

Project management establishes a structure to make sure project milestones are met on time and on budget. The goal of project management is to mobilize and align employees and provide them with the tools they need to quickly function as a team and get things done. The goal is *not* to hold a microscope up to every little thing that is happening during large-scale changes. Project management is like being the conductor of an orchestra: You don't create the music, but you help make sure all the music is aligned.

A good project-management office does three things: Creates a road map of critical phases, coordinates project planning and schedules, and manages change acceptance.

Creating a road map of critical phases

First, the project manager creates a road map that's aligned to the bigger vision of the change project that helps people work together on common problems. A road map is bigger than a timeline or project plan. It walks teams through critical phases of major change and then links these common activities together over the course of the initiative.

Coordinating project planning and schedules

Second, the project manager facilitates agreement on key activities and due dates. Aligning the road map to various project plans helps make sure things get done. But project management works best when the focus is not just on getting things done but also on making sure critical milestones and activities are coordinated with each other and contribute to the large-scale change as best they can. Imagine how chaotic it would seem to employees to have multiple communication messages and training invitations bombarding their e-mail inboxes.

A project manager acts as a shelter from being overwhelmed, aligning dates for key training, messages, and activities so employees aren't confused about what's expected from them.

Managing change acceptance

Finally, project management works best when the manager goes out and monitors the overall organizational acceptance of the multiple changes. When multiple changes are underway, change leaders are most likely focused on one or two key initiatives that impact their department or team. A project manager looks across the board to see how one initiative may be impacting another or how one success may help propel success in other areas.

Being a good project manager

Now that you have a good understanding of how and when project management works, you want to find a fabulous change leader to lead the project management effort. Here's the job description:

- ✔ Working with the team to create processes and templates for the overall change. A project manager can take the best of all change worlds and help facilitate knowledge sharing from one team to the next.

- ✔ Giving input to teams and frequently checking in with senior leadership to make sure all the changes are on track.

- ✔ Keeping track of resources and frequently reviewing the outcomes of change along the way.

- ✔ Working with change teams to develop repeatable processes and templates for future and ongoing changes.

- ✔ Gathering information and feedback from employees and providing this information to senior leadership. Project managers tend to take the pulse of the organization from an objective point of view.

A project-management office does not take the place of change leaders or project managers. Nor should it try to dictate what employees do. Rather, it should support functions during large-scale change. When introducing company-wide information systems or significant changes to how work is done, the project office can help the local leadership take ownership of the changes by giving them tools, templates, and plans to make the change happen. Local and team leaders already have a full-time job, so the project office must be seen as a way to make the change easier, not as an extra layer of bureaucracy.

Project management can also work effectively by capturing lessons learned from the changes and then developing a change process that works for the company. A project manager can facilitate the lessons learned workshops, compile all the information, and distribute it throughout the organization to increase the collective knowledge of the company on what does and doesn't work.

When overall timelines are established and milestones are tracked, leadership time is freed up to concentrate on the overall performance and results of the project, not the nitty-gritty details.

Organizing manageable but complex change

One of the big things leaders note when they are going through complex change is that they want to make sure work continues to get done, even though the change needs to be fast and efficient. Many leaders want to make the change happen quickly and efficiently, a bit like ripping off a bandage: It is painful when happening but soon over. The alternative is to feel like the company is suffering death by a thousand fish bites, or many small changes that may not be that painful but just keep on coming and coming until the organization can take no more. Quickly ripping off a bandage helps teams move to the future state of change and minimizes disruption from multiple initiatives.

Organizing change management is a balancing act. Change leaders need to work within the constraints of business realities but also make sure that projects don't go so slowly that they lose steam. *Manageable complex change* means looking at the changes your organization is going through as a system that needs to keep flowing.

Seeing chaos as mere complexity

What may look like chaos is more likely just complexity. Your role is to manage the complexity so that you and your organization can adjust to changes rationally.

Think of the New York subway system: With more than 420 operating stations, more than 200 miles of track (over 300 kilometers), and an average of 5 million riders on weekdays, you don't need a book to tell you that it looks like chaos at times (especially rush hour). People are running this way and that, but for the most part everyone gets to where they need to go, when they need to get there. The system seems chaotic, but it has order.

Although you may not want your change to have any chaos, there will always be something you can't control (financial markets tumbling down, an irrational customer, internal turnover). These things are part of everyday business, but when paired with multiple changes they can feel a bit like chaos. Your job as a change leader is to manage as much of the change as you can through a controlled and systematic approach. Your goal is as follows when managing multiple projects, multiple changes, and the perception of chaos: Be sure order is underneath it all.

Figure 5-1 shows how you can bring chaos into control and even alignment by managing patterns and creating acceptable and unacceptable rules for operating.

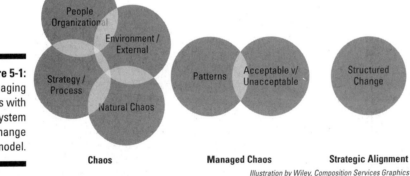

Figure 5-1: Managing chaos with a system change model.

Chaos   Managed Chaos   Strategic Alignment

Illustration by Wiley, Composition Services Graphics

The more complex change is, the more it may *seem* like chaos. In Figure 5-1, chaos can come in four main forms:

✔ **People and organization:** People may be changing jobs, not sure of what their jobs are, and not really sure who they report to or who they will report to in the future.

✔ **Strategy/process:** When a strategy is seen as unclear or when processes seem to continually change, no amount of change management is going to make the organization operate better. Without a clear vision or plan, the organization will be running around chasing whatever is thrown its way.

✔ **Environment/external:** This type of chaos comes from customers, shareholders, or other people outside of the organization. Is everyone in a panic, selling shares of the company because the stock market plunged? This situation can be seen as chaos. Did a giant snowstorm in an unusual area cause everyone to run for cover, thinking the world is coming to an end? Another external source of chaos.

✔ **Natural chaos:** You just have to deal with this type of chaos, because it doesn't go away. Some things just don't work out, and people or organizations panic. This is just the natural level of chaos out in the world; the important thing is to manage as much of the change and chaos as you can so the organization can deal with them rationally.

Building scenarios and setting standards

Your job as a change leader is to identify all the major complexities in your organization and build possible scenarios. Start by using the four major categories just mentioned. You don't need to list everything, just the big ones. After you list them, start managing these elements of the organization (that is, the system) by first identifying patterns in the complexities. You do this by collecting data and observing what is really going on from employees', customers', and external stakeholders' points of view. Then, with this data, you start doing something to set standards for what is acceptable and what is not during the change. Standards come in all forms, ranging from developing new answers for the sales process to new metrics to determine how a process is working to new performance management expectations of employees.

As a change leader, if you can find themes, the chaos begins to feel more organized. You can put the appropriate structure around it, which leads to the final step of managing chaos systematically: structuring it. After you're able to identify patterns in complexity (through observations, metrics, and review) and then use them to redefine how the business will operate in the future with new acceptable and unacceptable norms and processes, you can move the organization into a more structured change approach. Things calm down and people no longer feel like their world is being turned upside down, so you can take a deep breath and align all the changes, whatever their sources, to the strategy of the organization.

Example of managing complexity: A call center and its merger

To see what can happen when managing complex change, check out this example of a call center that's undergoing significant change. Delightful Benefits helps companies manage their benefits, like retirement, healthcare, and bonuses. Delightful was bought by Hue Healthcare, and together they're combining various centers to save costs, opening new operations across the globe, and changing how they sell products and services to customers. Here are a few of the complexities the acquisition change team identified:

- ✔ **People and organization:** Combining two different company cultures is creating tension, and some superstar performers are leaving the organization unexpectedly. Because the acquisition just closed, many people out in the field are still unsure of which centers are combining and what it means for their jobs.

- ✔ **Strategy/process:** People at Hue Healthcare are a little upset about the lack of process Delightful brought over to the new company. Delightful is a bit put off by the stringent processes for everything from getting a badge to posting information on the internal website. The future way of doing business is unknown because teams are still working to create those processes.

- ✔ **Environment/external:** Although Hue-Delight has been in a great space with few competitors, the market is quickly growing, which means more price competition and a demanding customer base. This change adds complexity to the sales cycle and a bit of chaos based on change in the market.

- ✔ **Natural chaos:** With the opening of locations around the globe, the company must deal with an expected bit of complexity with new government regulations and local cultures.

What did the call center do? Step one was to set up a project office, headed by a senior leader in the organization. Step two was to re-communicate the vision and shared need of the acquisition. Employees from the two companies had vastly different perspectives on the change, and executive leaders went back to talk with their employees about WIIFM ("What's in it for me?"). With visible leadership at the sites, the project manager continued to work on creating a change road map that addressed the risks of each of the two areas as well as how success would be measured in each area.

Next, senior leaders in the two companies were partnered with one another and signed up to own one of the four areas in addition to their regular jobs:

- ✔ One team of senior leaders went to each of the major call centers and talked about the people and cultural issues to find out what could potentially help or hurt the merger.

- ✔ Another team took on strategy and spoke with managers and executives across the company to make sure strategies and goals were tied together from the top to the bottom of the organization.

✔ Another team of senior leaders took on working with customers and gauging the external market to understand what additional external or environmental complexity may be on the horizon.

✔ The last team addressed the natural chaos expected from multiple regions, governments, and cultures.

These four teams, working together with executive leaders and reporting their ideas, concerns, and recommendations to the project manager office, put significant structure around a potentially chaotic merger. Within one year of the merger, productivity was 20 percent higher than before the merger, and 90 percent of employees said the merger was a change for the better. But managing complexities didn't stop there: The senior leadership team continued to find patterns in complexity and how to manage this complexity in the future. The following sections detail how.

Step one: Identifying patterns in complexity

The acquisition team quickly got to work by identifying patterns in an increasingly complex environment. One of the first patterns they saw was in the customer feedback on sales calls. Customers continued to demand more technical capabilities, one-stop-shops for their employees to call when they had questions, and the metrics to prove everything was working as the sales team promised. These unmet needs gave a sense of chaos because none of the old client contracts mentioned Internet or web access to serve clients. Customers calling in were no longer happy waiting for something to come in the mail or being told to go find something on an outdated website. They wanted to have all the answers without having to call multiple times.

When leaders at Hue Healthcare started talking about these complexities, Hue's employees began voicing similar concerns of not really knowing what they were supposed to be doing when they did not know the answer to customer questions.

Step two: Defining acceptable and unacceptable complexity and chaos

With these patterns of complexity coming at the organization from every angle, the sales group and customer service team invited a few key clients to discuss what the best approach would be to refine what was satisfactory (acceptable) service and what was not. The joint team came up with a comprehensive list of when it was okay to send customers to the website and when customer service team members should give personalized care. They also made the website more user-friendly so clients didn't even need to call if they preferred to have self-service from the website. The sales team was then able to translate all these items into a new standard offering for potential clients.

Businesses that strategically place competent change leaders throughout the organization are the ones that change quickly and remain competitive. However, business change can't just be a bunch of high-potential people running around changing whatever they feel needs changing — that would just be chaos.

Developing organizational knowledge during complex change

Knowledge management is not a separate part of change — it is one of the key ingredients of creating a sustainable structure. Managing knowledge across an organization means putting knowledge out there, building agreements to share knowledge, and equipping employees with tools to make it happen. These three steps put a structure in place for capturing all the information and make sure the information is available long after the changes happen.

Book VI

Managing Business Change

1. **Put knowledge out there.** With so many changes flying around at once, you'll have plenty of questions and concerns to address. This first step in harnessing knowledge is about getting knowledge out there. Whether you're talking about change, encouraging discussions on how work is done, or trying to figure out what to do after an unexpected change falls in your lap, keeping it all in someone's head benefits no one (and probably gives that person a big headache).

   Reward employees for discussing and documenting old and new work processes to help make changes transparent. An internal blog can help employees share information; social media is another effective option.

2. **Build agreements to share knowledge.** Too many leaders assume that employees know exactly what they're supposed to do during change or assume that knowledge is being shared perfectly. Get people in a room and let employees help define what knowledge needs to be shared and how it can be shared more effectively. As a change leader, one of your greatest feats will be facilitating these initial agreements.

   Sharing information is not just going to happen overnight if the company has never had a structure in place for sharing knowledge. Helping employees build relationships with one another is the first step to making sure they are talking with one another — and talking leads to sharing.

3. **Prepare and equip employees to leverage and harness knowledge.** Even the best-laid structure of knowledge management can go by the wayside if it isn't supported by the right tools. If none of the systems "talks" with one another, getting teams to actually converse will be an uphill battle. If you currently have a knowledge-sharing database with

hundreds of naming conventions and even more ways of storing information, you may need a better approach. A company wiki site, searchable blogs, or weekly informational webinars or podcasts are all tools that can help spread knowledge in the organization.

Knowledge is best shared when it is easy to do so. If an employee has to request software, learn how to use it, and then go off and search for the information in an unending maze of drop-down menus, the system probably needs to be more user-friendly. Here you have a perfect chance to include employees. Do any of your employees have a skill for creating interesting videos? Ask them to help create informational videos on lessons learned during the change. Do you have employees who love social media? Make it part of their job to socialize the knowledge internally. Involve employees who can affect the success of the initiative so they can take action to support knowledge sharing.

When processes aren't documented, some employees may feel they have job security because they're the only ones who know the entire process. This situation is obviously not good for the company, and it puts those employees on their guard because they always feel like they need to hoard information to protect it. When you involve these employees from the beginning and give them some control or leadership opportunity, they do come around.

Keeping Interest High

Sometimes structure can have an unwanted result: the *flavor-of-the-month syndrome,* the employee belief that the company initiates a new change practically every month and none of them matter after a while. This evil stepsister of chaos brings the perception of multiple changes coming at employees from some project office in the sky, and some employees will just think, "Well, if I wait around long enough, another change will come flying at me and this one, which I'm not too fond of, may just go away."

To avoid or get over the flavor-of-the-month syndrome, start by answering these two questions (honestly, please):

- ✔ How have most change projects or new programs ended up in your organization? Were the outcomes sustained and are they still living, or did they fizzle out when the project teams disbanded?

- ✔ Is anything different about the change you are working on or are about to embark on? If so, what makes it different from the past projects?

The answers to these questions tell you a lot about where your current path toward change may end up if you keep going about change in the same way. You have to do something different to expect different results.

To make changes memorable, some organizations like to brand change with clever acronyms or inspirational thoughts. Take the branding path with caution. Branding or fun names are fine, but every change does not need to be branded for memorability, and branding can lead to a bad taste in employees' mouths (especially if too much money is being spent on "marketing" to employees if jobs or other benefits may eventually be cut out of the budget). Communication is important, but a sincere discussion from leadership can mean more to employees than a creative slogan.

Solving problems, not generating them

Book VI

Managing Business Change

Some change programs start with an in-depth review of what is wrong with the company, which can lead to a negative start. What is the alternative? Why not start solving problems on day one? Going out and collecting a bunch of data takes time, money, and energy. You probably could have gotten the same result days or weeks sooner with a problem-solving approach, not a problem-generating approach.

A problem-*generating* approach to change tries to uncover as many problems as possible, takes people out of their day-to-day jobs to do so, and then delivers results in 6 to 12 months. A problem-*solving* approach to change finds out what the biggest pain point is quickly, begins working on problems to generate momentum, and gathers more information along the way. The problem-solving approach gets you away from the flavor-of-the-month feeling because within a month, things are getting done. Things are different, which builds momentum to continue on with the changes.

To get you started on solving problems on day one, here is what the first six weeks will look like for your change when you focus on solving problems from day one:

Week 1: Change leaders coach teams on what the change toolkit is (see Chapter 2 of this Book) and then create their own change plan using these tools.

Week 2: Change leaders hold a process-mapping session on the biggest pain point. Real changes that need to happen are identified.

Week 3: Project teams work on the quick hits, identifying the real cause of problems.

Week 4: Teams present their findings back to one another, learn from one another, and start brainstorming solutions.

Week 5: In-depth solutions begin to be developed, quick wins are implemented, and additional problems are captured in real time from leaders and employees.

Week 6: Visible results banish most fears of the flavor-of-the-month syndrome.

Breaking out of the annual cycle

The problem-solving approach gets momentum and helps employees feel that the change is real and that something is different this time. Change leaders should continually tie this approach to the strategy and vision. A good model is to start with a vision and initial change toolkit, earn credibility through real improvement, and then revise the vision and toolkit as needed to get ready for future changes. This approach means teams will need to break from a traditional annual planning cycle and adjust change plans in real time (more on that in a second).

Most companies are really good at reviewing their business models, employee performance, and finances every year. An annual cycle is needed for financial reasons, but not for change. During change, the review cycle needs to happen more quickly in order to keep momentum going for the long haul while insuring that the change plan reflects and anticipates reality.

A good tool to use during change is the *Plan, Do, Check, Act* method (PDCA):

1. **Plan the change (your change toolkit).**

2. **Do some of the changes.**

3. **Check how the changes are accepted by employees, customers, and external stakeholders.**

4. **Act on those results.**

This method is simple, but it works. The cycle may happen on a six-week basis or quarterly basis, but let the change, not the calendar, dictate the timeline.

Climbing out of chaos: Using a belay system

Thomas Edison had it right when he said, "Good fortune is what happens when opportunity meets with planning." Everyone knows that he who fails to plan, plans to fail. Yes, it pays to plan ahead. So now it's time to talk about how to combine this notion of continuous change with smart planning.

Ideal change links goals, roles, processes, and people skills, something that takes a significant amount of planning and coordination. Successful change also takes into account all the moving pieces that can create a domino effect down the road. Combining real-time change and planning is a lot like climbing a mountain. You have to plan your course in order to get from the base to the summit, but you may not be able to see some obstacles or opportunities from where you are starting. Similarly, you will start out on your change with a solid road map, great vision, and a capable team. But things will happen and you'll have to adjust course.

The way you stop adjustments from seeming like changes to the core vision or plan (and therefore causing confusion, chaos, or that horrible flavor-of-the-month taste) is to do what mountaineers do: Use a belaying system. The *belay* is a spike or other device securely anchored to the rock every few vertical feet that prevents the climber from falling too far if he happens to fall. During large-scale change, you create a change road map with "belays" built into it that prevent the change from falling back to square one (or falling off the map completely) if and when changes need to occur.

The pattern to support the balance of real-time change and planning is this: Plan and make decisions (belay), take action (climb), adjust plans as necessary and make new decisions (belay), and take more action (climb). You get the idea. You and your change team continue this pattern throughout all the changes your organization is undertaking.

Here is what your organizational change belay system may look like in a bit more detail:

1. **First belay:** Vision is set for the change.

2. **Climb:** Create some quick wins aligned with the vision and start uncovering patterns in the complexity and chaos (people/organizational, strategy/process, external, natural).

3. **Second belay:** Adjust the plan and decide (and agree) on what to do with the information the teams have gathered based on quick wins and initial reactions to the vision.

4. **Climb:** Communicate what's happening (again), gather feedback on how initial changes are going, and begin to create solutions to problems.

5. **Third belay:** Use the feedback to revisit the communication plan and identify any gaps in how leaders or employees may be supporting the change.

6. **Climb:** Go out and implement the next round of changes, all aligned to the initial vision the team created.

These planning and decision points can be incredibly useful in keeping change teams on track, engaging the wider employee population, and adjusting plans to fit with the current realities of the business while staying aligned to the vision for the change. Teams can come together to make decisions and plan, but they don't need to solve everything on their own. After the planning, teams go back out among the people who are affected by the change and draw them into the change process.

The belay method of securing a place on the change road map and then moving forward has an added benefit: You don't often need to bring everyone together to make decisions along the way because the change team is going out into the world frequently to coordinate action and facilitate results in real time. It is much easier to continue making forward progress and keep moving up to the next level when you don't fall back to the starting point whenever a decision is questioned or a concern is raised. The process has no closed doors or ivory towers because information is flowing in and out of the core change team on a frequent (not just annual or quarterly) basis.

Embedding Complex Change within the Culture

The more complex an organization, the more likely it is to feel chaotic during change. This chapter has talked about some highly visible, massive changes, but change doesn't come only with a high-profile name or event. Think about some of the changes that may be impacting all businesses, big and small, over the next decade:

- **Technology:** Even if your company isn't implementing a large technology product, technology is changing. Fans, friends, tweets, and professional networks are changing business at a near-constant pace.

- **Global businesses:** Customers, partners, and maybe even employees can be in different time zones, countries, and continents.

- **Regulations:** From Sarbanes-Oxley in 2002 to the Dodd-Frank Act of 2010, from Medicare changes to uncertainty of international markets, a number of regulations and political decisions mean real change for companies.

- **Employee base:** Some markets, like the United States, are facing an aging workforce. Other markets, like India, are helping to create the new middle class.

More likely than not, your company has faced or is facing a few, if not all, of these changes. You can embed the ability, will, and energy to work through change in your culture by creating a structure that controls what you can control, plans for what you can't control, and resolves conflict productively to reduce the stress associated with change.

Controlling what you can

One thing that's always in your control is your own behavior. And through your actions, you can influence the behavior of others. When employees see leaders doing their jobs differently and making the changes they're talking about, employees are more likely to believe the changes are real and will start acting differently as well.

In the midst of complex change, you can define and clarify the vision, scope, ownership, organizational structure, and leadership. Yes, that leadership word again — specifically, visible leadership. During large-scale, multiple-focus changes, you can take action and control how some aspects of the project turn out by doing the following things:

Book VI

Managing Business Change

- ✔ **Get leaders talking.** The best way to do this is to create agreements with the leadership team regarding the vision for the changes, how decisions will be made, and who will make them.

- ✔ **Understand ownership and scope.** If you can make sure the financial, people, and time requirements that will be necessary for the change are clearly understood and agreed on by leadership in the company, as well as making sure everyone is on board with the role they will play in the change, you will be controlling a large aspect of change.

- ✔ **Agree on key messages.** Although you can't control how communication will be received, you can control the messages you and the rest of the leadership team will send. Before the changes start happening, agree on key messages that need to go out to all the stakeholder groups. Put a communication structure in place for the duration of the change.

Planning for what you can't control

During times of change, some things are out of your control. For example, the economy, though predictable for some analysts, is not controllable for the most part. Few people can predict, let alone control, what country's currency will be the next to put pressure on international markets. Closer to home, you can't always control employee satisfaction and acceptance, customer buying behavior, or how the communities in which the business operates will respond when faced with a tragedy or emergency. Planning for what you and the organization cannot control means assessing your risks accordingly and adjusting course as needed.

When dealing with complex change, you absolutely must plan for risks. When you realize or are planning to go through substantial change, stop and do a change assessment to identify where your highest risks are. You can use the risk assessment in Chapter 2 of this Book to start focusing on the specific risks associated with your project, but the change assessment is a bigger, broader view. Conduct your assessment with quantitative answers (ranking how you are doing), and then dig deeper with more discussion.

Table 5-1 shows an example of a change assessment. Score yourself by answering the questions on a scale of 1 to 5:

1 = We are very vulnerable in this area (high risk).

2 = We are doing some things right, but the area still has many concerns (high/medium risk).

3 = We are doing okay in this area — not great, but no major shortfalls (medium risk).

4 = We are proficient, and if nothing else is done, we would be just fine (low risk).

5 = We are experts in this area.

Table 5-1	Change Assessment
Question	*Score*
Building a sustainable structure	
Are rewards set up to help change happen quickly and productively?	_____
Do we have a plan to adjust processes in order to make changes sustainable?	_____
Is training in place to support both short- and long-term needs?	_____
Do we have resources to implement all the changes?	_____
Creating two-way communication	
Are people satisfied with the amount of information about the change?	_____
Are conflicts dealt with proactively?	_____
Are solutions to problems communicated?	_____
Is feedback encouraged and happening?	_____
Working from your customer's point of view	
Do customers see a convincing need for the change?	_____

Question	Score
Are customers aware of any changes directly impacting them?	_____
Making change (and life) easier for your employees	
Do employees expect and want the change to flourish and last?	_____
Do employees have ample opportunities to participate in the changes?	_____
Does everyone who will be impacted by the changes know about them?	_____
Have employees been actively involved in making any process changes that directly impact their jobs?	_____
Visible leadership: Getting leadership to talk and walk the change	
Do we have a clear vision tying all the changes together?	_____
Can leaders state the purpose of the change?	_____
Do leaders know the benefits and expectations of the change?	_____
Do all changes have one clear sponsor?	_____
Shareholders: Ensuring the change makes sense to external parties	
Will the change benefit external stakeholders and shareholders?	_____
Are measurements in place to track the expected outcome of changes?	_____

After the results are in, add up all the scores and then discuss the details. Using the 1 (We are very vulnerable in this area) to 5 (We are experts in this area) scale, here is how you can interpret the results:

- ✔ **Fewer than 36 points:** Although your organization may have a few people who really want change to happen, the structures, communication channels, and leadership are not ready to make the commitment necessary to make change last. Does this change really need to happen? Is the change part of the strategic goal? Work with senior leaders to determine whether the change is necessary and whether the organization is willing to commit the resources to make it happen. If so, go back and start creating the structure for change so the change will be meaningful and last long after the change is complete.

- ✔ **36–72 points:** Change doesn't need to be perfectly planned out in advance, but not having a plan and not having senior leaders visibly supporting the change can make the entire process an uphill battle. Find ways to communicate with employees, identify the best way to train people on the change, and ask leaders to define the benefits of change for employees. Even though the change may be urgent, sometimes it is in the best interest of the organization to slow down, put the change structure in place, and then move full speed ahead.

- ✔ **73–99 points:** You have some of the change tools ready; others may just be starting. Go back and make sure your leadership is all in agreement with the change and what the change will mean to your company. Next, make sure employees have ways to give real-time feedback to senior leaders about how the change is going. With open channels for communication and a committed group of leaders, your change will have the basic structure it needs to get the change going.

- ✔ **100 points:** You are off to a great start for change. With the majority of change tools in process or already complete, your employees, customers, and other stakeholders have a good understanding of why the change needs to happen, what change is happening, and how they can make the change happen. Keep tracking progress, and you are on your way to change success.

Remember, the lower the number, the more risk there is in making change happen.

Take some time with your change team to review some of the risks associated with change, especially complex change. This step can't be done in an e-mail. But don't sweat the time it will take to sit down with the change team or one on one with senior leaders — reviewing the change-assessment questions will deliver exponential time savings in the long run.

The second part of planning for what you can't control is setting a vision and then adjusting accordingly. Your business change will work out in the end, not because you control everything and stay the course no matter what's thrown your way but because you change plans and goals often, if not continuously. However, the one constant of these plans and goals must be that they are aligned to your vision and continuously communicated. Staying the course is admirable, but so is changing it when it makes sense. An organization can't plan for everything, but the vision for the future should not be changing constantly.

Resolving conflict productively: The four As

The four As of conflict resolution — awareness, agreement, acceptance, and action — become especially important when everything is changing. You have plenty of opportunities to resolve conflicts because many of them occur while people adjust to new challenges and modify their work processes.

Keep in mind that not all resistance or conflict is bad. In fact, it can lead to new and better ideas than you had planned. Here are a few tricks to leveraging resistance and resolving it proactively before it turns into a political battle within the organization:

- ✔ **Awareness:** Awareness during complex change and complex conflict starts by saying the conflict exists. Acknowledge that differences exist as soon as you know they do. This awareness is not about blame or finger pointing; it is simply observing that differences exist.

- ✔ **Agreement:** Agree to the bigger goals of the project and what you are trying to achieve (outcomes, objectives), and recognize that you can reach desired outcomes in multiple ways. Take the time to develop multiple options to achieve the desired outcome, identify the pros and cons of each, and then decide how to get to the acceptance of the solution.

- ✔ **Acceptance:** Acceptance during change is not just about nodding yes or no. It gets down to having everyone state personal preferences, even if they are different than the way the group wants to go, and then identifying what everyone can and can't support. The proactive resolution to conflict (or even just differences of opinion) doesn't need to be a unanimous decision, but everyone must be willing to visibly support the outcome and communicate it to employees and other stakeholders where necessary.

- ✔ **Action:** When everyone is in agreement, put a plan in place and move on, but remember that this is not a one-time-solves-everything deal. Conflict will come up again, and as a change leader your goal is to handle it proactively so you can grow and maintain relationships. Maybe the solution isn't exactly what you think it should be, but if all the people involved can support it and take action, you have created a sustainable structure for change and conflict resolution.

Book VI

Managing Business Change

When resolving conflict, make sure all parties involved visibly take ownership of the accepted and agreed-on solution, use two-way communication to solve the problem, and make solving conflict part of the way business is done. If the action plan takes into account the viewpoints of employees, shareholders, and customers, success will surely come your way.

Index

• E •

• **F** •

• *M* •

About the Authors

Ken Lloyd, PhD (Encino, CA), is a nationally recognized consultant, author, and newspaper columnist with specialties in organizational behavior, communications, and management development. His frequent television and talk-radio guest spots have included *Good Morning America*, CNN, and *Morning Edition* on NPR. Dr. Lloyd has taught several courses in the MBA Program at the UCLA Anderson School of Management, and he continues to lecture at various universities and speak before numerous organizations and associations. He is a member of the American Psychological Association and the Society for Industrial and Organizational Psychology.

Christina Tangora Schlachter, PhD, is the author of *Critical Conversations For Dummies* and co-author of *Are You Ready for the Top Job? Practical Advice for Getting the Executive Promotion You Deserve.* As Managing Partner of She Leads, she has coached thousands of emerging leaders and senior executives on how to master the art of leading meaningful change in the workplace. She is a certified Master Black Belt in Six Sigma, lectures at Colorado State University's Executive Education program, and is a Fellow with the Fielding Institute for Social Innovation. Additionally, she is the founder of Junior Journalists, a nonprofit focused on improving literacy and communication skills with elementary school students. Download change tools and watch videos on how to master leading business change at www.drchristinas.com.

Marshall Loeb is the daily columnist for CBS MarketWatch.com and an award-winning editor and broadcaster.

Stephen Kindel is a former senior editor at Forbes.

Marty Brounstein is based in the San Francisco Bay area and runs the management consulting firm The Practical Solutions Group, specializing in leadership and organizational effectiveness. He has authored eight books, including *Managing Teams For Dummies, Communicating Effectively For Dummies,* and *Coaching & Mentoring For Dummies,* and was a contributing author to *Thriving in the Workplace For Dummies.*

Dr. Bob Nelson, PhD (San Diego, CA), is considered one of the leading authorities on employee recognition, motivation, and engagement. He is president of Nelson Motivation Inc., a management training and consulting company that specializes in helping organizations improve their management practices, programs, and systems. He serves as an Executive Strategist for HR Issues, has worked with 80 percent of the Fortune 500, and previously worked with Dr. Ken Blanchard (of *The One Minute Manager* fame) for ten years as his chief of staff, vice president, and primary writer.

Peter Economy (La Jolla, CA) is The Management Guy on Inc.com and best-selling author and ghostwriter of more than 65 books on business and other topics.

Marilee Sprenger (Peoria, Illinois) is an international educational neuro-science consultant and an adjunct professor at Aurora University where she teaches brain-compatible strategies and memory courses. Marilee is a member of the American Academy of Neurology, the Cognitive Neuroscience Society, and the Learning and Brain Society. She is nationally known for her keynote speeches and presentations.

Vivian Scott (Snohomish, WA) is a Certified Mediator and a Certified Member of the Washington Mediation Association, and she manages her private medi-ation practice serving King and Snohomish Counties.

Terry Hildebrandt MA, MA, PCC (Denver, CO), is the founder and CEO of Terry Hildebrandt and Associates, LLC, an executive coaching and organiza-tional development company. Dr. Hildebrandt has worked with the leaders of global business units and their teams to design and implement organiza-tional change initiatives, resulting in increased revenue, greater market share, improved executive team effectiveness, and alignment of organizational culture with new business strategies. He is a catalyst for individuals and organizations to realize their full potential by providing facilitation, coach-ing, and organizational consulting. Prior to starting his own business in 2008, Terry worked at HP for over 22 years in a number of positions in engineer-ing, management, and internal consulting. He earned his PhD in Human and Organizational Systems from the Fielding Graduate University.

Publisher's Acknowledgments

Acquisitions Editor: Stacy Kennedy

Project Editor: Joan Friedman

Compiler: Traci Cumbay

Technical Editor: Aimee Dars Ellis, PhD

Project Coordinator: Rebekah Brownson

Cover Photos: © iStockphoto.com/PeskyMonkey

ple & Mac

ad For Dummies,
h Edition
8-1-118-49823-1

hone 5 For Dummies,
Edition
8-1-118-35201-4

acBook For Dummies,
Edition
8-1-118-20920-2

X Mountain Lion
r Dummies
8-1-118-39418-2

ogging & Social Media

cebook For Dummies,
Edition
8-1-118-09562-1

m Blogging
r Dummies
8-1-118-03843-7

terest For Dummies
3-1-118-32800-2

rdPress For Dummies,
Edition
3-1-118-38318-6

siness

mmodities For Dummies,
Edition
3-1-118-01687-9

esting For Dummies,
Edition
3-0-470-90545-6

Personal Finance
For Dummies,
7th Edition
978-1-118-11785-9

QuickBooks 2013
For Dummies
978-1-118-35641-8

Small Business Marketing Kit
For Dummies,
3rd Edition
978-1-118-31183-7

Careers

Job Interviews
For Dummies,
4th Edition
978-1-118-11290-8

Job Searching with
Social Media
For Dummies
978-0-470-93072-4

Personal Branding
For Dummies
978-1-118-11792-7

Resumes For Dummies,
6th Edition
978-0-470-87361-8

Success as a Mediator
For Dummies
978-1-118-07862-4

Diet & Nutrition

Belly Fat Diet For Dummies
978-1-118-34585-6

Eating Clean For Dummies
978-1-118-00013-7

Nutrition For Dummies,
5th Edition
978-0-470-93231-5

Digital Photography

Digital Photography
For Dummies,
7th Edition
978-1-118-09203-3

Digital SLR Cameras &
Photography For Dummies,
4th Edition
978-1-118-14489-3

Photoshop Elements 11
For Dummies
978-1-118-40821-6

Gardening

Herb Gardening
For Dummies,
2nd Edition
978-0-470-61778-6

Vegetable Gardening
For Dummies,
2nd Edition
978-0-470-49870-5

Health

Anti-Inflammation Diet
For Dummies
978-1-118-02381-5

Diabetes For Dummies,
3rd Edition
978-0-470-27086-8

Living Paleo For Dummies
978-1-118-29405-5

Hobbies

Beekeeping
For Dummies
978-0-470-43065-1

eBay For Dummies,
7th Edition
978-1-118-09806-6

Raising Chickens
For Dummies
978-0-470-46544-8

Wine For Dummies,
5th Edition
978-1-118-28872-6

Writing Young Adult Fiction
For Dummies
978-0-470-94954-2

Language &
Foreign Language

500 Spanish Verbs
For Dummies
978-1-118-02382-2

English Grammar
For Dummies,
2nd Edition
978-0-470-54664-2

French All-in One
For Dummies
978-1-118-22815-9

German Essentials
For Dummies
978-1-118-18422-6

Italian For Dummies,
2nd Edition
978-1-118-00465-4

 **Available in print and e-book formats.**

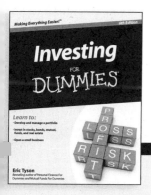
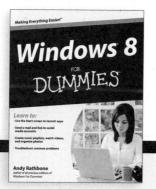

Math & Science

Algebra I For Dummies,
2nd Edition
978-0-470-55964-2

Anatomy and Physiology
For Dummies,
2nd Edition
978-0-470-92326-9

Astronomy For Dummies,
3rd Edition
978-1-118-37697-3

Biology For Dummies,
2nd Edition
978-0-470-59875-7

Chemistry For Dummies,
2nd Edition
978-1-1180-0730-3

Pre-Algebra Essentials
For Dummies
978-0-470-61838-7

Microsoft Office

Excel 2013 For Dummies
978-1-118-51012-4

Office 2013 All-in-One
For Dummies
978-1-118-51636-2

PowerPoint 2013
For Dummies
978-1-118-50253-2

Word 2013 For Dummies
978-1-118-49123-2

Music

Blues Harmonica
For Dummies
978-1-118-25269-7

Guitar For Dummies,
3rd Edition
978-1-118-11554-1

iPod & iTunes
For Dummies,
10th Edition
978-1-118-50864-0

Programming

Android Application
Development For
Dummies, 2nd Edition
978-1-118-38710-8

iOS 6 Application
Development For Dummies
978-1-118-50880-0

Java For Dummies,
5th Edition
978-0-470-37173-2

Religion & Inspiration

The Bible For Dummies
978-0-7645-5296-0

Buddhism For Dummies,
2nd Edition
978-1-118-02379-2

Catholicism For Dummies,
2nd Edition
978-1-118-07778-8

Self-Help & Relationships

Bipolar Disorder
For Dummies,
2nd Edition
978-1-118-33882-7

Meditation For Dummies,
3rd Edition
978-1-118-29144-3

Seniors

Computers For Seniors
For Dummies,
3rd Edition
978-1-118-11553-4

iPad For Seniors
For Dummies,
5th Edition
978-1-118-49708-1

Social Security
For Dummies
978-1-118-20573-0

Smartphones & Tablets

Android Phones
For Dummies
978-1-118-16952-0

Kindle Fire HD
For Dummies
978-1-118-42223-6

NOOK HD For Dummies,
Portable Edition
978-1-118-39498-4

Surface For Dummies
978-1-118-49634-3

Test Prep

ACT For Dummies,
5th Edition
978-1-118-01259-8

ASVAB For Dummies,
3rd Edition
978-0-470-63760-9

GRE For Dummies,
7th Edition
978-0-470-88921-3

Officer Candidate Tests,
For Dummies
978-0-470-59876-4

Physician's Assistant Exam
For Dummies
978-1-118-11556-5

Series 7 Exam
For Dummies
978-0-470-09932-2

Windows 8

Windows 8 For Dummies
978-1-118-13461-0

Windows 8 For Dummies
Book + DVD Bundle
978-1-118-27167-4

Windows 8 All-in-One
For Dummies
978-1-118-11920-4

Available in print and e-book formats.